EDWARD HOPPER

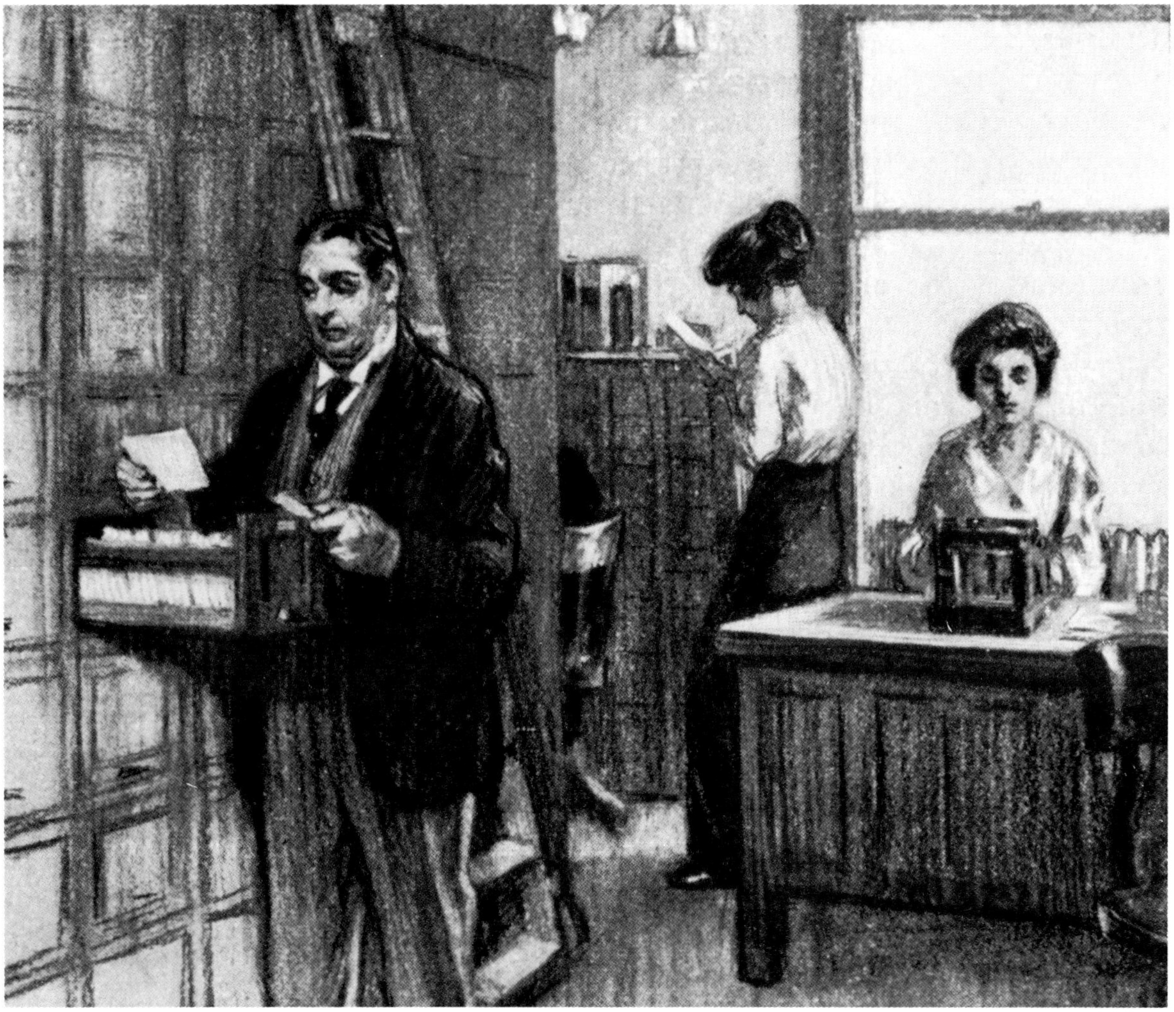

EDWARD HOPPER

AS ILLUSTRATOR

GAIL LEVIN

W · W · NORTON & COMPANY · NEW YORK · LONDON

IN ASSOCIATION WITH THE

WHITNEY MUSEUM OF AMERICAN ART

First Edition

BOOK DESIGN BY ANTONINA KRASS
LAYOUT BY BEN GAMIT

Typography by Fuller Typesetting of Lancaster
Four-color printing by Eastern Press Inc.
Black-and-white printing and binding
by The Murray Printing Company

Frontispiece: Pl. 53. Edward Hopper, illustration for *System*, March 1913, p. 231.

Library of Congress Cataloging in Publication Data

Levin, Gail
Edward Hopper as illustrator.

Published in association with the Whitney Museum of American Art.
1. Hopper, Edward, 1882–1967. I. Whitney Museum of American Art, New York. II. Title.
NC975.5.H66L48 1979 741'.092'4 79-12577
ISBN 0-393-01243-3
1 2 3 4 5 6 7 8 9 0

CONTENTS

FOREWORD

In January 1920, the first one-man exhibition of Edward Hopper's paintings was held at the Whitney Studio Club, founded in 1915 by Gertrude Vanderbilt Whitney. Hopper was finding little support for his work during these years and was earning his living through commercial art and illustrating. Mrs. Whitney's help came at a time when American artists were receiving little recognition; her support for Hopper's work was carried on by the Whitney Museum of American Art from its founding in 1930 until the artist's death in 1967. When his wife, Jo, died a year later, she left to the Museum their entire artistic estate, the largest bequest of the work of an American artist ever made to a public institution.

In 1976 the Andrew W. Mellon Foundation provided a generous grant to support curatorial research of the Hopper Bequest that will culminate in a four-volume catalogue raisonné of Edward Hopper's paintings, drawings, prints, and illustrations, to be published in 1982 by W. W. Norton & Company, Inc., in association with the Whitney Museum. Gail Levin was appointed Associate Curator of the Hopper Collection to conduct this research and to prepare two major and definitive exhibitions of Hopper's work. The first is *Edward Hopper: Prints and Illustrations,* for which this book and *Edward Hopper: The Complete Prints* serve as catalogues; the second will present Hopper's paintings and drawings. These exhibitions are planned also to celebrate the fiftieth anniversary of the founding of the Whitney Museum. The first exhibition is supported by Philip Morris Incorporated and the National Endowment for the Arts, the second by Philip Morris. These two sponsors are the largest supporters of exhibition activities at the Whitney Museum. It is a pleasure to express our appreciation to them for their association in this endeavor so closely identified with our history. Over the years their efforts have made each of them a major aspect of the ongoing life of the Whitney Museum.

Edward Hopper was an exceedingly private person who, through his own efforts and the watchful protectiveness of his wife, sought to determine how much of his life and what part of his art would enter history. His attitude toward his prolific work as an illustrator was never positive, and he rather successfully discouraged discussion and study of it. This, therefore, is the first presentation of Edward Hopper as an illustrator. Gail Levin's diligent research was aided by information from the Reverend Arthayer Sanborn and Clyde Singer. Their cooperation throughout preparation of this catalogue of Hopper's illustrations was invaluable to Dr. Levin and the Whitney Museum.

All research on Hopper builds upon the work of Lloyd Goodrich and his intimate knowledge of the artist from their association more than fifty years ago when Hopper was a member of the Whitney Studio Club and Goodrich was an editor of *The Arts,* a publication supported by Mrs. Whitney. Goodrich, now an Honorary Trustee of the Museum, became a curator in 1935 and was Director from 1958 to 1968. His and the Whitney Museum's continuous recognition of Hopper's work, particularly in the major retrospective exhibitions Goodrich organized in 1950 and 1964, resulted in the Hopper Bequest to the Museum. Goodrich's observations of the artist's life and work, published in books, meticulously recorded in papers and notes, and simply remembered, are also a resource of primary importance. We are deeply indebted to him for this and for his enthusiastic support and assistance for our present project.

It is a personal pleasure to be associated with a museum which is able to carry forward a commitment to an artist and sustain the enthusiasm of the founder. I hope artists will note that the Whitney Museum's involvement with Hopper may serve as a model for any public institution that is dedicated to the work of living artists and which then continues this commitment for the life of the institution.

Tom Armstrong
Director
Whitney Museum of American Art

PREFACE

This volume is a prelude to the catalogue raisonné of Edward Hopper's total production of paintings, drawings, prints, and illustrations, to be published in four volumes. It became apparent in the early stages of research for the catalogue that much of Hopper's work as an illustrator had survived (in the originals, as proofs, or in their published form) his own harsh evaluation of its quality. Extensive investigation and searching turned up many more examples of Hopper's published illustrations, making it possible to identify most of the collection of proofs he saved.

Hopper himself left no written records of his career as an illustrator, making research all the more difficult. While I hope that I have located all extant examples of his published illustrations and original artwork, additional examples may come to light—more of the original drawings or paintings for those illustrations published here, or illustrations which appeared in publications not known to have contained his work. Perhaps some of the dates and places of publication for the commercial advertisements, now known only in proofs, may yet be ascertained.

Further information on Hopper's commissions, such as how he obtained them, would also help to illuminate the story of his years as an illustrator. I was fortunate in locating and interviewing Elsie Scott and Milton Cederquist, who commissioned illustrations from Hopper during the 1910s; although they were invaluable sources of information, most of the details of Hopper's career as an illustrator have been lost with the passing of his generation.

Besides the usual problems of locating, identifying, and dating Hopper's illustrations, one of the major difficulties in completing this study has been whether to define as illustrations those original drawings or paintings not known to have been published. Hopper often sketched and even doodled on illustration board, but much of this work can only be classified as miscellaneous drawing often produced, it would seem, with no specific end in mind.

There are numerous works, particularly in the Hopper Bequest to the Whitney Museum of American Art, which were certainly intended to be illustrations and are thus included in this volume. It is probable, however, that some of these were produced as student exercises for illustration class, while others may have been submitted but not accepted for publication. Still other works, such as the illustrations for Victor Hugo's *L'Année Terrible,* may possibly have been made in hopes of interesting a publisher. Some of these undated or unidentified illustrations may actually have been published, but if so, I have not yet been able to locate them in published form. Inevitably, certain of Hopper's works not included in this volume might be classified as probable illustrations or unfinished illustrations. These, however, will be treated in the catalogue raisonné of drawings or watercolors.

In the process of compiling the catalogue raisonné, I have attempted to collect all of the Hoppers' correspondence. Either original manuscripts or copies of all the letters from the artist or his wife referred to in this volume are in the Hopper archives at the Whitney Museum of American Art.

I am especially grateful to Tom Armstrong, Director of the Whitney Museum of American Art, for entrusting to me so important a project as the catalogue raisonné of Edward Hopper and for his encouragement and continuing support of this endeavor. I wish to thank the Andrew W. Mellon Foundation which has generously supported research for the catalogue raisonné of Hopper's work.

I gladly acknowledge the invaluable help of Lloyd Goodrich, whose writings on Hopper as well as his unpublished notes from extensive interviews provide an essential resource. He has always generously made himself available to me. His early and lasting interest in Hopper's work, continuing Gertrude Vanderbilt Whitney's original commitment to this artist, resulted in the Hopper Bequest to the Whitney Museum.

I wish to thank the entire staff at the Whitney Museum for their day-to-day help. Tom Hudspeth has assisted me on this project in many ways, including helping me organize the illustrations. Doris Palca has enthusiastically added her support to this project from its inception. Anita Duquette was helpful in arranging for photography. Terry Hubscher, my secretary, helped conscientiously and typed this manuscript. I am also grateful to Jennifer Fiur and Tara Reddi, who volunteered their time, and to Julie Goodman and Dorian Rogers, two summer interns who excelled in searching for obscure data on Hopper.

I would like to express my appreciation to others who have helped in very important ways: Patrice Bachelard, Alice K. Bradford, Lawrence A. Fleischman, Arthayer R. Sanborn, Charles Scribner III, Clyde Singer, and Helen Tittle. Walter Zervos of the New York Public Library, William Sartain of the Library of Congress, Robert L. Mowery of the Library of Wittenberg University, Diana Haskell of the Newberry Library, Pat Sheidt of the Arts Club of Chicago, and Albert W. Gendebien and Daniel Evans of Lafayette College deserve special thanks.

I appreciate the efforts of James Mairs, both as editor and for locating Hopper's illustrations in rare extant examples of the *Farmer's Wife* which, coincidentally, his grandfather published. I also thank Margaret Aspinwall for her conscientious help in editing this manuscript. Antonina Krass, who had the challenging task of designing this volume, also deserves my thanks.

I have had valuable conversations with John Clancy, Barbara Novak, and Brian O'Doherty, who knew the Hoppers well and generously shared their reminiscenses with me. I also wish to thank all those who through their personal recollections have helped me to know Hopper better.

I have learned much from John I. H. Baur and Milton W. Brown, both of whom took time from their own work to read this manuscript and make important suggestions, for which I am very grateful. I also benefited from discussions with Leo Steinberg.

For the content and conclusions of the book, I am, of course, responsible. I hope that the publication and accompanying analysis of these previously unknown illustrations will add to the understanding of the development of Edward Hopper as they are an integral part of his complete oeuvre. Already deservedly famous as one of America's major representational artists of the twentieth century, Hopper should also be recognized as the creator of a distinctive group of popular illustrations with lasting appeal.

Gail Levin
December 12, 1978

INTRODUCTION

> In every artist's development the germ of the later work is always found in the earlier. The nucleus around which the artist's intellect builds his work is himself; the central ego, personality, or whatever it may be called, and this changes little from birth to death. What he was once, he always is, with slight modification. Changing fashions in methods or subject matter alter him little or not at all.[1]

In spite of Edward Hopper's statement in 1935 of his belief that an artist's mature development is linked to the work of his formative years, almost no attention has been given to the many illustrations Hopper worked on during the twenty years from 1906 to 1925. Published references to Hopper's career as an illustrator are scant. None of the books or exhibition catalogues on American illustration of this period have considered or even acknowledged his illustrations, probably because the authors have not known of their existence. Hopper himself dismissed this aspect of his career—in fact, he covered it up. If he spoke of his work as an illustrator, it was with great reluctance.

Given this attitude toward his illustrations, it is remarkable that Hopper saved such a large group of them, as well as many of the proofs he was sent along with the various periodicals containing his illustrations. A number of his original drawings and paintings done as illustrations were included in the Hopper Bequest to the Whitney Museum of American Art, and a few other originals have survived. However, most of the originals for Hopper's illustrations have disappeared and were probably destroyed. Some illustrations exist only in published reproductions. A few of these publications are so rare that there is only one extant copy. Others are available only on microfilm. When various publications moved their art departments to new locations, they often shipped original drawings and proofs to pulp mills.[2] (Publishers rarely returned the original drawings to the artists unless they were important enough to insist on it.) Some magazines even sold the originals to their subscribers.[3]

Today, none of the publications known to have reproduced Hopper's illustrations can locate any of the originals. Most have moved more than once, often to different cities, and Hopper's illustrations were lost in the process. Of the originals Hopper saved, most were done in the 1920s during his last years as an illustrator and at the time of his growing reputation as a painter, and most of these are from *Everybody's* magazine and *Scribner's Magazine.*

Hopper said that he was good at commercial art because, unlike most commercial artists, he could draw human figures.[4] Mrs. Hopper (Josephine Verstille Nivison, known as Jo) contradicted, or at least corrected, him when she exclaimed: "He never could do pretty girls." [5] Hopper insisted: "Illustration didn't really interest me. I was forced into it in an effort to make some money. That's all. I tried to force myself to have some interest in it. But it wasn't very real." [6]

In 1935 Hopper claimed to have been a poor illustrator because he was not interested in the right subjects: "I was always interested in architecture, but the editors wanted people waving their arms." [7] Defending his need to illustrate for a living, Hopper insisted: "I don't know a single man in this country who hasn't had to teach, paint signs, shovel coal or something." [8]

Later Hopper reiterated, "I was a rotten illustrator—or mediocre, anyway," and explained that he was not interested in drawing people "grimacing and posturing. Maybe I am not very human. What I wanted to do was to paint sunlight on the side of a house." [9] Another time Hopper revealed his ambivalence about working as an illustrator: "Sometimes I'd walk around the block a couple of times before I'd go in, wanting the job for money and at the same time hoping to hell I wouldn't get the lousy thing." [10] Hopper admitted that he had worked as a commercial artist and as a magazine illustrator for *Scribner's, Adventure,* and other periodicals, but that he had never aspired as high as the *Saturday Evening Post.*[11]

In his essay for the catalogue of Hopper's retrospective exhibition at the Museum of Modern Art in 1933, Alfred Barr wrote of Hopper: "He is now famous but for twenty years his career as an artist was obscure to the point of mystery. . . . He is now famous as a painter of landscape and architecture but his student years were devoted exclusively to figure painting and illustration." [12] Barr also noted:

> He was too uncompromising to make a successful illustrator. . . . After a mediocre summer's work in 1915 he began to devote most of his time to pot boiling illustration. In his spare time he learned to etch.[13]

Although he wrote Barr a polite letter about it, Hopper was evidently displeased with the tone and some of the inaccuracies in Barr's essay, but Jo Hopper was outraged. She wrote a long letter expressing her indignation to Alice Roullier, the chairman of the exhibition committee of the Chicago Arts Club, where the exhibition was to travel after its New York showing at the Museum of Modern Art. She insisted that they allow Hopper "some dignity," imploring, "If you have any control over the publicity, we'd be so relieved if you could prevent all this sob-sister stuff in newspapers about being neglected for twenty years—a poor illustrator—so discouraged, etc. . . . nothing of the sort." As to Hopper's pot-boiling illustration, Jo commented:

> He certainly did do plenty of pot boiling—but was never a wage slave. He had no one to support and could live such manner of frugal life as he pleased. He was so accomplished a draftsman that he could easily turn his hand to illustration—such illustration as he could get without compromise—he never did that and could not do pretty girls—he'd get locomotives etc. Did covers of ship yards [*The Dry Dock Dial*]—express companies etc. [*Wells Fargo Messenger* and *Express Messenger*]—all very much in character. *Scribner's* were wonderful to him—let him go his own gait—careful not to give him things not his kind to do. He did work hard—when he was working—but no one could make him work more than three days a week—the rest he painted in his own studio to suit himself. His illustration or any of his commercial work was a thing a part—only pot boiling—and strictly his own affair. Same as our washing the dishes or washing out silk underwear—nobody's business—not our career. He didn't even runabout with the illustration profession. His friends were the painters. . . .

She also revealed that Hopper "doesn't like at all all this playing up of his being an illustrator and having people see only illustration in his pictures where it isn't." [14]

Few artists who knew Hopper ever remarked on his early career as an illustrator. One, Nathaniel J. Pousette-Dart, did so publicly with a certain amount of condescension. Hopper wrote a letter to the magazine *The Art of Today* in 1935 to protest Pousette-Dart's assertion in an article that Hopper had been strongly influenced by the work of his contemporary Charles Burchfield, causing Pousette-Dart to reiterate his point: "Personally I see two major influences in Edward Hopper's work. The first one is Winslow Homer's, which is basic; the second one is Charles Burchfield's, which is directional." [15] Pousette-Dart had become acquainted with Hopper's work in St. Paul, Minnesota, when he was art director of a publication called *Farmer's Wife,* for which Hopper made drawings. Pousette-Dart also pointed out that in 1922, when he was art director of the George L. Dyer Company, Hopper had done some illustrations for his firm.[16]

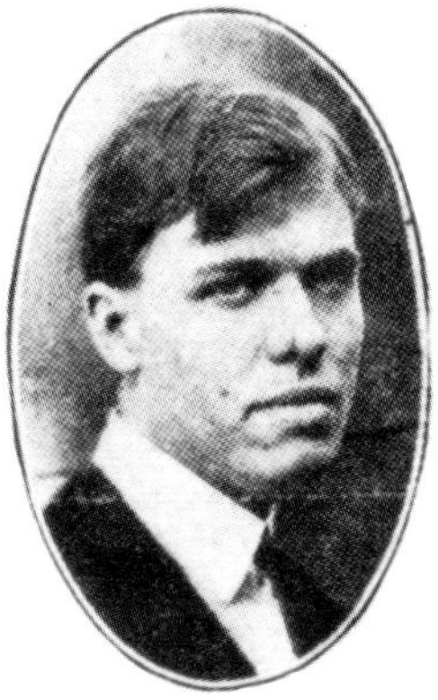

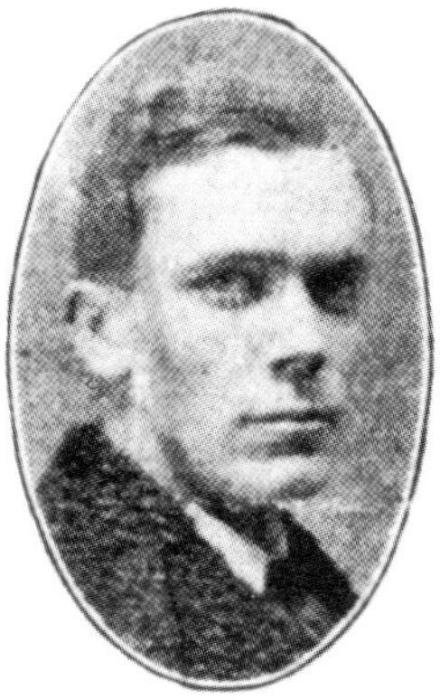

Edward Hopper and Walter Tittle, neighbors at 3 Washington Square North and illustrators for the *Farmer's Wife,* were the subject of a feature article in that magazine in April 1915.

Another artist to remark on Hopper's work as an illustrator was Walter Tittle, a former classmate at the New York School of Art who, beginning in January 1914, lived for more than thirteen years in the studio adjoining Hopper's at 3 Washington Square North. In his unpublished autobiography, Tittle, who also worked as an illustrator, remembered:

> He made his living at this time by the doing of odd commercial jobs, the American Express Company [actually the Wells Fargo Company] being one of his clients. He designed some of the posters that were used on the sides of their wagons. Occasionally he had some illustrations to do, and, being well in touch with that field, I recommended him to editors, sometimes with success. I succeeded in getting him a bit of work from *Scribner's* magazine almost by brow-beating my old friend Chapin, insisting that here was a man really too good for him. Though his drawings for this publication were small and few, I was amused to see one of them carefully included in the fiftieth anniversary number of *Scribner's* magazine that appeared a few years ago [Pl. 312b]. Hopper's later success caused them to claim him as an asset, though at the time the stories were given almost in a spirit of charity, which is all to the credit of the givers.[17]

To comprehend Hopper's subsequent dismissal of his illustrations, one must examine both the changing attitudes toward illustration and what relationship, if any, Hopper's illustrations have to the paintings of his maturity. Gradually, as photography replaced illustration in representing reality in most adult books and periodicals, opportunities for illustrators became increasingly limited to children's literature and fantasy. And the art world's distinction between illustration and "fine art" or "art for art's sake" became increasingly clear. Yet in 1922, a year when Hopper had reached his peak as an illustrator, James B. Carrington seriously, if defensively, contended in *Scribner's:*

> No one who follows the development of modern art can afford to overlook the work of the men and women who draw for illustration, for the time has long since past when illustration may be considered beneath the dignity of the most ambitious art student.
>
> Some of the most admired painters of our time were known in their early days as successful illustrators, and they found the work of illustrating a thorough test of their technical equipment. and discovered that the line between the illustration and the painting was often hard to define.[18]

Carrington added: "Kenyon Cox once said that Michael Angelo and Veronese were the greatest illustrators that ever lived." [19]

Hopper brought to his art and to illustration a cool detachment reflecting the reserve with which he dealt with the world around him. His personality, especially his shyness, did not lend itself to illustrating fiction that was either overly sentimental or involved with fantasy. Hopper preferred to depict what he observed in the most matter-of-fact manner. When he had to illustrate to earn a living, he found greater freedom in the illustration of nonfiction topics, particularly for trade publications.

Nonetheless, Hopper was frustrated at having to illustrate at all. His attitude was the antithesis of that of the popular illustrator Norman Rockwell, who even preferred to produce work on assignment and insisted that he was not a "fine arts" man.[20] Rockwell, who from 1916 produced many covers for the *Saturday Evening Post,* summarized what Hopper must have resented most about having to illustrate:

> You've got to be obvious. You've got to please both the art editor and the public. This makes it tough on the illustrator as compared with the fine artist, who can paint an object any way he happens to interpret it.[21]

Hopper rejected not only Rockwell's kind of sentimental evocations but also the picturesque fantasies of illustrators like Howard Pyle, N. C. Wyeth, and Maxfield Parrish, as well as the elegant subjects and styles of fashionable illustrators like Charles Dana Gibson and Howard Chandler Christy. Hopper's preference for depicting what he observed limited the market for his illustration: photography and the technical development of printing processes had begun to make representations of reality easily available, offering a cheaper and less complicated alternative to commissioning illustrations.

At issue is just how much Hopper was able to define "the line between the illustration and the painting" in his own work. Although illustration can be defined as a visual image linked to a text, narrative painting often utilizes many of the same conventions: gesture, facial expression, setting, and costume.[22] The difference, of course, is that the illustrator must complement the words of the author, while for the narrative painter the only story is the one he chooses to reveal in the painting itself. For this reason the painter's story is usually less anecdotal and less specific. This is particularly true where the artist, as in Hopper's case, does not utilize the title of the painting as a substitute caption. Nonetheless, as Carrington asserted:

> Painting, we are told, has nothing to do with story-telling, but what a lot of stories have been told by the painters, from the days of the old primitives down to our own times.[23]

Hopper's paintings and etchings are usually evocative of a certain mood and often do seem to convey events isolated from an unknown narrative. This is consistent with a statement Hopper made in 1956:

> I look all the time for something that suggests something to me. I think about it. Just to paint a representation or a design is not hard, but to express a thought in painting is. Thought is fluid. What you put on canvas is concrete, and it tends to direct the thought. The more you put on canvas the more you lose control of the thought. I've never been able to paint what I set out to paint.[24]

Artists during the period Hopper worked as an illustrator often developed specializations in certain types of subject matter. Maxfield Parrish, for example, rendered dreamy landscapes, while N. C. Wyeth portrayed vigorous, active characters. Jay Hambidge and John Sloan depicted lower-class city life, William Glackens portrayed the middle classes, while Arthur Keller, one of Hopper's illustration teachers at the New York School of Art, created visions of the life of the wealthy. Hopper's own specializations—the subjects in which he was especially prolific as an illustrator—included offices, ships, railroads, and hotel and restaurant scenes. This is of particular significance because all of these became themes of major importance in the paintings of his maturity.

Despite Jo Hopper's remarks that *Scribner's* allowed Hopper to "go his own gait" and that they were "careful not to give him things not his kind to do,"[25] it is evident from published excerpts of a letter he wrote to the editor of this magazine in 1927 that even there he found much fiction unsatisfactory:

> I want to compliment you for printing Ernest Hemingway's "The Killers" in the March *Scribner's*. It is refreshing to come upon such an honest piece of work in an American magazine, after wading through the vast sea of sugar coated mush that makes up the most of our fiction. Of the concessions to popular prejudices, the side stepping of truth, and the ingenious mechanism of trick ending there is no taint in this story.[26]

Indeed, looking at the varied illustrations Hopper produced for *Scribner's*, it is difficult to believe that his exotic illustrations for stories such as "The Buddha" in August 1923 or "The Distance to Casper" in February 1927 were "his kind to do" (Pls. 314, 333).

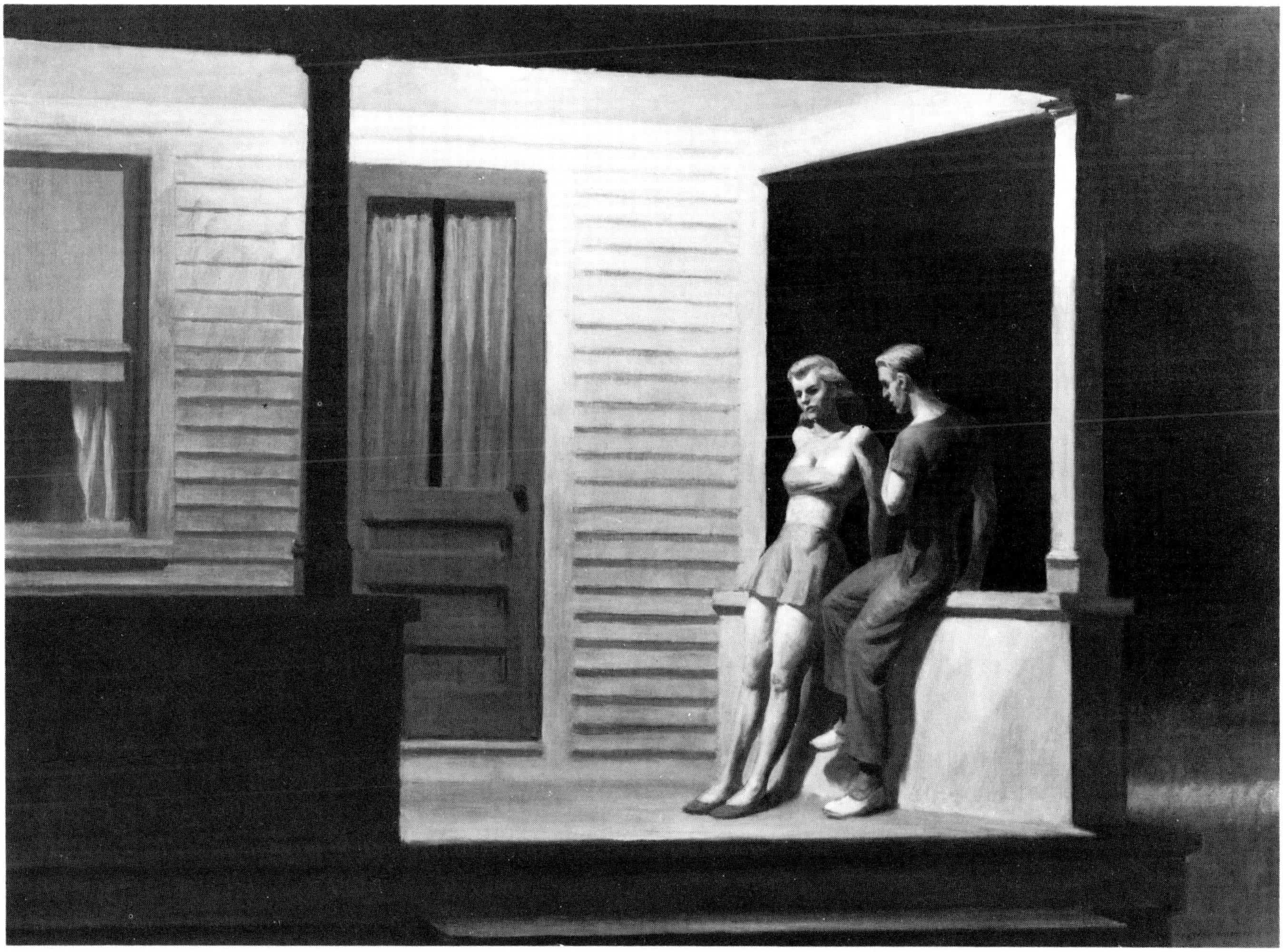

Fig. 1. Edward Hopper, *Summer Evening*, 1947. Oil on canvas, 30 × 42 inches. Private collection.

In an interview in 1955, Hopper summed up his attitude toward illustration: "Partly through choice, I was never willing to hire out more than three days a week. I kept some time to do my own work. Illustrating was a depressing experience. And I didn't get very good prices because I didn't often do what they wanted." [27] Yet, the fact is that Hopper was able to produce and sell a large number of illustrations. It would be telling to know what Hopper was saying about this work at the time he earned his living by illustrating, but unfortunately no such letters or other documents have appeared.

One must consider that in the years subsequent to Hopper's work as an illustrator, the prestige of illustrators changed as the competition from photography lessened the demand for their portrayal of reality, forcing them to turn almost exclusively to fantasy and humor. Simultaneously, as Hopper's own reputation grew, he became more and more defensive about his earlier years as an illustrator. Furthermore, as abstraction challenged realism as the leading mode of painting in America, it became too easy to label and therefore dismiss a realistic painting with the pejorative term "illustrative."

Hopper was particularly sensitive when a critic remarked of his romantic oil painting *Summer Evening,* of 1947, that it would do for an illustration in "any woman's magazine" (Fig. 1).[28] He responded defensively that he had had the painting in the back of his head

> for 20 years, and I never thought of putting the figures in until I actually started it last summer. Why, any art director would tear the picture apart. The figures were not what interested me; it was the light streaming down, and the night all around.[29]

HOPPER'S CAREER AS AN ILLUSTRATOR

In 1899, after graduating from high school in his hometown of Nyack, New York, Hopper commuted to New York City daily to study illustration at the Correspondence School of Illustrating at 114 West Thirty-fourth Street. His parents had not objected to his becoming an artist, but they encouraged him to study commercial illustration which offered a more secure income. This must have seemed more practical to his father, who owned a dry goods store in Nyack and would have been familiar with advertising illustrations. The next year he began to attend the New York School of Art on West Fifty-seventh Street (formerly called the Chase School, after its founder William Merritt Chase) where he remained until 1906. He continued to study illustration with Arthur Keller and Frank Vincent Du Mond, and then studied painting with Kenneth Hayes Miller and Robert Henri (Fig. 2).

Hopper may have first met John Sloan as early as April 1904, just after Sloan's move to New York where he lived in the same building as Robert Henri, but certainly by 1906 when Sloan substituted for Henri for one month at the New York School of Art. For Hopper, Sloan represented one artist he could respect who prior to 1916 had worked regularly as a commercial illustrator.[30] Sloan's influence is particularly visible during Hopper's formative years.[31]

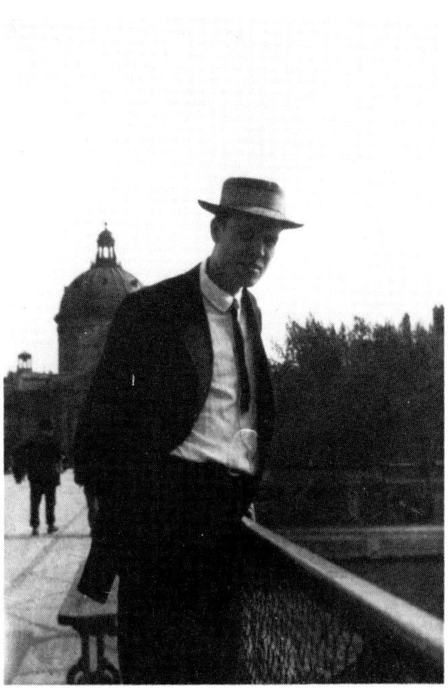

Fig. 3. Edward Hopper in Paris, 1907.

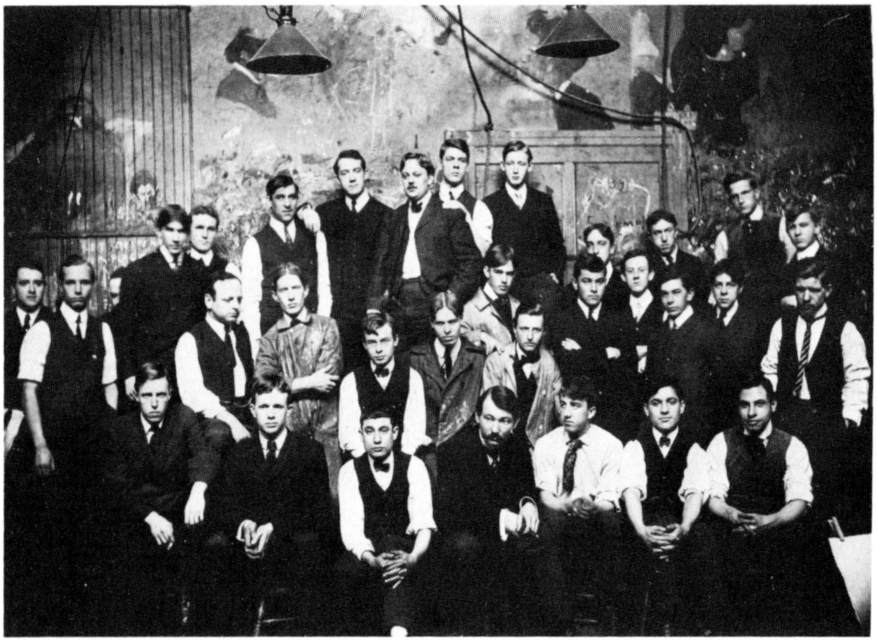

Fig. 2. Robert Henri's Men's Afternoon Life Class at the New York School of Art, 1903. Hopper is the sixth from the left in the second row from the front. Arthur Cederquist, wearing a smock, is standing behind him, and Henri is seated in the center of the front row.

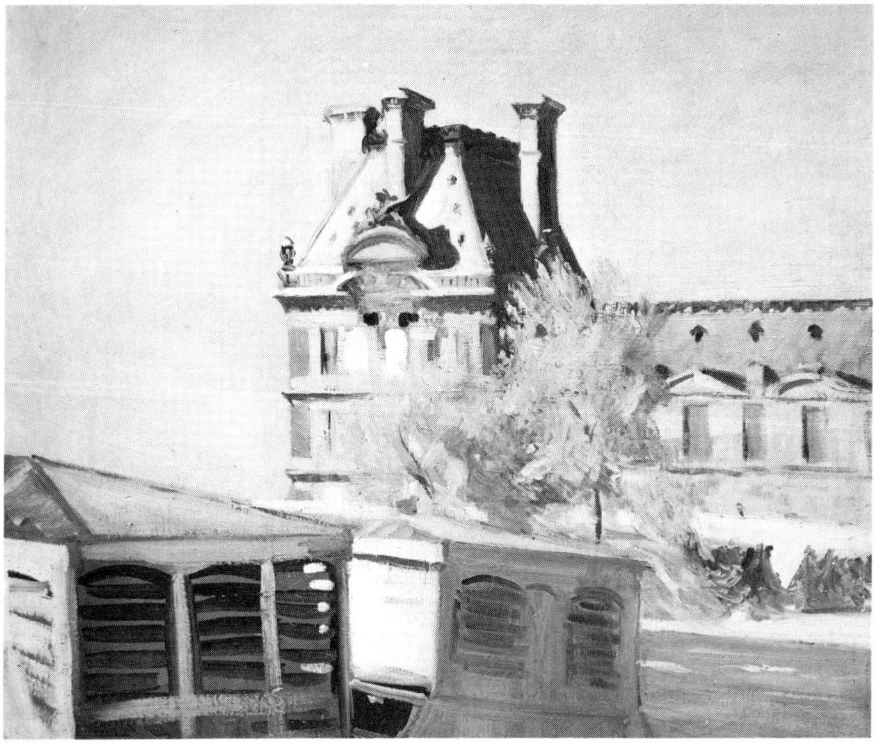

Fig. 4. Edward Hopper, *Le Louvre (Le Pavillon de Flore)*, 1909. Oil on canvas, 23 × 28 inches. Whitney Museum of American Art, New York; Bequest of Josephine N. Hopper. 70.1174.

Hopper had heard Henri praise the work of European artists such as Daumier, Courbet, Degas, Manet, Renoir, Rembrandt, Hals, Velásquez, Goya, and El Greco, and like so many other of Henri's students, felt he should travel to Europe to see the works of these great masters first-hand. So, with his parents' help, he left for Paris in October 1906 and did not return until the following August (Fig. 3).

Upon his return, Hopper worked for an advertising agency three days a week earning money to help pay for two additional trips abroad in 1909 and 1910. In New York Hopper had his first two opportunities to show his work in art exhibitions during this period. During March 9–31, 1908, he exhibited with several other Henri students—including Arnold Friedman, Glenn O. Coleman, George Bellows, Rockwell Kent, and Guy Pène du Bois—in rented space at the old Harmonie Club building at 43–45 West Forty-second Street. He showed *The Louvre,* one of his Paris oil paintings, in the Exhibition of Independent Artists organized by Sloan, Henri, and Arthur B. Davies held April 1–27, 1910, on West Thirty-fifth Street (Fig. 4). After his last trip to Europe he settled in New York City and supported himself through commercial art and illustrating.

Hopper's generation of illustrators was the first initially trained to draw or paint work intended to be reproduced by the photographic process of transfer. Using the half-tone screen, this process offered the artist freedom to create a drawing or painting of any size, for it could be enlarged or reduced by the camera as the editor desired. Illustrators' tasks were simplified by no longer having to rely on complications such as the abilities of wood engravers, who previously cut the designs artists submitted for reproduction.

Hopper worked in various media in producing his illustrations. At times he drew in charcoal, pencil, crayon, or pen and ink. He painted in watercolor, such as his illustration *New York and Its Houses* (Pl. 459), in gouache, or in oil on canvas, such as his illustrations for *Everybody's* in 1921 (Pls. 25a, 26a). In these black-and-white illustrations for *Everybody's,* he worked in white, black, and shades of gray which enabled him better to approximate the tonal values of the eventual reproduction. On certain illustrations, such as one crayon drawing for *Scribner's,* Hopper utilized a white paint for corrections which did not show up when the drawing was photographed (Pls. 323a, 323b). This white substance, however, has turned gray over the years, now adding a strange unintentional character to some of these drawings.

Art editors did not hestitate to alter Hopper's designs by cropping them or printing them reversed, as in *System* where the same design often appeared in variously altered versions in different articles (Pls.

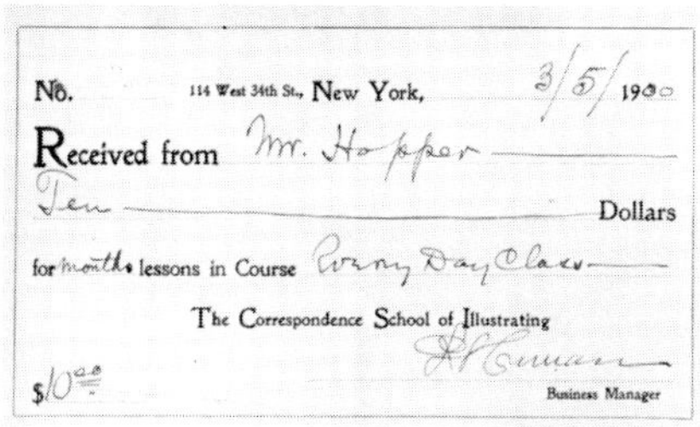
No. 114 West 34th St., New York, 3/5/1900
Received from Mr. Hopper
Ten Dollars
for months lessons in Course Evening Day Class
The Correspondence School of Illustrating
$10.00
Business Manager

A receipt for Hopper's tuition from the Correspondence School of Illustrating, 1900.

42a, 42b, 47a, 47b). *Scribner's* actually divided a drawing photographically and printed two smaller reproductions on two pages (Pls. 323a, 323b). Although the original art for all of his magazine covers is lost, it is safe to assume that some alteration of color resulted in the printing process.

Hopper illustrated for several trade or business publications including *System, Wells Fargo Messenger,* the *Express Messenger, Hotel Management, The Morse Dry Dock Dial,* and *Tavern Topics.* These required factual representations of the daily activities relevant to the periodical's focus and generally allowed more artistic freedom than the illustrations he produced for fiction in magazines such as *Adventure, Everybody's,* and *Scribner's.* Probably the most specific demands were the commercial advertisements. These appear to have been Hopper's first income-producing assignments as an illustrator, allowing him his first economic independence.

Regardless of whether he was responding to the unpredictable demands of fiction writers or producing a series of covers for a trade journal, Hopper excelled when the editor required what can be called a more "painterly" illustration. Rather than conforming to the style of simple linear drawings published in magazines such as *Adventure,* Hopper was at his best when he painted or drew more elaborate pictures such as the covers for *Hotel Management* and *The Morse Dry Dock Dial* or the full-page illustrations for *Scribner's* or *Tavern Topics.*

Although Hopper's forte was depicting reality rather than representing some author's imaginary fantasy, it appears that he never received an assignment as an illustrator-reporter, the kind of newspaper illustration practiced by Henri, Sloan, William Glackens, Everett Shinn, and others during the 1890s. His greatest degree of expressive freedom in illustration appears in various series of painterly covers for trade publications.

The demanding pace of meeting art editors' arbitrary publication deadlines, to which all illustrators are inevitably and routinely subjected, was incompatible with Hopper's manner of working. To the question "When do you paint?" Hopper replied, "When I can force myself to." [32] Mrs. Hopper added, "Eddie always waits for it and it isn't until it knocks him over that he gets up and stretches a canvas." Hopper then remarked, "So many people say painting is fun. I don't find it fun at all. It's hard work for me." [33]

The most significant events shaping Hopper's development during his formative years were three trips to Europe, particularly the lengthy stays in Paris. There, in October 1906, Patrick Henry Bruce, whom Hopper had known since 1903 when they were both in Henri's class at the New York School of Art, "introduced him to the work of Impressionists, especially Sisley, Renoir, and Pissarro." [34] Hopper undoubtedly came to admire firsthand the work of Degas, Manet, and Renoir whose work he had previously learned of in Henri's class. It was probably during his stay in France that he became familiar with the art of Courbet and Daumier and discovered the work of the etcher Charles Meryon who had produced such enchanted views of Paris. These French artists, more than any other influences, provided Hopper with inspiration in his work both as an illustrator and as a painter and etcher. As late as 1962 Hopper said, "I think I'm still an impressionist." [35] While in Europe, Hopper also visited Holland where he became acquainted with Rembrandt and the other Dutch masters, and Spain where he saw the work of Goya and Velázquez.

The years following his last trip to Europe in 1910 were a time of economic and aesthetic struggle for Hopper. Much later, he admitted, "It seemed awfully crude and raw here when I got back. It took me ten years to get over Europe." [36] During the 1910s and 1920s, he submitted his paintings to the conservative exhibitions of the National Academy of Design only to have them repeatedly rejected.[37] Hopper did manage to exhibit his prints regularly and sold them for modest prices, although except for the one oil purchased from the Armory Show in 1913, he sold no paintings until 1924. In these lean years, the fees he earned for his illustrations represented a much-needed source of income.[38]

Given his financial needs, it is no wonder that Hopper was willing to conform, however reluctantly, to the aesthetic demands of various editors and advertising agencies. Thus, his illustrations in a particular periodical such as *Adventure* or *Everybody's* usually present a more consistent style than would a comparison of several contemporary examples of his work for different magazines. While some editors were more sympathetic to the artistic integrity of the illustrator, others obviously insisted on more than just a specific format and subject.

Among Hopper's earliest attempts to sell his illustrations are three unpublished covers he produced for the *Bulletin of the New York Edison Company* in 1906 before he left for Paris. A stamp on the back of these illustrations indicates that he submitted these to C. C. Phillips & Company, an advertising agency located at 24 East Twenty-second Street in New York, founded by Clarence Coles Phillips (Fig. 5).[39] Like Hopper, Coles Phillips had also been a student at the New York School of Art during 1905 and this is probably how they met, although Phillips

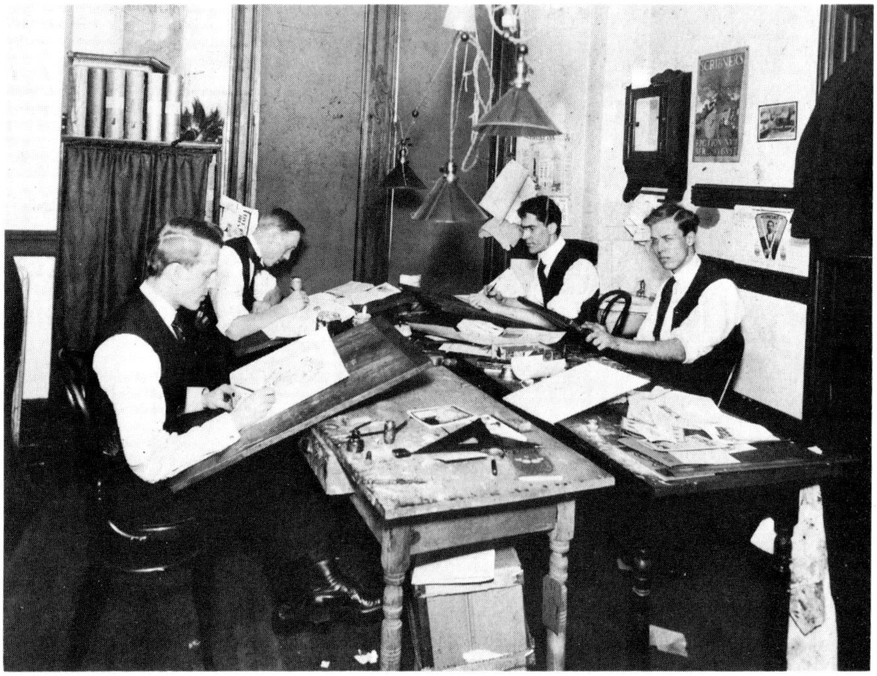

Fig. 5. Edward Hopper (*right foreground*) at work in the C. C. Phillips Agency in 1906. Coles Phillips is seated across from him.

was only enrolled in the night class. While Phillips started his agency in 1906, and closed it early the next year, the *Bulletin of the New York Edison Company* ceased publication with the issue for November 1907, perhaps indicating why Hopper's charming covers were never published. Soon after closing his agency, Coles Phillips began a very successful career as an illustrator.

The earliest datable published illustration by Hopper is an advertisement for Brigham Hopkins straw hats for the season of 1909, produced sometime during 1908 (Pls. 392, 394).[40] Although one might never guess that this unsigned advertisement is by Hopper, the proof was inscribed in Jo Hopper's hand: "Lettering by E. H. & silhouette," evidently so that this would be clear for posterity. This indicates that Hopper was responsible for all but the representation of the hats. The advertisement for the Sherman & Bryan advertising agency of New York and Chicago was one of several other assignments during the next few years. Hopper's use of silhouettes to depict various men wearing straw hats and his overall layout for the advertisement are reminiscent of other art nouveau designs of the period. This early work shows that he had not yet developed his own distinctive style, although it demonstrated a certain refinement.

The next datable illustration, also produced for Sherman & Bryan, was an announcement for buyers of a catalogue for the Wearing Apparel Show held in Madison Square Garden in New York on January 19–26, 1910, and therefore must have been drawn in the latter part of 1909 (Pl. 403). Hopper's black-and-white design, featuring a crowd of buyers in winter dress, has quite a bold graphic sense with its very shallow depth and careful use of pattern.

The next dated illustration, also for Sherman & Bryan, is an advertisement for "The Wearing Apparel, Textile and Fashion Show" which took place in Chicago on March 2–9, 1910 (Pl. 404). Again, as this advertisement was aimed at potential exhibitors, it was probably produced in late 1909. Hopper's design featured an Atlas figure holding up the sign announcing "A Colossal Exposition of national scope . . ." with muscles decoratively indicated by patterns of line.

Many of Hopper's commercial illustrations produced for Sherman & Bryan were clothing ads, obviously a preoccupation of this agency. From its style, the advertisement "Variety Is The Spice Of Life" for Fashion Clothes also appears to date from Hopper's employment at Sherman & Bryan (Pl. 422). Another of Sherman & Bryan's accounts, Brandegee, Kincaid & Co., clothing manufacturers with tailor shops in Utica, New York, provided Hopper with numerous assignments which are related in style to his other work for this agency. None of this identifiable work for Sherman & Bryan is very closely related to Hopper's later style, but rather represents him in his earliest phase as an illustrator and would-be artist.

Hopper produced a series of illustrations for the *Melange,* the yearbook of Lafayette College in Easton, Pennsylvania, in 1912. He made these as a favor for his friend, the artist and illustrator Arthur Cederquist (1884–1954) who had been in his class with Henri (Fig. 6). Cederquist's younger brother, Milton Oliver Cederquist was supervising art editor for the yearbook and his illustrations, under the name "Seedy," are published along with those by other students and the three by Hopper.[41] Hopper was not paid for his illustrations, which included one he subtitled "Greetings" for the title page, a title page for the section "Atheletics" where he misspelled the word, and a title page for the section entitled "Society" (Pls. 383, 384, 385). These are datable to late 1911 or before February 28, 1912, when the yearbook went to press. The engravings for the yearbook were made by the Electric City Engraving Company in Buffalo, New York. The original drawings were discarded years ago.[42]

For the athletics section, Hopper depicted an Atlas-like figure, dressed in gym shorts and shirt, who kneels and holds a Lafayette College

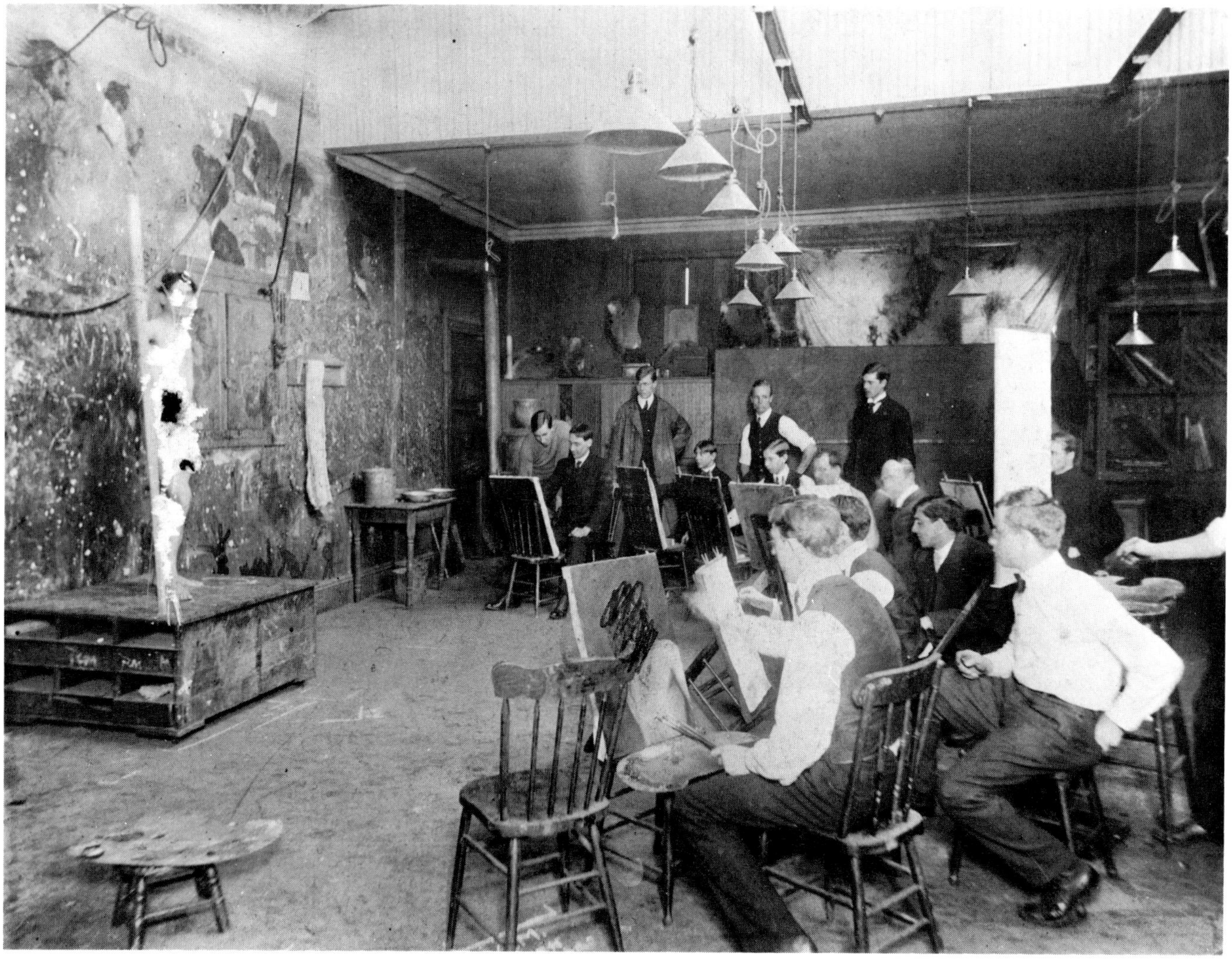

Fig. 6. Robert Henri's class at the New York School of Art, c. 1903–04. Hopper is third from the left. To his left stand Rockwell Kent and Arthur Cederquist. George Bellows leans over the first easel on the left.

emblem above his head in place of the usual planet earth. The flat black-and-white motifs for this yearbook are related to his earlier work for the Sherman & Bryan agency, yet these designs are often more complicated and more innovative.

Several related illustrations not included in the Lafayette yearbook also exist in proofs (Pls. 386, 391). These may have been for another yearbook, for Milton Cederquist recalls that he was delighted with Hopper's illustrations and used all that the artist sent him. Hopper's figure for "Basket Ball" is animated by a large emphatic shadow which has a graphic presence of its own. The illustration entitled "The Dial Vol. IX" probably indicates that Hopper made a set of drawings for a second college yearbook which has not yet been identified.

By 1912, Hopper managed to obtain work illustrating for several periodicals including *Sunday Magazine, The Metropolitan Magazine,* and *Everybody's* magazine. At this time *Everybody's* published fiction, entertainment, and general information articles. During 1911–14, Trumbull White was editor, having moved there from *Adventure* where Hopper would first publish his illustrations in the issue of March 1916. Hopper initially illustrated various fiction stories in *Everybody's,* but for the issue of January 1915 he produced depictions of soldiers in the war for a report from the magazine's correspondent on the European front (Pl. 11). Hopper did not accompany the war correspondent, but he had visited Berlin for several days during his stay in Europe in 1907. Hopper's illustrations began to appear regularly in *Sunday Magazine,* which was included weekly in newspapers in cities all around the country.

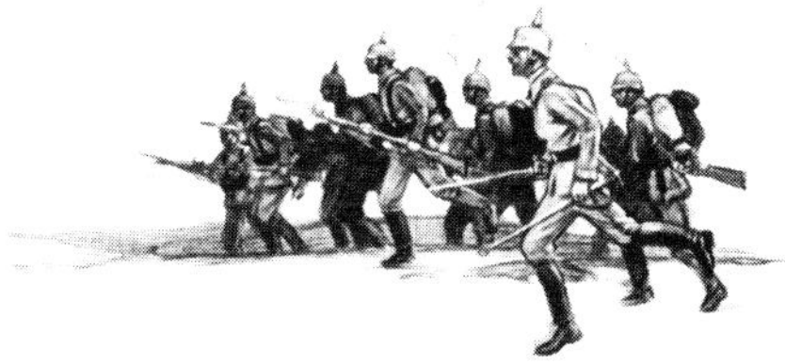

Pl. 11. Edward Hopper, illustration for *Everybody's,* January 1915, p. 75.

More important was *System, the Magazine of Business,* a forerunner to *Business Week,* where he published illustrations from 1912 until 1916. The articles in *System* frequently required illustrations of people in offices, a subject Hopper found so appealing that he later pursued it in paintings like *Office at Night* of 1940 (Fig. 7), *Office in a Small City* of 1953, and *New York Office* of 1962. In writing an explanation of his painting *Office at Night,* Hopper noted: "My aim was to try to give the sense of an isolated and lonely office interior rather high in the air, with the office furniture which has a very definite meaning for me."[43] Perhaps the "very definite meaning" of the office furniture refers to his earlier illustrations for *System* magazine, which provided him with much-needed income during very lean years.

In his first illustrations for *System* and *Everybody's* in 1912, Hopper developed his pictorial conceptions much beyond the simple emblematic ads he had produced for Sherman & Bryan (Pls. 4, 46). His designs are often related compositionally to the art of American expatriate James McNeill Whistler, Edgar Degas, and other French impressionists who had been influenced by Japanese prints. This interest in impressionism was shared with painters who were his contemporaries, including William Glackens and Everett Shinn, who also illustrated. An example is his illustration in *Everybody's* for March 1912, where Hopper utilized a long narrow space defined by a sharp diagonal on the left side with the floor tilted out toward the viewer. This is quite a departure from the shallow space of the frieze-like motifs he did for Sherman & Bryan. The spatial organization of Hopper's illustration is related to that in both Whistler's etching *The Kitchen* of about 1858 and his paintings such as *Harmony in Green and Rose: The Music Room* of 1860 (Figs. 8, 9). Hopper's illustration for *System* in September 1912

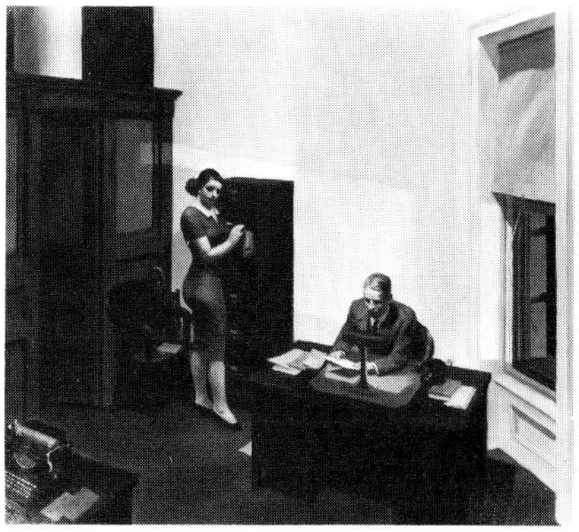

Fig. 7. Edward Hopper, *Office at Night,* 1940. Oil on canvas, 22⅛ × 25 inches. Walker Art Center, Minneapolis.

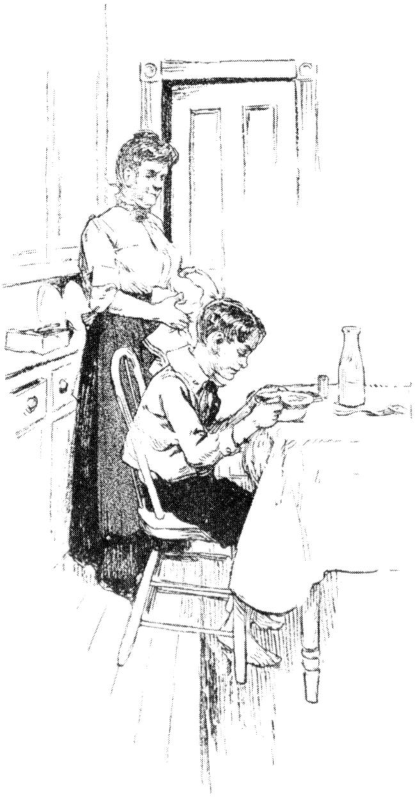

Pl. 4. Edward Hopper, illustration for *Everybody's,* March 1912, p. 422.

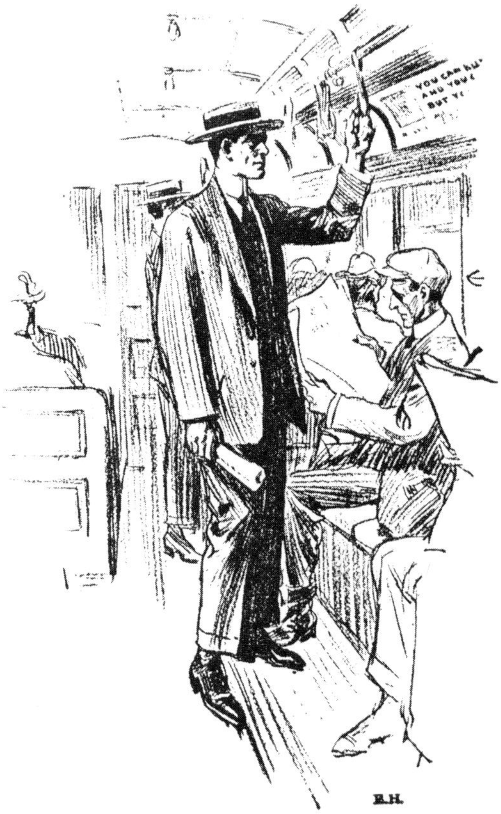

Pl. 46. Edward Hopper, illustration for *System,* September 1912, p. 237.

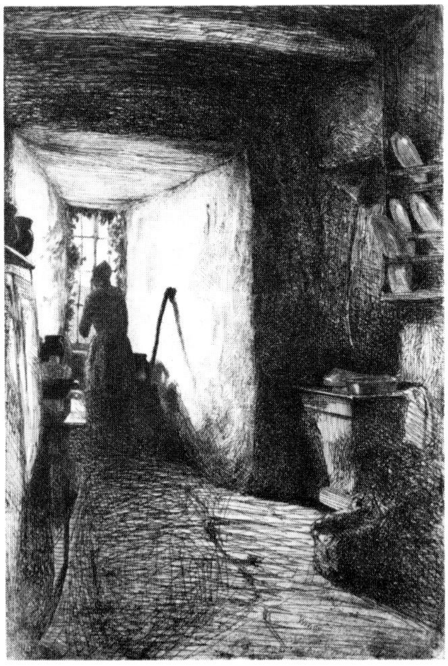

Fig. 8. James McNeill Whistler, *The Kitchen,* c. 1858. Etching, $8\frac{15}{16} \times 6\frac{3}{16}$ inches. Freer Gallery of Art, Smithsonian Institution, Washington, D.C.

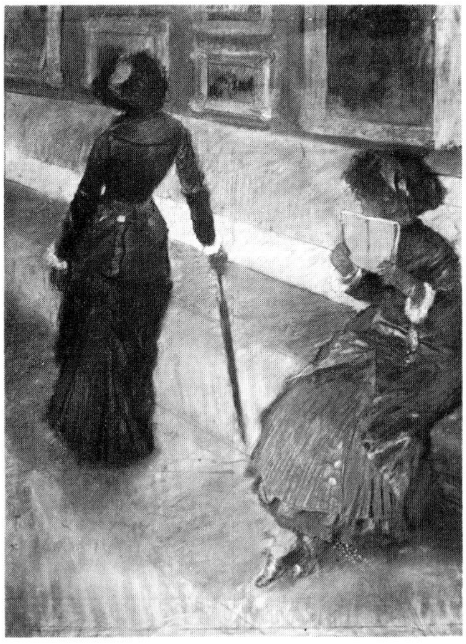

Fig. 9. James McNeill Whistler, *Harmony in Green and Rose: The Music Room,* 1860. Oil on canvas, $37\frac{5}{8} \times 27\frac{7}{8}$ inches. Freer Gallery of Art, Smithsonian Institution, Washington, D.C.

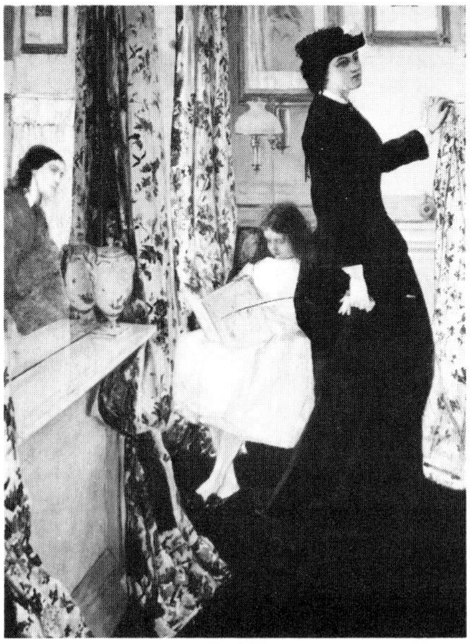

Fig. 10. Edgar Degas, *Mary Cassatt at the Louvre,* 1879–80. Pastel on paper. Private collection.

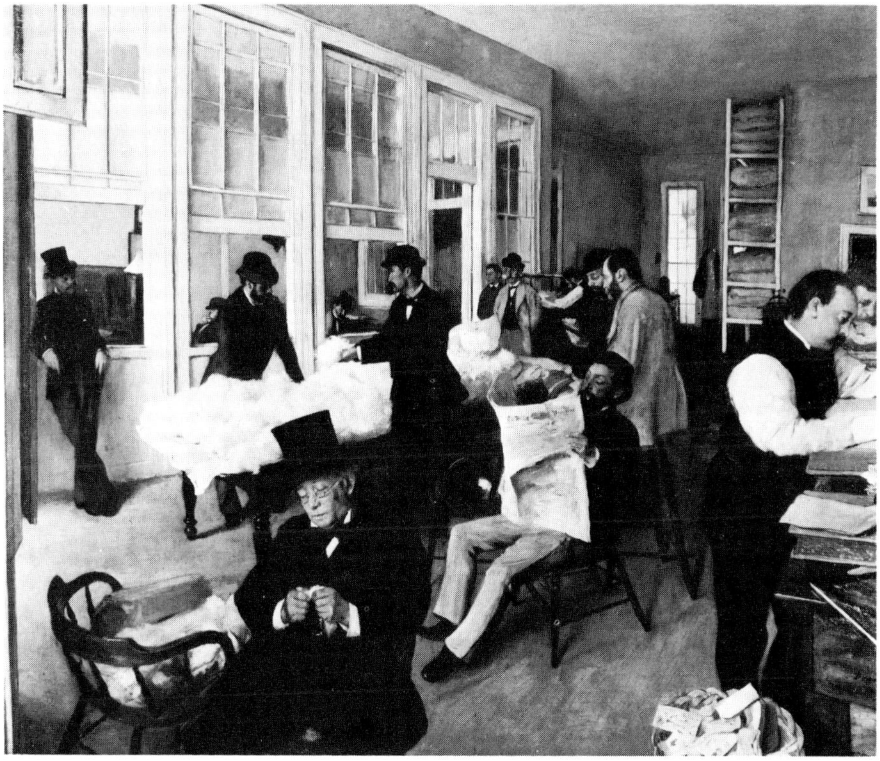

Fig. 11. Edgar Degas, *The Cotton Exchange, New Orleans,* 1873. Oil on canvas, 29⅛ × 36¼ inches. Museum of Pau, France.

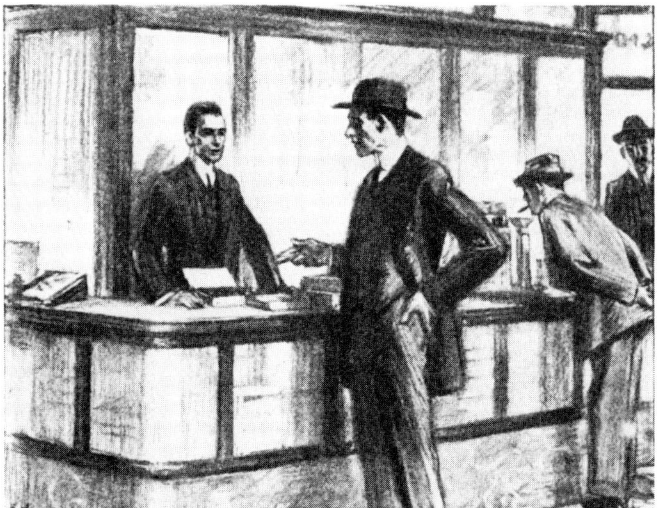

Pl. 60. Edward Hopper, illustration for *System,* May 1913, p. 471.

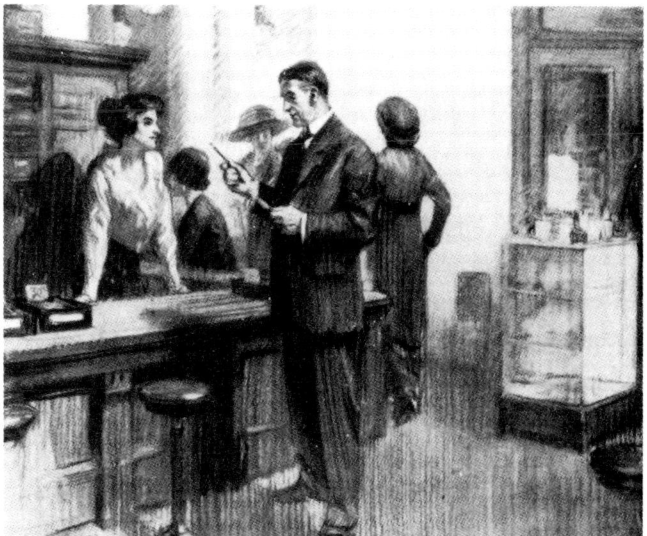

Pl. 54. Edward Hopper, illustration for *System,* March 1913, p. 233.

recalls compositions by Degas such as *Mary Cassatt at the Louvre* where again the floor tilts outward and the wall is angled sharply along the right side (Fig. 10).

A look at several of his illustrations of offices and shops in *System* hints that Hopper may have studied Degas's *The Cotton Exchange* of 1873, one of the best known paintings of an office interior, a theme not seen nearly so frequently as domestic interiors in the history of art (Fig. 11; Pls. 54, 60, 64, 67). Like Degas, Hopper, in an illustration of May 1913 for *System,* utilized the spatial device of windows receding into the picture's depth on a diagonal along the left side (Pl. 60). As in *The Cotton Exchange,* Hopper used the strong vertical and horizontal accents and the rectangular shapes of the windows to frame the posturing figures of businessmen. In an illustration for the *System* of March 1913, the positions of the female clerk leaning forward on a counter and the manager with whom she speaks are comparable to the stances of the two male figures negotiating over a table laden with cotton (Pl. 54). Not only is the placement of these two figures close to Degas, but so is the picture's overall spatial arrangement, including the diagonal angle of the counter, the doorway, and the cabinet, and the floor tilted forward. In several office interiors, such as one for "The Spur of Pay and Promotion" in the June 1913 issue of *System,* Hopper used a similar type of curved slat-back wooden office chair seen in Degas's *The Cotton Exchange* as well as Degas's familiar device of a "picture within a picture" seen in works such as *Sulking* of 1869–71, another office interior (Fig. 12; Pl. 64).[44]

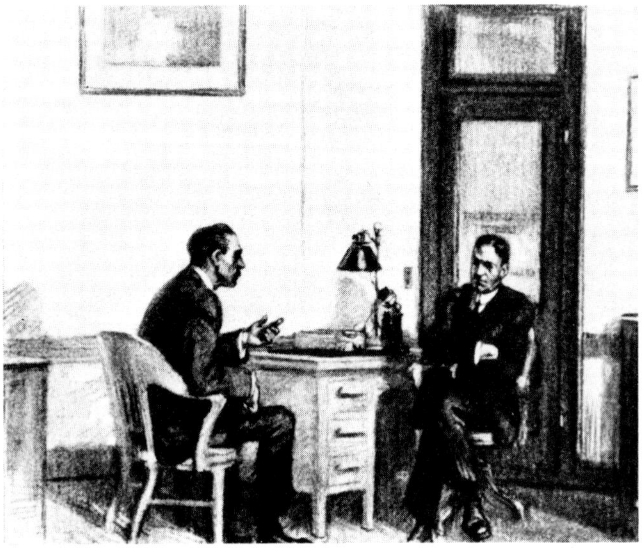

Pl. 64. Edward Hopper, illustration for *System,* June 1913, p. 569.

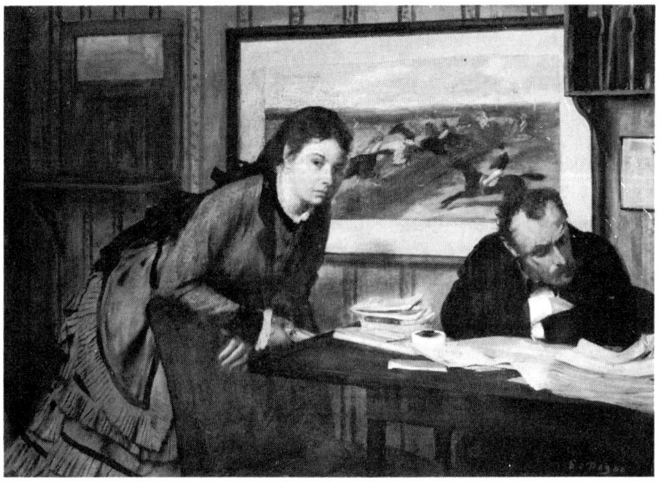

Fig. 12. Edgar Degas, *Sulking,* 1869–71. Oil on canvas, 12¾ × 18¼ inches. The Metropolitan Museum of Art, New York; The H. O. Havemeyer Collection, bequest of Mrs. H. O. Havemeyer, 1929.

Hopper's arrangement of a seated and standing figure in his illustration for *System* magazine of July 1913 recalls Degas's composition in *The Bellelli Family* of about 1860 (Fig. 13; Pl. 67). Hopper, like Degas, makes use of physical distance to express psychic tension. He again utilized Degas's compositional devices such as a "picture within a picture" and a curved chair to contrast with the strong horizontal and vertical accents which organize the picture.

Hopper's illustration for "Tales from the Road" for *Sunday Magazine* on November 16, 1913, is reminiscent of Shinn's *Sixth Avenue Elevated,* a pastel of 1899 (Fig. 14; Pl. 103). This illustration resembles the Shinn in both its composition and theme and is evidence of Hopper's roots in the aesthetics of Henri and other artists of his circle.

During 1915, Hopper continued to illustrate for *System* and *Everybody's* and began to contribute his work to *Farmer's Wife,* published in St. Paul, Minnesota, where Nathaniel J. Pousette-Dart was art editor. He depicted typical domestic themes for *Farmer's Wife,* a monthly magazine which catered to the interests of the rural home-oriented woman.

The quality of Hopper's draftsmanship is particularly strong in the illustrations he made for *System* and *Farmer's Wife.* For example, a comparison of Hopper's illustration in the issue of *Farmer's Wife* for

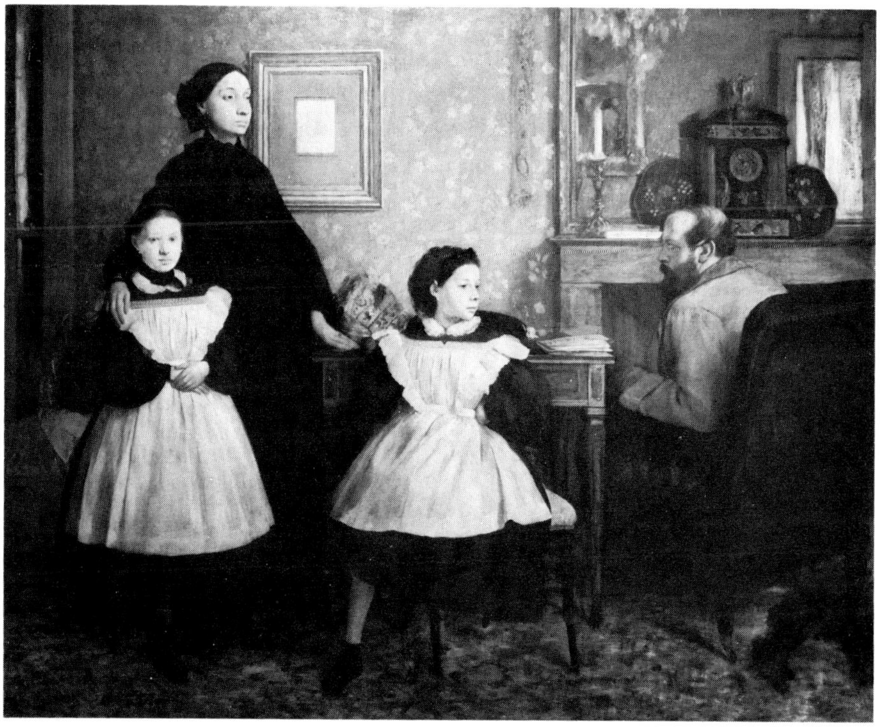

Fig. 13. Edgar Degas, *The Bellelli Family,* c. 1860. Oil on canvas, 78¾ × 99⅝ inches. Musée du Jeu de Paume, Paris.

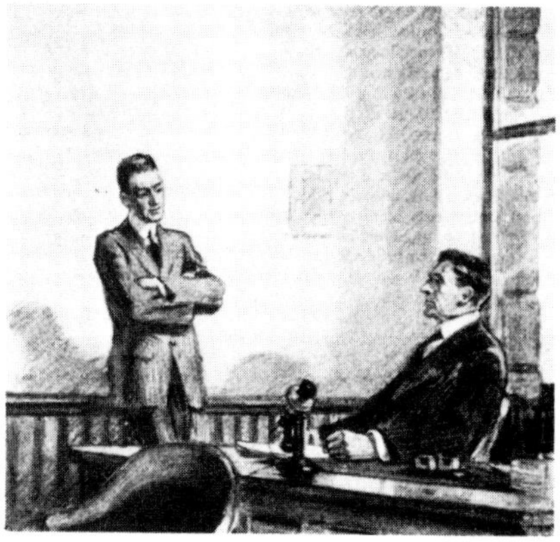

Pl. 67. Edward Hopper, illustration for *System,* July 1913, p. 13.

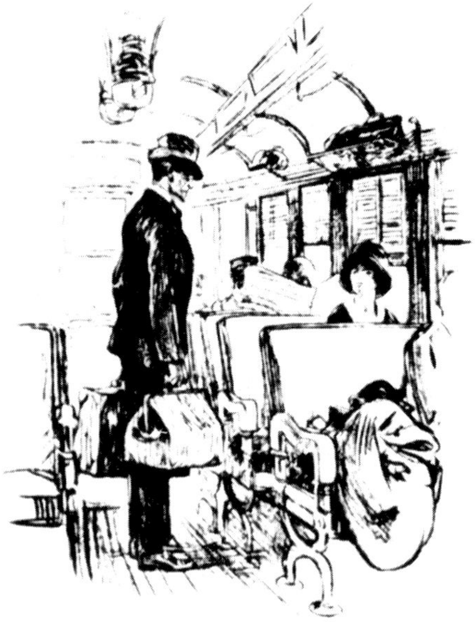

Pl. 103. Edward Hopper, illustration for *Associated Sunday Magazine,* November 16, 1913, p. 9.

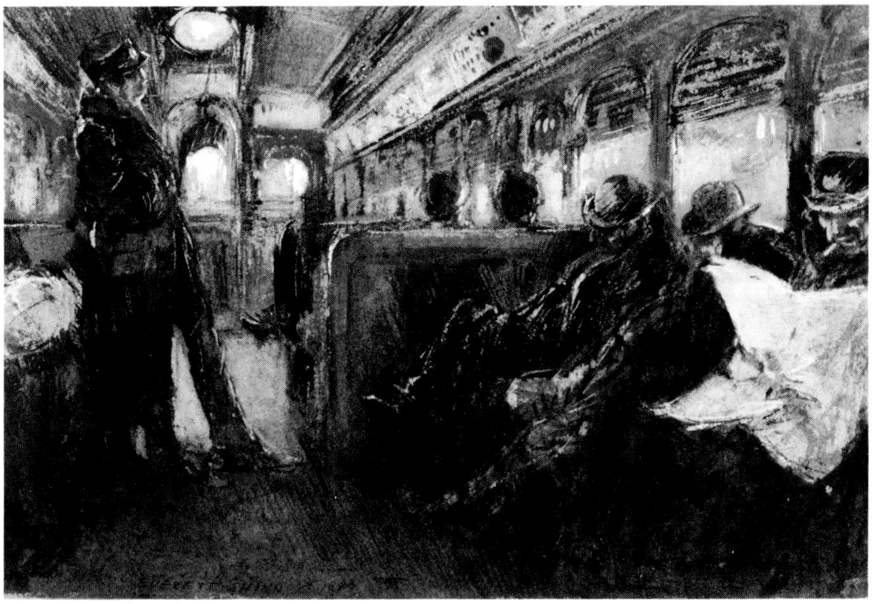

Fig. 14. Everett Shinn, *Sixth Avenue Elevated,* 1899. Pastel on paper, 8 × 12½ inches. Collection of Arthur G. Altschul.

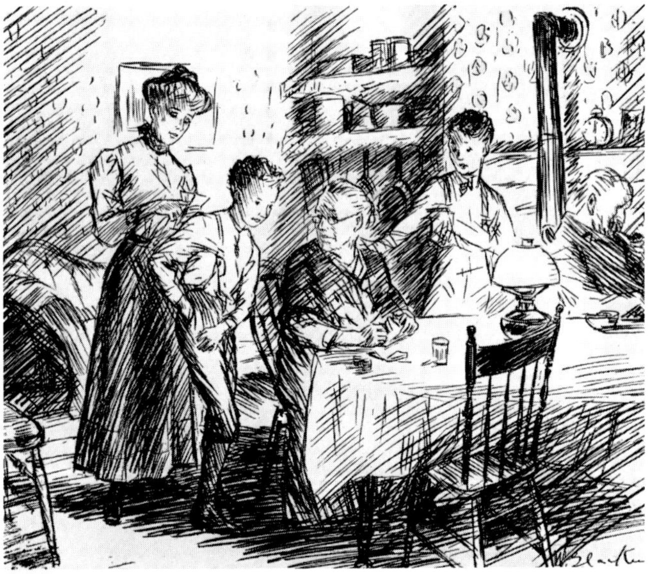

Fig. 15. William Glackens, illustration for *McClure's,* July 1909, p. 273.

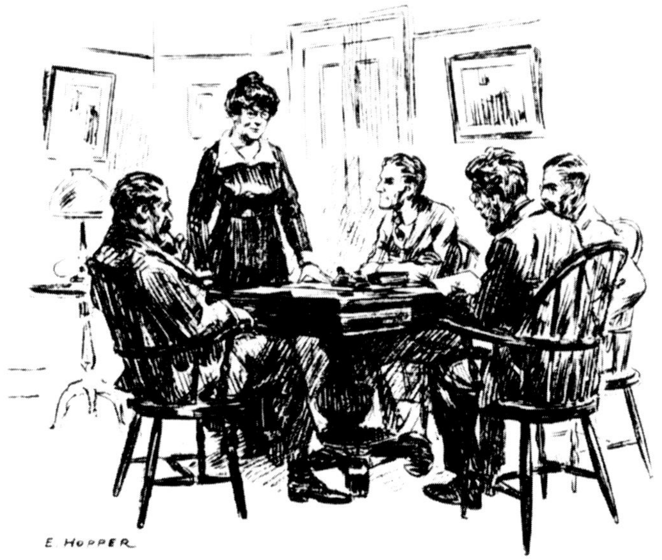

Pl. 162. Edward Hopper, illustration for *Farmer's Wife,* January 1918, p. 174.

January 1918 to one of a similar theme by William Glackens for *McClure's* in July 1909 demonstrates Hopper's more careful, controlled approach (Fig. 15; Pl. 162). Where Glackens's lines appear to be spontaneously slashed across his composition, Hopper's lines and details are spare and precise. His theme, however, is reminiscent of Glackens's interior, again linking him to the earlier attitudes of the artists in Henri's circle.

In 1916, Hopper began to illustrate for *Country Gentleman,* the *Wells Fargo Messenger,* and *Every Week. Country Gentleman,* a national agricultural weekly catering to farm families, was at this time published in Philadelphia by the Curtis Publishing Company. It included popular fiction but focused on farming, country life, outdoor living, and domestic how-to articles such as those Hopper illustrated in 1917 on home canning (Pls. 259, 260). Hopper's illustrations were for articles aimed at the female readership. His illustrations for *Country Gentleman* are painted in grisaille, rather than his more usual method of drawing with pencil or pen and ink (Pls. 244, 245). They are simplified with flat areas of various shades of gray within forms crisply outlined in black. Again the subjects are domestic scenes, including family gatherings, picnics, and women working at home.

Hopper first sold his work to the *Wells Fargo Messenger,* a magazine for that company's employees, by just walking into its editorial offices where he met Elsie Scott who recalled that she purchased his illustrations for ten dollars each, a price that he was happy to get.[45] Hopper's illustrations for the *Wells Fargo Messenger* include domestic and office scenes as well as various depictions of trains. His rendition of a French street corner with the bank Société Générale is in the spirit of scenes of American streets by artists such as Sloan, Shinn, and Glackens (Pl. 429).

In 1917, Hopper began to produce covers in color for the *Wells Fargo Messenger* and by 1918 he was also making them for *The Dry Dock Dial,* the employee magazine of a shipbuilding company (Pls. 230, 274). He may have recalled the art of the mid-nineteenth-century French realists such as Gustave Courbet, Honoré Daumier, and Jean François Millet when he was called upon to depict workers including shipbuilders for *The Morse Dry Dock Dial,* company employees for the *Wells Fargo Messenger* and its successor the *Express Messenger,* and factory workers for *System* magazine during the 1910s. Yet Hopper, who grew up in a comfortable family and was always a political conservative, never shared the French realists' desire to dignify laborers and the lower classes. Indeed, he presented these groups with the same matter-of-fact attitude he was to take with the upper-class wealth he featured on the covers of *Hotel Management* during 1924–25.

Political and social statements were evidently not on Hopper's mind, as he indicated in a comment on his etching *East Side Interior* of 1922 made in a letter of 1956: "No implication was intended with any ideology concerning the poor and oppressed . . . nor is there any derivation from the so called 'Ash Can School' with which my name has been erroneously associated." [46] Unlike his friend John Sloan, whose work certainly influenced Hopper's early development, he found no need to express political viewpoints in either his illustrations or his paintings.

Evidently he never wanted to contribute to *The Masses,* a radical, socially conscious, anticapitalist magazine where Sloan served as art editor from December 1912 through April 1916. Interestingly, another Henri student, Jo Nivison, whom Hopper was to marry in 1924, did contribute illustrations to *The Masses.*[47] Since he illustrated for income rather than out of choice, Hopper certainly had no need to work for a magazine that could not afford to pay him. Although Sloan's aesthetics interested Hopper, his humanitarian, Socialist politics did not. Nonetheless, Hopper's respect for Sloan was profound, as he expressed in his article "John Sloan and the Philadelphians" in 1927:

> Sloan's chief interest is humanity, but the architecture or landscape in which his figures live is always a part of the plastic whole and is never the slight and casual thing it so often is to humorists and satirists. . . . In the drawings made for *The Masses* Sloan's satire was harnessed to a practical purpose. As in most propaganda of this sort, society is offered strong medicine for malignant maladies. The sincerity of Sloan's work for this magazine can not be questioned and he made some of his very finest drawings for it. In his work generally and above all in the extensive chronicle of New York that he has made, Sloan is the inheritor of the tradition of Daumier, Gavarni and Manet and the great movement in French art to which they belong.[48]

Hopper's intentions are vastly different from the kind of revolutionary political consciousness Millet sought to convey in his depictions of peasants. One can contrast the French artist's painting *Planting Potatoes* of 1861–62 to Hopper's illustration for the *Wells Fargo Messenger* of June 1917, "The Wells Fargo Man Does His Bit For Home and Country" (Fig. 16; Pl. 232a). Back-breaking effort now becomes patriotic duty; the setting is middle-class America complete with mother, child, and white picket fence.

Hopper made his most political illustration in 1918 for a wartime poster competition conducted by the United States Shipping Board (Pl. 283a). His design, entitled *Smash the Hun,* won the first prize of three hundred dollars in a contest of fourteen hundred posters. Yet, "Before the poster was reproduced, for distribution, the armistice was arranged and war posters were no longer needed." Believing that "the poster carries as vital a lesson to-day as it did at the time it was drawn," Bert Edward Barnes, the editor of *The Morse Dry Dock Dial,* arranged to use it as a cover for the issue of February 1919 (Pl. 283b).[49] This was particularly appropriate as Hopper had based the poster design

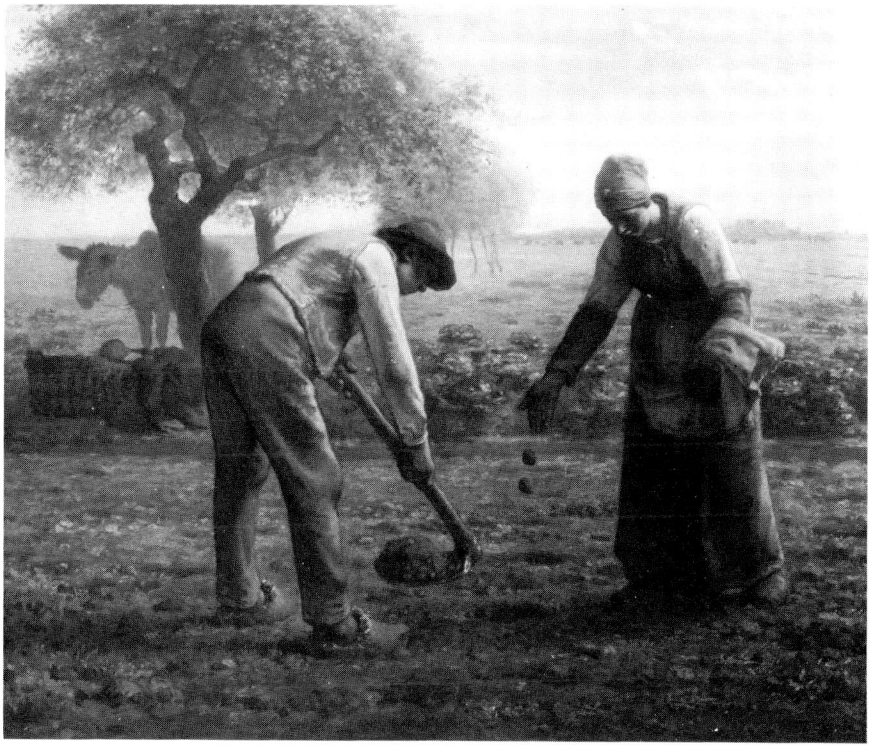

Fig. 16. Jean François Millet, *Planting Potatoes,* 1861–62. Oil on canvas, 32½ × 39¾ inches. Museum of Fine Arts, Boston; Gift of Quincy A. Shaw through Quincy A. Shaw, Jr., and Marian Shaw Houghton.

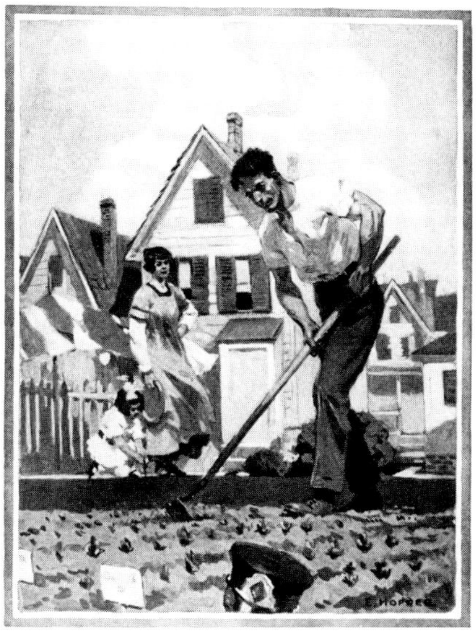

Pl. 232a. Edward Hopper, illustration for *Wells Fargo Messenger,* March 1917, back cover.

on a photograph of Peter Shea (one of the employees who worked on the angle slab in the shipyard) given to him by Barnes (Fig. 17).[50] Having visited the shipyard to experience the atmosphere among the shipworkers, Hopper captured in the poster a heroic sense of energy, toughness, and strength both in the human figure and in the American industrial war effort represented by the smokestacks and the linear forms of bridges in the distance.

Hopper's image *Smash the Hun* relates in its spirit to the industrial images and workers depicted by Joseph Stella in his illustrations for *The Survey* in 1907 and 1908. It also owes to images of the Industrial Revolution in Europe and in America. Among its American antecedents is *Ironworkers: Noontime* of about 1880–82 by Thomas Anshutz, who taught Hopper's teacher Henri (Fig. 18). Shinn had also depicted the energy and brawn of industrial workers in his portrayal of the Roebling steel mills for the Trenton, New Jersey, city hall in 1911.

Hopper must have found his work for *The Morse Dry Dock Dial* relatively pleasant (Pls. 278, 288). He had enjoyed representing ships since his youth in Nyack, New York, a Hudson River port where with wood provided by his father he had built himself a catboat to sail. In-

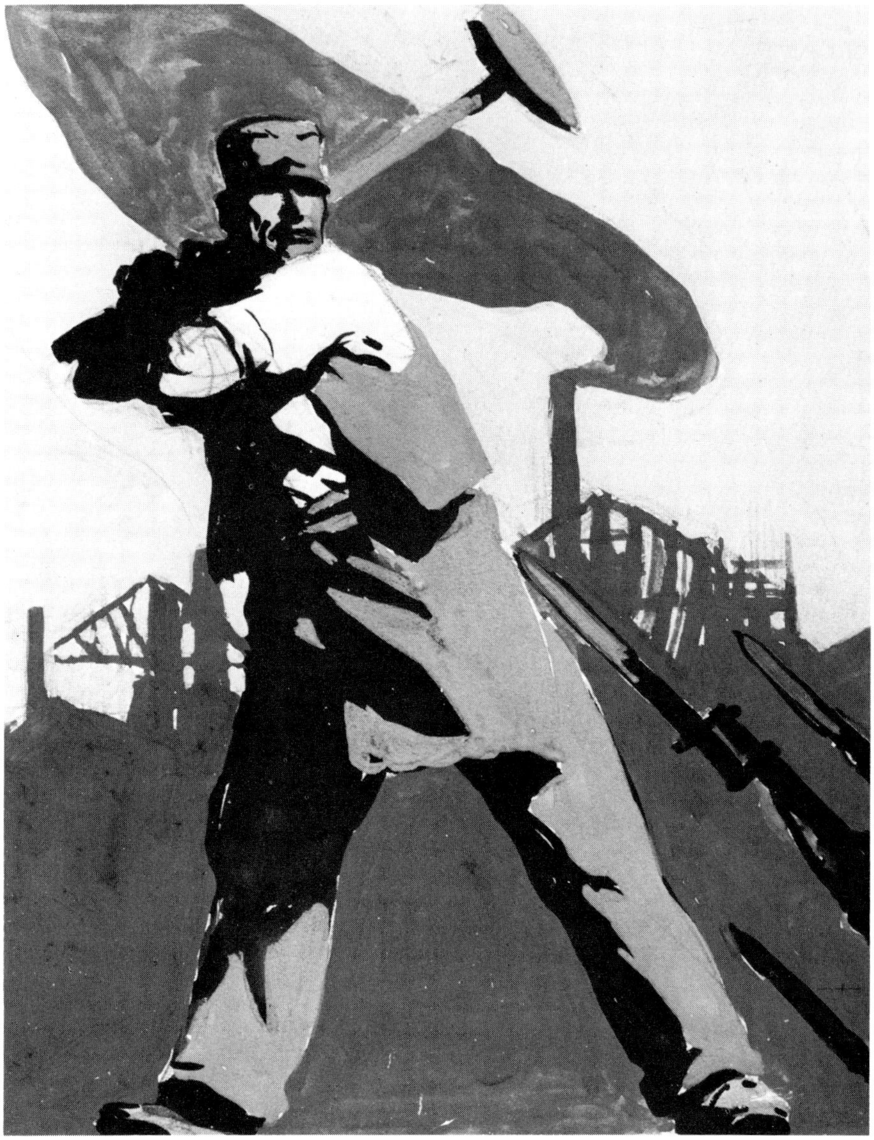

Pl. 283a. Edward Hopper, study for poster *Smash the Hun*, 1918. Gouache on illustration board, 9½ × 6⅜ inches. The Charles Rand Penney Collection.

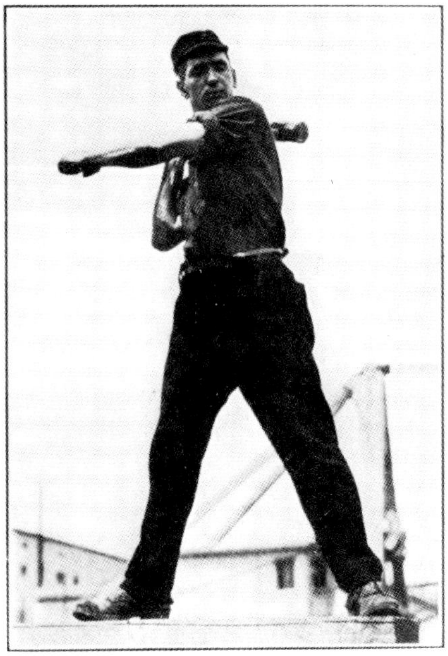

Fig. 17. Photograph of Peter Shea given to Hopper by Bert Edward Barnes, editor of *The Morse Dry Dock Dial*.

deed, many of these cover illustrations are simply more sophisticated conceptions of the same subjects in his childhood drawings and paintings (Fig. 19).

Hopper's style for *The Morse Dry Dock Dial* covers appears to have been influenced by the German poster style of the 1910s. The use of flat areas of contrasting colors as shading to model three-dimensional forms and the bold placement of forms against a flat ground of contrasting color are characteristic devices. Hopper may have absorbed this style through some of his American contemporaries such as Adolf Treidler.

In designing his cover for *The Morse Dry Dock Dial* of July 1919 Hopper may have had in mind Courbet's famous painting *The Stone-Breakers* of 1849 (Fig. 20; Pl. 286). Two of Hopper's four shipbuilders have poses that are mirror images of the two stone-breakers, as if we are seeing the two figures from the opposite direction. Hopper praised Courbet's "mechanical strength," the "physical force and substance" of the French painter's work, stressing that Courbet had this quality more than any other nineteenth-century painter.[51]

Hopper's commercial illustration for "Presto! A convertible Coat Collar" must date after June 5, 1917, when this collar design was registered with the United States Patent Office (Pl. 428). His style here resembles the famous "Arrow Collar Man" by Joseph Christian Leyen-

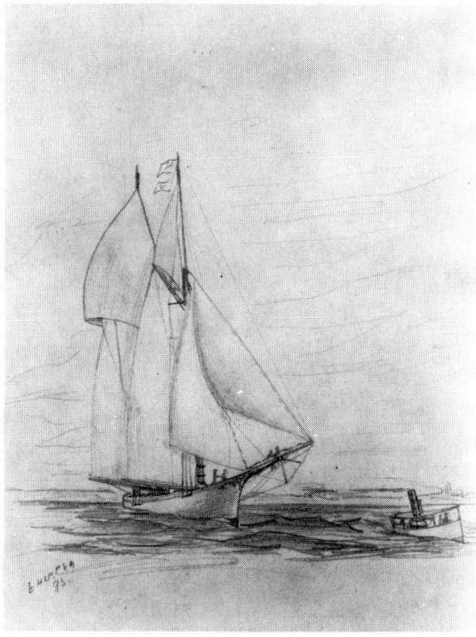

Fig. 19. Edward Hopper, *Yacht,* 1895. Pencil on paper, 5 × 3⅞ inches. Kennedy Galleries, Inc., New York.

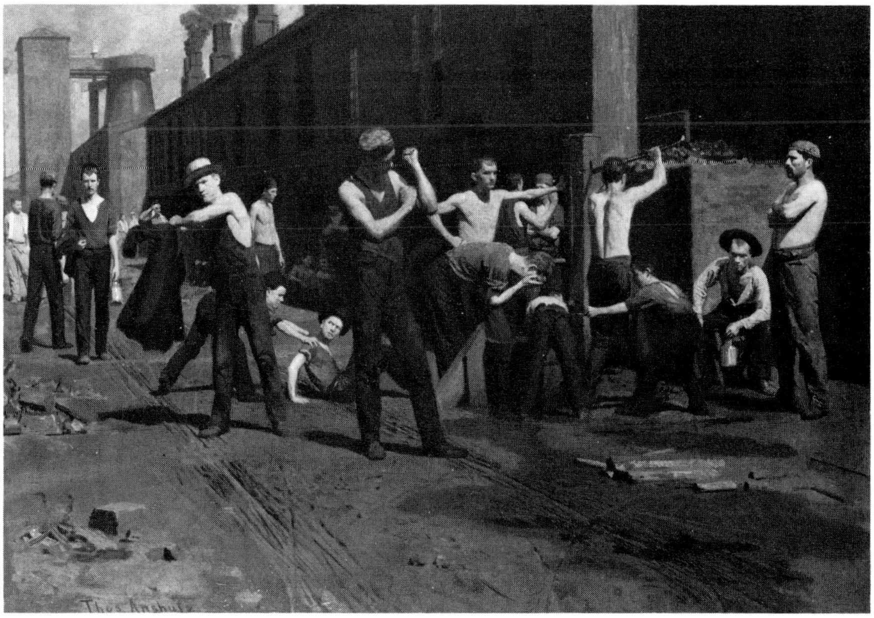

Fig. 18. Thomas Anshutz, *Ironworkers: Noontime,* c. 1880–82. Oil on canvas, 17 × 24 inches. Collection of Mr. and Mrs. Howard N. Garfinkle.

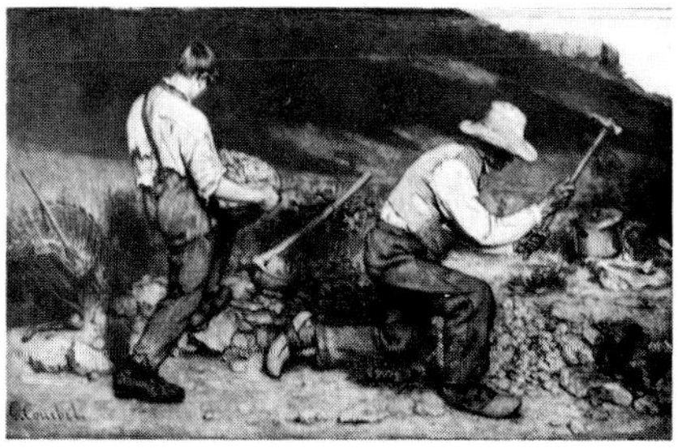

Fig. 20. Gustave Courbet, *The Stone-Breakers,* 1849. Destroyed, formerly Gemäldegalerie, Dresden.

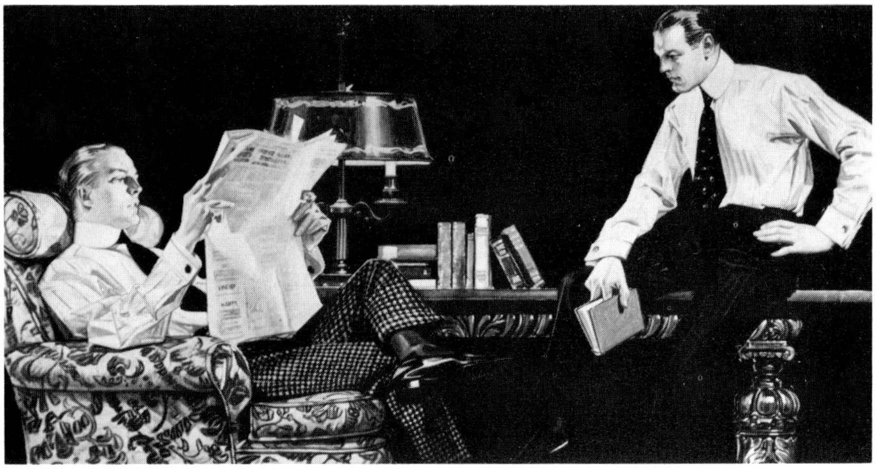

Fig. 21. Joseph Christian Leyendecker, detail from an advertisement for the Arrow Collar Man. Courtesy of The Arrow Company, New York.

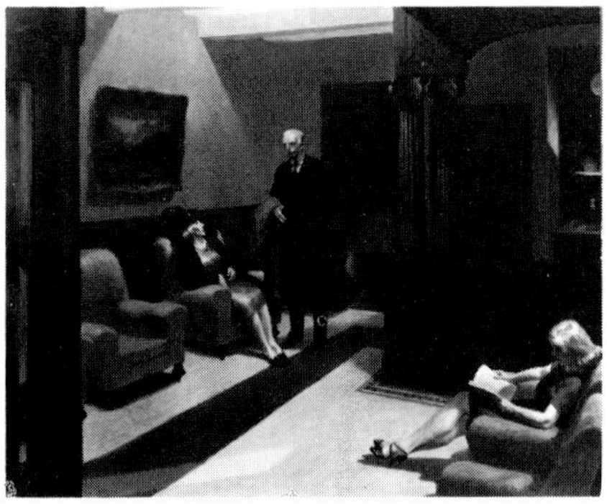

Fig. 22. Edward Hopper, *Hotel Lobby,* 1943. Oil on canvas, 32 × 40 inches. The Indianapolis Museum of Art.

decker in advertisements published about 1910 (Fig. 21). Hopper seems to have adapted Leyendecker's pictorial device of striated facial shading as well as the calm elegance of his Arrow shirt advertisements.

Hopper felt positively enough about his ad for "Knothe Unseen Suspenders" of about 1917–20 that he kept the original painting on illustration board (Pl. 427a). The image is related to various stiff male figures who appear in his later paintings such as *Office at Night* of 1940 and *Hotel Lobby* of 1943 (Figs. 7, 22).

Hopper's love of things French extended beyond his admiration of nineteenth-century painting. He was able to design two covers for *La France,* the American magazine on French culture, during 1919 and 1920. For the issue of November 1919, Hopper chose the image of one of Viollet-le-Duc's gargoyles from the north tower of Notre-Dame with a panorama of the city beyond (Pl. 334). He may have been inspired by reading a chapter in Victor Hugo's *Notre-Dame de Paris* entitled "A Bird's-Eye View of Paris."

Hopper's interest in Hugo's writing probably began before his travels to France. He produced a design for a cover or frontispiece to an edition of Hugo's *Les Misérables* which was most likely done as an assignment for his illustration class (Pl. 436). Even his pencil sketch for this cover design survives (Pl. 435). Later, probably just after his first trip to France in 1906–7, he painted an impressive series of watercolor illustrations for an unpublished edition of Hugo's book of poems about the Paris commune entitled *L'Année Terrible,* originally published in 1872 (Pls. 445, 446, 447). Hopper's close friend, the artist Guy Pène du Bois, wrote of him: "Something about the French appeals to him. He has studied their language and knows their literature to an extent exceedingly rare among Americans." [52]

In designing his cover for *La France* for November 1919, Hopper certainly was aware of a similar view in Charles Meryon's etching *Le Stryge* or *The Vampire* of 1853, one of the artist's best known works (Fig. 23). But Hopper's cover is much closer to a view of the familiar gargoyle captured by Charles Nègre in his famous photograph of around 1851 of *Henri Le Secq at Notre-Dame* (Fig. 24). On his cover, Hopper has replaced the dark figure of Henri Le Secq with the silhouette of an owl perched on top of the gallery rail just behind the gargoyle. Like the Nègre photograph, Hopper's panorama omits the large tower of the destroyed medieval church Saint-Jacques-de-la-Boucherie which figures so prominently in Meryon's etching. Possibly Hopper consulted still other sources in creating his cover which so successfully captures the romance of Paris.

For his cover of *La France* for the issue of April 1920, Hopper looked closer to home for his inspiration (Pl. 335). At Ninety-third Street and Riverside Drive in New York City, he found Anna Hyatt Huntington's bronze equestrian sculpture *Joan of Arc* which was placed there in 1915 and won the Purple Rosette from the French government (Fig. 25). Hopper's choice to utilize this work by one of his contemporaries might indicate his respect for the award that Huntington (who was only six years his senior) won from the French government while he was still a struggling illustrator, as well as his own previous notice of Joan of Arc. While living in Paris in 1909, Hopper had written to his mother: "All

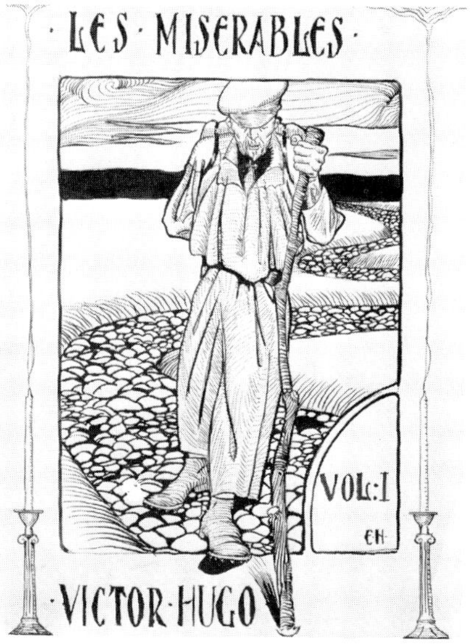

Pl. 436. Edward Hopper, unpublished illustration for Victor Hugo's *Les Misérables,* c. 1900–09. Pencil on paper, 8 × 5¾ inches. Whitney Museum of American Art, New York; Bequest of Josephine N. Hopper 70.1565.74.

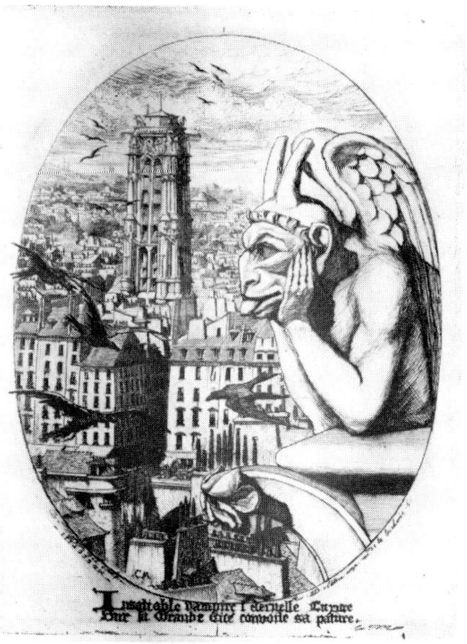

Fig. 23. Charles Meryon, *Le Stryge* (*The Vampire*), 1853. Etching, 6⅝ × 5 inches. Yale University Art Gallery, New Haven, Connecticut.

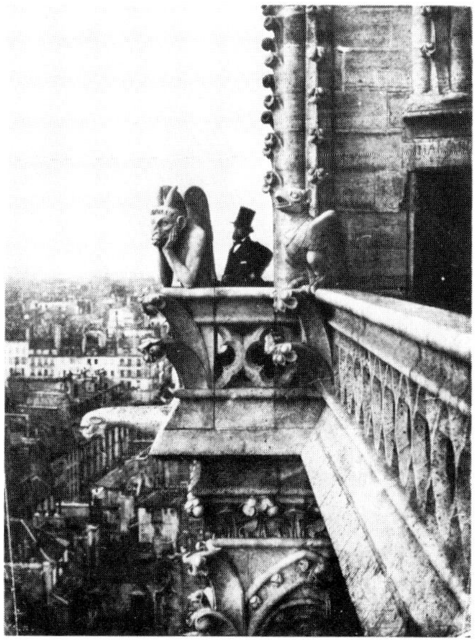

Fig. 24. Charles Nègre, *Henri Le Secq at Notre-Dame,* 1851. Photograph, 13⅛ × 9¼ inches. The Metropolitan Museum of Art, New York.

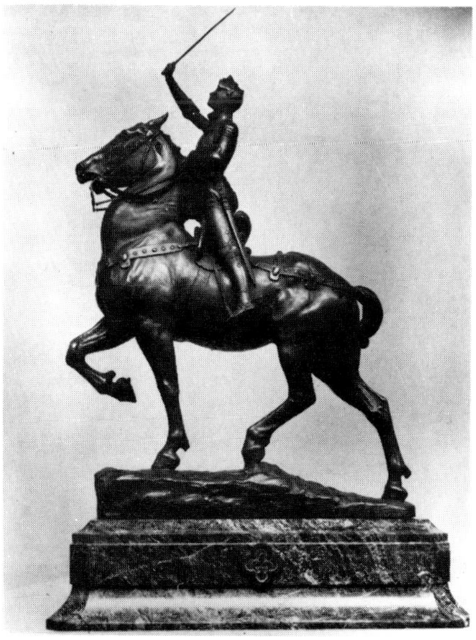

Fig. 25. Anna Hyatt Huntington, *Joan of Arc,* 1915. A version of the bronze statue at Riverside Drive at Ninety-third Street, New York.

Paris is decorated in honor of Jeanne d'Arc as she has recently been canonized in Rome." [53] About this time he produced his own illustration of Jeanne d'Arc, which was probably never published (Pl. 449).

Hopper produced a number of magazine covers and other illustrations with restaurant and theater scenes, subjects popular with both the French impressionists and his American contemporaries, particularly Glackens, Shinn, and Sloan. His illustrations for *Tavern Topics,* a magazine given away to visitors in hotels in New York and Philadelphia, featured these themes (Pls. 336, 341). For example, the issue of February 1920 includes a restaurant. This illustration is notably close in its composition to Glackens's illustration for *A Broad Prairie Mating* of August 31, 1912 (Fig. 26; Pl. 336). The similarity of shape and placement of the table and the tilt and checkerboard design of the floor indicate that Hopper may have known the Glackens illustration and learned from it. Yet Hopper's use of light and shadow, even at this early date, is more subtle than that of Glackens. His cover for *Tavern Topics* of March 1921, depicting a box at the theater, recalls such impressionist paintings as Mary Cassatt's *Woman in Black at the Opera* of 1882 or Renoir's *The Loge* of 1874 (Figs. 27, 28; Pl. 341).

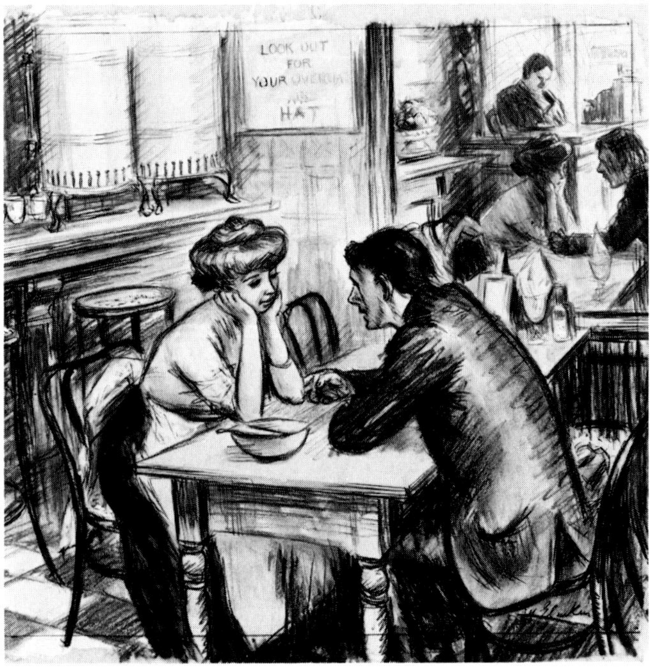

Fig. 26. William Glackens, illustration for *A Broad Prairie Mating,* August 31, 1912. Chalk, black ink, heightened with white on paper, 11½ × 12¾ inches. Collection of Mr. and Mrs. Ira Glackens.

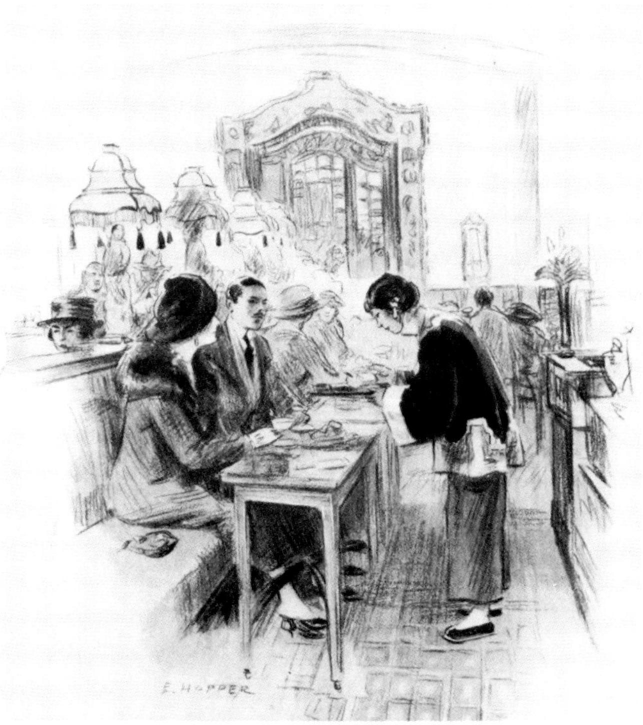

Pl. 336. Edward Hopper, illustration for *Tavern Topics,* February 1920, p. 6.

For the cover of *Tavern Topics* for April 1923, Hopper utilized a photograph as the basis of his design, just as he had for his prize-winning poster *Smash the Hun* (Pl. 342). Included in the issue of *Tavern Topics* for February 1923 was a photograph of Fifth Avenue at Forty-second Street for a feature entitled "Controlling Traffic" (Fig. 29). Hopper seems to have worked from this photograph, although the magazine's editor, Elsie Scott, may have given him another view of this site which was not actually published.

Hopper has borrowed many of the photograph's architectural forms for his cover including the traffic control tower featured in the center and several church towers on the right side. He depicted a city bus with passengers visible on the open top deck and a policeman gesturing in the composition's foreground. While both the bus and policeman are present in other views in the published photograph, Hopper appears to have invented his own versions for his cover.

The only sales records of Hopper's illustrations to turn up so far are those for *Scribner's,* where Hopper sold his drawings in 1918–25. These records, now in the Brandywine Museum in Chadds Ford, Pennsylvania, provide a picture of the variable time gaps between the sale of an illustration and its actual publication. For example, Hopper sold his first two drawings to *Scribner's* on September 27, 1918, and they were published the following December for Henry Van Dyke's story "The Hearing Ear" (Pls. 307, 308). However, his final sale to *Scribner's* of three drawings was on September 29, 1925, and these were not published until the issue of February 1927, making them the last of his illustrations to appear in print (Pls. 331, 332, 333). He received a total of $100 for his first two drawings sold to *Scribner's* and $175 for each of the articles that followed. The originals were returned to him.

Joseph Hawley Chapin, *Scribner's* art editor who commissioned illustrations from Hopper, was by all accounts an exceptionally likable and accessible editor. In his memoirs, Chapin noted his own openness to new work:

> It was my aim to maintain a sympathetic attitude toward the artist and especially toward the beginner, hoping to at least make a friend for the house even if we failed to do business together. For years I made a practice of seeing all callers, because one never knew when one might find in a portfolio the makings of a future celebrity.[54]

Thus Chapin, who published the work of Howard Pyle and his students such as N. C. Wyeth and Maxfield Parrish, also managed to publish the last illustrations by Hopper, who had been recommended to

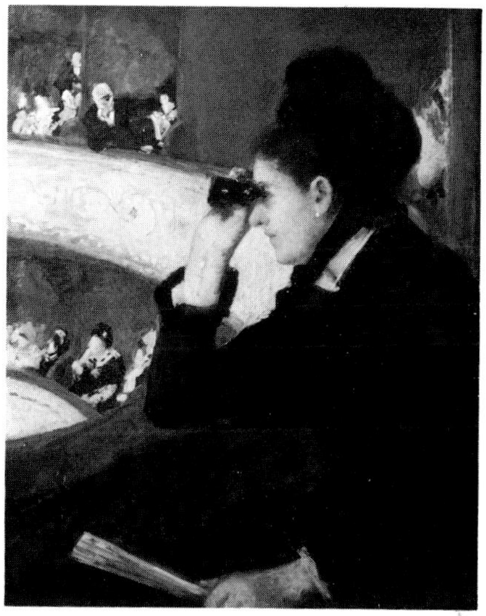

Fig. 27. Mary Cassatt, *Women in Black at the Opera,* 1880. Oil on canvas, 32 × 26 inches. Museum of Fine Arts, Boston; Charles Henry Hayden Fund.

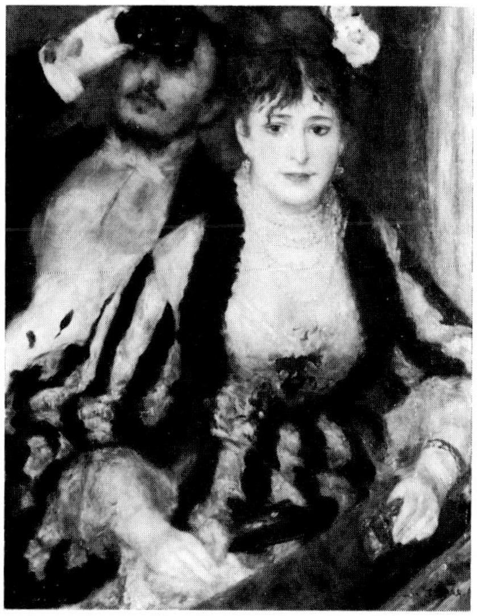

Fig. 28. Pierre Auguste Renoir, *The Loge,* 1874. Oil on canvas, 31½ × 25 inches. Courtauld Institute Galleries, London.

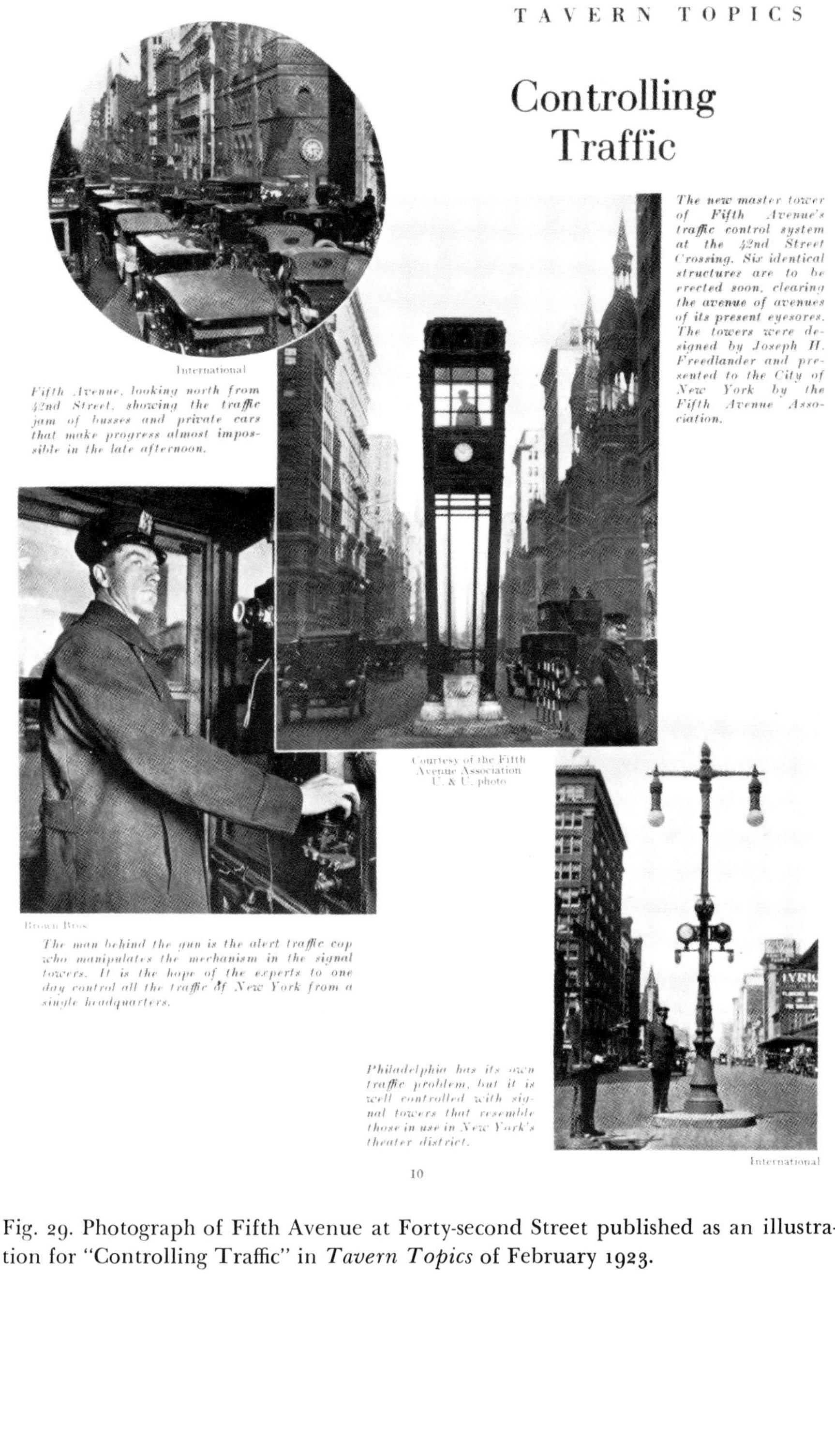

TAVERN TOPICS

Controlling Traffic

International

Fifth Avenue, looking north from 42nd Street, showing the traffic jam of busses and private cars that make progress almost impossible in the late afternoon.

The new master tower of Fifth Avenue's traffic control system at the 42nd Street Crossing. Six identical structures are to be erected soon, clearing the avenue of avenues of its present eyesores. The towers were designed by Joseph H. Freedlander and presented to the City of New York by the Fifth Avenue Association.

Courtesy of the Fifth Avenue Association
U. & U. photo

Brown Bros

The man behind the gun is the alert traffic cop who manipulates the mechanism in the signal towers. It is the hope of the experts to one day control all the traffic of New York from a single headquarters.

Philadelphia has its own traffic problem, but it is well controlled with signal towers that resemble those in use in New York's theater district.

International

10

Fig. 29. Photograph of Fifth Avenue at Forty-second Street published as an illustration for "Controlling Traffic" in *Tavern Topics* of February 1923.

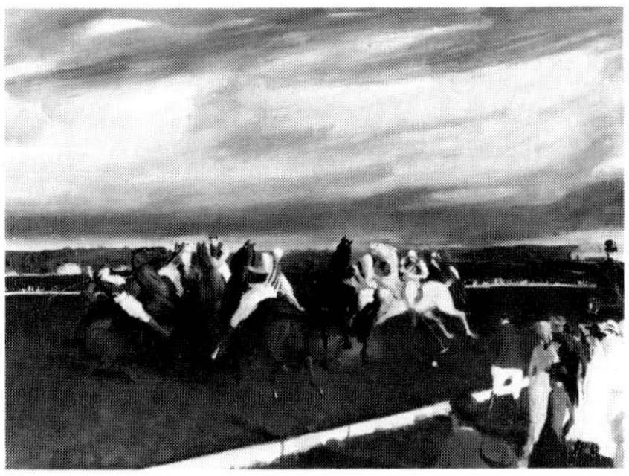

Fig. 30. George Bellows, *Polo at Lakewood,* 1910. Oil on canvas, 45 × 63 inches. The Columbus Gallery of Fine Arts, Columbus, Ohio.

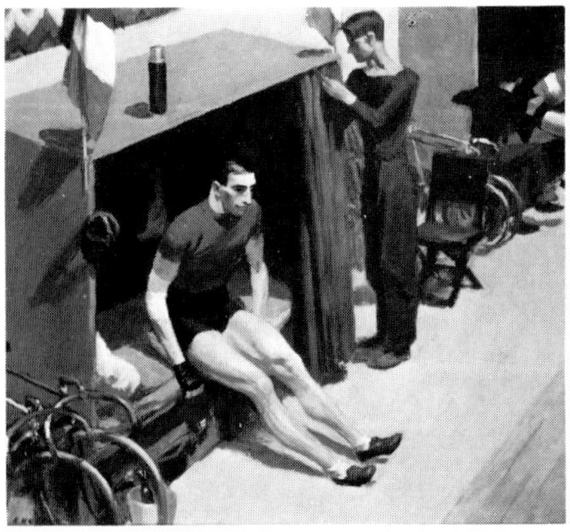

Fig. 31. Edward Hopper, *French Six-Day Bicycle Rider,* 1937. Oil on canvas, 19½ × 17½ inches. Collection of Mr. and Mrs. Albert Hackett.

him by Walter Tittle. On the threshold of his success as a painter, Hopper sold work to Chapin as late as 1925, evidently encouraged by the editor's fairness and forthright manner.[55]

During the years Hopper illustrated for *Scribner's* the magazine became increasingly interested in realistic fiction, the genre of story most appropriate to his style. Contemporary American writers who could deal with reality were most appealing to Hopper. Nonetheless, his own assignments at *Scribner's* still required that he capture many overly dramatic situations (Pls. 327, 330).

Hopper's choices of subject matter for the covers in the series he produced during 1924 and 1925 for *Hotel Management,* a trade magazine, are consistent with his earlier fascination with impressionism. All of these covers show scenes the impressionists favored: people at leisure out-of-doors. Similar themes were also popular in the work of other American artists whom Hopper knew. For example, his cover for *Hotel Management* for October 1924 depicted polo players, recalling the painting *Polo at Lakewood* of 1910 by George Bellows who had been Hopper's classmate under Henri (Fig. 30; Pl. 347).

One of the themes peculiar to Hopper's illustrations is the depiction of athletic activity seen particularly on the covers he designed for *Hotel Management.* Although some of his later paintings included athletic scenes, he rarely again dealt with such vigorous motion. In Hopper's *French Six-Day Bicycle Rider* of 1937, he chose to show the rider at rest (Fig. 31). His various sailing pictures seem rather static. While his covers of *Hotel Management* for October 1924 and April 1925 successfully present equestrian subjects in motion, by contrast the three horses in *Bridle Path,* his painting of 1939, appear rather frozen and the proportions distorted (Fig. 32; Pls. 347, 353). Perhaps at the insistence of his editor, Hopper repeatedly chose uncharacteristic action themes for these *Hotel Management* illustrations. We can only speculate that he may have looked to the work of various artists such as Sloan, Bellows, and Renoir for inspiration in an endeavor to produce a series of covers with subjects which were alien to his sensibilities.

By this time he was already painting watercolors which he began to sell in 1924, making illustration seem increasingly irrelevant. The colors he employed for these covers are surprisingly bright, yet compatible with the open-air themes. Their linear style is probably also influenced by contemporary art deco poster design.

For his delightful cover of *Hotel Management* for June 1925, Hopper may have recalled Renoir's *The Luncheon of the Boating Party* of 1881 (Fig. 33; Pl. 355). Like Renoir, Hopper chose a festive outdoor scene with relaxed men and women eating and drinking. His renewed inter-

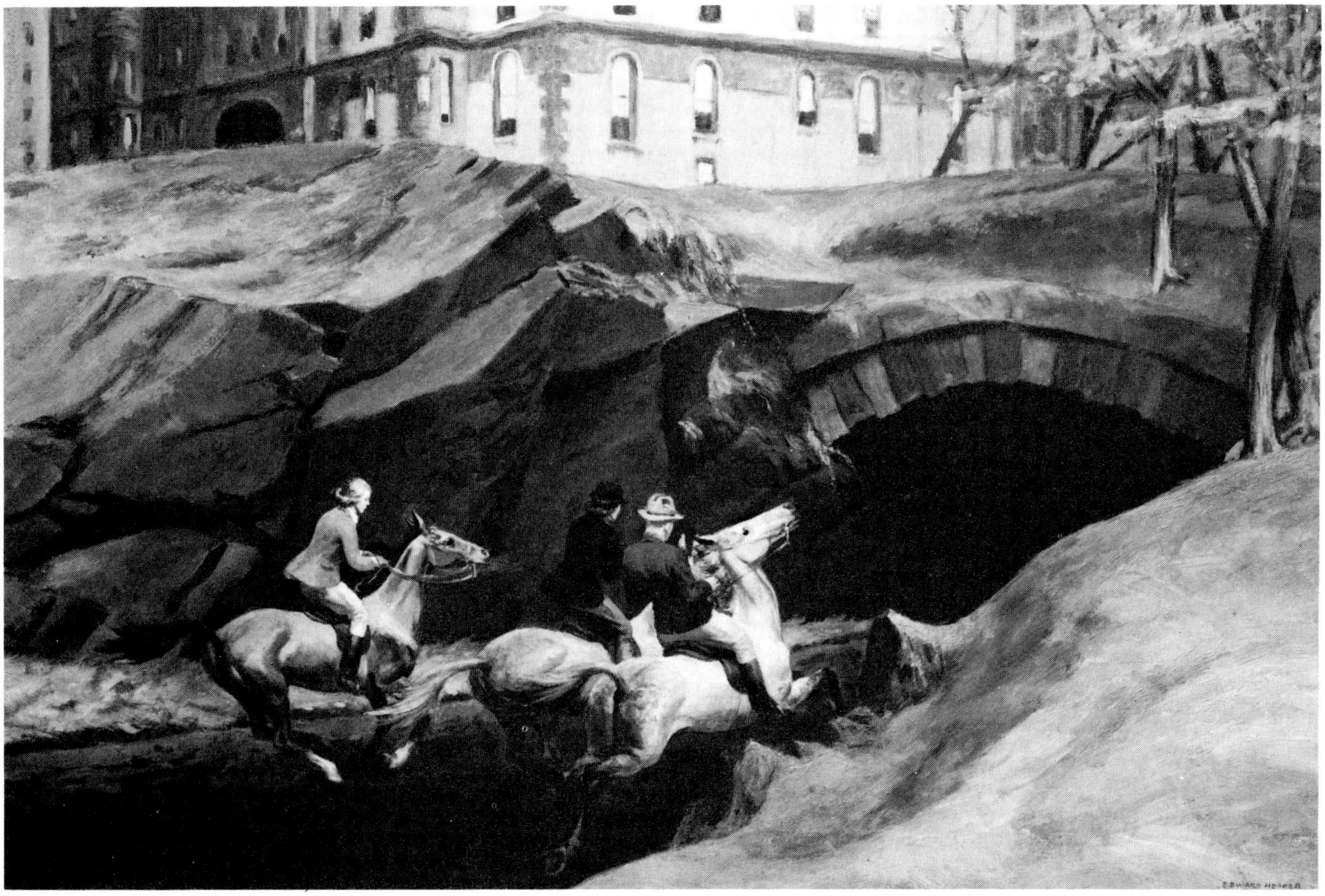

Fig. 32. Edward Hopper, *Bridle Path,* 1939. Oil on canvas, 28 × 42 inches. The San Francisco Museum of Modern Art.

est in Renoir, whose work he had known in Paris, may have been sparked by a visit to the exhibition of the artist's work at the Durand-Ruel Galleries in New York in 1922 and by the subsequent attention paid to Renoir in local art publications.[56] Renoir's masterpiece, *The Luncheon of the Boating Party* of 1881, was featured in this exhibition and several articles reproducing the painting followed.[57] The organization of Hopper's composition is close to Renoir's receding diagonal axis which extends from the lower left corner into the middle ground of the picture space. This diagonal line is marked by the placement of two poles supporting the gaily striped scalloped awning in both Renoir and Hopper. In both compositions the tables are tilted outward and the spectator views the scene from above. In the design of his composition and in the sunny theme itself, Hopper's illustration is reminiscent of Renoir.

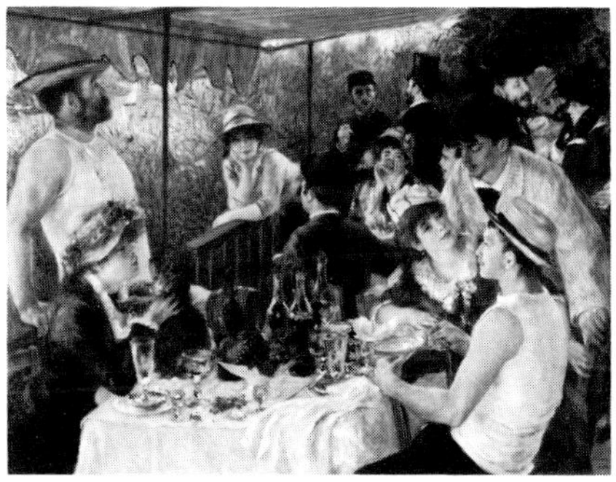

Fig. 33. Pierre Auguste Renoir, *Luncheon of the Boating Party,* 1881. Oil on canvas, 51 × 68 inches. The Phillips Collection, Washington, D.C.

Hopper's cover for *Hotel Management* of July 1925, featuring a woman playing tennis, appears remarkably similar in its theme and composition to Sloan's illustration *On the Court at Wissahickon Heights* for the *Philadelphia Inquirer* of February 12, 1892 (Fig. 34; Pl. 356). Certainly Hopper was familiar with some newspaper illustrations from his own illustration classes and from later years after he had become well acquainted with Sloan. The overall angle of vision is quite close, as is the profile and back view of the woman playing tennis. Hopper's illustration is in color while Sloan's was done in black ink for linecut reproduction. Even so, Hopper's is notably flat, like Sloan's design emphasizing the outline contours of people and scenery. As in Sloan's illustration, the crowd of spectators stretches in a near-horizontal band across Hopper's entire composition and is topped on the right side by curving horizontal lines indicating the surrounding foliage. Hopper enlarged the female player in the foreground and minimized the importance of her male partner and the couple competing on the opposite side of the court. In Sloan's illustration the game is singles, but the opponent is also shown small, emphasizing the elegant form of the player in the foreground.

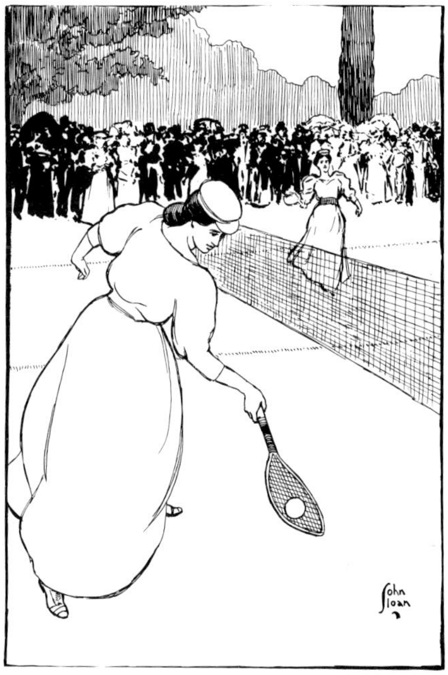

Fig. 34. John Sloan, *On the Court at Wissahickon Heights,* illustration for the *Philadelphia Inquirer,* February 12, 1892. John Sloan Trust, Delaware Art Museum, Wilmington.

Sloan's ability, like Degas's, to convey the graceful dynamism of athletic activity may well have served as inspiration for Hopper when he designed his *Hotel Management* illustrations. Although Sloan was adept at a flat, patterned poster style influenced by Japanese prints and art nouveau which was far from Hopper's overriding concern with three-dimensionality, his work may have provided general clues for the simplification necessary for Hopper to produce such direct and emphatic covers. One can compare, for example, Sloan's illustration for both a poster and book cover for William Lindsey's *Cinder-Path Tales* of 1896 with Hopper's cover for *Hotel Management* of August 1925 (Fig. 35; Pl. 357). Sloan showed a running male athlete, arms extended, leaping a hurdle with lyrical ease. Hopper depicted in a similar linear fashion a male and female bather, arms extended, gracefully running into the sea. Hopper's angle of vision is straight ahead rather than Sloan's off-center approach. Hopper simplified and flattened his design but never to the extent of Sloan's decorative manipulations. Yet less than two years later, Hopper expressed in writing his deep admiration for Sloan:

> Sloan is one of t ose rarely fortunate artists who distort unconsciously and to the point and without obvious process. His is the distortion that looks like truth and not that which looks like distortion. . . . His figures have the unaffected gestures of the human animal when unobserved. The object drawn is seen first before one becomes conscious of its design or the linear structure which holds the various units together. . . . Sloan's design is the simple and unobtrusive tool of his visual reaction. It attempts tenaciously and ever the surprise and unbalance of nature, as did that of Degas.[58]

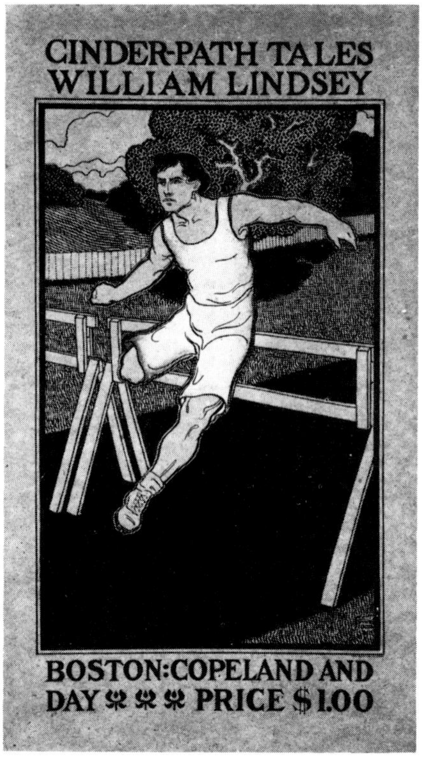

Fig. 35. John Sloan, illustration for poster and book cover of William Lindsey's *Cinder-Path Tales,* 1896. Photomechanical lithograph in black and brown ink on brown paper, 17¼ × 11⅛ inches. John Sloan Trust, Delaware Art Museum, Wilmington.

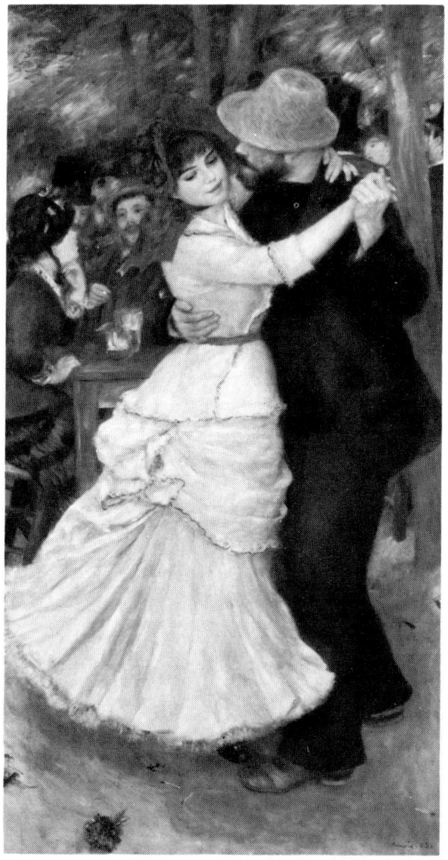

Fig. 36. Pierre Auguste Renoir, *Dance at Bougival,* 1883. Oil on canvas, 70⅞ × 38½ inches. Museum of Fine Arts, Boston.

For his cover design of *Hotel Management* for September 1925, Hopper again may have recalled one of Renoir's impressionist masterpieces (Pl. 358). Renoir's *Dance at Bougival* of 1883 may have inspired Hopper's own version of an elegant outdoor dancing scene (Fig. 36). Like Renoir, Hopper focused his composition on a couple dancing in the central foreground and tilted the ground plane out toward the spectator, again creating the sensation that we view the scene from slightly above. In the middle ground Hopper has repeated Renoir's choice of fashionable people seated at a table drinking and talking. Hopper also placed the feathery foliage of trees at the top of his composition as in Renoir's scene. Yet Hopper's space extends beyond the narrow space of Renoir to achieve a broader, more expansive feeling. Even if inspired by Renoir's paintings, Hopper's sensibility is strikingly different. While Renoir depicts his dancing couple in an intimate, warm relationship, Hopper's couple appears stiff and wooden. The man's legs do not move sensuously to the music as in the Renoir work, but are rather unnatural and unresponsive.

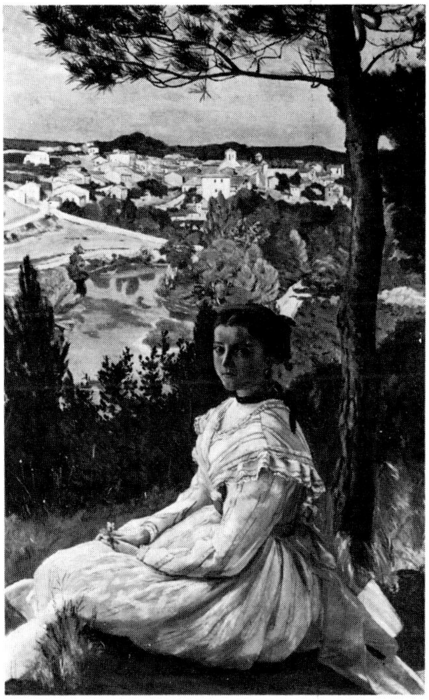

Fig. 37. Frédéric Bazille, *View of the Village,* 1868. Oil on canvas, 52⅛ × 35⅝ inches. Musée Fabre, Montpellier, France.

Hopper's cover of *Hotel Management* for October 1925 represents three figures on a hilltop overlooking a panoramic view of a village or a very large hotel located by a body of water (Pl. 359). It is strikingly reminiscent of another impressionist painting, Frédéric Bazille's *View of the Village* of 1868 (Fig. 37). In Bazille's painting one also sees beyond the figure on the hilltop to the water and the village below. Hopper's composition, like Bazille's, is divided into registers of hilltop, water, village, the land beyond, and the sky. Whether Hopper knew Bazille's picture or not, here his aims and approach are similar to those of the impressionists.

In 1924 Hopper experienced his first financial successes as a painter when in January the Brooklyn Museum purchased one of his watercolors and in November his first exhibition at the Frank K. M. Rehn Gallery sold out. Only three years later, in 1927, his last published illustration appeared in *Scribner's.* That same year in his article on John Sloan, Hopper wrote a passage that applies to himself as well as to Sloan, revealing his attitude toward his own career:

> John Sloan's development has followed the common lot of the painter who through necessity starts his career as a draughtsman and illustrator: first the hard grind and the acquiring of sufficient technical skill to make a living, the work at self-expression in spare time, and finally the complete emancipation from the daily job when recognition comes. This hard early training has given to Sloan a facility and a power of invention that the pure painter seldom achieves.[59]

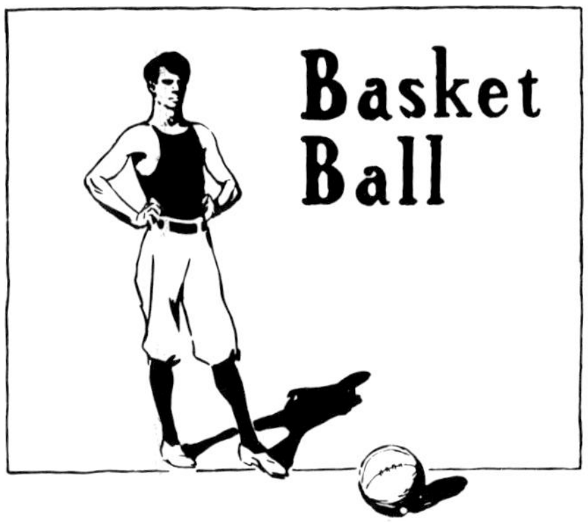

Pl. 386. Edward Hopper, "Basket Ball," c. 1911–12. Proof of illustration, publication unknown. Private collection.

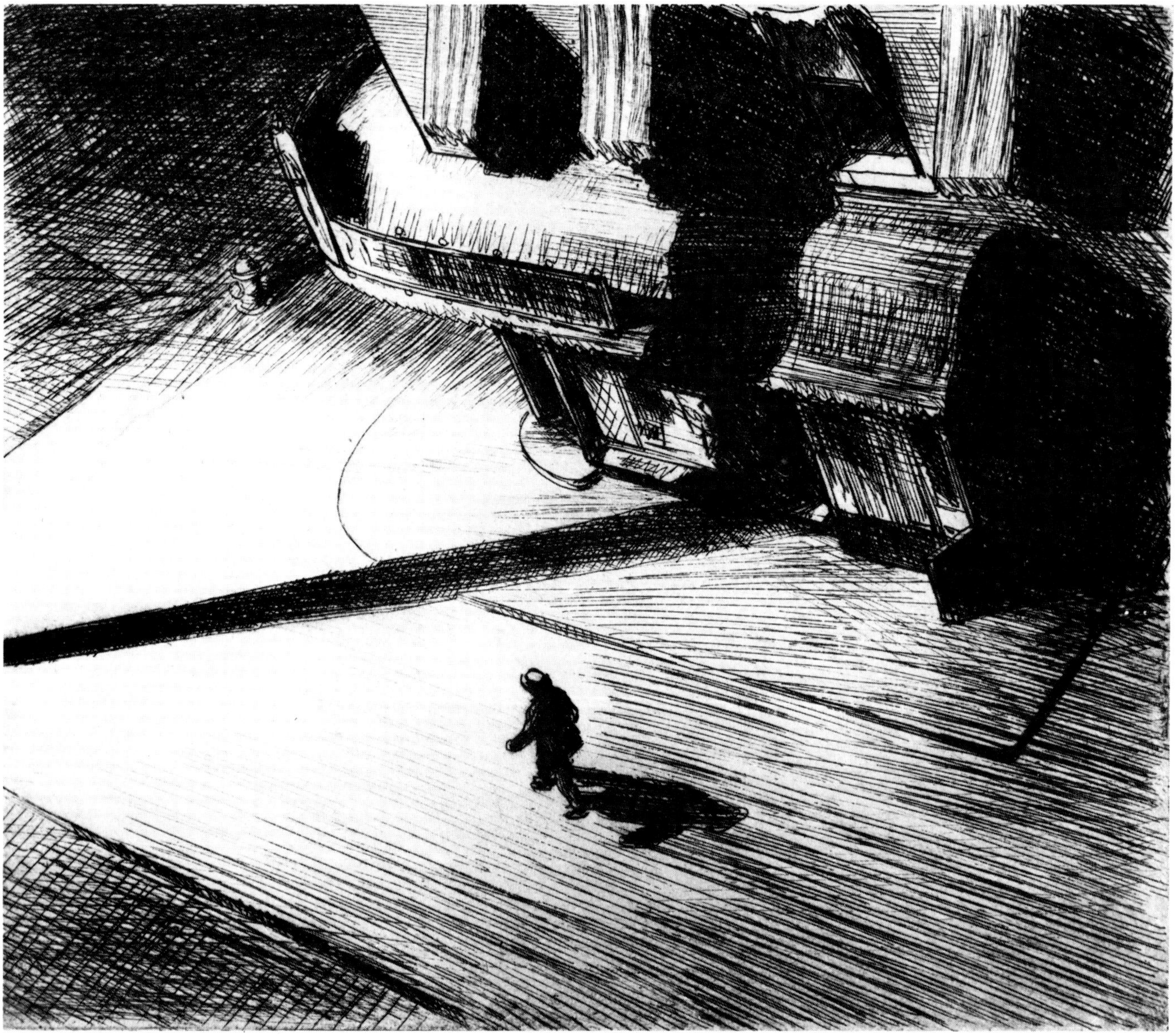

Fig. 38. Edward Hopper, *Night Shadows,* 1921. Etching, 6⅞ × 8¹⁵⁄₁₆ inches. Whitney Museum of American Art, New York; Gift of Gertrude Vanderbilt Whitney 31.691.

ILLUSTRATION AND HOPPER'S MATURE STYLE

In spite of Hopper's negative attitude toward the work, his early experiences as an illustrator undoubtedly exerted some influence on his mature art. During his formative years as an artist he was necessarily preoccupied with illustration. The relationship of both his later subject matter and style to his illustration must be examined and defined in order to establish a clear picture of Hopper's development as an artist.

Since his career as an illustrator coincides with and encompasses the years he devoted to making etchings, it is necessary to consider what relationships there are between the two. Certainly there are common motifs and subjects. Several themes occur first in Hopper's illustrations and later in an etching. For example, Hopper's yearbook illustration "Basket Ball" deals with the issue of the obvious shadow which becomes the focus of his etching *Night Shadows* of 1921 (Fig. 38; Pl. 386). In all probability Hopper produced this undated illustration around 1912, preceding the etching by nearly a decade.

One of his illustrations for a story entitled "A Fresh Start," which appeared in the January 1914 issue of *Everybody's,* depicts a solitary man by deserted park benches, a theme refined to poignancy in Hopper's etching of 1921 *Night in the Park* (Fig. 39; Pl. 7). Other illustrations such as that from *Associated Sunday Magazine* of November 16, 1913, and *Farmer's Wife* of December 1917 represented the interior of a train, a theme which Hopper developed in his etching *Night on the El Train* of 1920 and in *House Tops* of 1921 which depict elevated trains in New York City (Figs. 40, 41; Pls. 103, 161). In an illustration for *Associated Sunday Magazine* of May 4, 1913, train tracks cut horizontally across the composition while men walk into its depths (Pl. 93). In Hopper's etching *American Landscape* of 1920, the tracks again cut the composition, but cows now tread where men walked in the illustration (Fig. 42). Several illustrations of trains for the *Wells Fargo Messenger* during 1917 and 1918 precede Hopper's etching *The Locomotive* of 1923, but here drawings done in France during the period 1906–9 are the precedent for both the illustrations and the etching (Figs. 43, 44, 45; Pls. 230, 235).

Perhaps Hopper's most successful etchings were *East Side Interior* of 1922 and *Evening Wind* of 1921; both of these reveal a contemplative woman in an interior setting. Hopper's illustration for *System* magazine of January 1913 had shown the contemplative woman in the domestic interior with a picture on the wall and curtained doorway behind her similar to that in *East Side Interior,* although he presents a

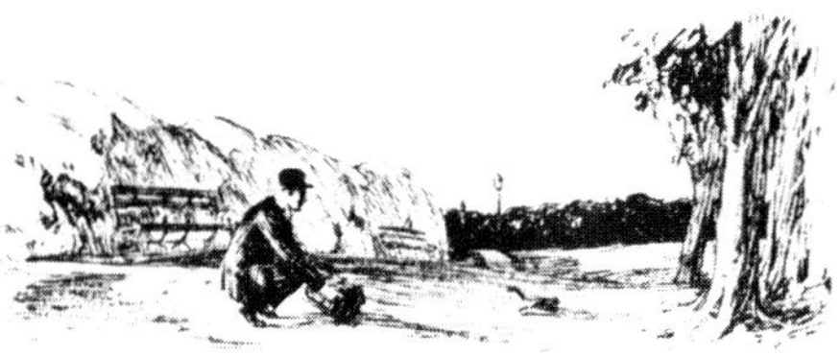

Pl. 7. Edward Hopper, illustration for *Everybody's,* January 1914, p. 102.

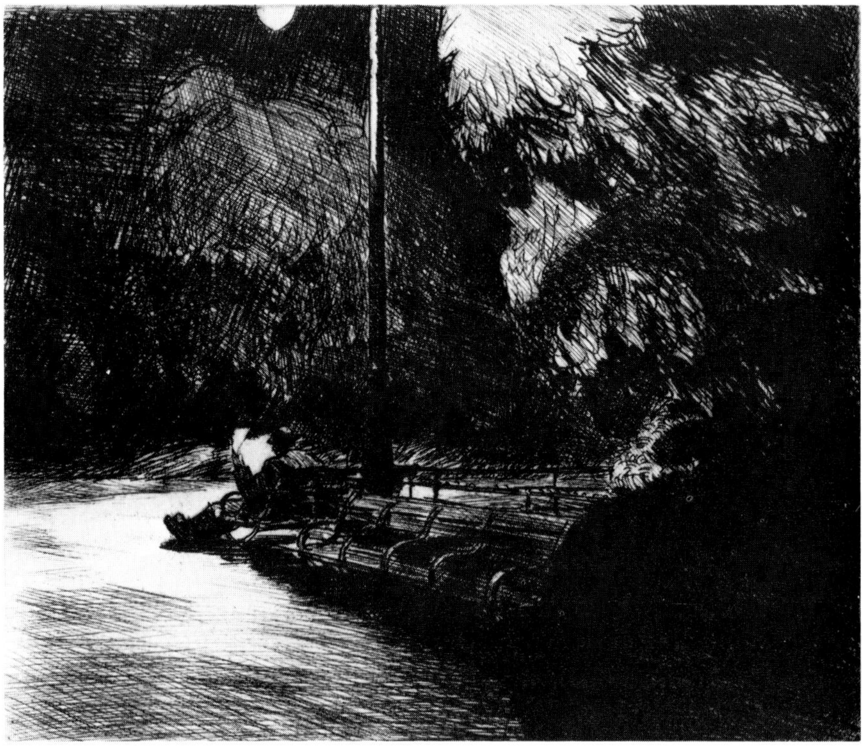

Fig. 39. Edward Hopper, *Night in the Park,* 1921. Etching, 6⅛ × 8¼ inches. Whitney Museum of American Art, New York; Bequest of Josephine N. Hopper 70.1046.

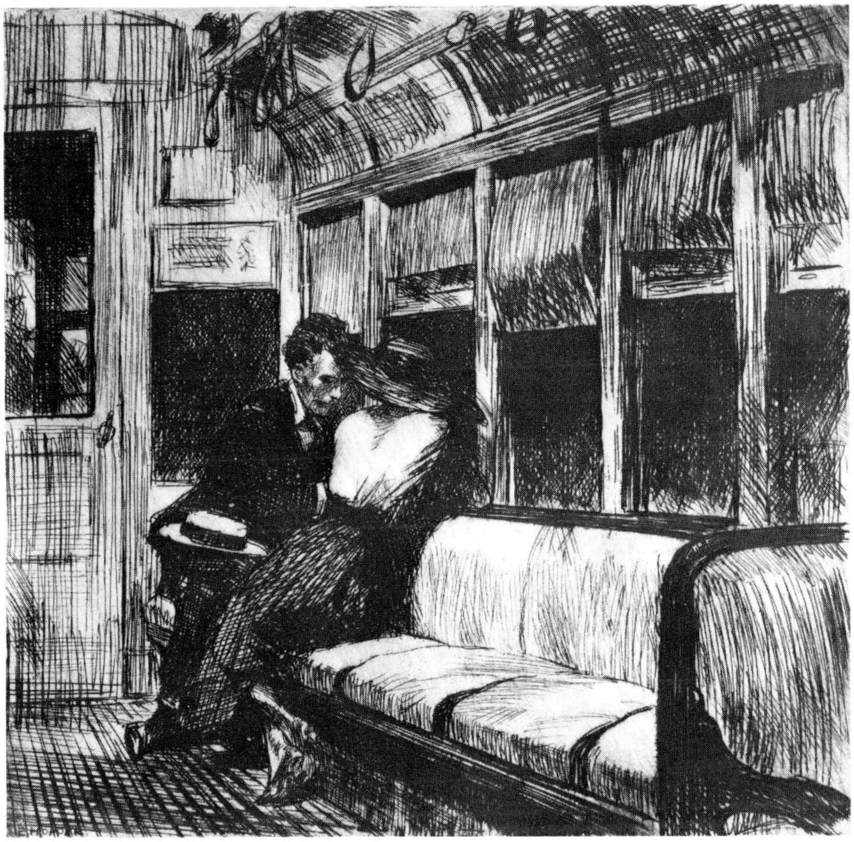

Fig. 40. Edward Hopper, *Night on the El Train,* 1920. Etching, 7½ × 8 inches. Philadelphia Museum of Art; purchased: The Harrison Fund.

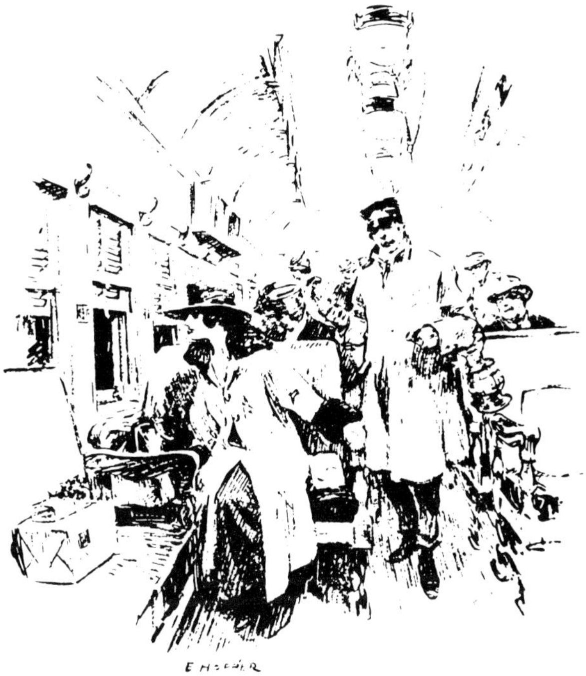

Pl. 161. Edward Hopper, illustration for *Farmer's Wife,* December 1917, p. 151.

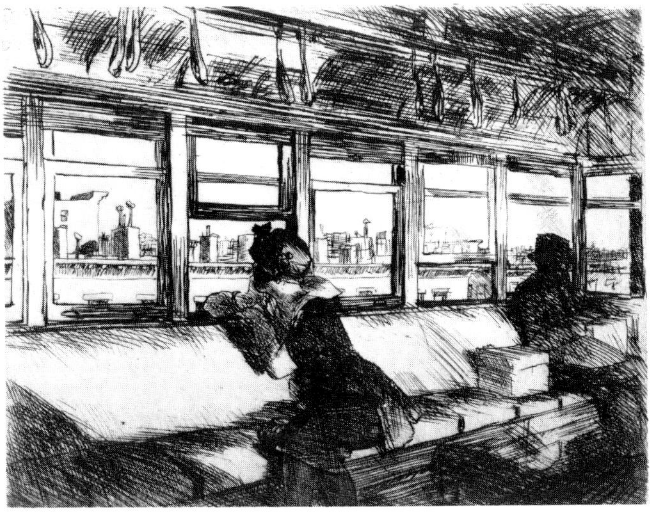

Fig. 41. Edward Hopper, *House Tops,* 1921. Etching, 6 × 8 inches. Philadelphia Museum of Art; purchased: The Harrison Fund.

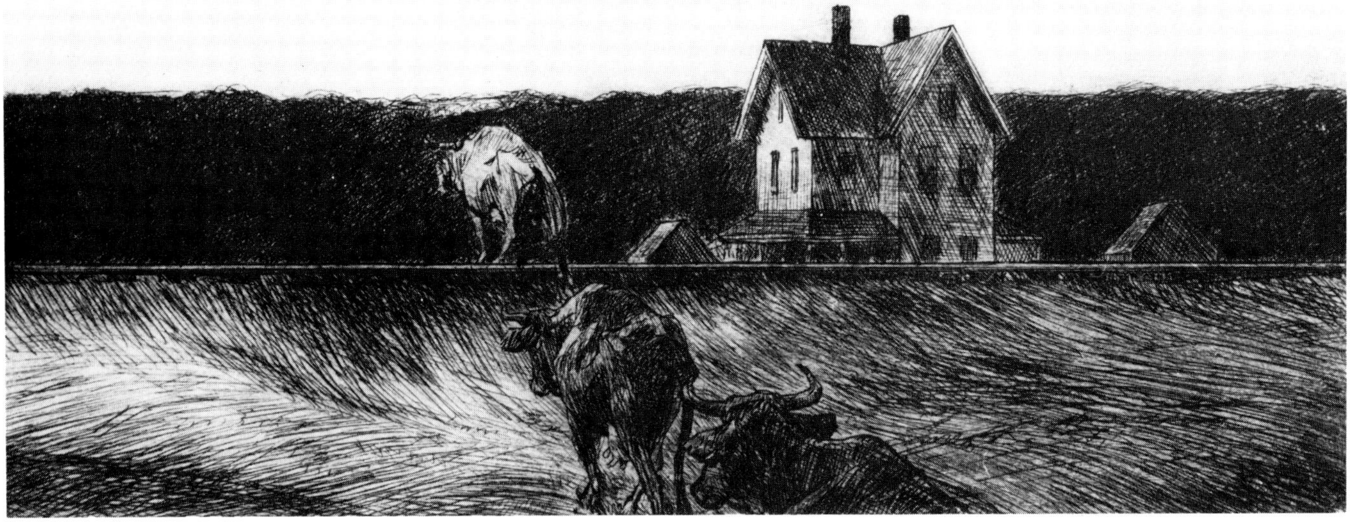

Fig. 42

Fig. 42. Edward Hopper, *American Landscape,* 1920. Etching, 7½ × 12½ inches. Whitney Museum of American Art, New York; Bequest of Josephine N. Hopper 70.1005.

Pl. 93. Edward Hopper, illustration for *Associated Sunday Magazine,* May 4, 1913, p. 10.

Fig. 43. Edward Hopper, *The Locomotive,* 1923. Etching, 7⅞ × 9⅞ inches. Whitney Museum of American Art, New York; Bequest of Josephine N. Hopper 70.1039.

Fig. 44. Edward Hopper, *The Railroad,* 1906/07 or 1909. Conte and wash with touches of white on illustration board. 17¾ × 14⅞ inches. Whitney Museum of American Art, New York; Bequest of Josephine N. Hopper 70.1049.

Fig. 45. Edward Hopper, *People by the Seine,* 1906/07 or 1909. Conte and wash on illustration board, 14½ × 11¾ inches. Whitney Museum of American Art, New York; Bequest of Josephine N. Hopper 70.1339.

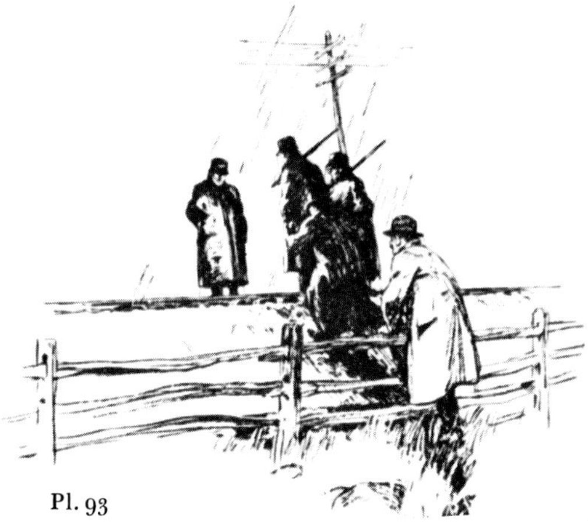

Pl. 93

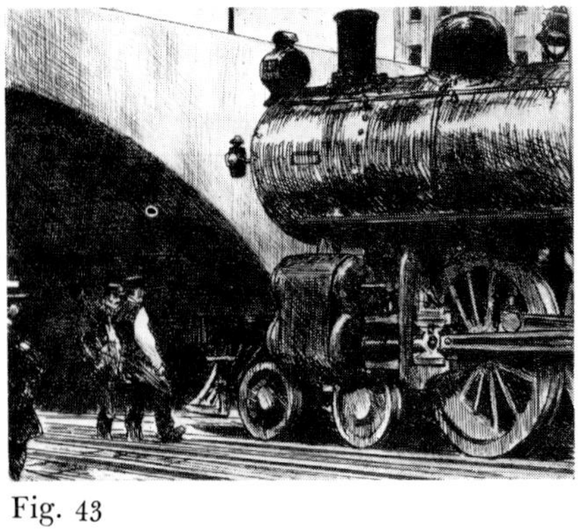

Fig. 43

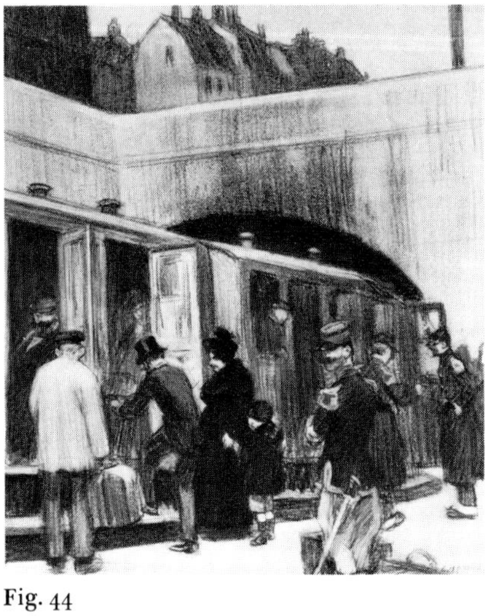

Fig. 44

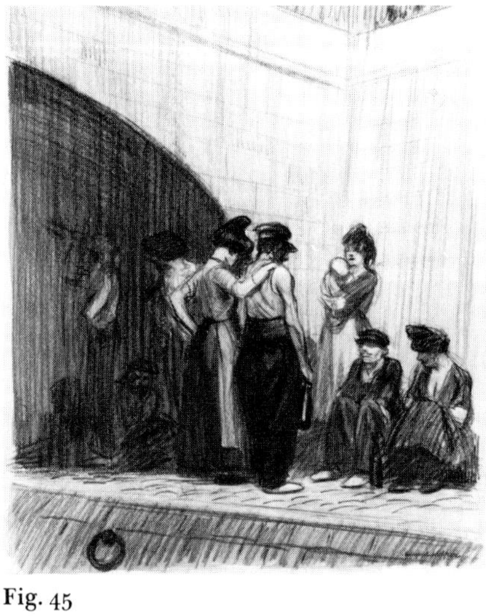

Fig. 45

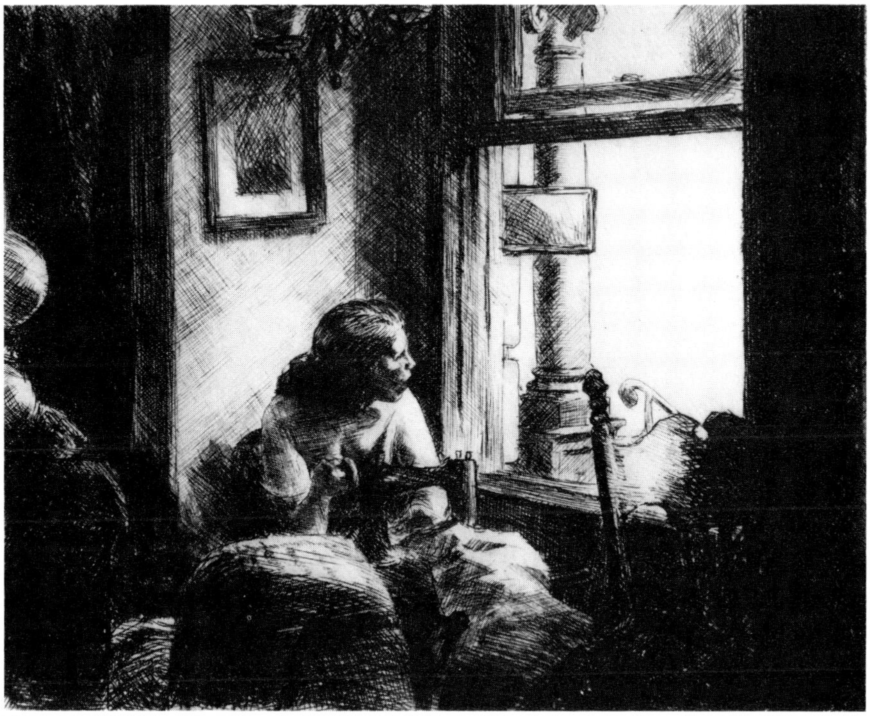

Fig. 46

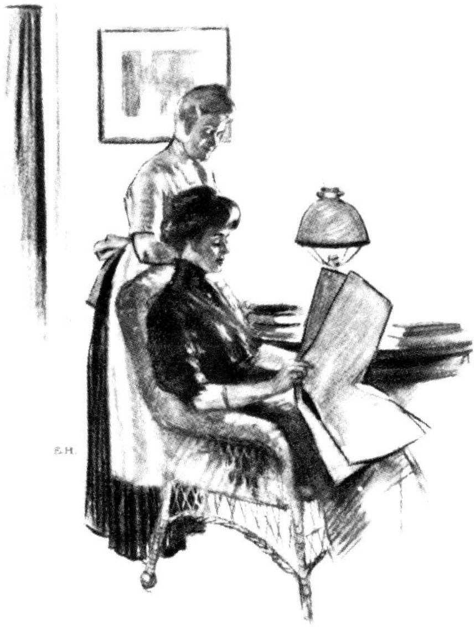

Pl. 50

Fig. 46. Edward Hopper, *East Side Interior,* 1922. Etching, 7⅞ × 9$\frac{13}{16}$ inches. Whitney Museum of American Art, New York; Bequest of Josephine N. Hopper 70.1020.

Pl. 50. Edward Hopper, illustration for *System,* January 1913, p. 18.

Fig. 47. Edward Hopper, *Evening Wind,* 1921. Etching, 6⅞ × 8¼ inches. Whitney Museum of American Art, New York; Bequest of Josephine N. Hopper 70.1022.

Pl. 18. Edward Hopper, illustration for *Everybody's,* September 1921, p. 5.

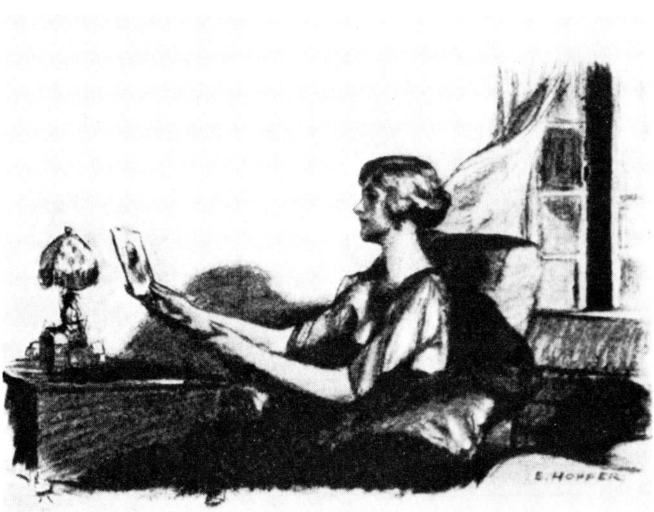

Pl. 18

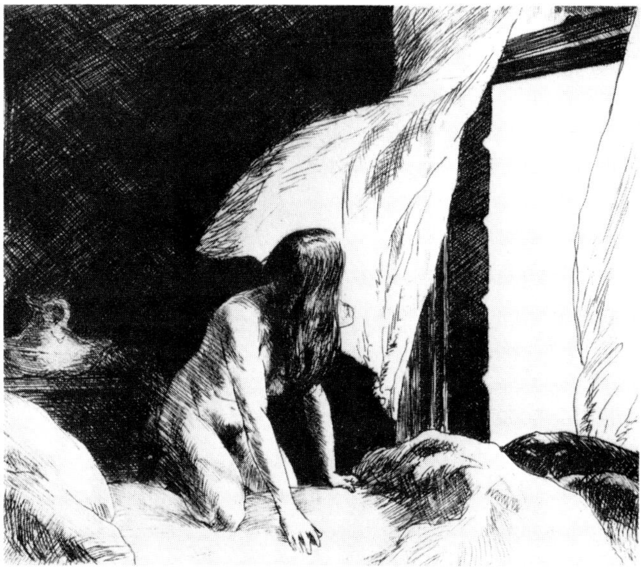

Fig. 47

very different social class and mood (Fig. 46; Pl. 50). In September 1921, for an article in *Everybody's,* Hopper portrayed a woman before an open window with the curtains blowing in the breeze, an environment similar to that in his etching *Evening Wind* of the same year (Fig. 47; Pl. 18). It is impossible to tell whether Hopper first produced the etching or the illustration, but the similarity is significant.

Sometimes themes appeared first in an etching and subsequently in an illustration. For example, Hopper etched *The Cat Boat* in 1922, and another sailboat *The Henry Ford* in 1923, while he used the motif of a sailboat for the cover of *Hotel Management* in September 1924 (Figs. 48, 49; Pl. 346). The compositional arrangement of this illustration is quite similar to that in *The Cat Boat.* Again, Hopper's outdoor cafe scene on the cover of *Hotel Management* for June 1925 relates to his etching *Les Deux Pigeons* of 1920 (Fig. 50; Pl. 355). While the sensuality of the couple embracing is now missing, the cafe setting with round tables, folding chairs, and standing waiter looking on is repeated.

But usually it was the illustrations that predicted Hopper's later work, as in the office interiors which evolved from various illustrations he made during the 1910s, particularly for *System* magazine. Theater scenes, focusing mainly on the audience, such as the cover of *Tavern Topics* for March 1921, recur in works such as *Two on the Aisle* of 1927, *New York Movie* of 1939, and *First Row Orchestra* of 1951 (Figs. 51, 52, 53; Pl. 341). Cabaret scenes such as the cover of *Hotel Management* for January 1925 later appear in *Girlie Show* of 1941 and in *Two Comedians* of 1965 (Figs. 54, 55; Pl. 350). Several restaurant themes occur in the illustrations such as that for *Everybody's* of January 1914, *Associated Sunday Magazine* of January 11, 1914, and *Tavern Topics* of February 1920, and again in paintings such as *New York Restaurant* of about 1922, *Automat* of 1927, *Chop Suey* of 1929, *Tables for Ladies* of 1930, and *Sunlight in a Cafeteria* of 1958 (Figs. 56, 57, 58, 59, 60; Pls. 8, 111).

A woman standing in a bedroom before an open window appeared as early as July 1912 as an illustration in *The Metropolitan Magazine,* then in Hopper's etching *Evening Wind* of 1921; this theme is also developed in paintings such as *Moonlight Interior* of about 1920–23, *Morning in a City* of 1944, and *A Woman in the Sun* of 1961 (Figs. 61, 62, 63; Pl. 33). Of course, in his etching and all of these paintings, the female figure is nude, a liberty Hopper could not take in his illustration. It is this lack of freedom in making illustrations that may have cramped Hopper's style and made him resent these endeavors.

The compositions of some of Hopper's best paintings were often pre-

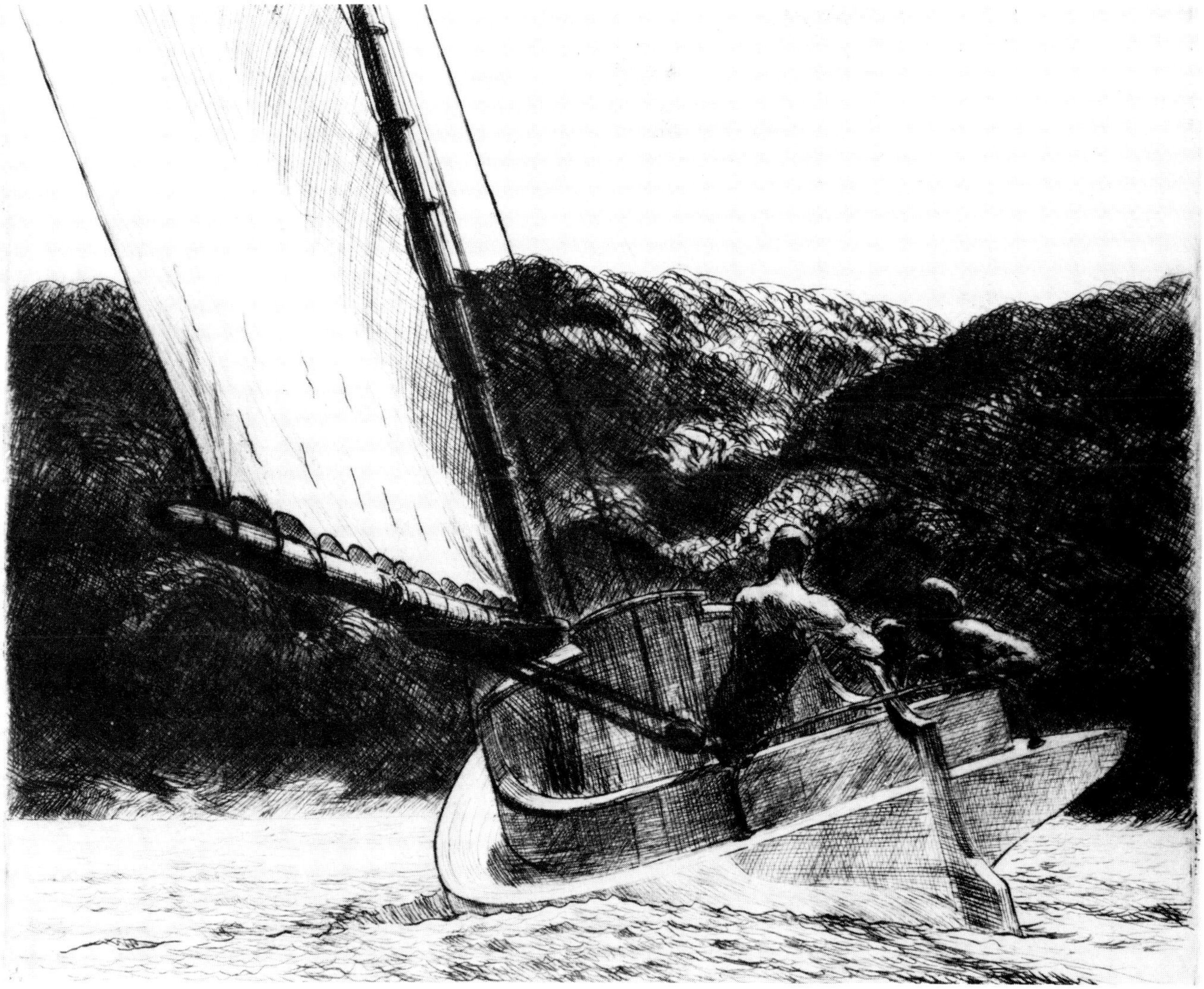

Fig. 48. Edward Hopper, *The Cat Boat,* 1922. Etching, 8 × 10 inches. Whitney Museum of Modern Art, New York; Bequest of Josephine N. Hopper 70.1008.

Fig. 49. Edward Hopper, *The Henry Ford,* 1923. Etching, 12 × 15 inches. The Art Institute of Chicago.

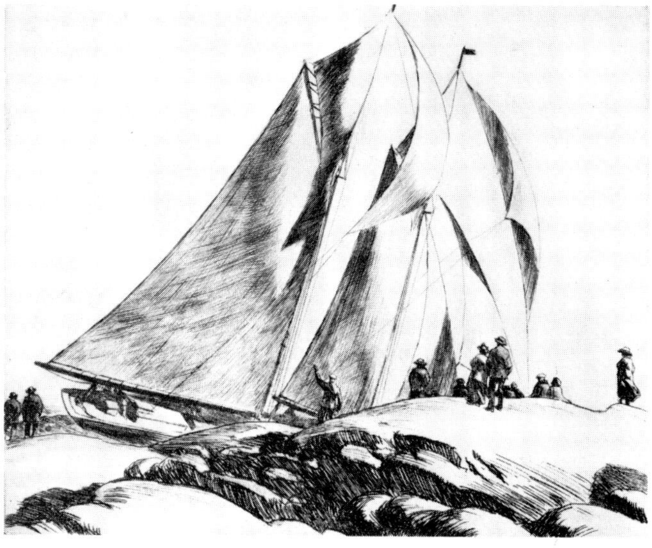

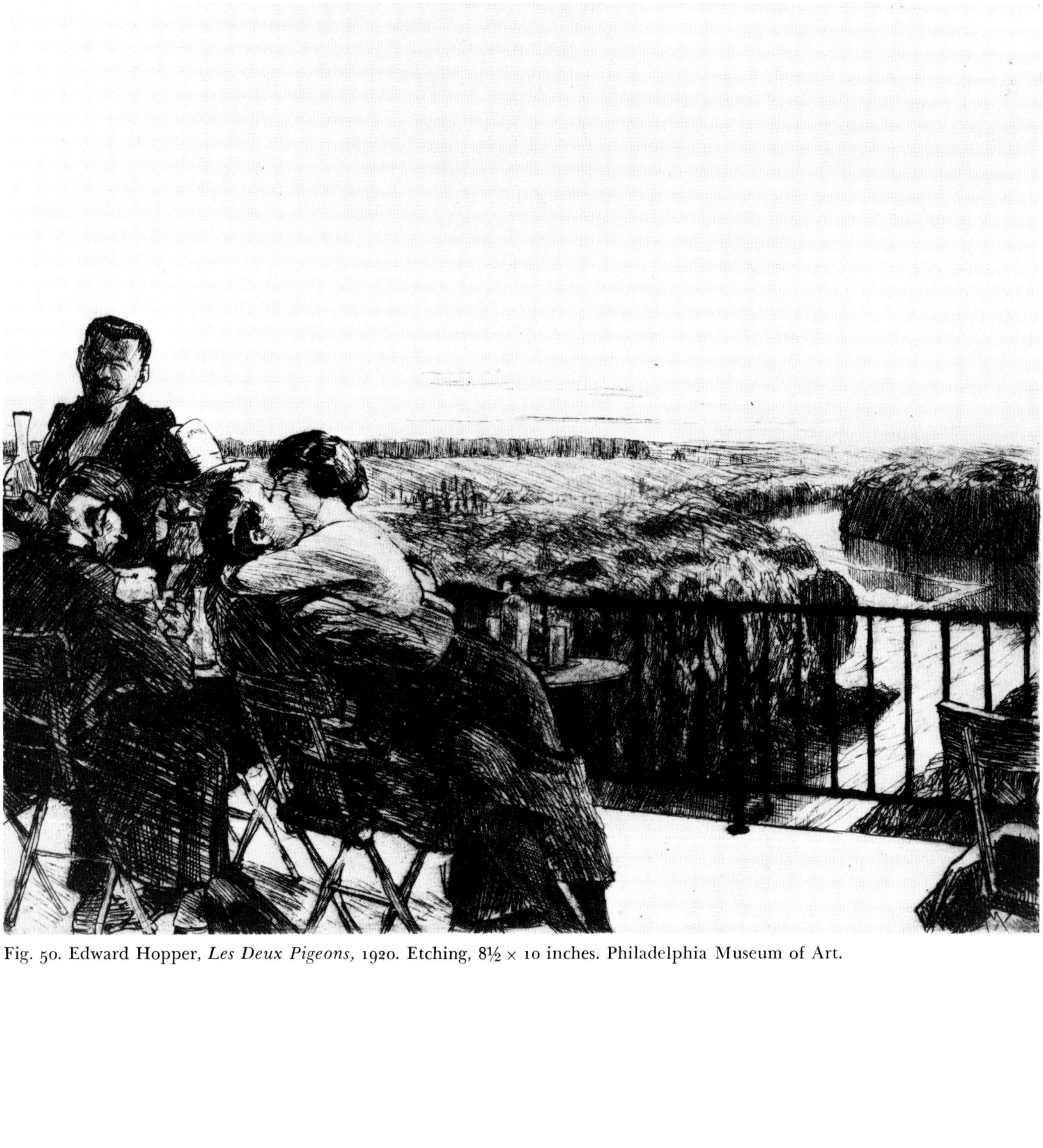

Fig. 50. Edward Hopper, *Les Deux Pigeons,* 1920. Etching, 8½ × 10 inches. Philadelphia Museum of Art.

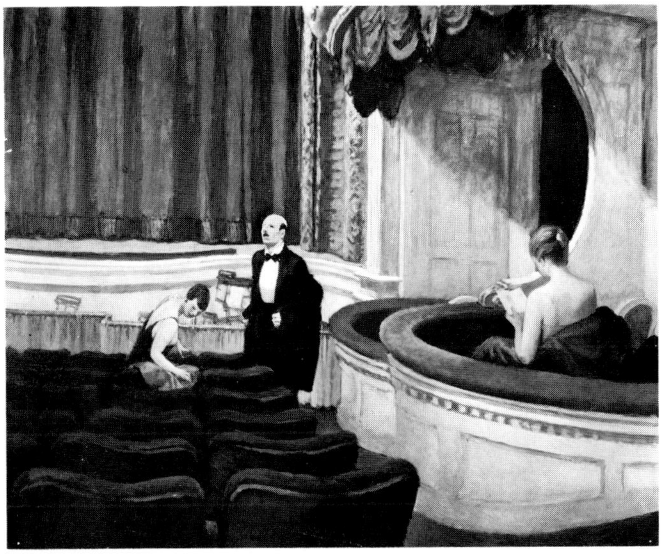

Fig. 51

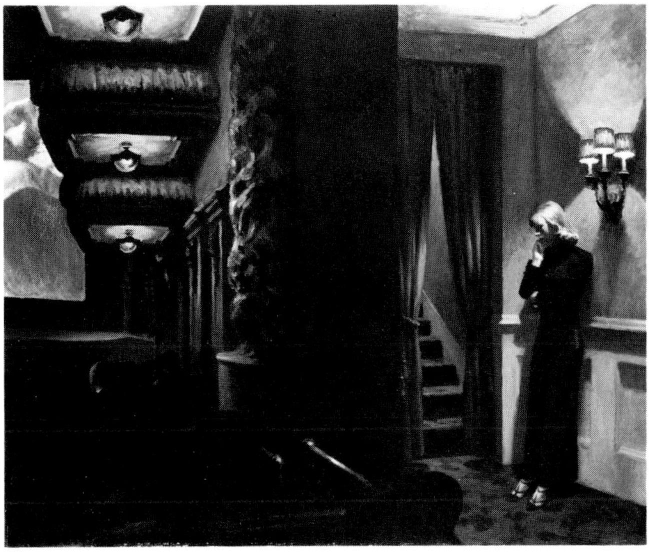

Fig. 52

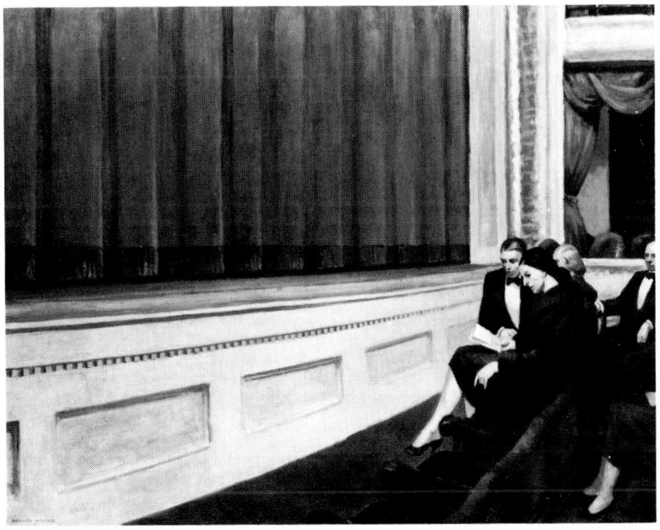

Fig. 53

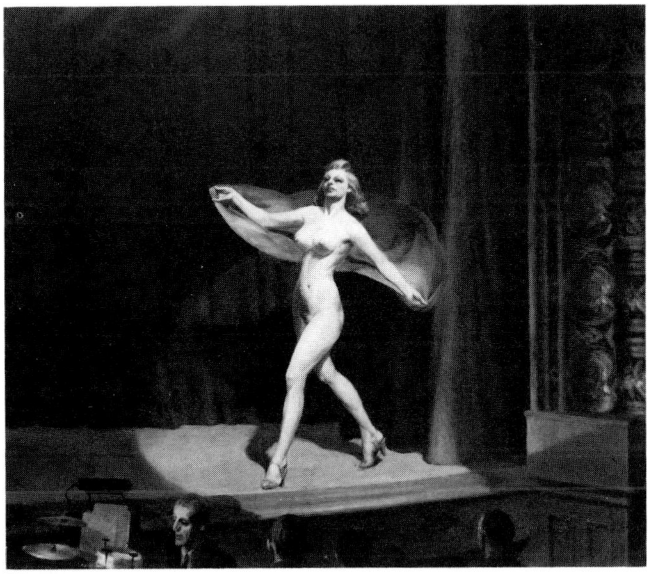

Fig. 54

Fig. 51. Edward Hopper, *Two on the Aisle,* 1927. Oil on canvas, 40¼ × 48¼ inches. The Toledo Museum of Art; Gift of Edward Drummond Libbey.

Fig. 52. Edward Hopper. *New York Movie,* 1939. Oil on canvas, 32¼ × 40⅛ inches. The Museum of Modern Art, New York.

Fig. 53. Edward Hopper, *First Row Orchestra,* 1951. Oil on canvas, 29 × 40 inches. The Hirshhorn Museum and Sculpture Garden, Smithsonian Institution, Washington, D.C.

Fig. 54. Edward Hopper, *Girlie Show,* 1941. Oil on canvas, 31 × 40 inches. Private collection.

Fig. 55. Edward Hopper, *Two Comedians,* 1965. Oil on canvas, 29 × 40 inches. Private collection.

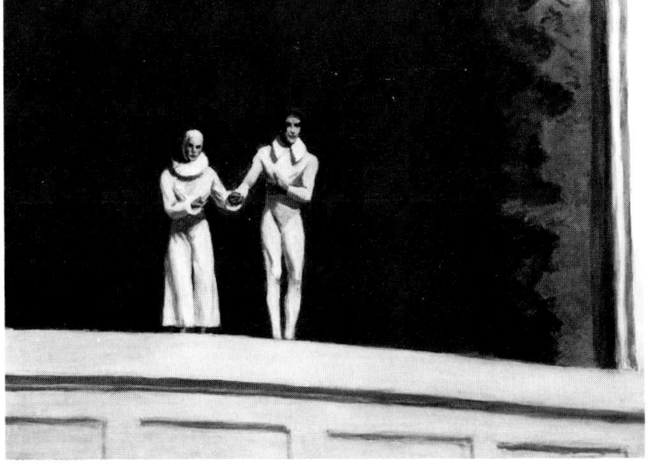

Fig. 55

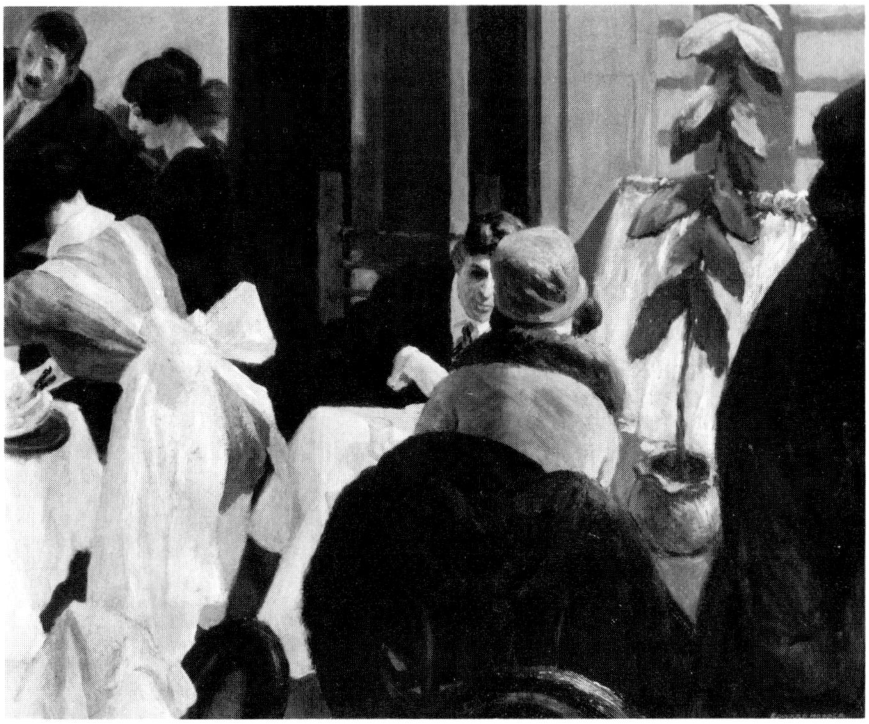

Fig. 56. Edward Hopper, *New York Restaurant,* 1922. Oil on canvas, 29¼ × 24¼ inches. Hackley Art Museum, Muskegon, Michigan.

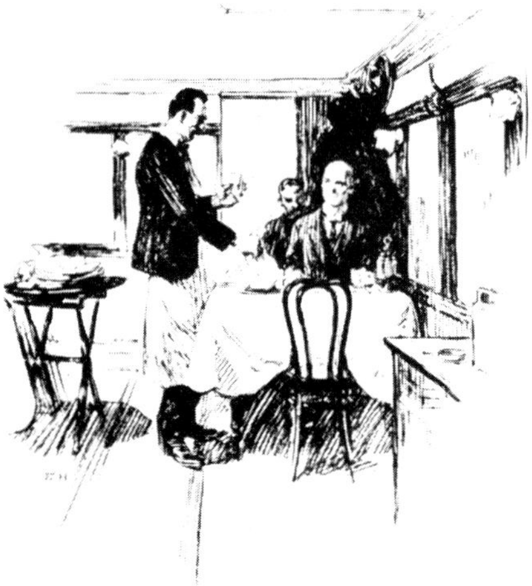

Pl. 8. Edward Hopper, illustration for *Everybody's,* January 1914, p. 103.

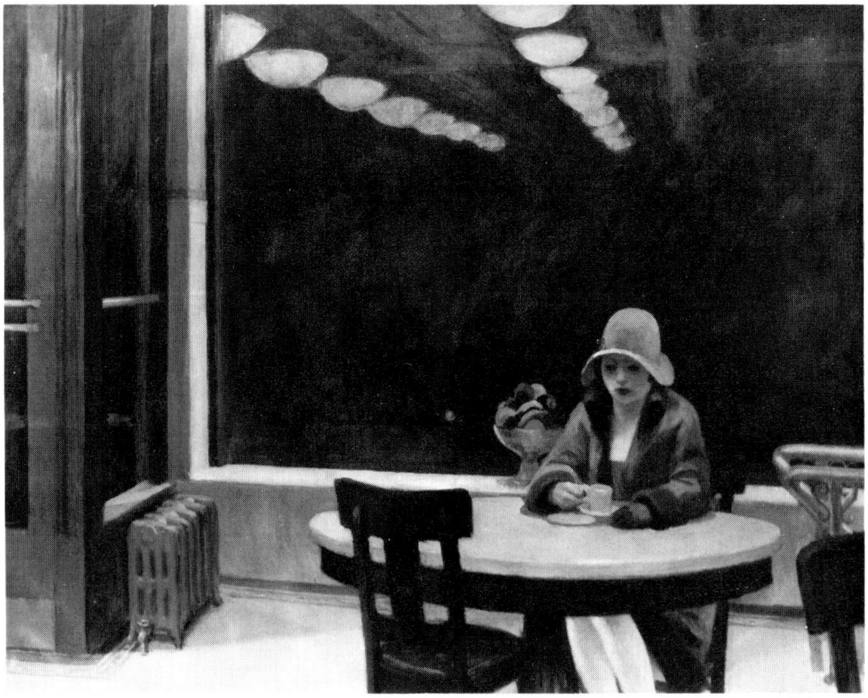

Fig. 57. Edward Hopper, *Automat,* 1927. Oil on canvas, 28 × 36 inches. Des Moines Art Center; Edmundson Collection.

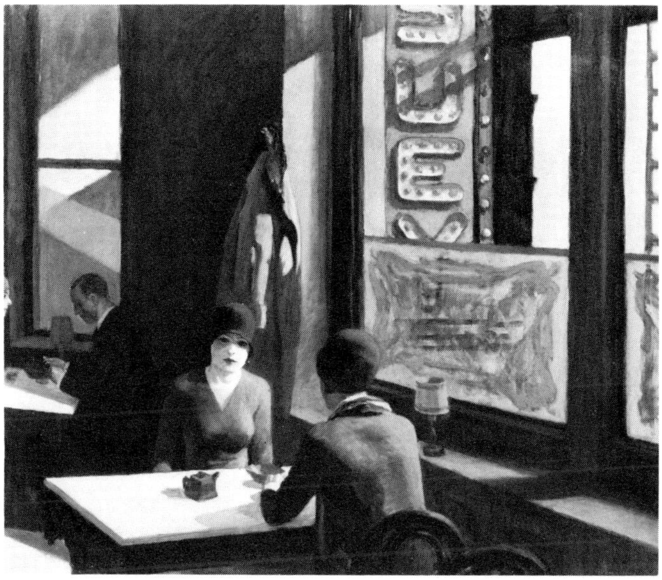

Fig. 58. Edward Hopper, *Chop Suey,* 1929. Oil on canvas, 32 × 38 inches. Collection of Barney Ebsworth.

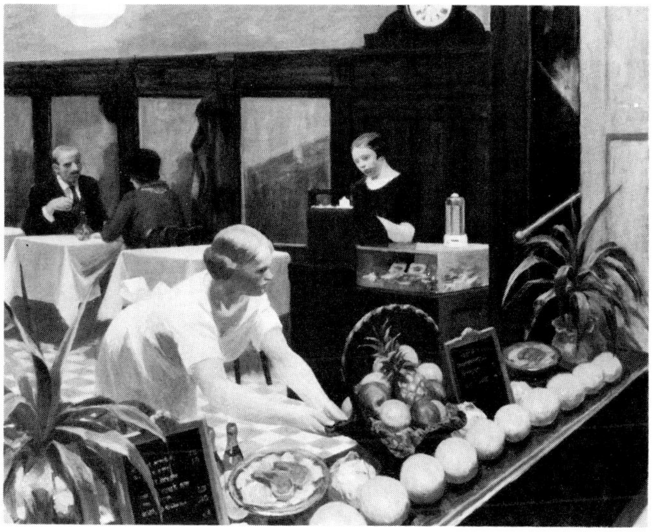

Fig. 59. Edward Hopper, *Tables for Ladies,* 1930. Oil on canvas, 48¼ × 60¼ inches. The Metropolitan Museum of Art, New York.

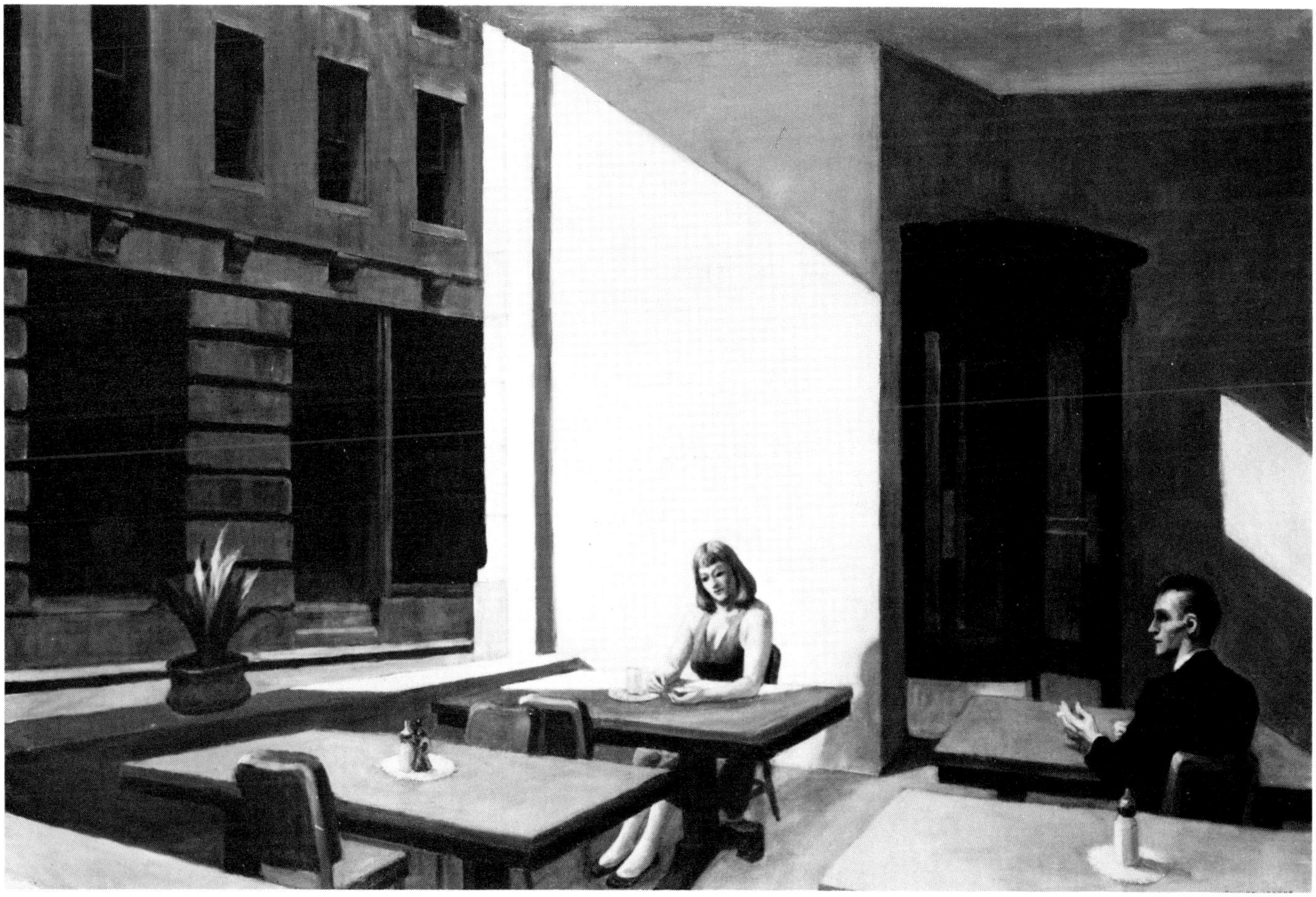

Fig. 60. Edward Hopper, *Sunlight in a Cafeteria,* 1958. Oil on canvas, 40¼ × 60⅛ inches. Yale University Art Gallery, New Haven, Connecticut; bequest of Stephen Carlton Clark.

dicted, even worked out, in various illustrations. For example, the space of the restaurant in *Chop Suey* relates to that in Hopper's illustration in *Everybody's* for January 1914 (Fig. 58; Pl. 8). In both, one looks down on a space formed by two walls. A table, the central focus of our attention, is placed in front of the corner where the two walls meet. Coats hang on hooks along the wall. The mood is quiet. The windows, counters, and table tops create sharp angles and divide the space. The softly curved backs of bentwood chairs are counterpoints to the otherwise angular shapes. Hopper's cover for *Hotel Management* for January 1925 features a couple sitting at a table in the foreground with another couple visible beyond them (Pl. 350). Hopper's method of arranging these figures is quite similar in this illustration and in *Chop Suey*. In both, one sees the back of the female in the foreground and focuses on the face of her companion. The woman in the background is shown only in profile, and part of her head and body are cut off by the border of the picture in a manner typical of Degas and other impressionist painters. A nearly identically posed couple to that in the foreground of this *Hotel Management* cover is visible in Hopper's painting *Tables for Ladies* of 1930 (Fig. 59).

Other compositional similarities between Hopper's illustrations and his paintings abound. An illustration for *System* magazine in January

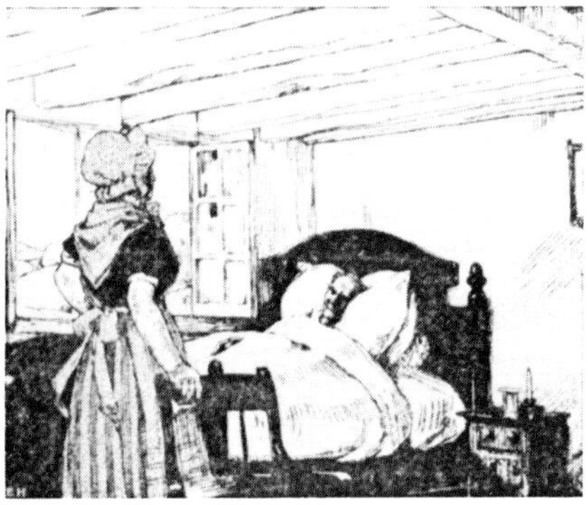

Pl. 33. Edward Hopper, illustration for *The Metropolitan Magazine,* July 1912, p. 45.

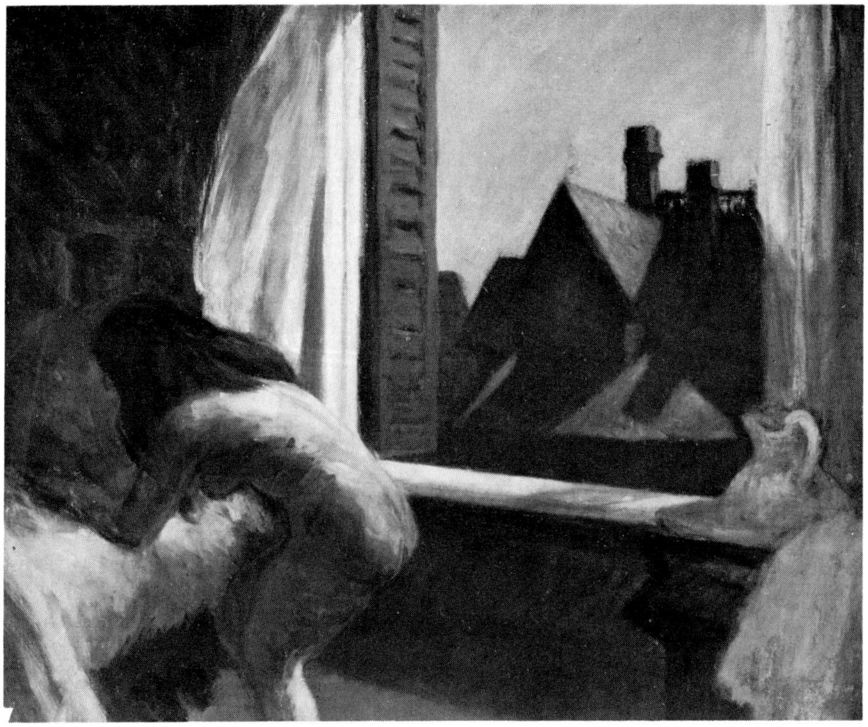

Fig. 61. Edward Hopper, *Moonlight Interior,* c. 1920–23. Oil on canvas, 24 × 29 inches. Private collection.

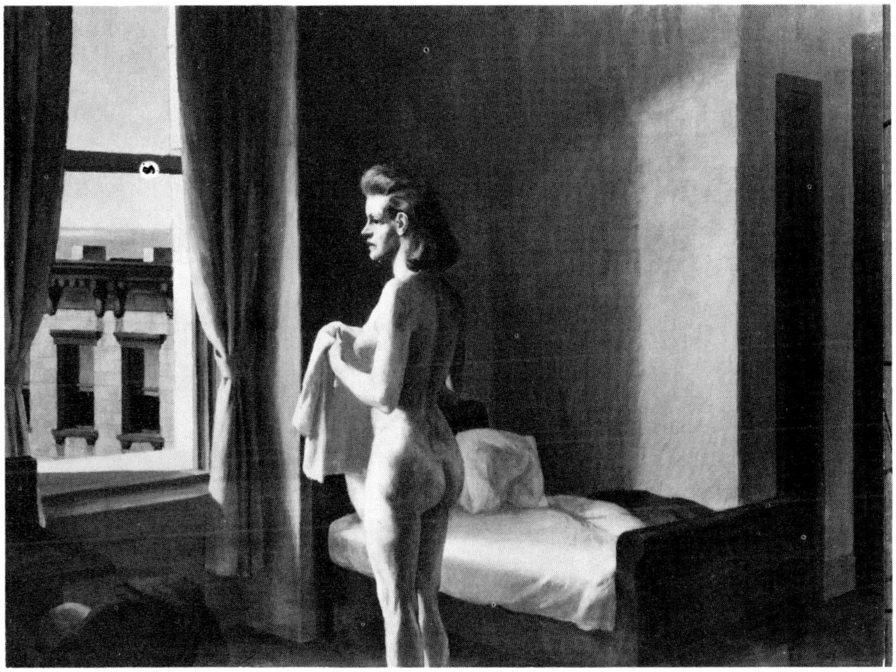

Fig. 62. Edward Hopper, *Morning in a City,* 1944. Oil on canvas, 44 × 60 inches. Williams College Museum of Art, Williamstown, Massachusetts.

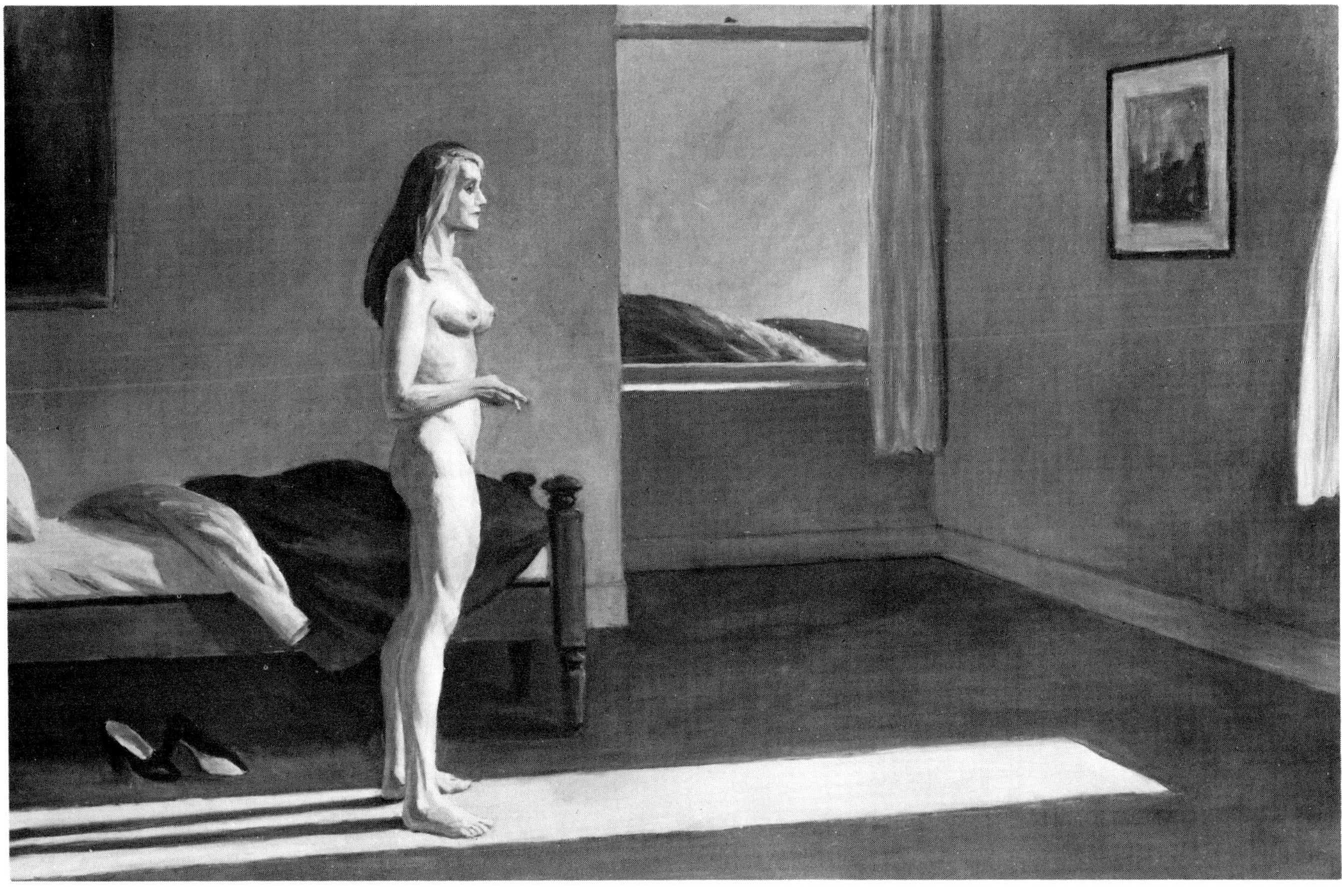

Fig. 63. Edward Hopper, *A Woman in the Sun,* 1961. Oil on canvas, 40 × 60 inches. Collection of Mr. and Mrs. Albert Hackett.

1913, for instance, depicts a woman in the open doorway of a white clapboard house similar to Hopper's painting *High Noon* of 1949 (Fig. 64; Pl. 49). A few unnecessary details like the man, the number and doorbell, and the potted plant have been eliminated in the oil painting which now encompasses the entire house, but the original conception of the illustration is quite similar in its design to part of the painting done thirty-six years later. The profundity of the mood has evolved, as has his use of light and shadow. Likewise, Hopper's illustration of 1917–18 for Wells Fargo & Company showing American soldiers before a French bank predicts his manner of depicting the corner storefront in his painting *Drug Store* of 1927 (Fig. 65; Pl. 429). Hopper's penchant for city architecture is evident in both compositions. In the painting, however, Hopper was able to choose the mood and message he sought to convey, and the figures, no longer necessary, were not included. Interestingly, Hopper's earlier oil of 1913, *Corner Saloon,* did include a number of figures (Fig. 66).

Thus, while there are compositional devices in Hopper's paintings that are quite close to his illustrations, he moved consistently toward simplification in his oil paintings. We can conclude that in order to convey the message necessary to the illustration, Hopper was often forced to include details he would never otherwise have chosen. Indeed, perhaps the essence of Hopper's urge to attain simplicity is summed up in his comment that what he wanted to do was "to paint sunlight on the side of a house" and in his monumental oil painting of 1963 *Sun in an Empty Room* (Fig. 67).

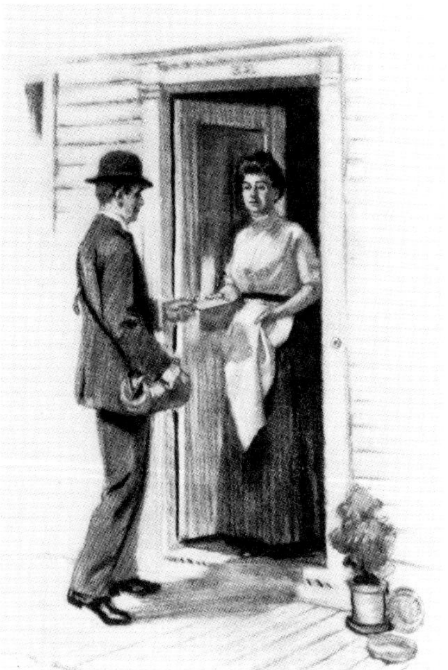

Pl. 49. Edward Hopper, illustration for *System,* January 1913, p. 17.

Although Jo Hopper claimed that Hopper never "compromised" on his illustrations, it is clear that some of the work he did was much more attuned to his sensibilities than that for certain other publications. Surely Hopper chose to apply for work on specific periodicals, particularly trade publications, because they offered a steady diet of more palatable and more predictable subjects. Thus, because of his long and deep love for ships, he tried out successfully for *The Dry Dock Dial.* His interest in trains no doubt encouraged his interest in the *Wells Fargo Messenger.* His work on *Tavern Topics* resulted from the demise of the Wells Fargo publications and the subsequent shift of Elsie Scott, who had bought his work, from their editorial office to that of *Tavern Topics.* Perhaps his past successes there inspired him to try another hotel-related periodical, resulting in his steady employment at *Hotel Management.* Certainly he found it attractive to illustrate for *La France* because of his enjoyment of French culture and pleasant memories of France.

Fiction, however, represented greater problems for the illustrator: the author's product was unpredictable and the illustrator's assign-

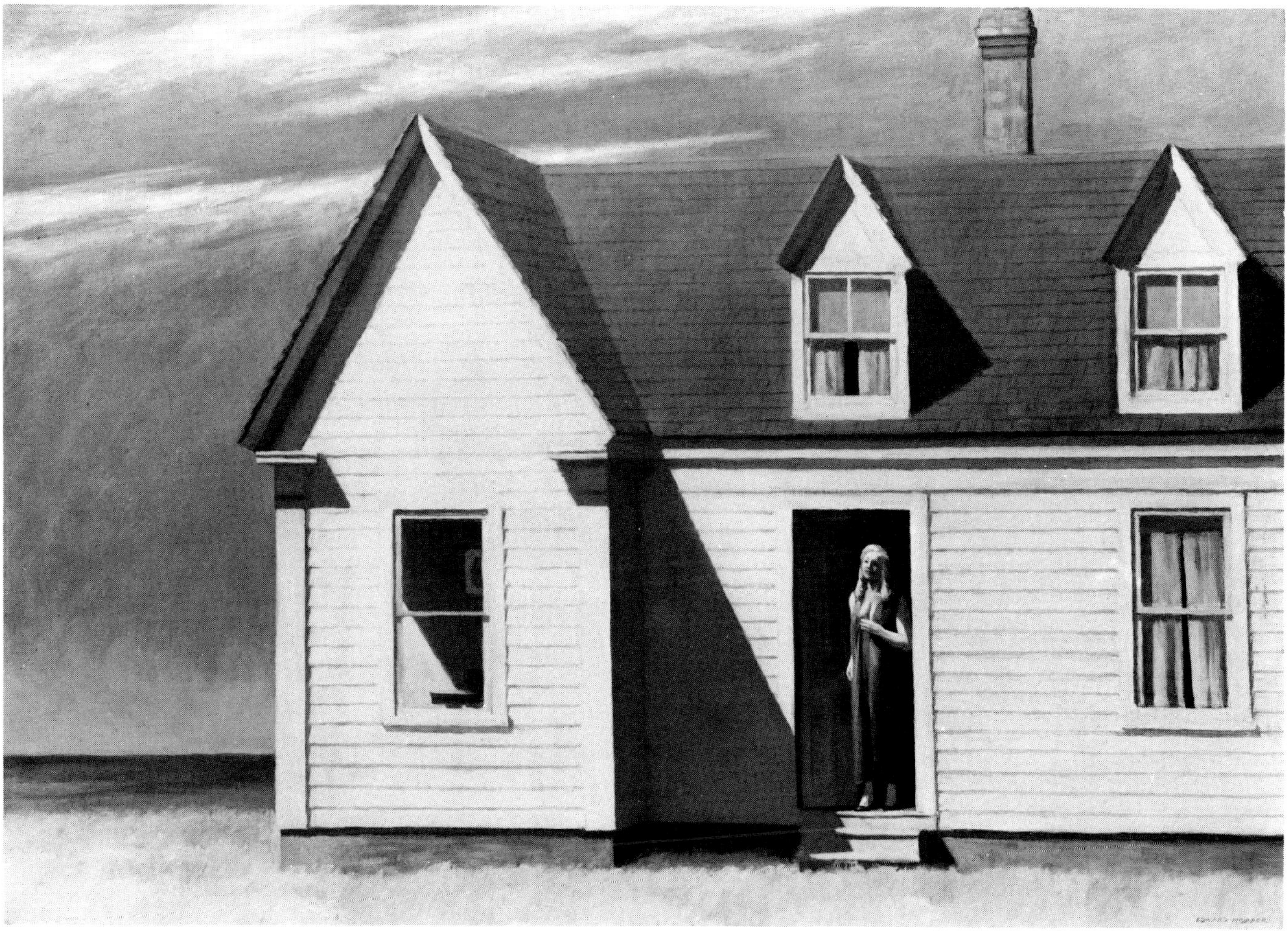

Fig. 64. Edward Hopper, *High Noon,* 1949. Oil on canvas, 28 × 40 inches. Collection of Mr. and Mrs. Anthony Haswell.

ment even more specific. The frustration experienced by many illustrators of contemporary fiction was aptly expressed by popular illustrator James Montgomery Flagg's article of 1915 entitled "A Challenge to Authors." [60] In his article Flagg lamented the difficult task of the illustrator by publishing his illustrations and inviting writers to "authorstrate" them. The Hopper illustrations which have the least relationship to his later art are those for fiction which appeared in *Adventure* and *Everybody's* (Pls. 168, 183). For example, among his illustrations for *Everybody's* in 1921 are depictions of African tribal warriors at battle, surely an alien topic for the quiet Hopper (Pl. 26).

Despite the older Hopper's defensiveness and generally negative attitude toward his early work in illustration, we can conclude that his experiences as an illustrator helped to shape his mature art. Many of the illustrations have a graphic strength and quality not indicated by his negative comments. Rather than take away from the unique quality of his work, Hopper's illustrations reveal one of the vital forces influencing the artist's development during his formative years. As Hopper admitted, "After I took up etching, my paintings seemed to crystallize." [61] What he was not so willing to admit was that in his work as an illustrator there are glimpses of the direction his art would take in the future. The embryonic Hopper who would become one of America's most outstanding realist painters is present in the illustrations even though he resisted total involvement with them. Indeed, it appears that there was an unconscious continuum from much of his commercial work through his mature art.

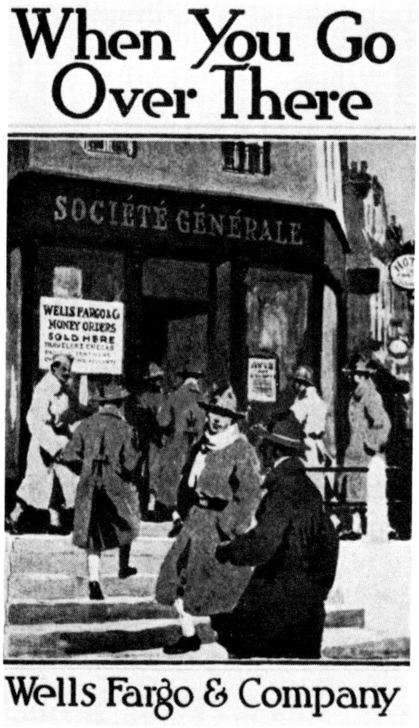

Pl. 429. Edward Hopper, illustration for Wells Fargo & Company brochure, 1917.

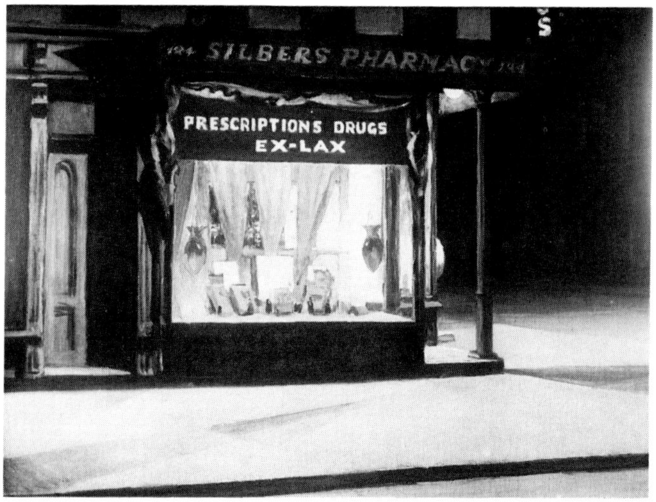

Fig. 65. Edward Hopper, *Drug Store,* 1927. Oil on canxas, 29 × 40 inches. Museum of Fine Arts, Boston.

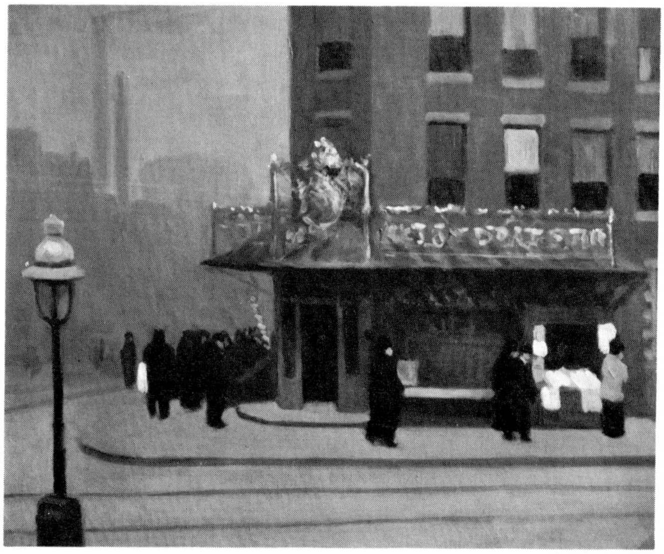

Fig. 66. Edward Hopper, *Corner Saloon,* 1913. Oil on canvas, 24 × 29 inches. The Museum of Modern Art, New York.

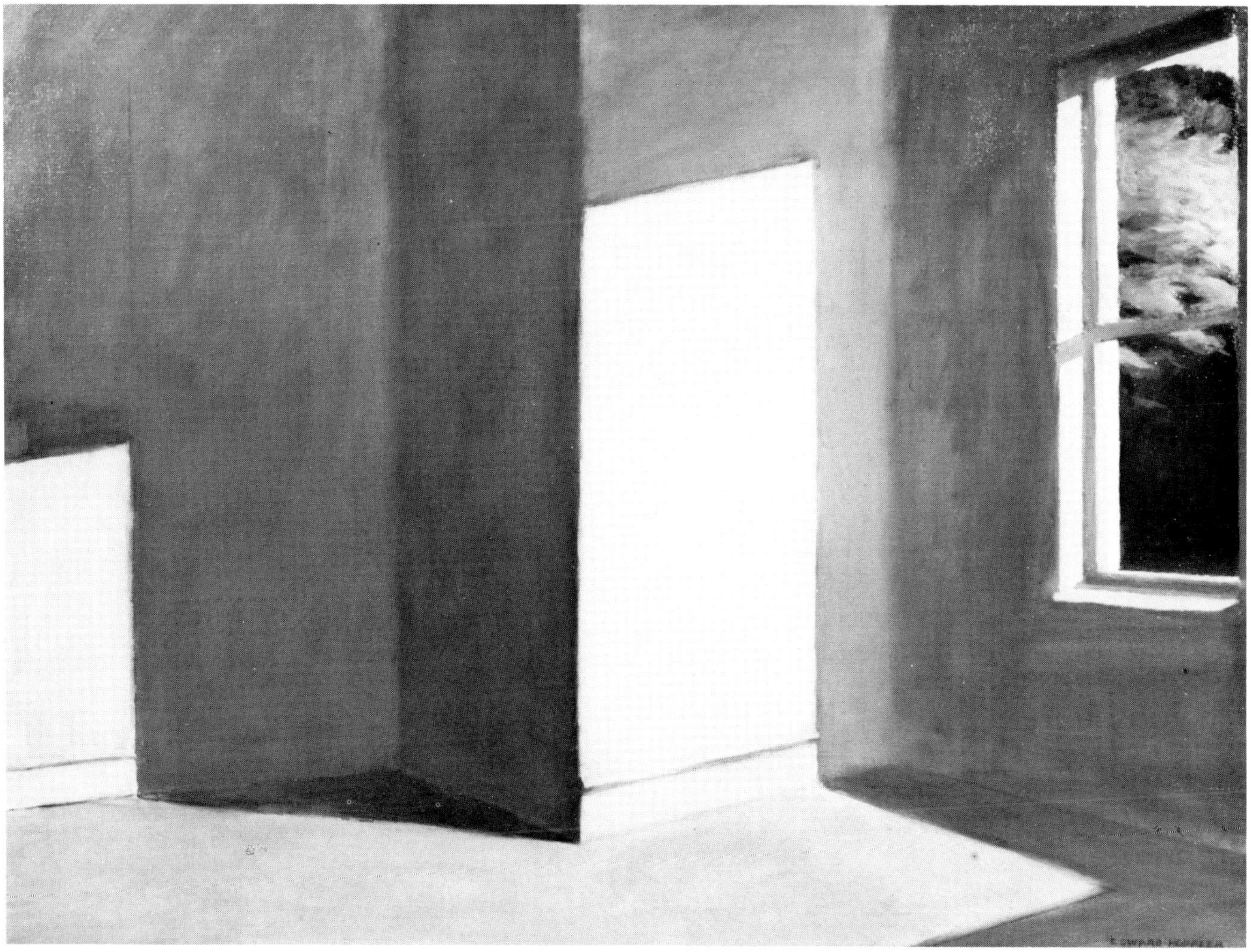

Fig. 67. Edward Hopper, *Sun in an Empty Room,* 1963. Oil on canvas, 29 × 40 inches. Private collection.

NOTES

1. "Edward Hopper Objects" [letter from Hopper to the editor, Nathaniel J. Pousette-Dart], *The Art of Today,* 6 (February 1935), p. 11.
2. Rowland Elzea, *The Golden Age of American Illustration 1880–1914,* exhibition catalogue (Wilmington: Delaware Art Museum, 1972), p. 17.
3. Ibid.
4. Lloyd Goodrich, notes of conversation with Edward Hopper, 20 April 1946, archives of the Whitney Museum of American Art, New York.
5. Brian O'Doherty, *American Masters: The Voice and the Myth* (New York: Random House, 1973), p. 16.
6. Ibid.
7. Archer Winsten, "Wake of the News. Washington Square North Boasts Strangers Worth Talking To," *New York Post,* November 26, 1935.
8. Ibid.
9. Lloyd Goodrich, *Edward Hopper* (New York: Harry N. Abrams, 1976), p. 31.
10. Quoted in Alexander Eliot, "The Silent Witness," *Time,* December 24, 1956, p. 37; reprinted in Alexander Eliot, *Three Hundred Years of American Painting* (New York: Time Incorporated, 1957), p. 297.
11. Carl Zigrosser, "The Etchings of Edward Hopper," in *Prints,* ed. Carl Zigrosser (New York: Holt, Rinehart and Winston, 1962), p. 157.
12. Alfred H. Barr, Jr., *Edward Hopper,* exhibition catalogue (New York: Museum of Modern Art, 1933), p. 9.
13. Ibid., p. 11.
14. Jo N. Hopper to Alice Roullier, 25 November 1933. This manuscript, found in Jo Hopper's papers, was not the letter actually sent; rather she mailed an abbreviated, toned-down version dated 25 and 26 November 1933, now in the Modern Manuscript Collection, The Newberry Library, Chicago. Also in this collection is a letter from Edward Hopper to Alice Roullier, 9 December 1933, which expresses his embarrassment over learning of Jo's letter and gives them permission to use Barr's essay if they wanted it for their catalogue.
15. Nathaniel J. Pousette-Dart, "Editorial Comment," *The Art of Today,* 6 (February 1935), p. 11. The article to which Hopper referred was "Thomas Craven: Prophet, Surgeon or Undertaker," by Pousette-Dart, *The Art of Today,* 5 (December 1934), pp. 7–9.
16. Pousette-Dart, "Editorial Comment," p. 11. These illustrations have not been located, but may be among the unidentified originals in the Hopper Bequest in the Whitney Museum of American Art.
17. Walter Tittle, "The Pursuit of Happiness," unpublished autobiography, Wittenberg University Library, Springfield, Ohio.
18. James B. Carrington, "American Illustration and the Re-

productive Arts," *Scribner's Magazine,* 72 (July 1922), p. 123.

19. Ibid., p. 126.
20. Norman Rockwell, *Norman Rockwell, My Adventures as an Illustrator, As Told to Thomas Rockwell* (Garden City, N.Y.: Doubleday, 1960), p. 359. Rockwell constantly emphasized the distinction between "a fine arts painter" and an illustrator "who has to satisfy his client as well as himself. He must express a specific idea so that a large number of people will understand it; and there must be no mistake as to what he is trying to convey. Then there are deadlines, taboos as to subject matter. . . . the proportions of the picture must conform to the proportions of the magazine" (ibid).
21. Quoted in the artist's obituary, "Norman Rockwell, Artist of Americana, Dead at 84," by Edwin McDowell, *New York Times,* November 10, 1978, p. A29.
22. Linda S. Ferber, "American Illustration: 1850–1920," in *A Century of American Illustration,* exhibition catalogue (New York: The Brooklyn Museum, 22 March–14 May 1972), p. 13.
23. Carrington, "American Illustration and the Reproductive Arts," p. 123.
24. Eliot, *Three Hundred Years,* p. 298.
25. Jo Hopper to Roullier, 25 November 1933.
26. Edward Hopper to the editor, *Scribner's Magazine,* 82 (June 1927), p. 706d.
27. Quoted in Suzanne Burrey, "Edward Hopper: The Empty-ing Spaces," *Arts Digest,* 1 April 1955, pp. 9 and 33.
28. "Traveling Man," *Time,* 19 January 1948, p. 60.
29. Quoted in ibid.
30. For John Sloan's illustrations, see Edgar John Bullard III, "John Sloan and the Philadelphia Realists as Illustrators, 1890–1920" (master's thesis, University of California at Los Angeles, 1968).
31. See Gail Levin, *Edward Hopper: The Complete Prints* (New York: W. W. Norton, 1979), for an analysis of the influence of Sloan's etchings on Hopper.
32. Quoted in O'Doherty, *American Masters,* p. 41.
33. Quoted in ibid.
34. Barr, *Hopper,* p. 10.
35. Quoted in Katharine Kuh, *The Artist's Voice: Talks with Seventeen Artists* (New York: Harper and Row, 1962), p. 135.
36. Quoted in O'Doherty, *American Masters,* p. 16.
37. Hopper was able to exhibit his etchings at the National Academy in 1921, 1922, 1923, and 1924. In 1932 he declined membership in this organization because it had consistently rejected his paintings in previous years.
38. This has been attested to by Walter Tittle in his unpublished autobiography, and by Elsie Scott in an interview with the author, 9 July 1976. Miss Scott worked as an editor in the advertising department at Wells Fargo & Company during the First World War. Reading in the *New York Times* about the Hopper project at the Whitney Museum, Miss Scott, then ninety-two, contacted me to report that she remembered buying Hopper's illustrations both for the *Wells Fargo Messenger* and when she worked for *Tavern Topics* after the *Express Messenger* had ceased publication.
39. For examples of illustrations by Coles Phillips and the source for facts about his career, see Michael Schau, *"All-American Girl" The Art of Coles Phillips* (New York: Watson-Guptill Publications, 1975).
40. The advertisement, which is aimed at retailers, reads: "There will be a decided change in styles for 1909, compared with 1908." Such advertising by wholesalers usually precedes the selling season.
41. I was fortunate to speak with Milton Cederquist, now eighty-nine years old, who remembers well the circumstances of Hopper's contribution to his college yearbook. Arthur Cederquist had felt that he was not familiar enough with college life to do the illustrations and persuaded Hopper to take the project.
42. The Electric City Engraving Company was later taken over by Niagara Frontier Engraving. The company never returned the originals to Cederquist and at some point discarded them (according to a letter of 29 March 1965 from Edward M. Sibble to Milton Cederquist).
43. Edward Hopper, explanatory statement accompanying a letter of 25 August 1948 to Norman A Geske, Walker Art Center, Minneapolis. For an analysis of this painting, see Gail Levin, "Edward Hopper's 'Office at Night,'" *Arts Magazine,* 52 (January 1978), pp. 134–37.
44. For additional examples of this device in Degas's work, see Theodore Reff, *Degas: The Artist's Mind* (New York: Metropolitan Museum of Art, Harper and Row, 1976), chap. 3, "Pictures Within Pictures," pp. 90–146.
45. See note 38. Hopper, it seems, would sell his illustrations at whatever price a periodical was willing to pay, sometimes, as in the case of *Scribner's,* getting more.
46. Edward Hopper to Miss Marian Ragan, 10 February 1956, collection of the Montclair Art Museum, Montclair, New Jersey.
47. Jo Nivison made illustrations for "Happy Valley," by John Reed, which appeared in *The Masses,* 5 (July 1914), pp. 14–17.
48. Edward Hopper, "John Sloan and the Philadelphians," *The Arts,* 11 (April 1927), p. 174.
49. "This Month's Cover," *The Morse Dry Dock Dial,* 2 (February 1919), p. 3.
50. There are only a few known instances of Hopper's work-

ing from a photograph. During this period, illustrators began to utilize photographs more often as an aid in their work.

51. Goodrich, notes of conversation with Edward Hopper, 20 April 1946.

52. Guy Pène du Bois, "The American Paintings of Edward Hopper," *Creative Art,* 8 (March 1931), p. 191.

53. Edward Hopper to his mother, Elizabeth Griffiths Smith Hopper (letter from Paris), 18 May 1909.

54. Quoted in Roger Burlingame, *Of Making Many Books: A Hundred Years of Reading, Writing and Publishing* (New York: Charles Scribner's Sons, 1946), p. 235.

55. Ibid., pp. 234–47. This text offers a lengthy account of Joseph Chapin's method of working, but makes no mention of Hopper. The location of his complete unpublished memoir, excerpted here, is unknown.

56. The catalogue *Seven Paintings by Renoir,* by Royal Cortissoz, was published by Durand-Ruel, Paris and New York, 1923.

57. For example, see Forbes Watson, "Le Dejeuner des Canotiers," *The Arts,* 5 (April 1924), p. 203. This painting received extra attention when purchased by Duncan Phillips in late 1923.

58. Hopper, "John Sloan," pp. 172–73.

59. Hopper, "John Sloan," p. 172.

60. James Montgomery Flagg, "A Challenge to Authors," *Everybody's,* 33 (October 1915), p. 417.

61. Quoted in Burrey, "Edward Hopper: The Emptying Spaces," p. 10.

LIST OF PERIODICALS

Adventure. Published twice a month by the Ridgeway Company, New York. Arthur Sullivant Hoffman, editor. A magazine of fiction, with special emphasis on western and sea adventures. (Plates 167–223)

American Magazine. With its first issue as "Frank Leslie's Popular Monthly" in 1876, the name was changed to *American Magazine* in 1906. The publisher was Philips Publishing, New York, from October 1906 to June 1916, and it was then taken over by Crowell Publishing, Springfield, Ohio, and New York. (Plate 140)

Associated Sunday Magazine. A tabloid issued weekly, cooperatively and simultaneously as part of the Sunday editions of the following newspapers: *Chicago Herald, Philadelphia Press, Pittsburgh Post, New York Tribune, Boston Post, Washington Star, Minneapolis Journal, Buffalo Courier, Detroit Tribune, Baltimore Sun, Cleveland Leader,* and *Cincinnati Commercial-Tribune.* The emphasis was on serialized fiction, with a small number of nonfiction articles. (Plates 85–139)

Bulletin of The New York Edison Company. Published by the electric company from 1902 through November 1907, when it ceased publication. The magazine contained articles discussing the use of electricity. It resumed publication in June 1908 as the *Edison Monthly* and continued publication through 1928. (Plates 440–442)

Country Gentleman. Purchased by the Curtis Publication Company in 1911. In 1916 it became a national weekly, circulation approximately 500,000. It contained fiction and nonfiction, both with emphasis on rural life. This publication is still in existence. (Plates 243–260)

Everybody's. Published monthly by the Ridgeway Company. From 1911 to 1914 Trumbull White was editor, and at this time the circulation was approximately 500,000. By 1921, when Sewell Haggard had become editor, the magazine became all fiction. Previously it was an entertainment magazine with an emphasis on serialized fiction. (Plates 1–31b)

Every Week. Published by Every Week Corporation, New York, from 1915 to 1918 as a weekly entertainment magazine. It was also issued as a supplement to a number of Sunday newspapers with the title of *Sunday Magazine.* (Plates 261–272)

Farmer's Wife. Published monthly from 1900 to 1939, it catered to the interest of the rural home-oriented woman. Originally founded at Winona, Minnesota, the publication had moved to St. Paul, Minnesota, by the time Hopper illustrated for it. Nathaniel Pousette-Dart was art editor at this time. (Plates 141–166)

Hotel Management. Published monthly by the Ahrens Publishing Company in New York with James S. Warren as its editor (1925). A trade publication dealing with the practical business problems of hotel management, including policies and methods of hotel organization and management throughout the world, contributed by a group of editorial advisors. (Plates 344–361)

La France, An American Magazine. Published monthly in New York by La France Publishing Corporation from August 1917 to August 1921 with Claude Rivière as editor-in-chief. It then became *New France* through May 1919, and from June through September 1919 was published as *Victory.* A magazine devoted to developing greater understanding of French history and culture in the United States, containing articles in both French and English. (Plates 334–335)

The Metropolitan Magazine. Published monthly by the Metropolitan Magazine Company, 286 Fifth Avenue, New York. A general-interest magazine combining popular fiction with diverse features covering such subjects as politics, the arts, and sports. (Plates 32–37)

The Morse Dry Dock Dial. A monthly magazine published by the Morse Dry Dock and Repair Company in Brooklyn, New York, from 1918 to 1923, for its Employees' Association and the general interests of the company. Bert Edward Barnes was editor. (Plates 273–306)

Profitable Advertising: The Magazine of Publicity. Boston, Massachusetts. "A Monthly magazine devoted exclusively to the interests of Advertisers and Publishers." Kate E. Griswald was publisher. (Plate 443)

Scribner's Magazine. Published monthly by Charles Scribner's Sons, New York, from January 1887 through May 1939. Robert Bridges was editor and Joseph Hawley Chapin was art editor during the time Hopper's illustrations were published. Fiction and articles on the fine arts were featured, but other topics included travel, biography, and public affairs. (Plates 307–333)

Survey Graphic. A magazine of social interpretation published monthly in New York from 1921 through 1948. "An illustrated magazine of social exploration, reaching out to whatever tides of a tenerous progress are astir." A monthly feature of the weekly *The Survey.* (Plate 343)

System, the Magazine of Business. Published by the A. W. Shaw Company, Chicago, Illinois, from 1900 to 1917. It contained articles discussing techniques of business management. It was superseded by *Magazine of Business* in 1928, which became *Business Week* in 1929. (Plates 38–84)

Tavern Topics. Published monthly in New York for distribution to hotel guests in New York and Philadelphia. Editorial staff included Elsie Scott. (Plates 336–342)

Wells Fargo Messenger. Published monthly in New York from Wells Fargo Headquarters at 65 Broadway from 1913 to June 1918 as a house organ for the company's employees. Succeeded by the *Express Messenger* in July 1918 after Wells Fargo merged with American Railway Express Company. The editor was Edward Hungerford and the editorial staff included Elsie Scott. (Plates 224–242)

PHOTOGRAPHIC CREDITS

Oliver Baker: Figs. 61, 67

Geoffrey Clements: Figs. 2, 5, 6, 15, 17, 38, 39, 43–48, 50, 55; Pls. 1–6, 10, 13–15, 25a, 26a, 28a, 34, 35, 38, 40, 41, 42b, 44–46, 47a–57, 58c, 62, 63a, 63b, 66, 76b, 79–82, 86, 87, 107, 121, 122, 125b, 126, 128, 129, 140, 228–234, 236–242, 245, 246, 261b, 262, 263, 264b, 265a, 266a, 266c, 268–271, 273–282, 283a, 283b, 284d, 285–288, 289b, 290–319b, 321a–333, 334b, 335, 337, 339, 342–349, 351–359, 393, 394, 401, 427a, 431, 432, 434–447, 449–456, 458–469, 471–473, 475–477, 479, 482–506

Tom Crozier: Pls. 7a, 7c, 8a, 9a, 11a, 12a, 17–24, 25b, 27, 29, 30, 32, 33, 42a, 43, 58a, 59a–62, 64, 65–78, 83–85a, 88a–92a, 96a, 98a–106a, 108a–113a, 116a, 117a, 119a, 120a, 123a, 124a, 133a, 136a, 138a, 139a, 141a–144a, 146a–155a, 158a–165a, 167a–227a, 235a, 243a, 244a, 247a–260a, 362–392, 395–400, 402–426, 427b, 428–430, 433

Deutsche Fotothek Dresden: Fig. 20

Peter A. Juley & Son: Figs. 1, 22, 32, 54, 57, 60, 62–64

Service de Documentation Photographique, Paris: Fig. 13

Claude O'Sughrue: Fig. 37

M.-L. Perony, Pau: Fig. 11

Taylor & Dull: Figs. 14, 58

Jann & John F. Thomson: Fig. 31

CATALOGUE OF ILLUSTRATIONS

COMPILED BY GAIL LEVIN WITH
THE ASSISTANCE OF TOM HUDSPETH

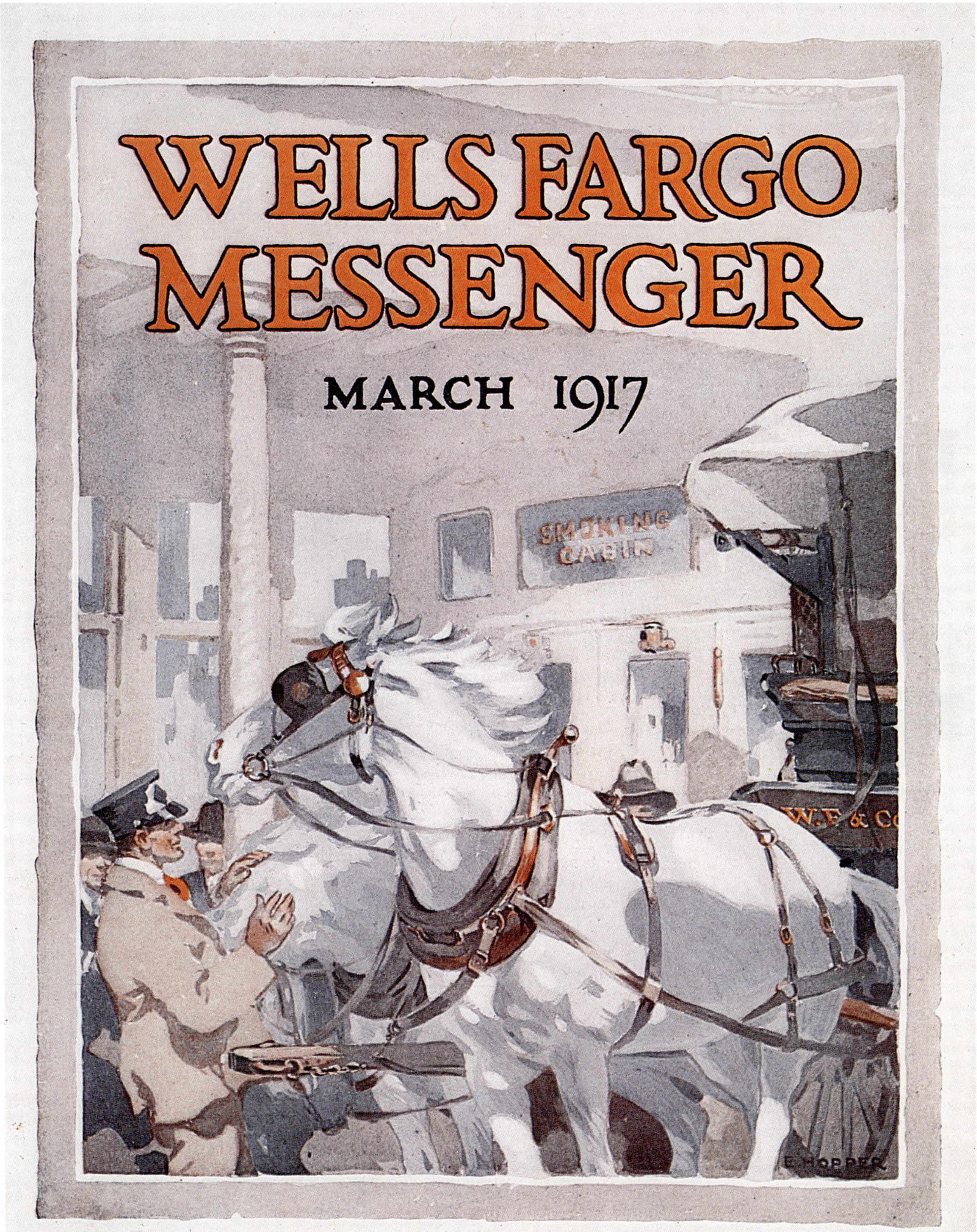
WELLS FARGO MESSENGER
MARCH 1917
SMOKING CABIN
W.F. & Co
E. HOPPER

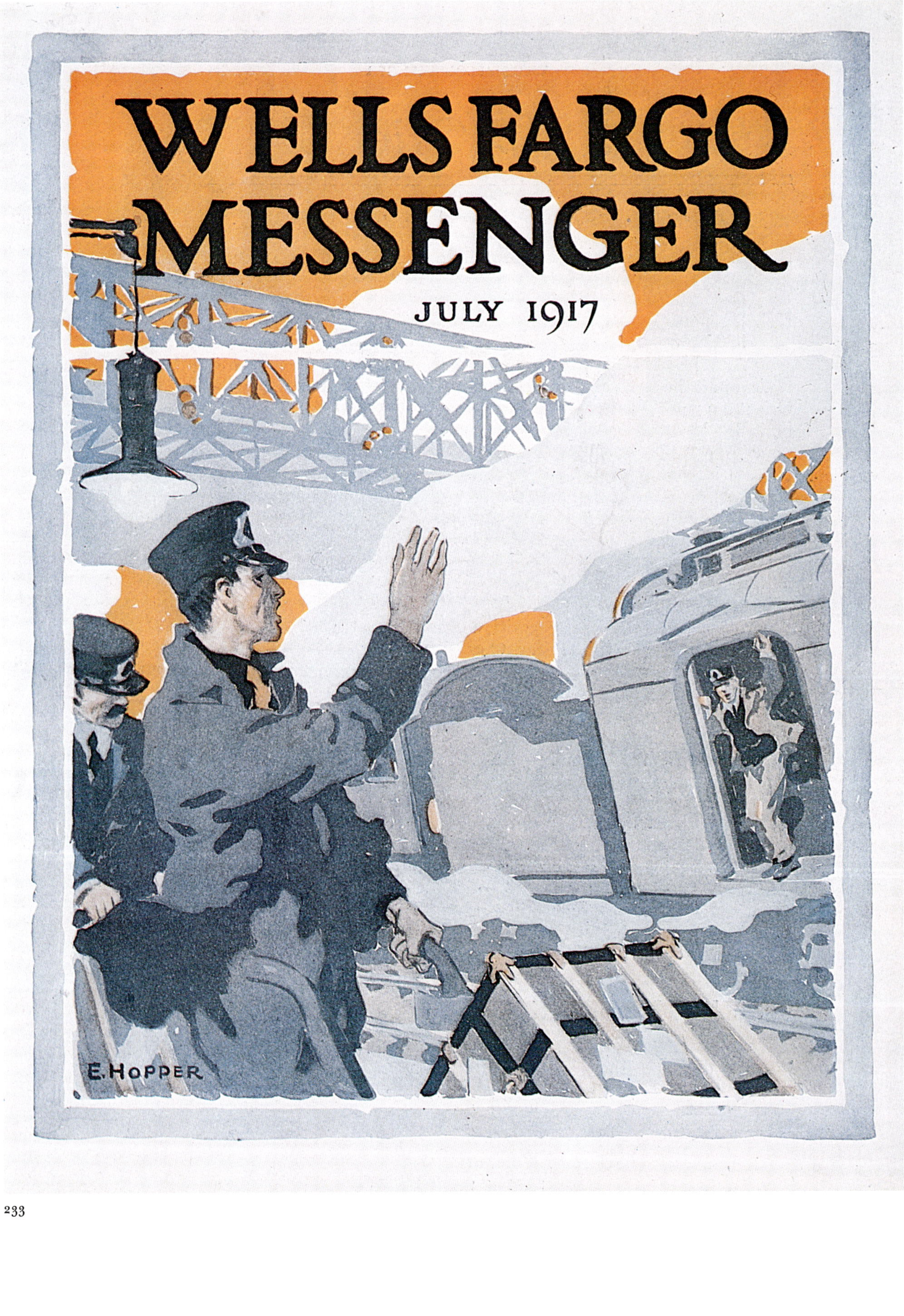
WELLS FARGO
MESSENGER
JULY 1917
E. HOPPER

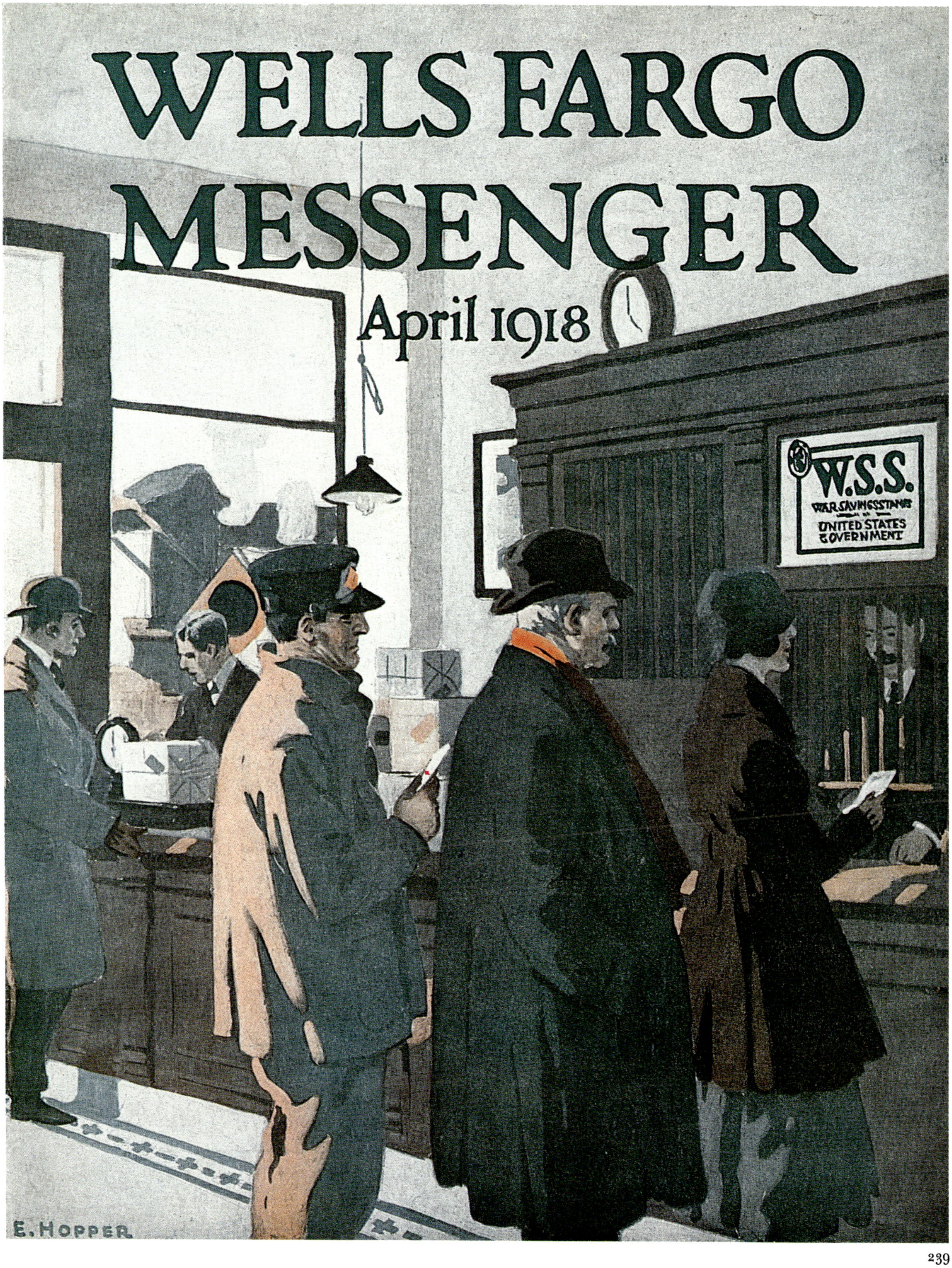
WELLS FARGO
MESSENGER
April 1918
W.S.S.
WAR SAVINGS STAMPS
UNITED STATES
GOVERNMENT
E. HOPPER

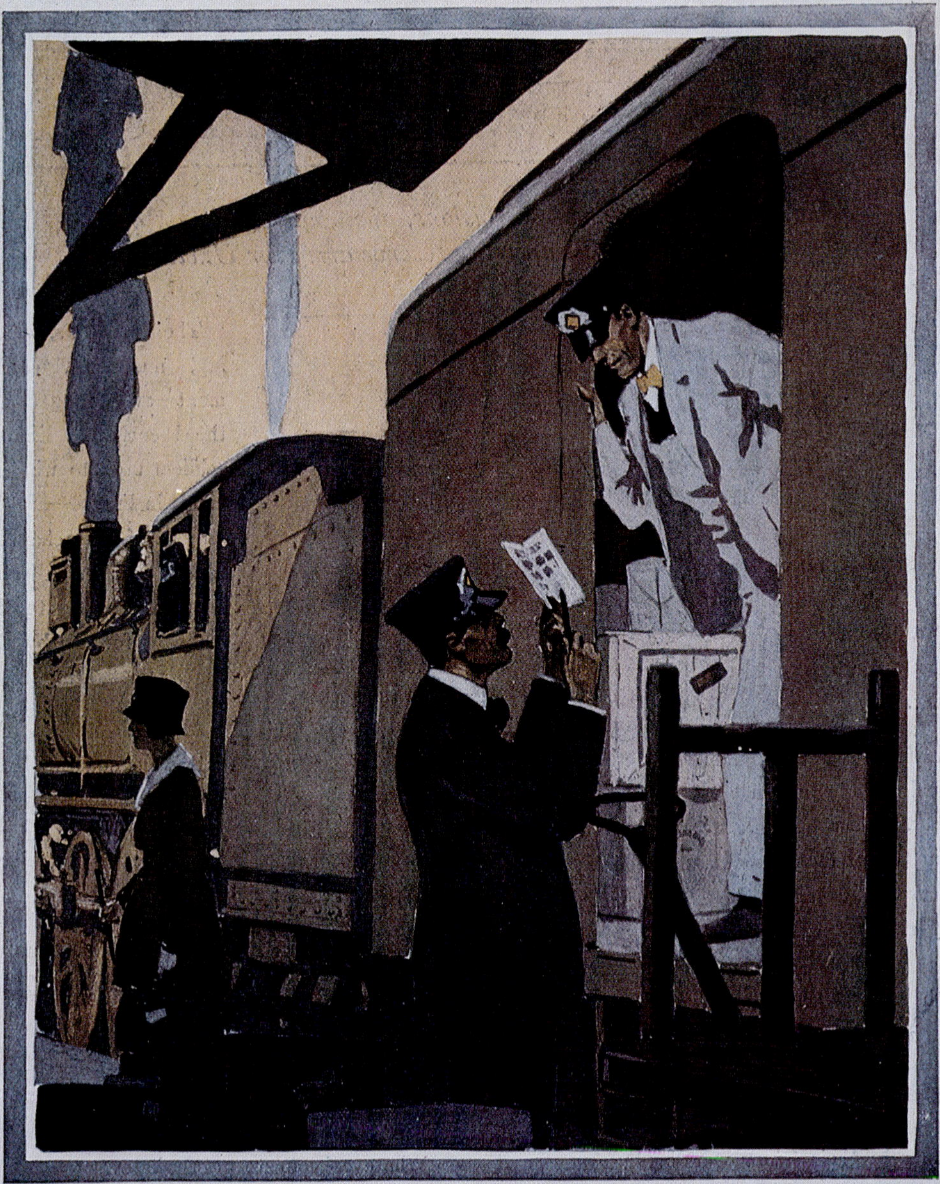

"See, my Thrift Card is almost filled!
How is yours coming along?"

"The First of May is Thrift Stamp Day in the U. S. A."

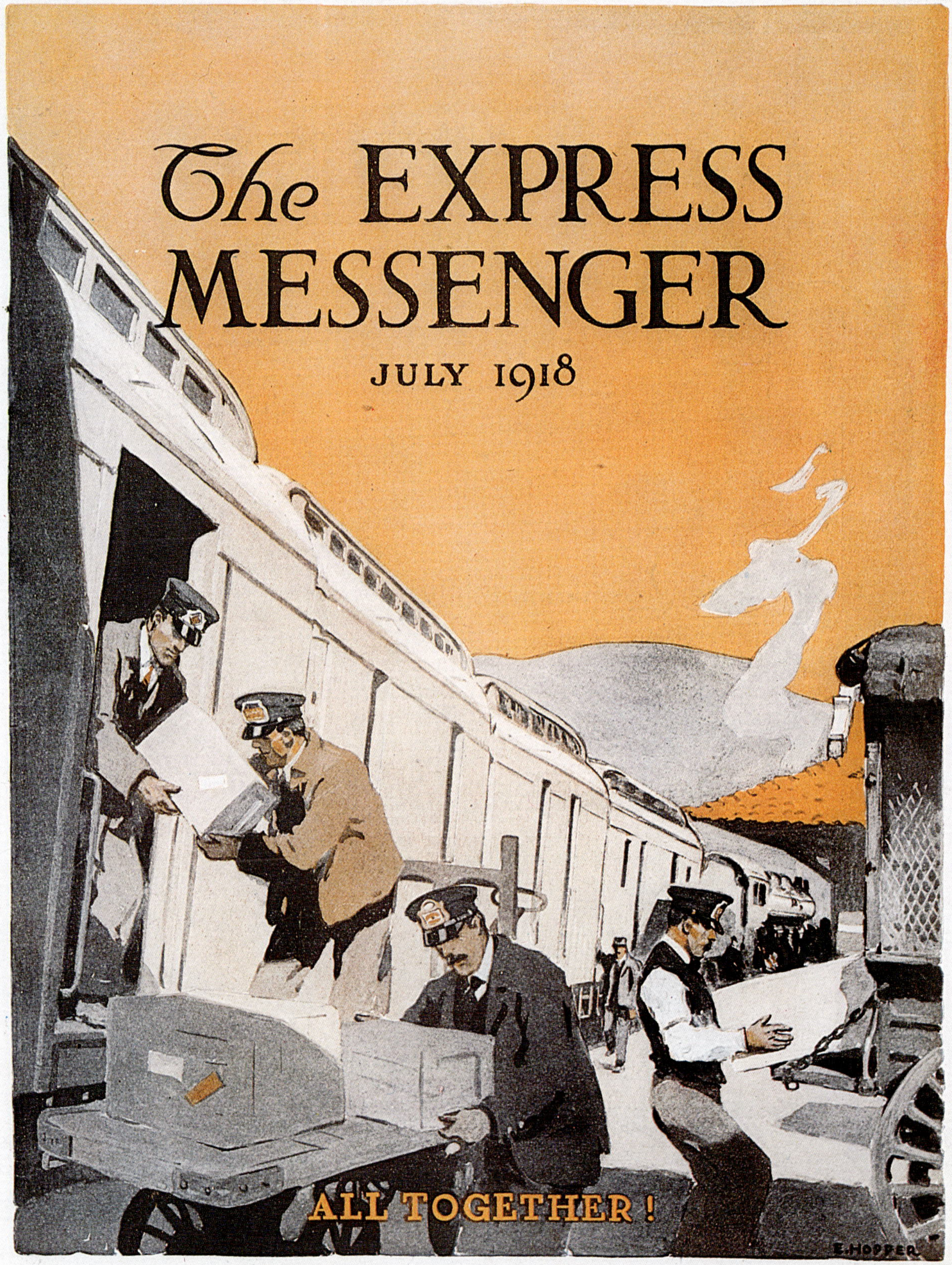
The EXPRESS MESSENGER
JULY 1918
ALL TOGETHER!
E. HOPPER

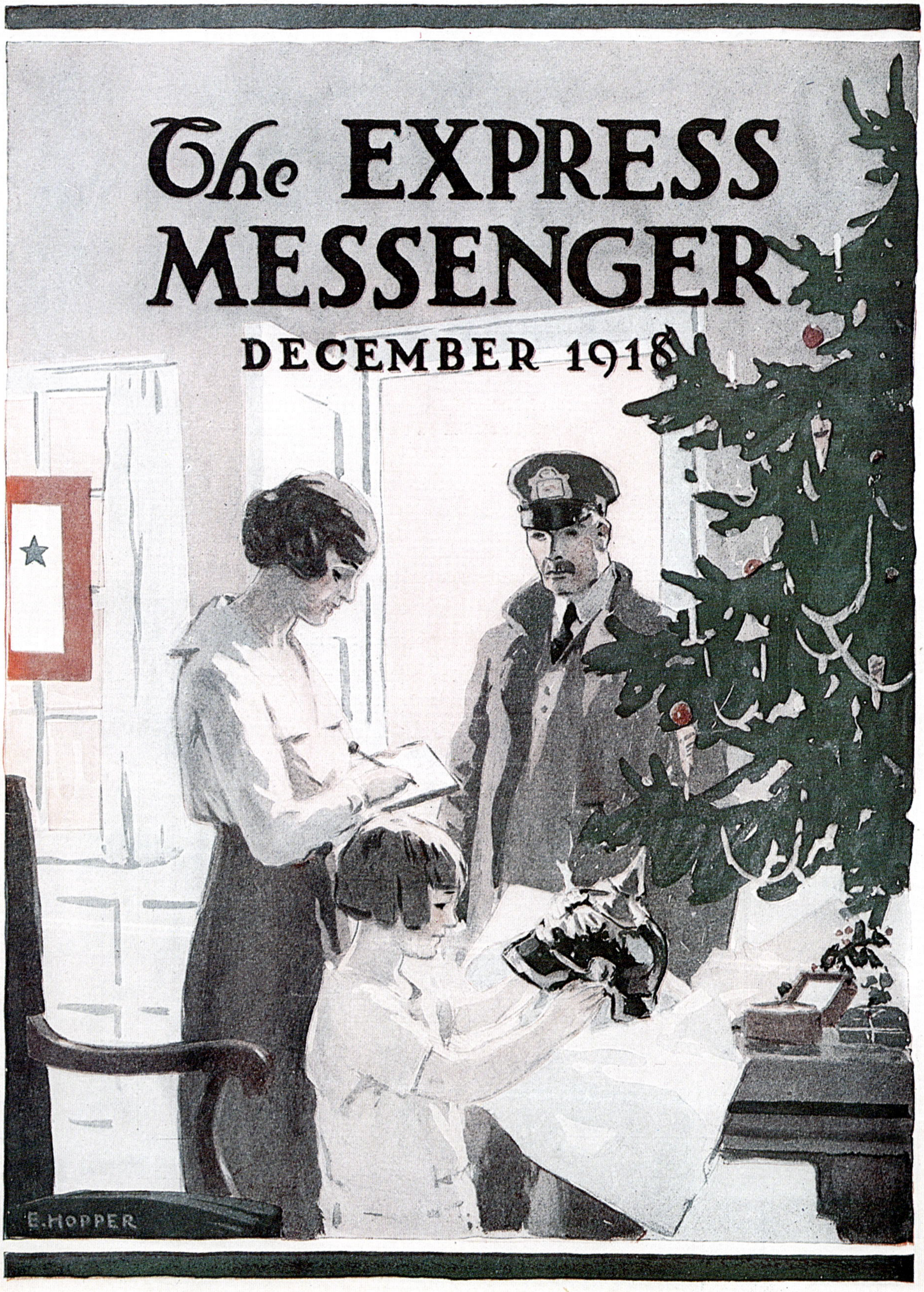
The EXPRESS MESSENGER
DECEMBER 1918
E. HOPPER

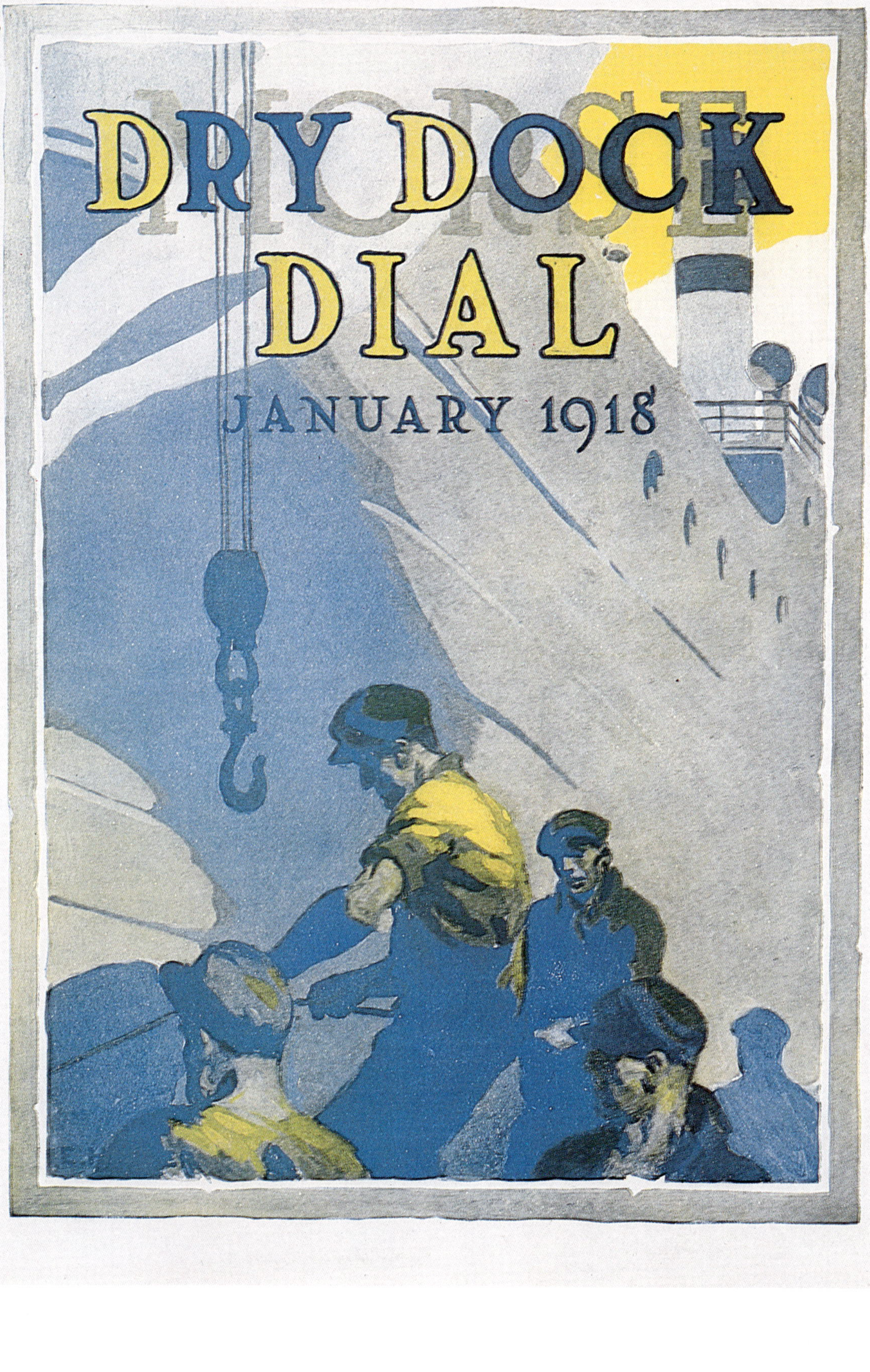
MORSE
DRY DOCK
DIAL
JANUARY 1918

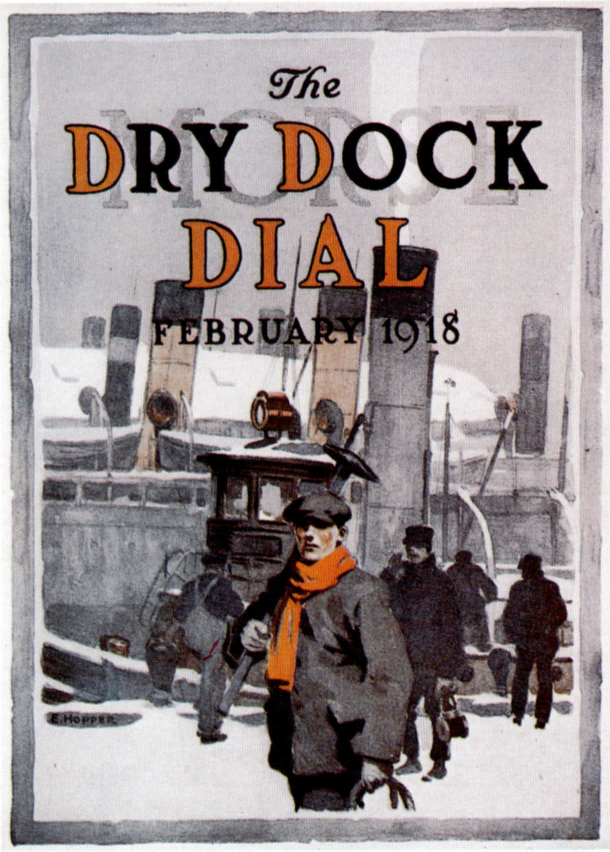

274

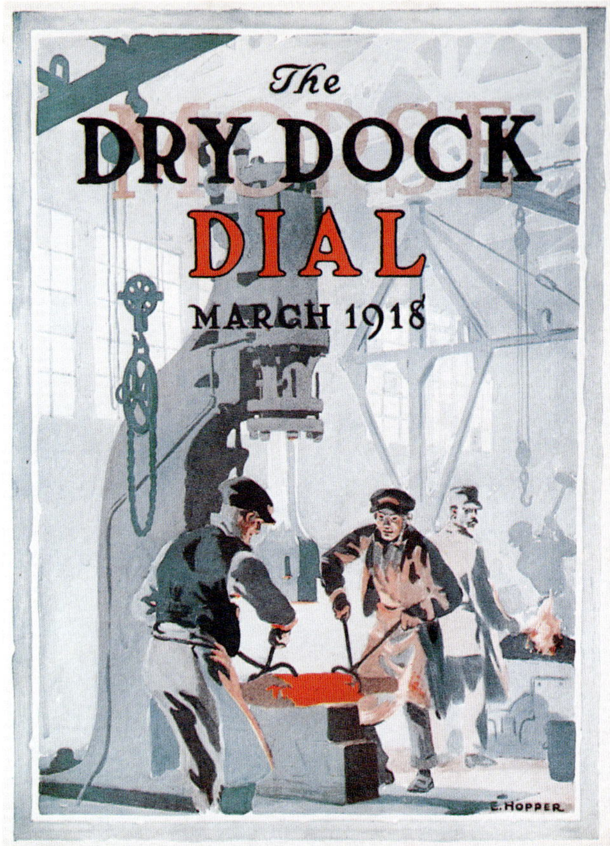

275

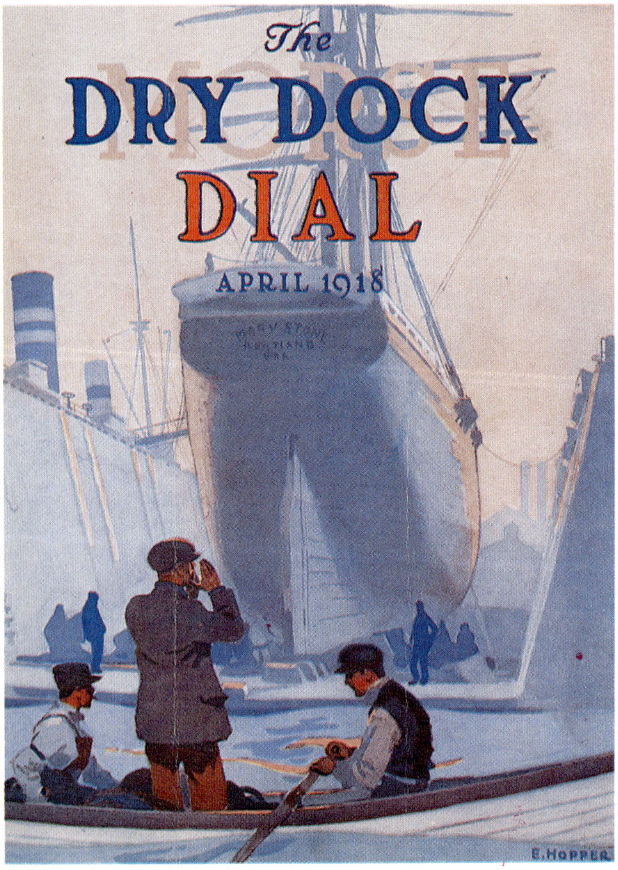

276

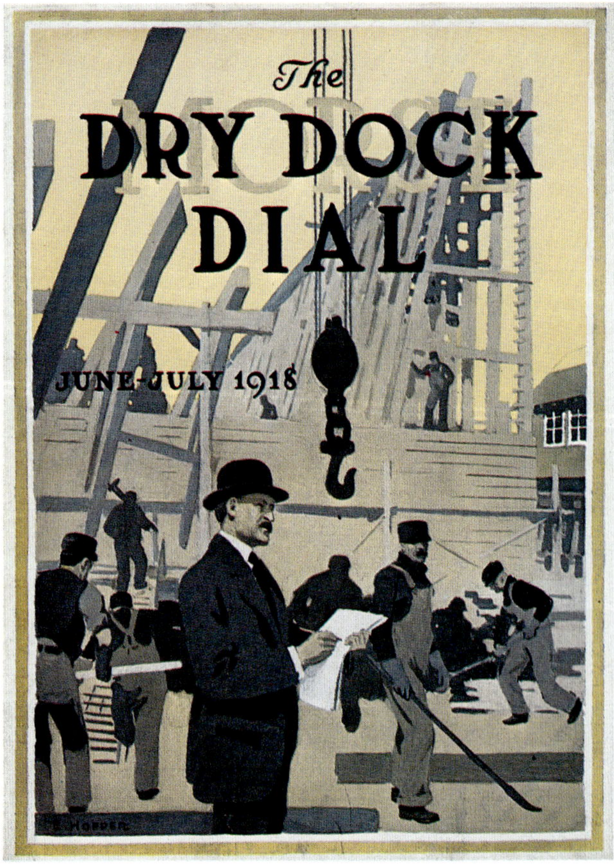

277

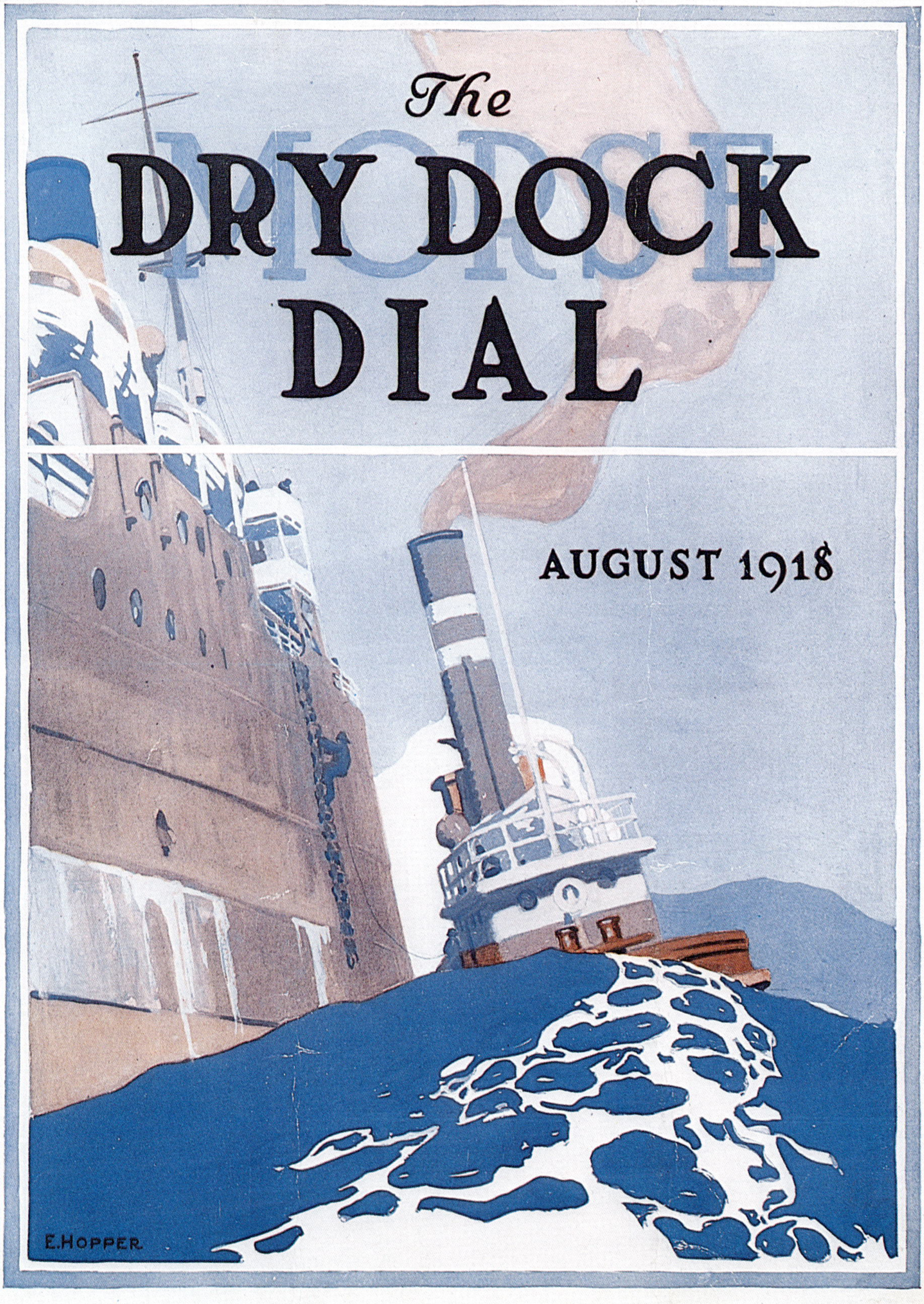
The
DRY DOCK
MORSE
DIAL
AUGUST 1918
E. HOPPER

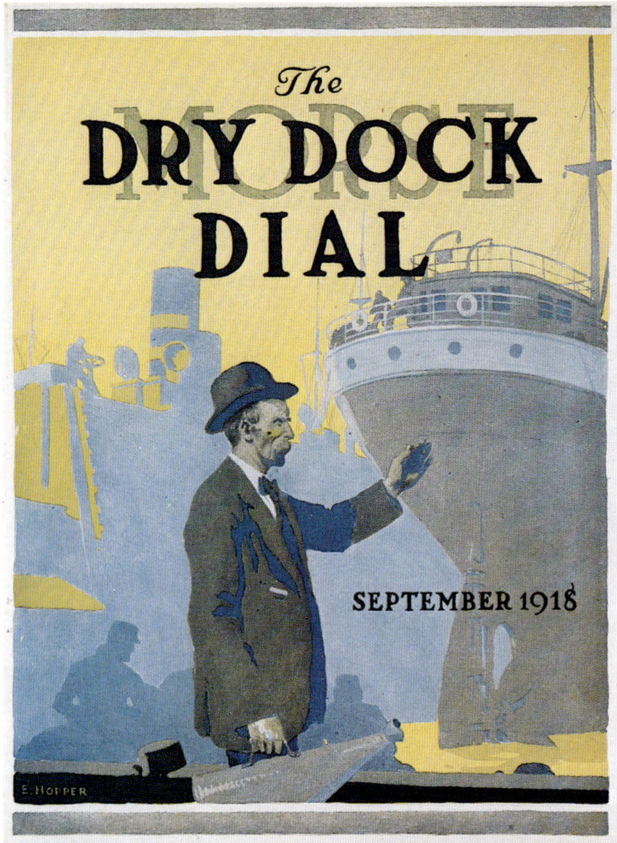

279

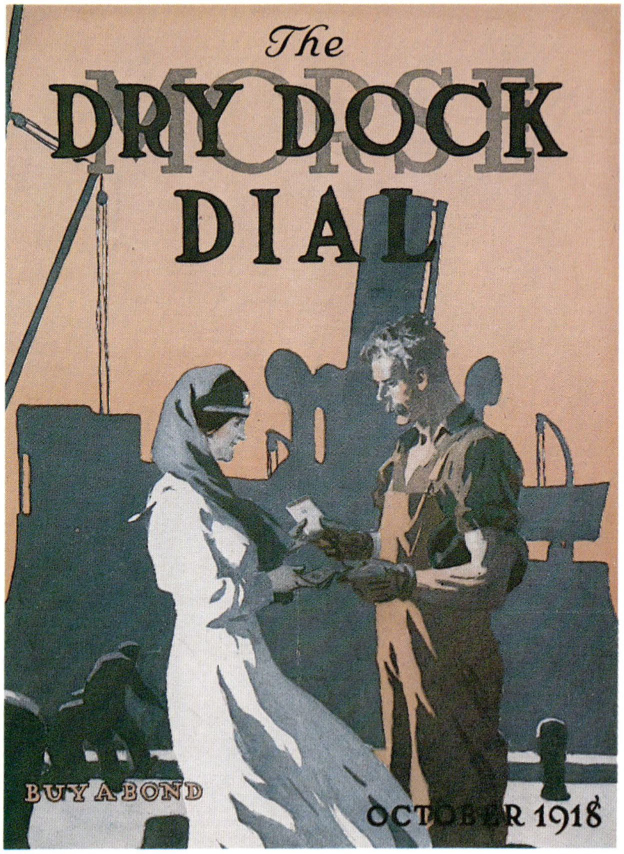

280

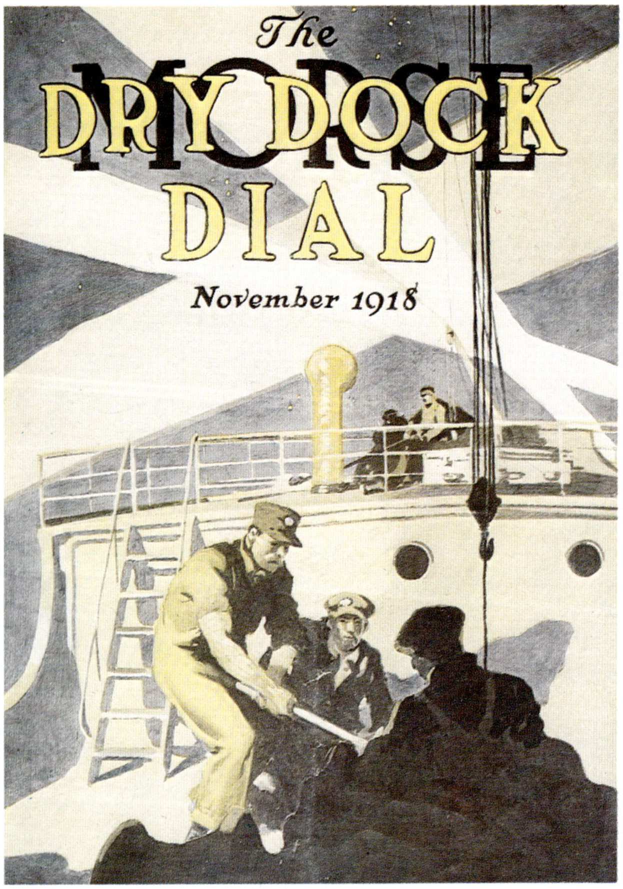

281

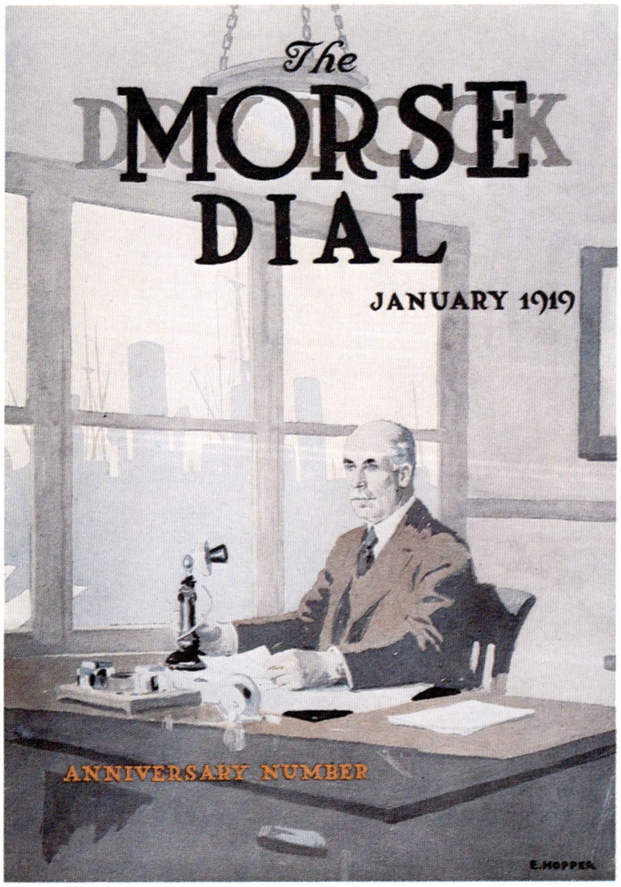

282

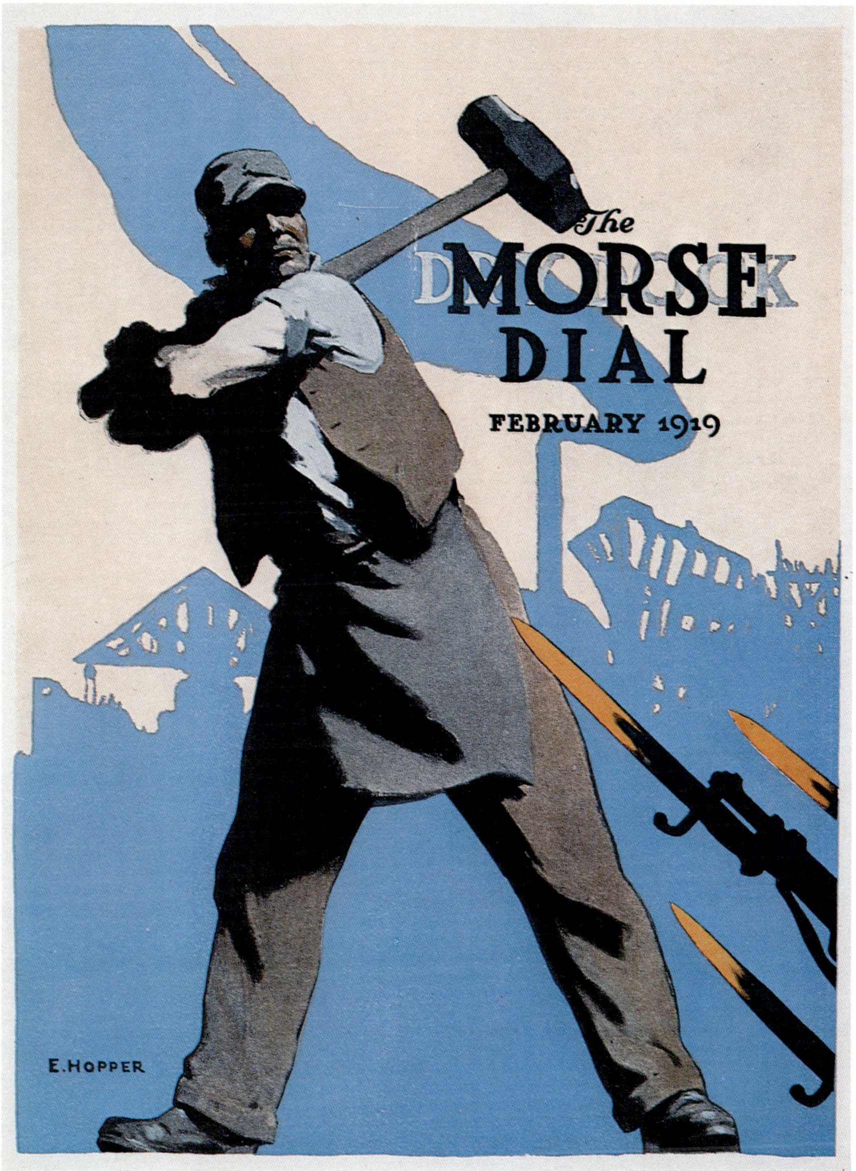

283b

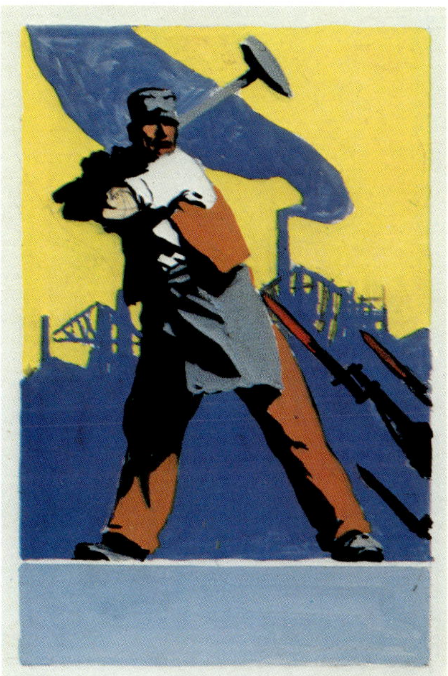
283a

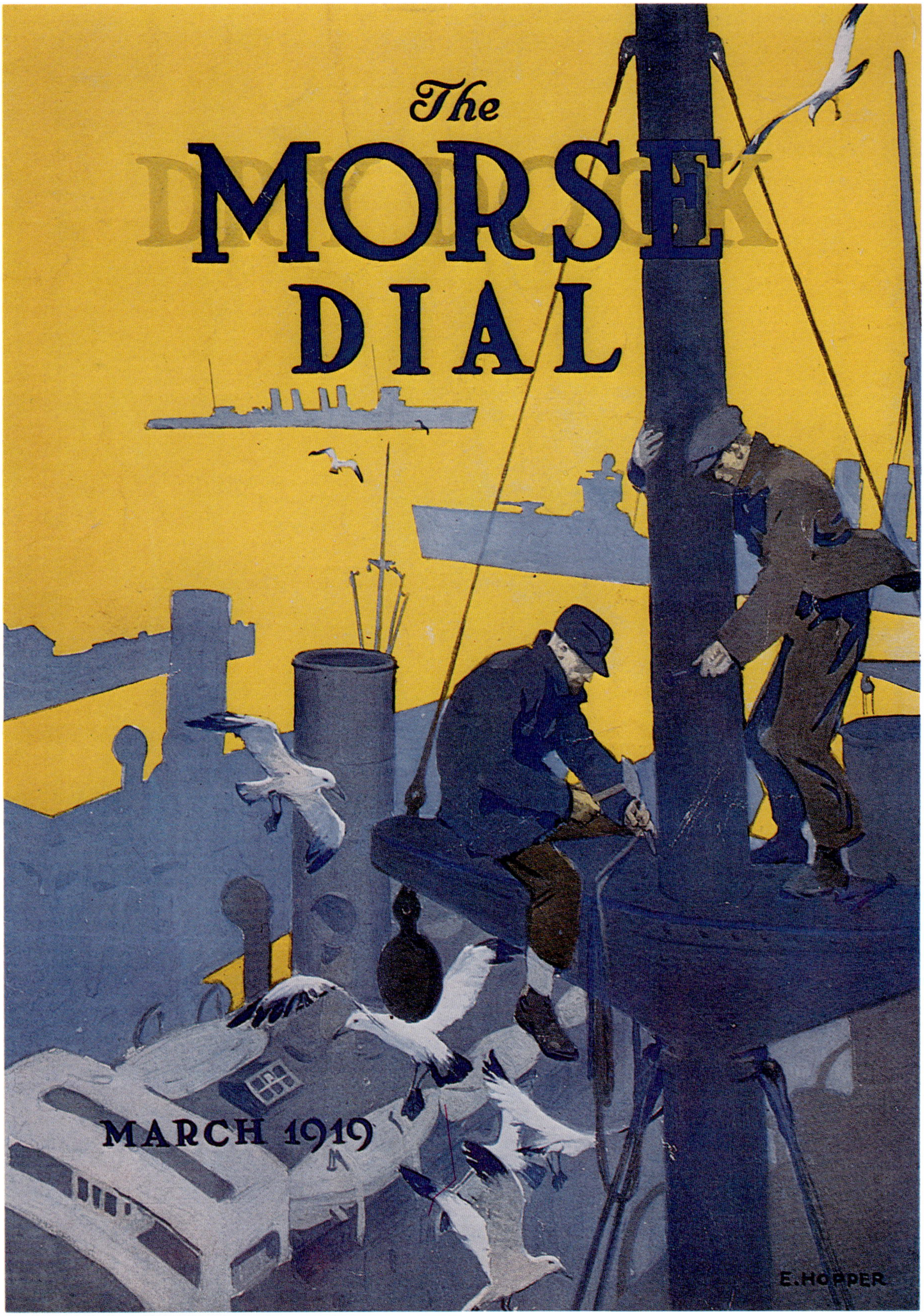
The
MORSE
DIAL
MARCH 1919
E. HOPPER

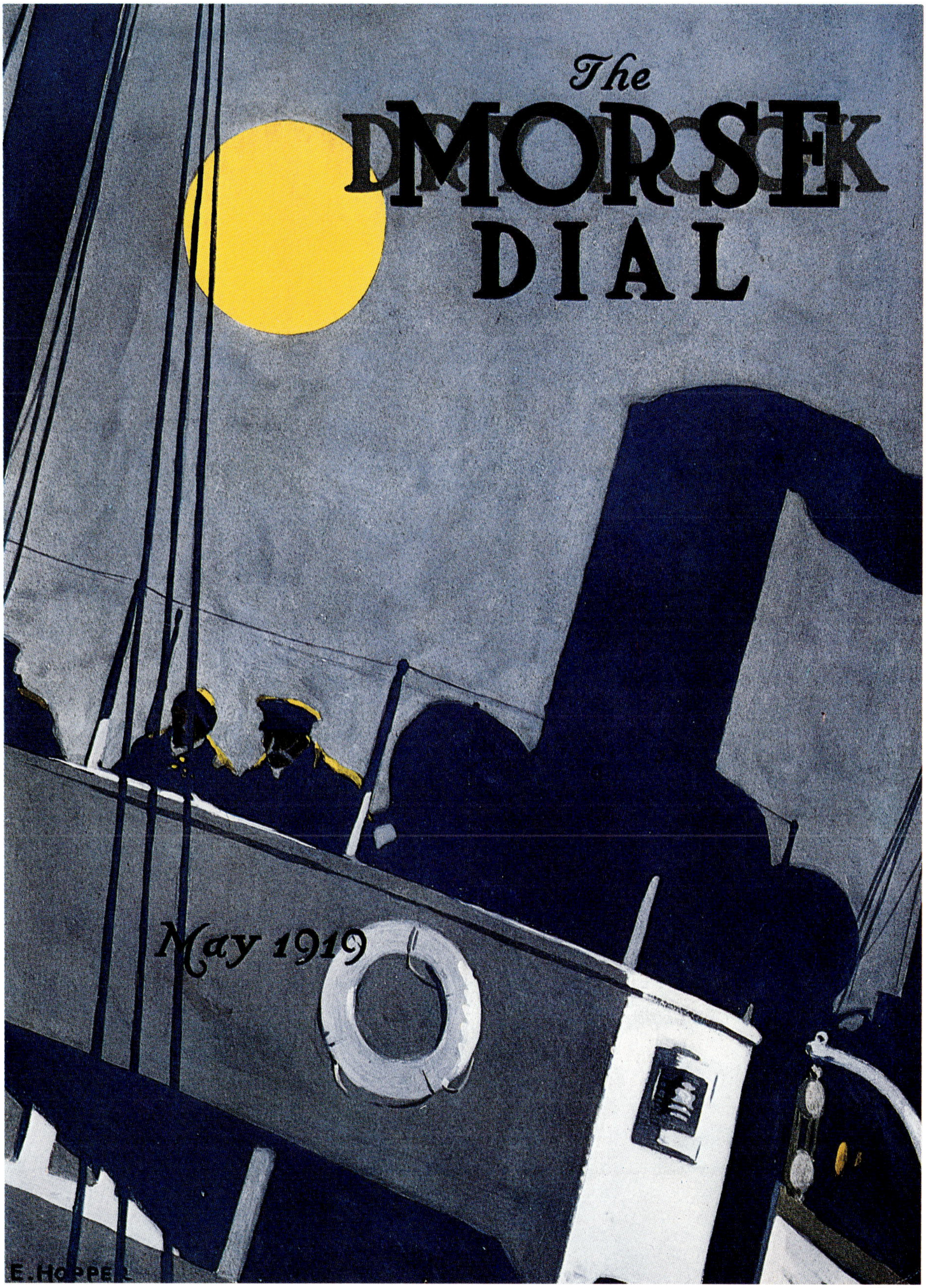
The
MORSE
DIAL
May 1919
E. HOPPER

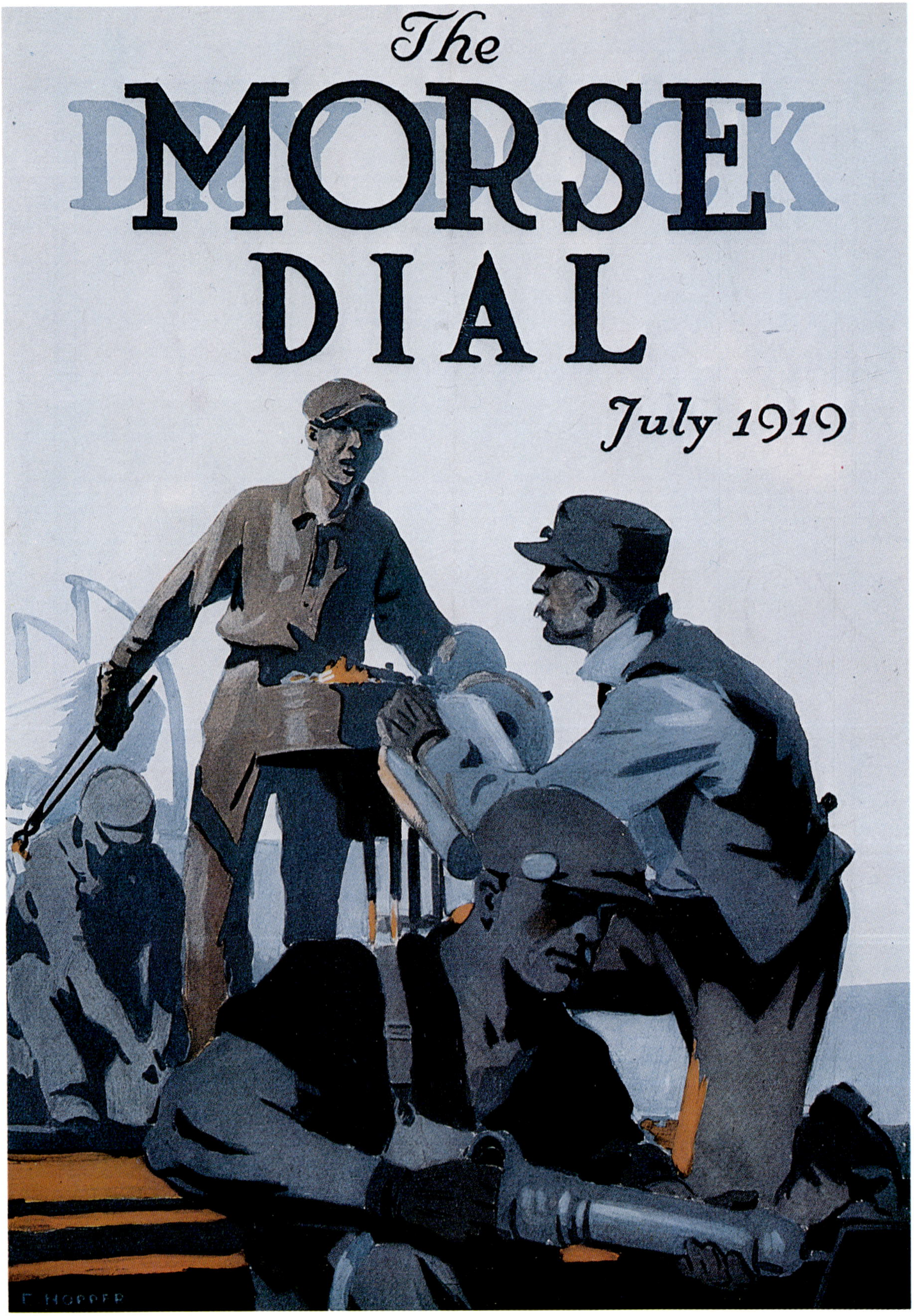
The
MORSE
DIAL
July 1919
E HOPPER

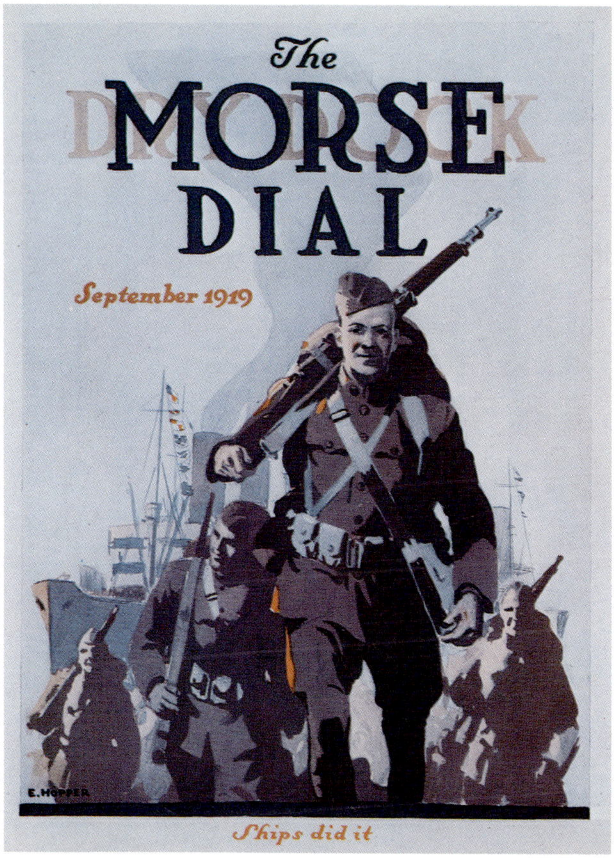

287

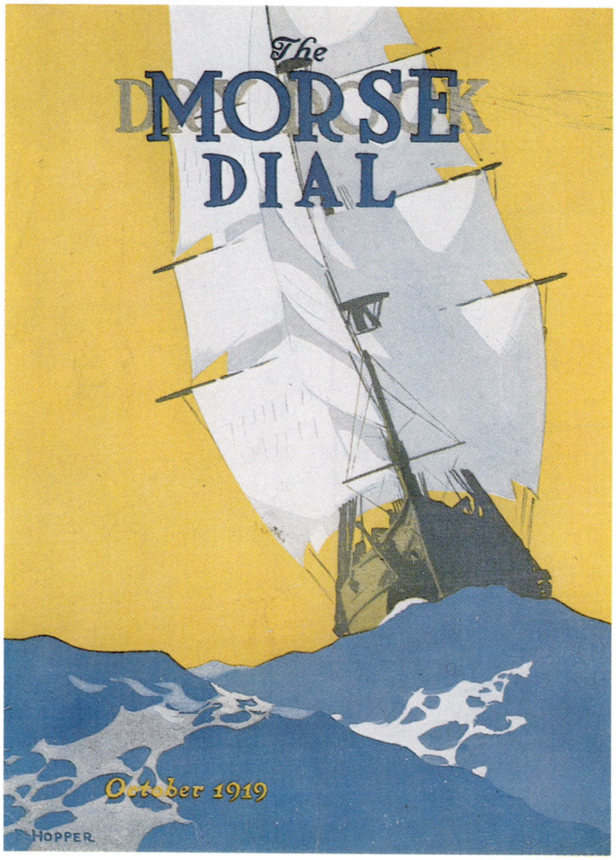

288

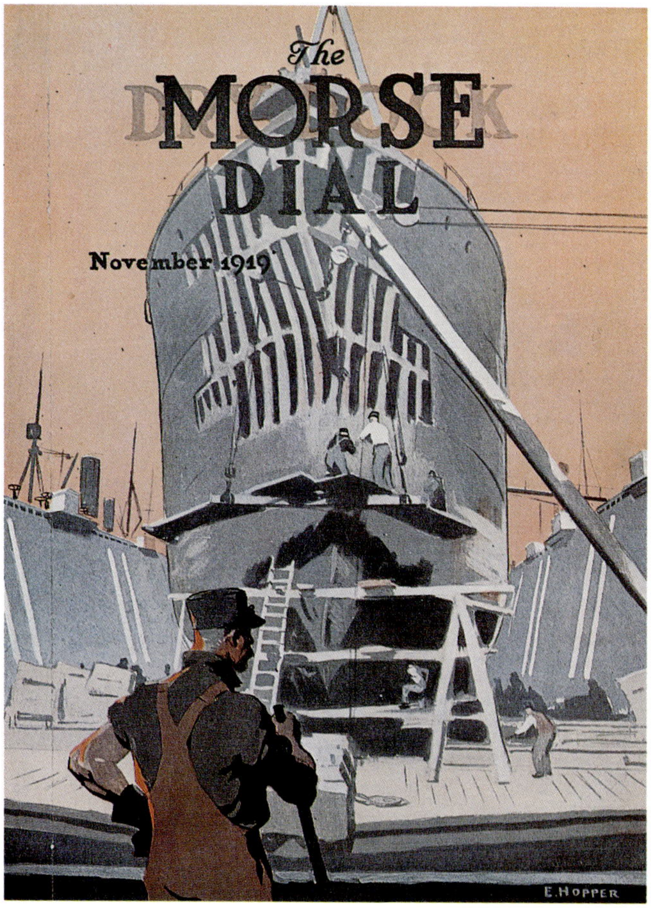

289

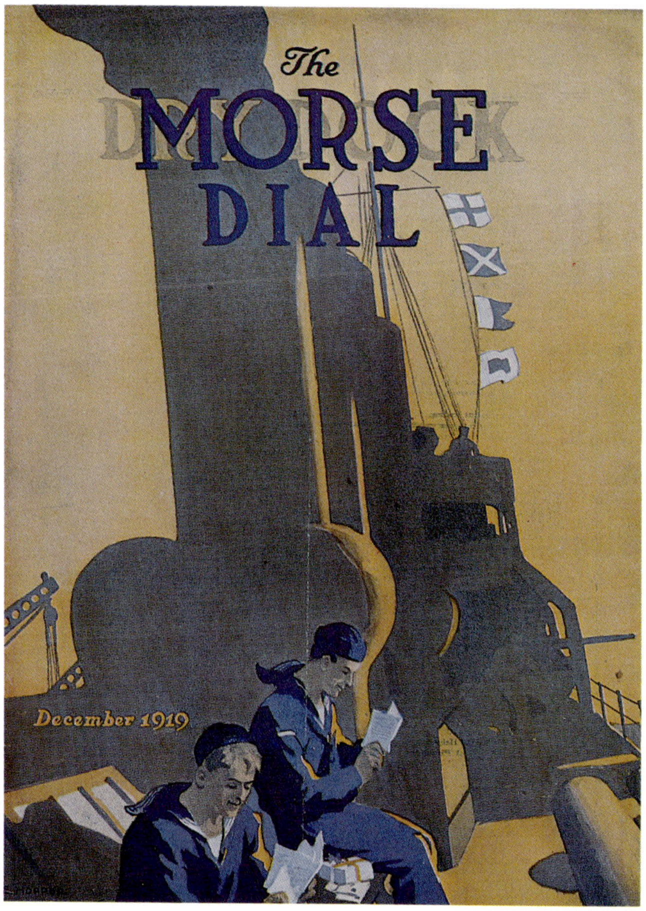

290

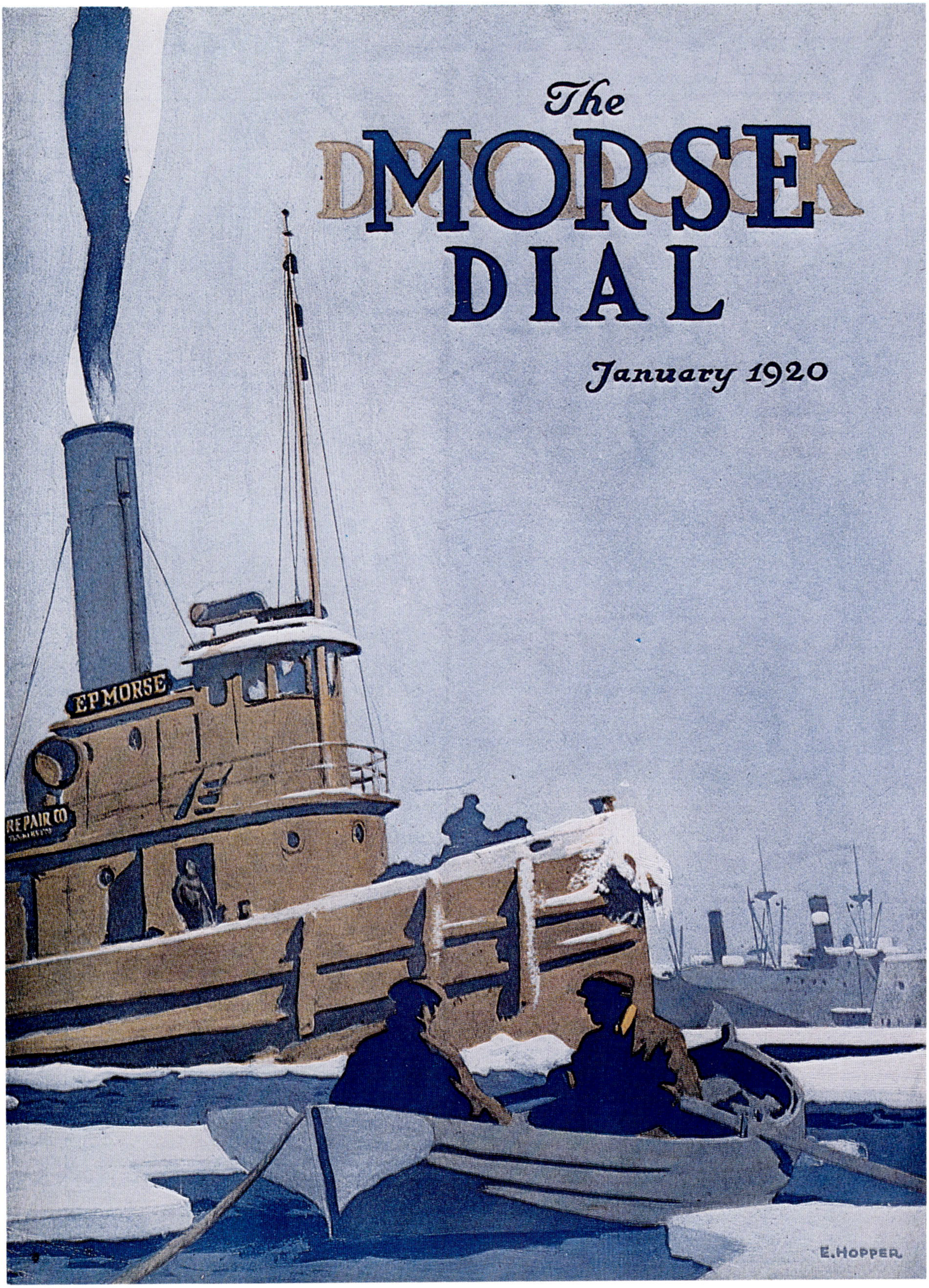
The
MORSE
DRY DOCK
DIAL
January 1920
EP MORSE
REPAIR CO
E. HOPPER

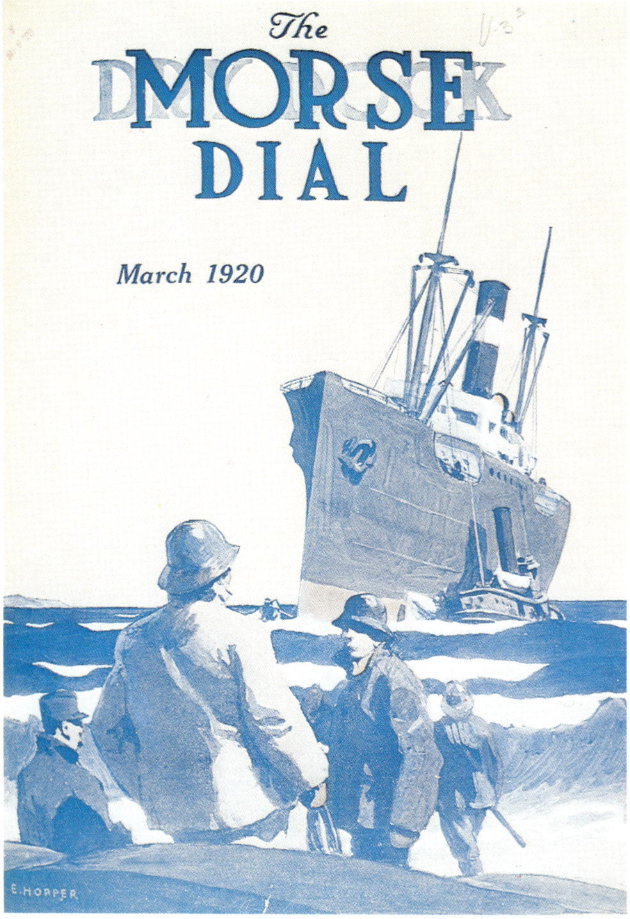

292

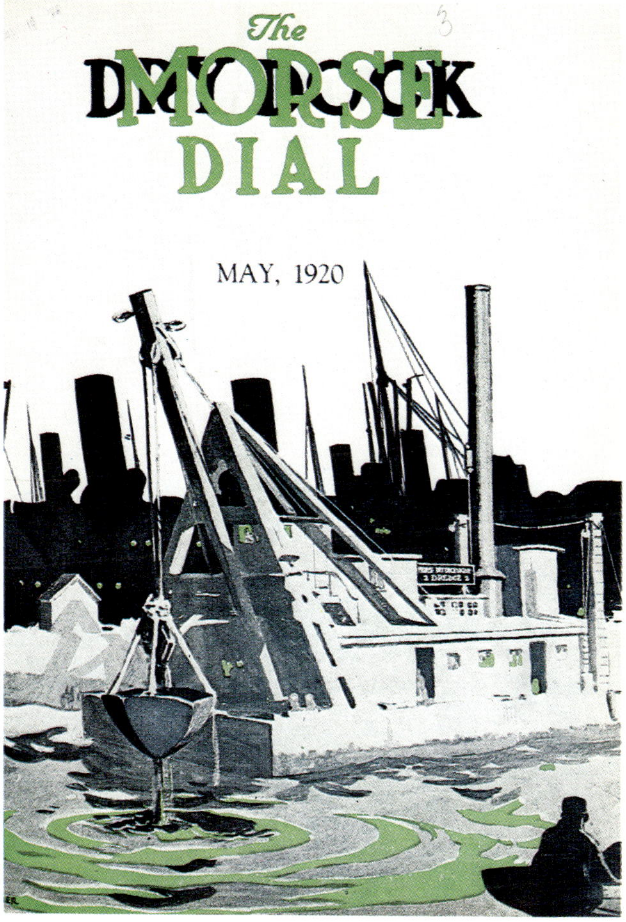

293

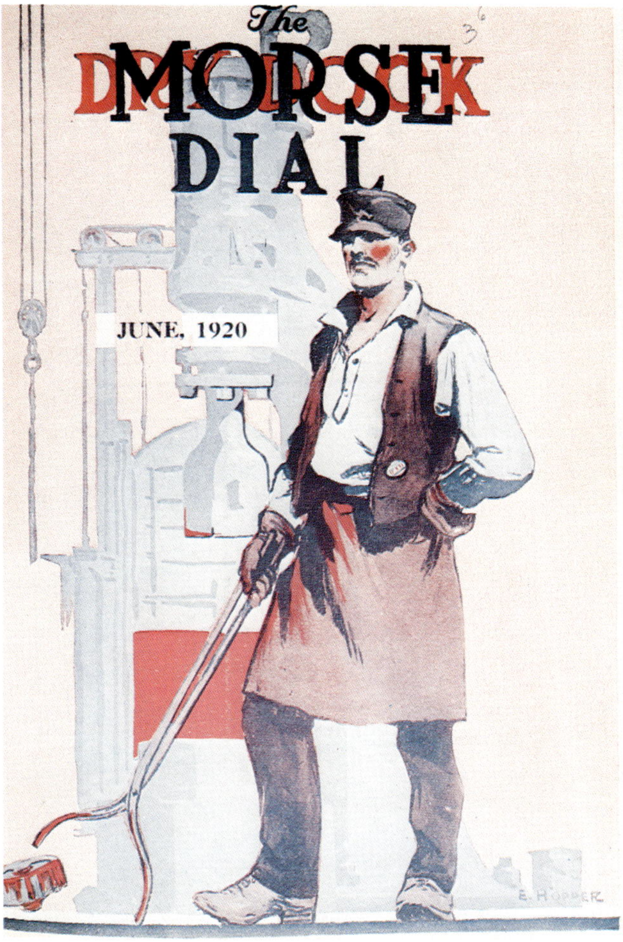

294

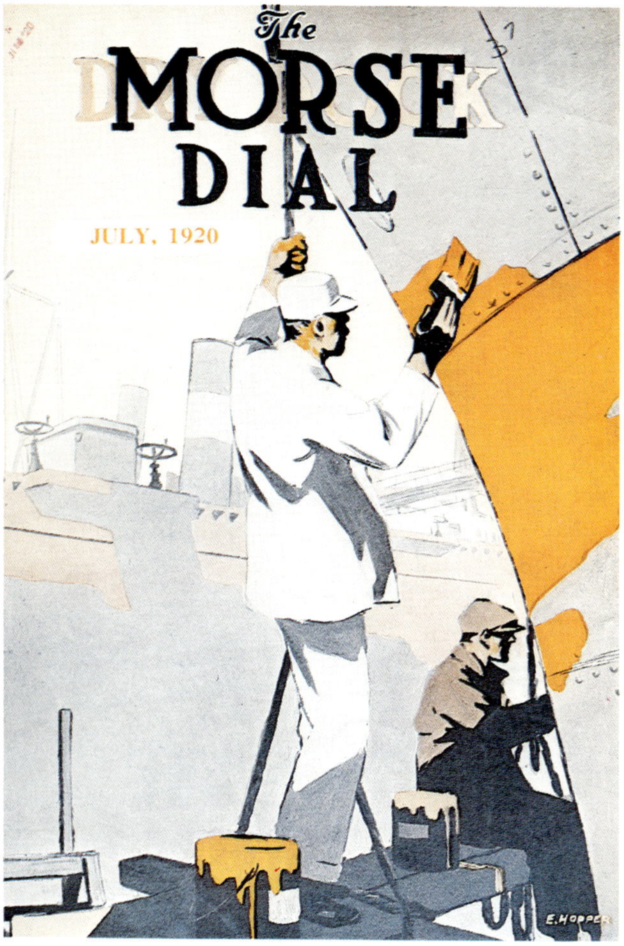

295

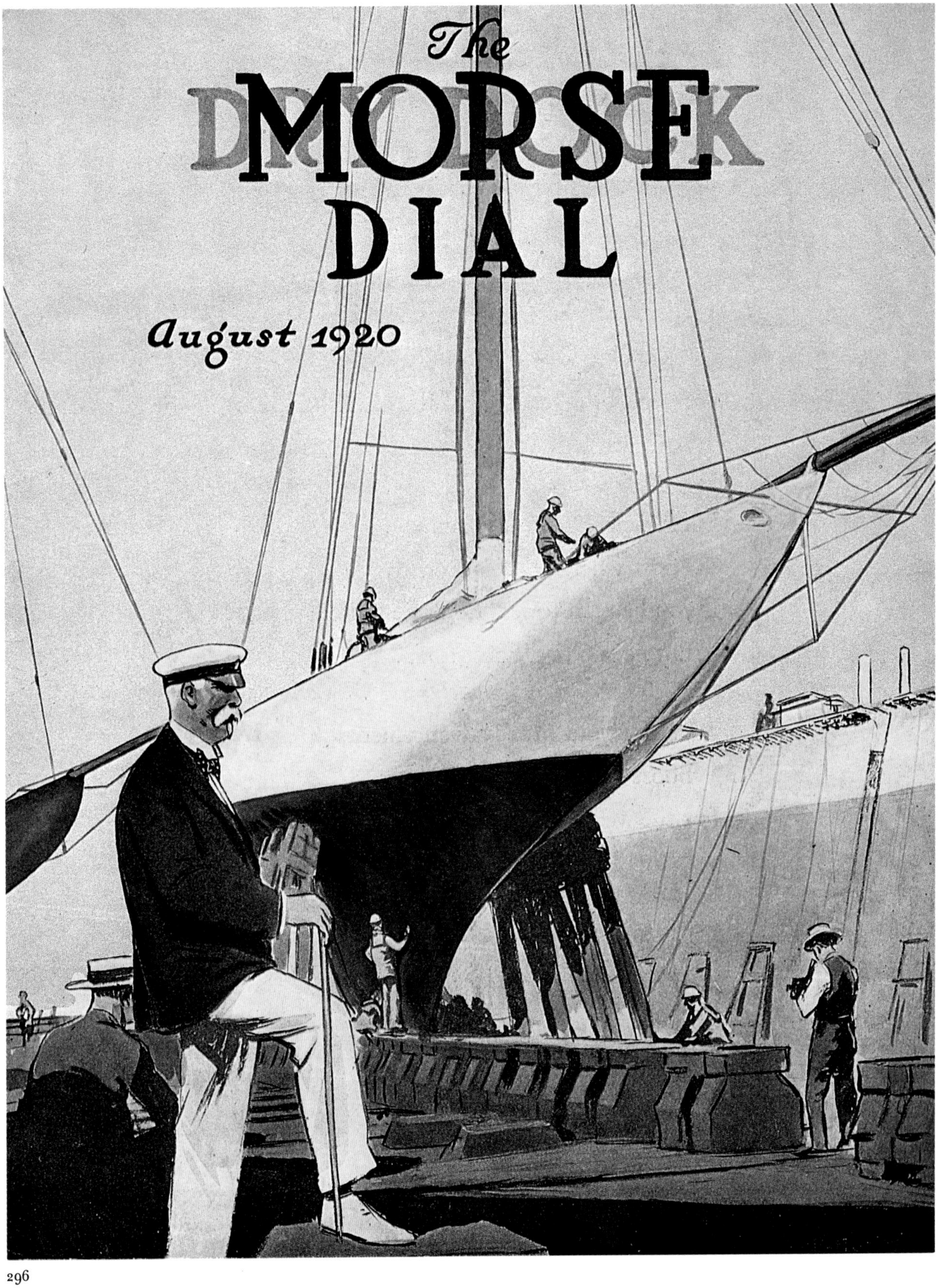
The
MORSE
DRYDOCK
DIAL
August 1920

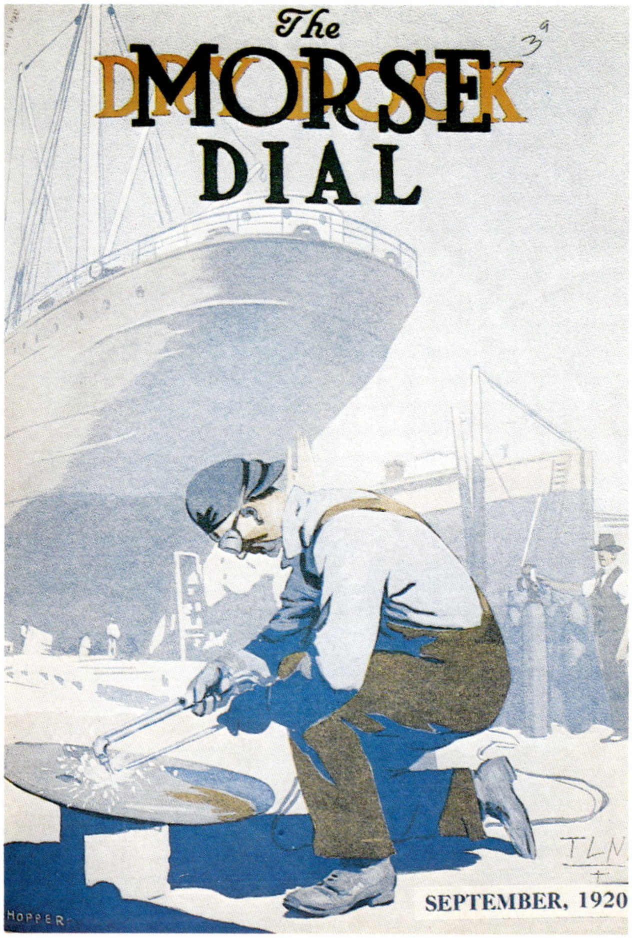

297

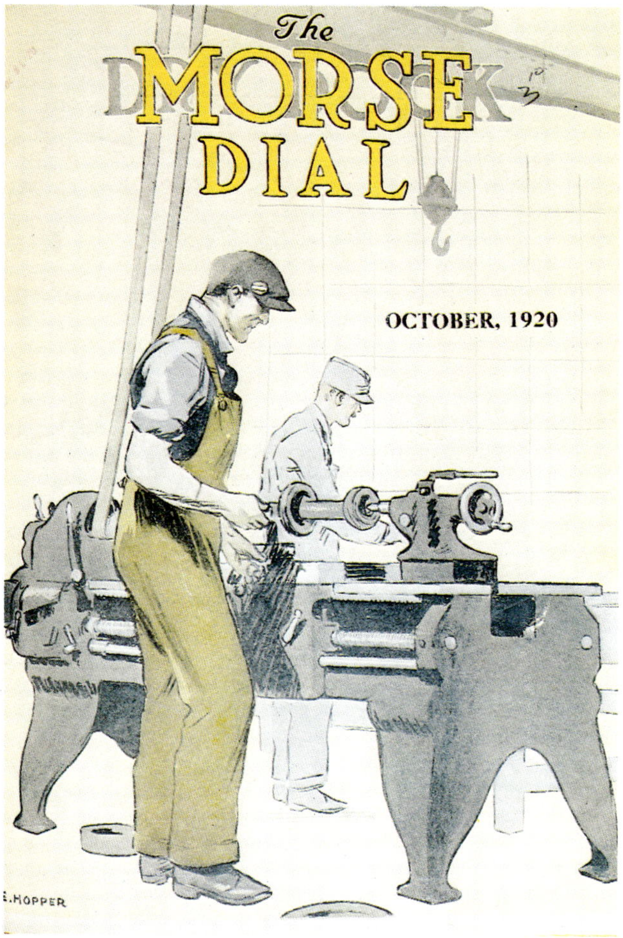

298

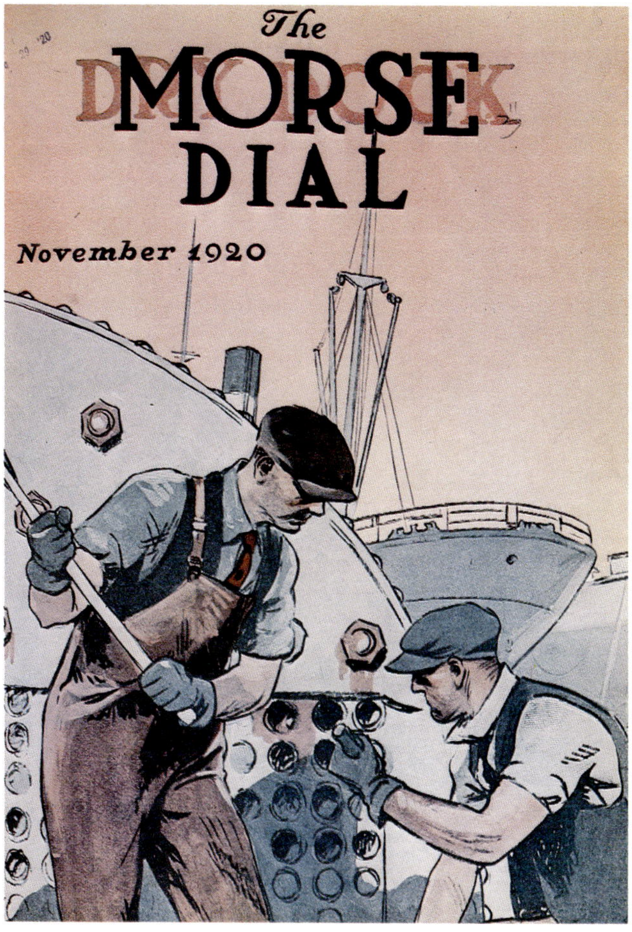

299

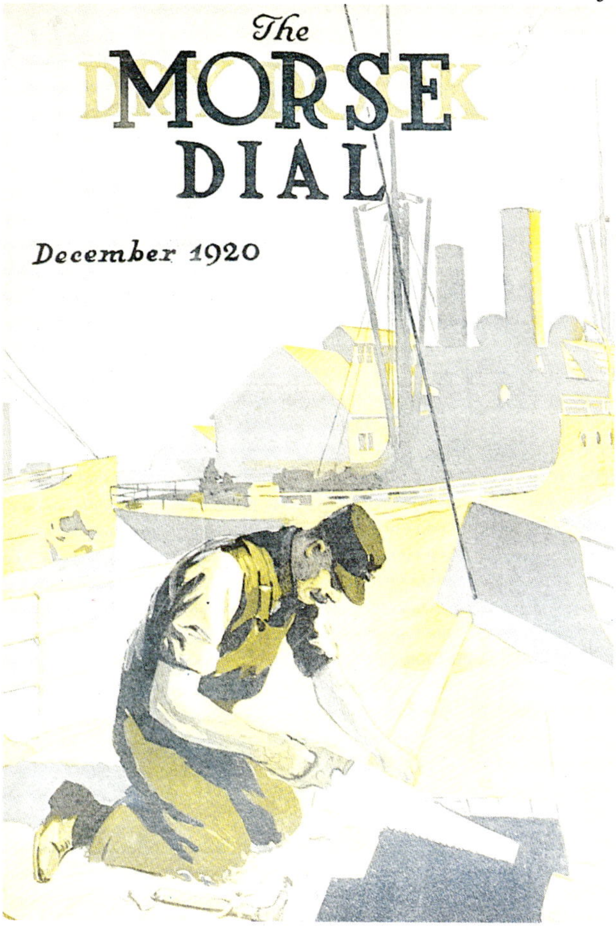

300

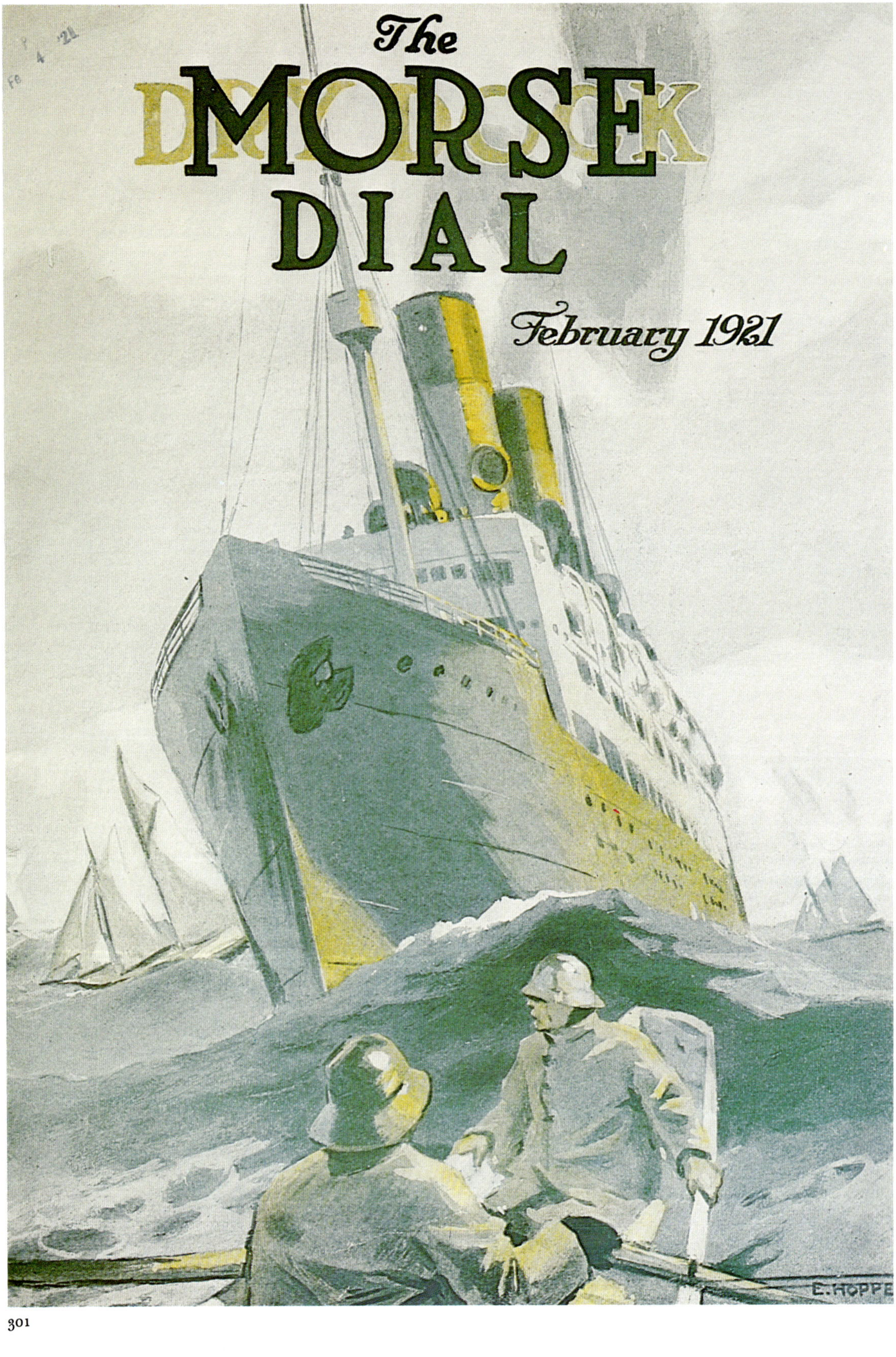
The
MORSE
DIAL
February 1921
E. HOPPE

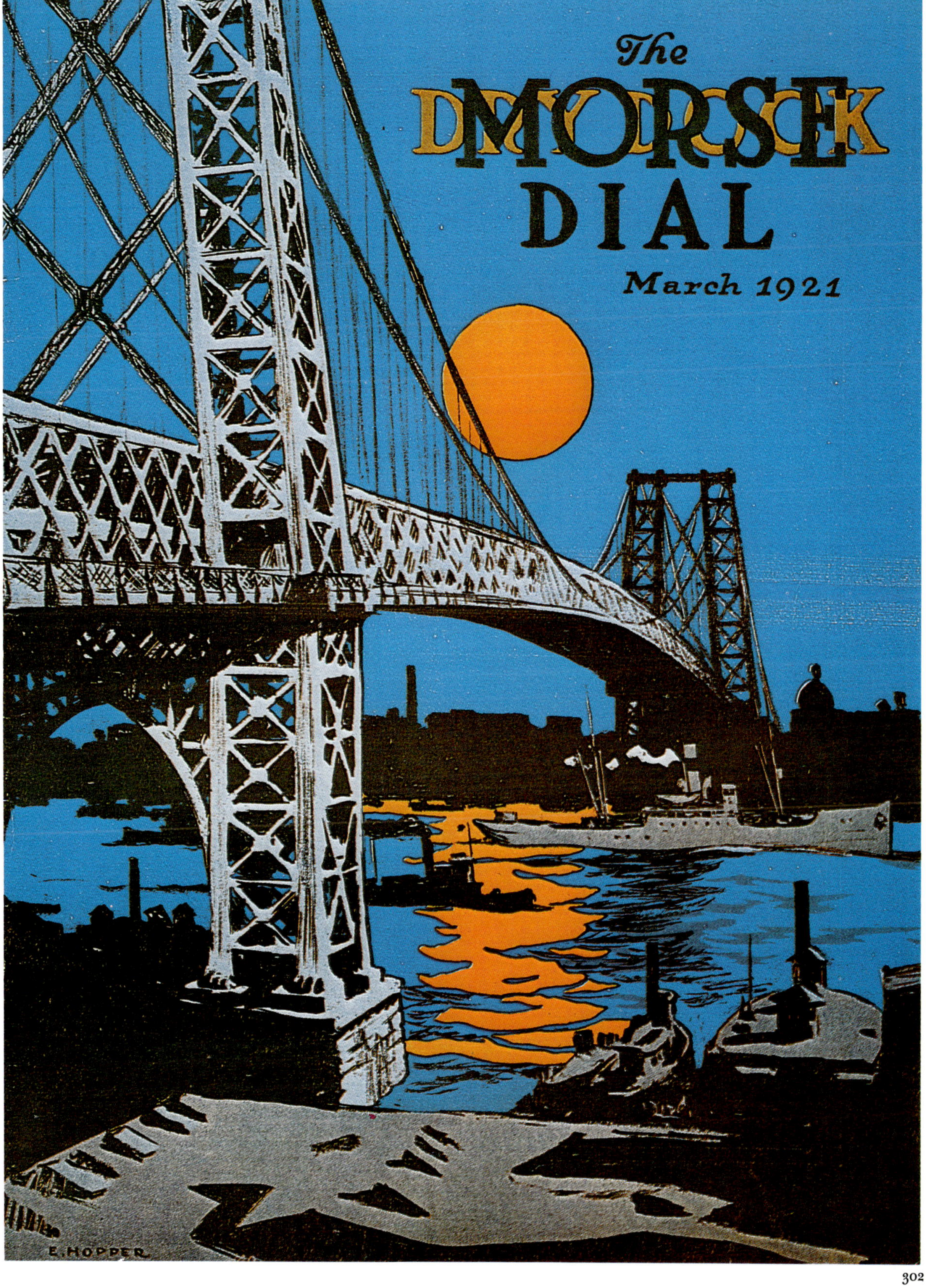
The
MORSE
DIAL
March 1921
E. HOPPER

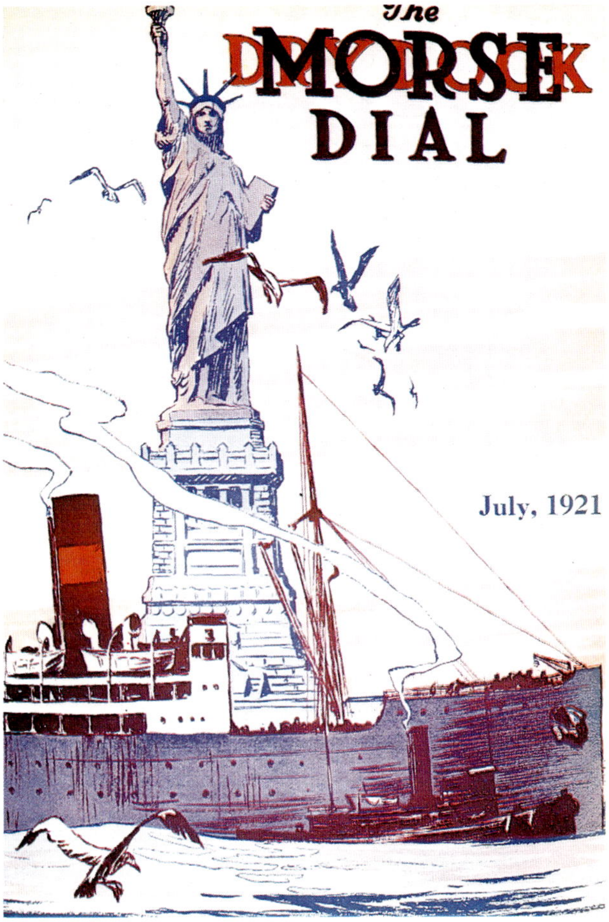

303

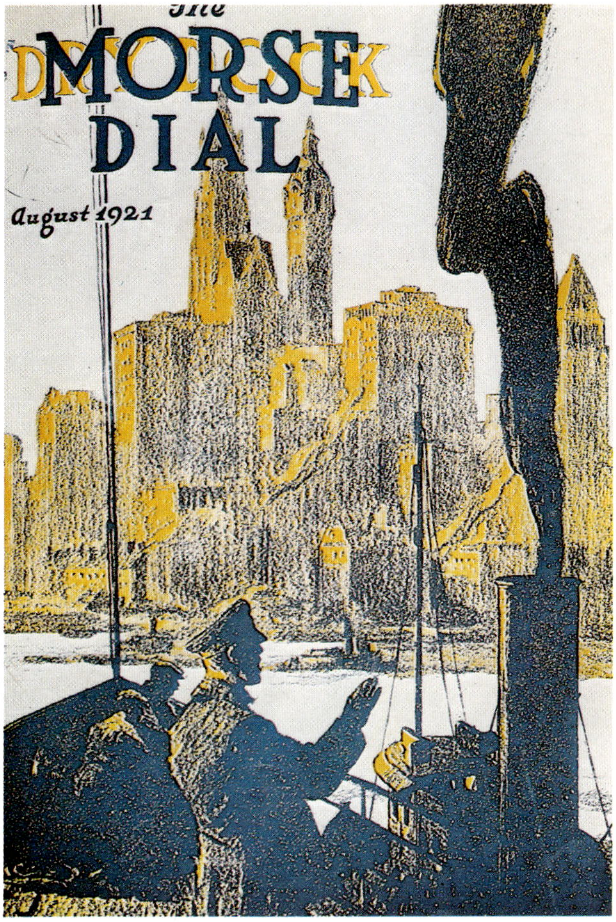

304

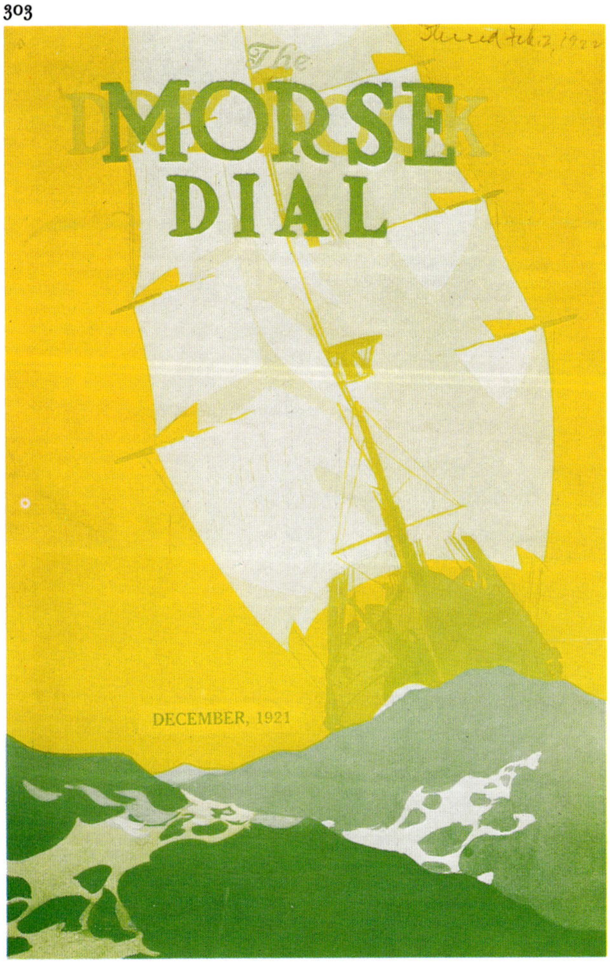

305

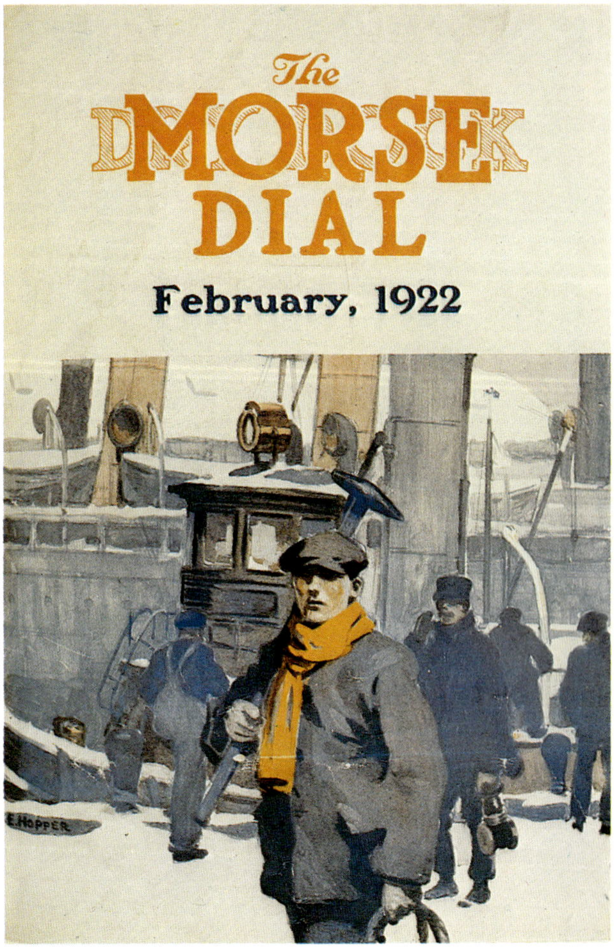

306

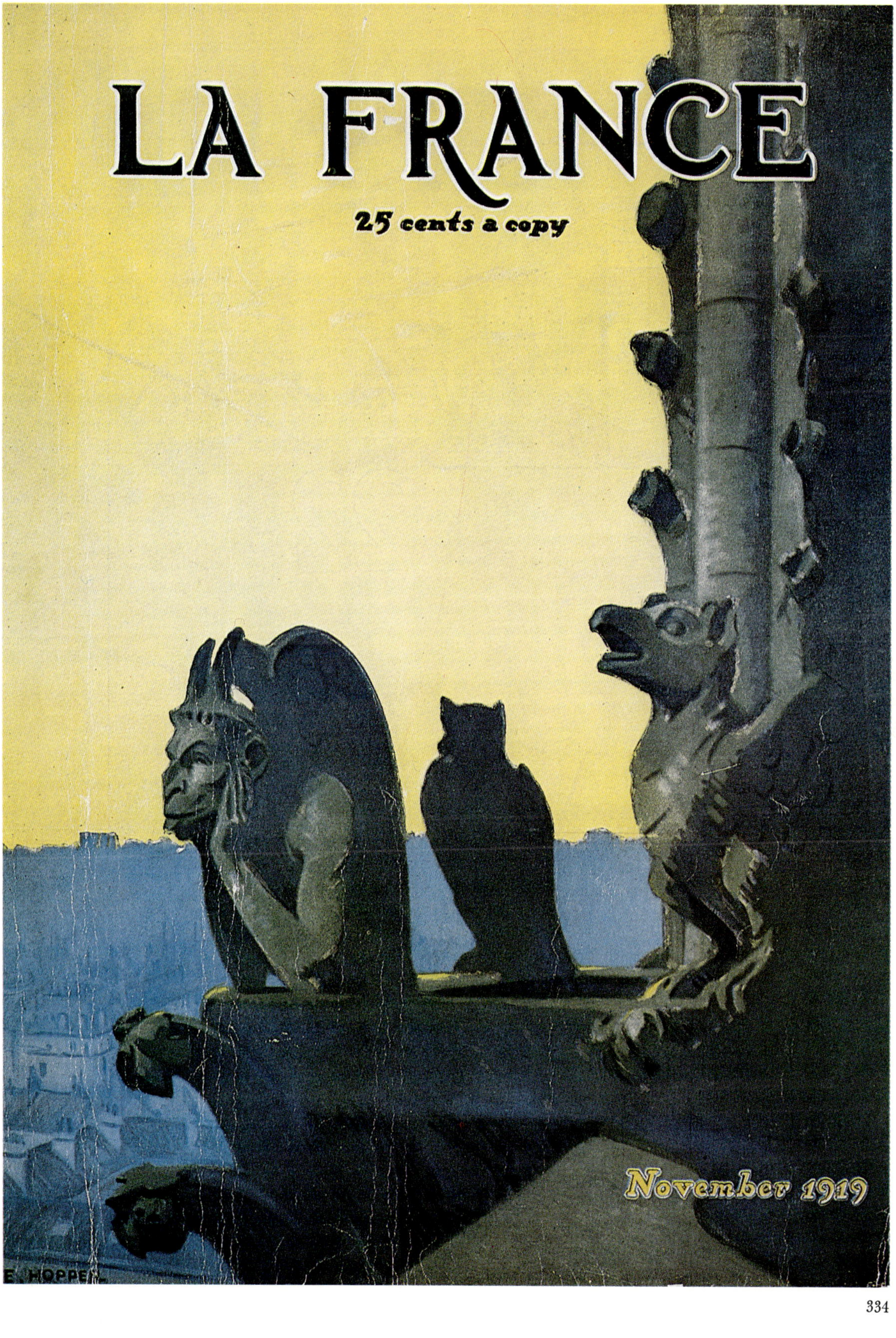
LA FRANCE
25 cents a copy
November 1919
E. HOPPER

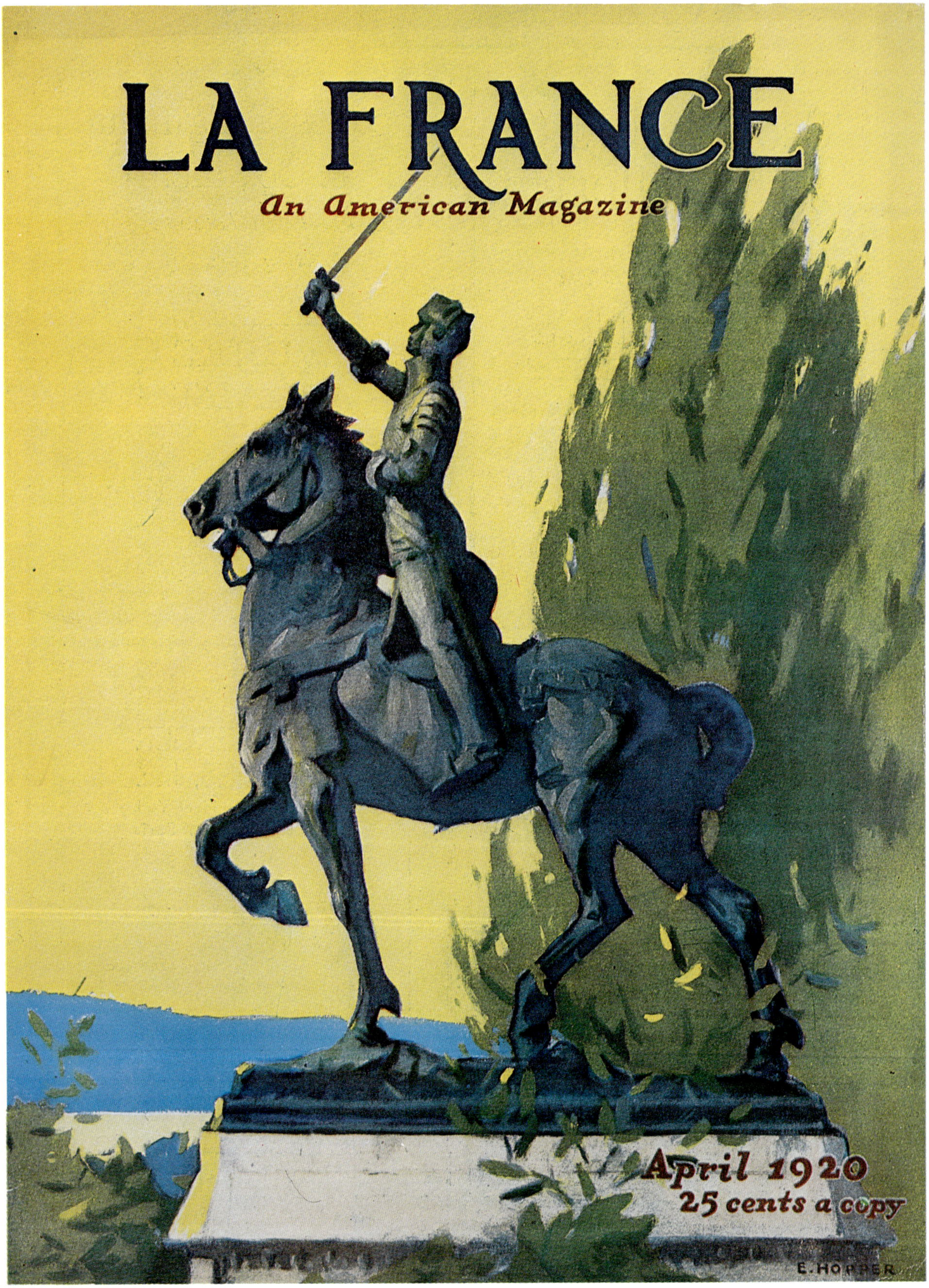
LA FRANCE
An American Magazine
April 1920
25 cents a copy
E. HOPPER

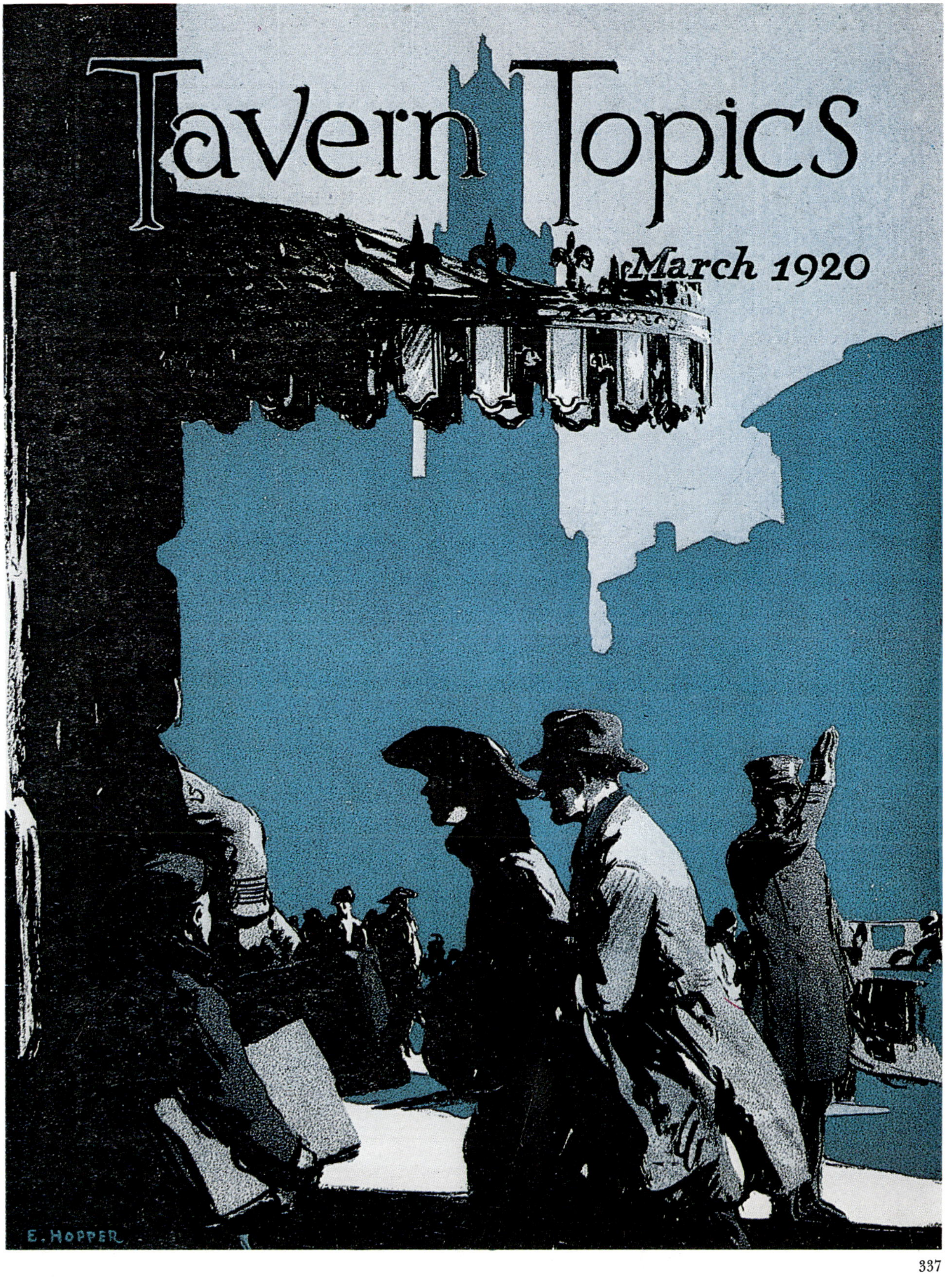
Tavern Topics
March 1920
E. HOPPER

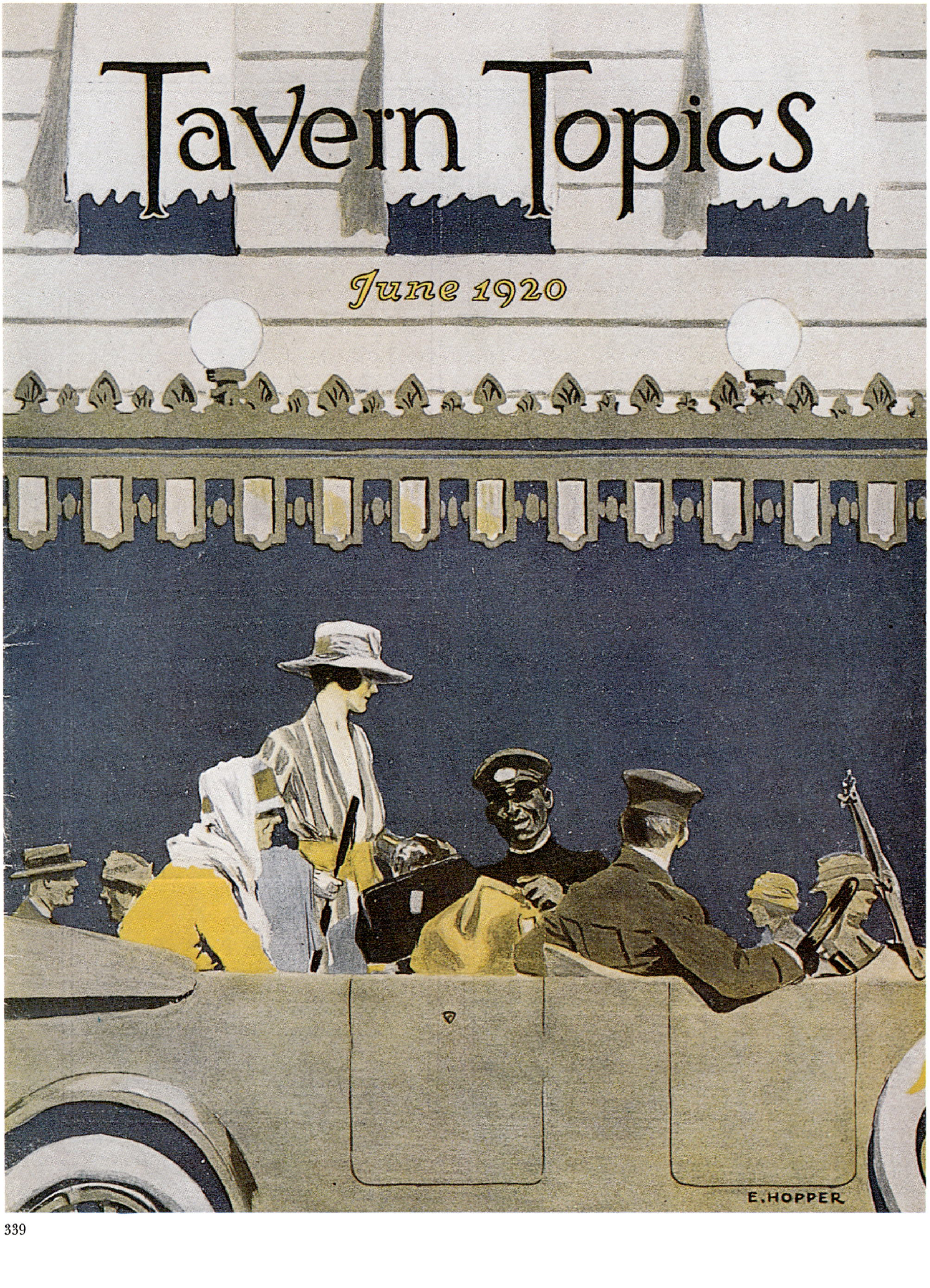
Tavern Topics
June 1920
E. HOPPER

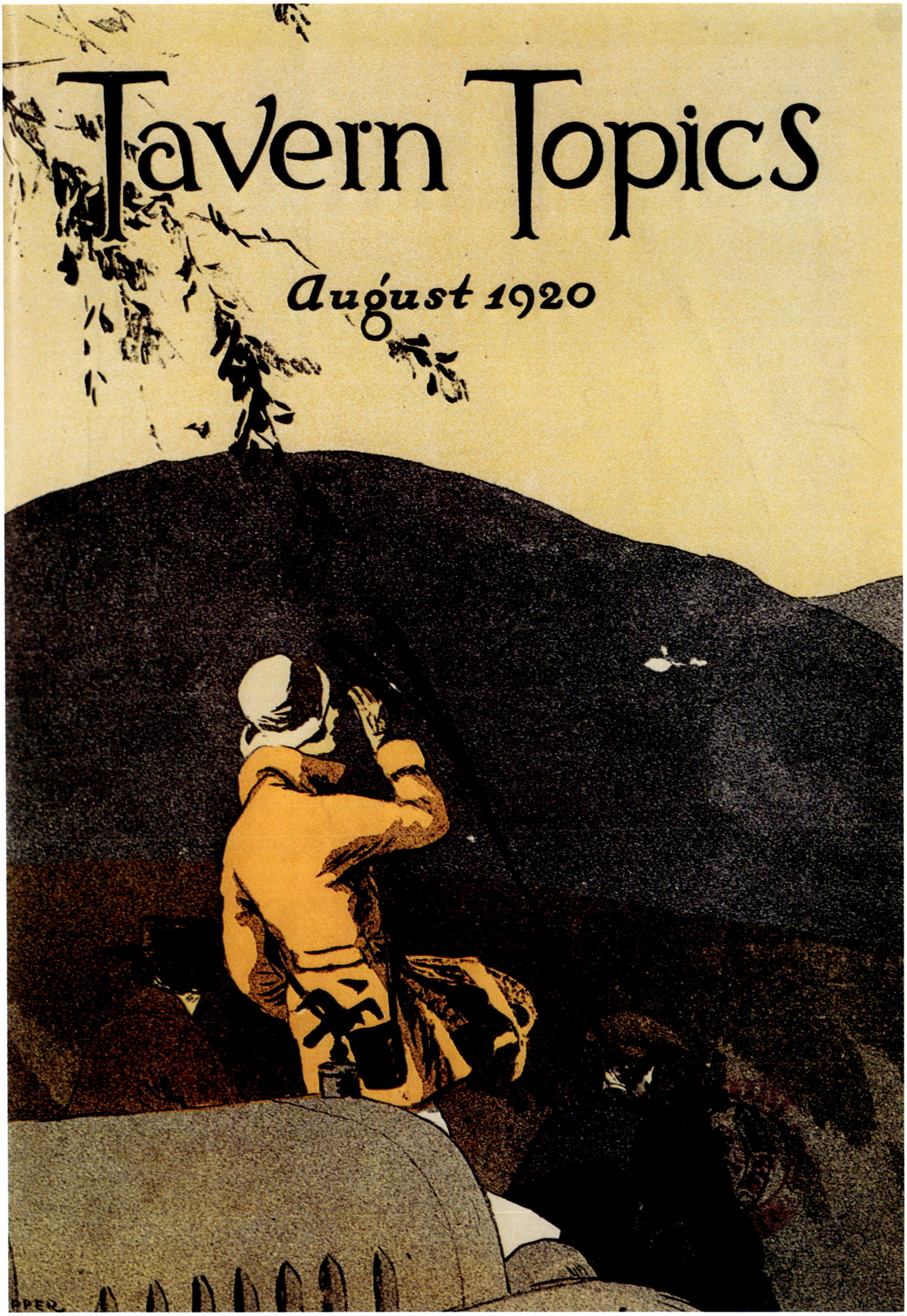
Tavern Topics
August 1920

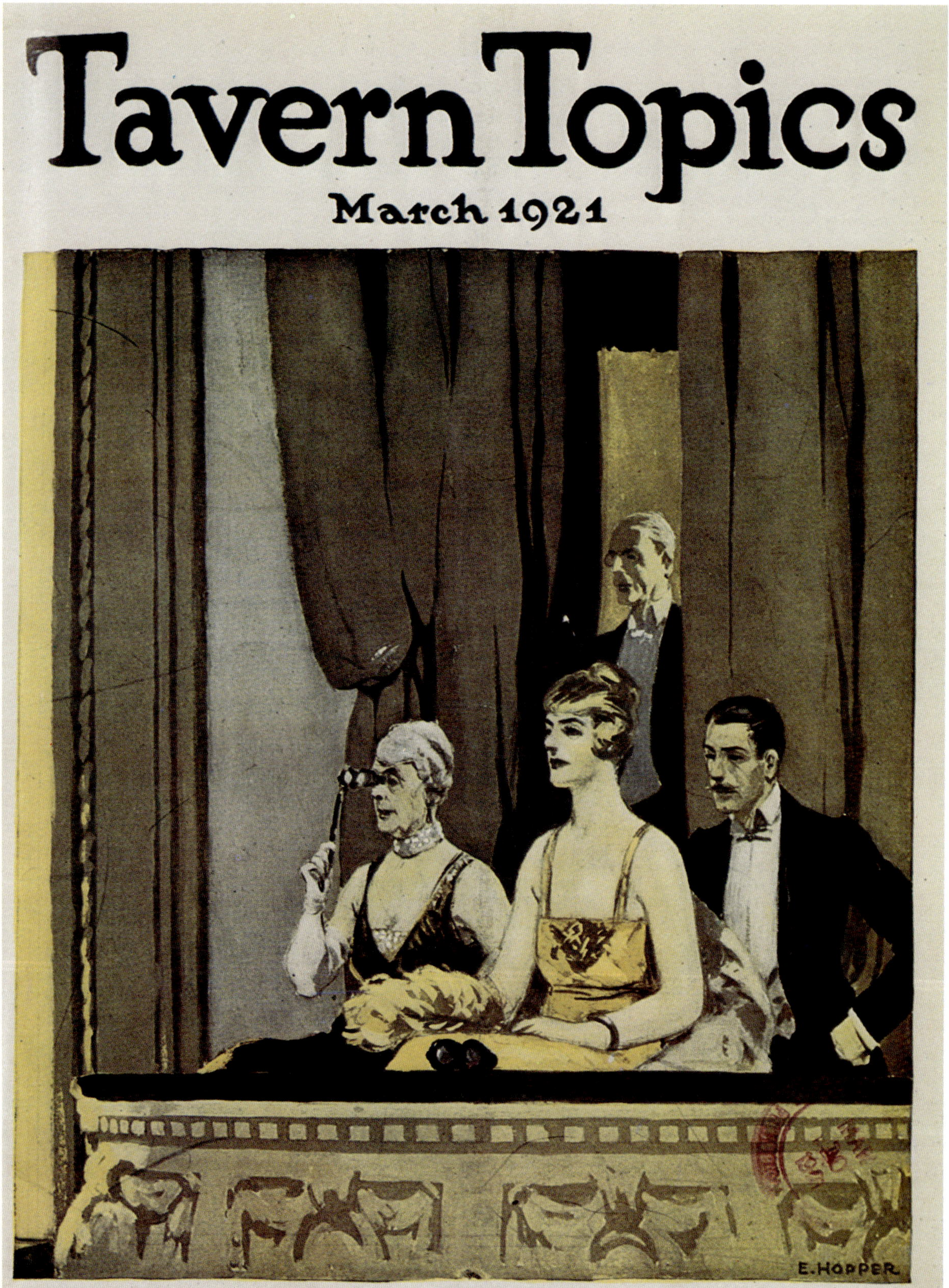
Tavern Topics
March 1921
E. HOPPER
10c Per Copy
Shops and Shows
Notas Hispano-Americanas
$1.00 Per Year

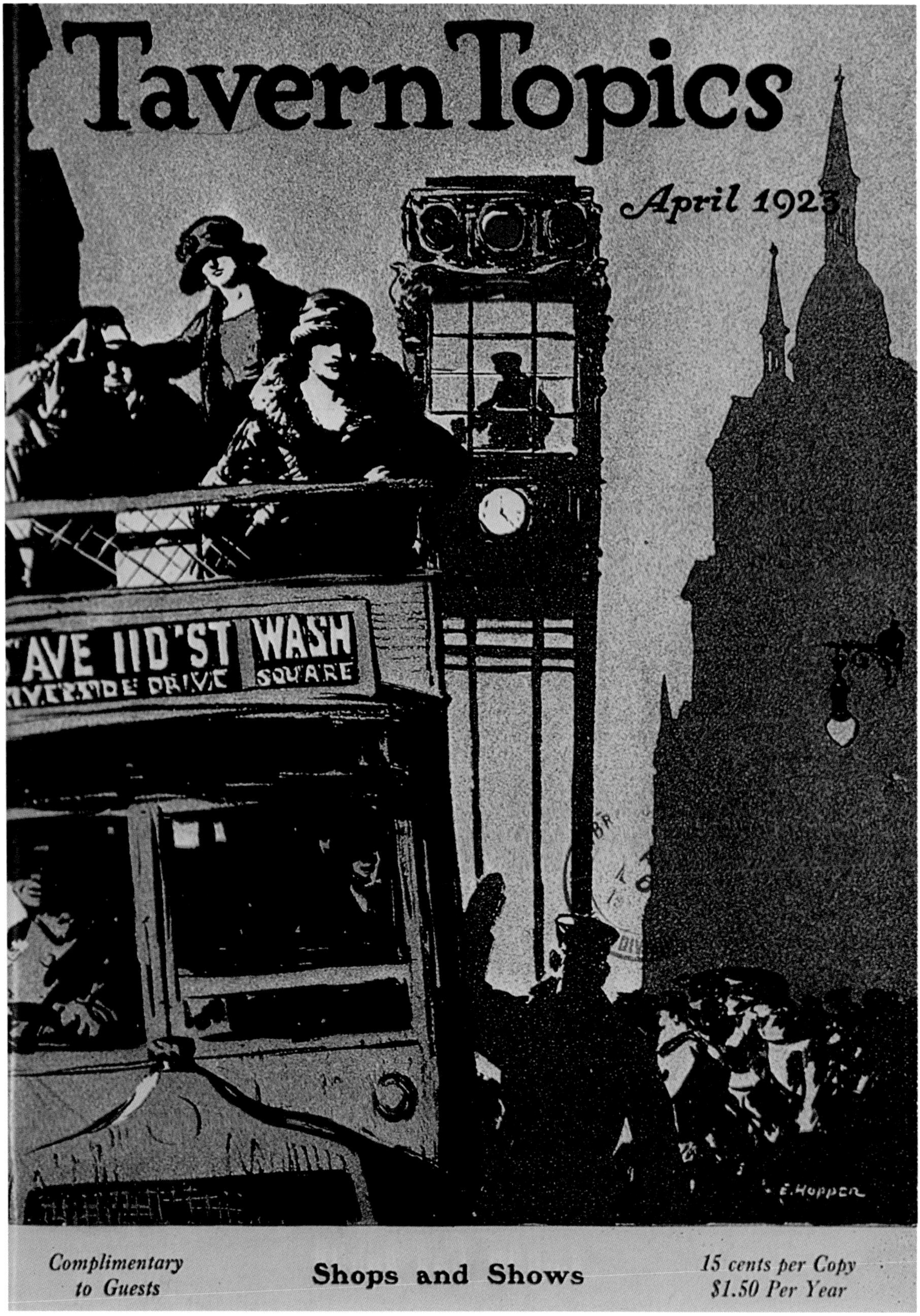
Tavern Topics
April 192
AVE 110'ST
WASH
SQUARE
E. Hopper
Complimentary
to Guests
Shops and Shows
15 cents per Copy
$1.50 Per Year

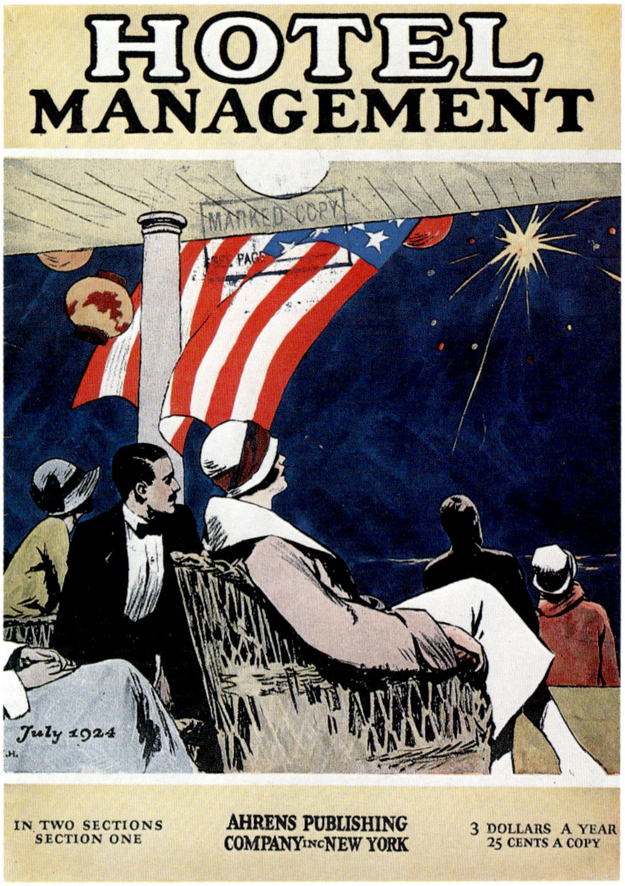

344

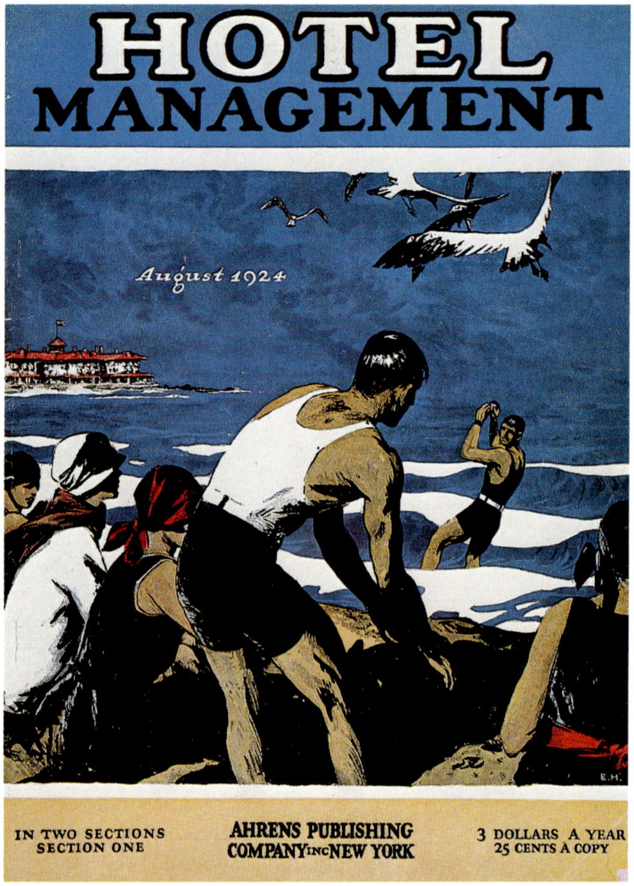

345

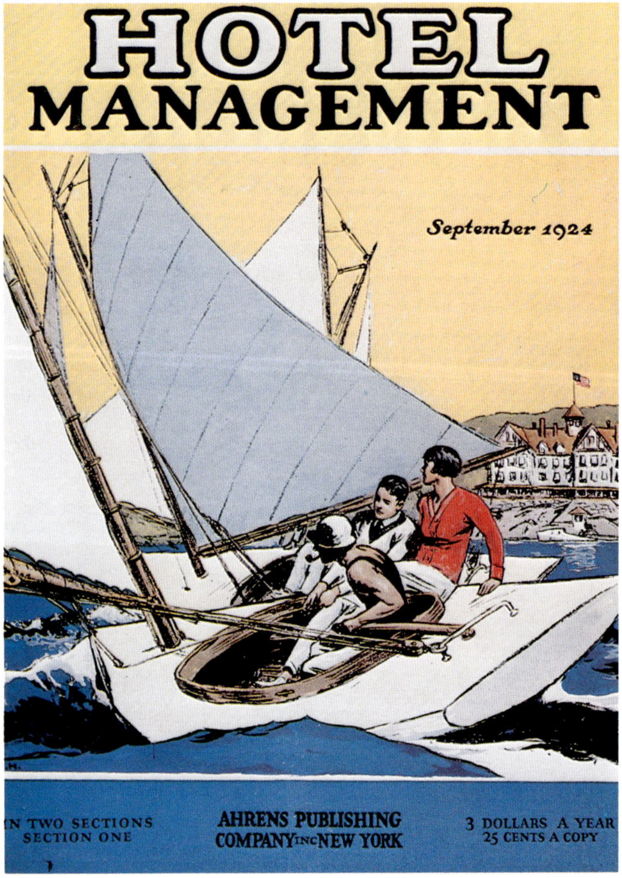

346

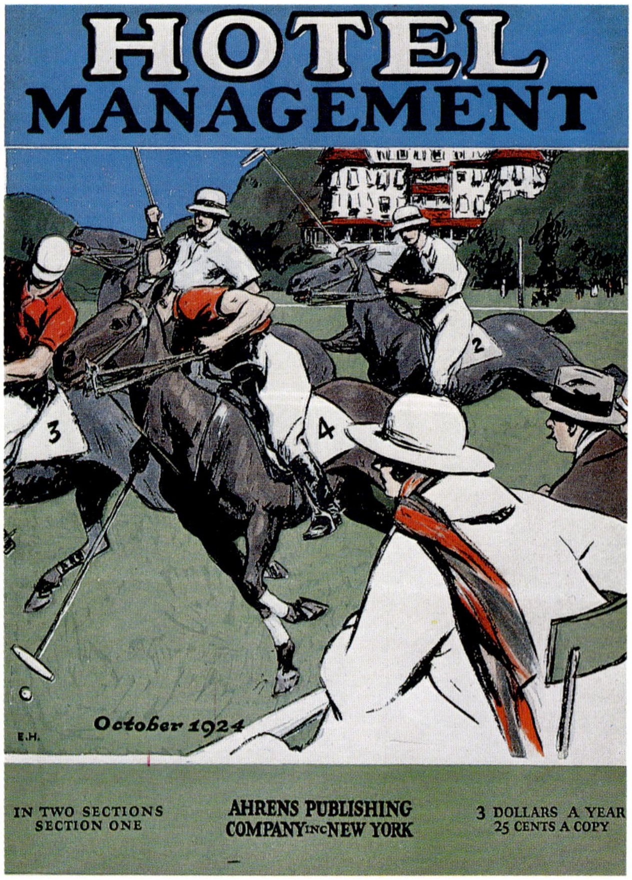

347

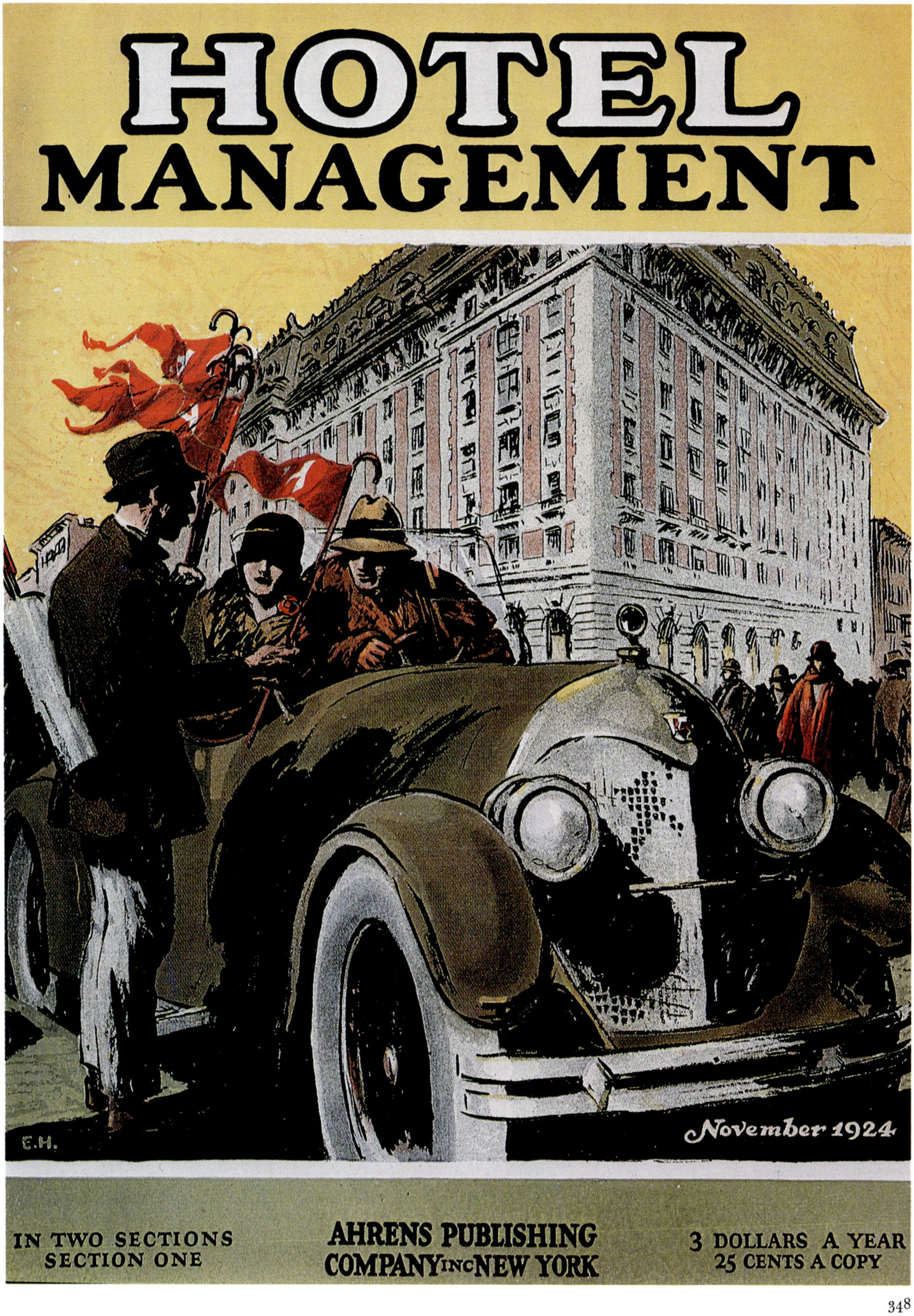
HOTEL
MANAGEMENT
E.H.
November 1924
IN TWO SECTIONS
SECTION ONE
AHRENS PUBLISHING
COMPANY INC NEW YORK
3 DOLLARS A YEAR
25 CENTS A COPY

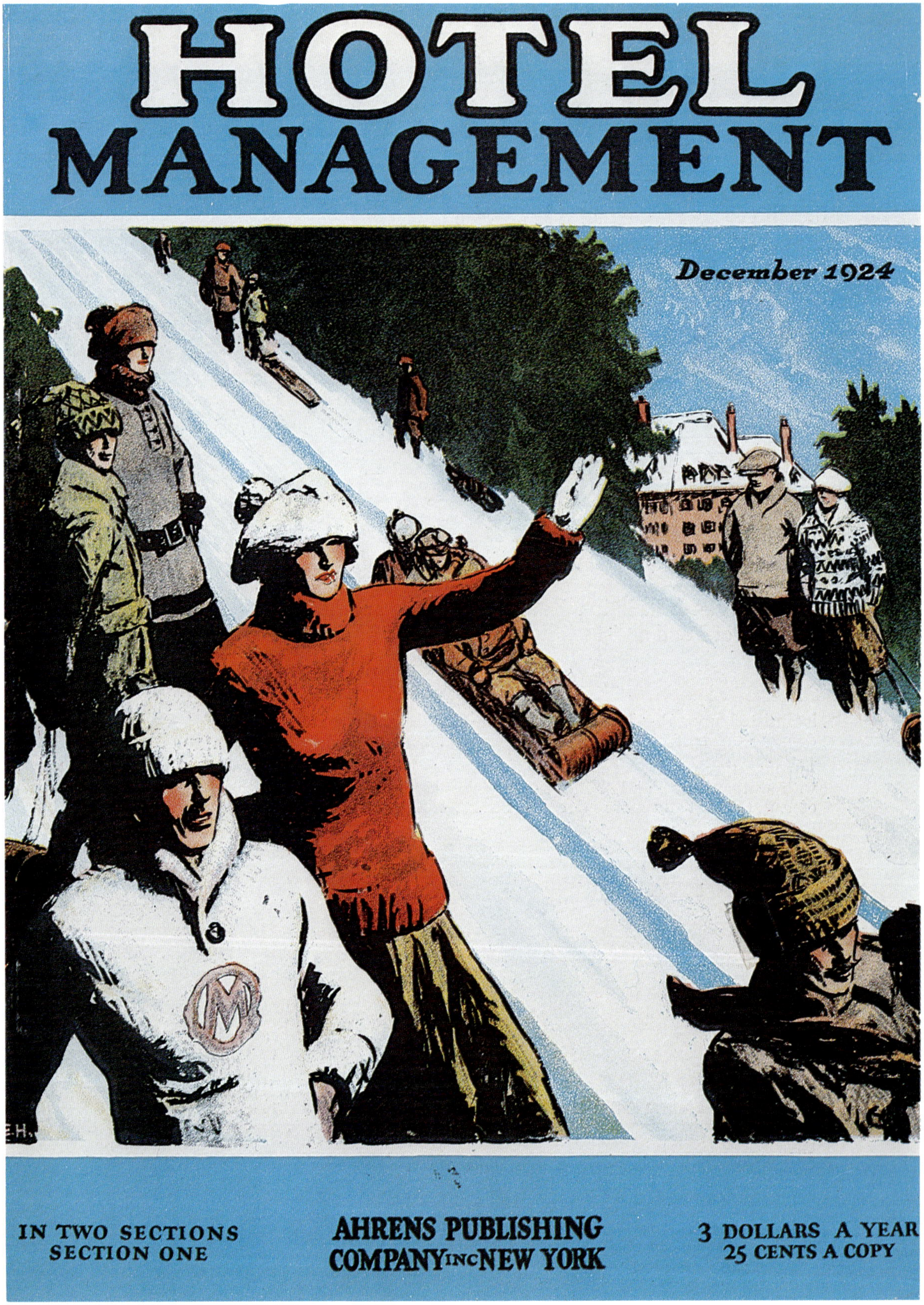
HOTEL
MANAGEMENT
December 1924
IN TWO SECTIONS
SECTION ONE
AHRENS PUBLISHING
COMPANY INC NEW YORK
3 DOLLARS A YEAR
25 CENTS A COPY

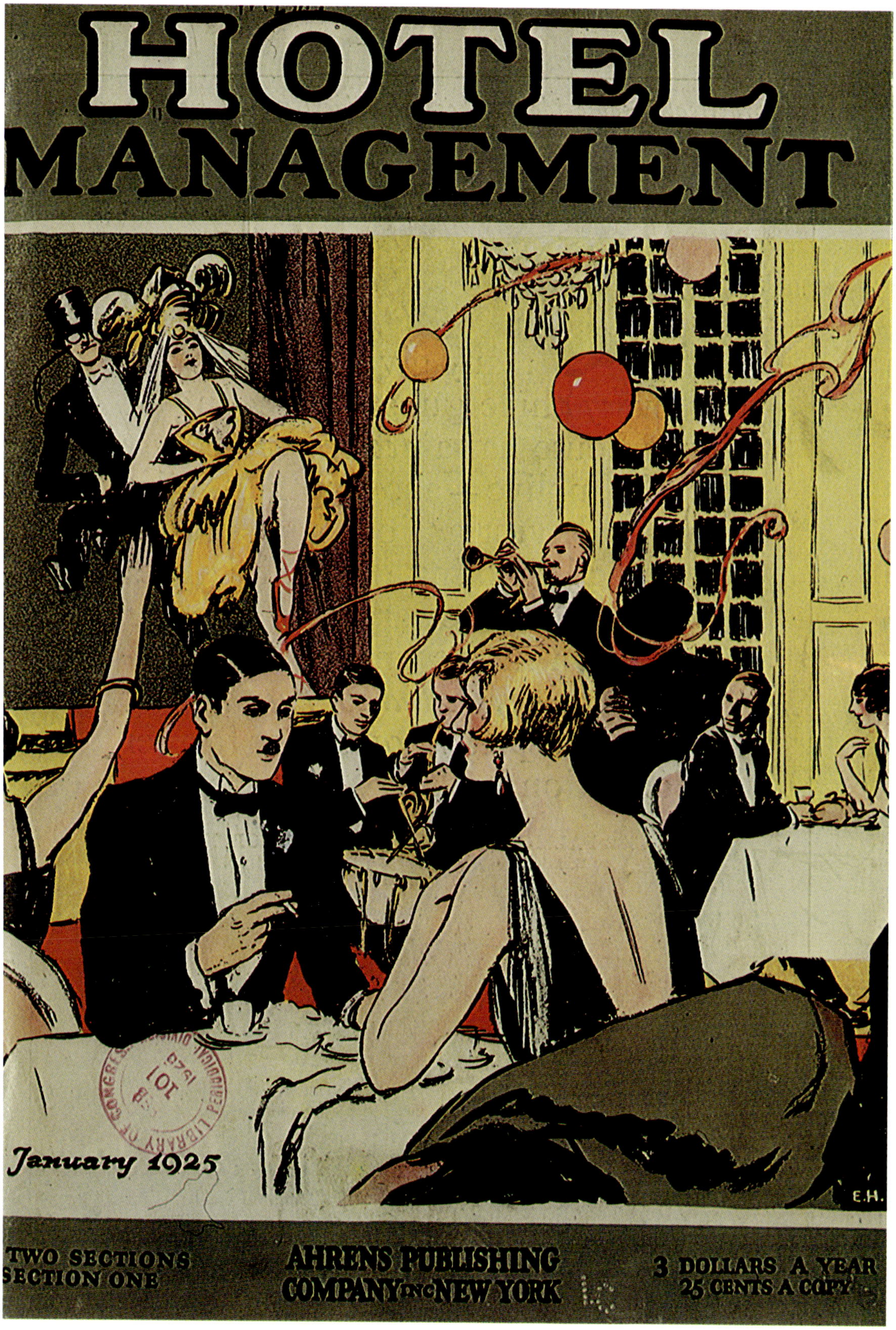
HOTEL
MANAGEMENT
January 1925
E.H.
TWO SECTIONS
SECTION ONE
AHRENS PUBLISHING
COMPANY INC NEW YORK
3 DOLLARS A YEAR
25 CENTS A COPY

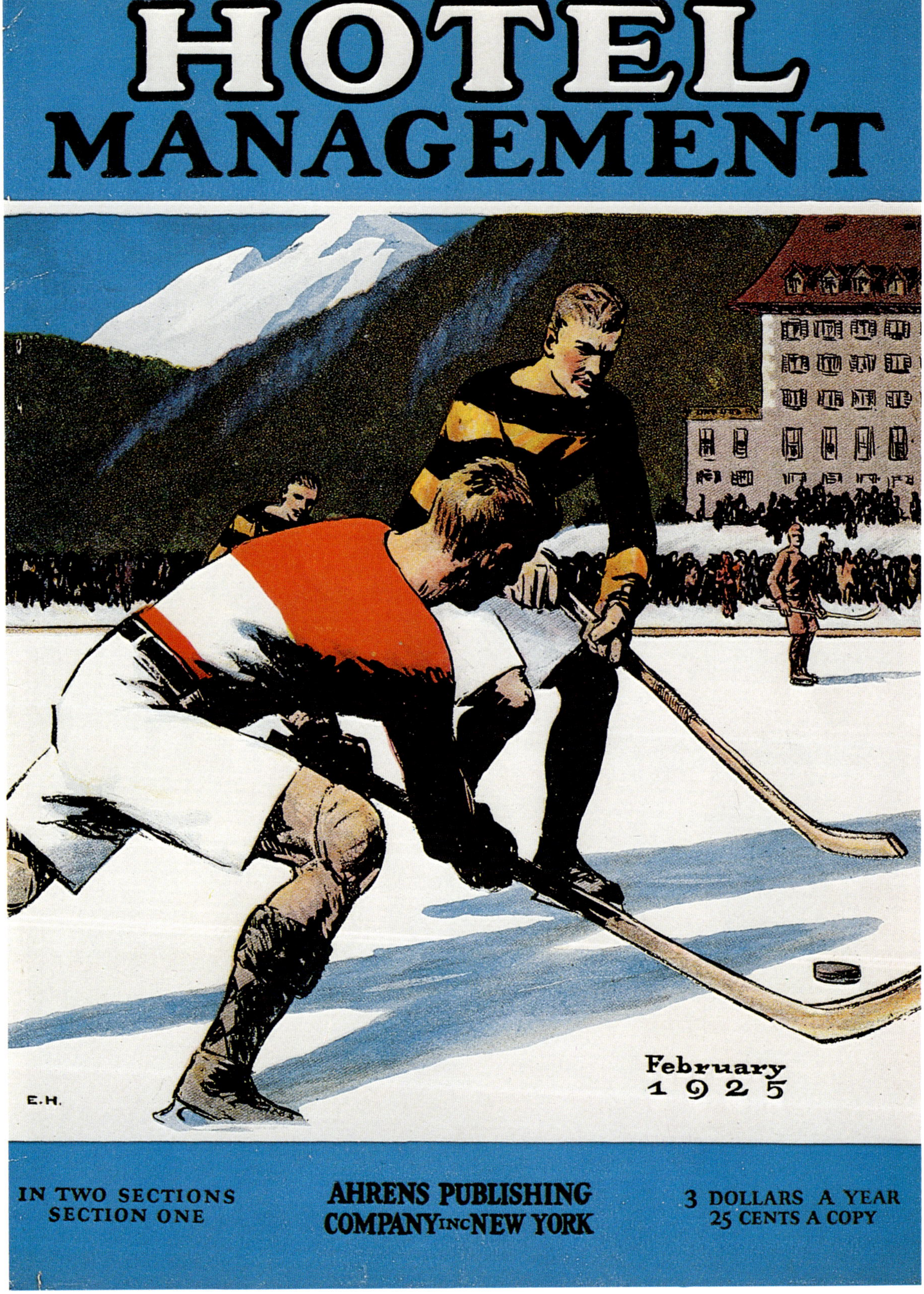
HOTEL
MANAGEMENT
February
1925
E.H.
IN TWO SECTIONS
SECTION ONE
AHRENS PUBLISHING
COMPANY INC NEW YORK
3 DOLLARS A YEAR
25 CENTS A COPY

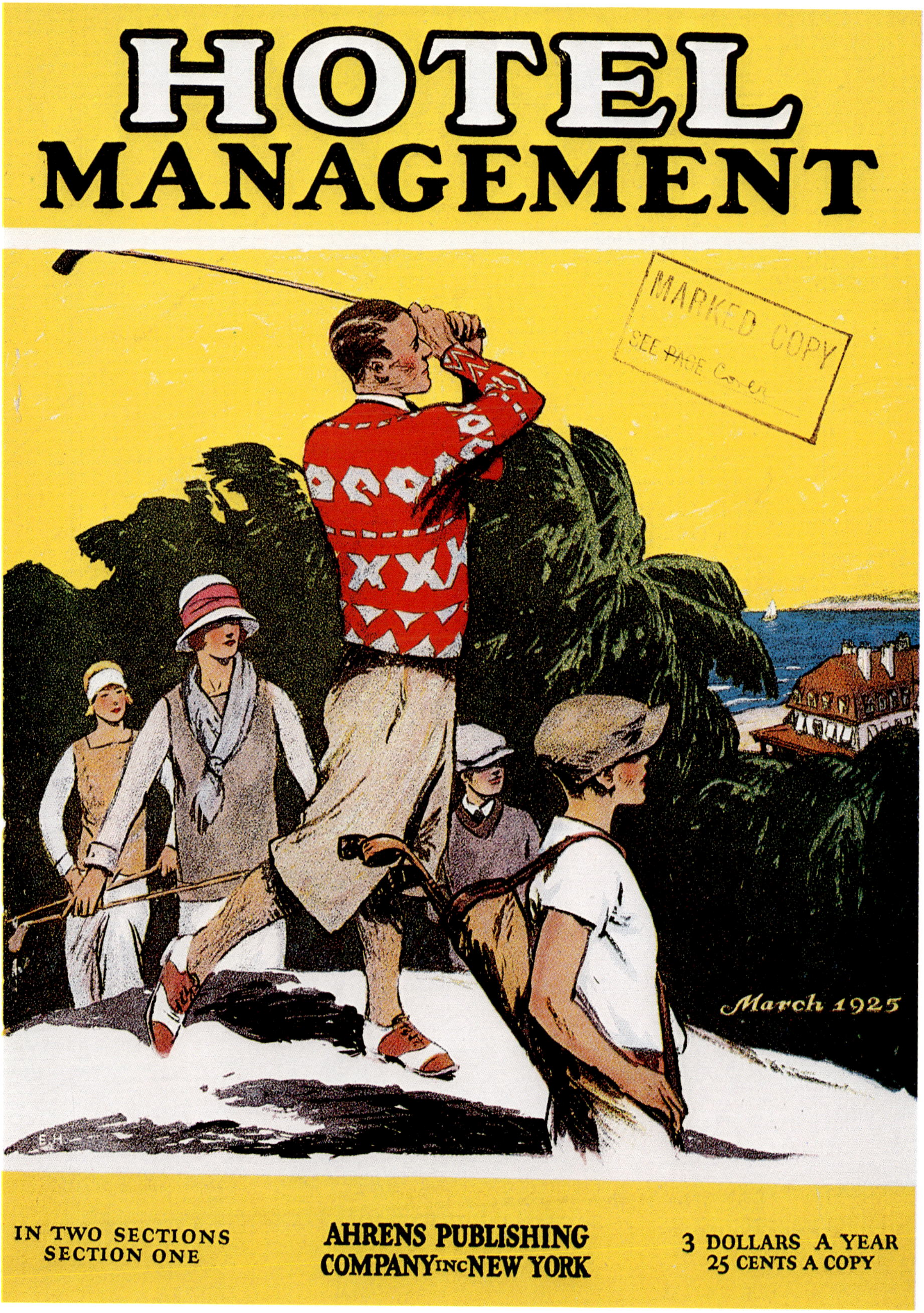
HOTEL
MANAGEMENT
MARKED COPY
SEE PAGE Cover
March 1925
IN TWO SECTIONS
SECTION ONE
AHRENS PUBLISHING
COMPANY INC NEW YORK
3 DOLLARS A YEAR
25 CENTS A COPY

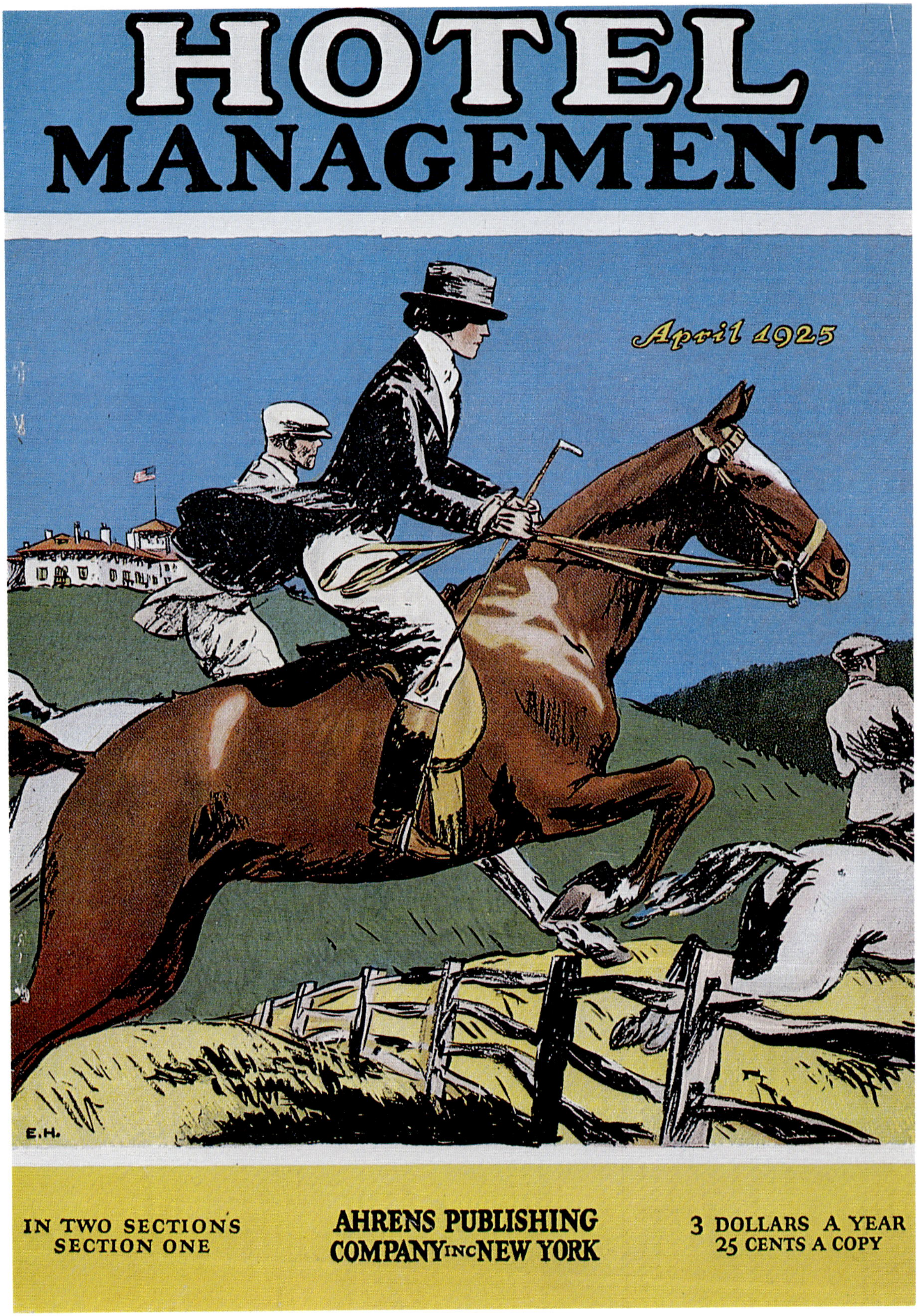
HOTEL
MANAGEMENT
April 1925
E.H.
IN TWO SECTIONS
SECTION ONE
AHRENS PUBLISHING
COMPANY INC NEW YORK
3 DOLLARS A YEAR
25 CENTS A COPY

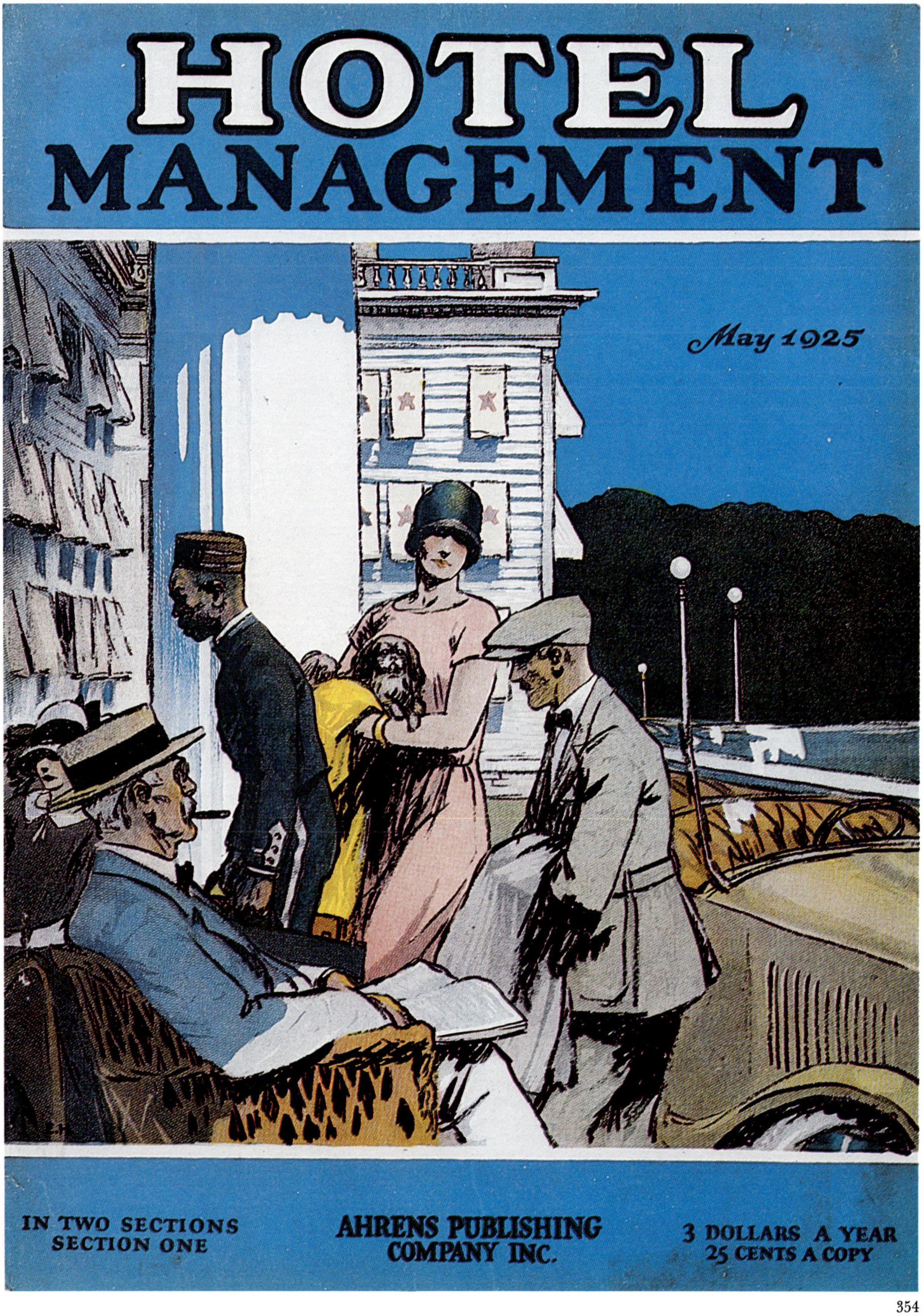
HOTEL
MANAGEMENT
May 1925
IN TWO SECTIONS
SECTION ONE
AHRENS PUBLISHING
COMPANY INC.
3 DOLLARS A YEAR
25 CENTS A COPY

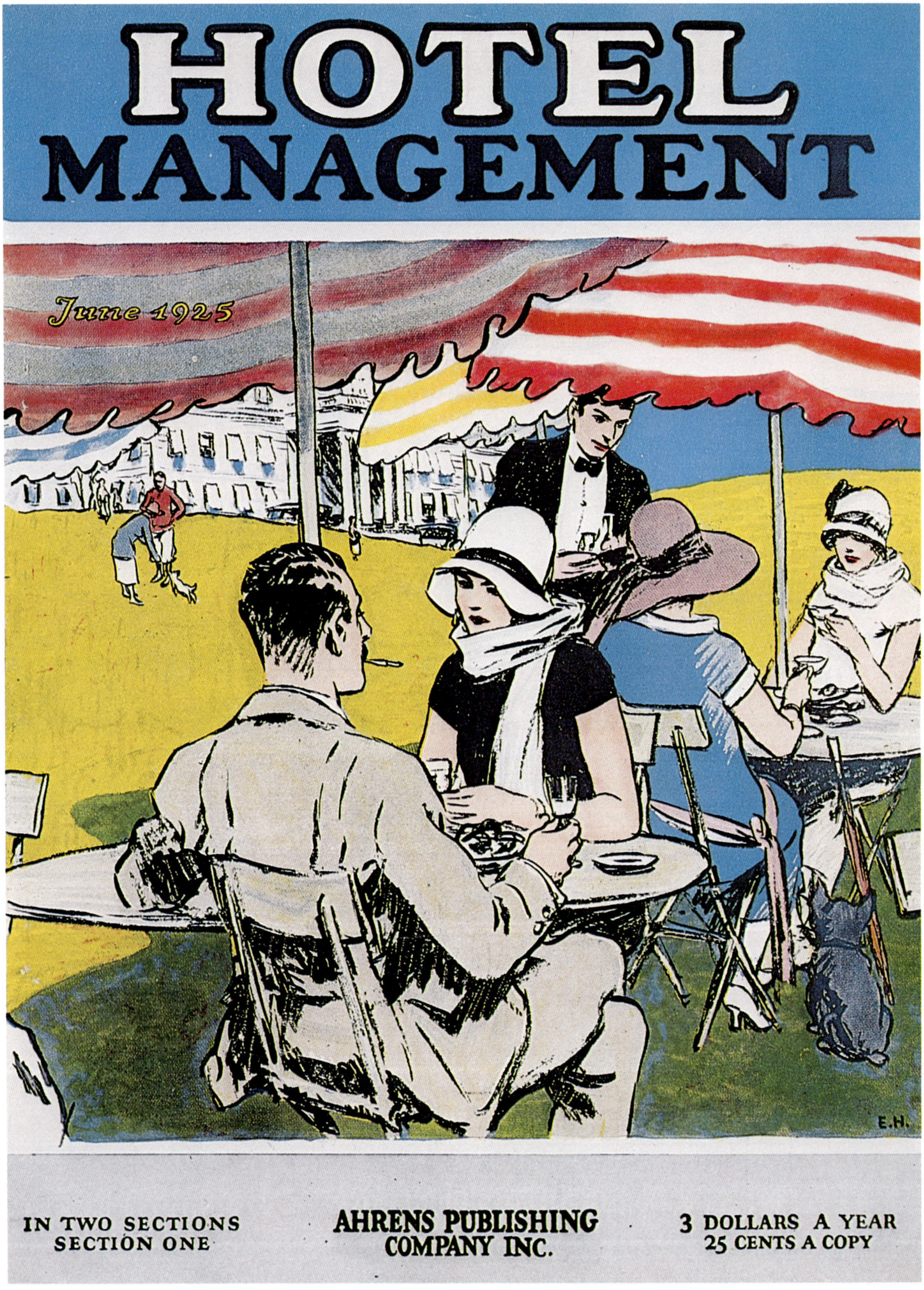
HOTEL
MANAGEMENT
June 1925
E.H.
IN TWO SECTIONS
SECTION ONE
AHRENS PUBLISHING
COMPANY INC.
3 DOLLARS A YEAR
25 CENTS A COPY

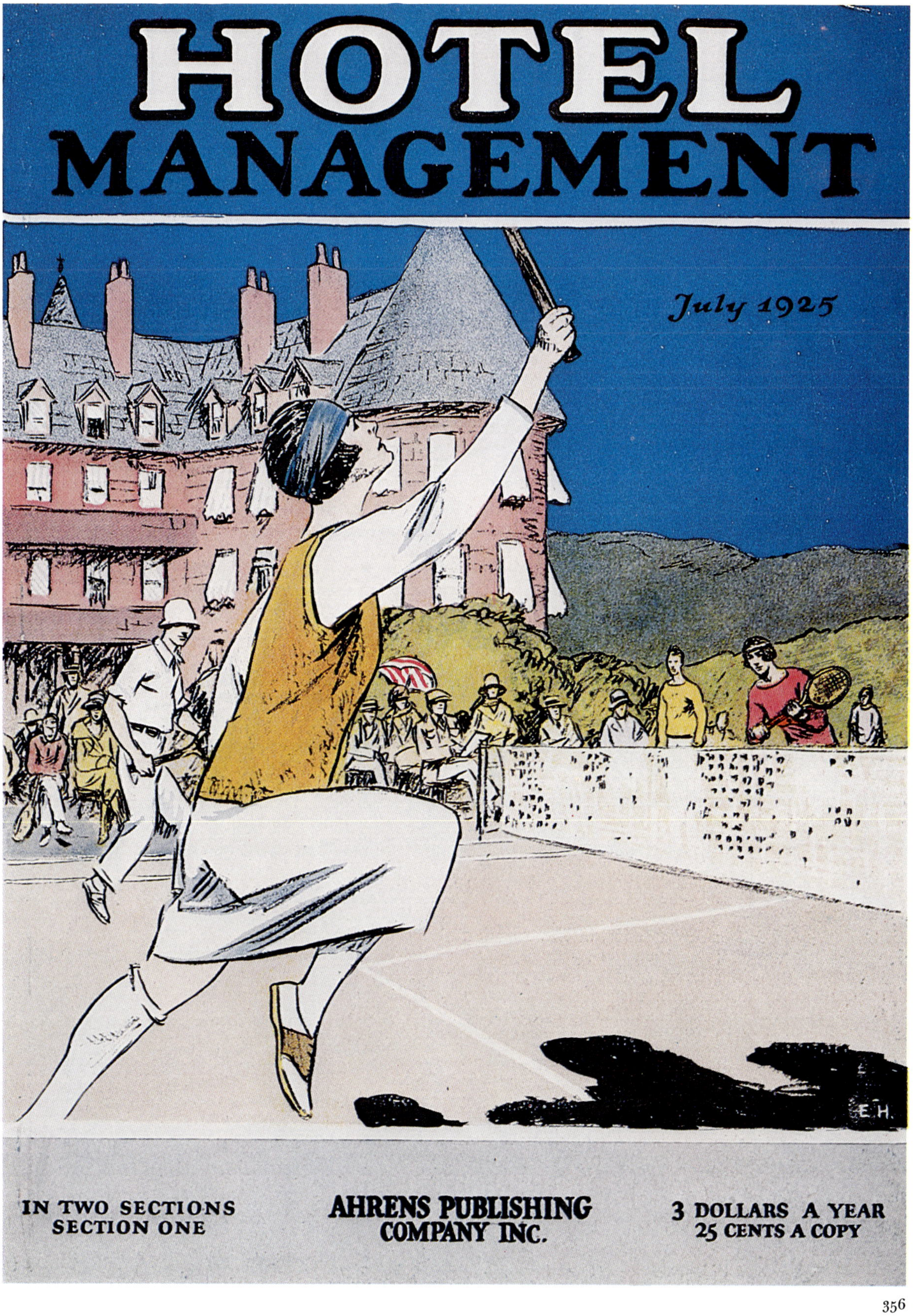
HOTEL
MANAGEMENT
July 1925
E.H.
IN TWO SECTIONS
SECTION ONE
AHRENS PUBLISHING
COMPANY INC.
3 DOLLARS A YEAR
25 CENTS A COPY

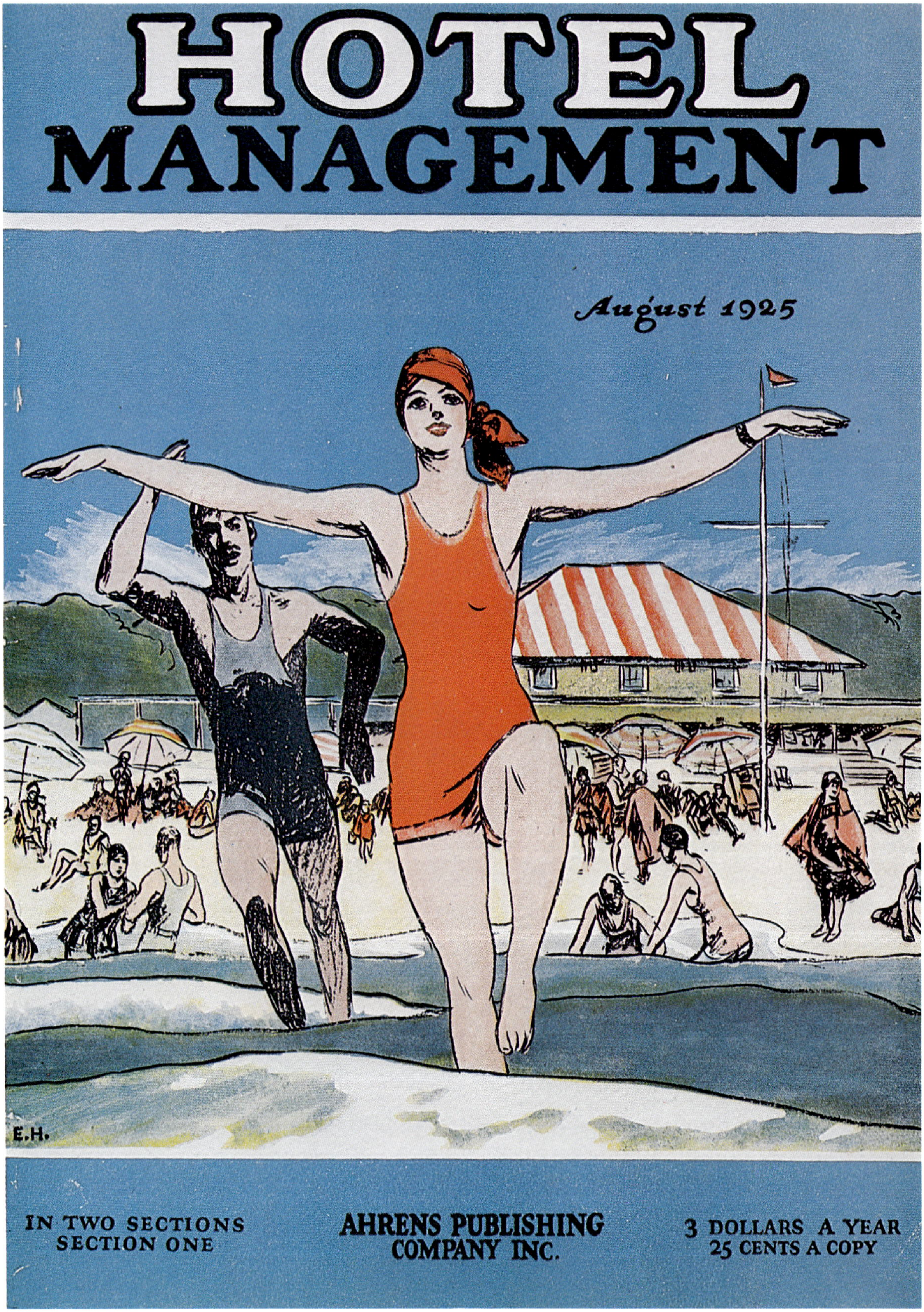
HOTEL
MANAGEMENT
August 1925
E.H.
IN TWO SECTIONS
SECTION ONE
AHRENS PUBLISHING
COMPANY INC.
3 DOLLARS A YEAR
25 CENTS A COPY

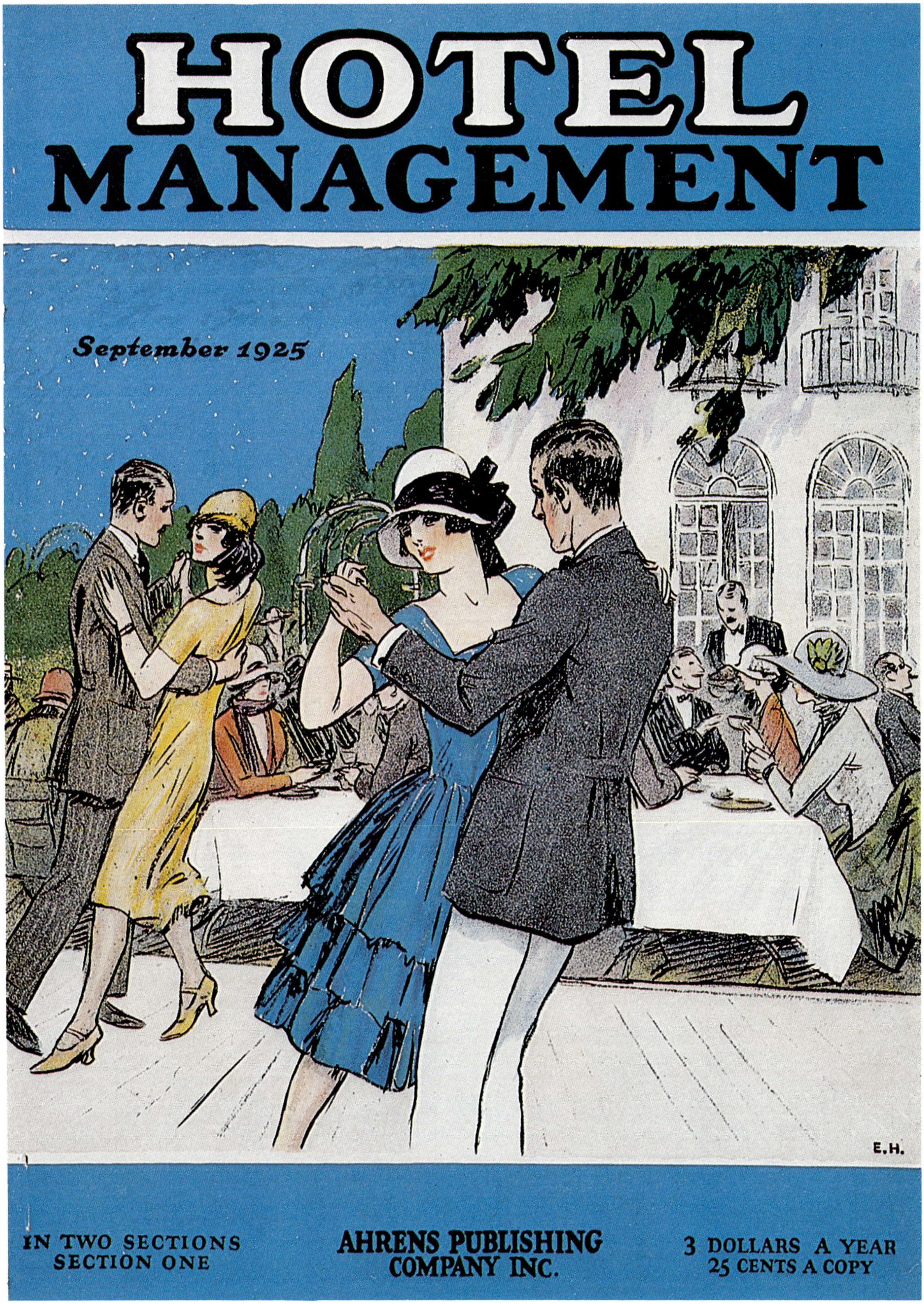
HOTEL
MANAGEMENT
September 1925
E.H.
IN TWO SECTIONS
SECTION ONE
AHRENS PUBLISHING
COMPANY INC.
3 DOLLARS A YEAR
25 CENTS A COPY

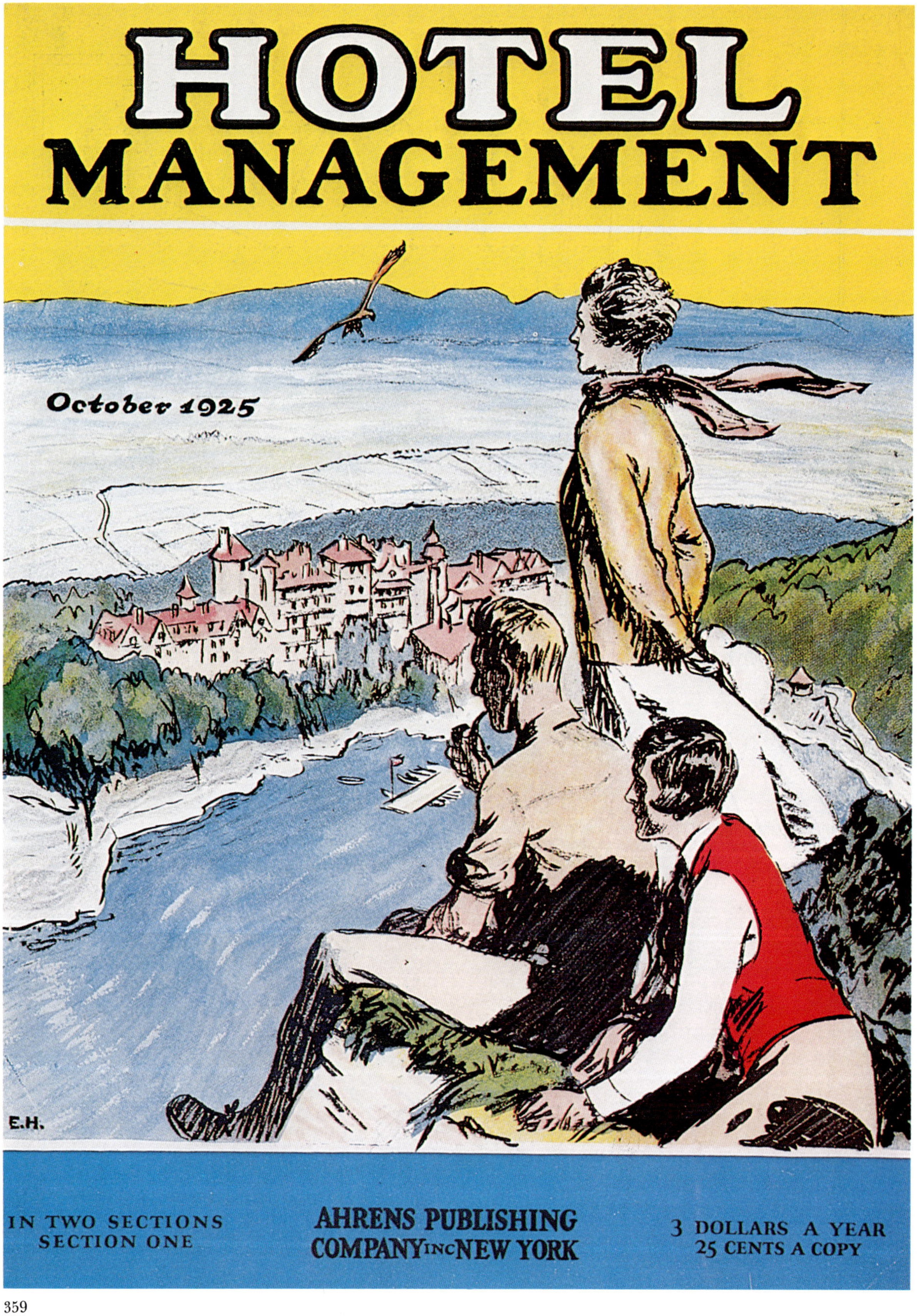
HOTEL
MANAGEMENT
October 1925
E.H.
IN TWO SECTIONS
SECTION ONE
AHRENS PUBLISHING
COMPANY INC NEW YORK
3 DOLLARS A YEAR
25 CENTS A COPY

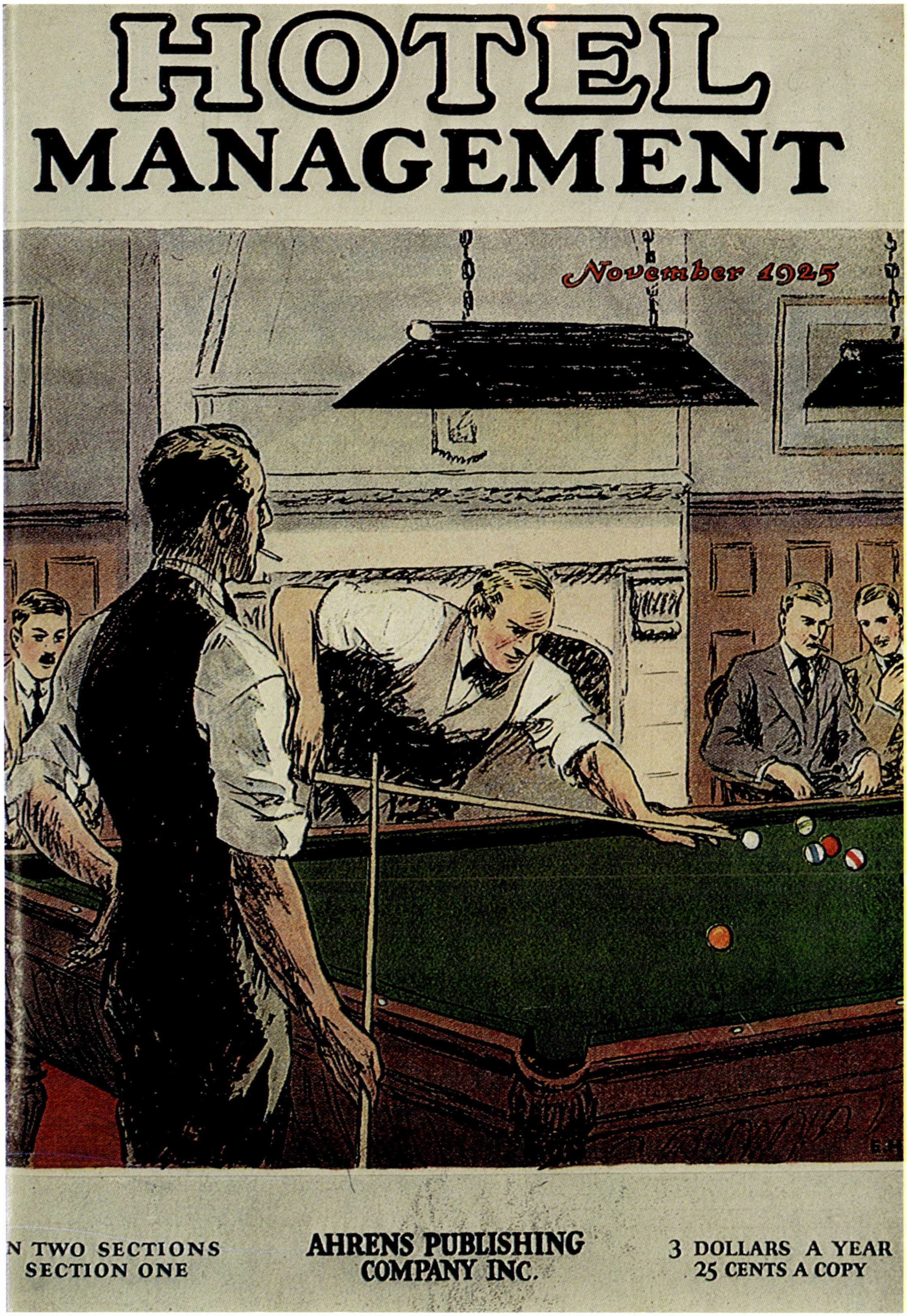
HOTEL
MANAGEMENT
November 1925
N TWO SECTIONS
SECTION ONE
AHRENS PUBLISHING
COMPANY INC.
3 DOLLARS A YEAR
25 CENTS A COPY

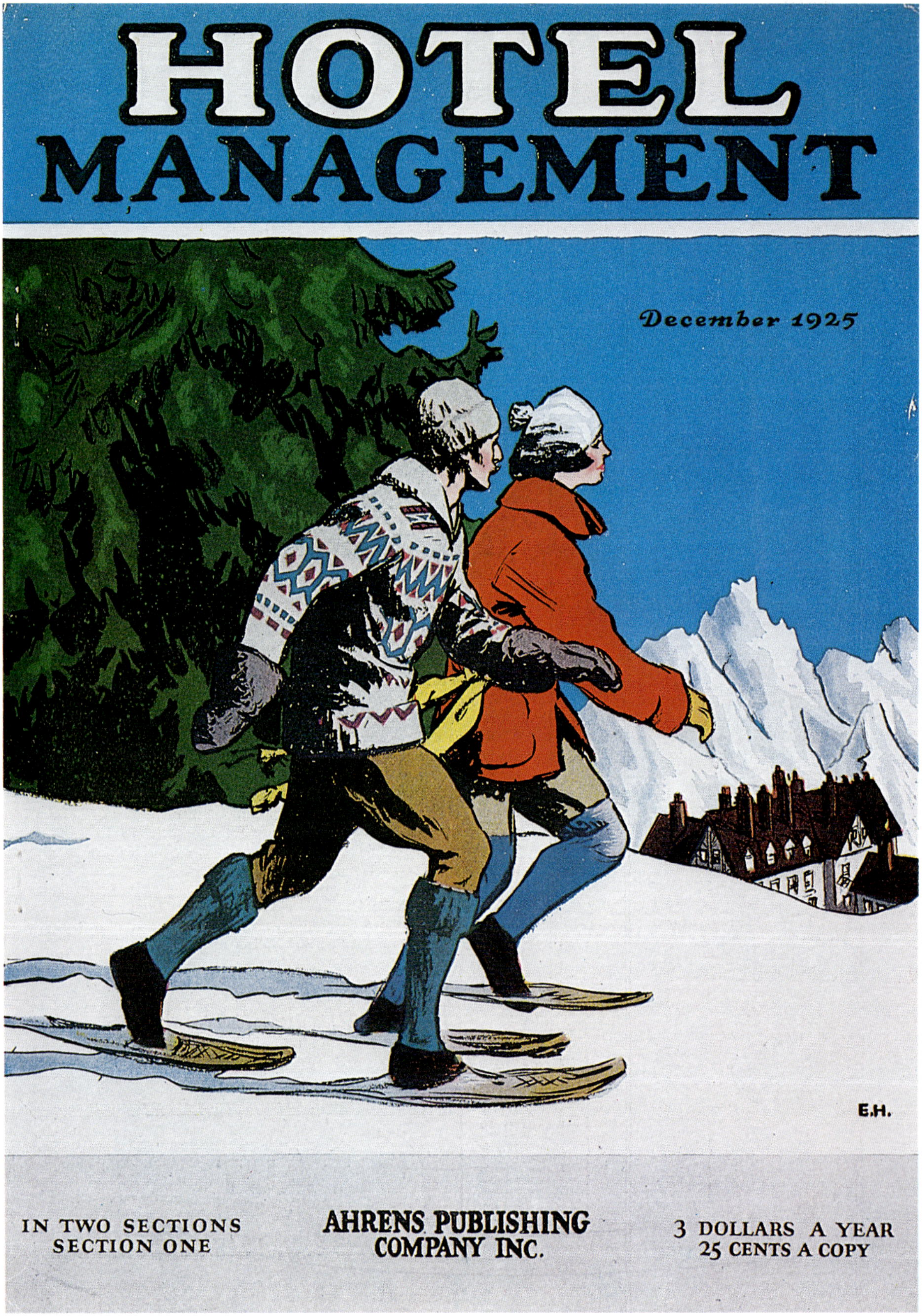
HOTEL
MANAGEMENT
December 1925
E.H.
IN TWO SECTIONS
SECTION ONE
AHRENS PUBLISHING
COMPANY INC.
3 DOLLARS A YEAR
25 CENTS A COPY

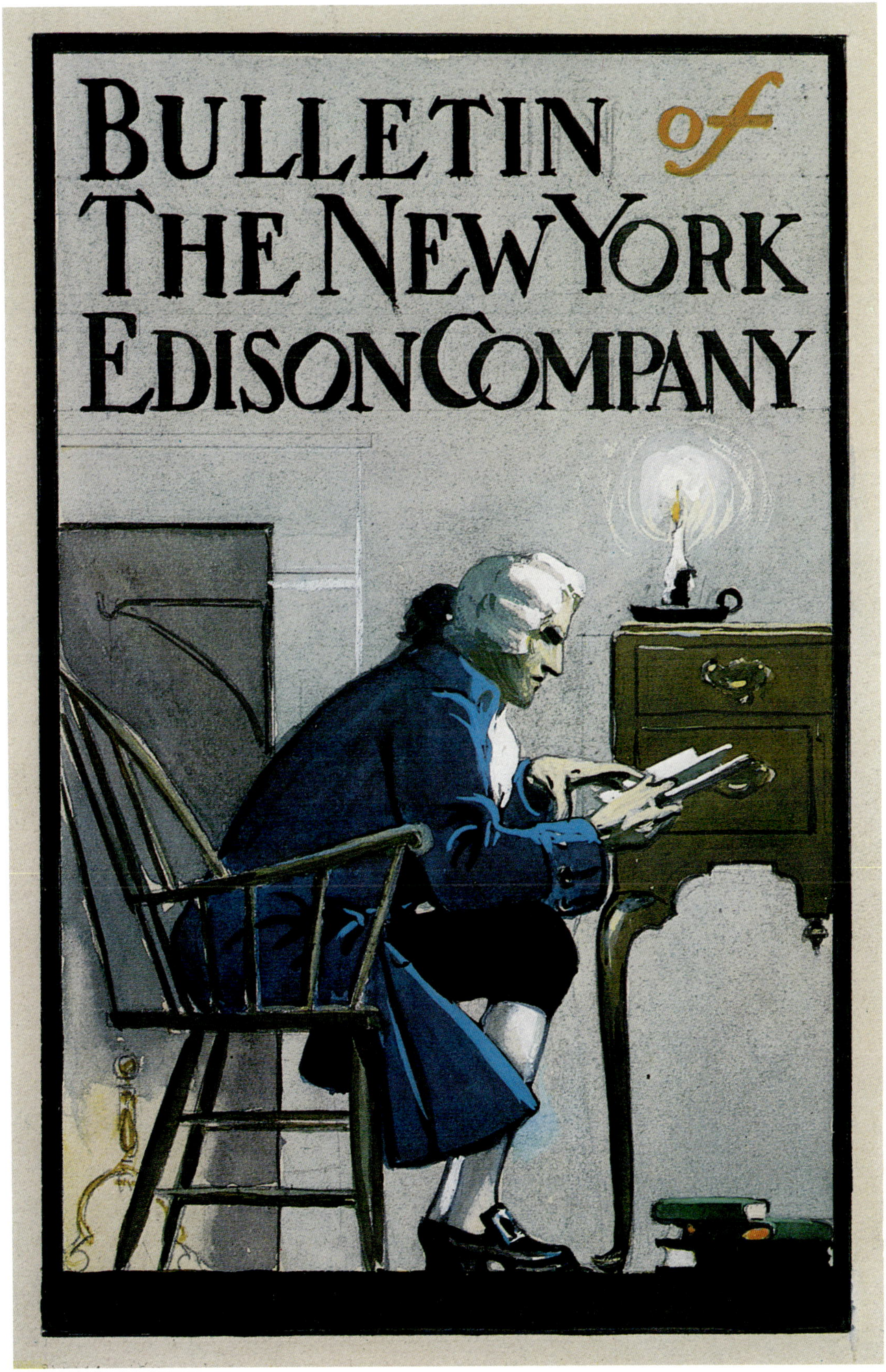
BULLETIN of
THE NEW YORK
EDISON COMPANY

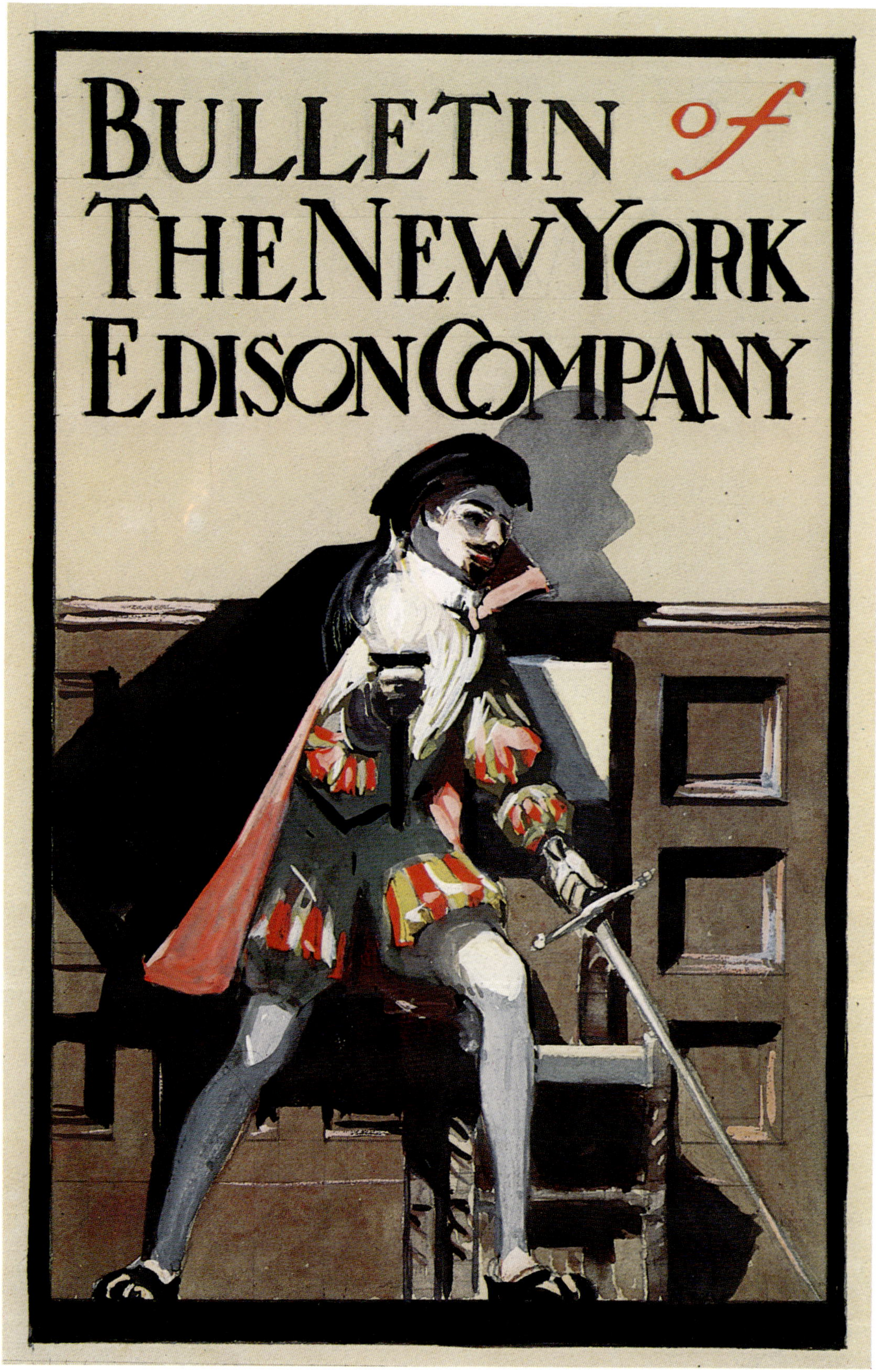

441

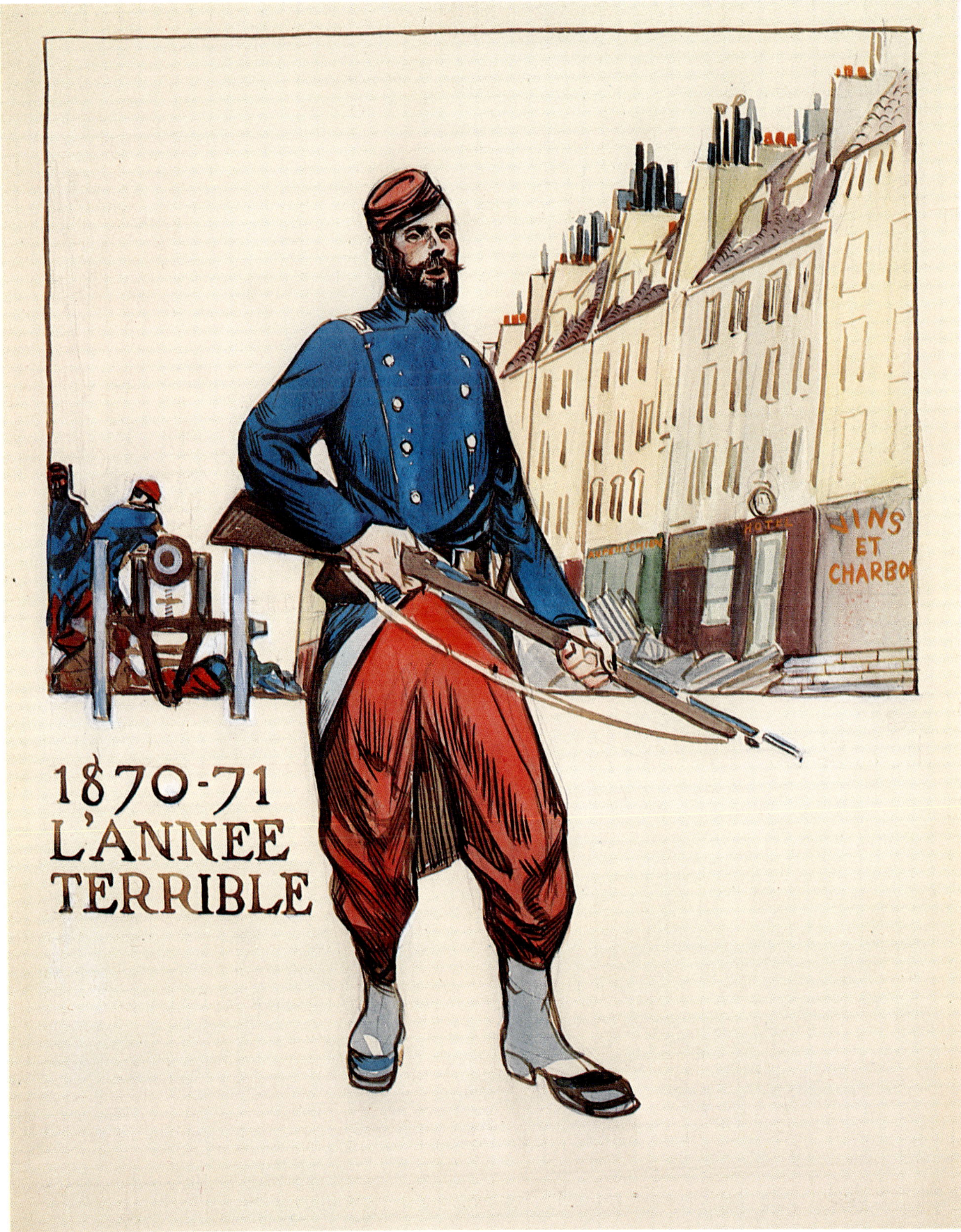
1870-71
L'ANNEE
TERRIBLE
VINS
ET
CHARBO

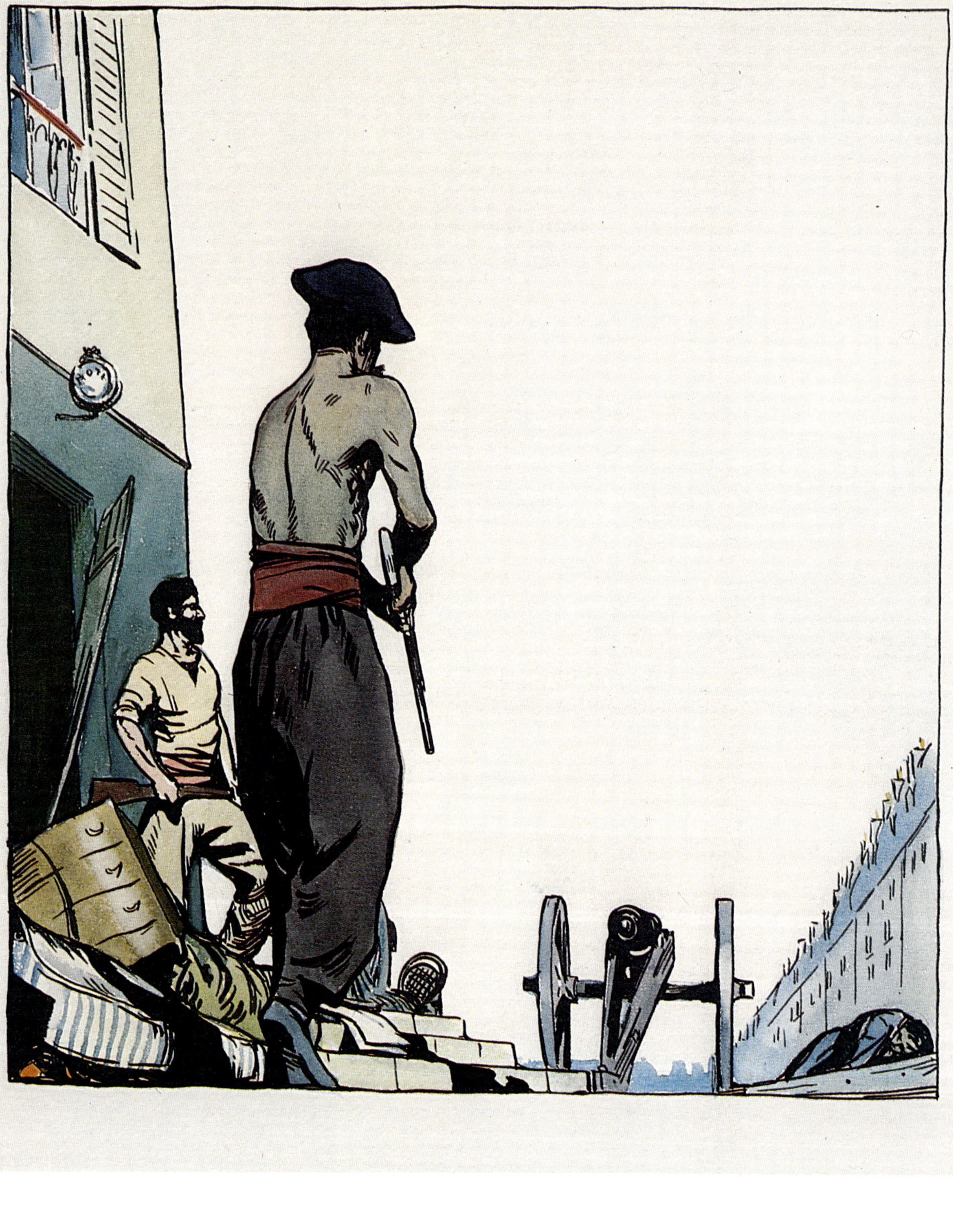

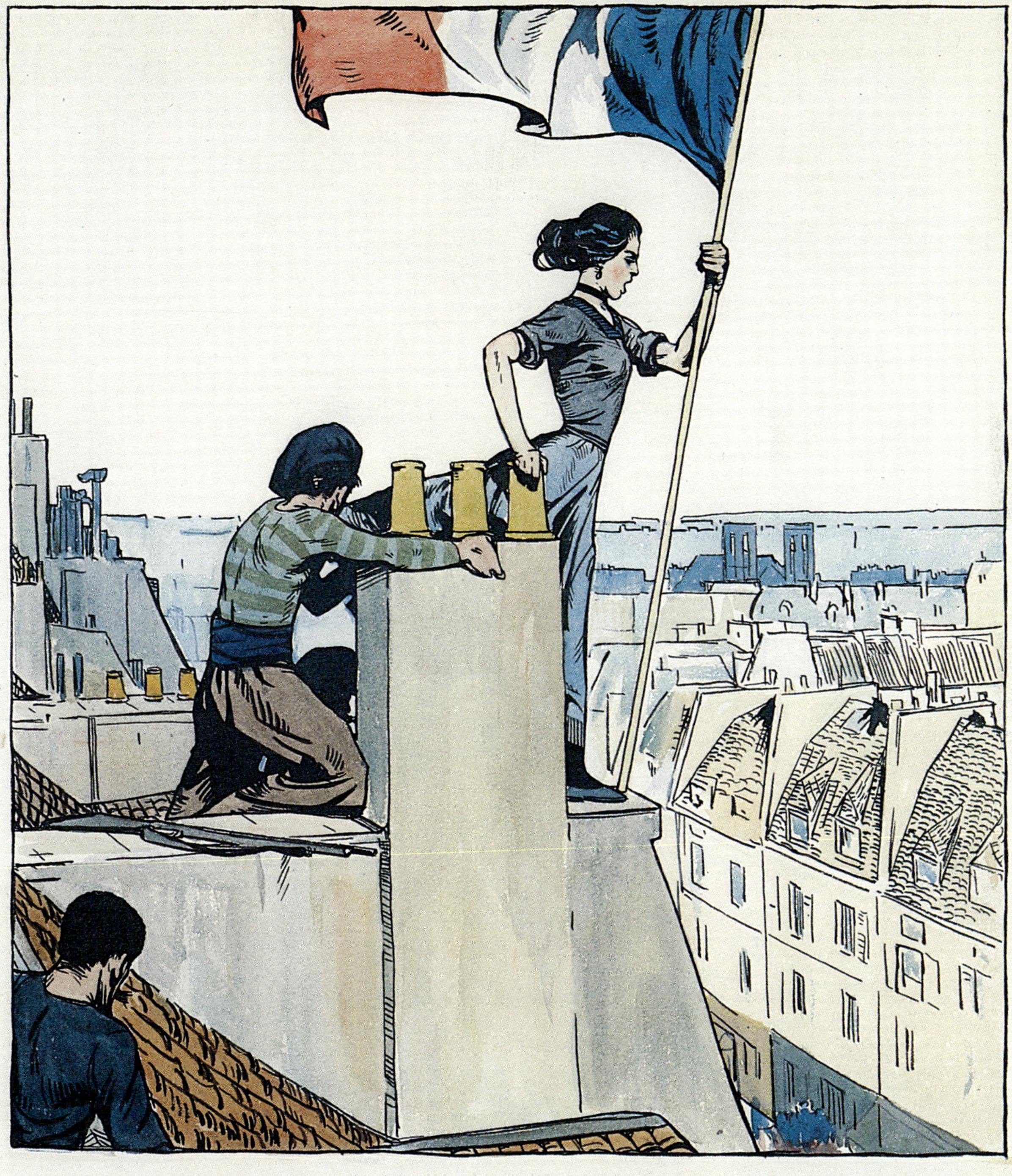

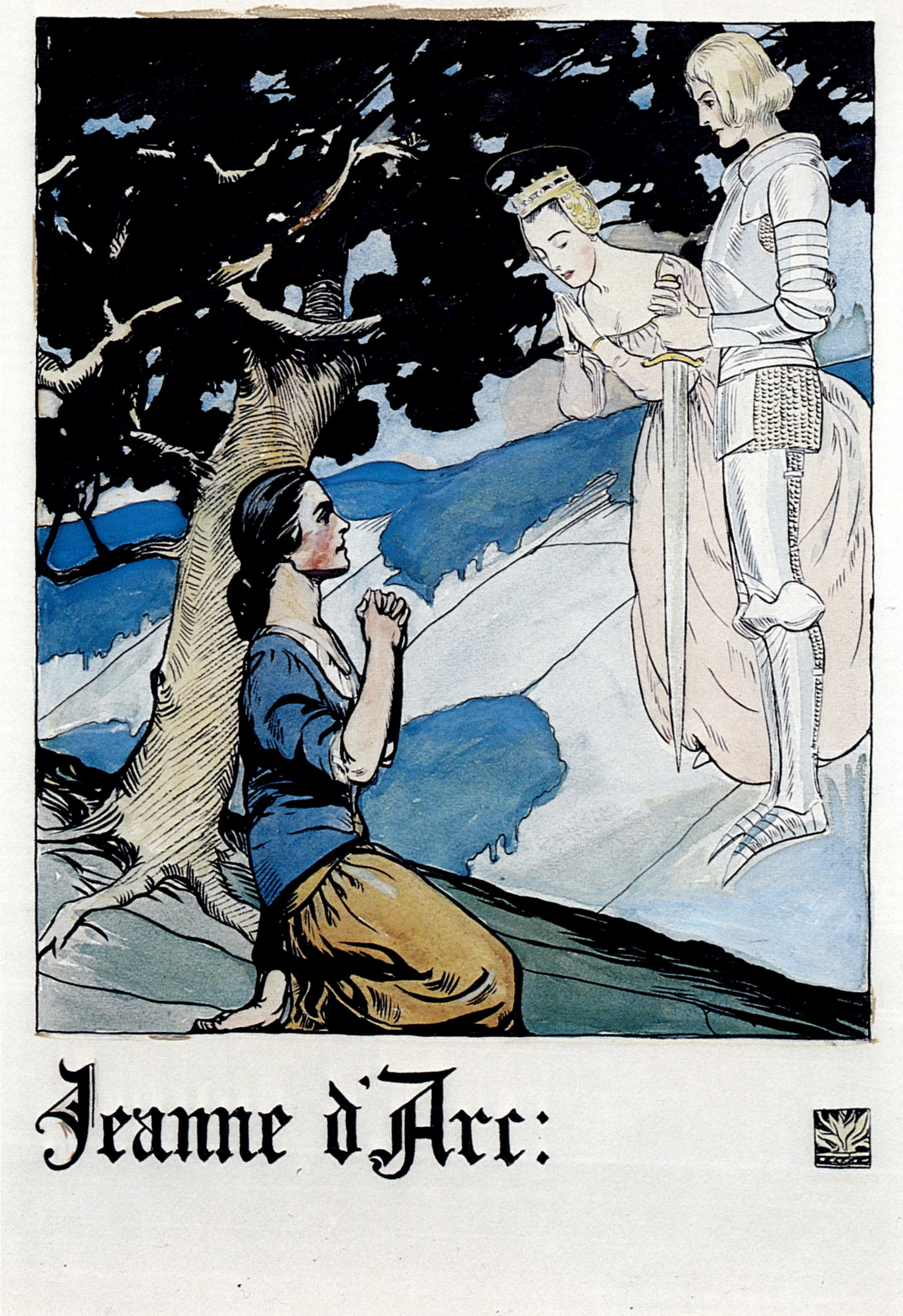
Jeanne d'Arc:

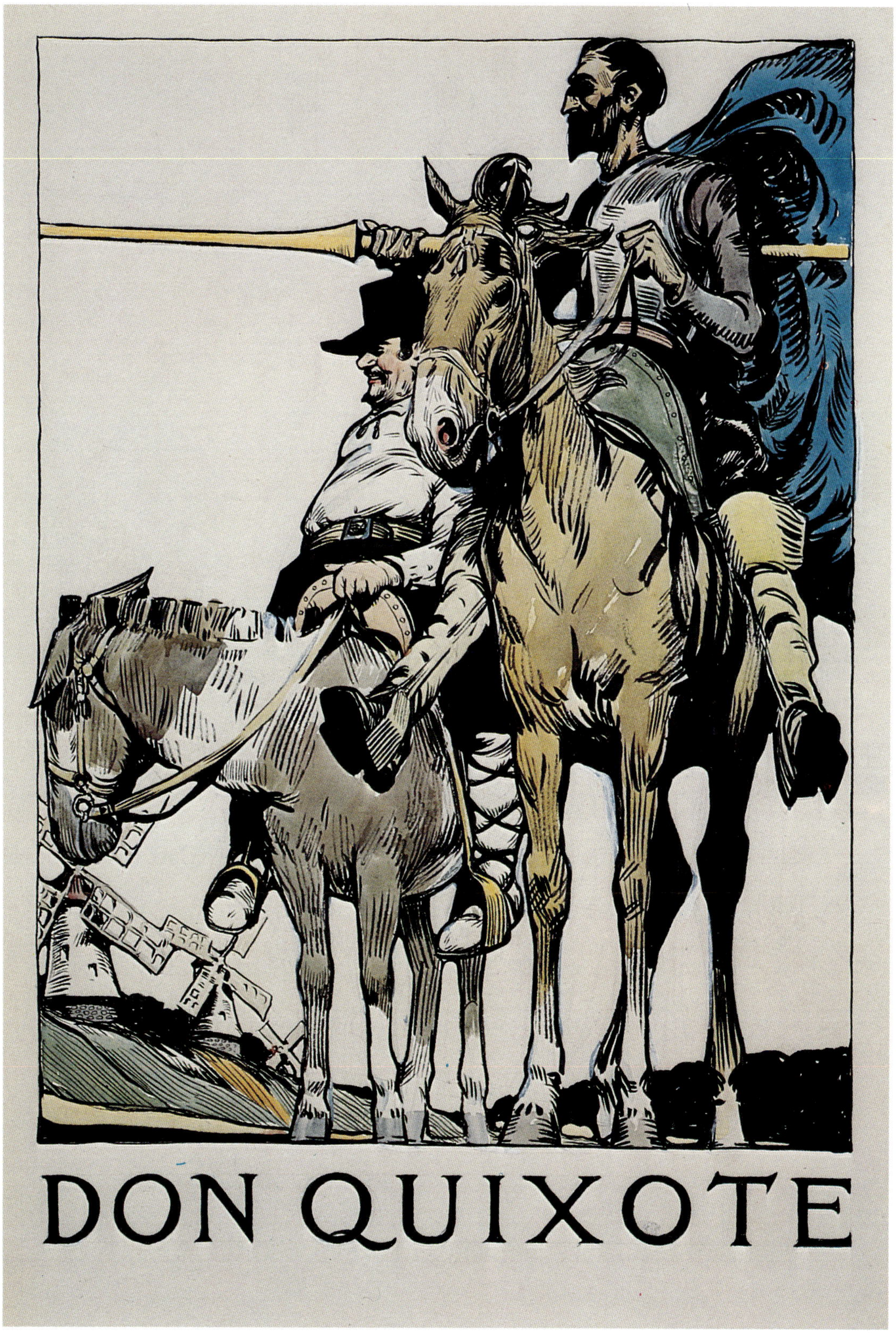
DON QUIXOTE

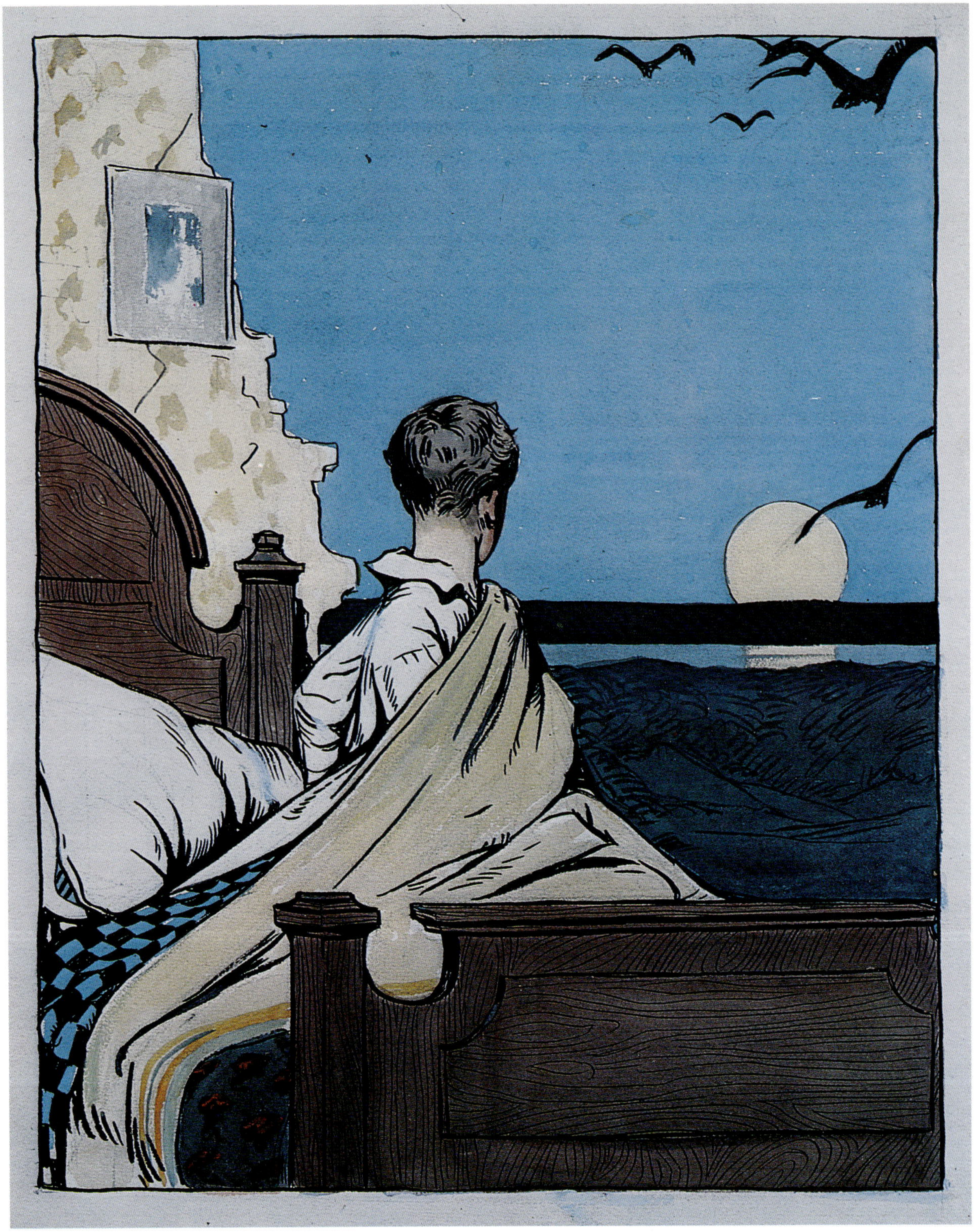

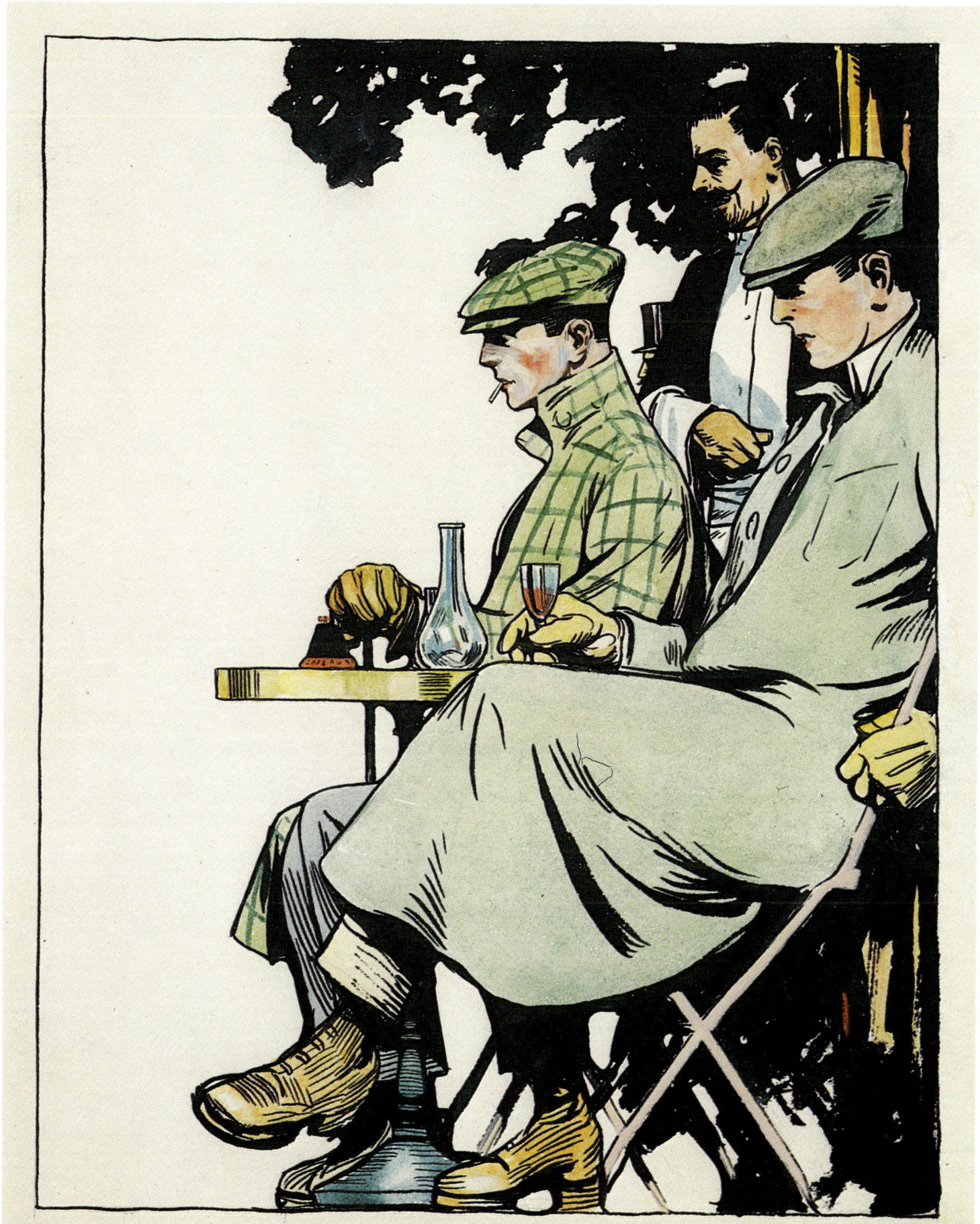

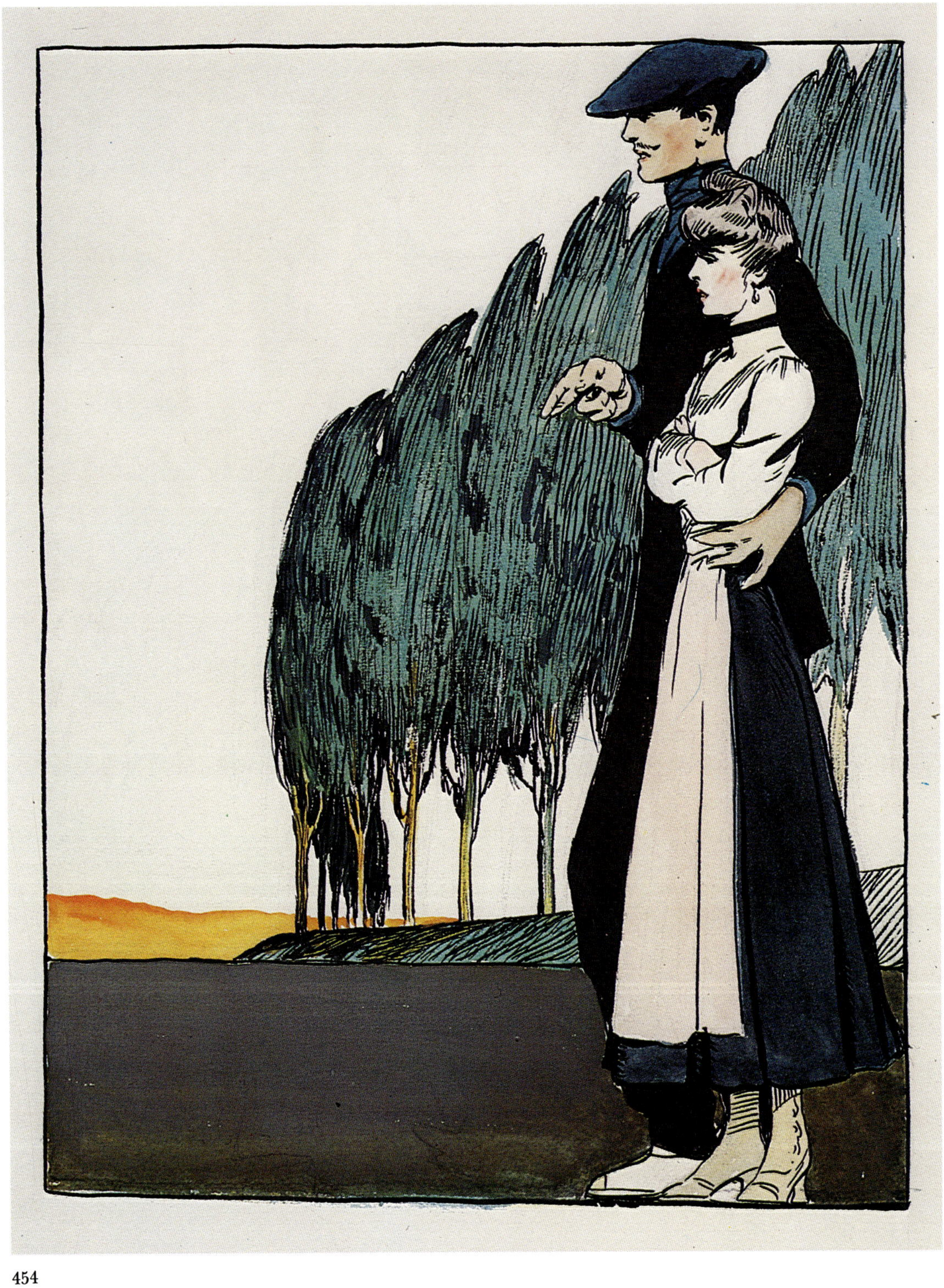

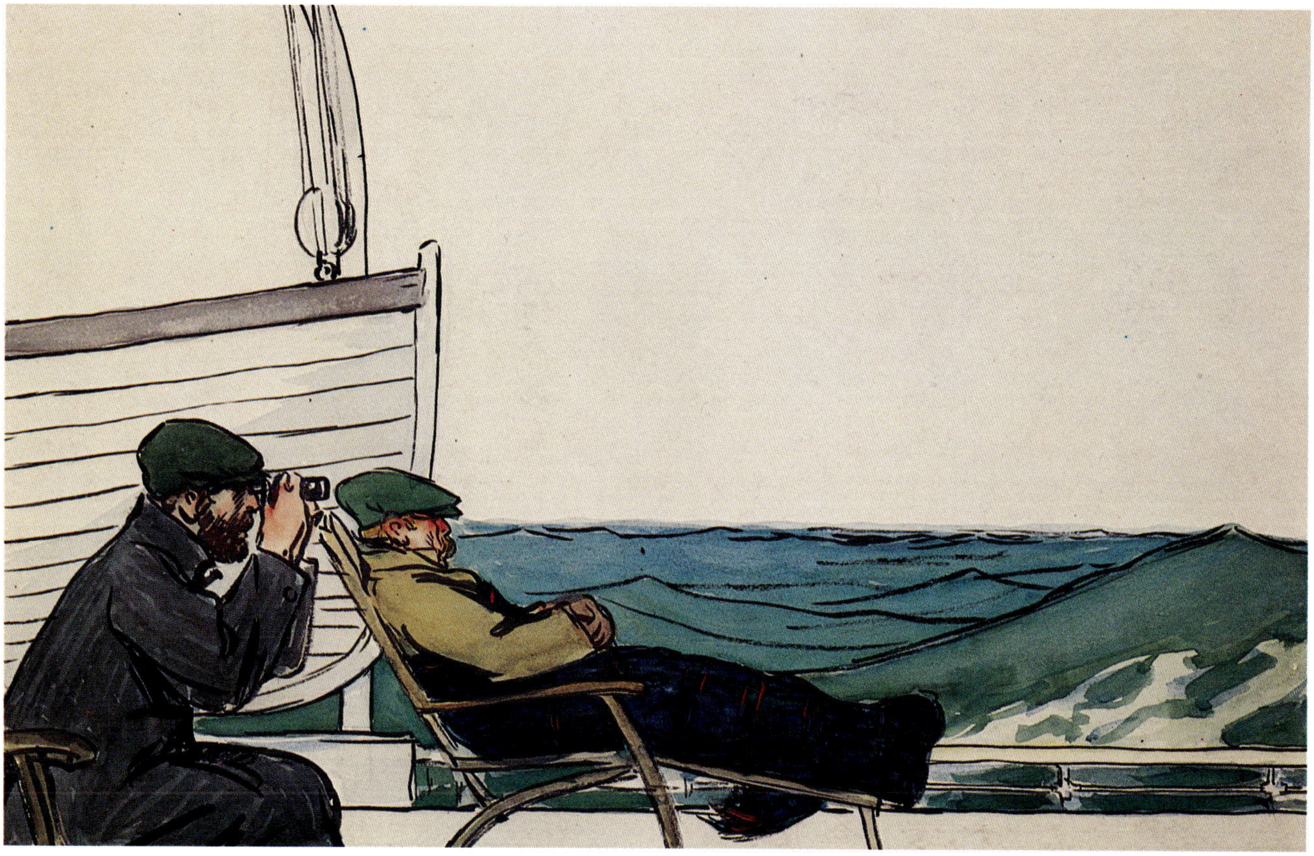

456

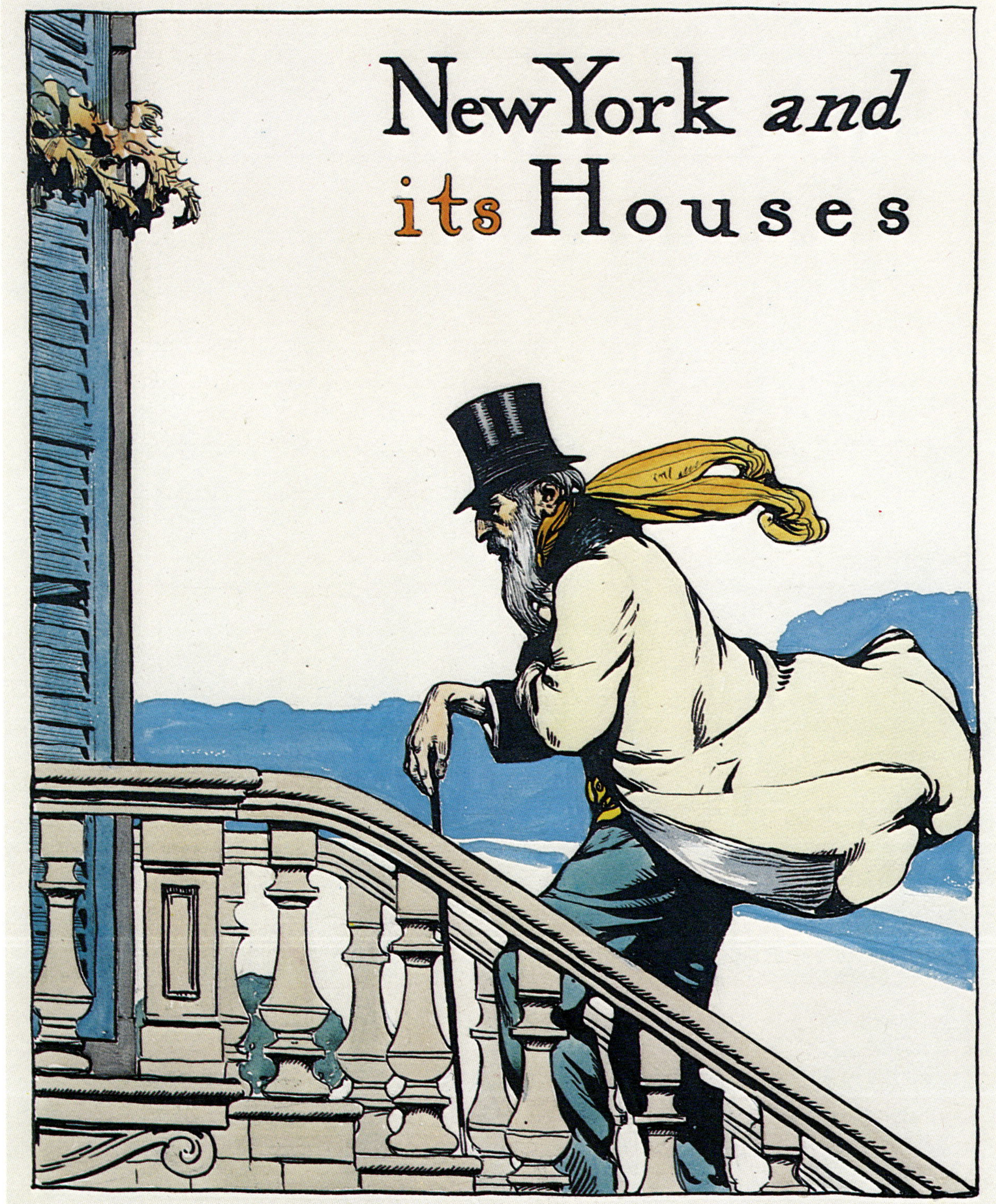
New York and
its Houses

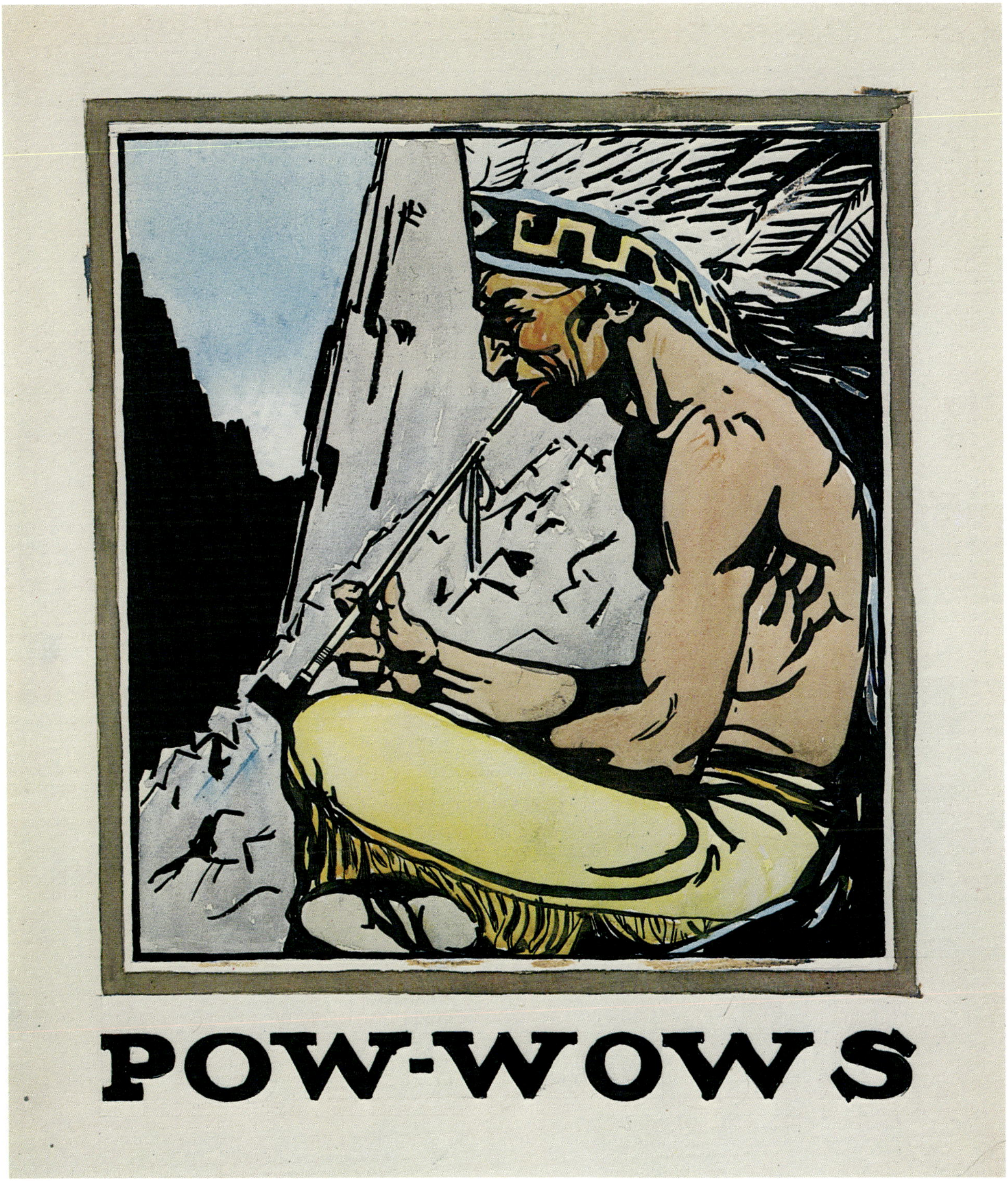
POW-WOWS

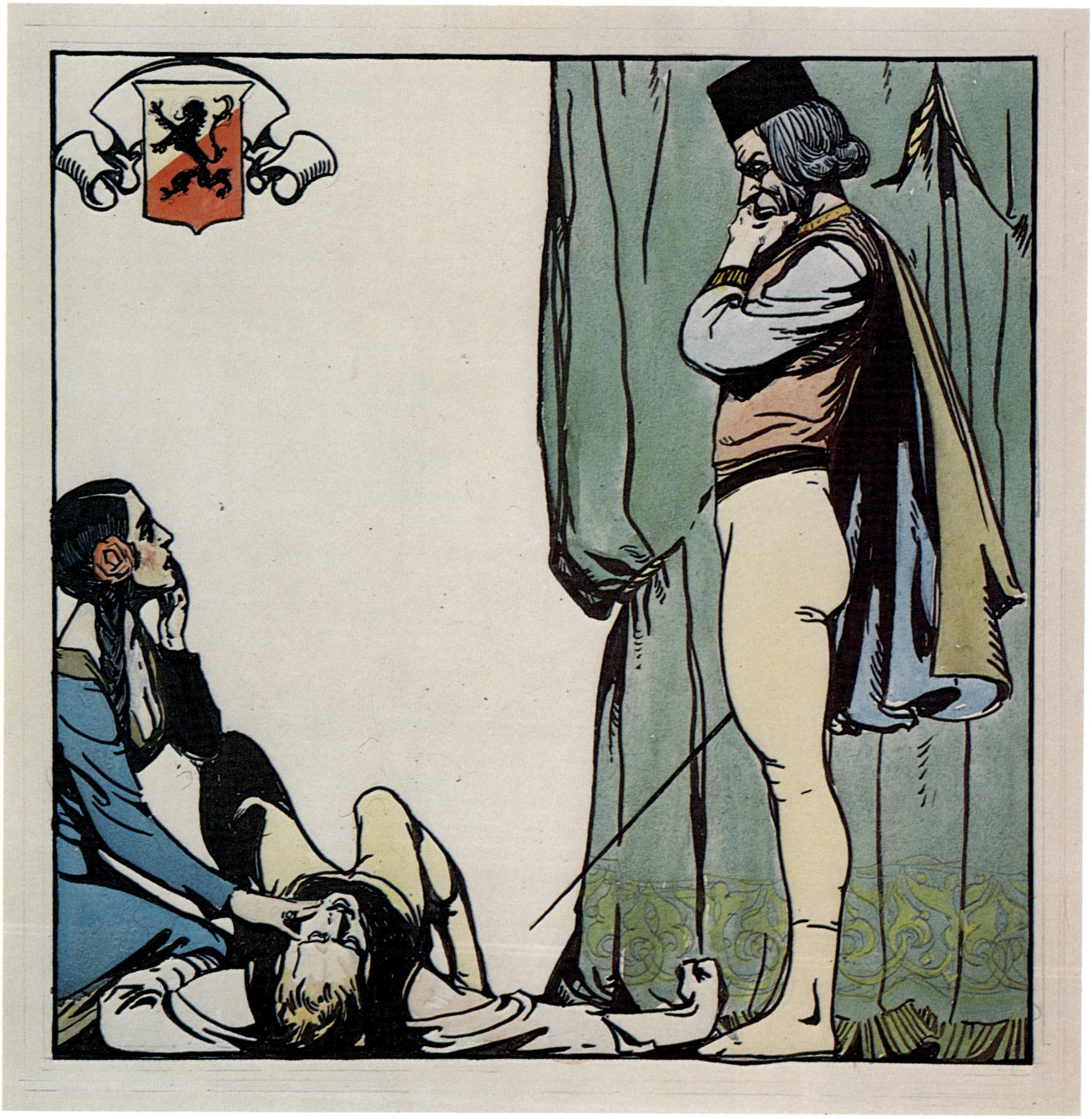

461

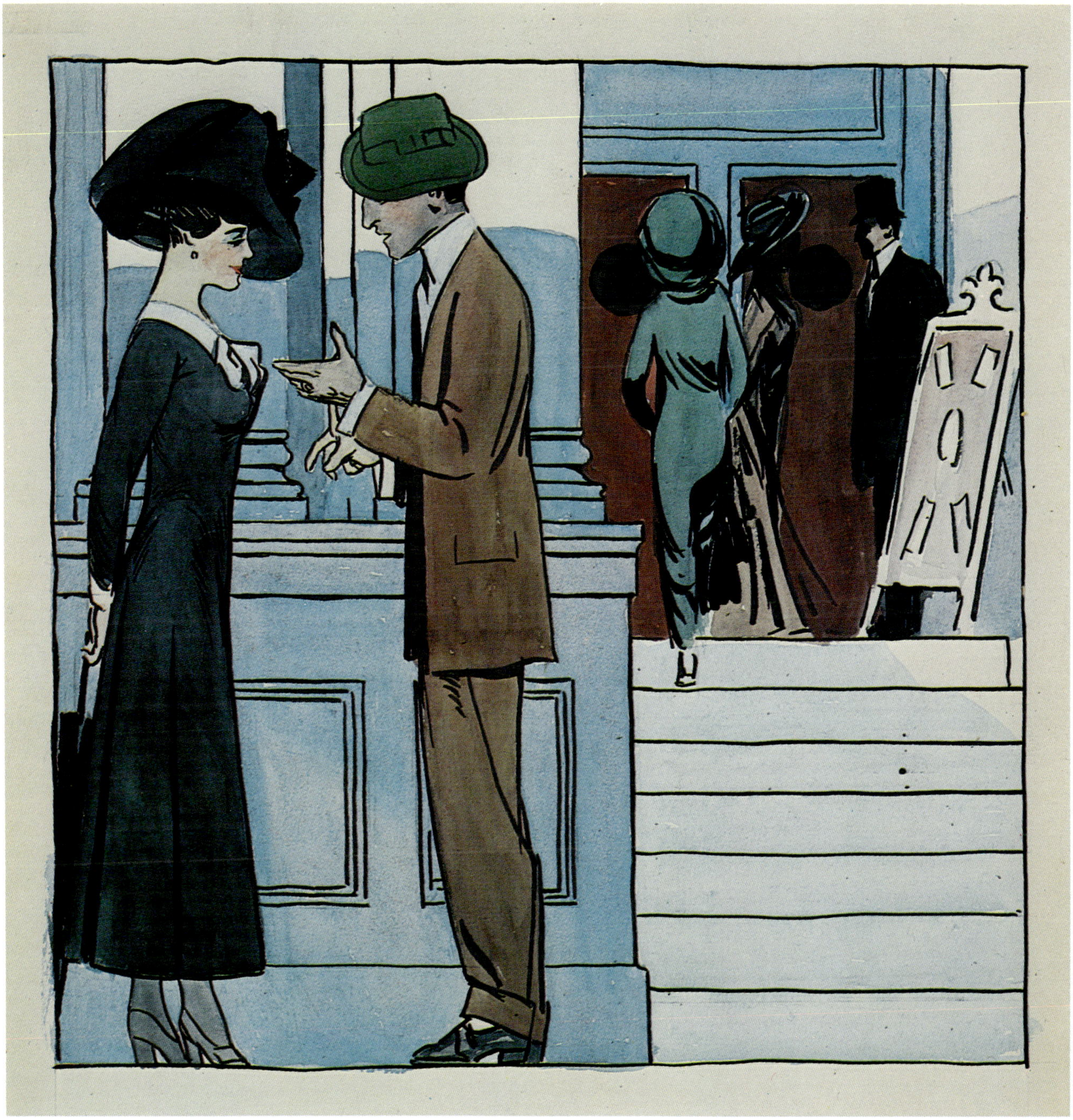

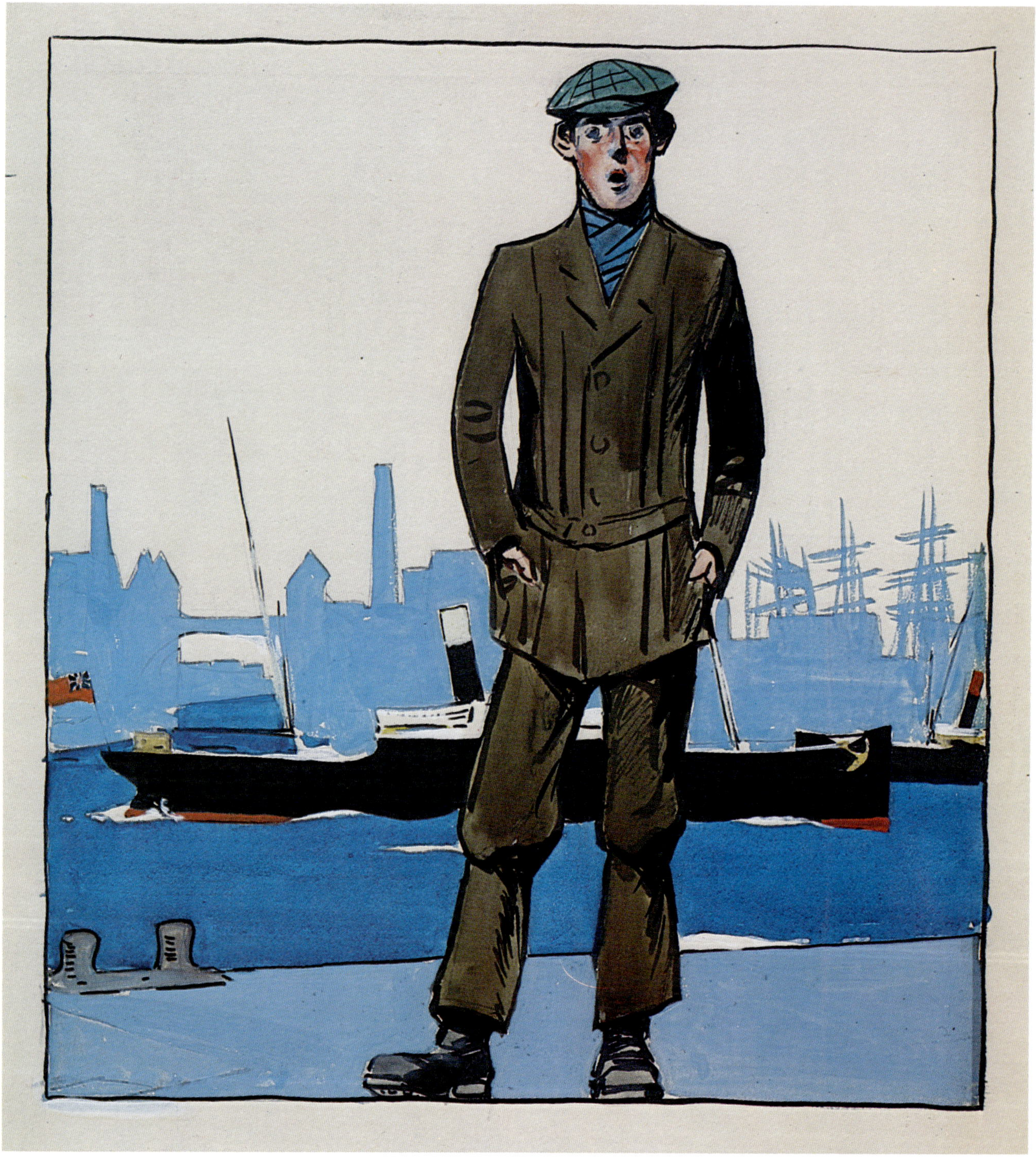

471

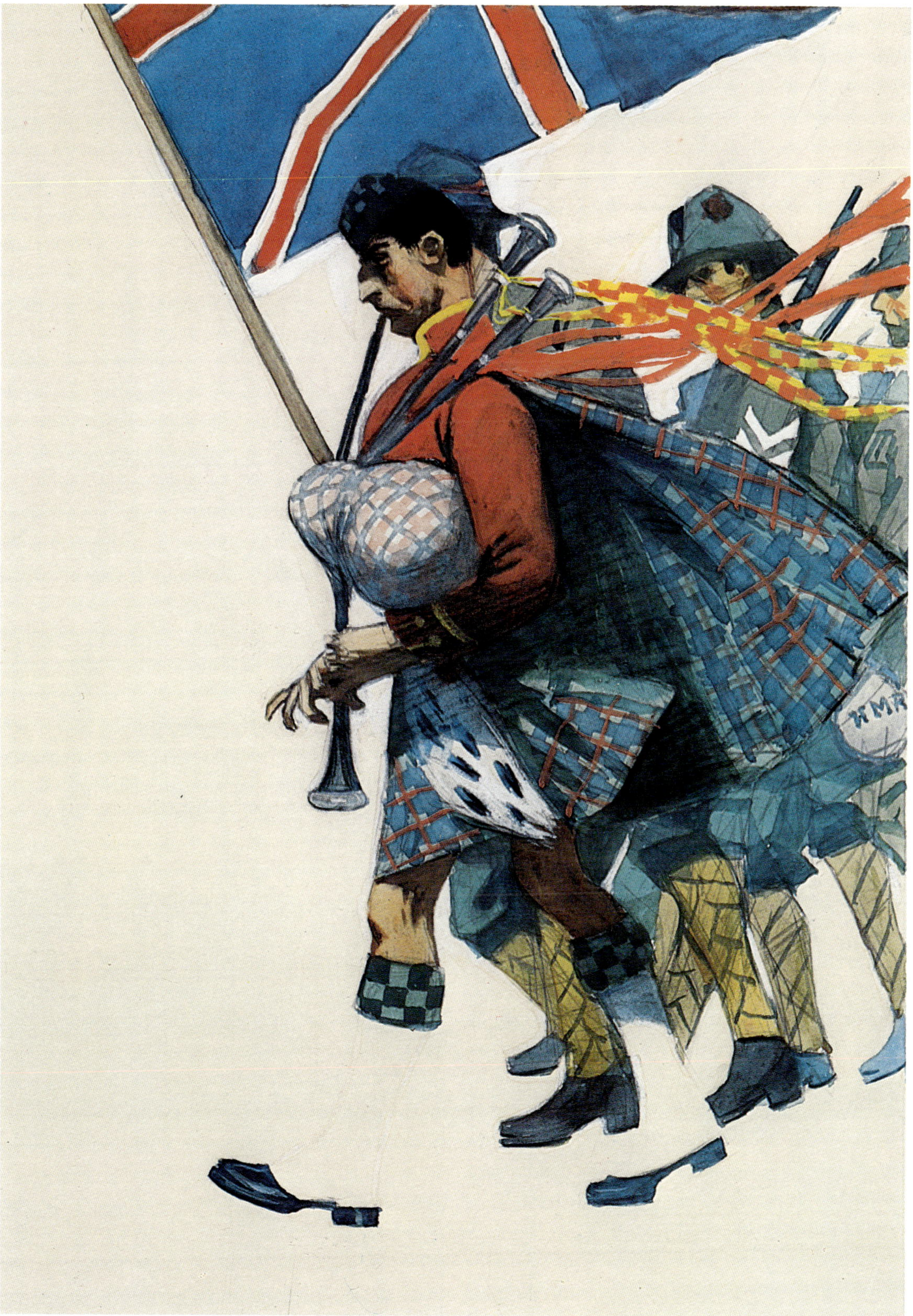

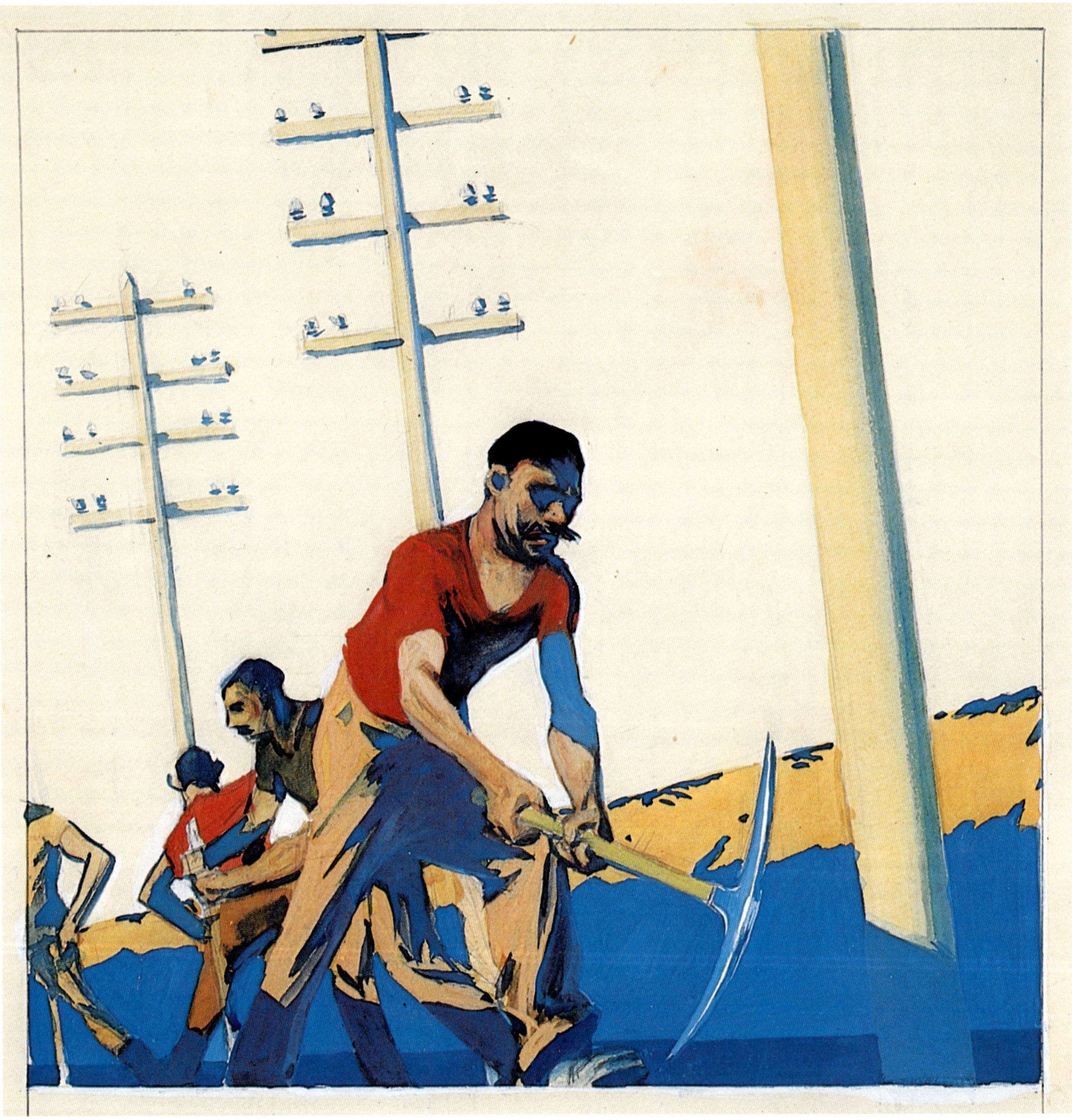

483

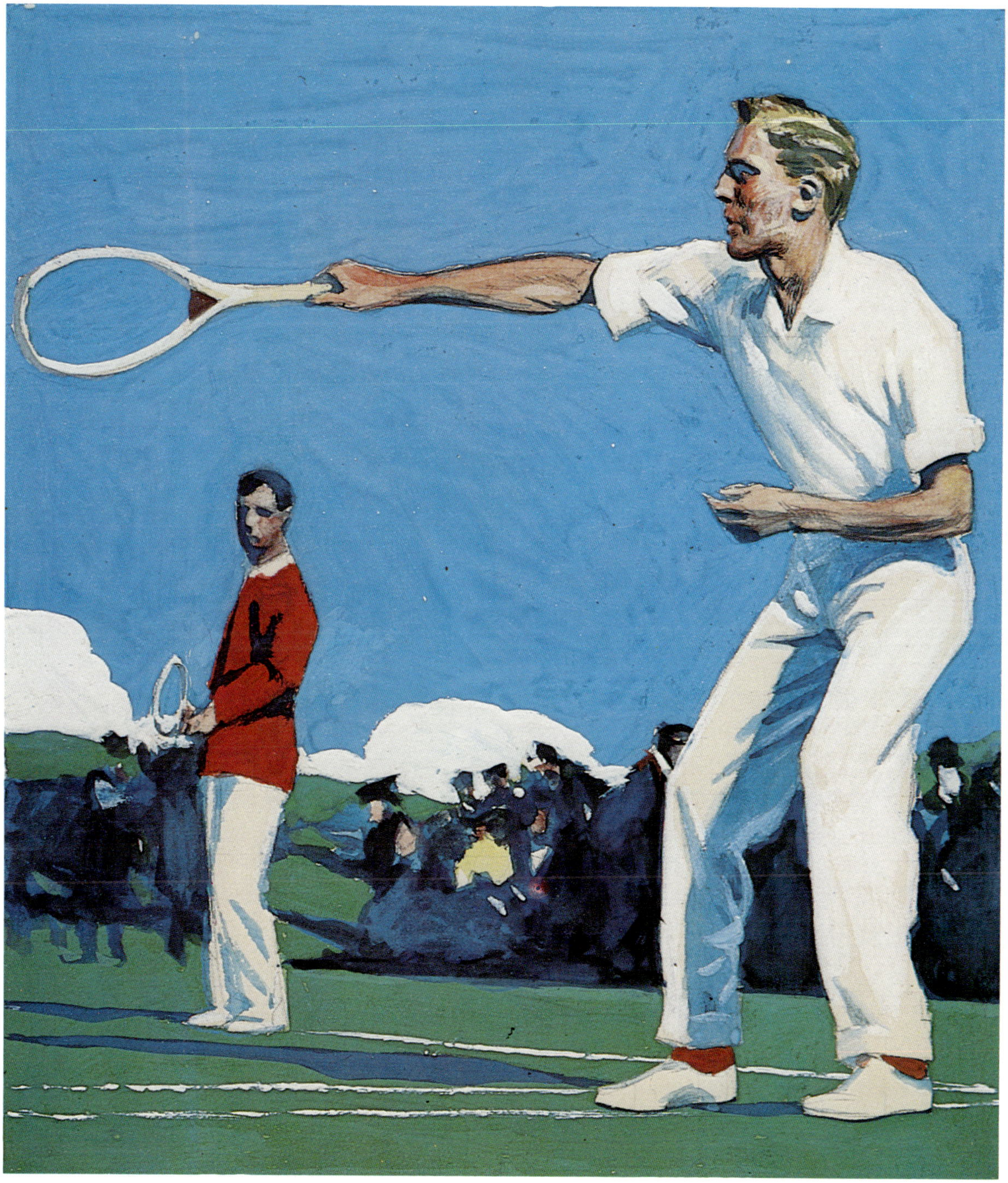

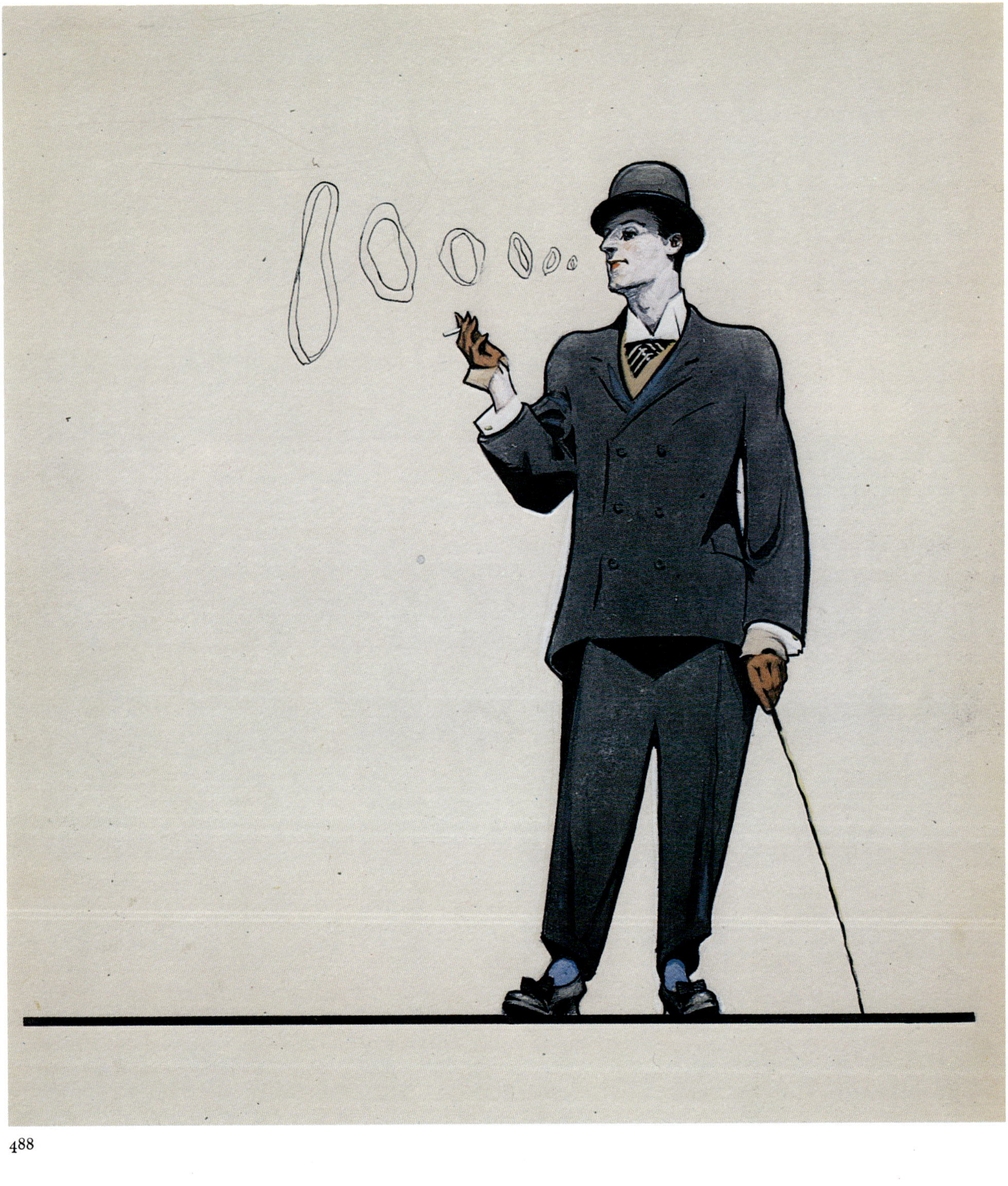

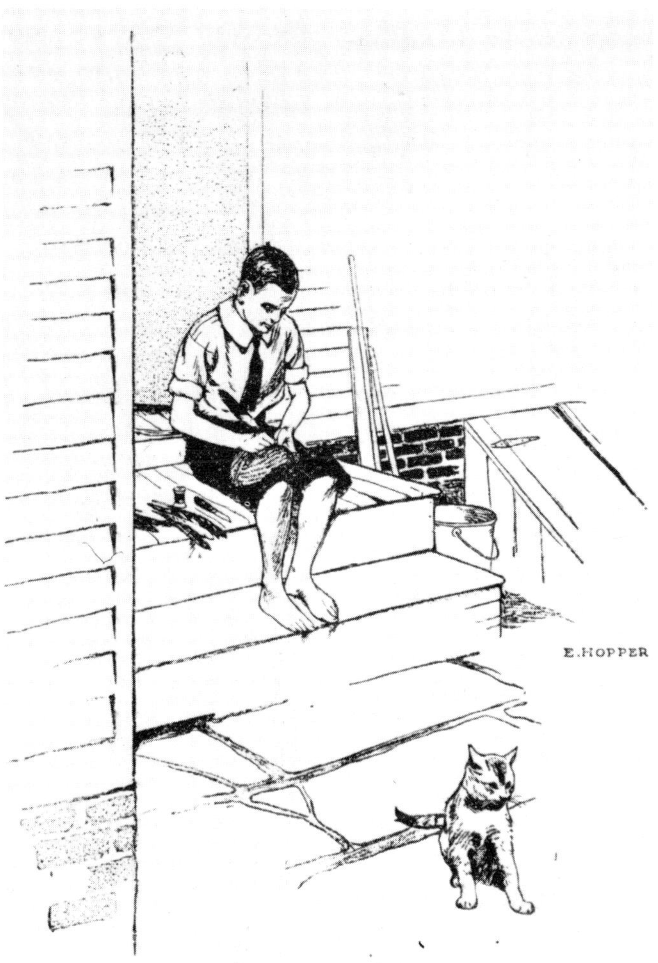

1

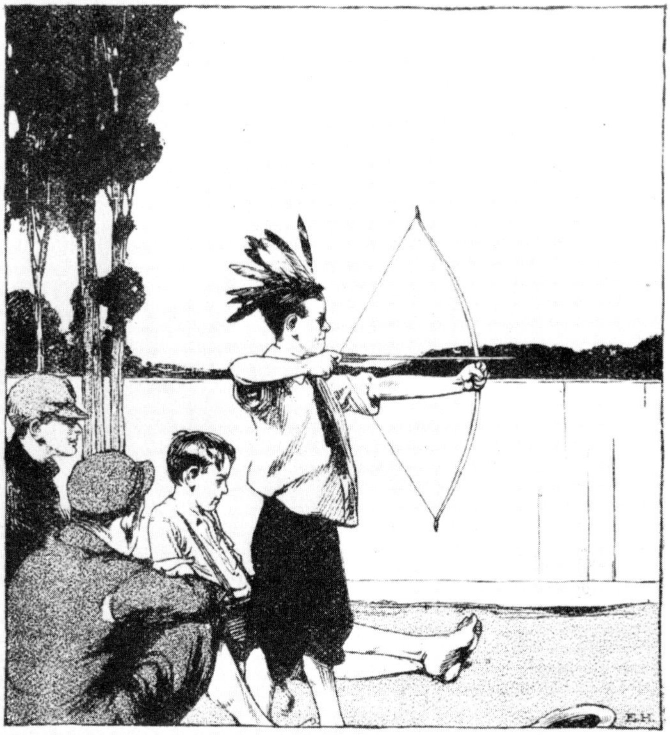

2

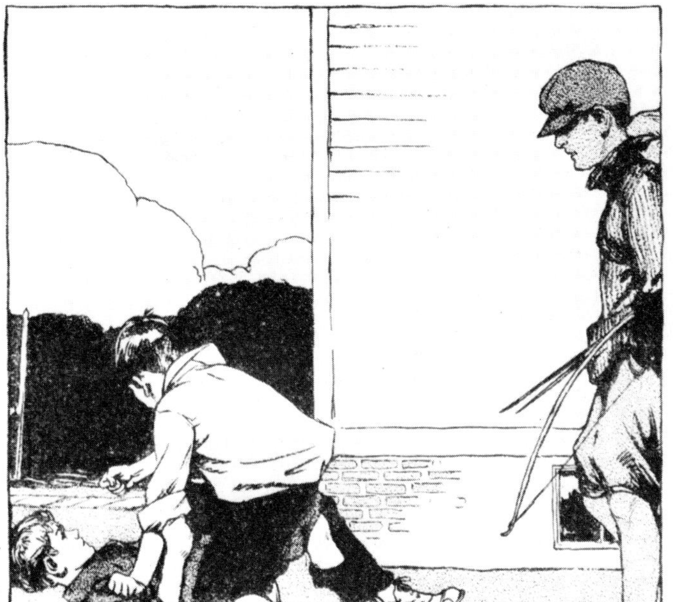

3

Illustrations for Ben Blow, "The New Boy," *Everybody's,* 26 (January 1912).

1. "Johnny Simmons fell to work, engaging in the manufacture of a war-bonnet," p. 130.

2. "Vast numbers of Indians were snuffed out by each one of the boys," p. 132.

3. "'Holler 'nuff,' he yelled. 'Dern me, I'll beat your face into a pulp,'" p. 133.

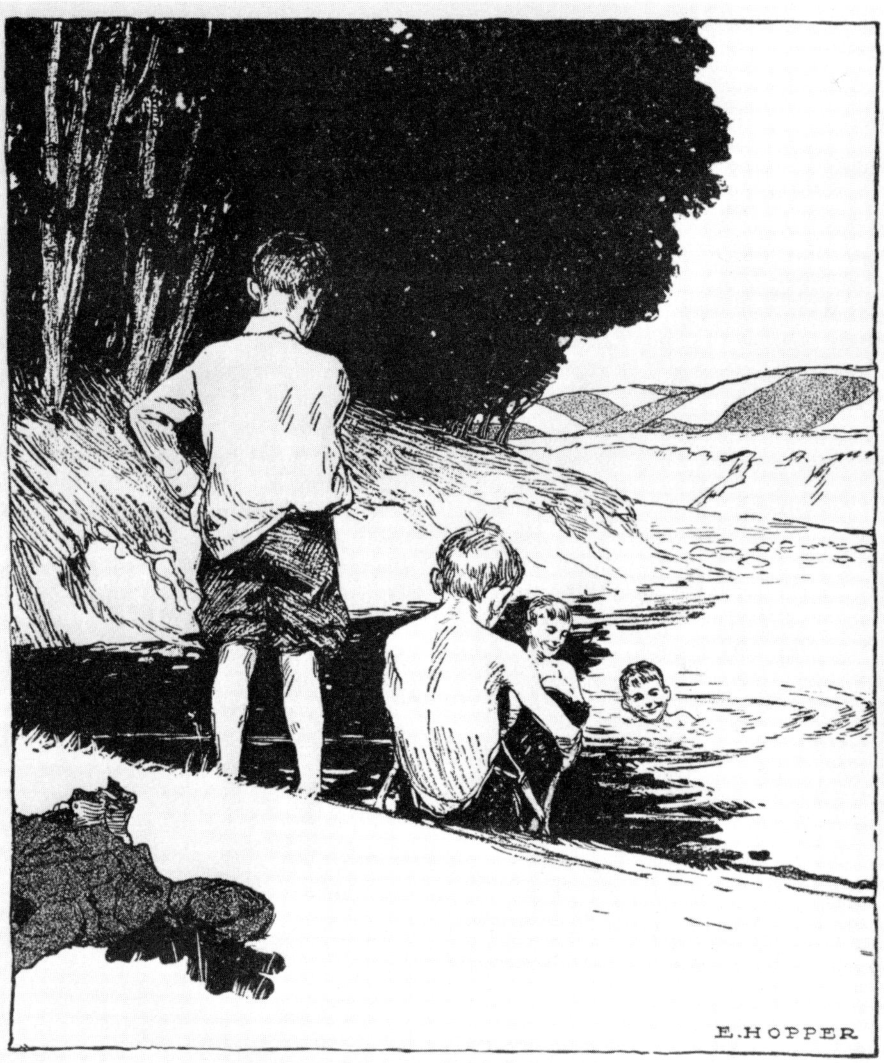

5

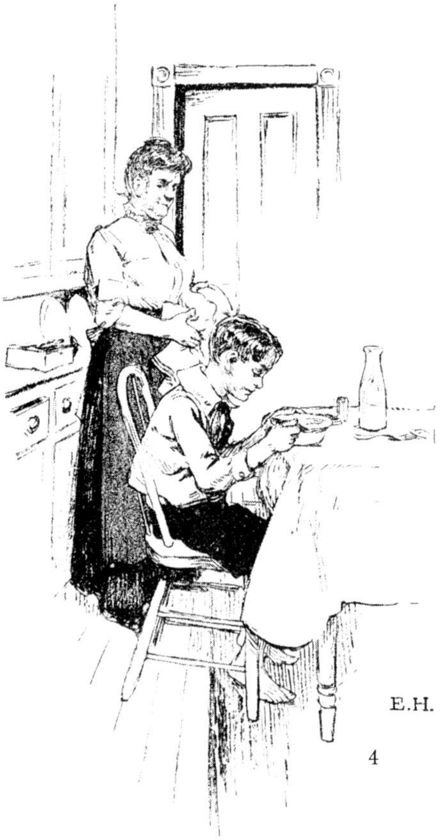

E.H.

4

Illustrations for Ben Blow, "Old Maje Departs," *Everybody's*, 26 (March 1912).

4. "Engaged himself pleasantly with a huge bowl of mush of milk," p. 422.

5. "With speed the newcomers cast off the curse of clothing. A water-splashing fight ensued, and mud was 'pasted,' " p. 423.

6. " 'What's the matter? Been gettin' into trouble, Henery?' Doc Henderson, astute observer, had noticed traces of tears on Fatty's cheeks," p. 425.

Illustrations for Emerson Taylor, "A Fresh Start," *Everybody's*, 30 (January 1914).

7a. Proof.

7b. P. 102.

7c. Unpublished proof.

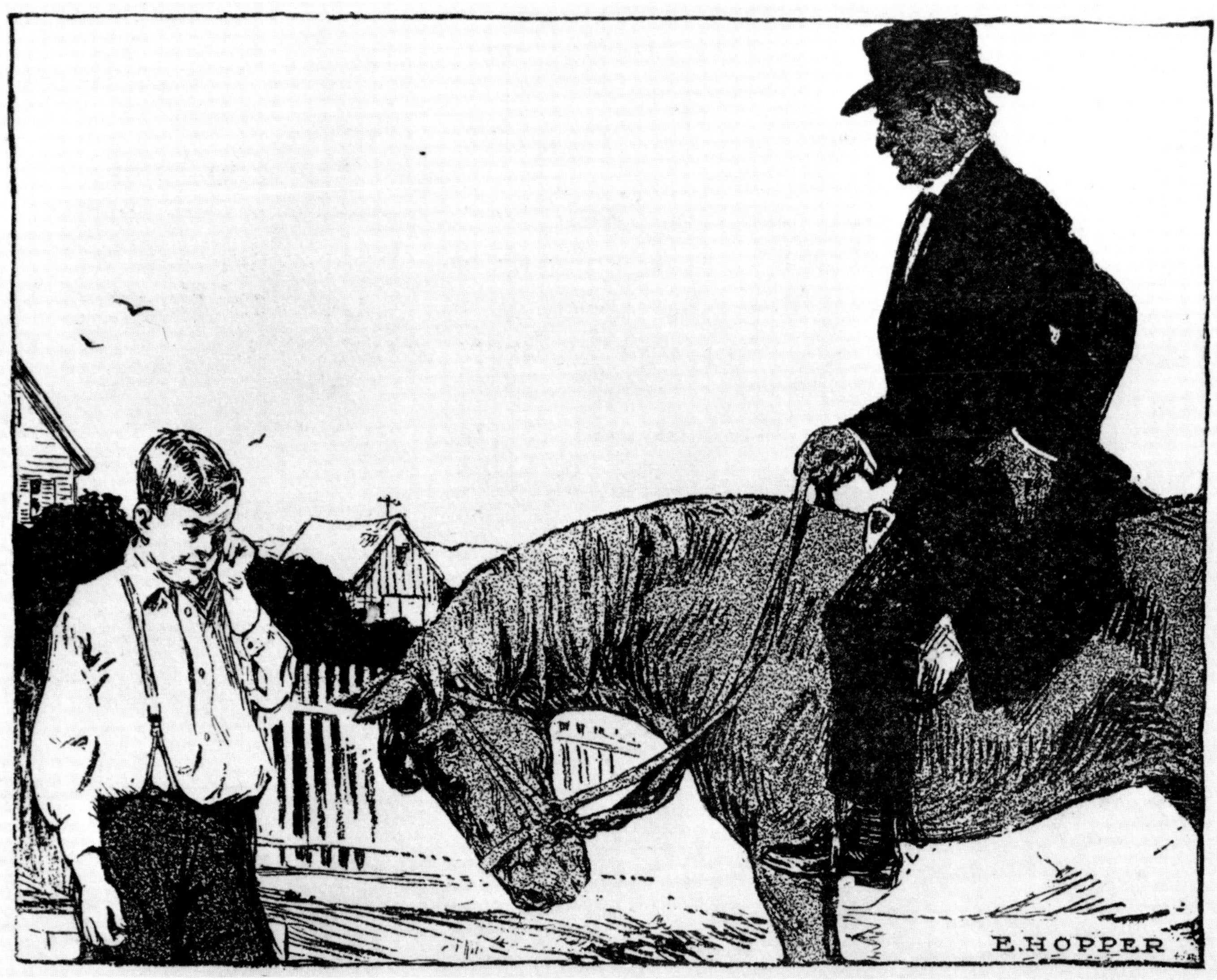

6

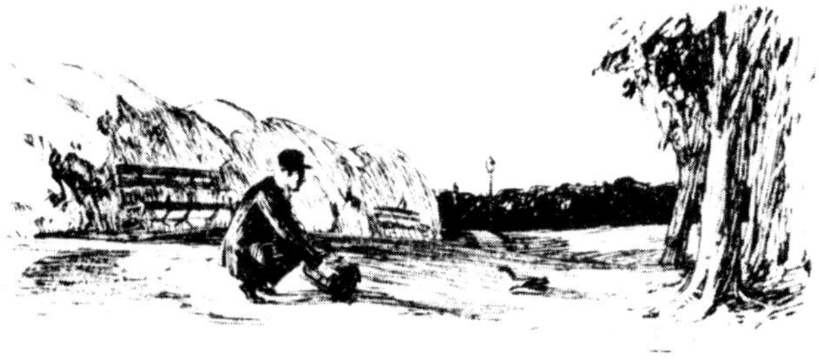

7b

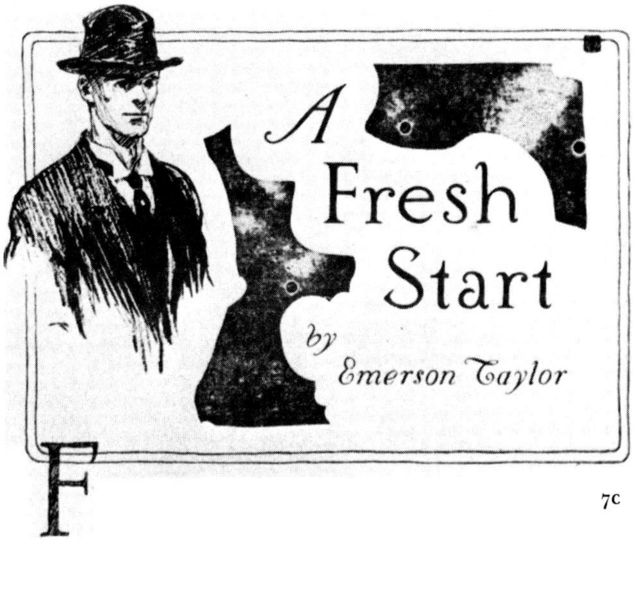

7c

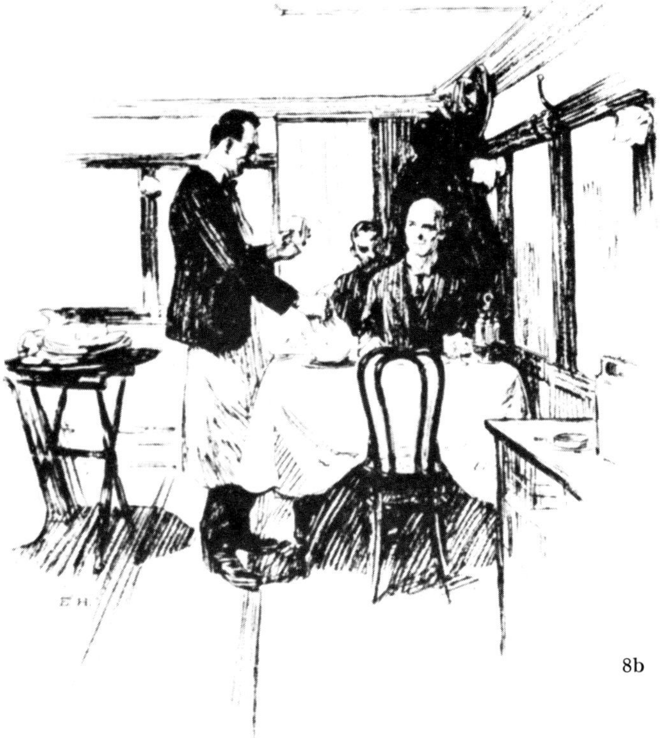

8b

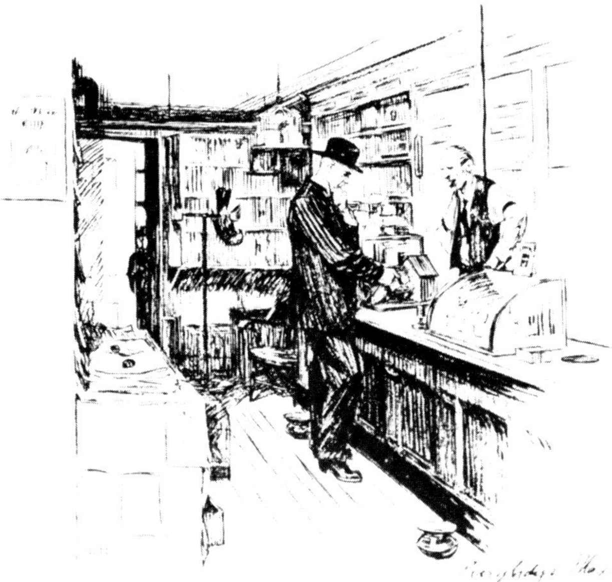

9a

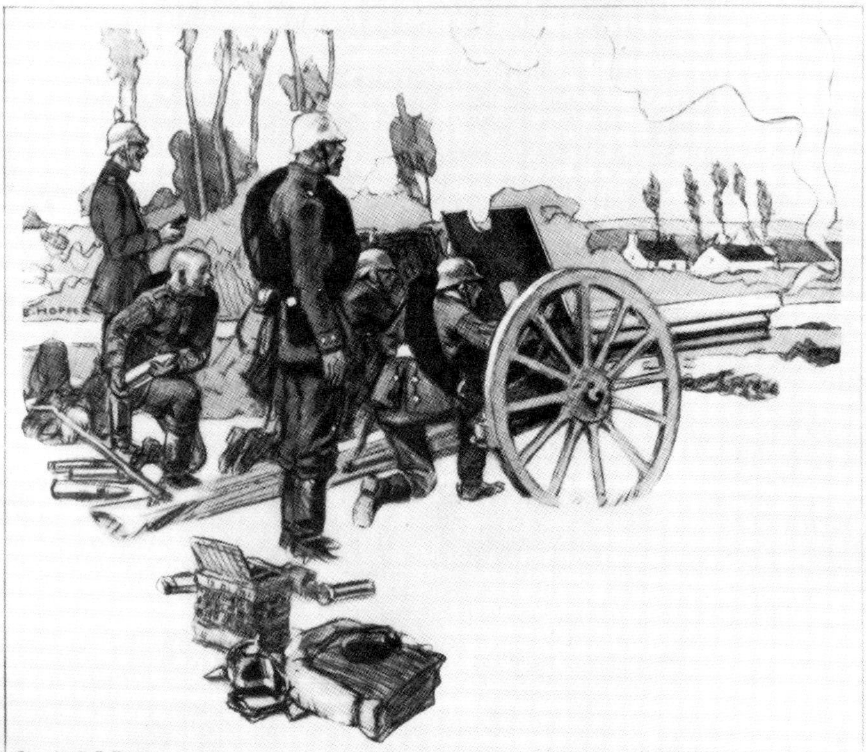

10

8a. Proof.

8b. "You look like a sailor—you do!" p. 103.

9a. Proof.

9b. "It ain't so hard, maybe, if you've never been free," p. 105.

Illustrations for Frederick Palmer, "Frederick Palmer in Germany: My Day at the Front," *Everybody's,* 32 (January 1915).

10. P. 72.

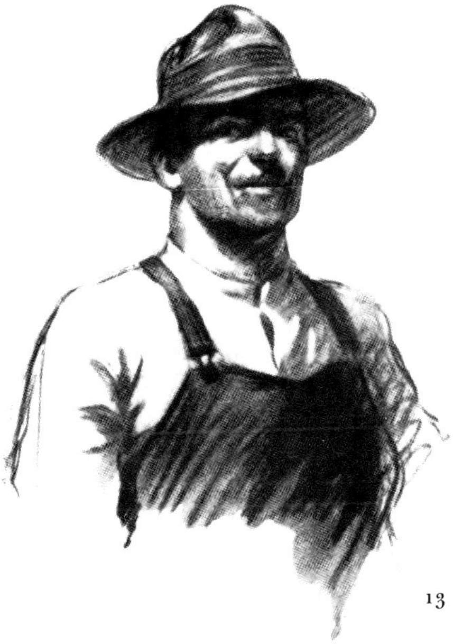

13

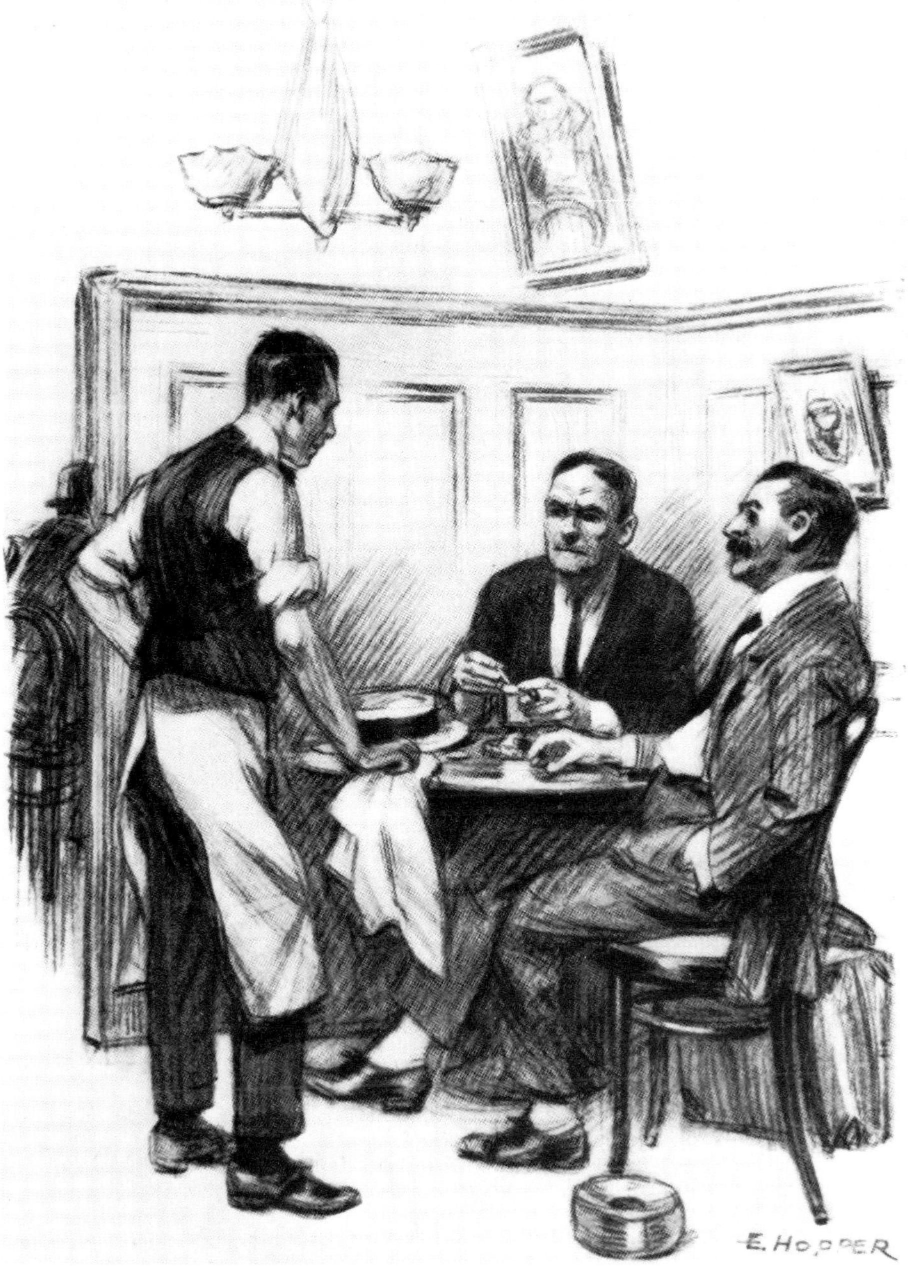

14

11a. Proof.

11b. P. 75.

12a. Proof.

12b. P. 78.

Illustrations for Edith R. Mirrielees, "The Hero Business," *Everybody's,* 32 (June 1915).

13. P. 751.

14. "The youth's eyes were fixed devouringly on O'Brien's face," p. 753.

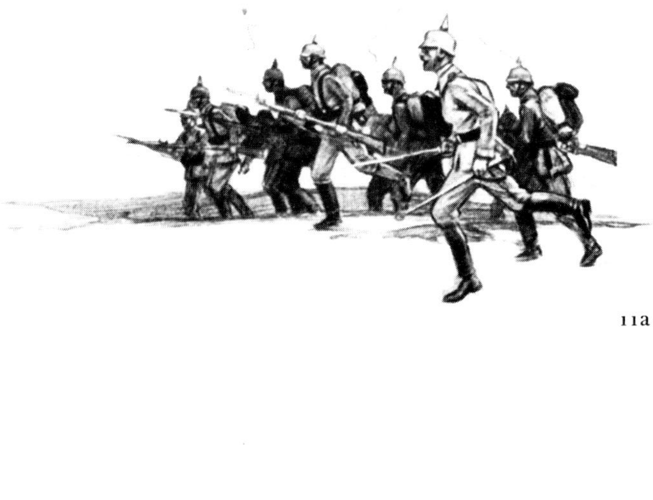

11a

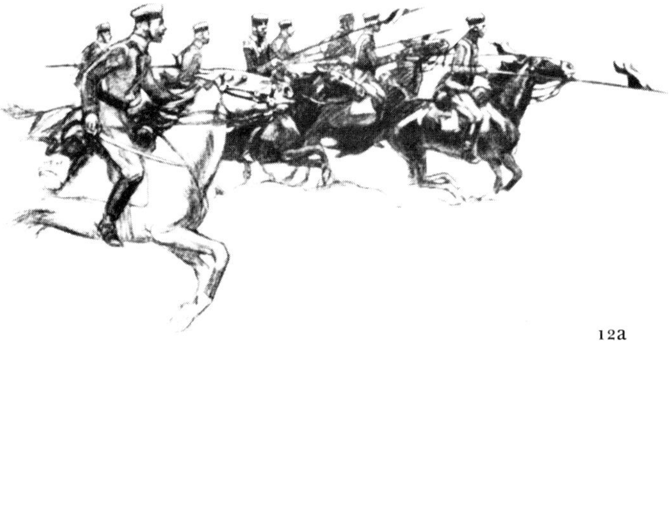

12a

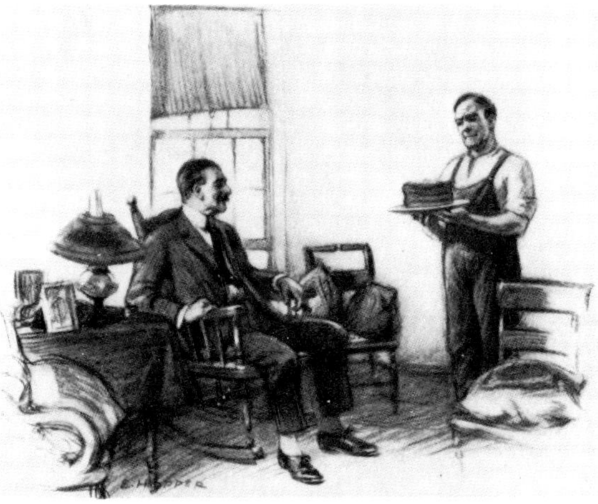

15

15. "Every time one of those sixty kids has a birthday—I get a cake," p. 755.

Illustration for Louise Closser Hale, "The House That Patty Built," *Everybody's*, 41 (July 1919).

16. "He ran ahead up the ragged sides of the crater, waving them on with a grenade in hand," p. 35.

Illustrations for Stephen French Whitman, "Sacrifice," *Everybody's*, 45 (September 1921). Part 1 of a five-part novel.

17. "At last it was yellow and crinkled, that magazine picture of the fair unknown which had become for him a living companion," p. 4.

18. "Lilla kept on her desk a magazine-picture of Lawrence Teck, the explorer, whom she had never seen," p. 5.

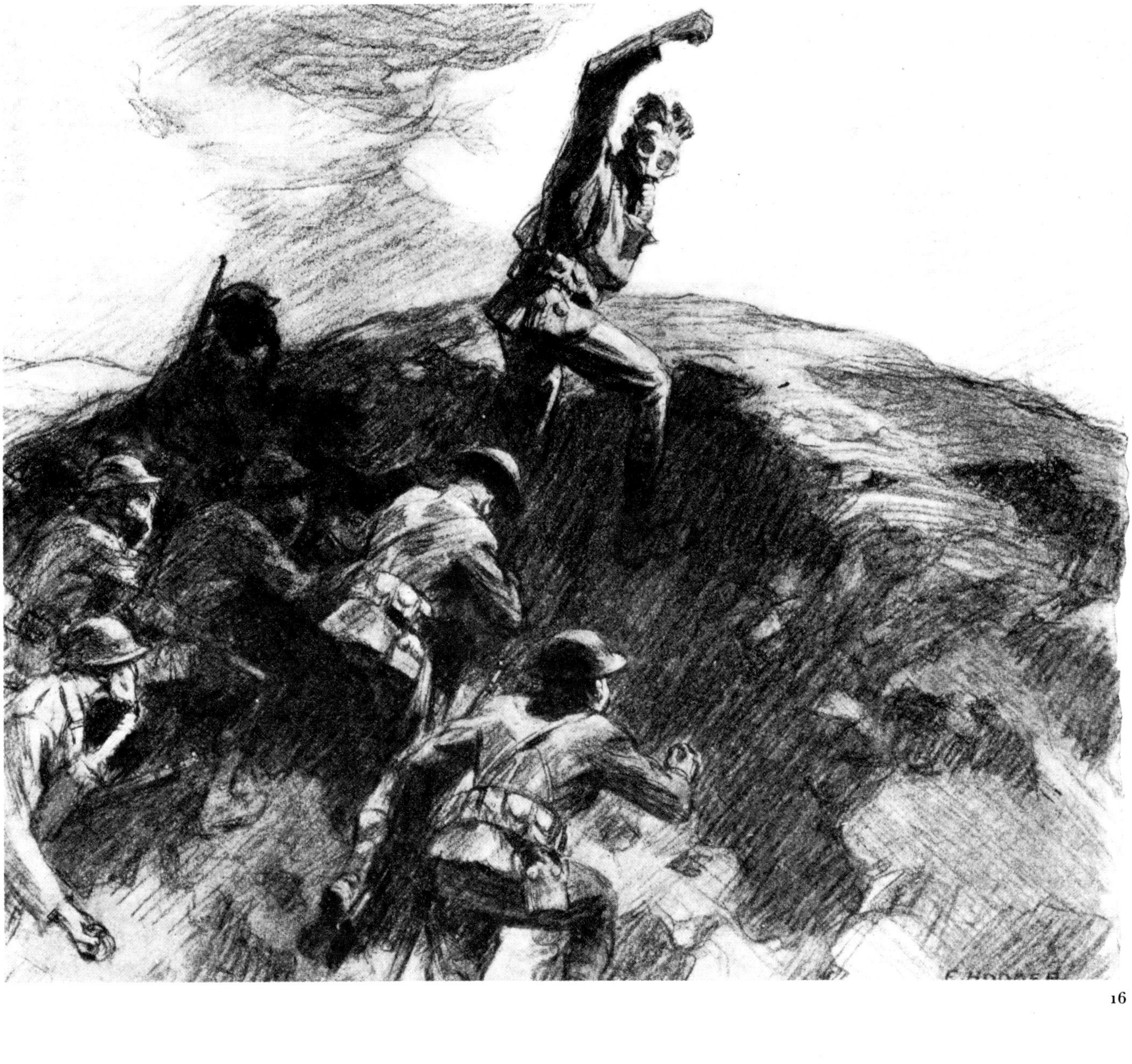

16

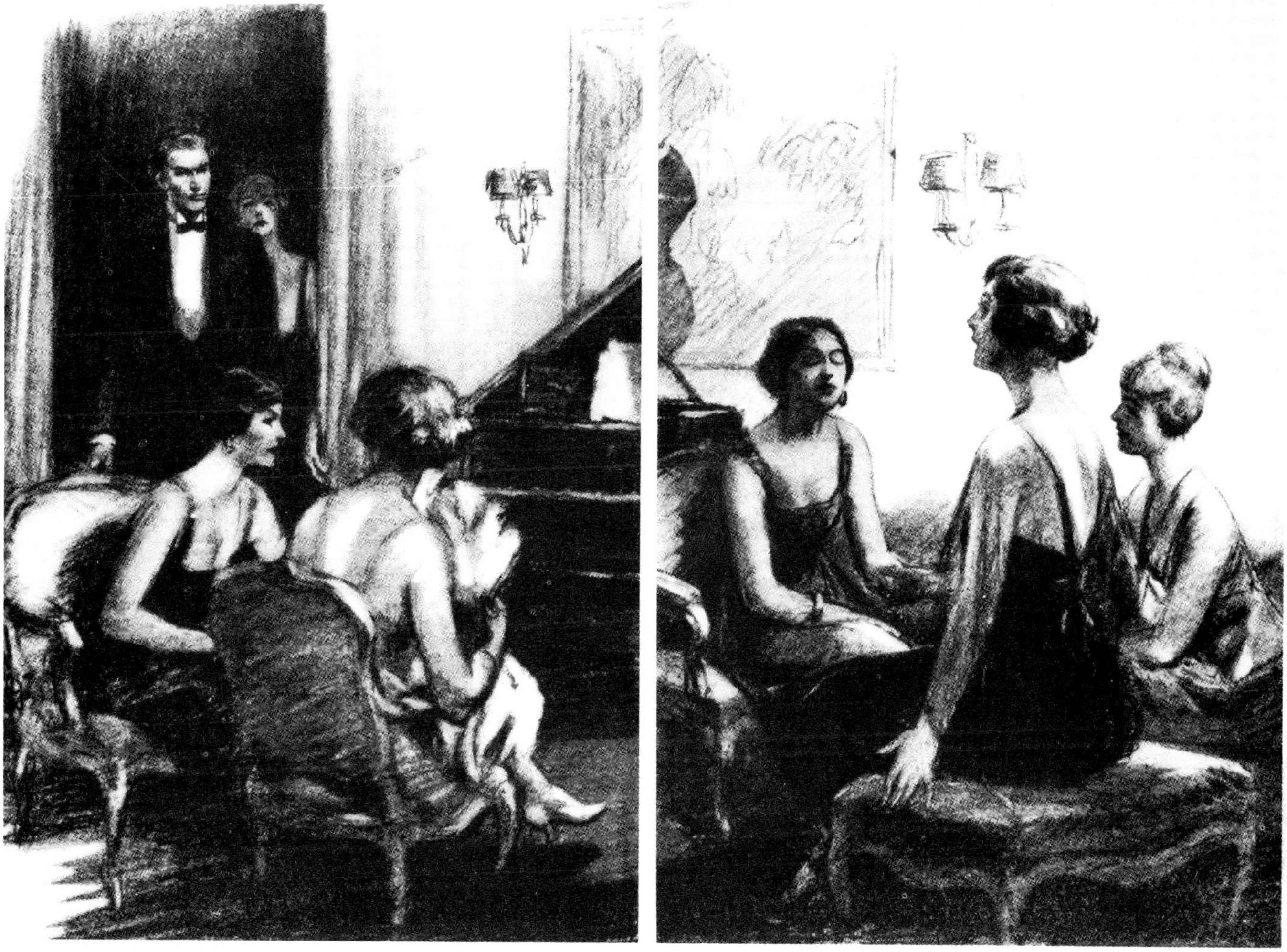

19

19. "Madame Zanidov, the clairvoyant, is telling Lilla's fortune. She sees a picture. 'The people in the clearing are black savages. They sit around a body that is stretched on the ground and covered with a cloth. I can not describe the one who lies in the midst of them. But I feel that it is some one who has loved you.' Lilla, raising her eyes, saw in the doorway a tall man, a stranger. It was Lawrence Teck, the explorer," pp. 10–11.

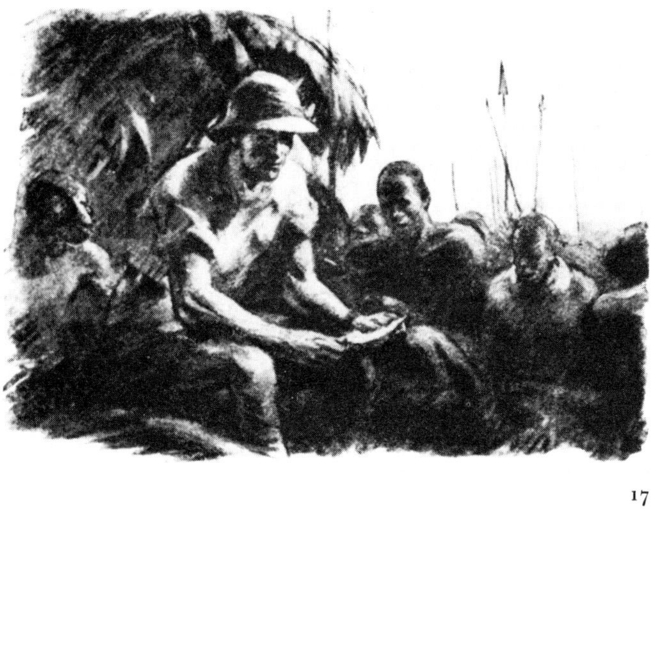

17

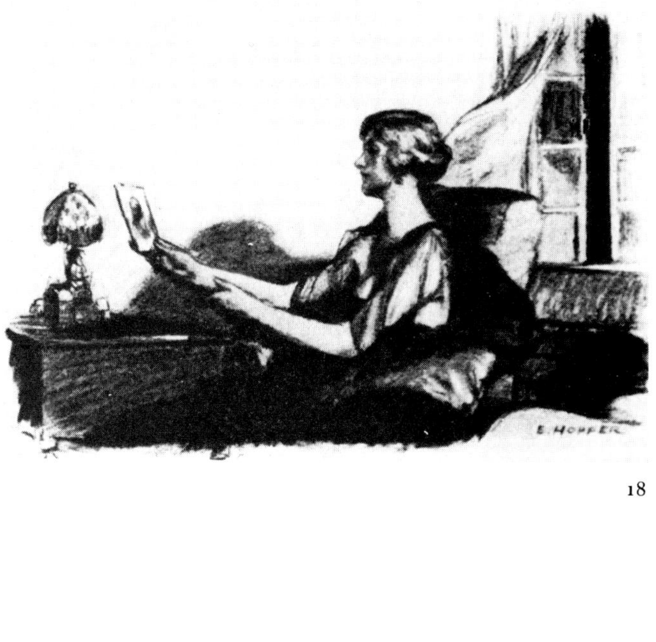

18

20

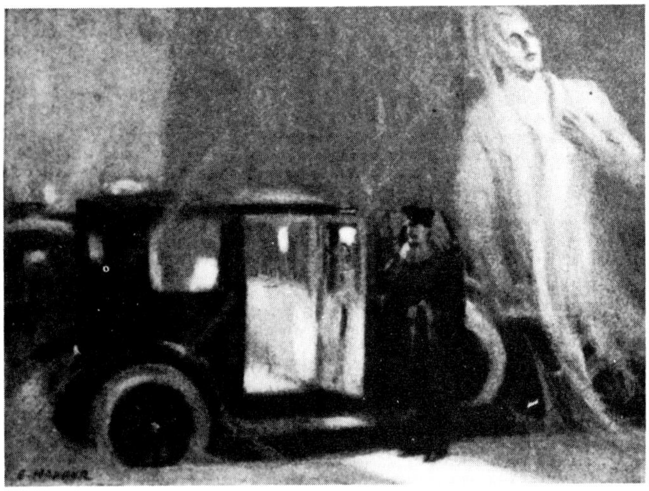

20

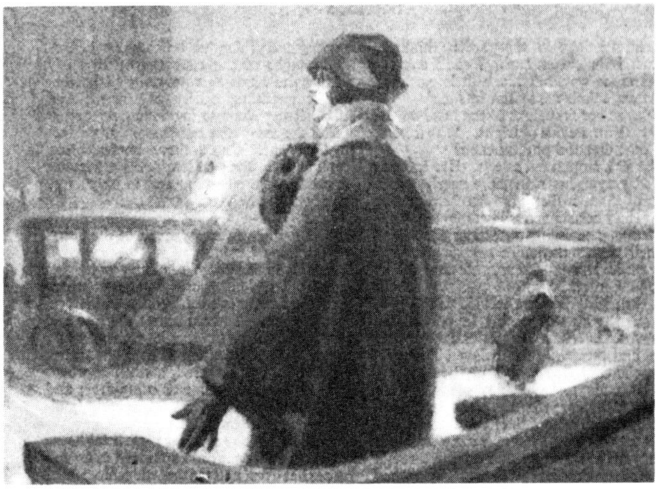

Illustrations for Stephen French Whitman, "Sacrifice," part 2, *Everybody's,* 45 (October 1921).

20. "As Lilla crossed the sidewalk to her car, an eddy of wind raised before her, head high, a whirl of snowflakes that resembled a wraith. A month later the newspapers published a dispatch reporting the death of Lawrence Teck at the hands of savages," pp. 30–31.

21. "Now and then for a moment she forgot his infirmity; he became the hero of an idyllic scene. But unlike those heroes he spoke only of the moment, since it was only the moment of which he could be sure. 'You are here,' his eyes said to her. 'I have this hour at least. Nothing else matters,'" pp. 40–41.

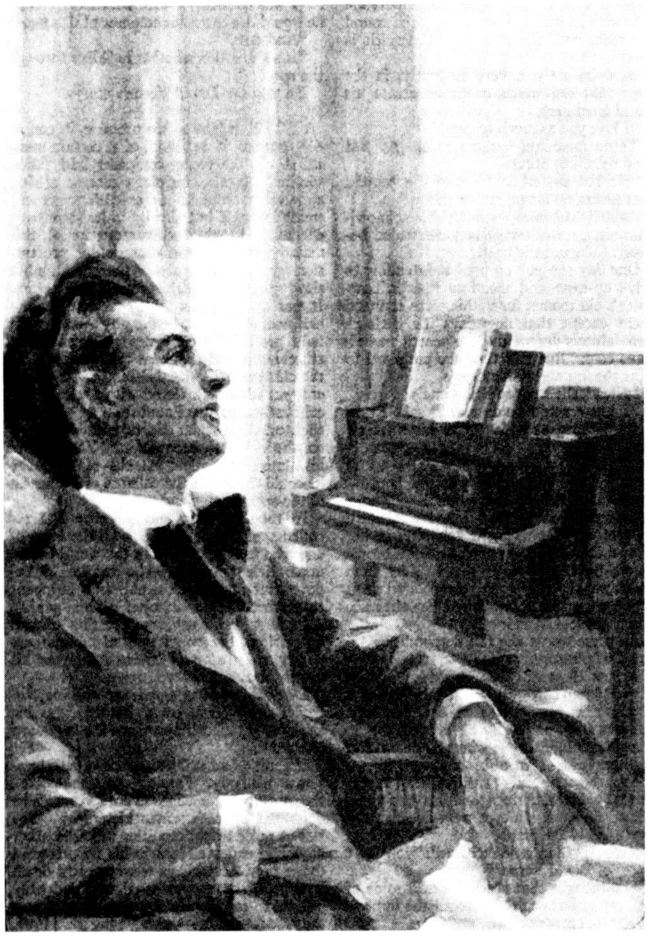

21

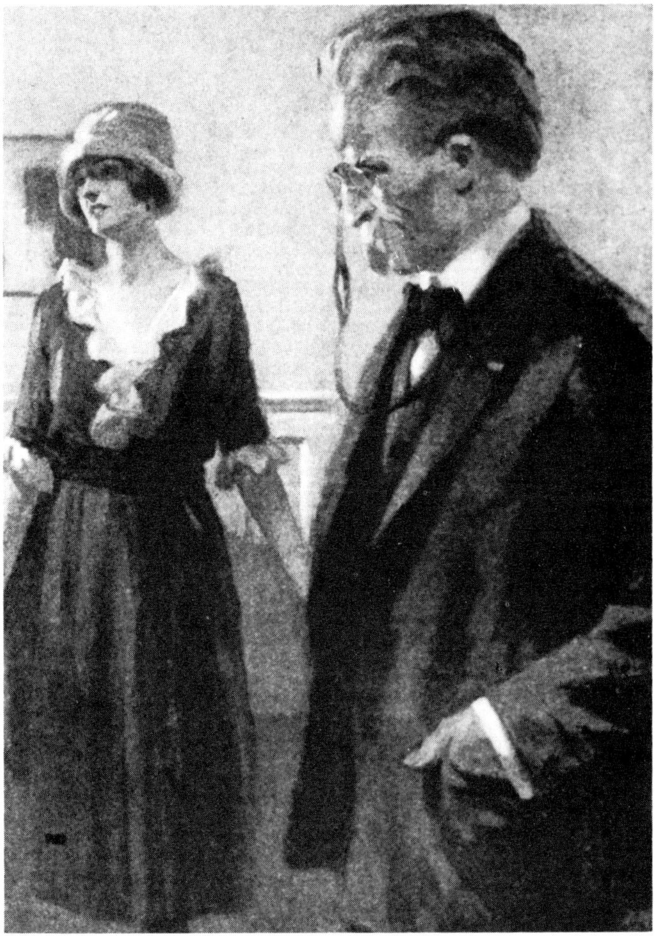

21

22

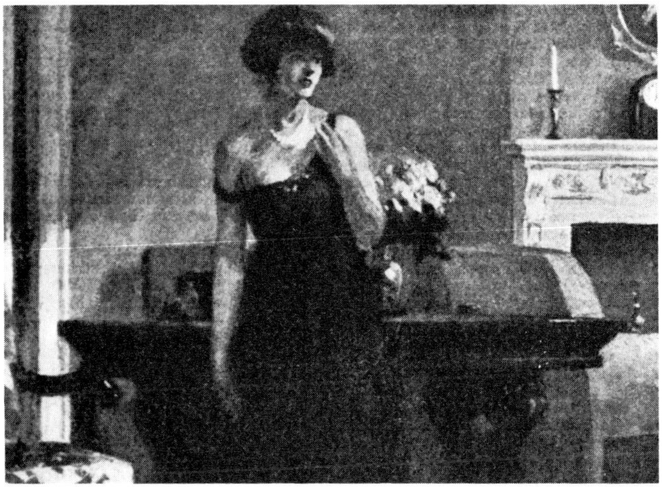

22

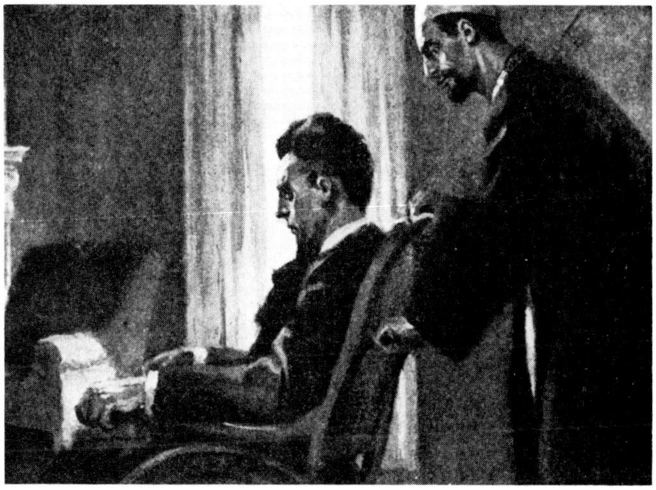

Illustrations for Stephen French Whitman, "Sacrifice," part 3, *Everybody's,* 45 (November 1921).

22. " 'What is it?' she exclaimed, and turned to catch her reflection in a mirror. She saw herself in a curious aspect also, white and a little wild. One of her shoulder-straps had slipped down across her arm. David carefully pronounced the words, 'That was Rysbroek,' wasn't it? 'Yes. He brought me bad news,' " pp. 138–39.

23. "In the equatorial forests where the Mambava spearmen dwelt unconquered, the black king, Muene-Motapa, sat in the royal house listening to a story-teller. At the story-teller's gestures—since gestures were needed to explain these wonders—chains clanked on his wrists," pp. 152–53.

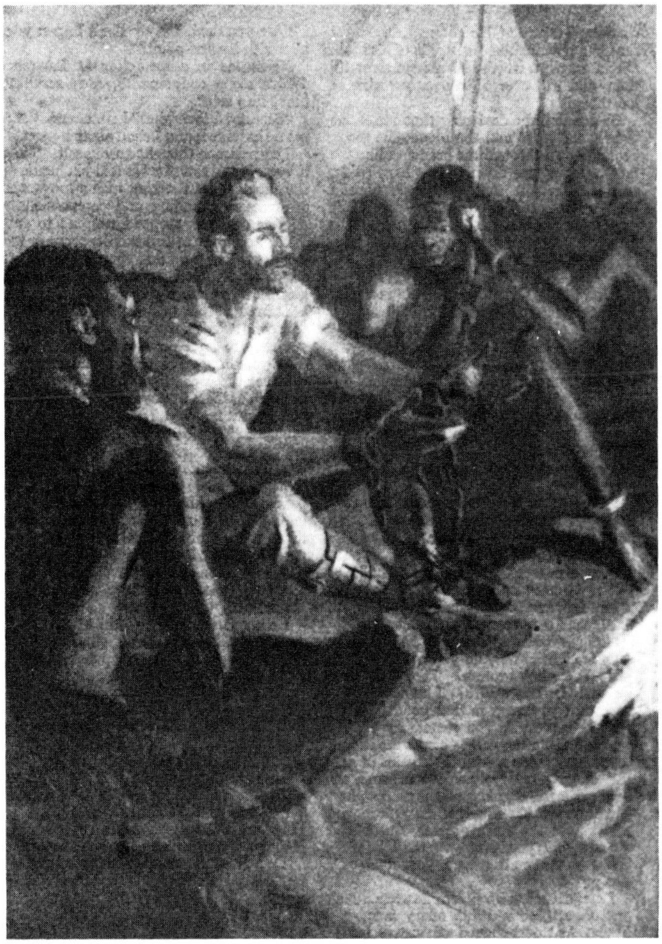

23

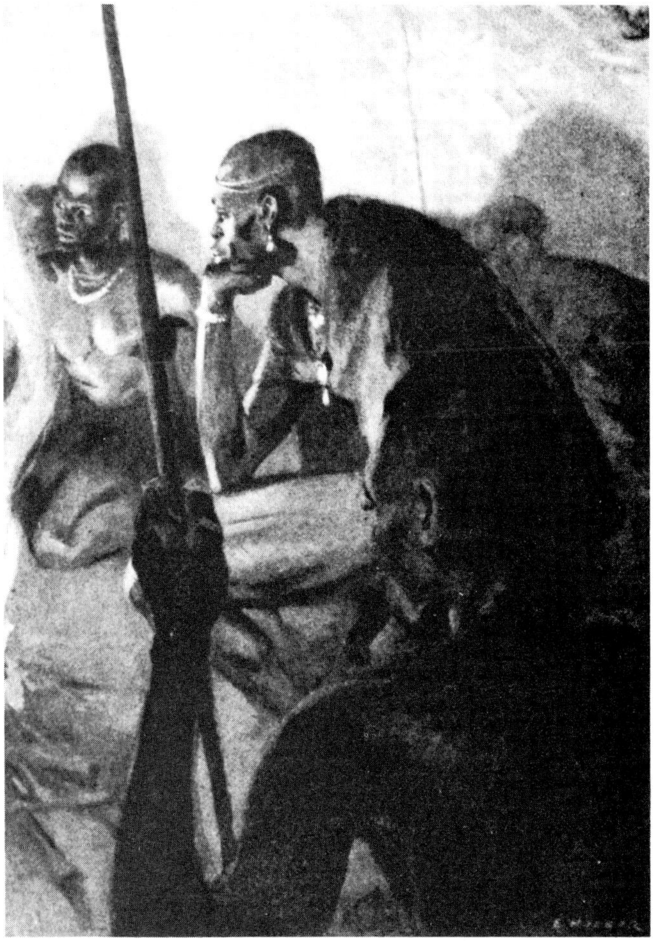

23

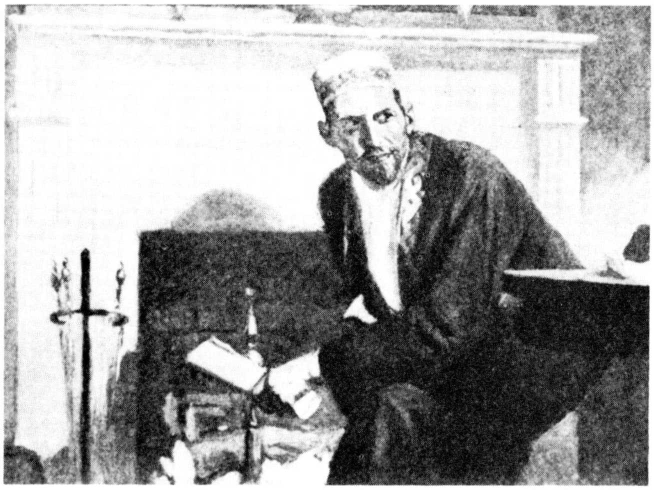

24

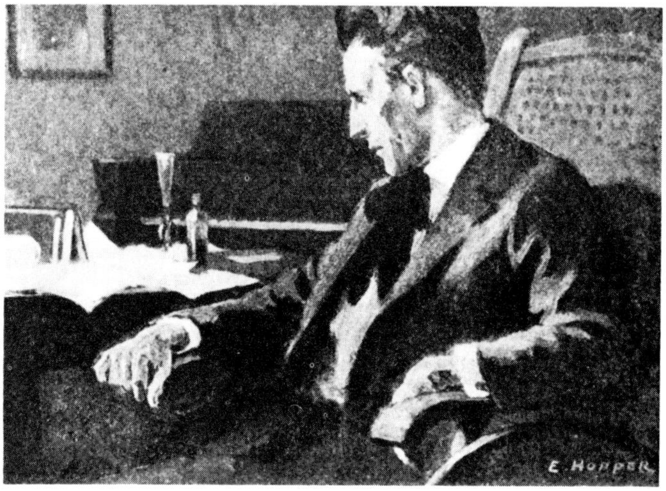

24

Illustrations for Stephen French Whitman, "Sacrifice," part 4, *Everybody's*, 45 (December 1921).

24. "Still kneeling on the hearth, Hamoud contemplated the other as though he were seeing him now for the first time. Of a sudden, the habit of protection grappled with his resolve, and might have conquered had he not recalled the sufferings of the beloved. The newspaper was in his left hand," pp. 116–17.

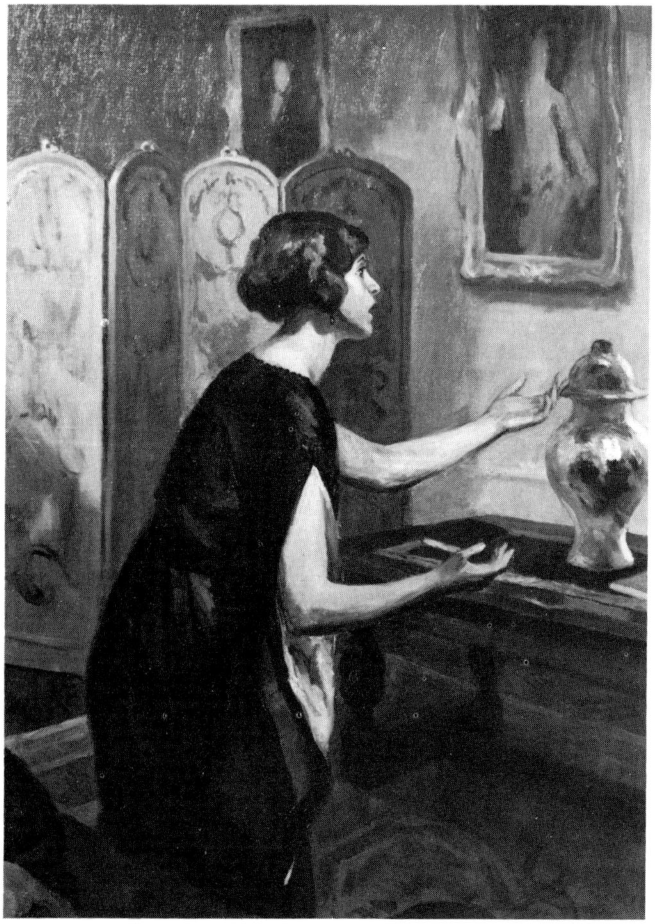

25a

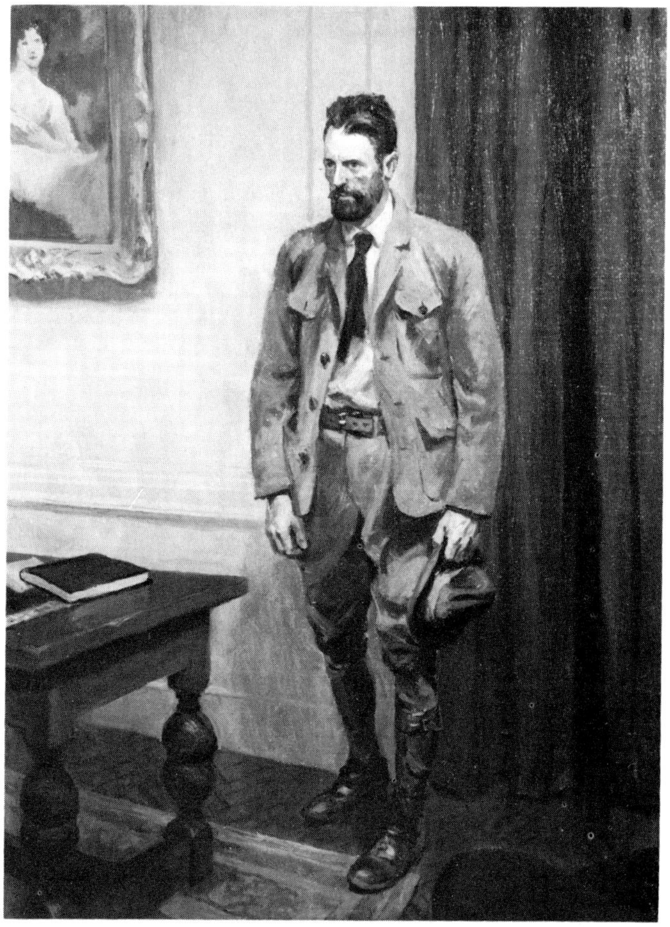

25a

25a. Illustration, 1921. Oil on canvas, 27 × 39 inches. Whitney Museum of American Art, New York; Bequest of Josephine N. Hopper 70.1168.

25b. "Lilla began to float toward him over the floor that she no longer felt beneath her feet, so that her disembodied spirit might be merged with this other spirit. But abruptly an invisible force seemed to check her progress midway, and she stood before him with her arms lifted in what appeared to be a frozen gesture of horrified denial," pp. 132–33.

Illustration for Stephen French Whitman, "Sacrifice," part 5, *Everybody's,* 46 (January 1922).

26a. Illustration, 1921. Oil on canvass, 27 × 39 inches. Whitney Museum of American Art, New York; Bequest of Josephine N. Hopper 70.1167.

26b. "Then without warning, came the charge. Lilla became aware of an apparition—a sort of naked harlequin, magnified by a towering head-dress. Another followed, crouching parallyzed before that inexorable advance," pp. 168–69.

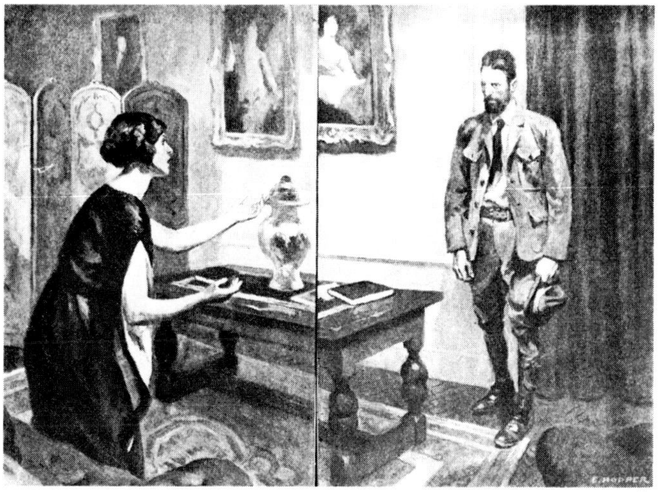

25b

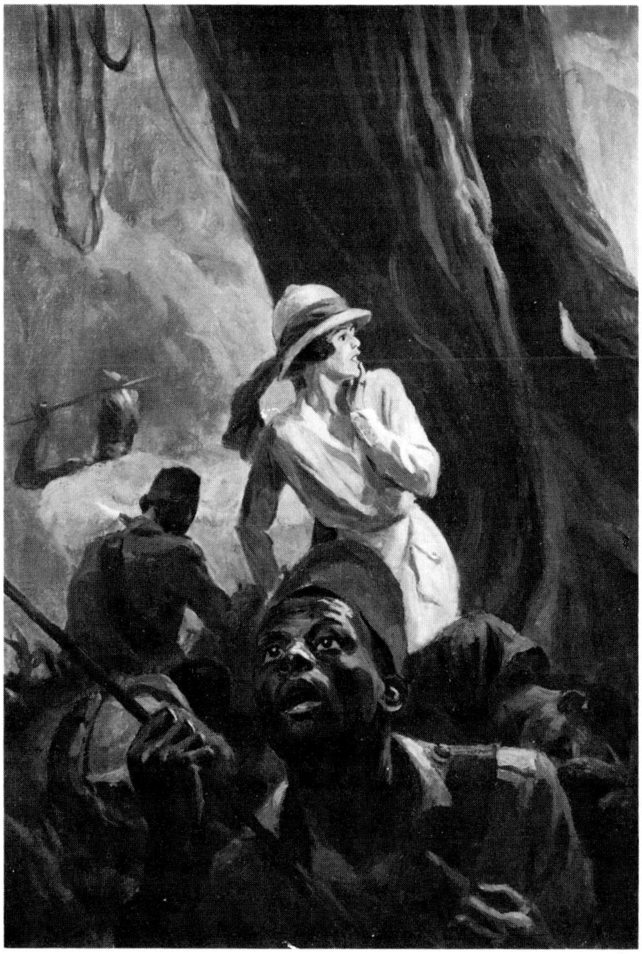

26a

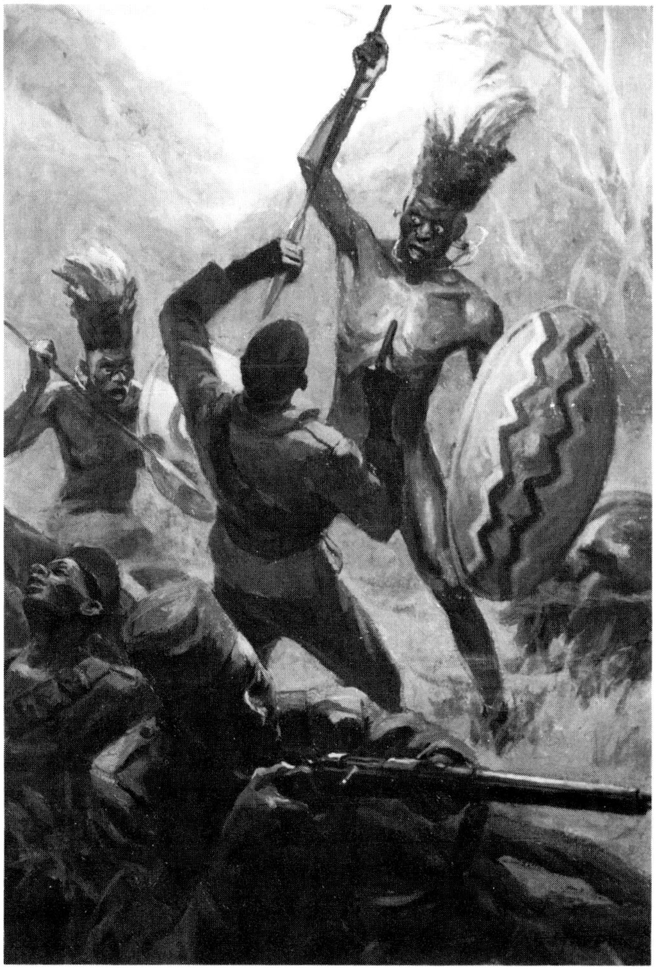

26a

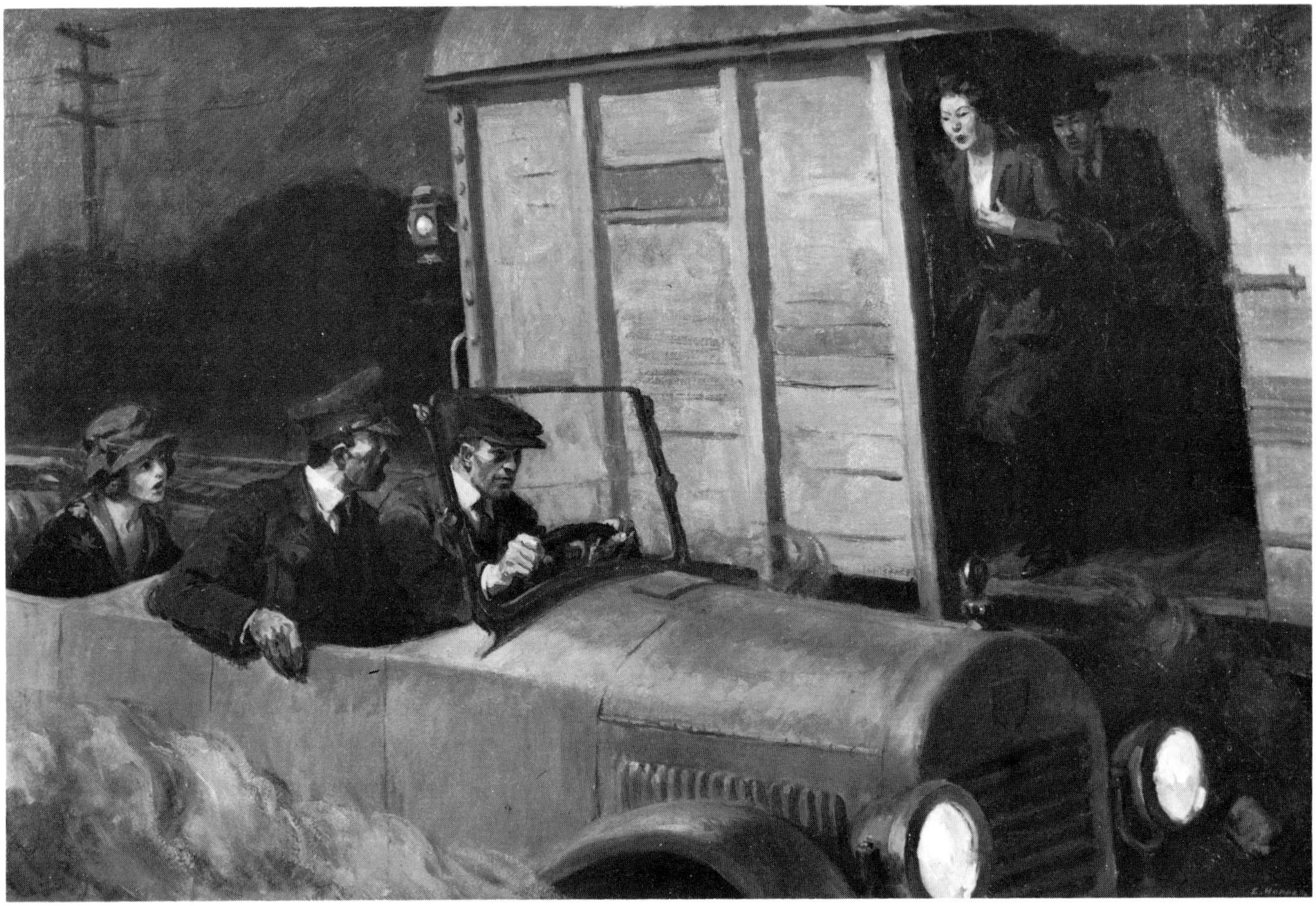

28a

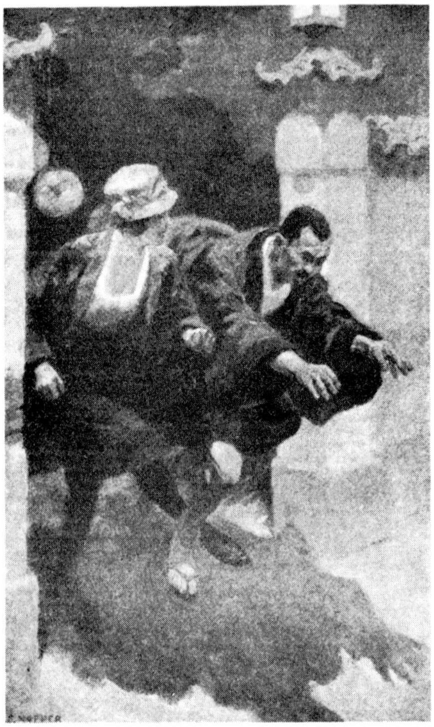

27

Illustrations for Walter De Leon, "Everything Save Honor," *Everybody's*, 46 (May 1922).

27. "As we raced through the gate, I inserted my foot between Kitanoya's pudgy knees," p. 36.

28a. Illustration, 1921–22. Oil on canvas, 27 × 39 inches. Whitney Museum of American Art, New York; Bequest of Josephine N. Hopper 70.1169.

28b. "Skilfully Paul drew the auto abreast of them and edged it close, perilously, recklessly close to the rocking, rumbling, freight-car," pp. 42–43.

Illustrations for Philip Gibbs, "The Game of Poverty," *Everybody's*, 46 (June 1922).

29. "Her next performance was to break a piece of bread from her roll and throw it with unerring aim at a one-armed young man at the other side of the room," p. 40.

30. "Janet stood full in the lamplight. She was wearing a little diamond crown, like a princess. Paul made a sudden step forward, and I put my hand on his arm and said, 'Steady, old man!' " p. 47.

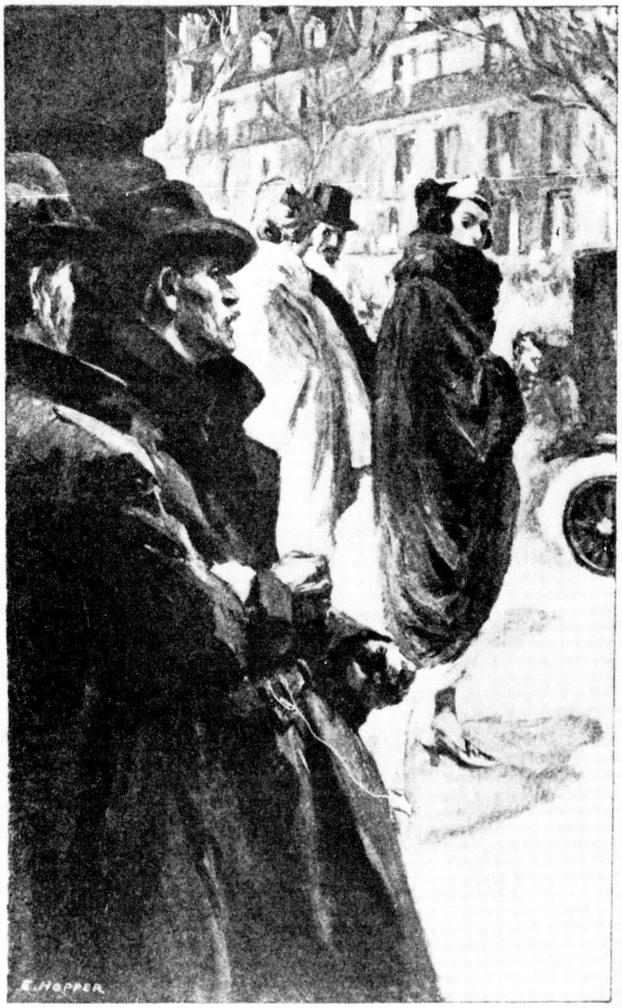

30

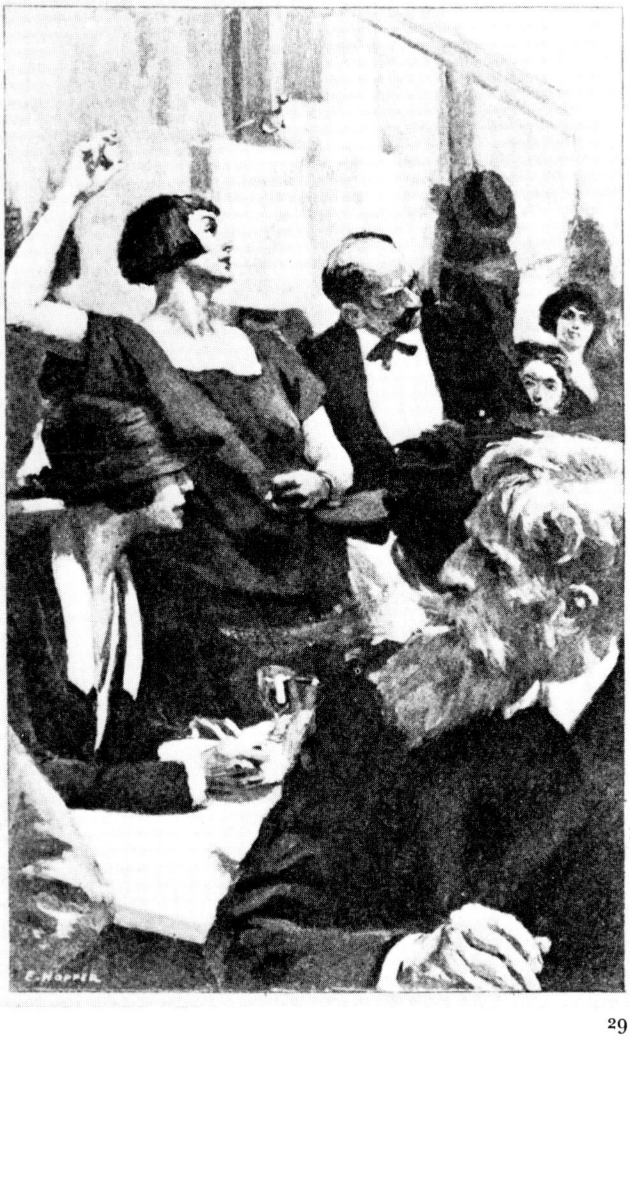

29

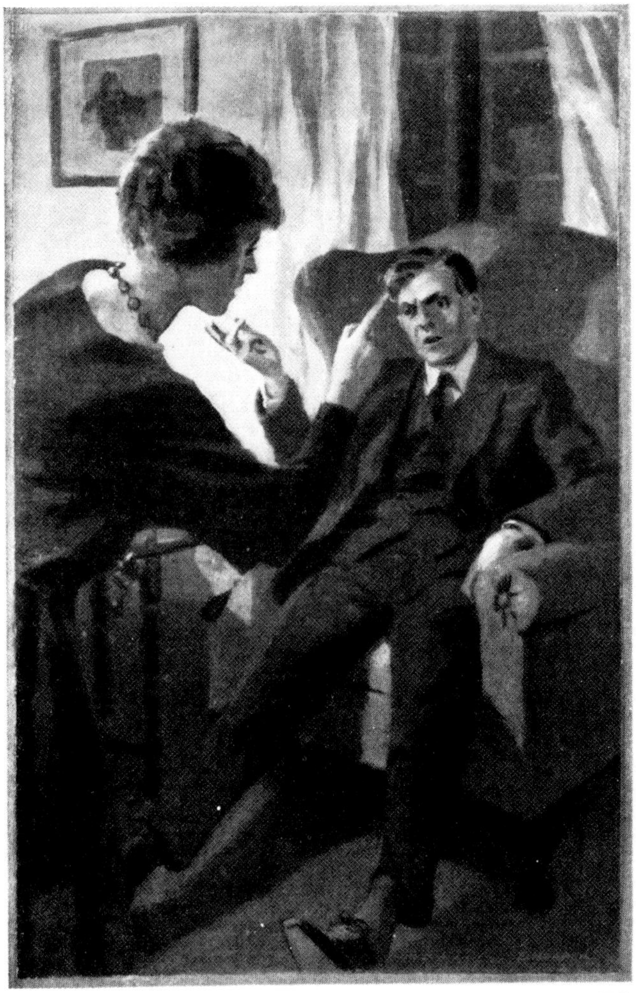

31a

Illustrations for Louis Lee Arms, "On and On," *Everybody's,* 48 (January 1923).

31a. " 'You have made a statement. You are going to stand by it, make or break.' She gazed at him tragically. 'Don't you see, Jimmy?' " p. 4.

31b. " 'Well, think it over,' said Bodie, stepping out of the car," p. 13.

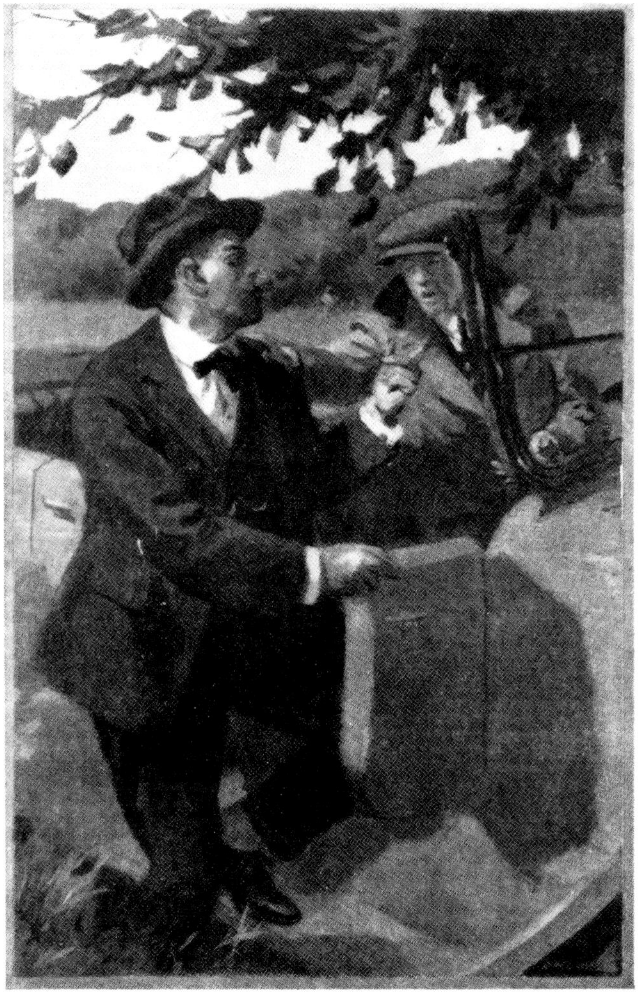

31b

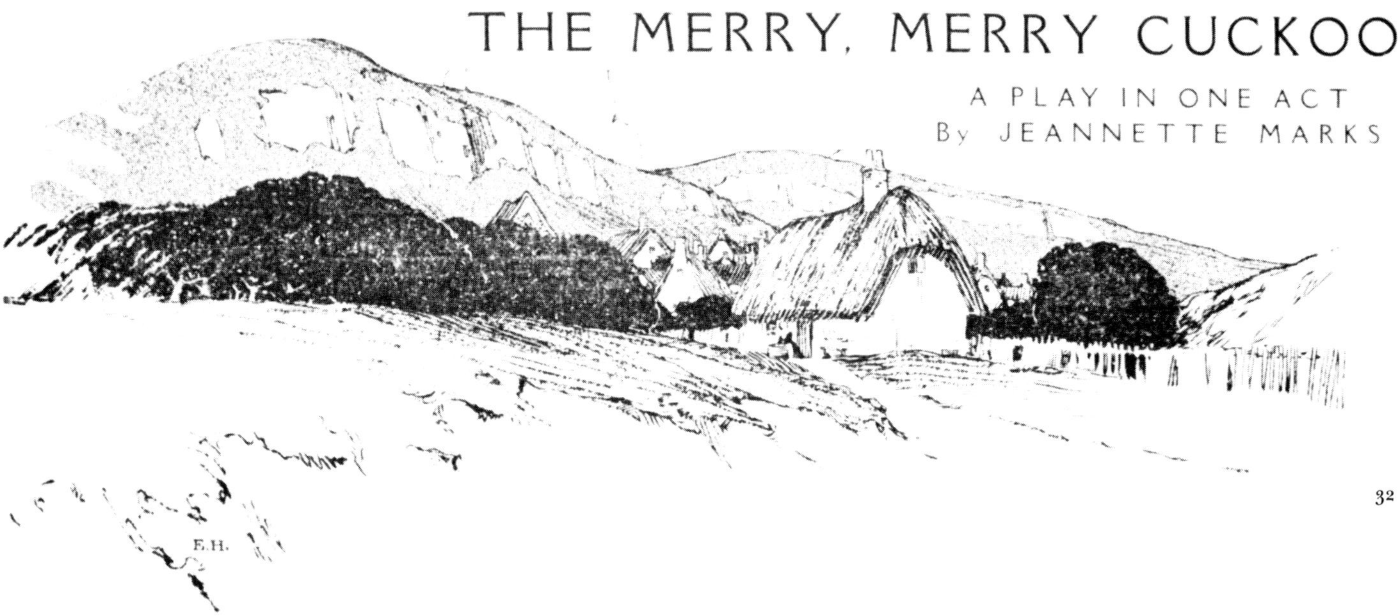

32

Illustrations for Jeannette Marks, "The Merry, Merry Cuckoo," *The Metropolitan Magazine,* 36 (July 1912).

32. P. 45.

33. "Annie, sweetheart, did ye hear the cuckoo singin'?" p. 45.

34. "Ye're neglectin' chapel and forgettin' the Lord, Annie Dalben," p. 45.

35. "She waits a moment—the heads are well above the wall now in amazement," p. 46.

33

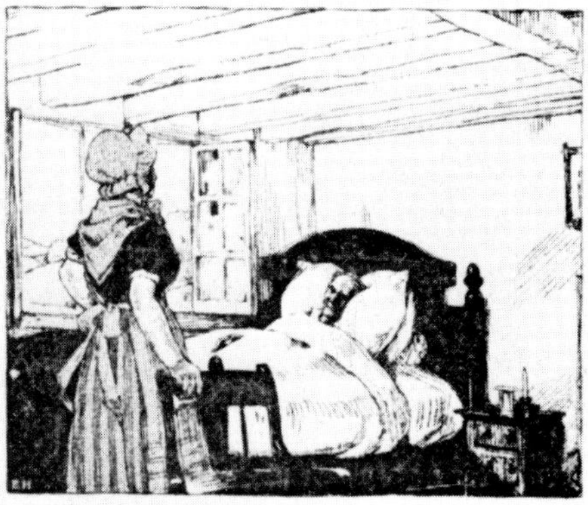

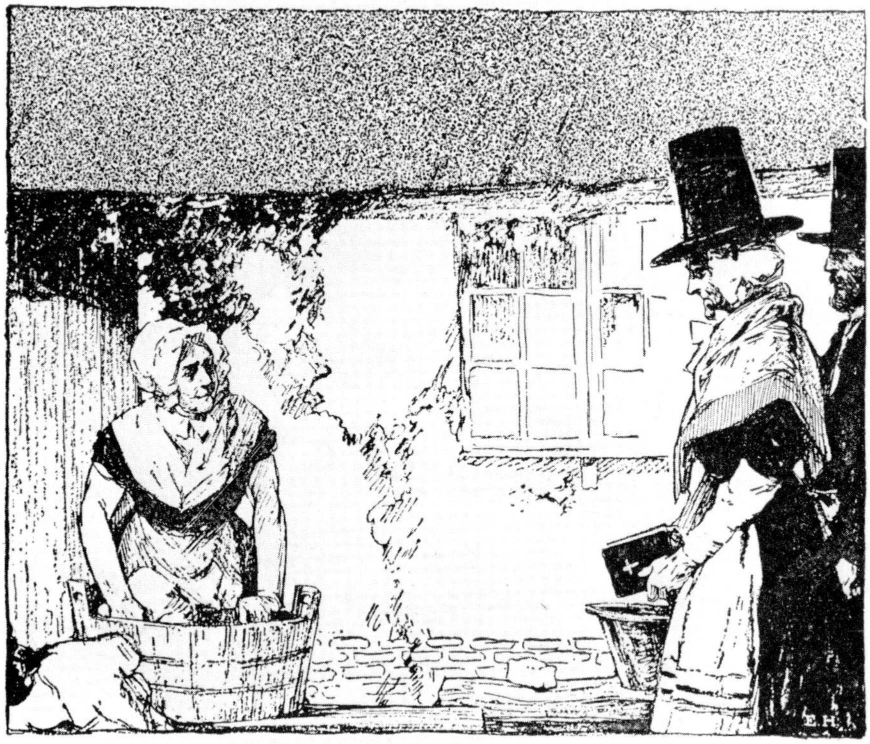

34

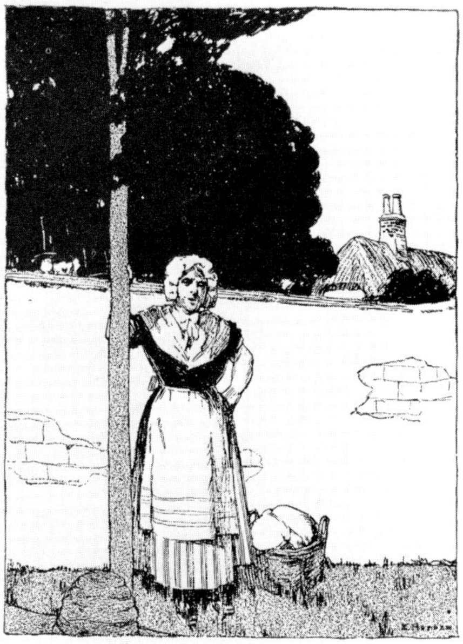

35

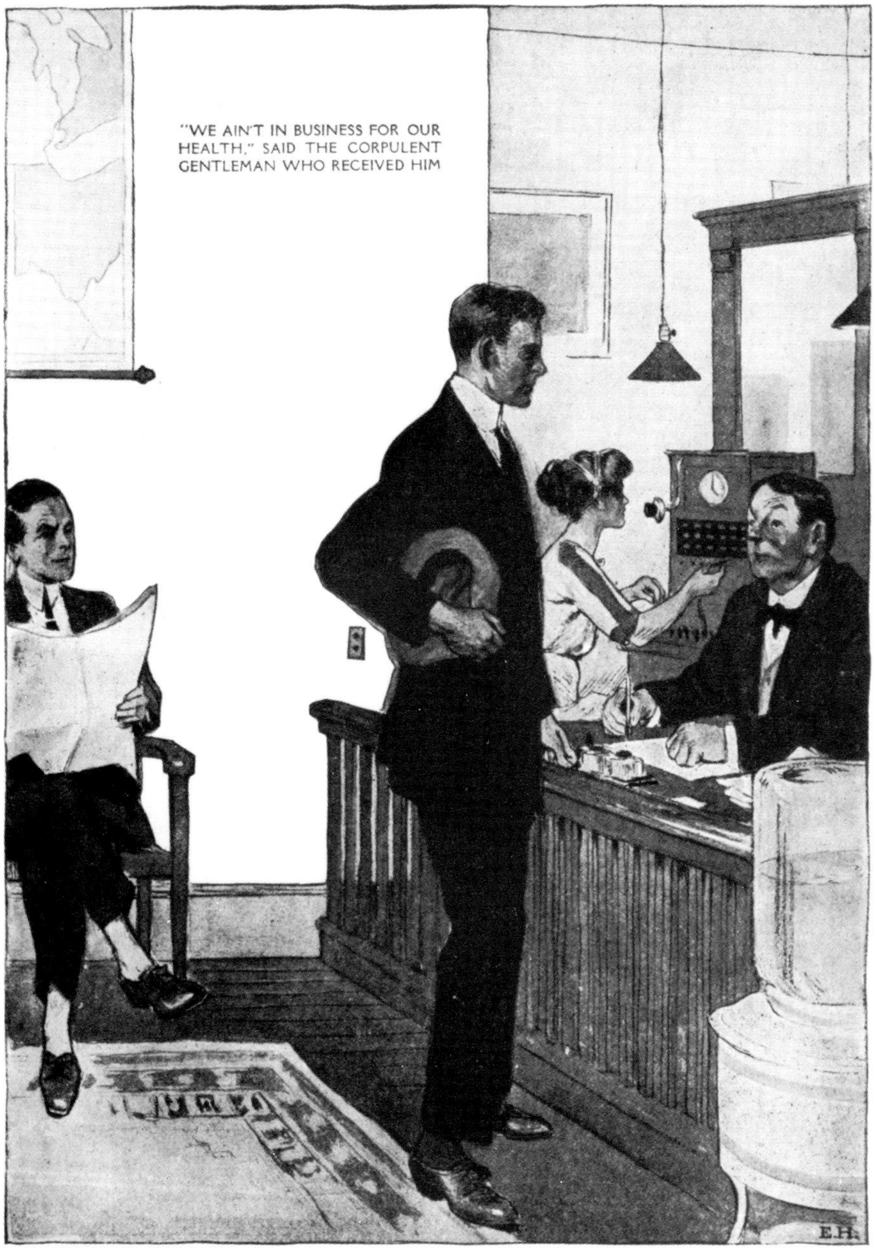

37b

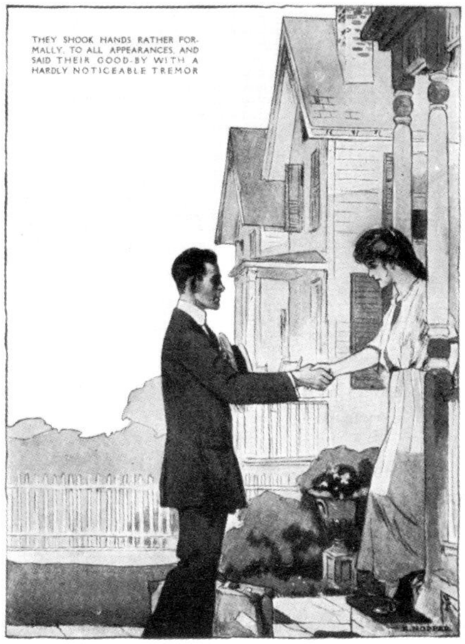

36b

Illustrations for Philip Prescott Frost, "The Knock of Opportunity," *The Metropolitan Magazine,* 37 (March 1913).

36a. Proof.

36b. "They shook hands rather formally, to all appearances, and said their good-by with a hardly noticeable tremor," p. 47.

37a. Proof.

37b. "'We ain't in business for our health,' said the corpulent gentleman who received him," p. 48.

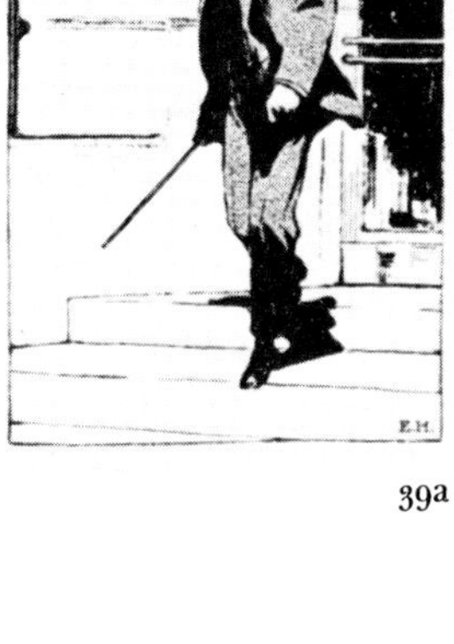

39a

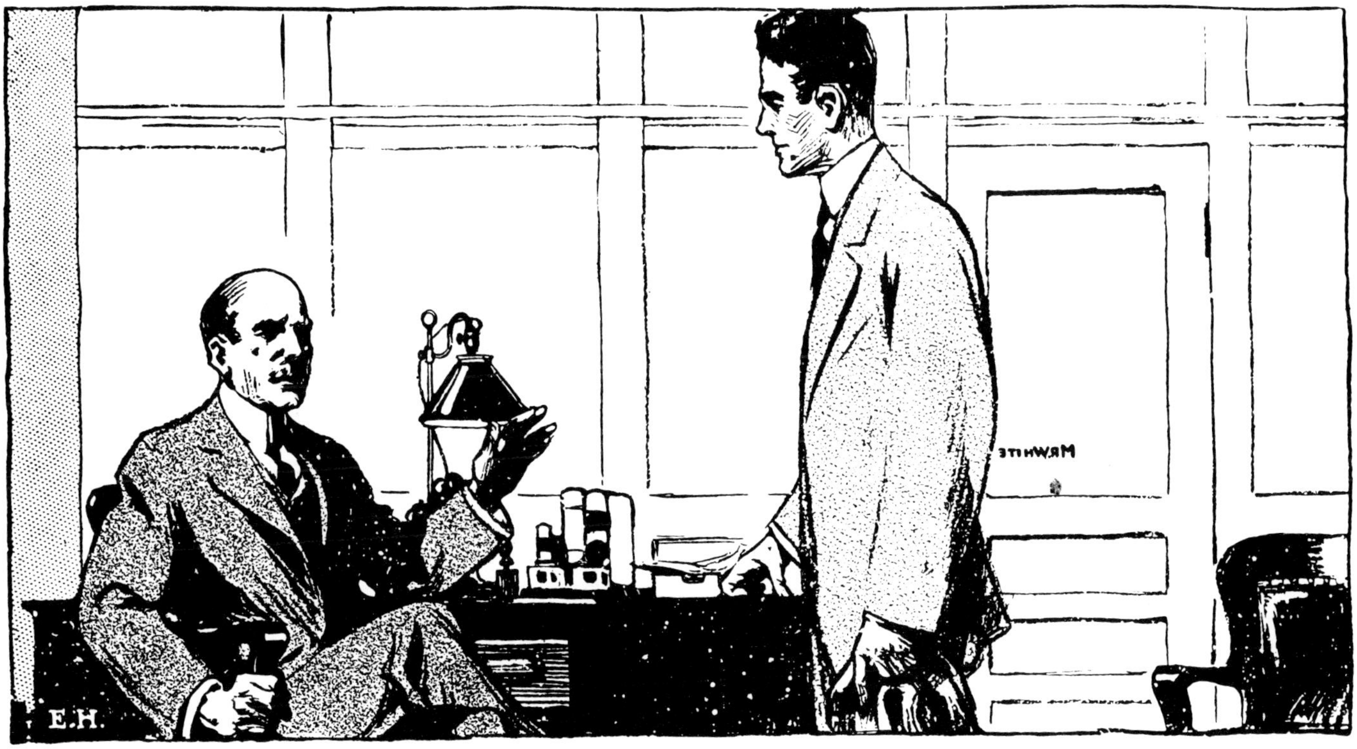

38

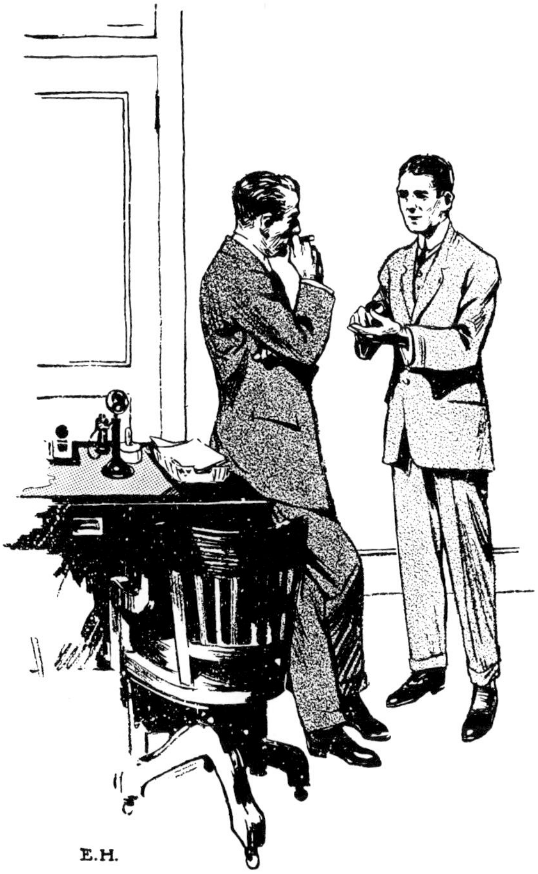

Illustrations for John I. Harden, "Fitting the Policy to the Prospect," *System,* 22 (August 1912).

38. "Take a $200,000 policy and you will be the most heavily insured man in my territory. When you pay the premium, I will advertise the fact in every county in the state," p. 162.

39a. Proof.

39b. "When it was pointed out to him that by an insurance policy on his own life he could protect the interests of his concern that borrowed money only because of his personal endorsement of its notes, he immediately put on his hat and went to the examiner," p. 164.

40. "The engineer who wanted an income after sixty-five took thirty policies of $1,000 each when he learned he could cash them for their paid up value as he needed the money," p. 166.

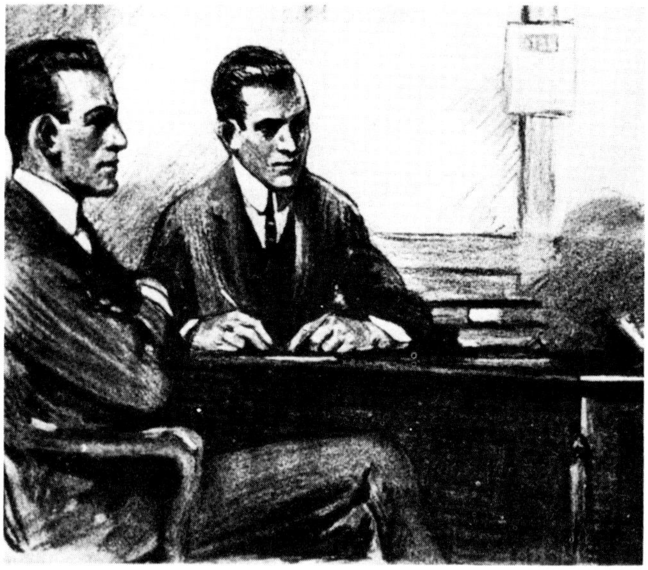

42a

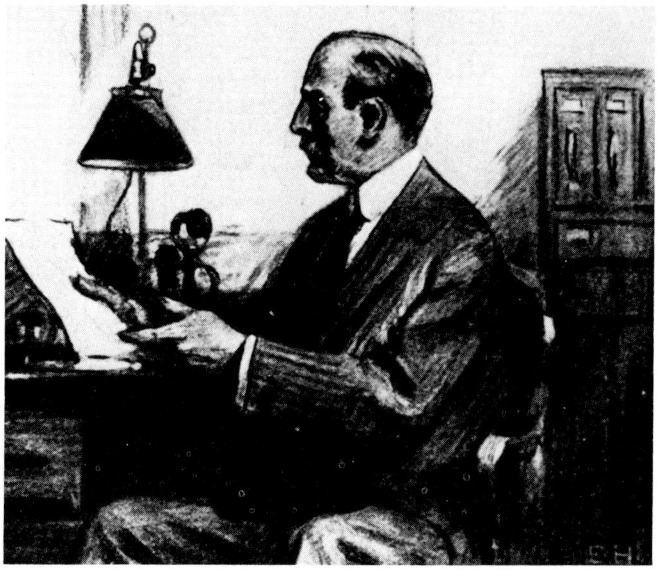

42a

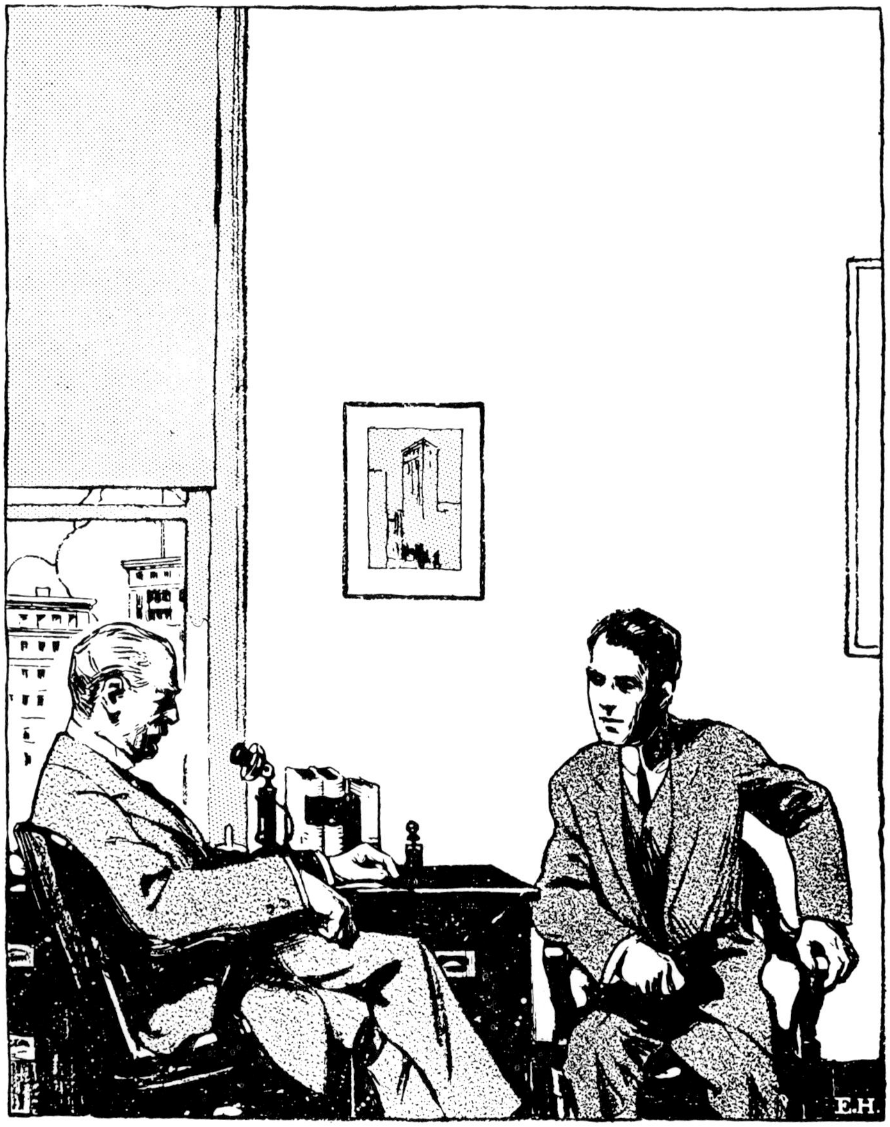

41

41. "In ten years this bank has lost four presidents, two by death and two by resignations, and has suspended once for lack of funds. If you were to die it would cost the stock holders $100,000 before you could be replaced. Isn't that sum worth protecting?" p. 169.

Illustrations for Carroll D. Murphy, "What Makes Men Buy?" *System,* 22 (September 1912).

42a. "The advertising manager's pencil had been busy. 'Isn't that what you mean?' he inquired, tossing a diagram across the table. 'I have followed the returns from copy of different types for the last five years and it seems to me there is a relation between my "reason why," descriptive or persuasive copy and the spontaneity of demand,'" pp. 228–29.

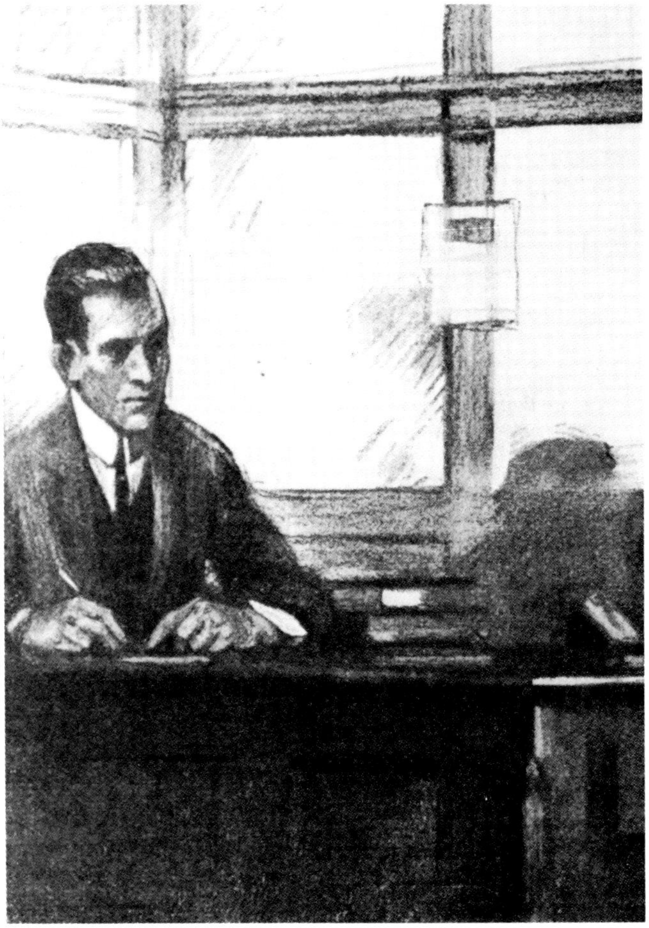

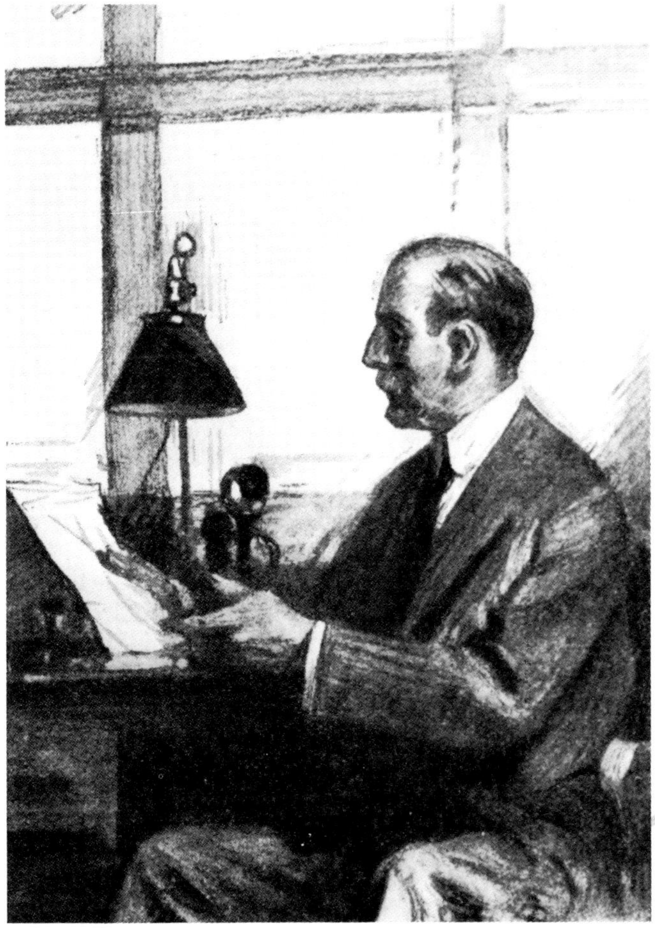

42b

42b

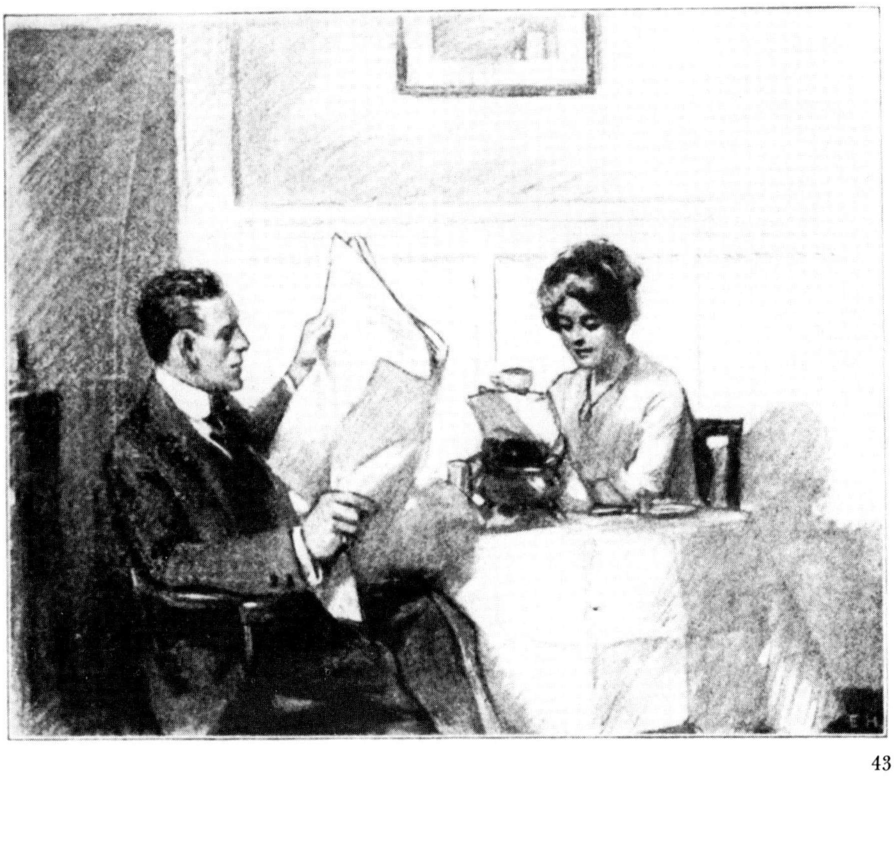

42b. Republished, *System,* 27 (March 1915), pp. 260–61. Right side and figure at far left cropped, and illustration extended at the top.

43. "His former appeal to their comfort and pride had nothing like the selling force of the appeal to the more potent motives of caution, foresight and parental love," p. 231.

43

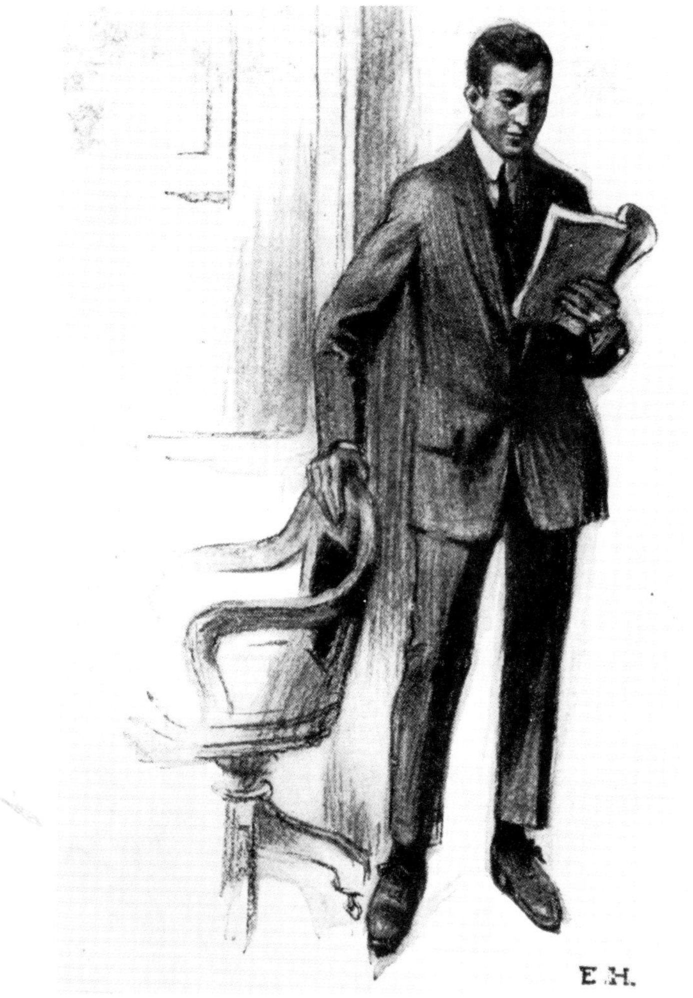

44

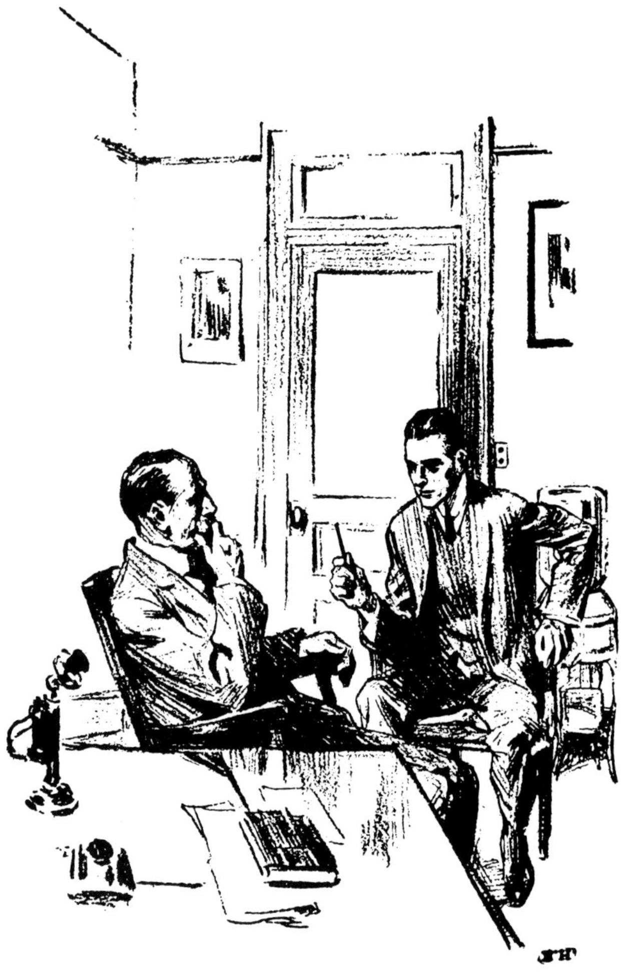

45

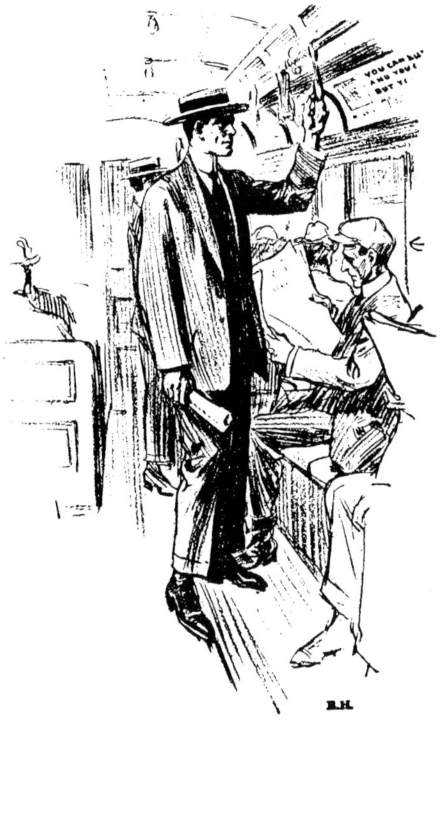

46

44. "He learns to make a mental purchase for the class of trade he seeks and to study the motives that impel his prospect to buy," p. 232.

45. "In every business interview there is a certain point to be carried. A certain result is aimed at and certain motives must be aroused to get that result," p. 235.

46. "Modern selling bears the other way. Nothing is too daring for it. It steam-whistles for attention and paragraphs with dynamite," p. 237.

Illustrations for W. C. Holman, "Keeping Retail Trade at Home," *System*, 23 (January 1913).

47a. "Your personal influence is a strong advertisement. So is the courtesy of your clerks," p. 13.

47b. Republished, *System*, 25 (May 1915), p. 461. Image flopped, mustache added to man's face, and price tags eliminated.

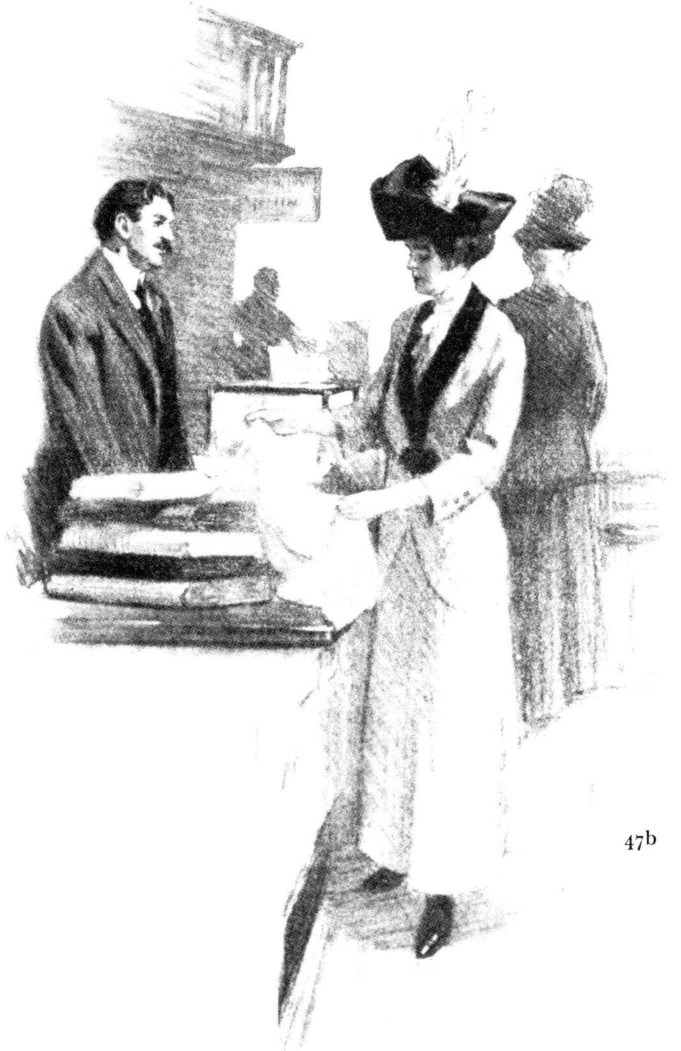

47b

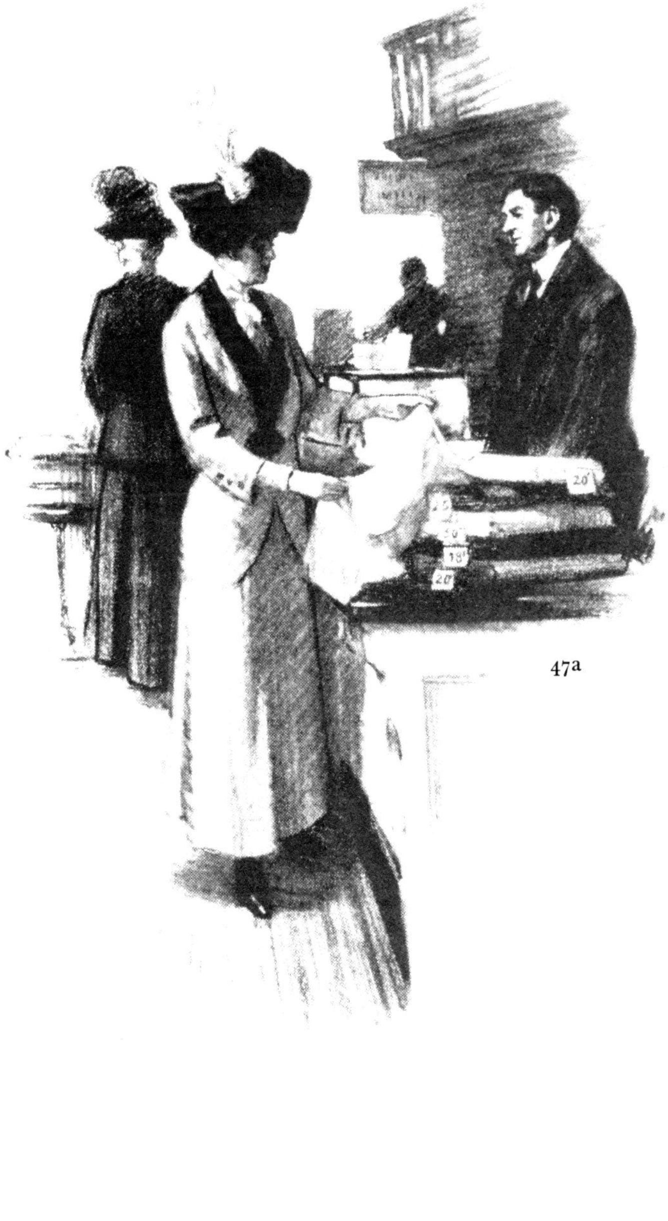

47a

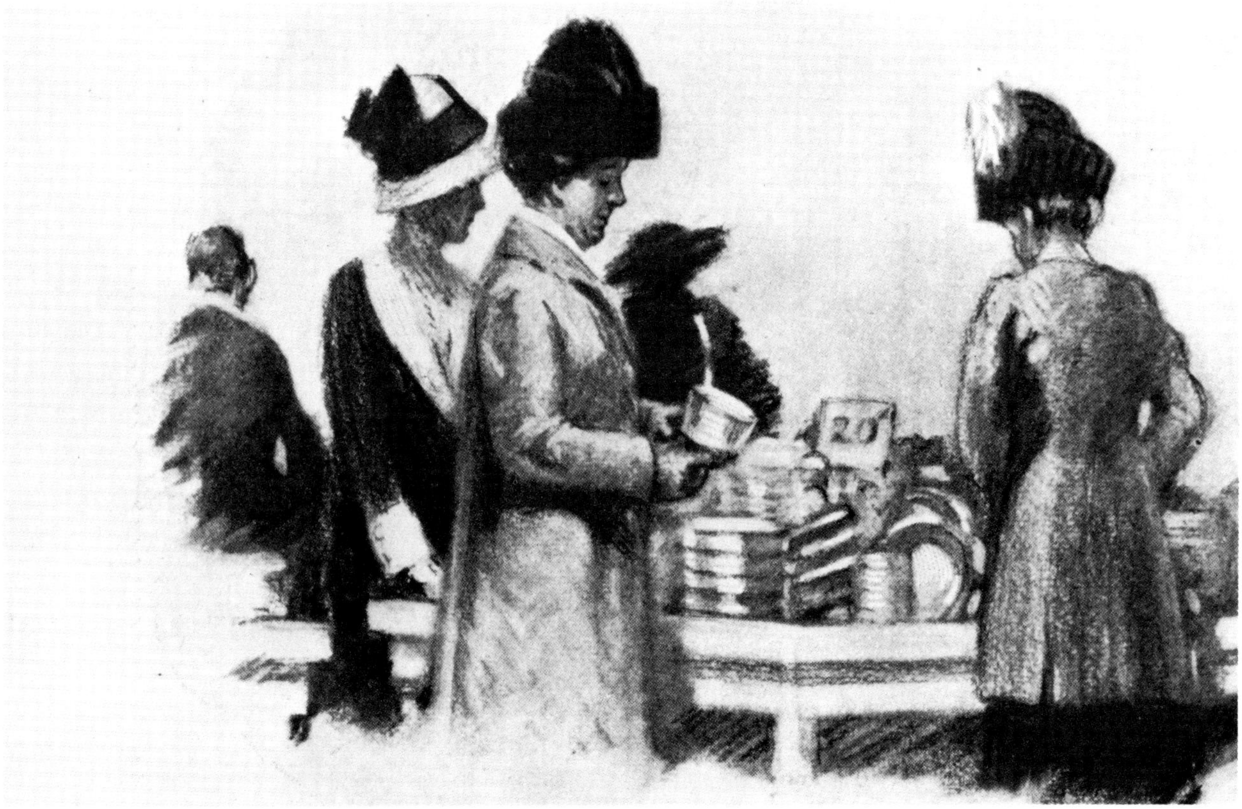

48 left

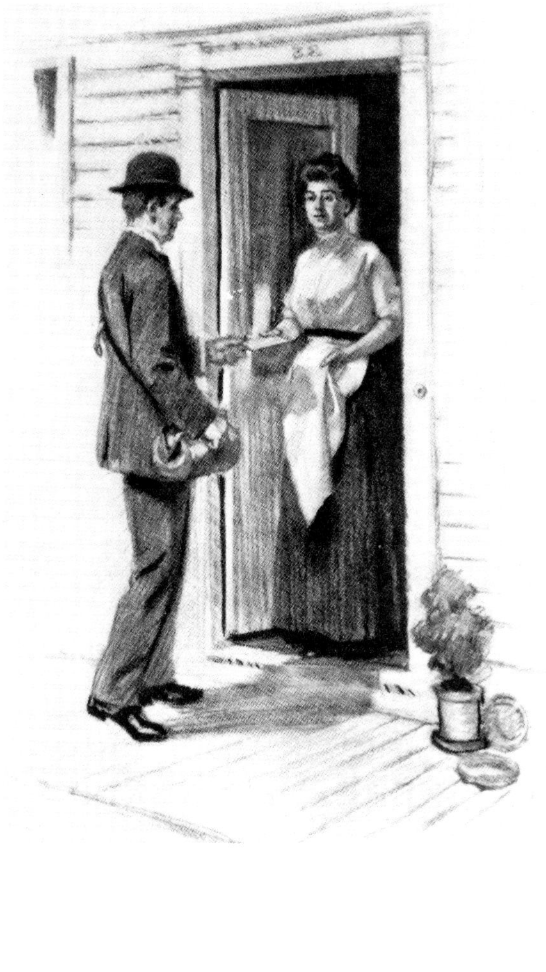

48. "Put price tags on the things you display. Many a woman who will not ask a clerk about the price, and will walk out without buying, will come forward and buy if she sees plain price tags," pp. 14–15.

49. "Better than all—since your selling efforts can be concentrated on a comparatively small field—you can have your clerk make calls on prospective customers in every direction. Or make them yourself," p. 17.

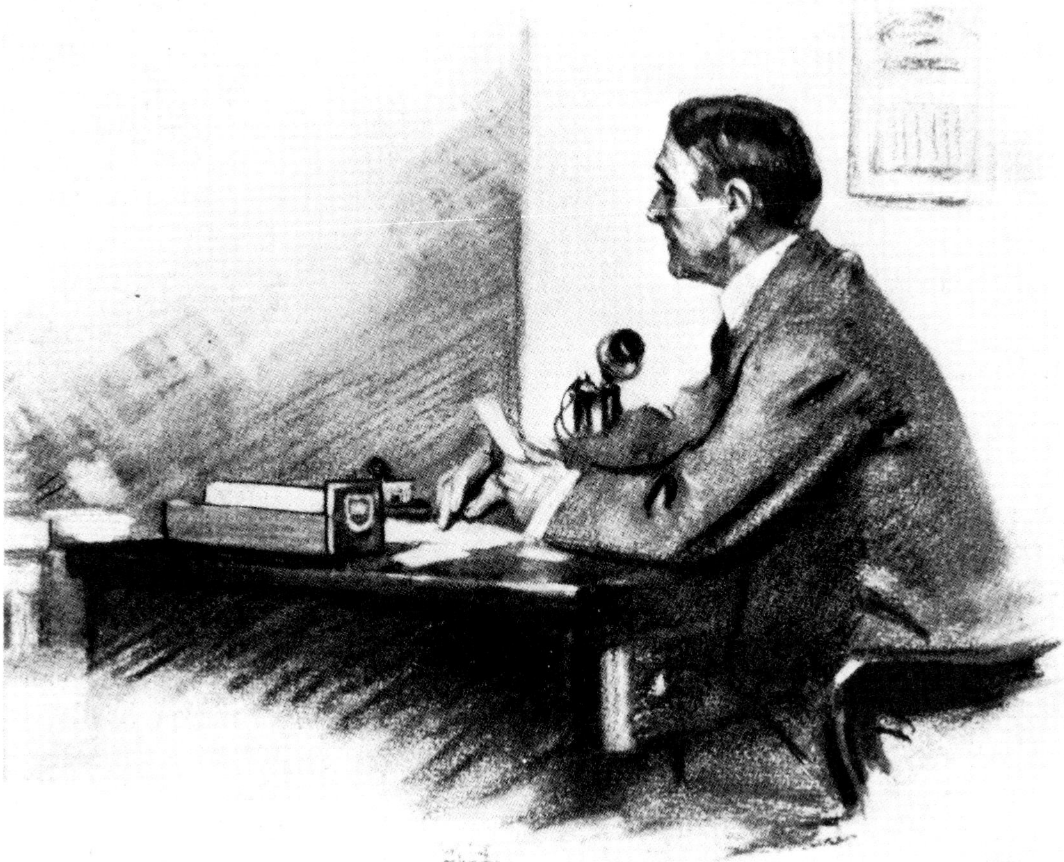

48 right

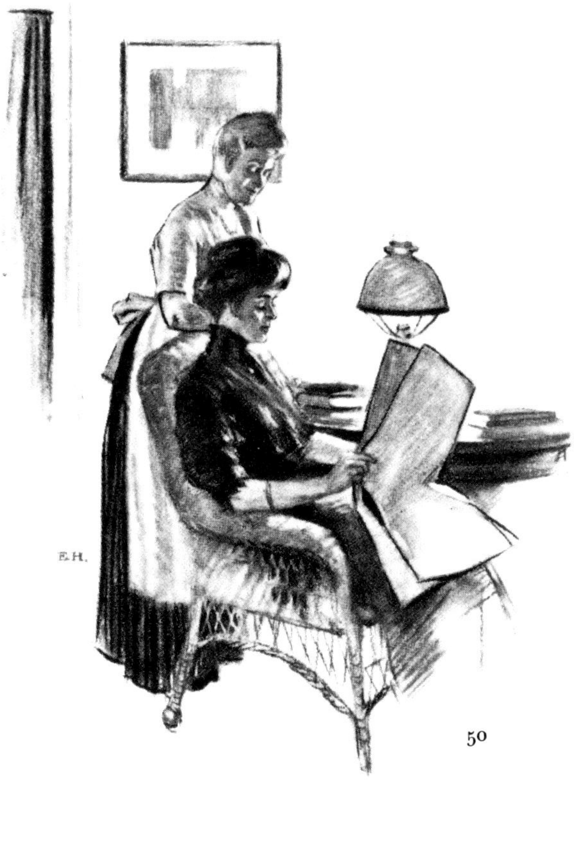

50

50. "In all your advertising, make your personality felt. Make your townspeople feel that you in person are talking to them. Make people wish to visit your store every day," p. 18.

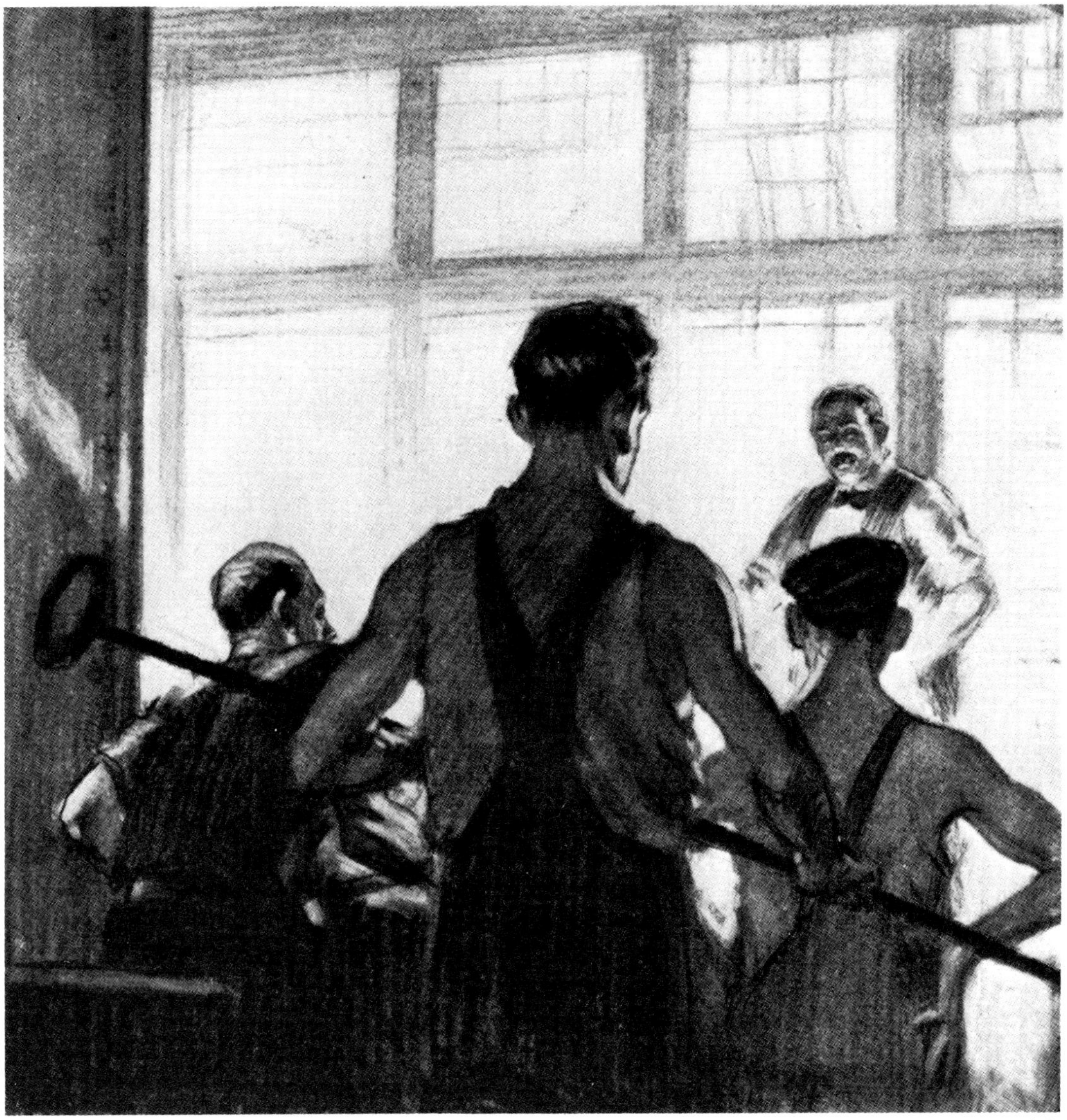

51 left

Illustrations for Carroll D. Murphy, "Buying More with Each Wage-Dollar," *System*, 23 (March 1913).

51. "There is pleasure, enthusiasm and the germ of individual growth in any work which a man can do well." / "Interest in the task is the key that unlocks the latent powers of workers; and interest means right placing," pp. 226–27.

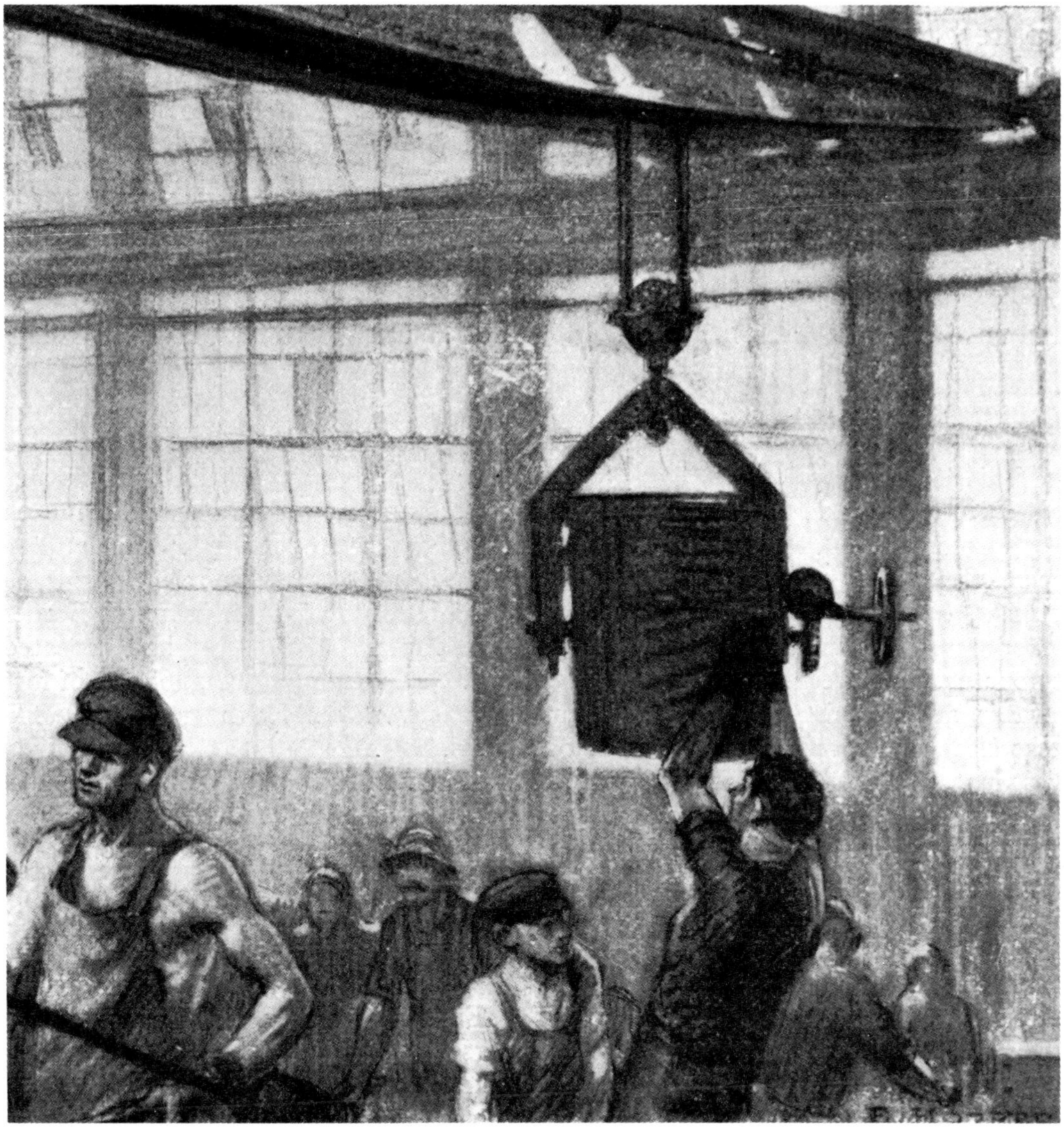

51 right

52. " 'Why not put him in charge of the pattern rooms,' suggested a foreman who had observed the knack for details which was developing in the German as he approached fifty-eight," p. 229.

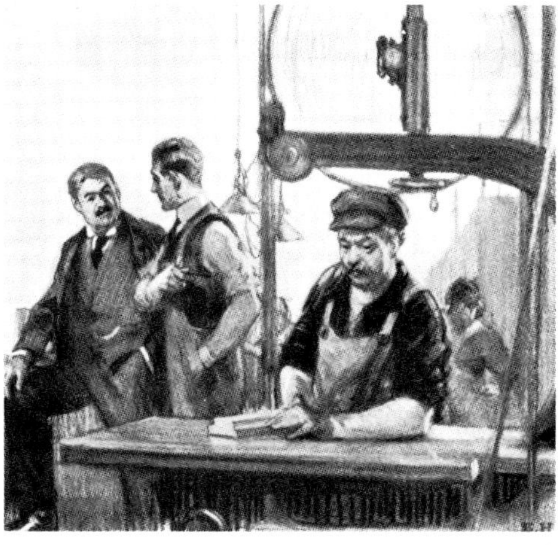

52

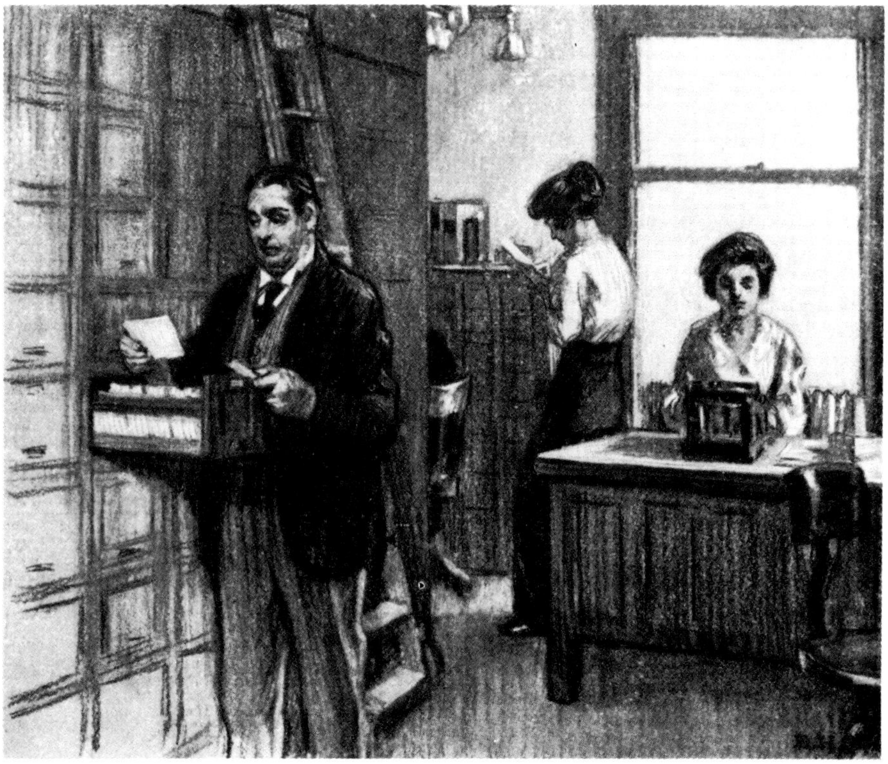

53

53. "The leak showed itself through Borden's own investigations. He had repeatedly noticed an experienced employee of forty-five at work among the girls at the filing cases. Efficiency was costing too much," p. 231.

54. "More than half this store manager's time is spent on the floor with his working force, and he thus maintains a personal bond with practically all of the rank and file of his organization," p. 233.

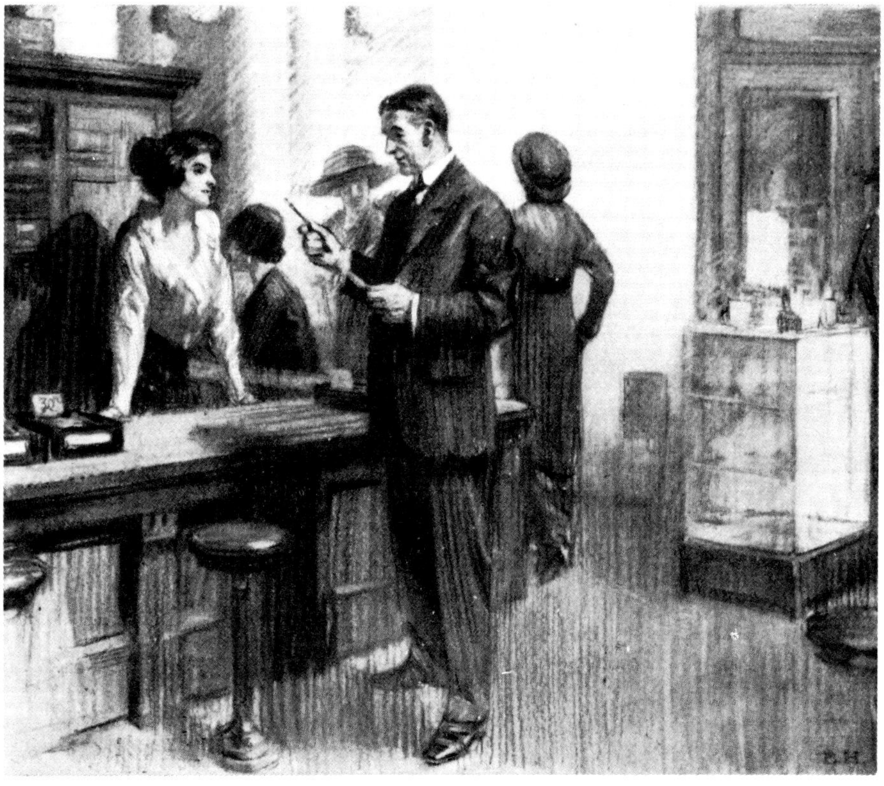

54

Illustrations for Carroll D. Murphy, "The Man for the Job," *System,* 23 (April 1913).

55. "Twenty minutes later, one of the boys handed in a neat and fairly accurate paper. The second applicant took an hour. . . . The time required to finish gave a line on each youngster's mental alertness," p. 402.

56. "He is expert in deciding between girls of the nervous type and steady workers who settle down when the rush hour comes and handle the work point by point regardless of how fast it pours in," p. 405.

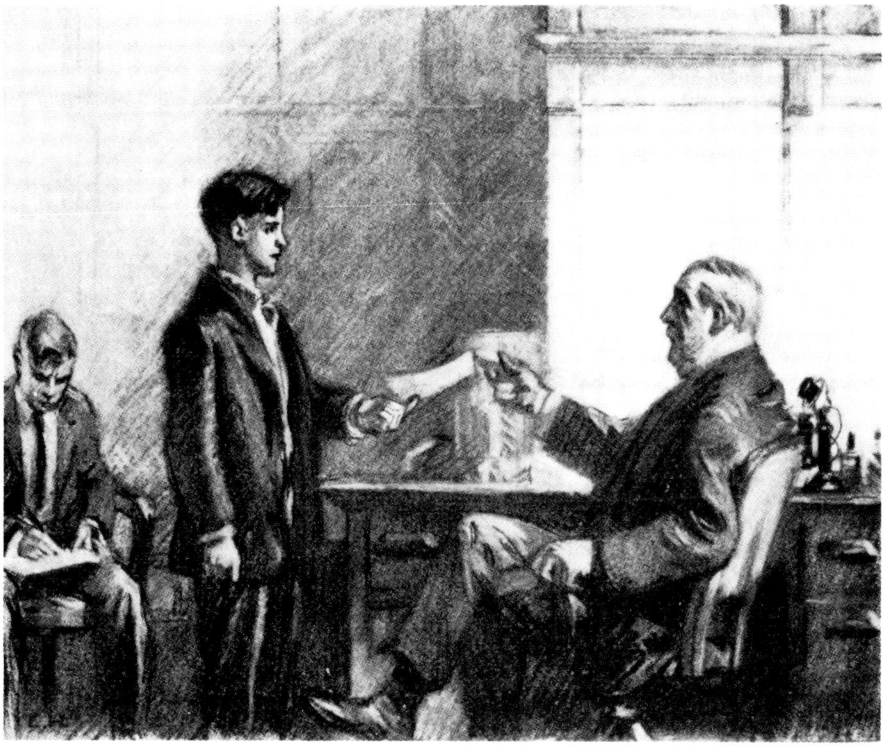

55

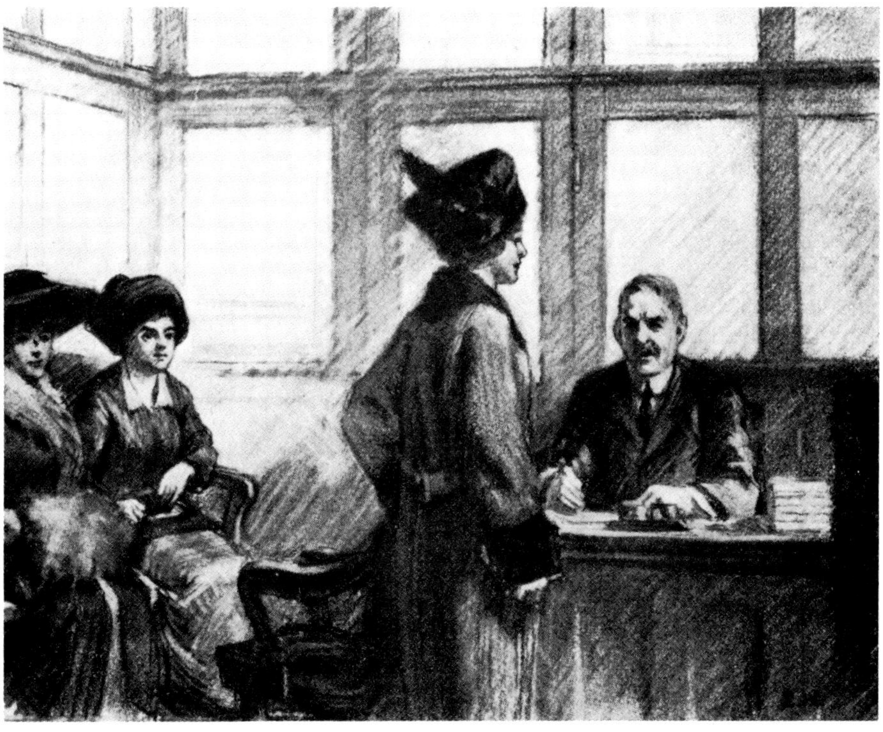

56

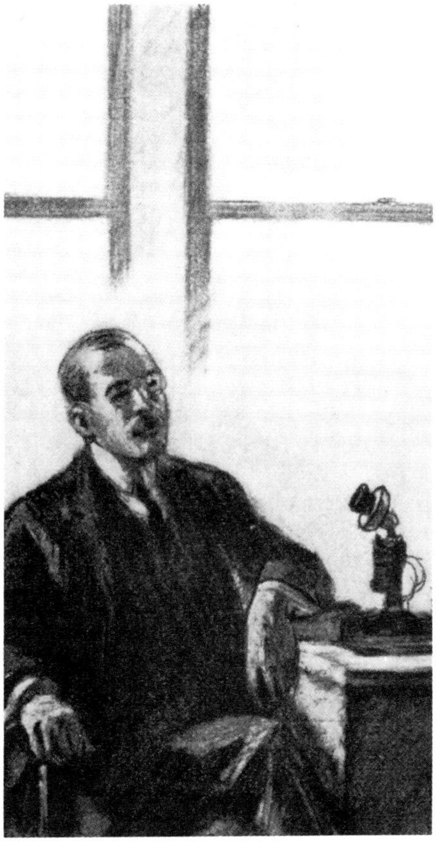

57

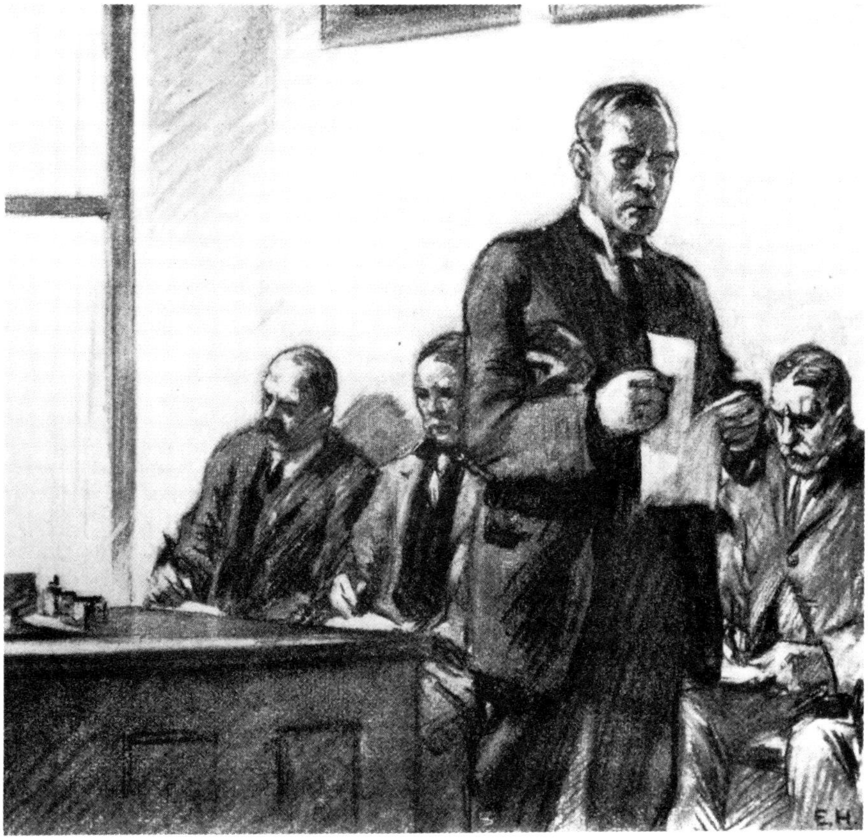

57

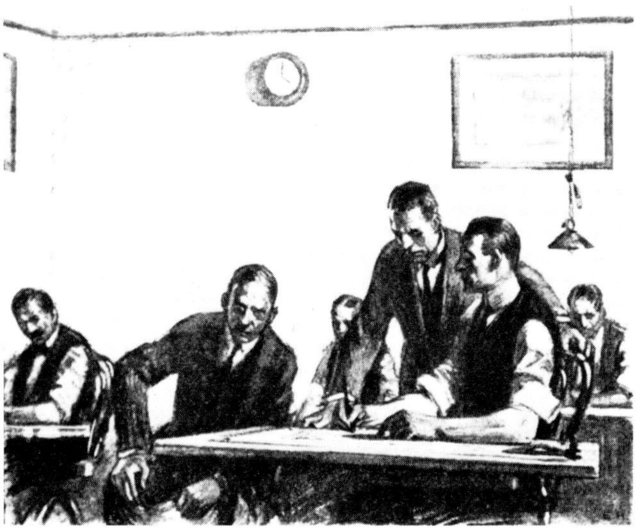

58a

57. "In many cases, too, intelligent and independent mechanics get out of patience trying to fathom the obscure queries of the application blank and quit in disgust," pp. 406–07.

Illustrations for Carroll D. Murphy, "Helping Men to 'Make Good,' " *System,* 23 (May 1913).

58a. Proof.

58b. "Assigned to the drafting room, he combined his practical and theoretical knowledge in a new design for the lathe on which he had worked. The design reduced the cost of one part sixty-five per cent," p. 466.

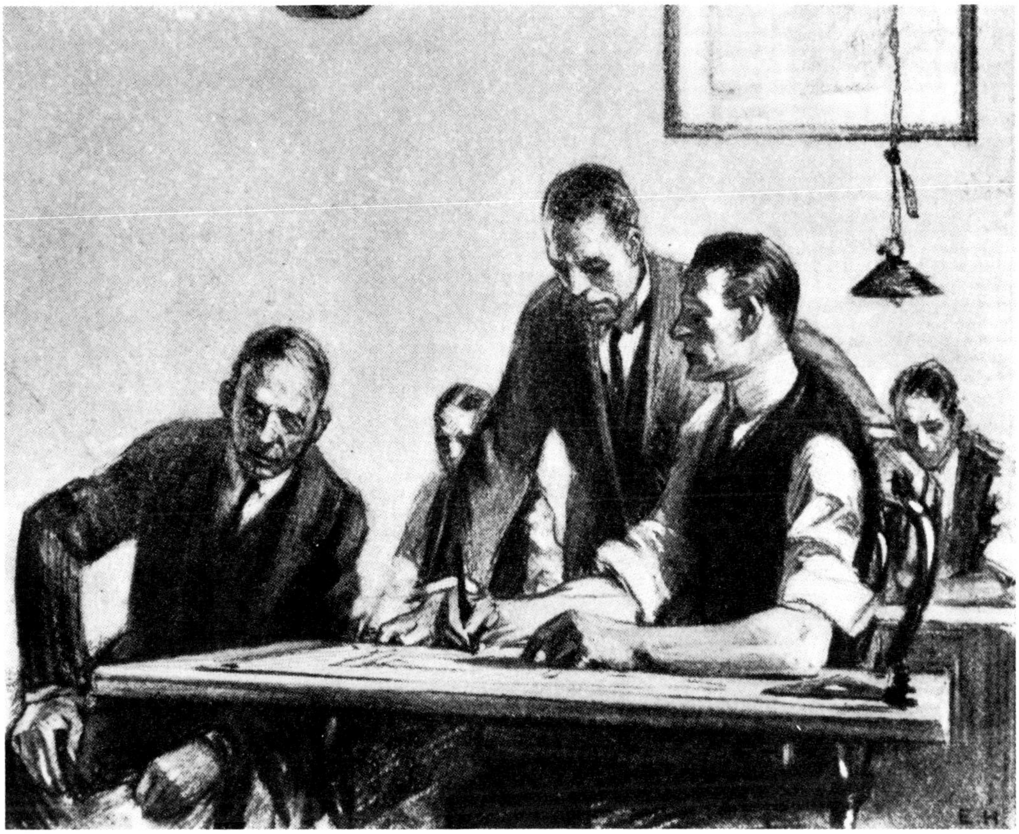

58c

58c. Republished, *System,* 26 (August 1914), p. 136. Cropped top and left.

59a. Proof.

59b. "In one organization, an employment committee informally checks the record of all the employees of a given grade whenever a vacancy is to be filled in the grade next above. The self-distrustful man thus comes in for consideration and help," pp. 468–69.

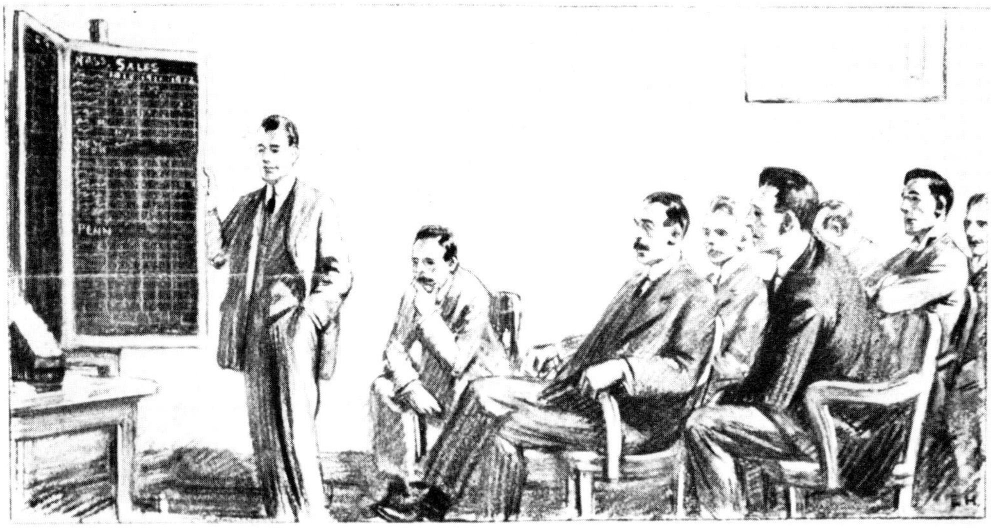

59a

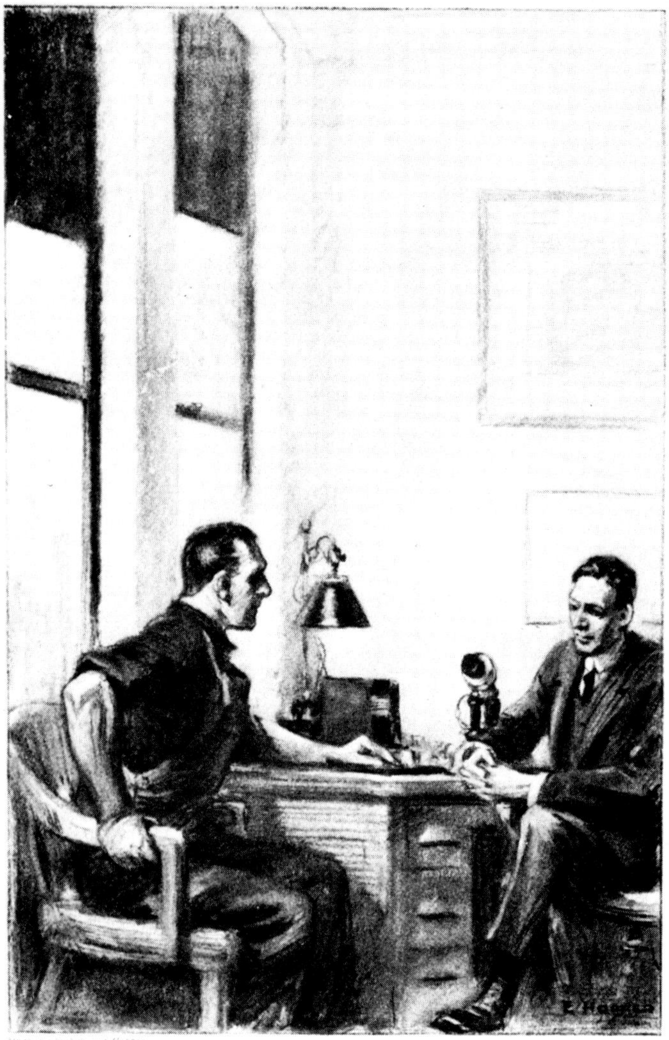

61

60a. Proof.

60b. "The sales manager makes himself welcome and spends a great deal of time in every shop. He counsels with rather than reprimands the buyer who orders too heavily or stocks locally unpopular brands," p. 471.

Illustrations for Carroll D. Murphy, "The Spur of Pay and Promotion," *System,* 23 (June 1913).

61. "'Just leave me where I am, Mr. Simpson,' replied the man whom he had called in to offer him an important promotion. 'I used to hope for this sort of thing and worked for it. Now, I guess, I am too old; the job looks too big for me to tackle,'" p. 562.

62. "The heads of the departments in which the candidates for promotion work are usually consulted. Often different candidates are invited to the employment office in order that personal judgment may reinforce or correct the testimony of their records," p. 565.

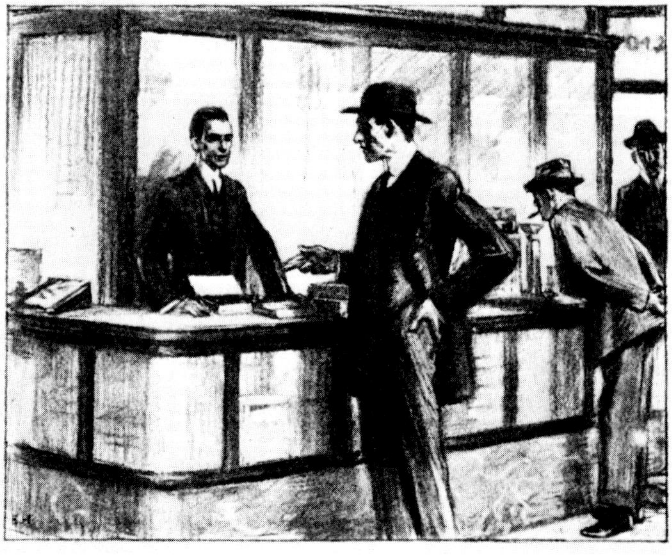

60b

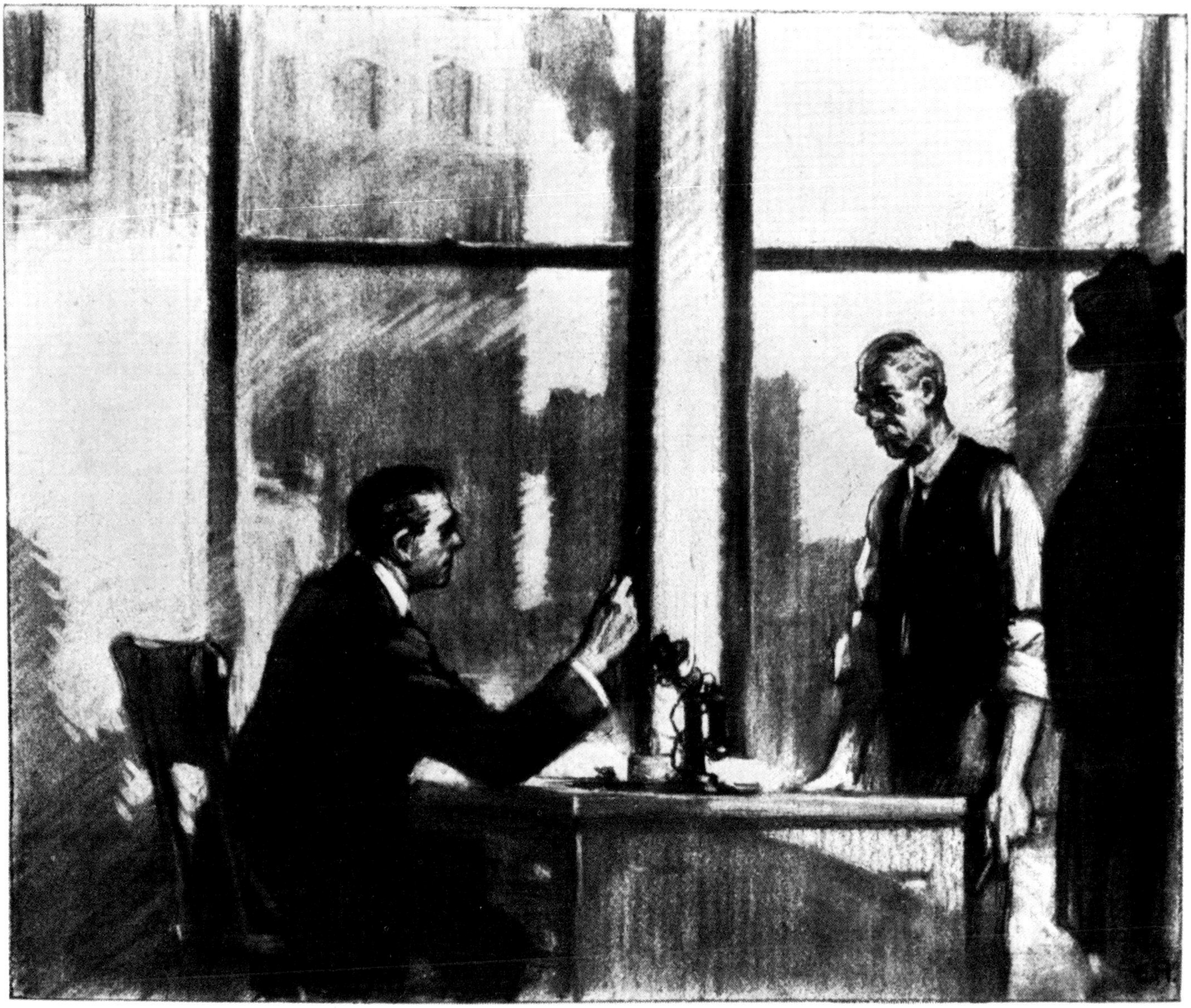

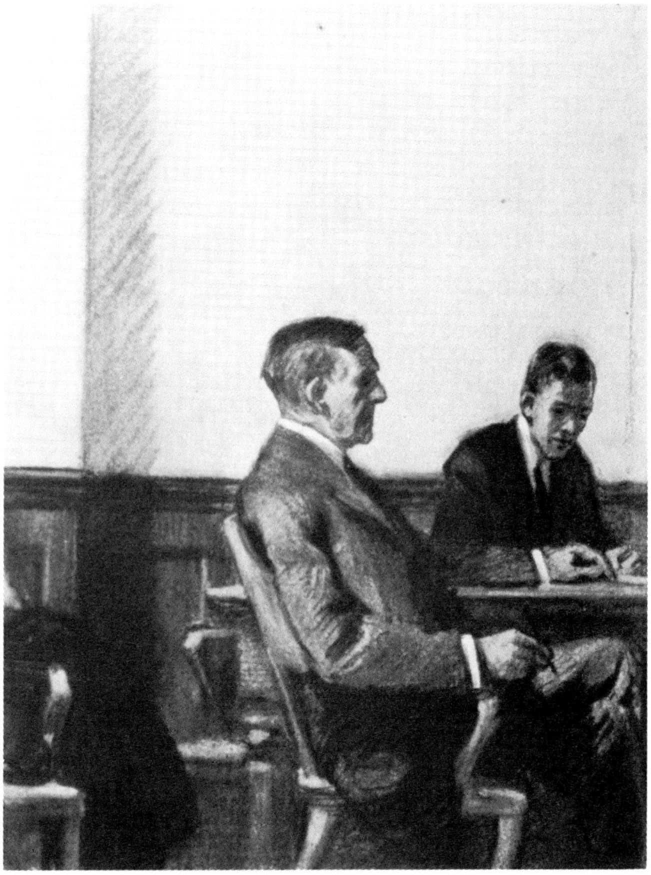

63a

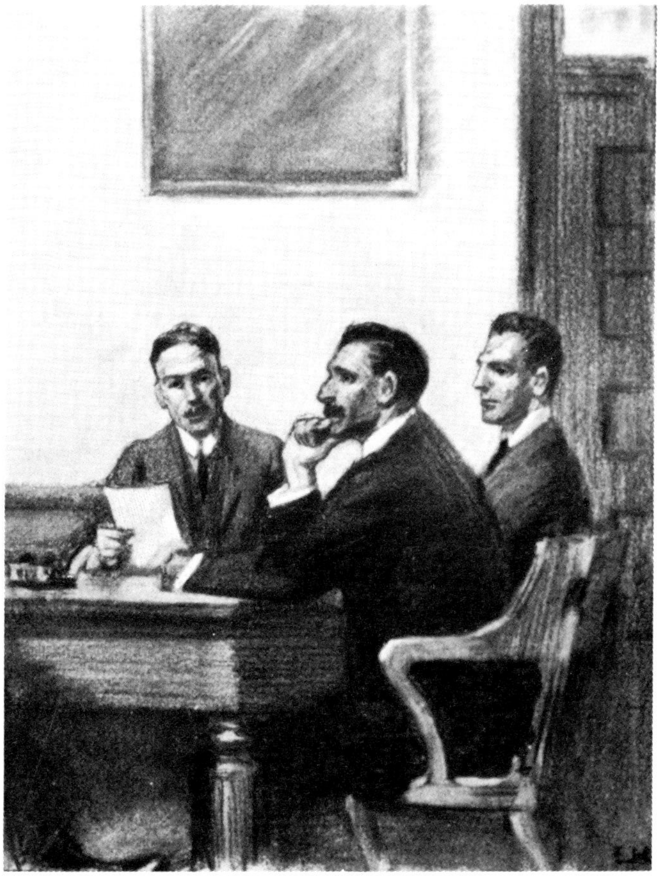

63a

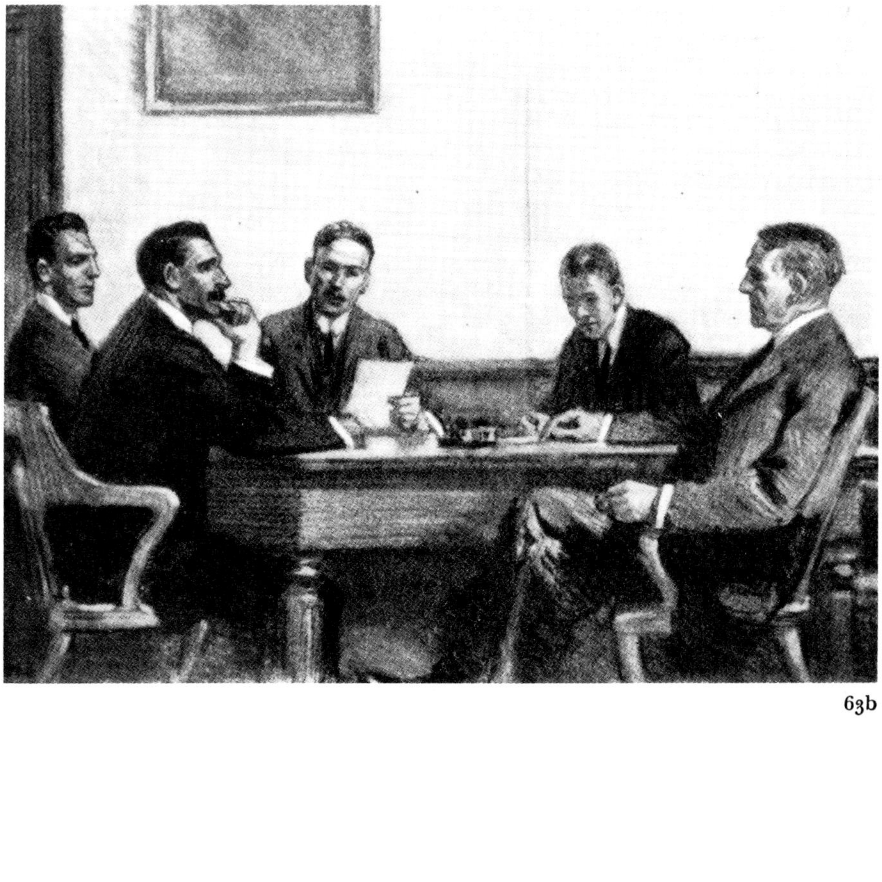

63b

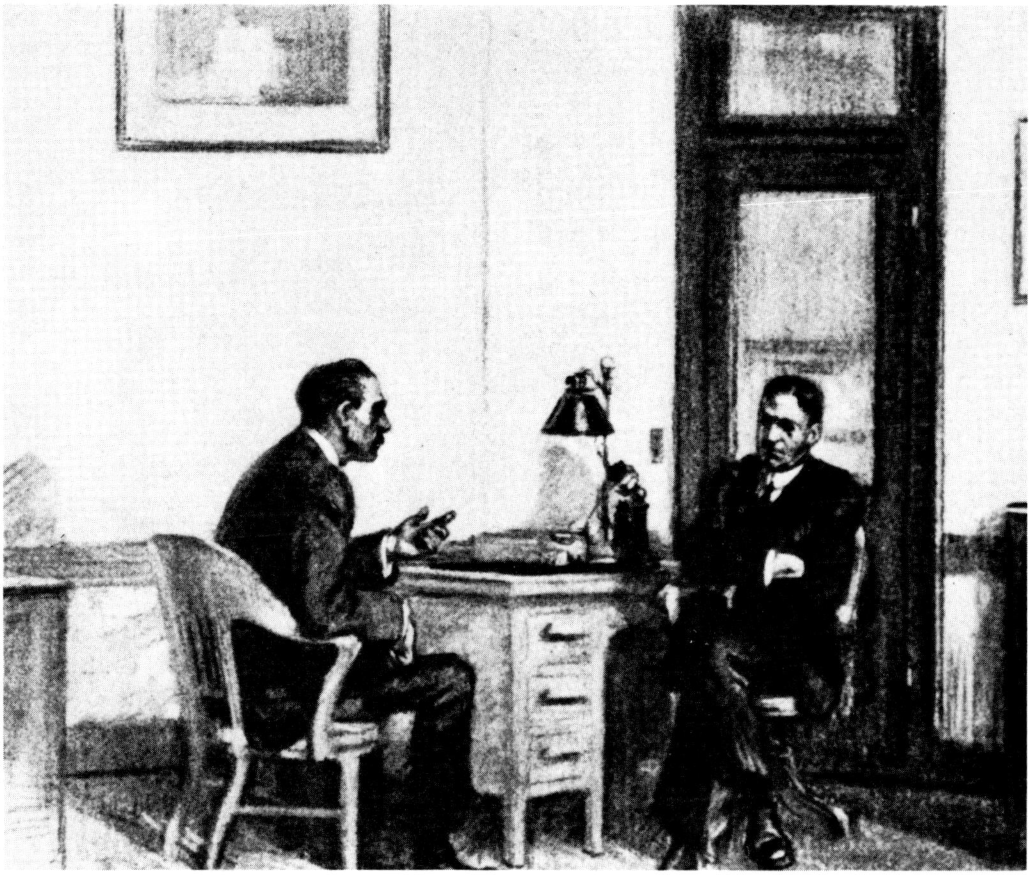

64

63a. "The committee put every position alongside the scale and ran it up or down to the point of identical value. Grade by grade, the ratings of the committee were tabulated, checked, proffered for objections and finally adopted," pp. 566–67.

63b. Republished, *System,* 26 (July 1914), p. 23. Flopped and cropped left, right, and top.

64. "I have not been in the department as many years as some others, but I have been taking care of my job by daylight and putting night study on the work of the chief. I figured that I could earn the first chance at his place if ever he is promoted, " p. 569.

Illustrations for Carroll D. Murphy, "Living up to Your Employment System," *System,* 24 (July 1913).

65. "The sales manager had no course but to suggest frankly that his assistant might fit into the vacancy in the other department," p. 18.

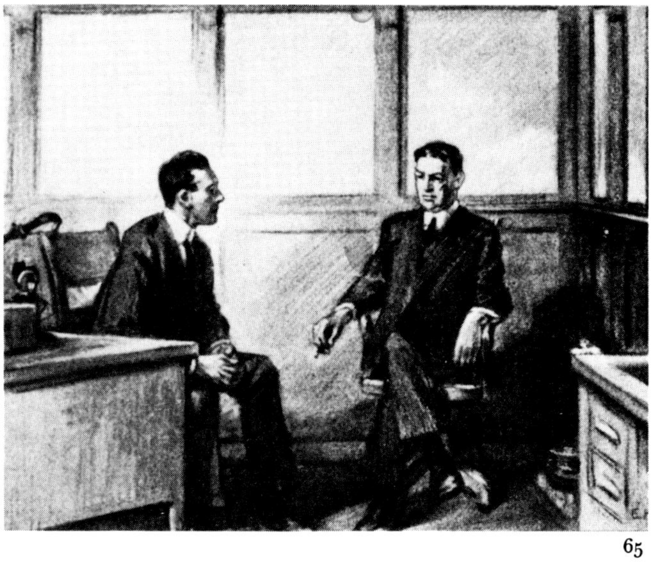

65

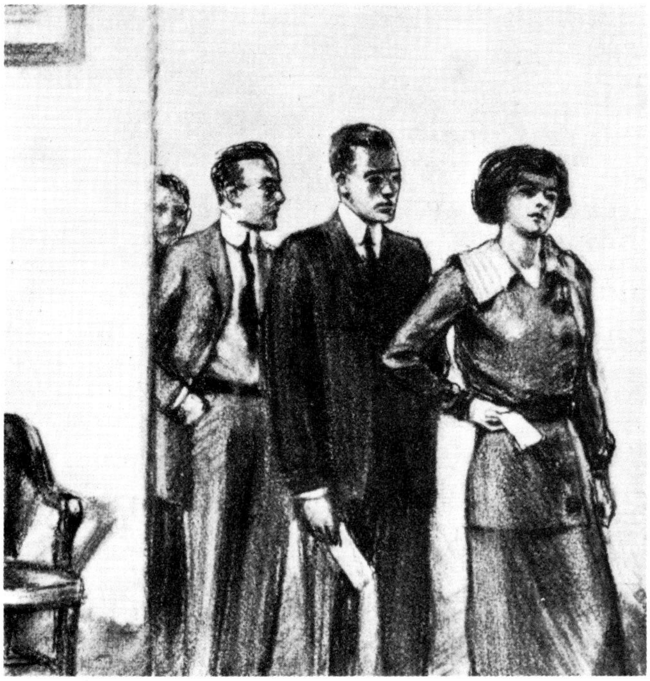

66

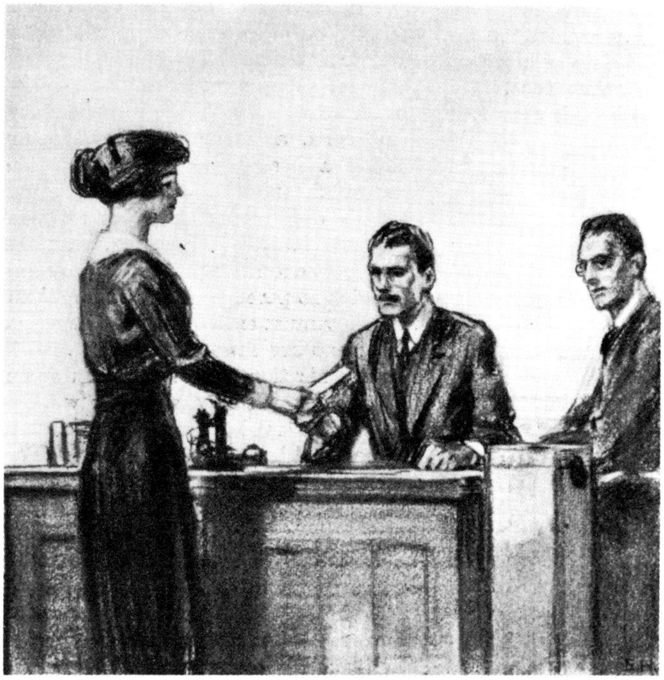

66

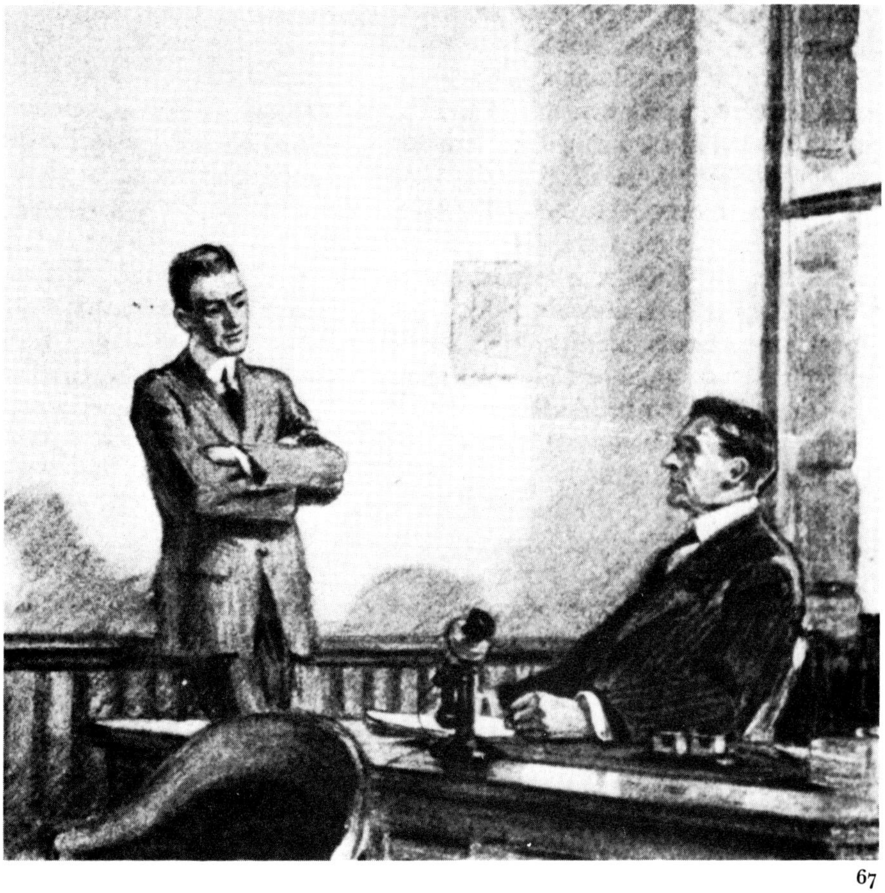

67

66. "By Australian ballot the employees elect members of an arbitration committee to hear serious complaints as to working conditions," pp. 20–21.

67. " 'Suppose you hold him over . . . and recommend him for some other territory. He's too valuable a man to let go,' the man from the factory suggested. 'I'm firing him' was the answer, doggedly given," p. 23.

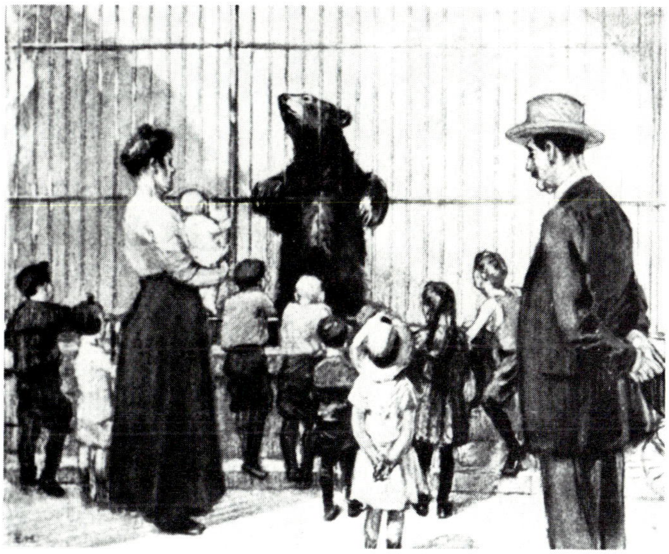

68

Illustrations for Wheeler Sammons, "Your Business Tomorrow," *System,* 24 (September 1913).

68. "The children unconsciously duplicated the movements of their four-footed friends. They would like dolls, therefore, representing animals, and permitting these fundamental motions," p. 231.

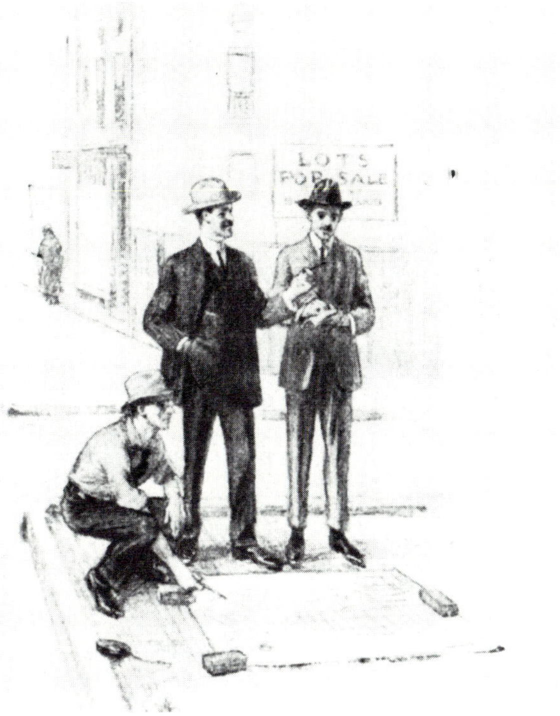

69

69. "On the basis of these canvasses and analyses, exchange buildings are located often in a locality and on such a scale as makes the residents wonder," p. 233.

70. Forty inventors, in forty locked, individually equipped little shops, are planning ahead to anticipate and satisfy demand," p. 235.

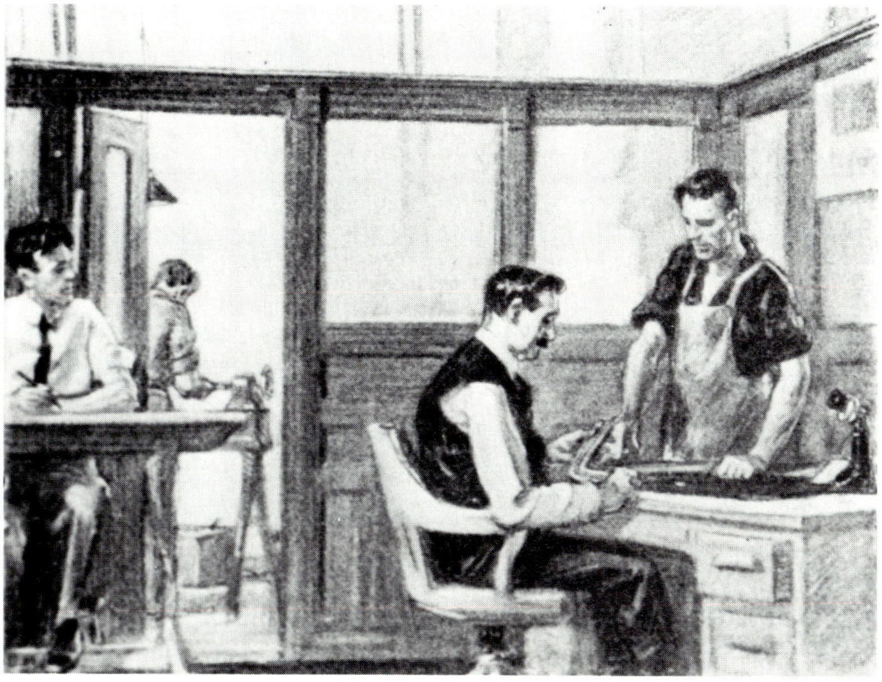

70

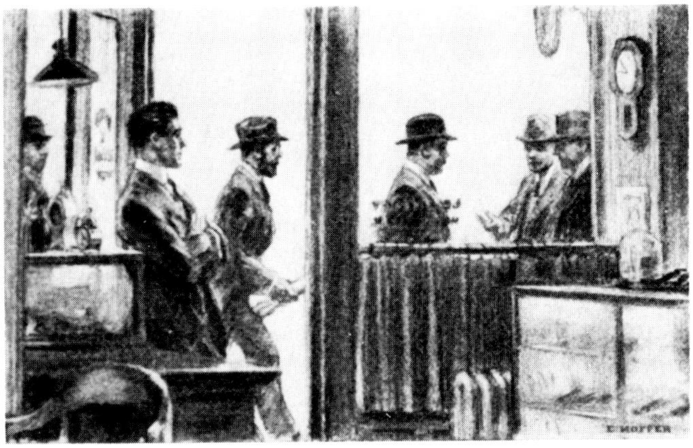

71

Illustrations for Charles Weinfeld, "How I Sell Life Insurance," *System,* 24 (November 1913).

71. There is a small jewelry store in one of my towns which I use as a place from which to reconnoiter. It is well located and from it I can watch the people going to their offices—I prefer to walk in on a man rather than to wait in his office for him," p. 477.

72. " 'I want to tell you something,' said my prospect when I told him I bought a certain brand of cigars by the box. 'I own stock in the factory where that cigar is made, and as long as you patronize me, I am going to reciprocate. You can write me up an application,' " p. 479.

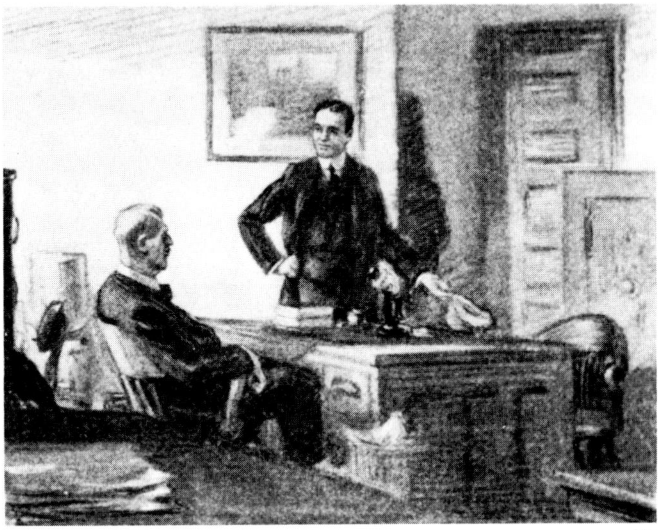

72

73. "I want to put a ten-thousand dollar bond in your safe among your other securities, for which I am going to charge you three per cent, or three hundred dollars a year. At the end of twenty years your payments cease and the bond is yours," p. 481.

Illustrations for Edward Mott Woolley, "Why I Bought of Them," *System,* 25 (May 1914).

74. "Our engineers had investigated the equipment of thirty odd mills, ascertained as closely as possible the performance

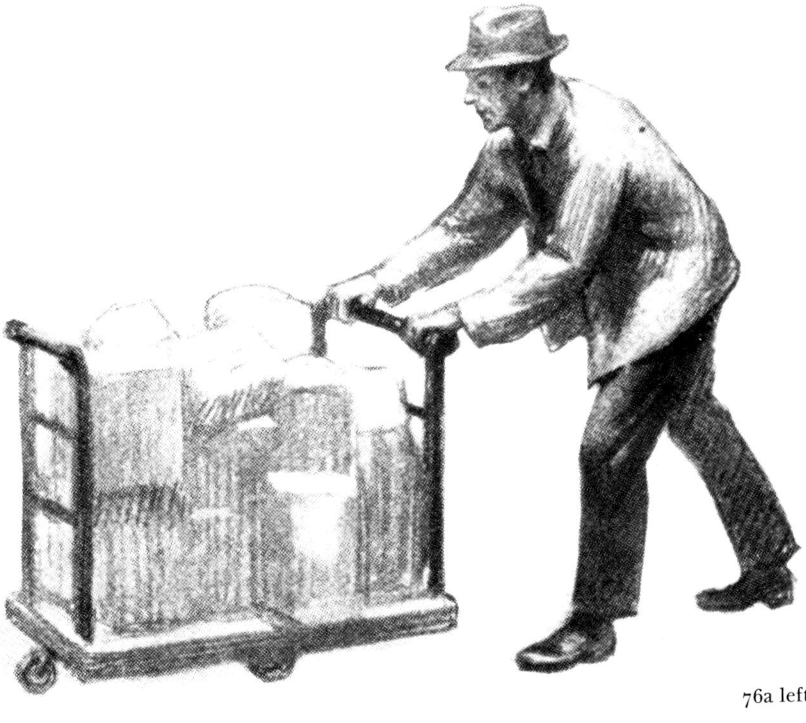

76a left

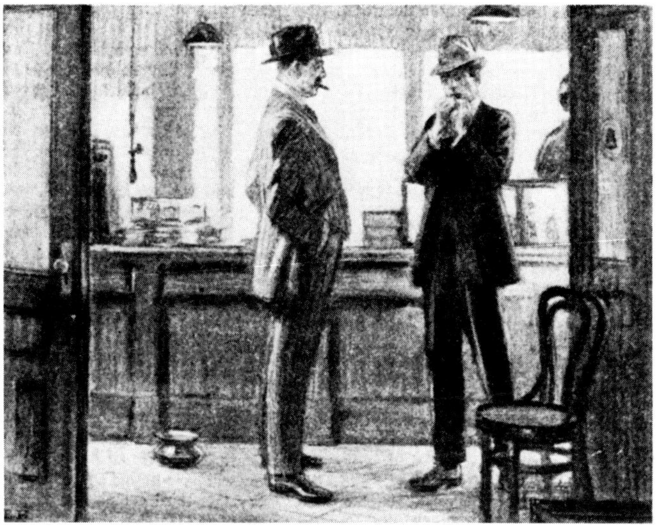

73

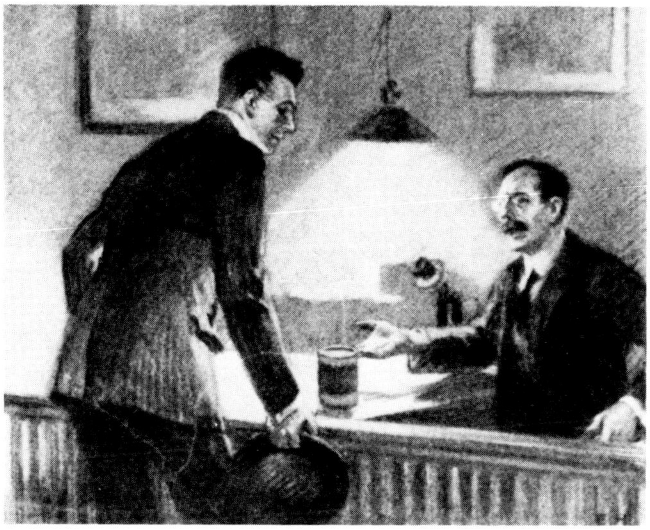

75

of the machinery in each, listened to the praise and the complaints, and made a record of them all," p. 462.

75. " 'What? Buy that stuff?' I said to his salesman. 'Not on your life! I don't know how to pronounce it myself. I will stick to the lines that I've handled and my customers know,' " p. 463.

76a. "I went back to the first house, which shipped every order on the day it was received and took advantage of the package car service," pp. 464–65.

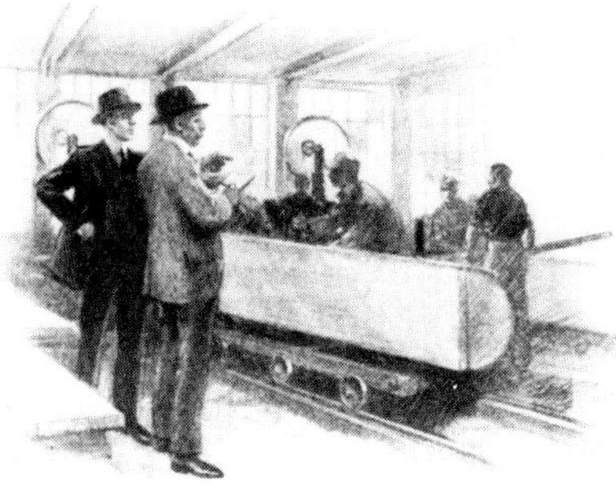

74

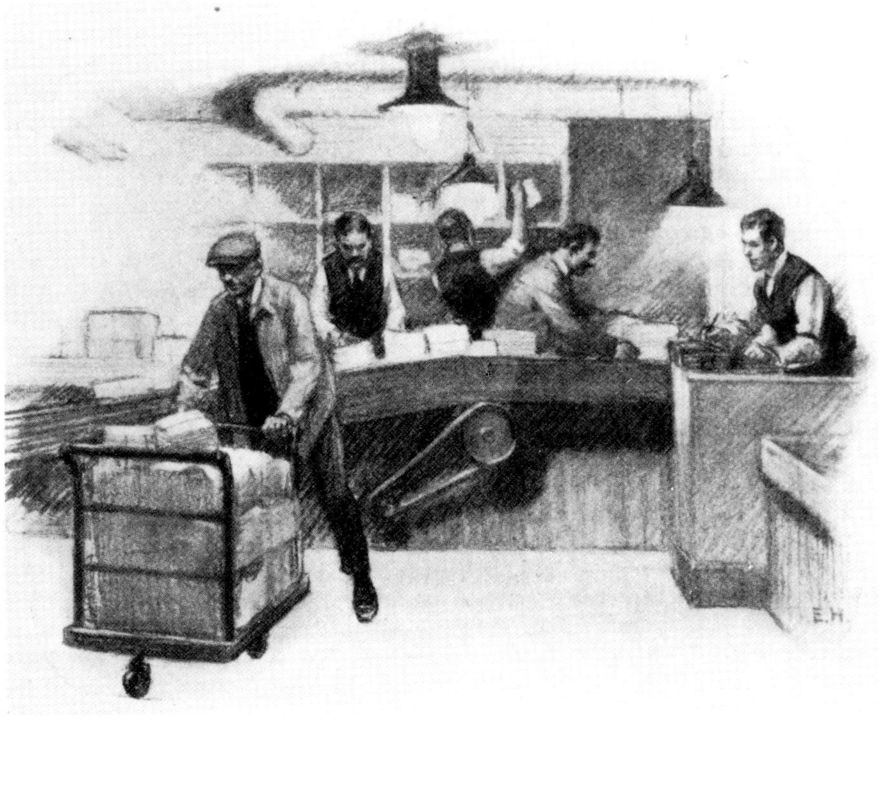

76a right

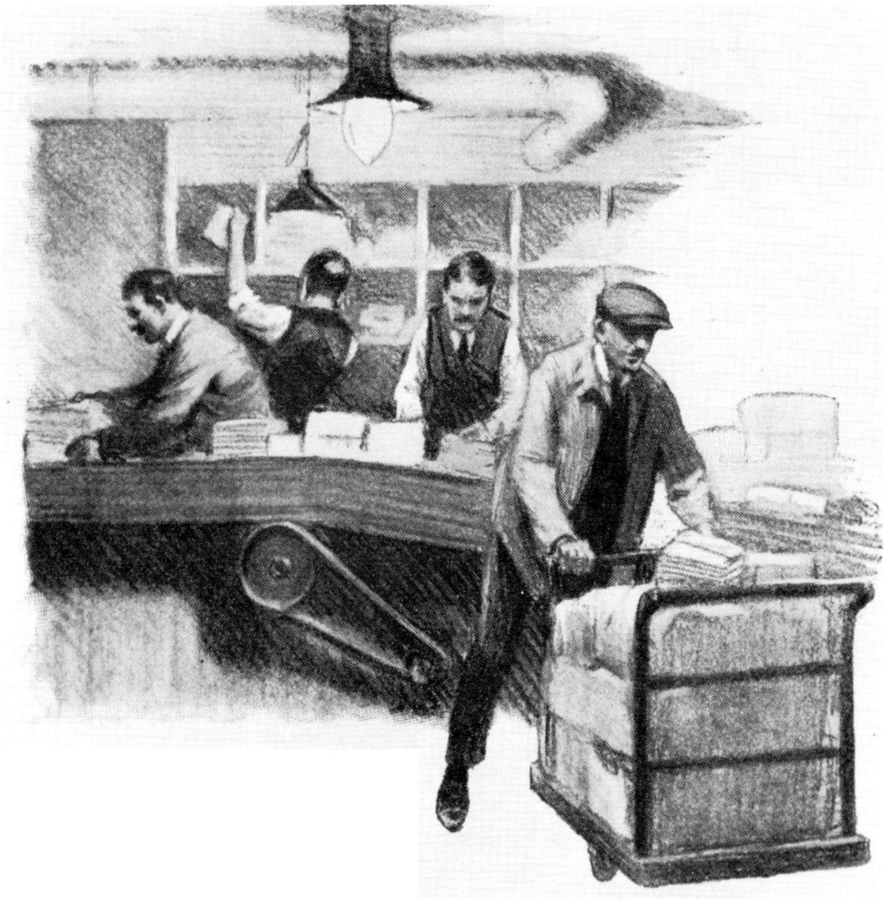

76b

76b. Portion of illustration on p. 465 republished, *System,* 26 (December 1914), p. 590. Flopped and cropped at right.

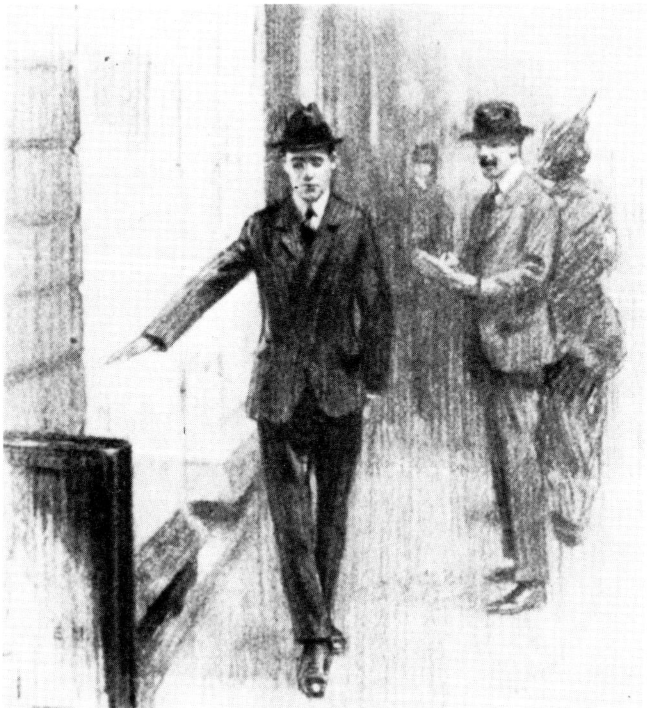

77

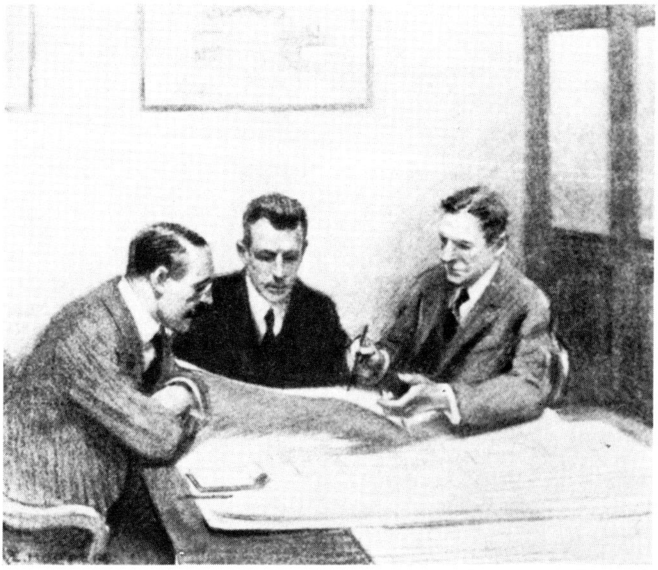

78

Illustrations for R. M. Graham, "Meeting Emergencies," *System,* 25 (June 1914).

77. "They measured some of the frontages, 'stepping them off' to learn the space requirements of each trade," p. 565.

78. "Step by step the vice-president, the superintendent and the cost man took the operations for the whole job apart," p. 567.

79. "To the surprise of the owner, he found that it cost him fifteen cents to handle any bundle," p. 568.

Illustration for H. Lad Landau, "Starting Trade with Latin America," *System,* 26 (November 1914).

80. "A five-months' trip, costing $2,000, should reach every worthwhile market in South America," p. 478.

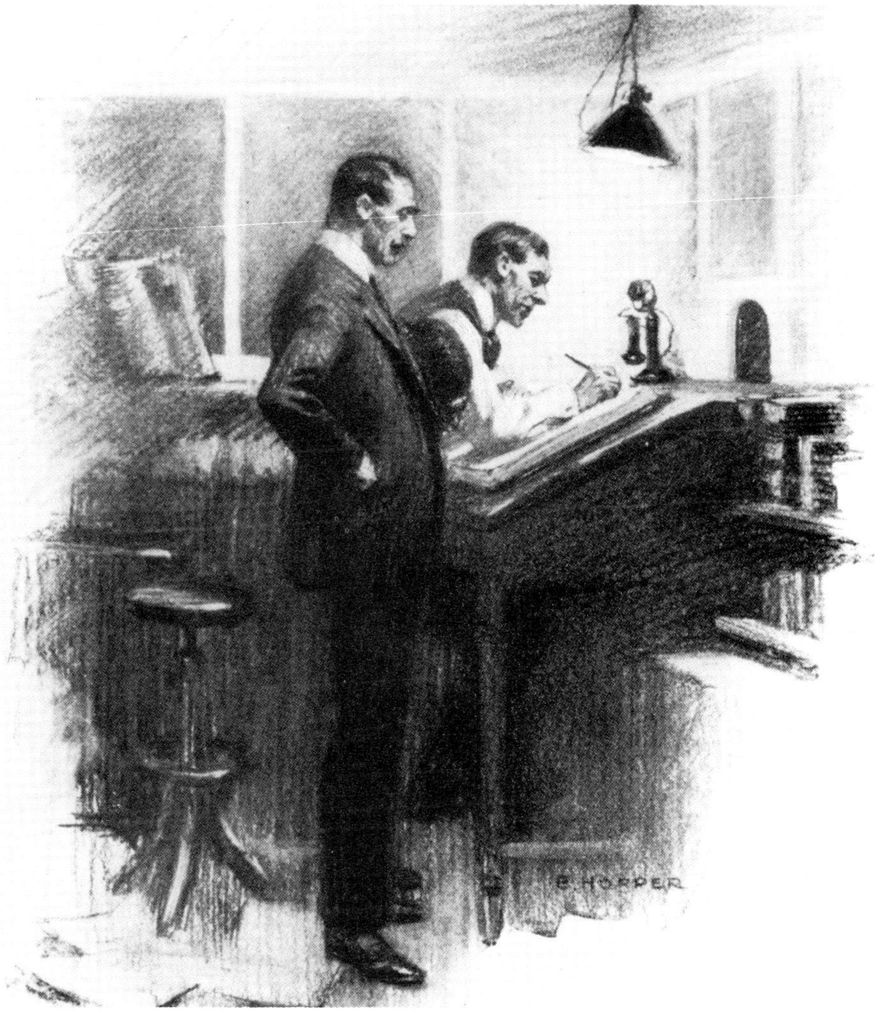

79

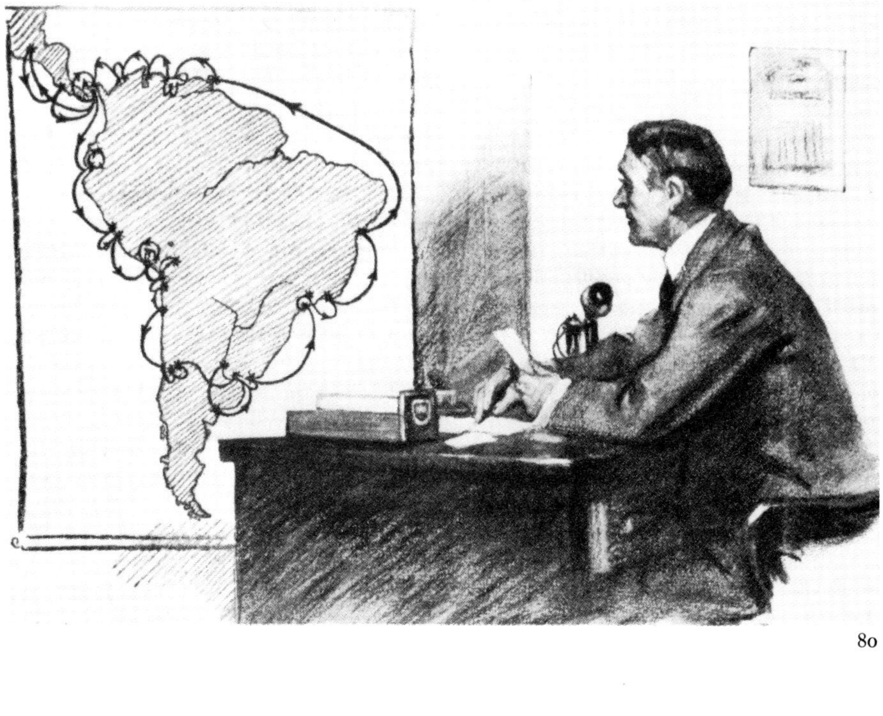

80

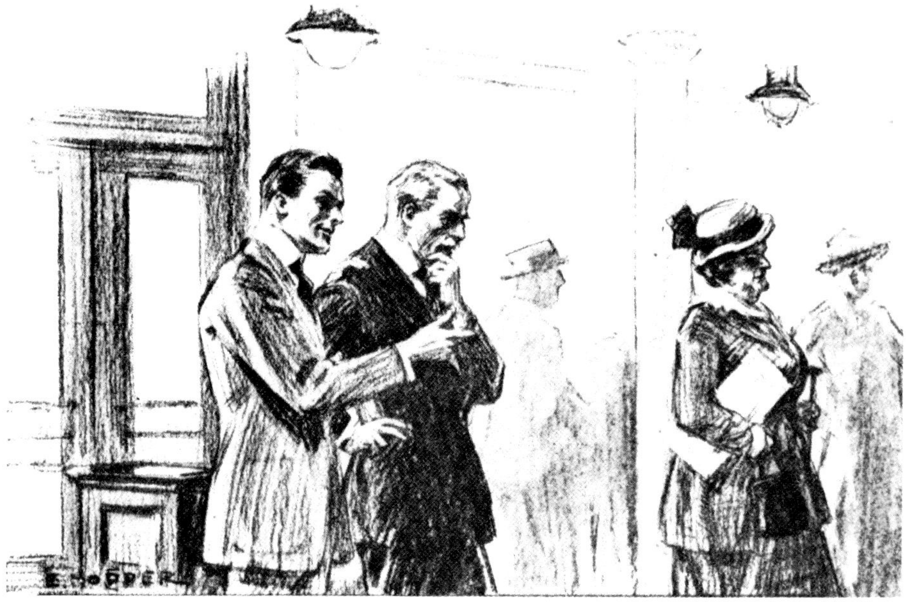

81 left

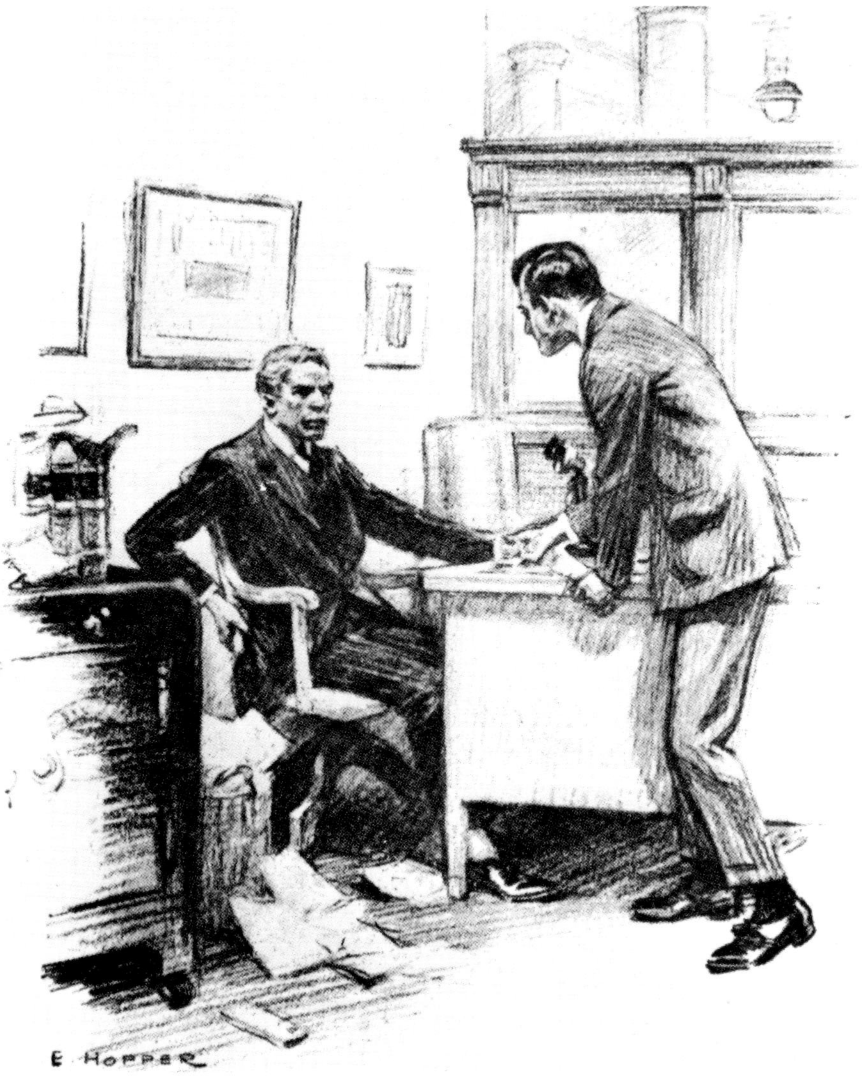

Illustrations for Camillus Phillips, "The Life of Trade," *System,* 28 (November 1915).

81. "When Jesse Thompson scanned his aisles after summoning each of his employees to his office for a severe curtain lecture intended to awaken keen enthusiasm, he could discern demureness on their faces, but nothing more," pp. 466–67.

82. " 'Whenever you choose to give me the authority to act for you,' Lem Barrow answered, 'I promise you I'll show results, Mr. Thompson,' " p. 471.

Illustrations for Carl H. Fast, "Customers' Wants *Versus* Buyers' Guesses," *System,* 30 (July 1916).

83. "The salesman reached for a pad of specially printed blanks and assured her he would have the brand looked up at once," p. 97.

84. "Each time a coat or suit was asked for, and none was in stock, the saleswoman recorded the price, color, material, size and style, all in tabulated form," p. 99.

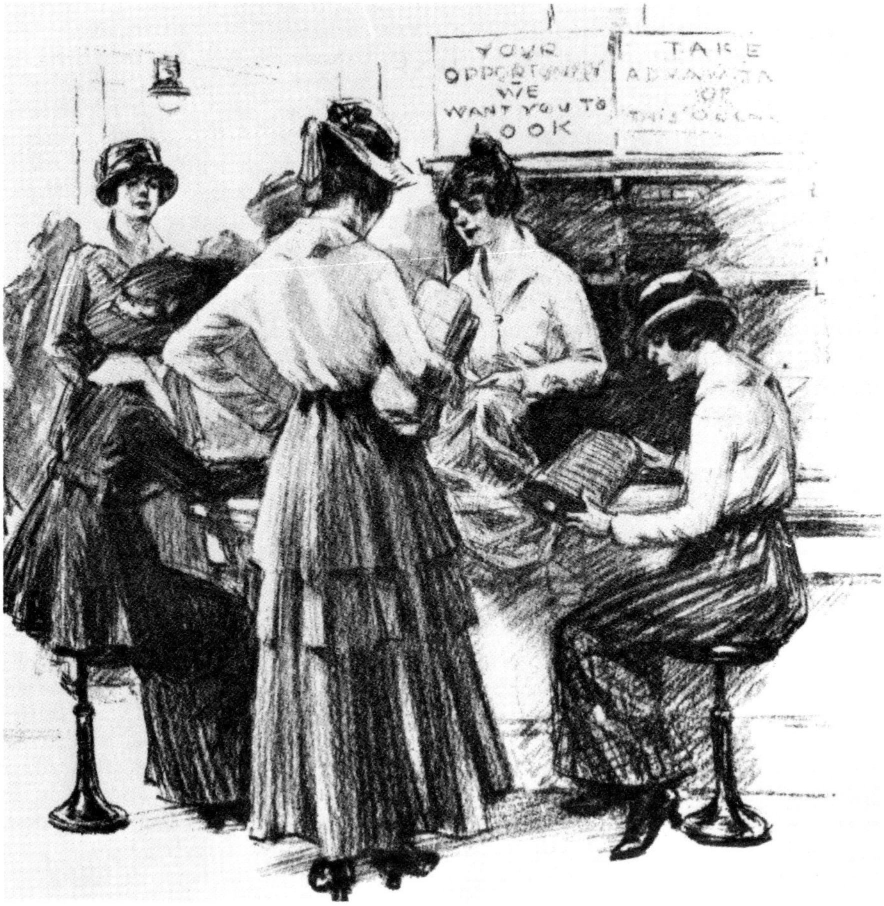

81 right

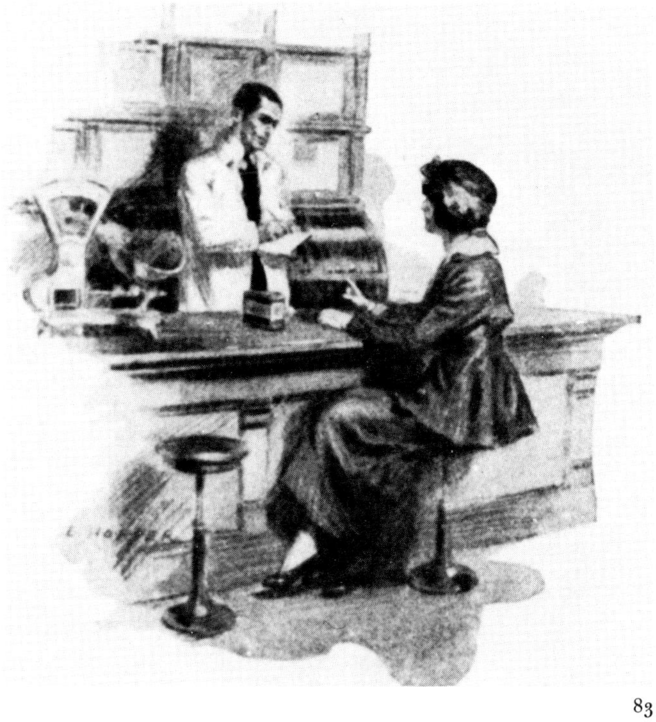

83

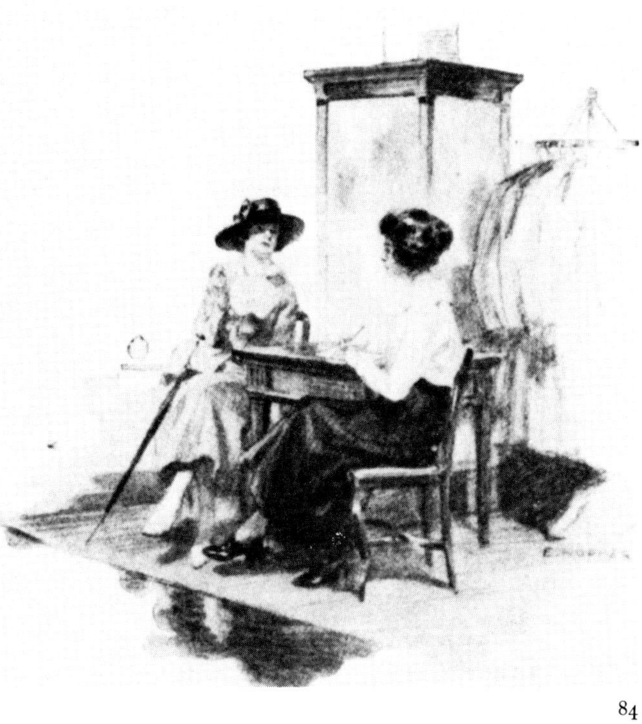

84

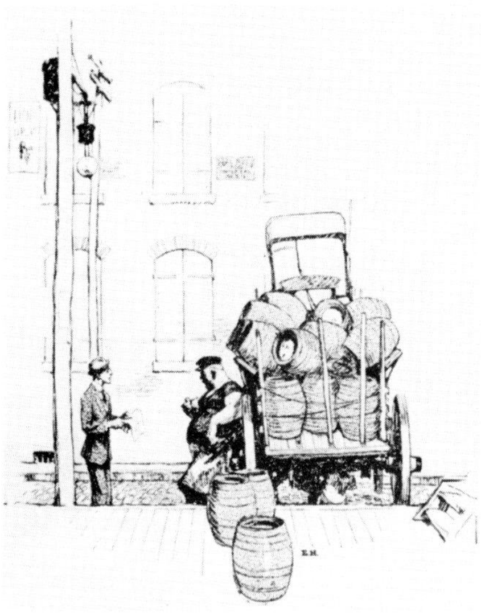

85a

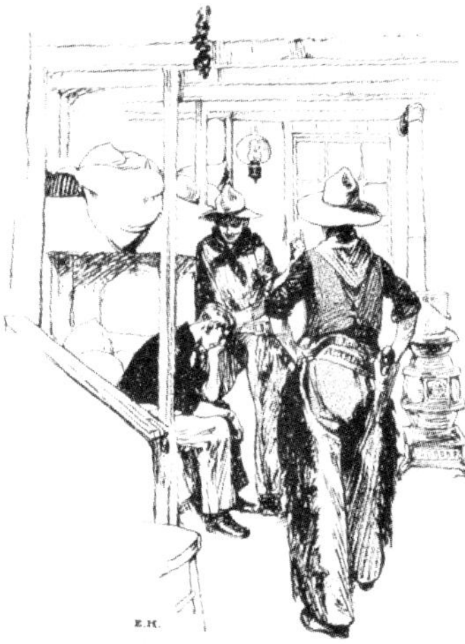

86

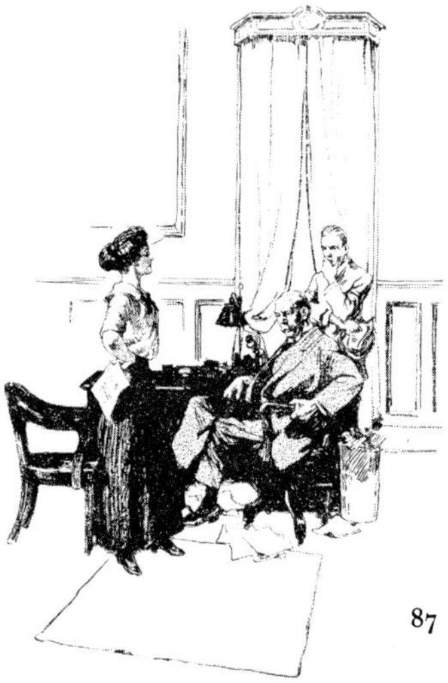

87

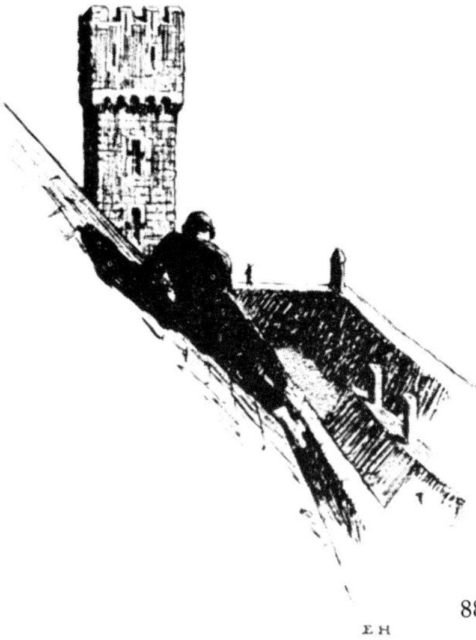

88a

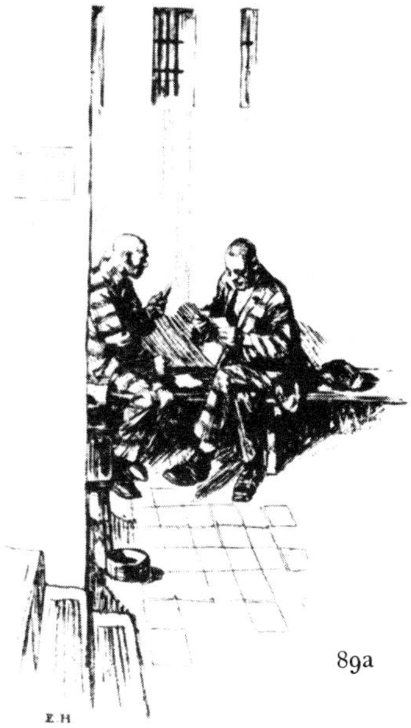

89a

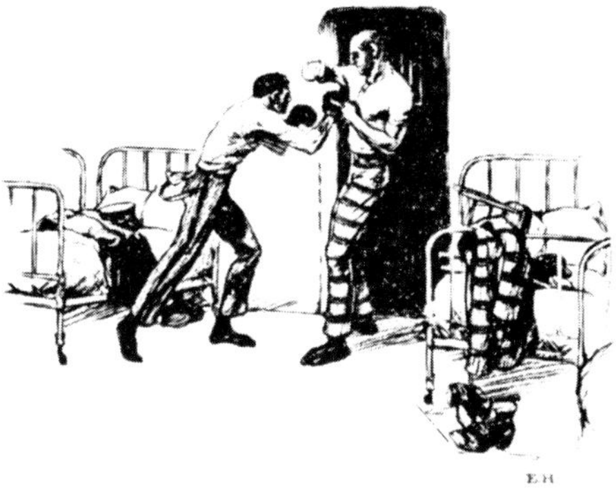

90a

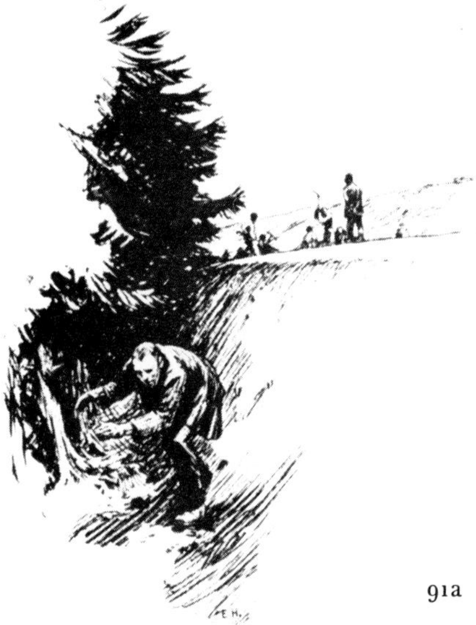

91a

Illustrations for Clarence L. Cullen, "Sudden Riches," *Associated Sunday Magazine,* December 29, 1912.

85a. Proof.

85b. "I would carry him off his feet with the great news," p. 6.

86. "Come here and have a peek at what's a Lord!" p. 7.

87. "I guess I'll resign my job right now," p. 7.

Illustrations for Edward Huntington Williams, M.D., "The People in the Walled City," *Associated Sunday Magazine,* March 23, 1913.

88a. Proof.

88b. "Individually they plan desperate means of escape," p. 8.

89a. Proof.

89b. "The forger may condescend to play cards with the sneak thief," p. 8.

90a. Proof.

90b. "The attendant was a crack boxer," p. 8.

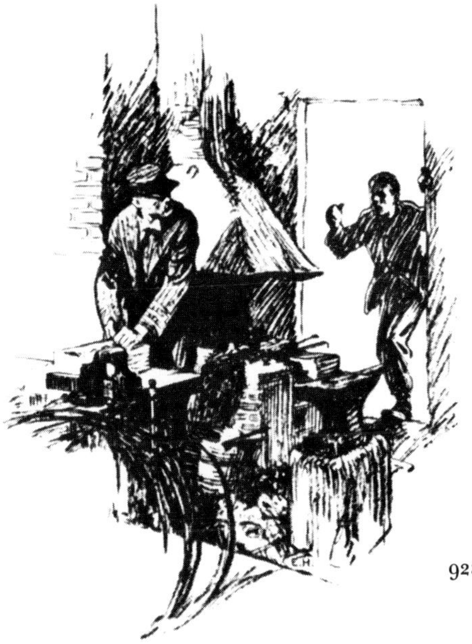

92a

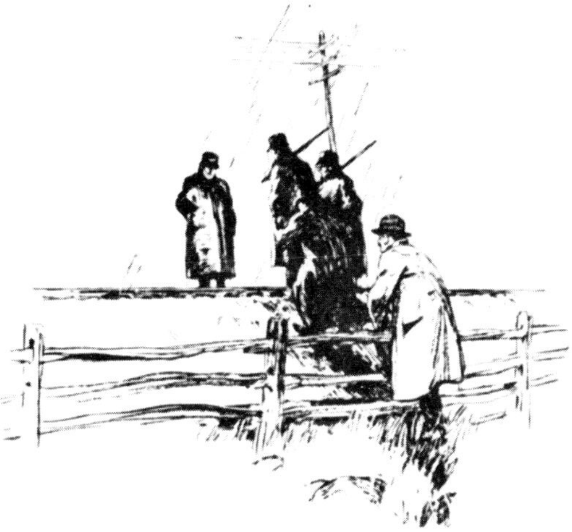

93

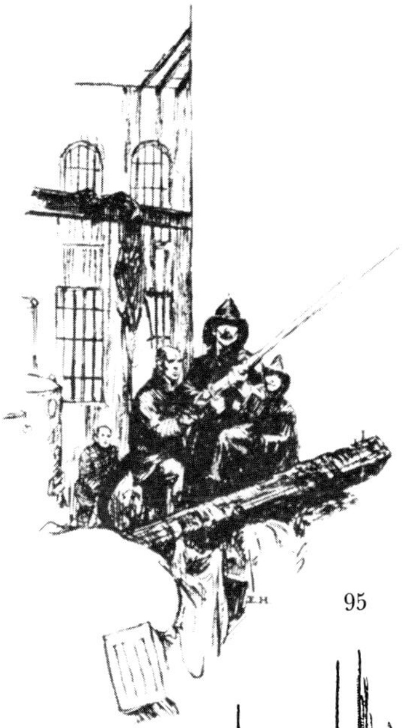

95

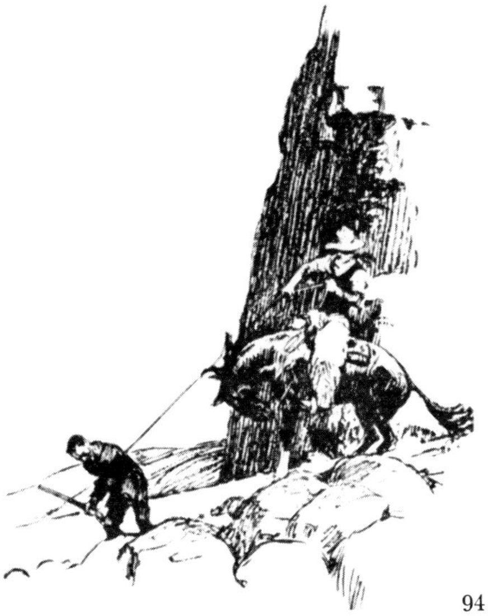

94

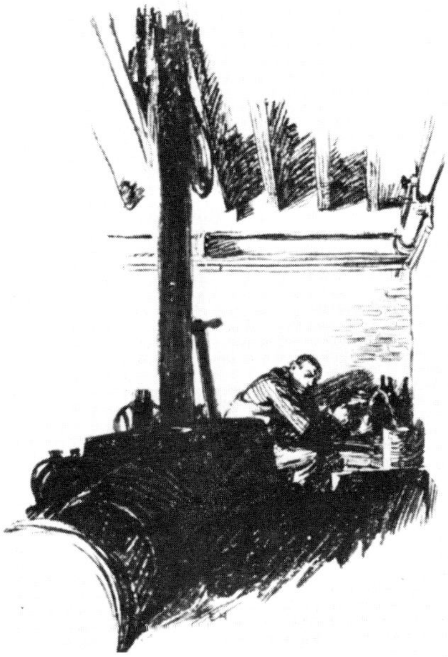

96a

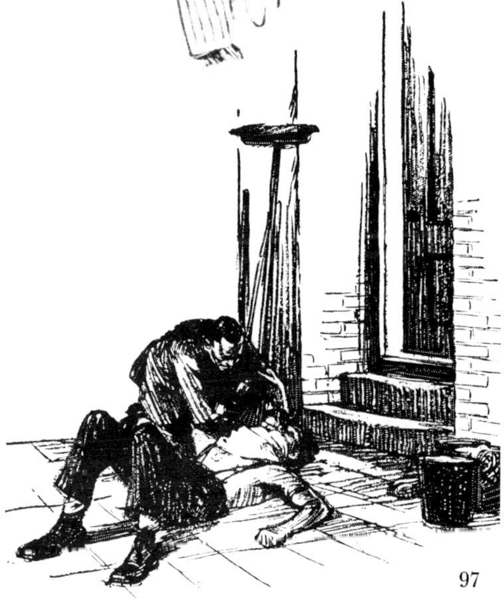

97

Illustrations for Edward Huntington Williams, M.D., "The Law's Long Arm," *Associated Sunday Magazine,* April 20, 1913.

91a. Proof.

91b. "One day he slipped into the bushes and disappeared," p. 7.

92a. Proof.

92b. "Yelling that Ryan had made a break for liberty," p. 7.

Illustrations for Edward Huntington Williams, M.D., "Wits Versus the Law," *Associated Sunday Magazine,* May 4, 1913.

93. "His telltale tracks led to the railroad," p. 10.

94. "He was captured in the end by a cowboy," p. 11.

95. "The most desperate characters in the place offered their services," p. 11.

Illustrations for Edward Huntington Williams, M.D., *Associated Sunday Magazine,* "Contented with Insanity," May 25, 1913.

96a. Proof.

96b. "Found the trusty running the still full blast," p. 12.

97. "The cook was soon tightly gagged," p. 12.

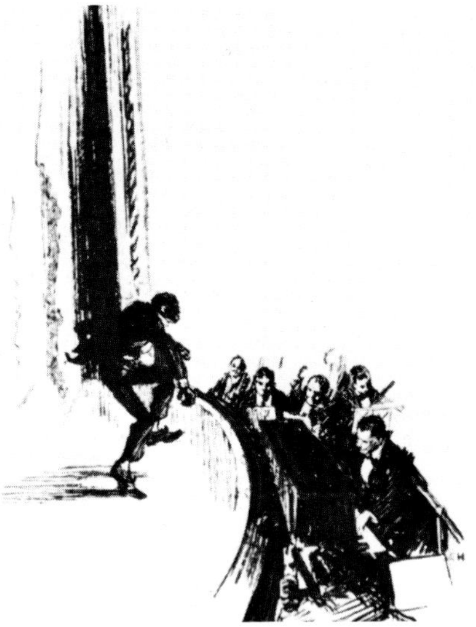

98a

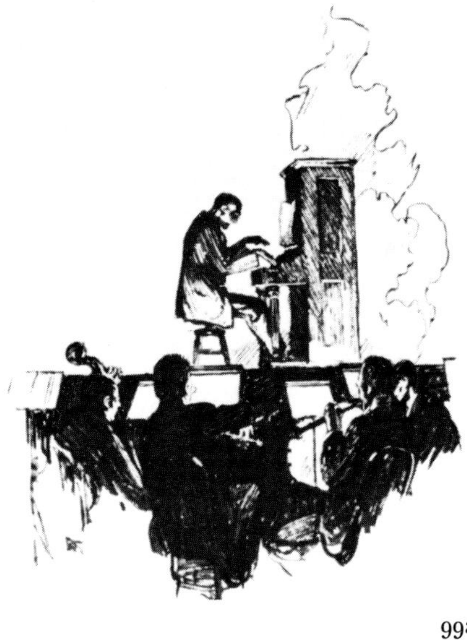

99a

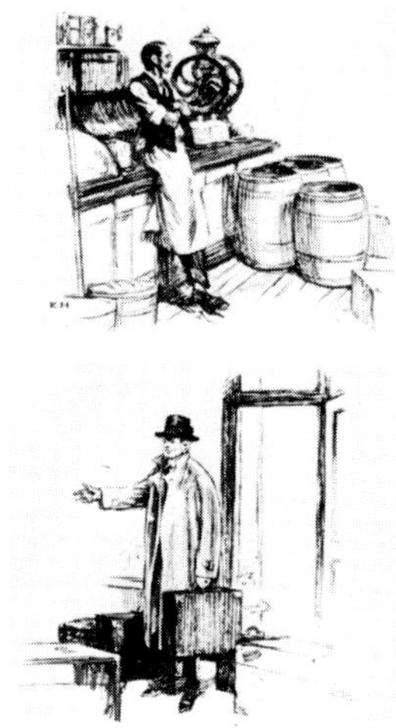

100a

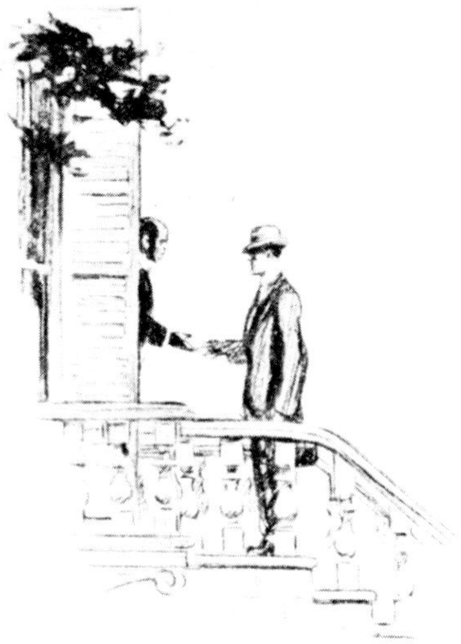

101a

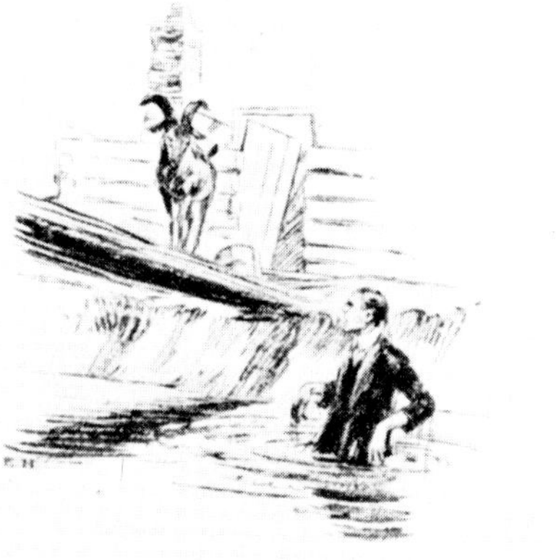

102a

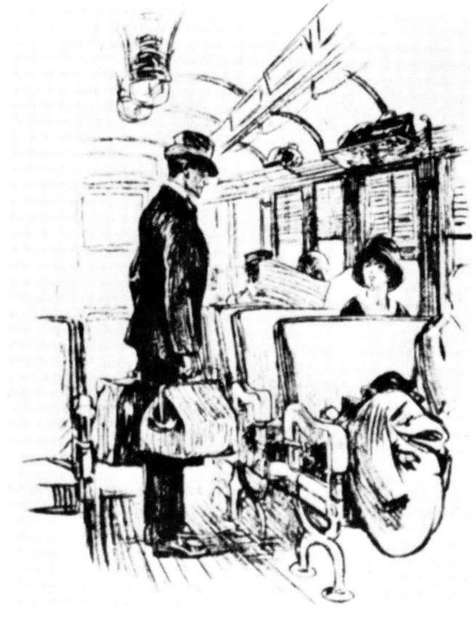

103a

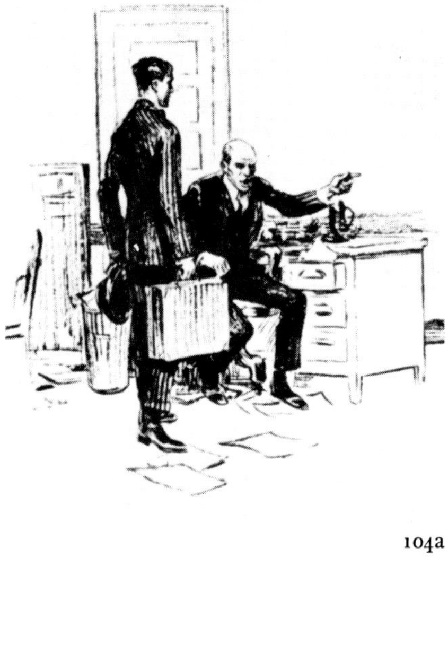

104a

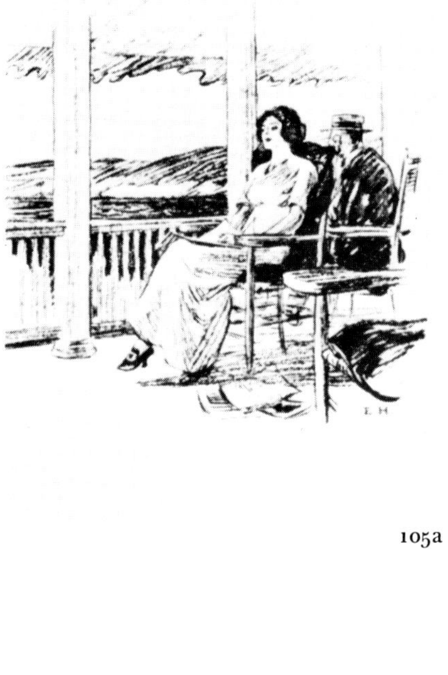

105a

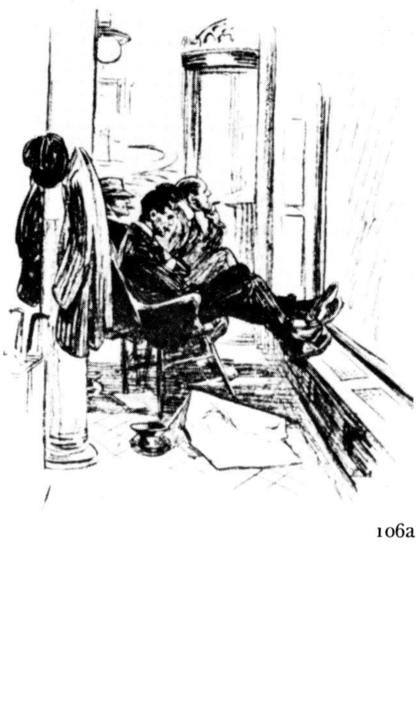

106a

Illustrations for Edward Huntington Williams, M.D., "The Insane at Play," *Associated Sunday Magazine,* June 22, 1913.

98a. Proof.

98b. "The Negro was furiously slapping the boards in one time while the orchestra played in another," p. 14.

99a. Proof.

99b. "Then Eddy would play his only solo," p. 14.

100a. Proofs.

100b. Illustrations for heading for weekly column, "Tales from the Road." First appeared in *Associated Sunday Magazine,* October 26, 1913, and the column ran every other week through the April 19, 1914 issue.

Illustrations for "Tales from the Road," *Associated Sunday Magazine,* November 2, 1913.

101a. Proof.

101b. "I selected an imposing brownstone house to make my first call." Charles E. Van Meter, "Knife Grinding as a Basis," p. 8.

102a. Proof.

102b. "If I started for the opposite bank, so would he; and if I turned to the other side, he would do likewise." William London King, "When the Goat Interfered," p. 14.

Illustrations for "Tales from the Road," *Associated Sunday Magazine,* November 16, 1913.

103a. Proof.

103b. "Big Tom asked nothing more than to share her seat." Horace Lytton Varian, "A Day Coach Samaritan," p. 9.

104a. Proof.

104b. "He pointed to the door and said get out." C. E. Brown, "The Ethics of Salesmanship," p. 14.

Illustrations for "Tales from the Road," *Associated Sunday Magazine,* November 30, 1913.

105a. Proof.

105b. "'Why didn't you tell me who you were?'" Hinson E. Stiles, "Cupid and Competitor," p. 13.

106a. Proof.

106b. "Hobbling down the street came a forlorn looking man." Crosby L. Smith, "Kindness Wins," p. 14.

Illustrations for "Tales from the Road," *Associated Sunday Magazine,* December 14, 1913.

107. "The old man hurrying back for another pocketful of earth." D. W. Fratcher, "Ferber's Transformation," p. 13.

108a. Proof.

108b. "I have to have it; so shell out!" I. Hamilton Faulkner, "Eliminating a Competitor," p. 14.

Illustrations for "Tales from the Road," *Associated Sunday Magazine,* December 28, 1913.

109a. Proof.

109b. "I tried to side-step the touch." R. F. W., "The Man Who Came Back," p. 14.

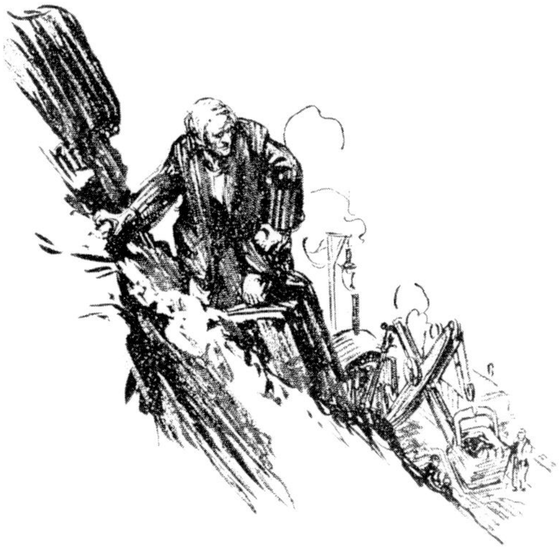

107

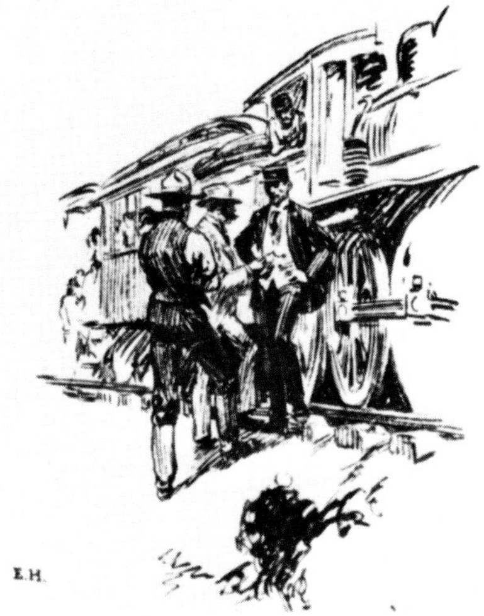

108a

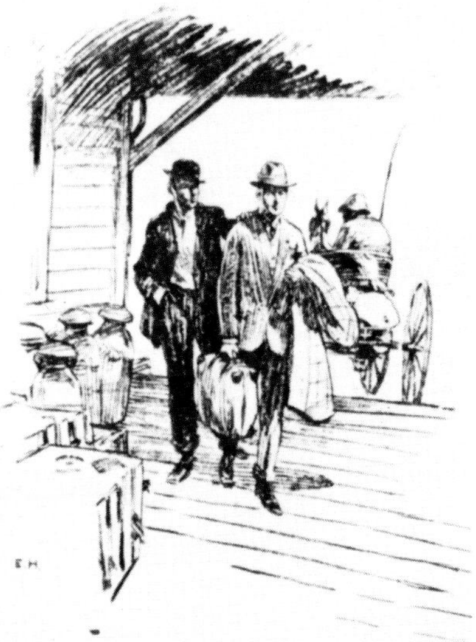

109a

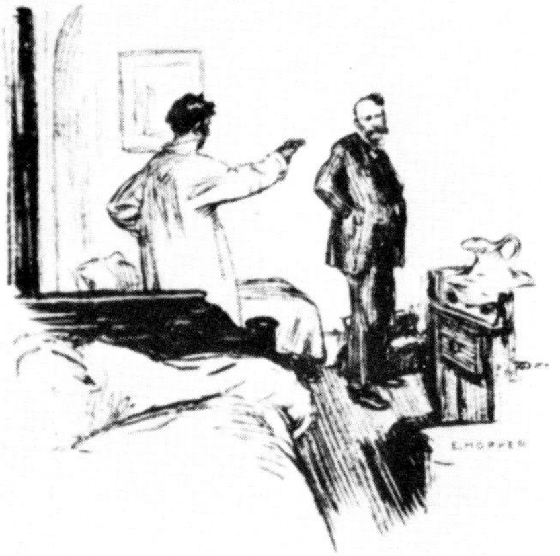

110a

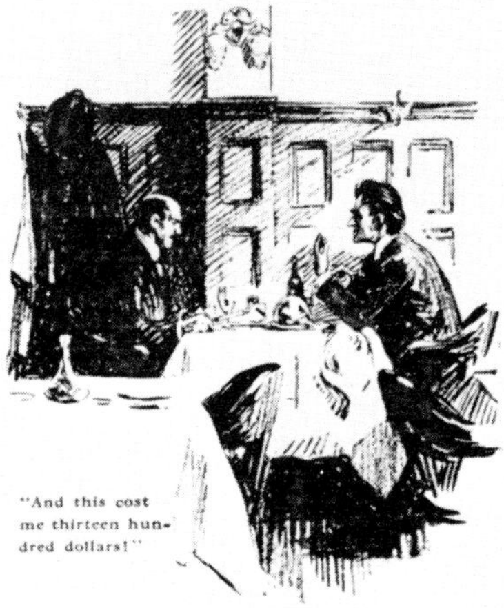

111

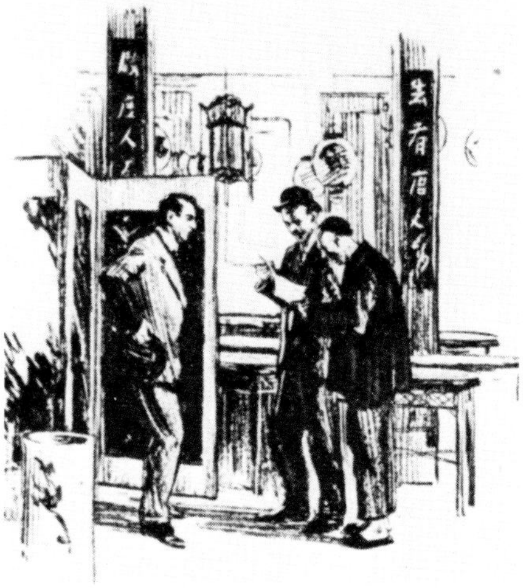

112a

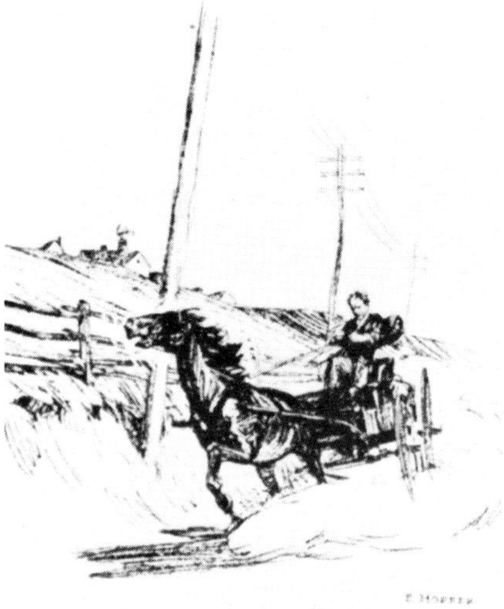

113a

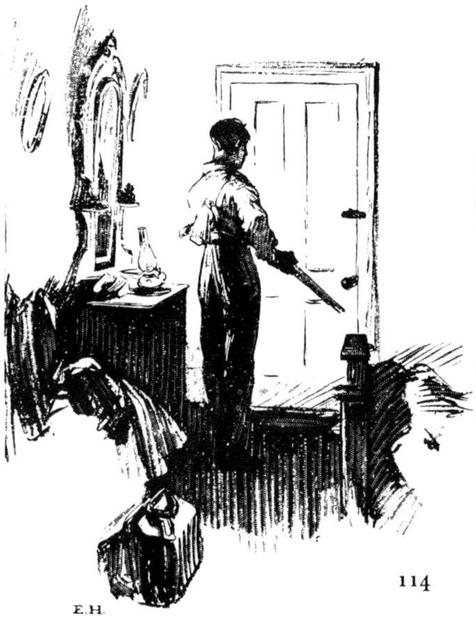

114

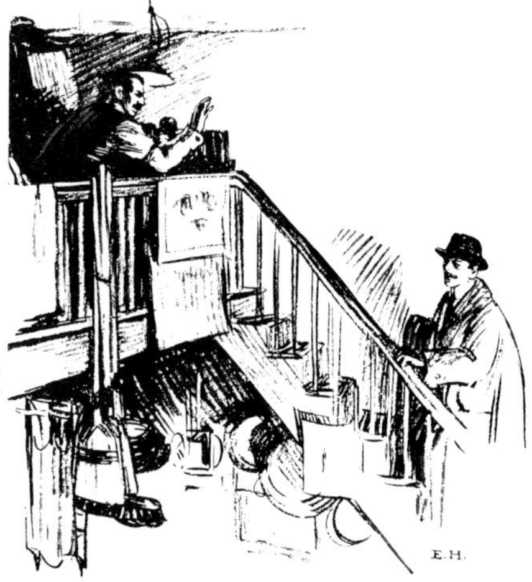

115

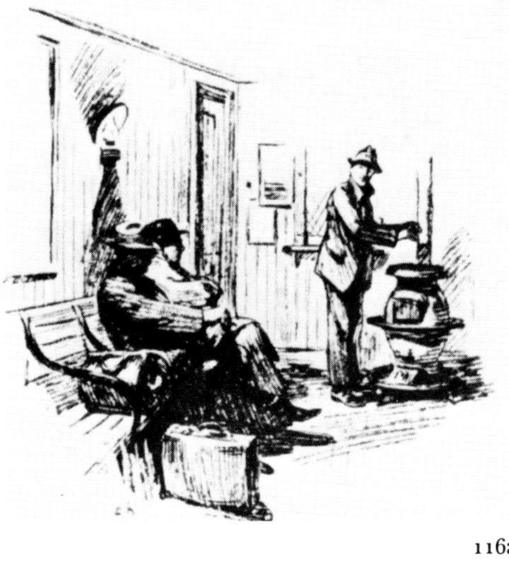

116a

110a. Proof.

110b. "If you stir another step it will be your last." P. J. MacFarland, "A Strange Roommate," p. 15.

Illustration for "Tales from the Road," *Associated Sunday Magazine,* January 11, 1914.

111. "And this cost me thirteen hundred dollars!" David W. Fratcher, "Diamonds and Junk," p. 12.

Illustrations for "Tales from the Road," *Associated Sunday Magazine,* January 25, 1914.

112a. Proof.

112b. "The Chinamen all agreed to use them." Robert James, "An Emergency Sideline," p. 10.

113a. Proof.

113b. "My only mishap was that the horse ran away for five miles." H. S. Hall, "Collecting on Christmas," p. 11.

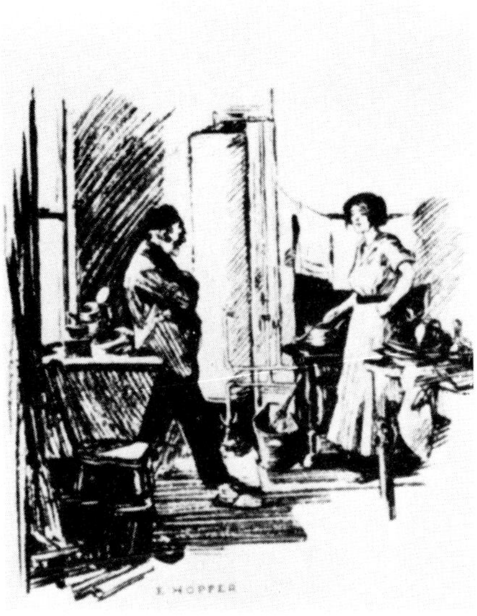

117a

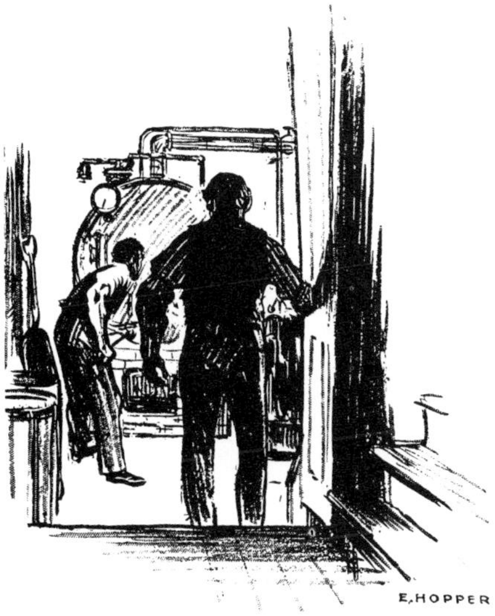

118

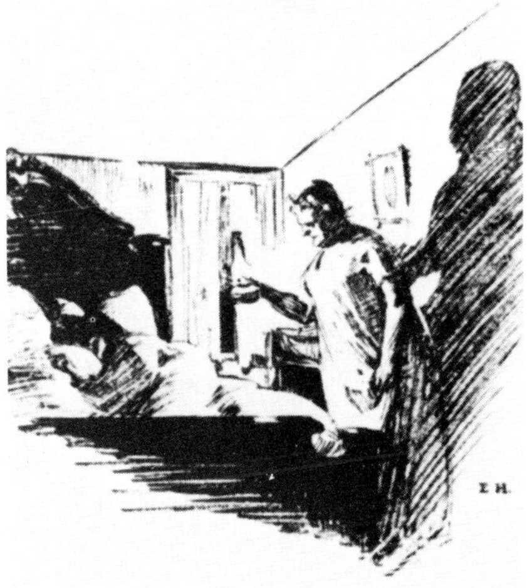

119

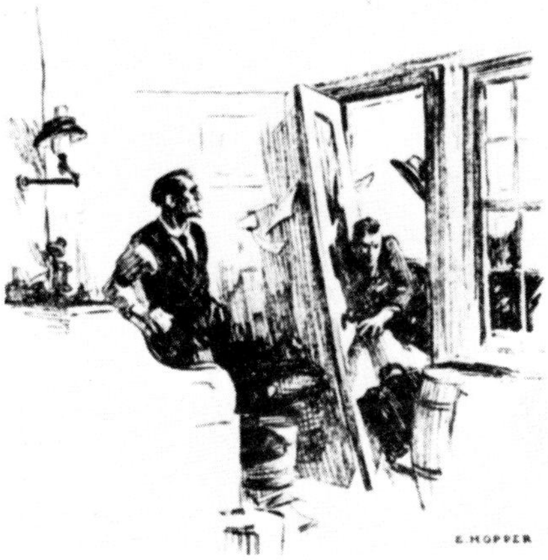

120a

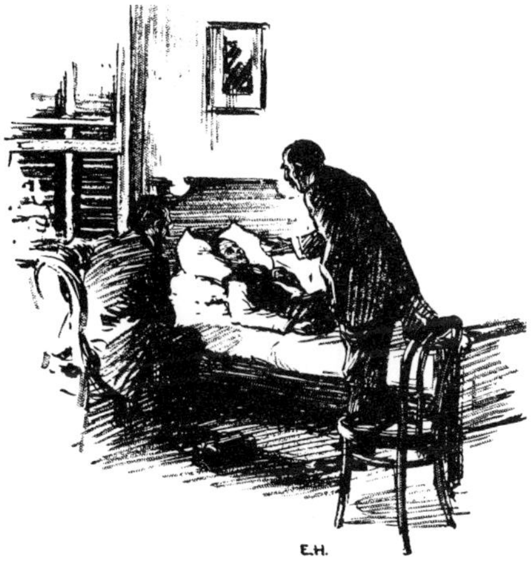

121a

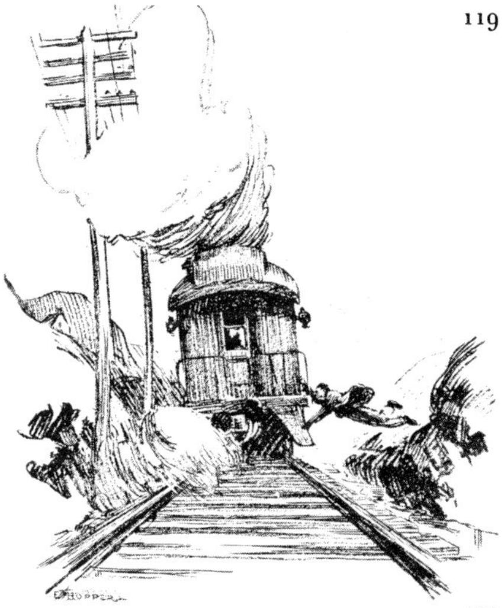

122

Illustrations for "Tales from the Road," *Associated Sunday Magazine,* February 8, 1914.

114. "The musket couldn't shoot; but it would scare 'em off." R. T. Delaney, "Shoes Shined Free," p. 13.

115. "Nothing doing—no time to waste —don't need anything—good day!" Hinson Stiles, "The Midnight Thieves," p. 13.

Illustrations for "Tales from the Road," *Associated Sunday Magazine,* February 22, 1914.

116a. Proof.

116b. "Could you stake me to the price of a meal?" Chester W. Billing, "A Favor Returned," p. 9.

117a. Proof.

117b. "The old man talked and I prepared the meal." Maud Francis, "Through his Stomach," p. 10.

Illustrations for "Tales from the Road," *Associated Sunday Magazine,* March 8, 1914.

118. "The old man followed me in, unable even to give suggestions." H. S. Hall, "The Leak," p. 10.

119. "When I awoke someone was trying to force whisky down my throat." Robert G. Wood, "An Eery Hunt for Gold," p. 11.

Illustrations for "Tales from the Road," *Associated Sunday Magazine,* March 22, 1914.

120a. Proof.

120b. "Then her mother knew she had been out." D. E. Terry, "The Haunted Engine," p. 13.

121a. Proof.

121b. "I shattered my way into the oil dealer's office." D. E. Terry, "The Haunted Engine," p. 13.

Illustrations for "Tales from the Road," *Associated Sunday Magazine,* April 19, 1914.

122. "I was afraid to breathe or move for fear of being dashed to the ground." D. W. Fratcher, "Taking Jerry's Measure," p. 9.

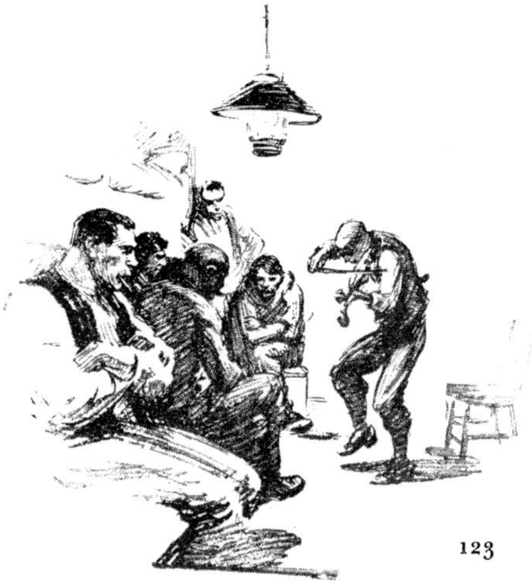

123

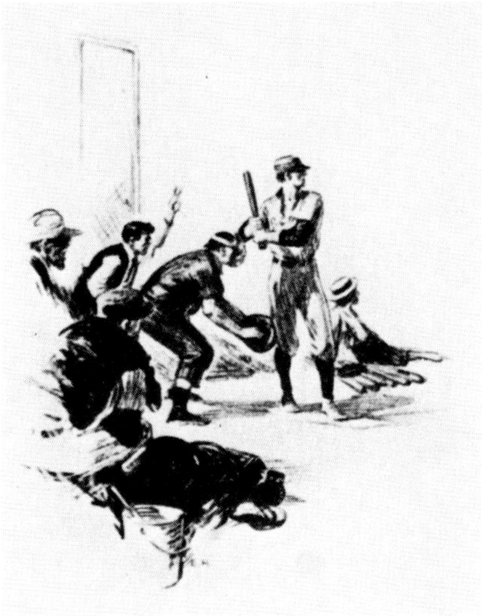

124a

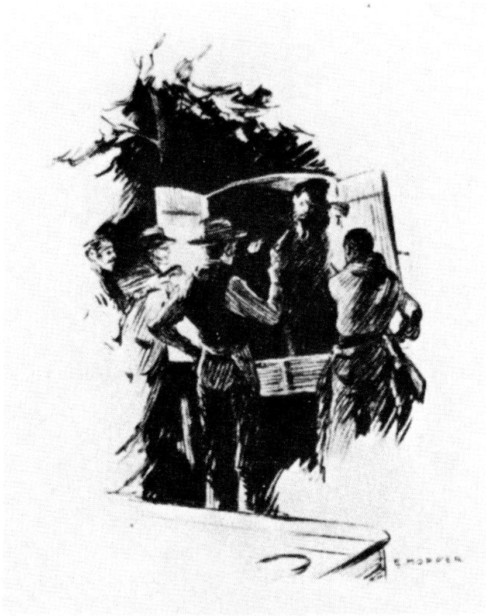

125a

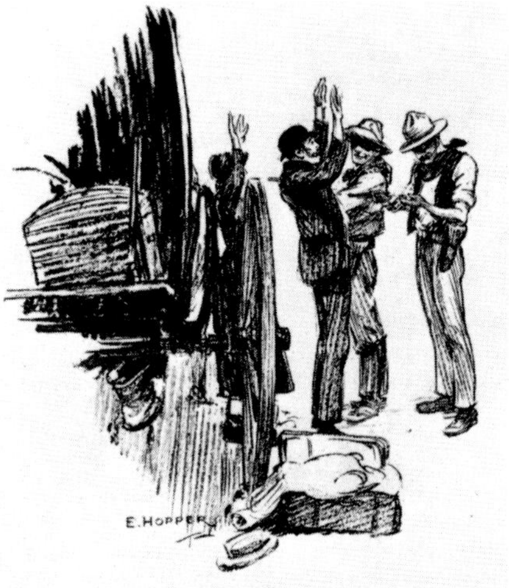

126

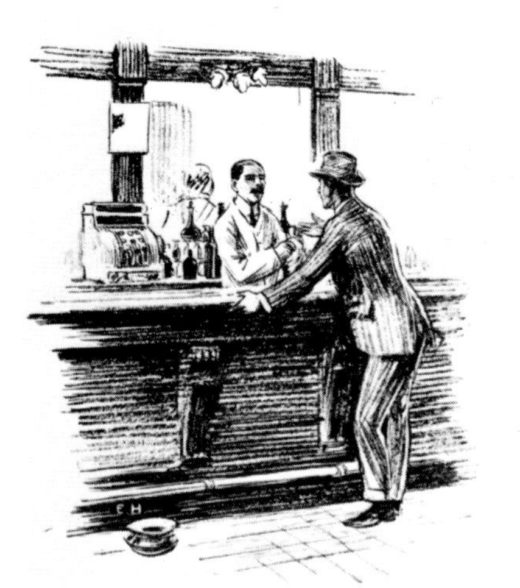

127

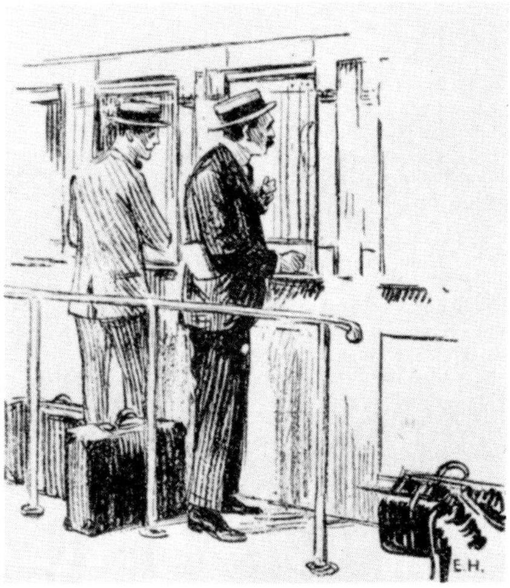

128

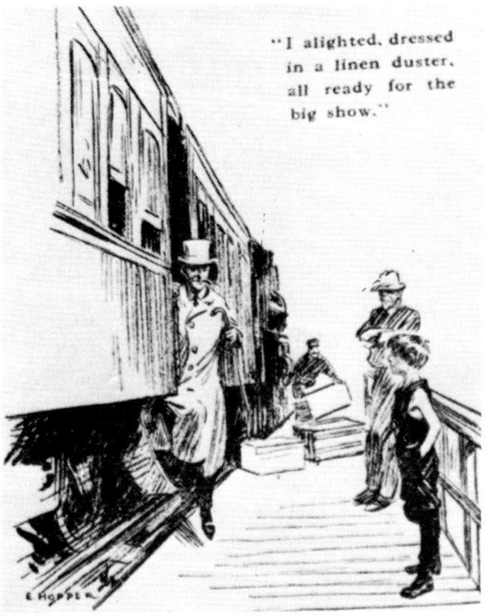

123. "And so the evening wore away." Richard S. Bates, "Home, Sweet, Home," p. 17.

Illustrations for "Tales from the Road," *Associated Sunday Magazine,* May 10, 1914.

124a. Proof.

124b. "Howled for Coggan to start something." L. D. Maxfield, "Baseball and Matches," p. 7.

125a. Proof.

125b. "There, cursing like a trooper, was Dick Hardhead!" Haddon Prentice, "How I Caught an Outlaw," p. 7.

Illustrations for "Tales from the Road," *Associated Sunday Magazine,* May 24, 1914.

126. Eugene Clay Ferguson, "A Texas Adventure," p. 12.

127. "That was the best piece of news I could learn." John A. Burton, "A Lost Order," p. 12.

(*Note:* The illustration on page 13 of this issue is not by Edward Hopper.)

Illustrations for "Tales from the Road," *Associated Sunday Magazine,* June 21, 1914.

128. "I watched the nervous man furtively." T. H. Baille, "Brick," p. 13.

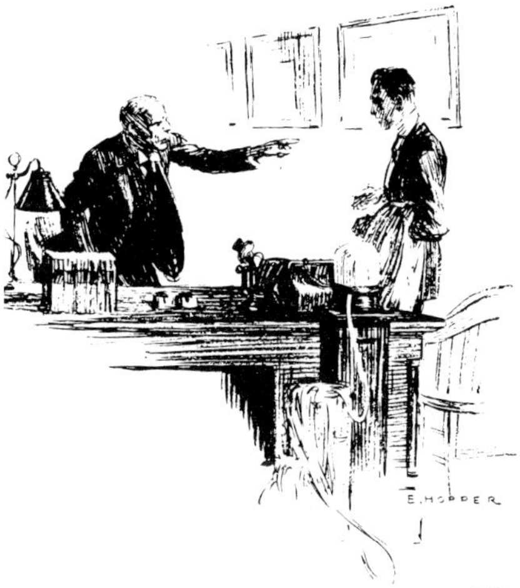

130

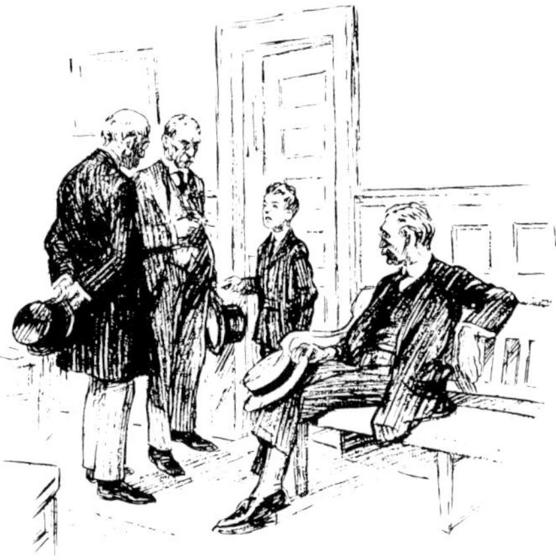

131

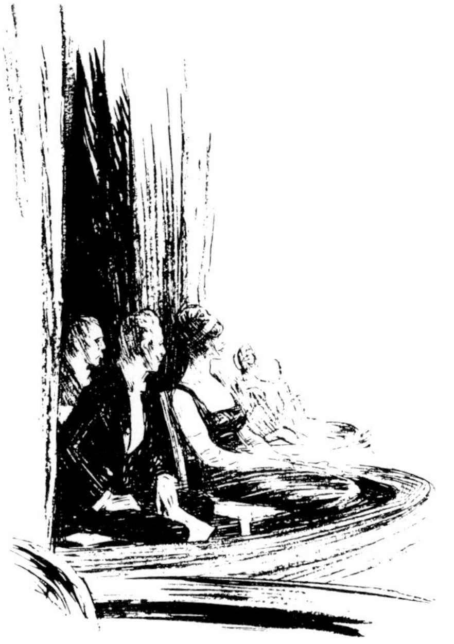

132

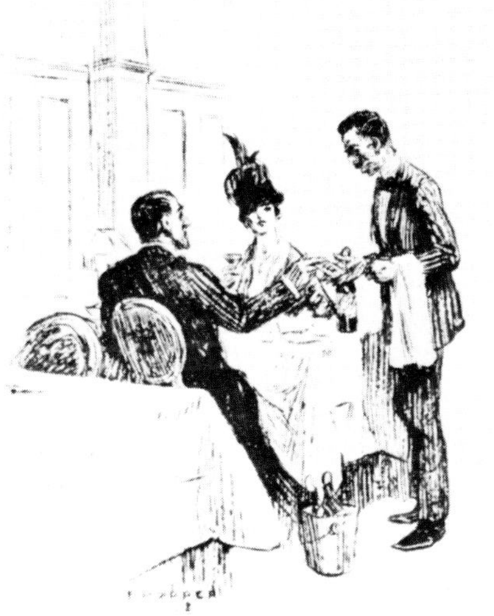

133a

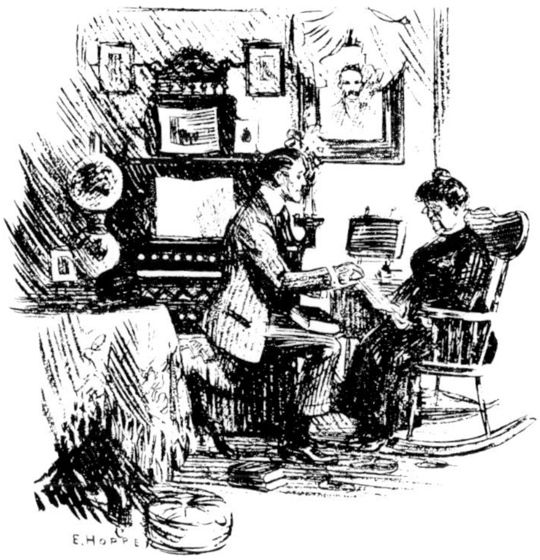

134

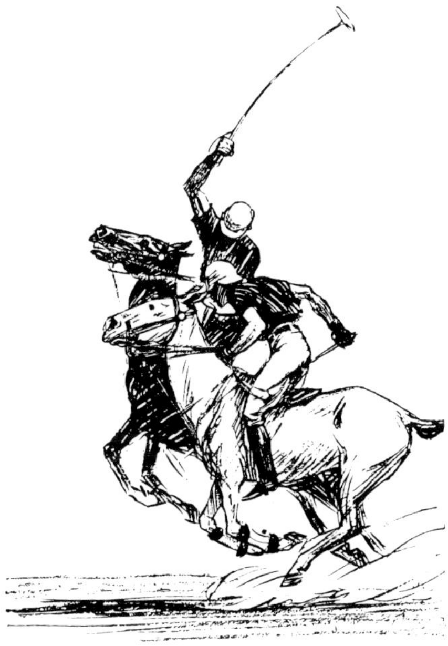

135

129. "I alighted, dressed in a linen duster, all ready for the big show." Lowell F. Maxwell, "My Lucky Day," p. 13.

Illustrations for Charles A. Collman, "Keeping Your Wits in Wall Street," *Associated Sunday Magazine,* September 27, 1914.

130. "The irate financier banished the young hopeful from his presence," p. 15.

131. "You ought to have witnessed the scenes in my office," p. 16.

Illustrations for Charles A. Collman, "Breaking Into Wall Street," *Associated Sunday Magazine,* October 11, 1914.

132. "The clerk was cordially entertained by the great Baring," p. 13.

133a. Proof.

133b. "Throws $50 tips at hotel waiters," p. 13.

Illustrations for Charles A. Collman, "What a Smile Is Worth in Wall Street," *Associated Sunday Magazine,* October 25, 1914.

134. "He had been a penniless book agent," p. 16.

135. "His directors await him in the boardroom," p. 16.

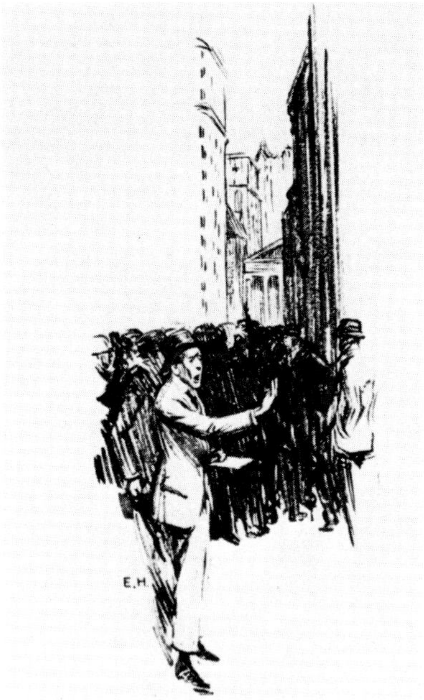

136a

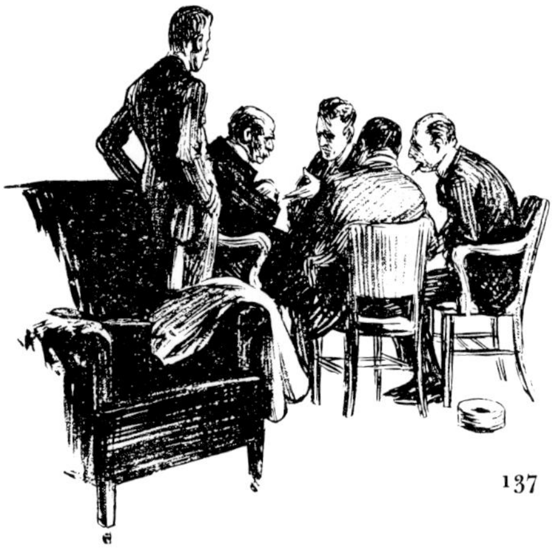

137

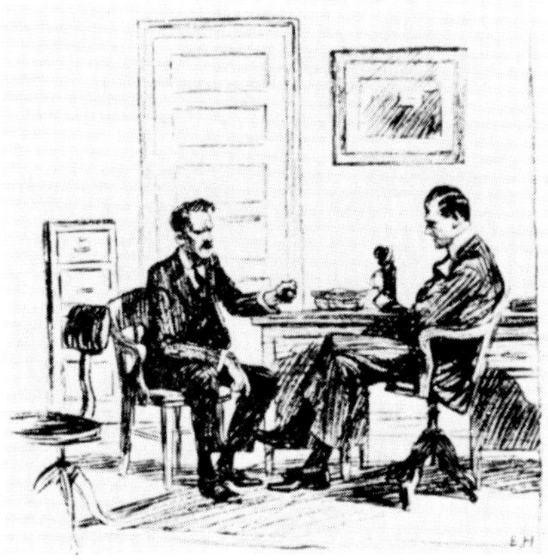

138a

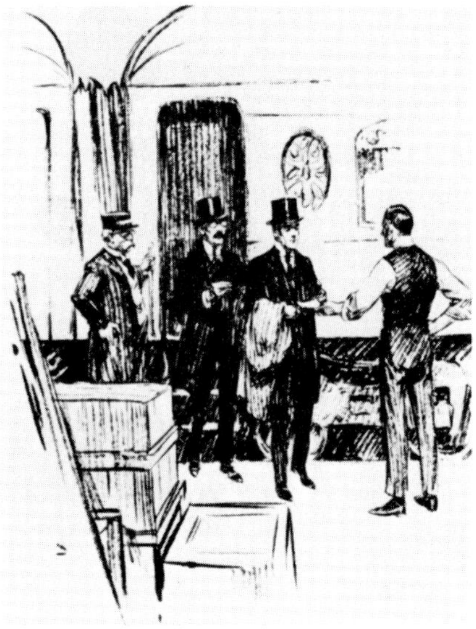

139a

Illustrations for Charles A. Collman, "The Wolves of Wall Street," *Associated Sunday Magazine,* November 22, 1914.

136a. Proof.

136b. "Mond knew how to boost the stock on the curb market," p. 14.

137. "The young directors were not frightened at the holdup," p. 14.

Illustrations for Charles A. Collman, "Making a Million in Wall Street," *Associated Sunday Magazine,* December 20, 1914.

138a. Proof.

138b. "No man is entitled to make a million," p. 16.

139a. Proof.

139b. "Offered him the presidency at $50,000 a year," p. 16.

Illustration for "How I Saved My Husband: A Temperance Document," *American Magazine,* 76 (August 1913).

140. "When I think, Philip, of what you might be and what you are, I realize I no longer love you," p. 67.

Illustrations for "Trail's End," chap. 1, by the Homesteader, *Farmer's Wife,* April 1915.

141a. Proof.

141b. "It took four bronchos to haul me, my dog, cat, crate of chickens, trunk, furniture, stove, water barrel and groceries ten miles across the hoof trailed plains," p. 312.

142a. Proof.

142b. "My pony 'went bad' a mile or so back and we had a mix-up," p. 313.

Illustration for "Trail's End," chap. 2, by the Homesteader, *Farmer's Wife,* May 1915.

143. " 'This is my boy,' said the woman simply. 'She's Miss Douglas from over yonder,' " p. 343.

Illustration for "Trail's End," chap. 3, by the Homesteader, *Farmer's Wife,* June 1915.

144a. Proof.

144b. "We ate our bacon and cold biscuits with zest," p. 7.

Illustration for "Trail's End," chap. 4, by the Homesteader, *Farmer's Wife,* July 1915.

145. "I looked up into his eyes, 'You may,' I whispered," p. 31.

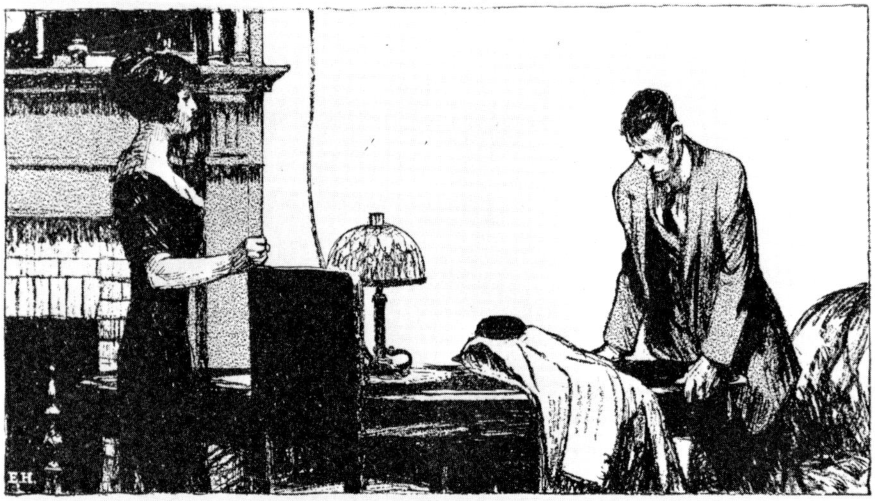

140

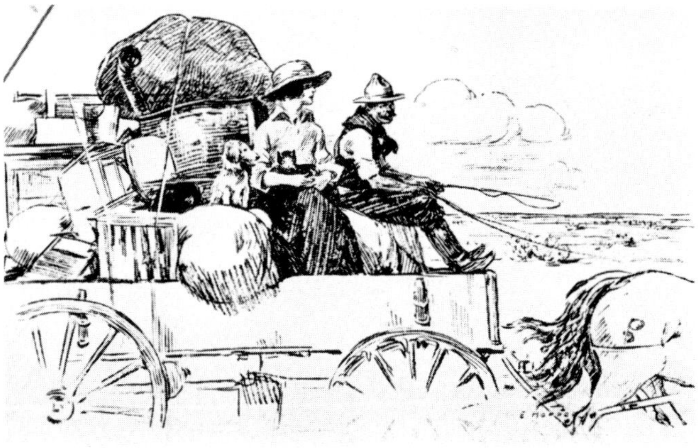

141a

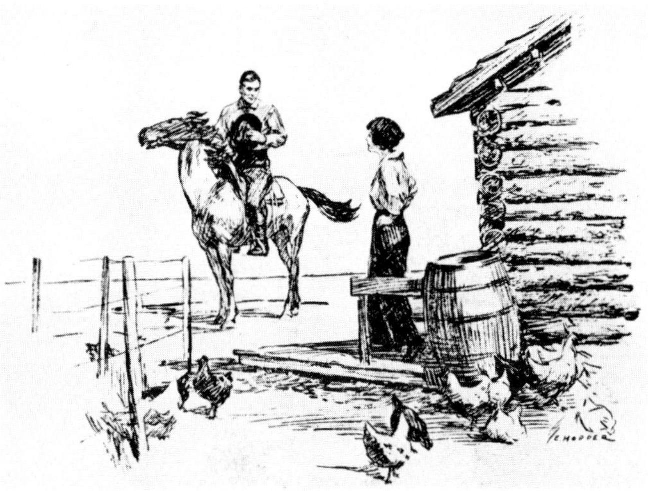

142a

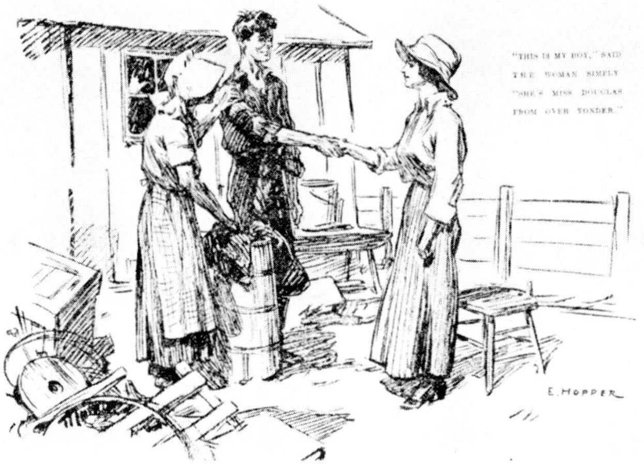

143

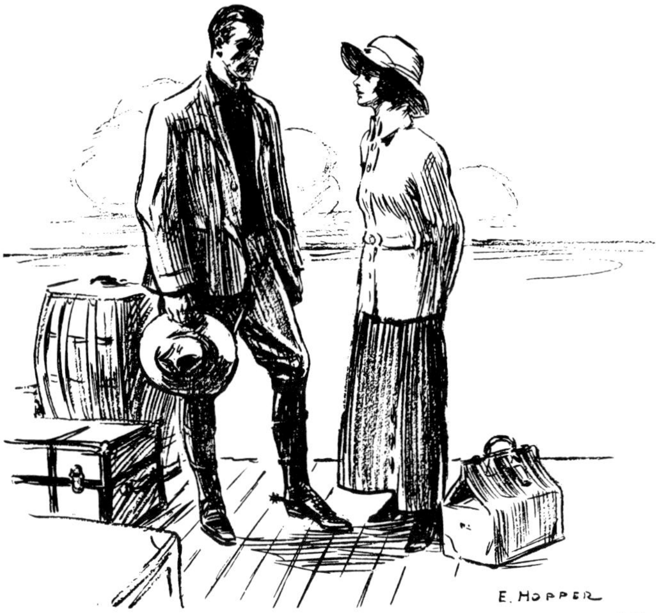

145

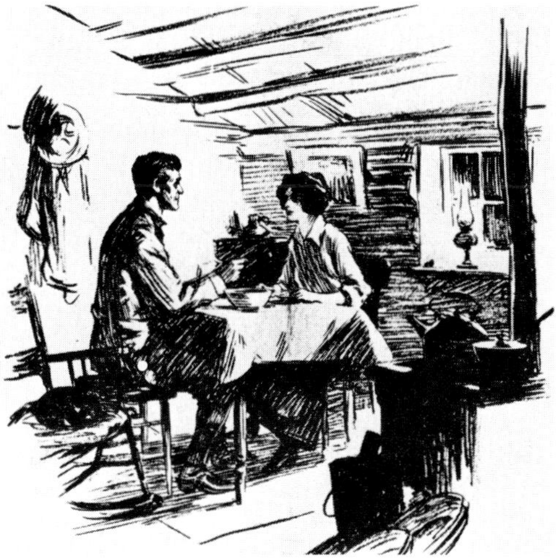

144a

Illustration for Robert T. Cole, "Santa Claus' Love Story," *Farmer's Wife,* December 1916.

146a. Proof.

146b. "In the afternoon when the Christmas dinner was settled, he took everybody out for a ride on the new bobsled," p. 145.

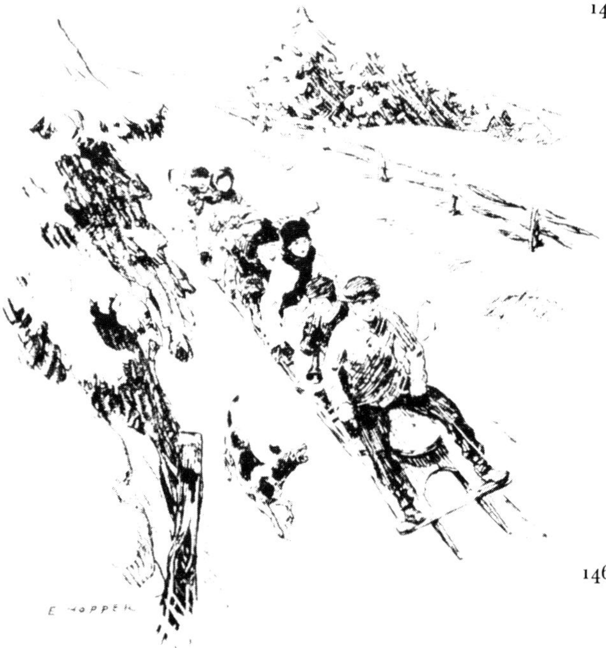

146a

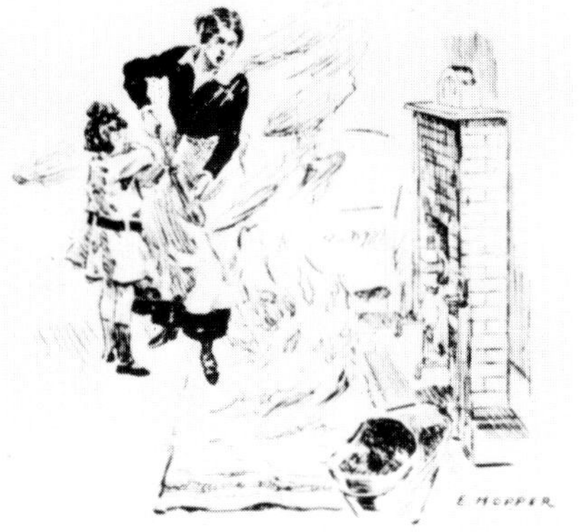

147a

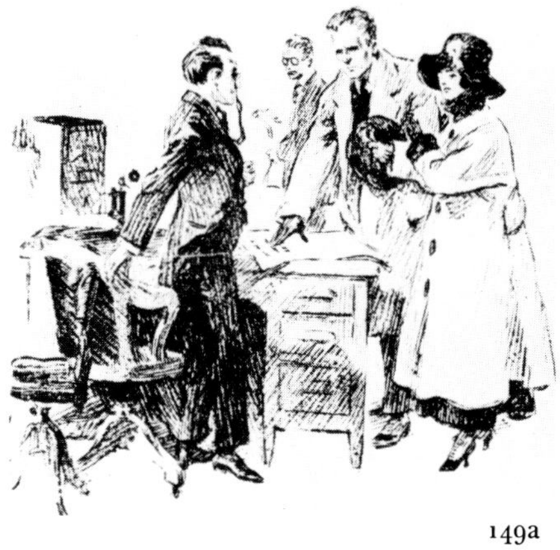

149a

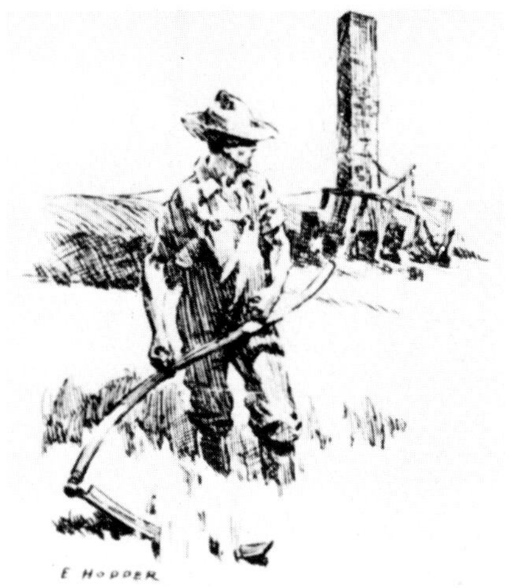

148a

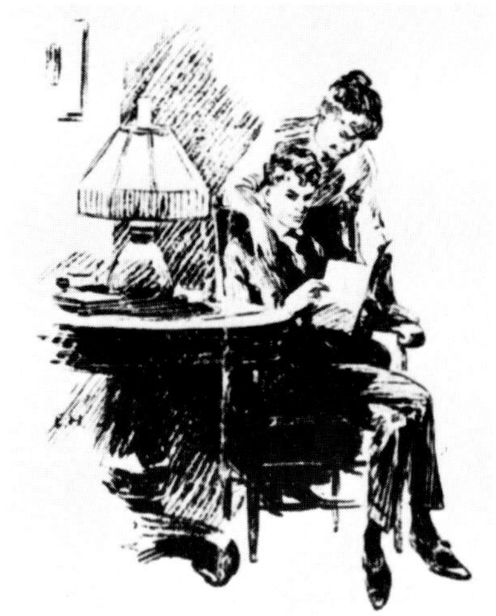

150a

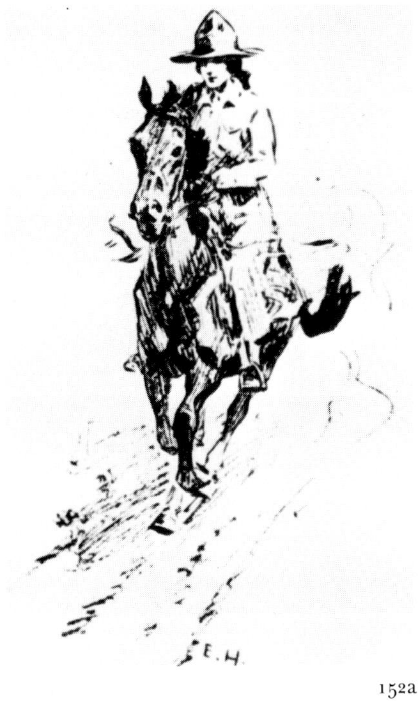

152a

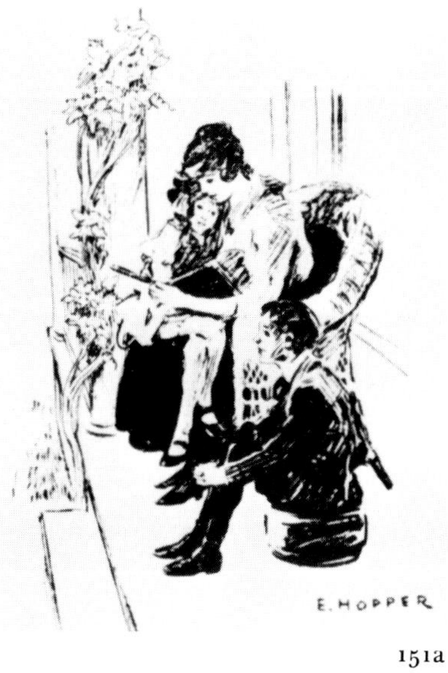

151a

Illustrations for Dorothy D. Calhoun, "Country Fire Protection," *Farmer's Wife,* January 1917.

147a. Proof.

147b. "Fireplaces should be protected by a screen of fine wire to prevent ignition by sparks," p. 168.

148a. Proof.

148b. "Twenty years gone up in smoke —was it necessary?" p. 168.

Illustration for Elva Cureton, "The Adjustment," *Farmer's Wife,* April 1917.

149a. Proof.

149b. "I know your employers, Saunders, and they have no liking for daylight. In to-morrow's issue you will retract that report and say that Mrs. Pendester's public work is heartily approved by her husband," p. 259.

Illustrations for Katherine Henry, "Then Contentment Reigns," *Farmer's Wife,* May 1917.

150a. Proof.

150b. P. 291.

151a. Proof.

151b. P. 291.

Illustrations for Katherine Henry, "Daughter Chooses the Farm," *Farmer's Wife,* June 1917.

152a. Proof.

152b. "A saddle horse would go far toward keeping her contented with life on the farm," p. 8.

153a. Proof.

153b. "A day's outing under the open sky will offset the busier hours of a period of stress like haying time. There must be periods of fun," p. 8.

Illustrations for Carmella E. L. Kenyon, "Lost Canyon," *Farmer's Wife,* August 1917.

154a. Proof.

154b. " 'Now,' said the engineer, 'the next number on the program will be a thirty-mile hike back to the hotel by the

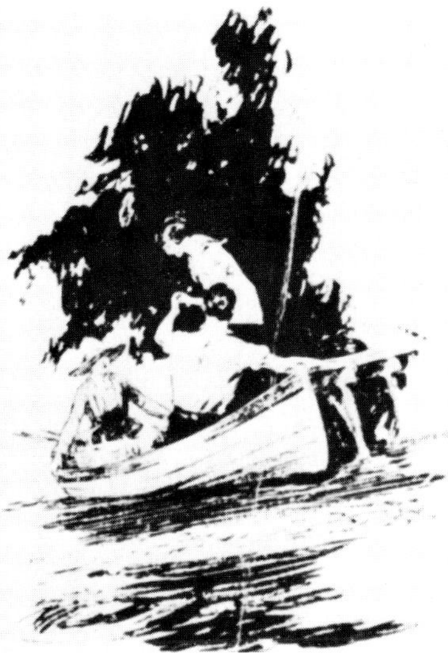

153a

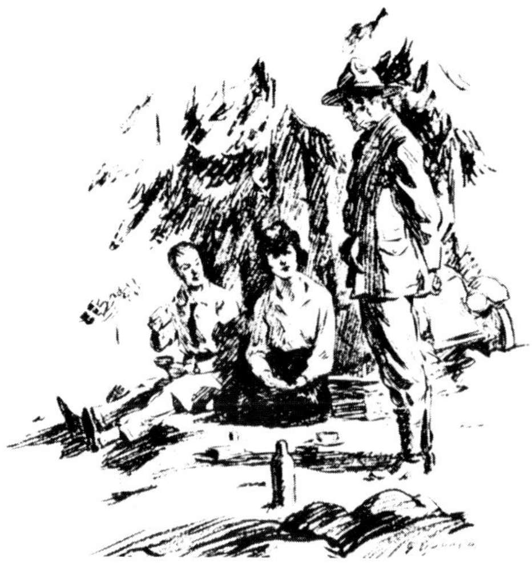

154a

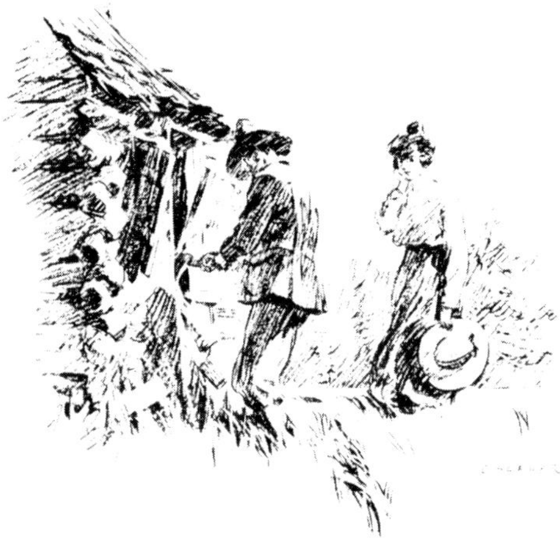

155a

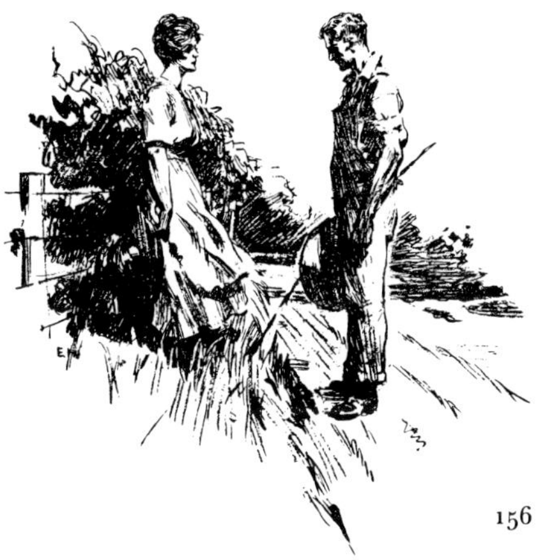

156

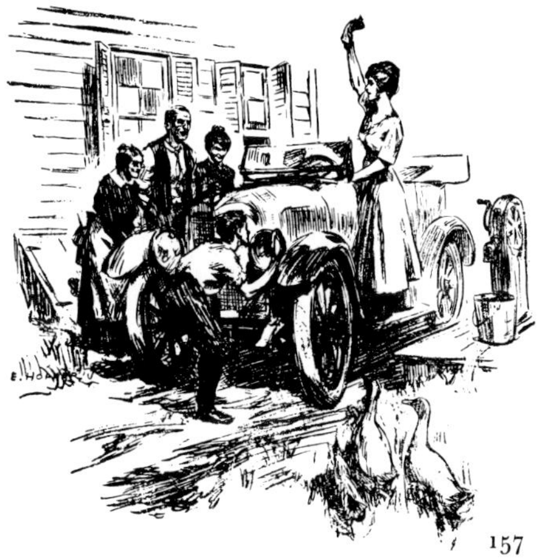

157

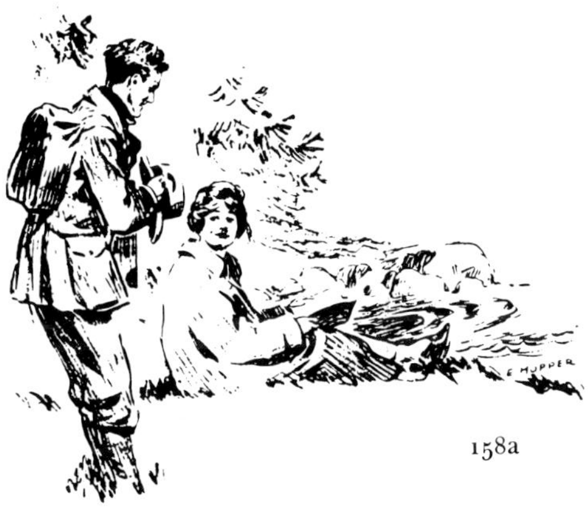

158a

well known hiker, Mr. Billy Stebbins,' " p. 51.

155a. Proof.

155b. "He repaired the old door as well as he could. I'll see to it that he has burial,' he said," p. 73.

Illustrations for Dorothy Donnell Calhoun, "The Legacy on Wheels," part 1, *Farmer's Wife,* September 1917.

156. " 'You can't ever—marry me?' The bewilderment on his honest face was drowned in a dull tide of red. 'But, Julie, why can't you ever?' 'Potatoes,' said Julie crisply. 'That's why,' " p. 68.

157. "Julie waved the blue check. 'Here's the money! I'll drive! I'll study the book and find out how to start and stop,' " p. 69.

158a. Proof.

158b. " 'You seem to be stuck. Is there anything I can do? I know quite a bit about this make of car.' Julie looked up into a pair of frank gray eyes. 'There are a hundred and sixty-three pages more! Oh, if you could! Uncle Henry is harder to start than old Peleg ever was,' " p. 95.

Illustration for Dorothy Donnell Calhoun, "The Legacy on Wheels," part 2, *Farmer's Wife,* November 1917.

159a. Proof.

159b. "In the midst of a heap of wretched household goods, broken chairs and tattered bedclothes, a woman sat rocking a wailing baby to her breast," p. 123.

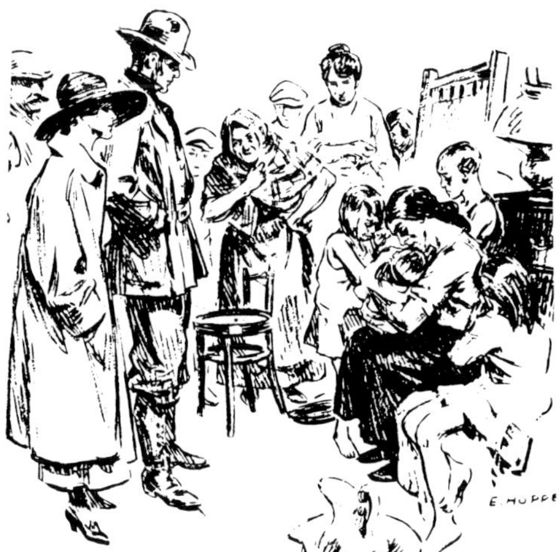

159a

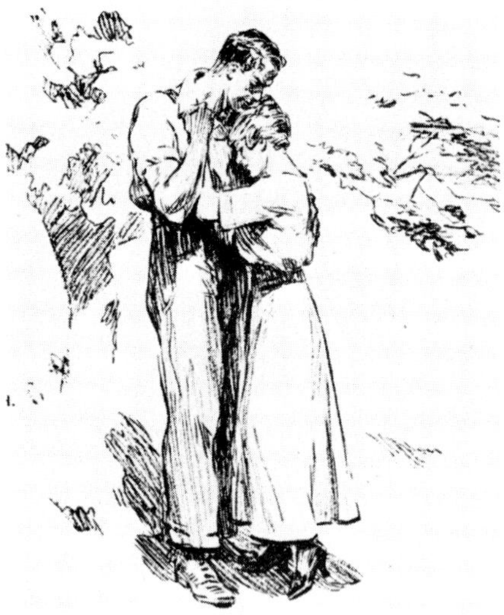

160a

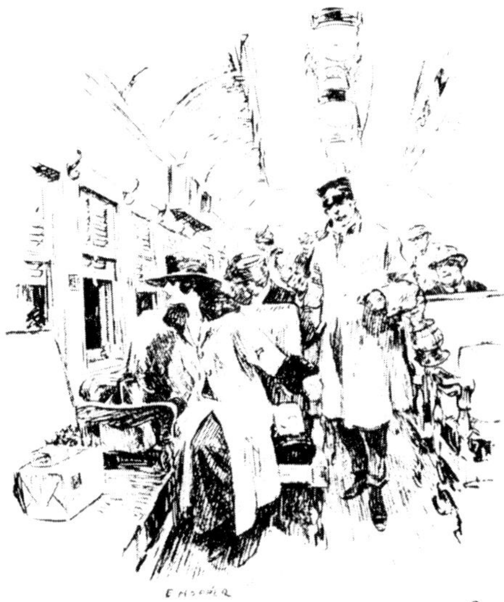

161a

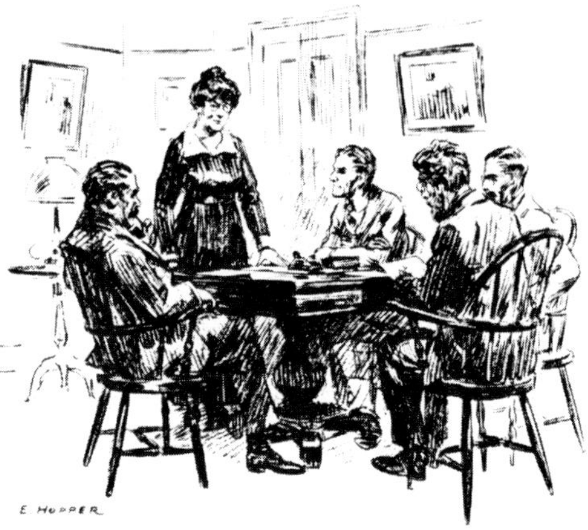

162a

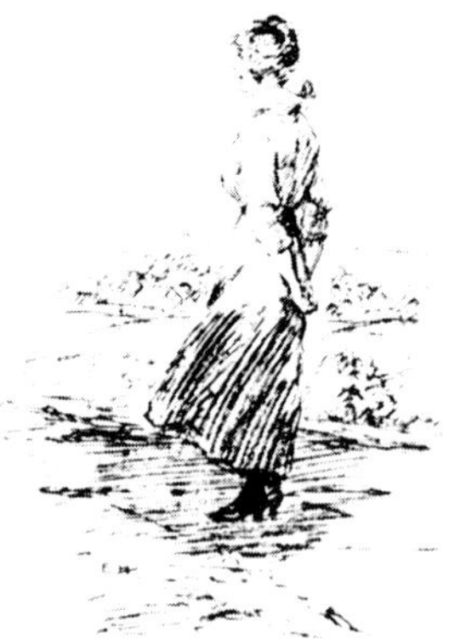

163a

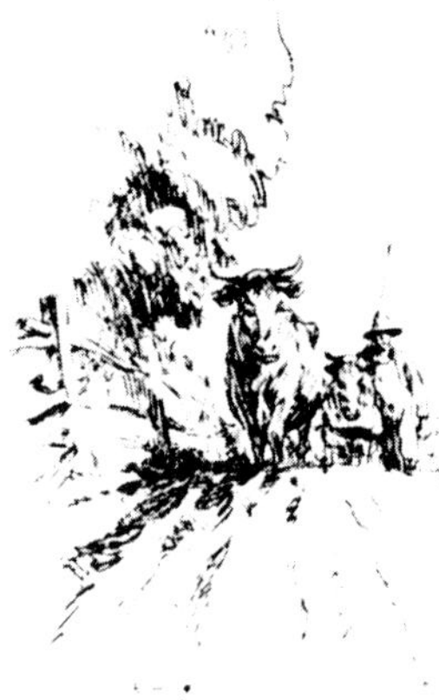

164a

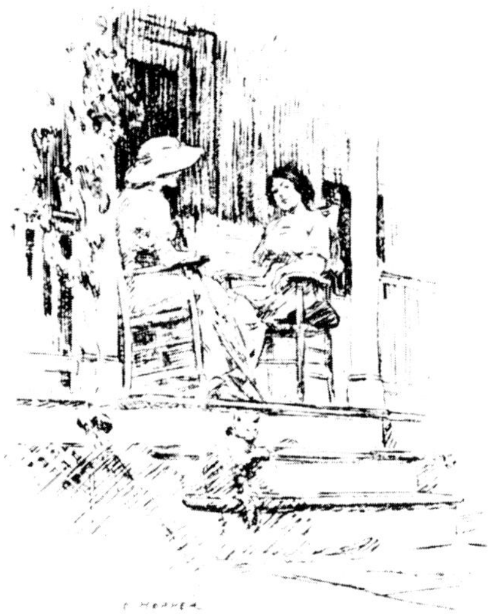

165a

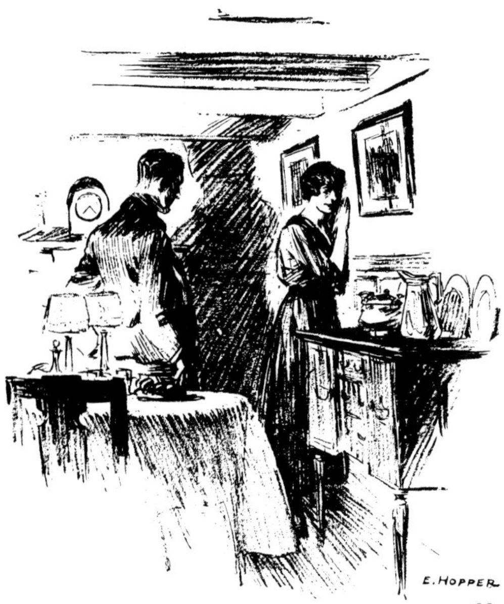

166

Illustration for Dorothy Donnell Calhoun, "The Legacy on Wheels," part 3, *Farmer's Wife,* December 1917.

160a. Proof.

160b. " 'Why!' cried Julie. 'I know what was the matter with me! I was homesick,' " p. 147.

Illustration for A. Donnell, "Father 'n Mothertown," *Farmer's Wife,* December 1917.

161a. Proof.

161b. " 'There's some kind of a big building out there if anybody wants to make a try for it,' " p. 151.

Illustration for Helen Bennett, "Mrs. Mayhew on the Board," *Farmer's Wife,* January 1918.

162a. Proof.

162b. " 'Before you judge, please read these letters,' she concluded," p. 174.

Illustrations for Alice Councilman, "Hail to Our Farm," *Farmer's Wife,* March 1918.

163a. Proof.

163b. P. 236.

164a. Proof.

164b. P. 236.

Illustration for L. D. Sterns, "Her Day," *Farmer's Wife,* May 1918.

165a. Proof.

165b. "She called on an old school friend and chatted until she felt like a girl again," p. 287.

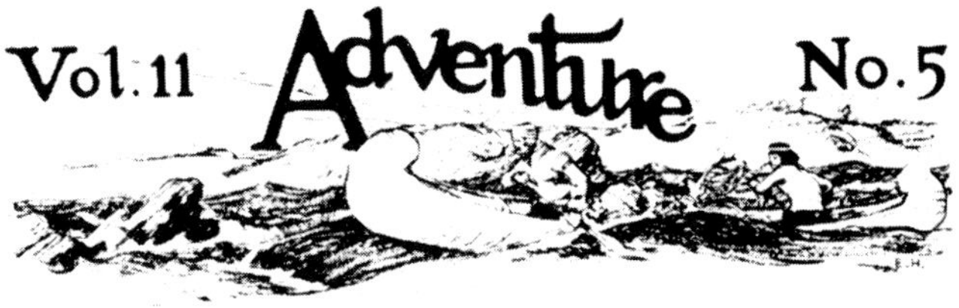

167a

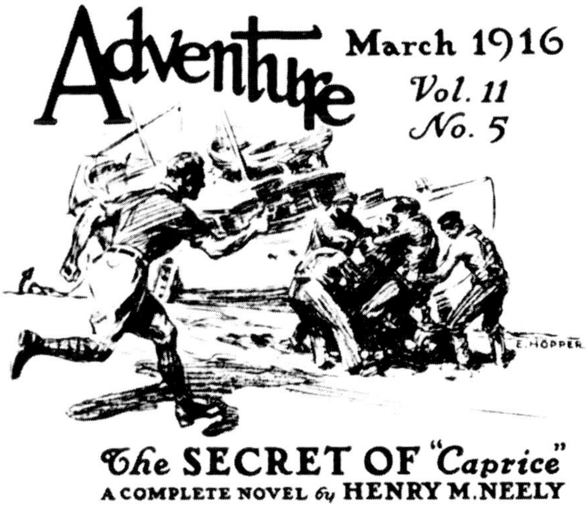

168a

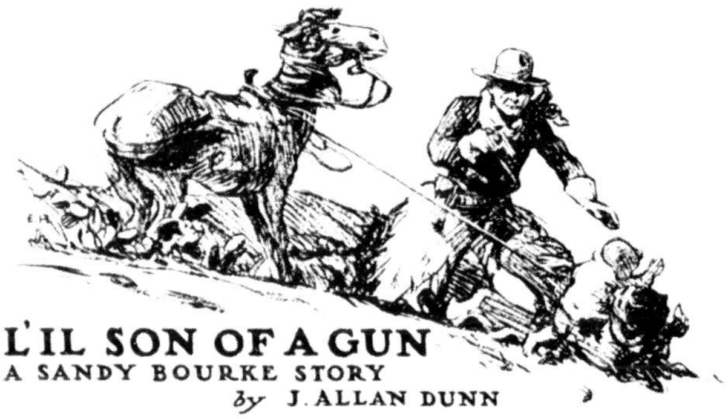

170b

Illustration for Dorothy Donnell Calhoun, "In a Crooked Little House," *Farmer's Wife,* March 1919.

166. " 'He did it just on purpose to frighten me,' she thought. 'I suppose he expects me to fall into his arms and beg him to forgive me. Well, I'm not going to, that's all,' " p. 228.

Illustrations for *Adventure,* 11 (March 1916).

167a. Proof.

167b. Illustration for heading of Contents, p. 1.

168a. Proof.

168b. Illustration for Henry M. Neely, "The Secret of 'Caprice,' " p. 3.

169a. Proof.

169b. Illustration for Edward Pilsworth, "The Pillar of Flame," p. 99.

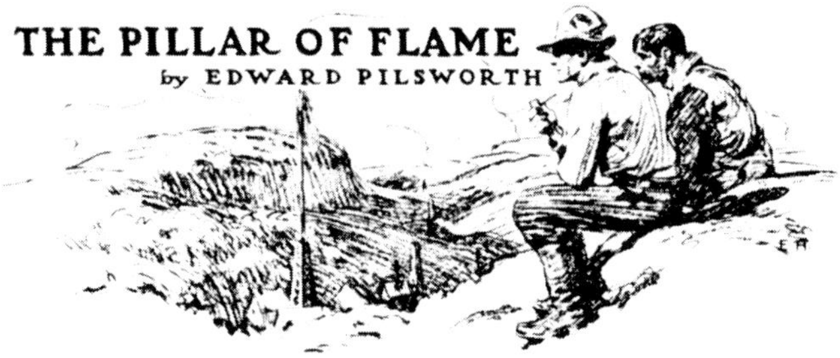

169b

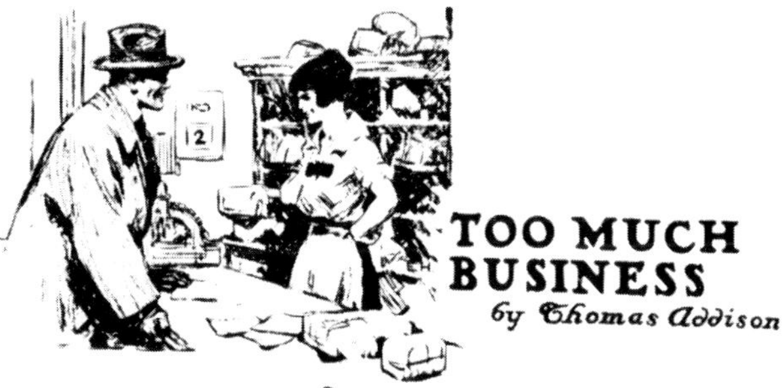

171a

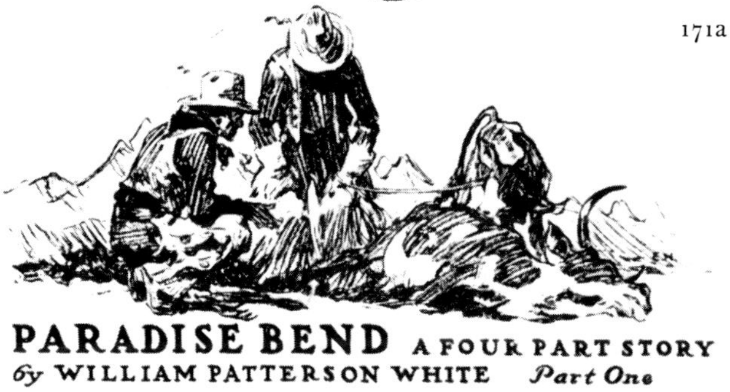

172a

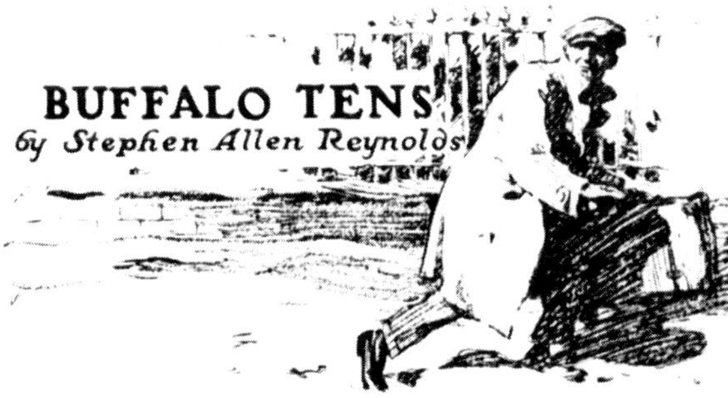

173a

170a. Proof.

170b. Illustration for J. Allan Dunn, "L'il Son of a Gun," p. 108.

171a. Proof.

171b. Illustration for Thomas Addison, "Too Much Business," p. 133.

172a. Proof.

172b. Illustration for William Patterson White, "Paradise Bend," part 1, p. 133.

173a. Proof.

173b. Illustration for Stephen Allen Reynolds, "Buffalo Tens," p. 164.

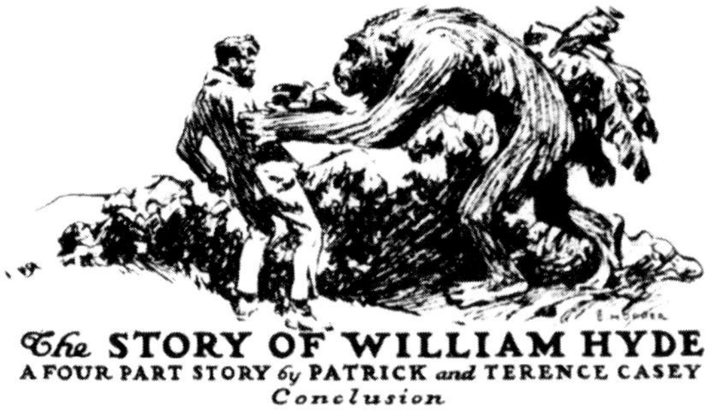

174a

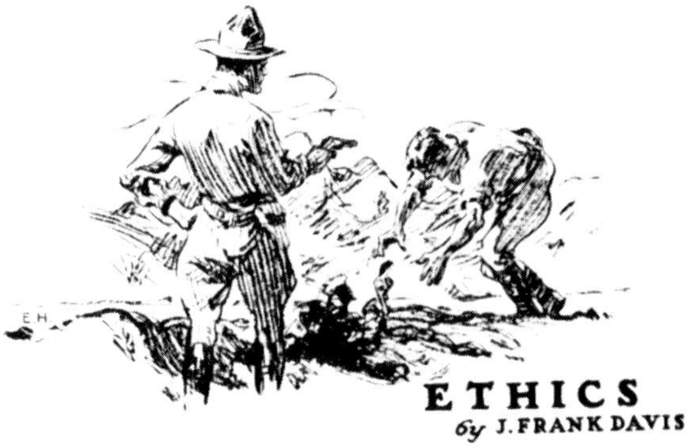

175a

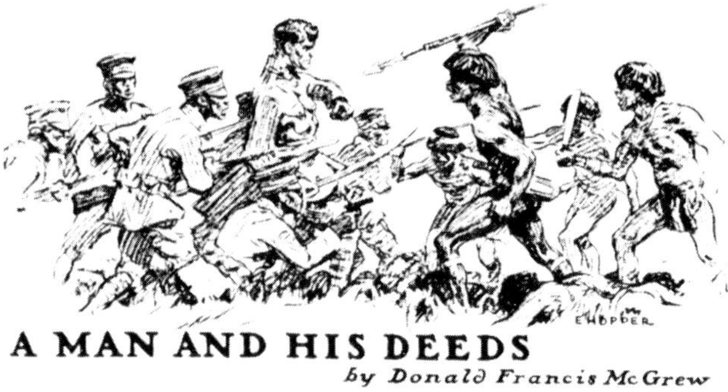

176a

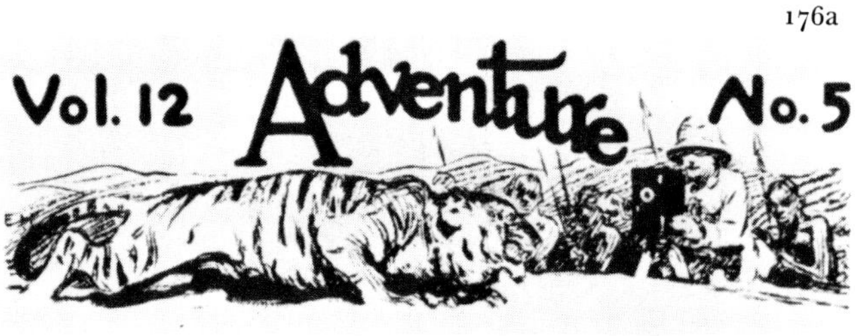

177a

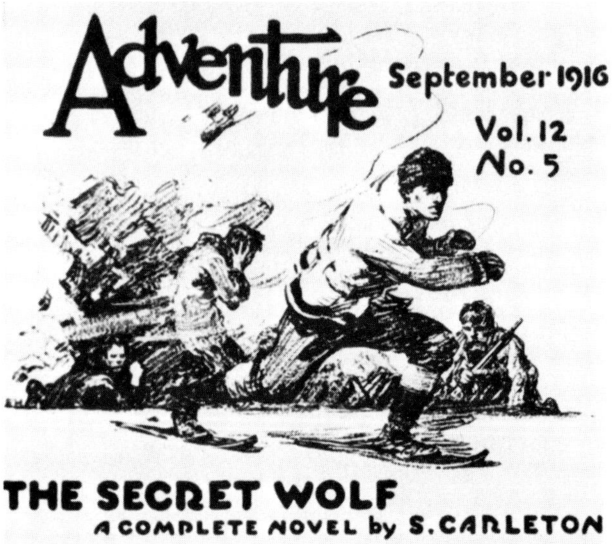

178a

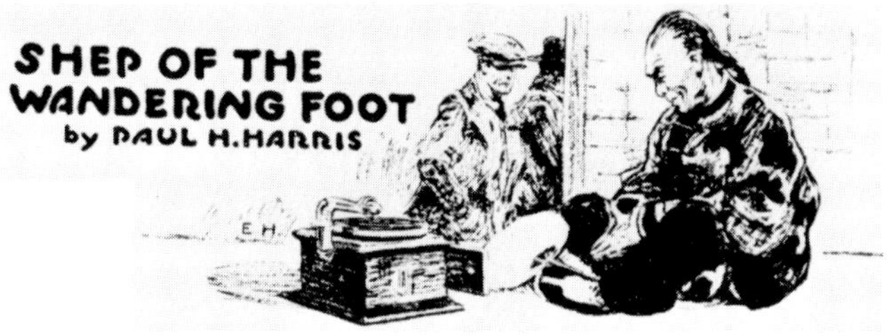

179a

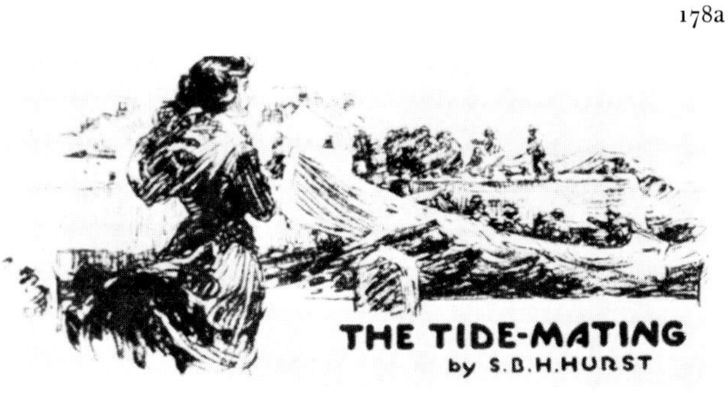

180a

174a. Proof.

174b. Illustration for Patrick and Terence Casey, "The Story of William Hyde," part 4, p. 170.

175a. Proof.

175b. Illustration for J. Frank Davis, "Ethics," p. 180.

176a. Proof.

176b. Illustration for Donald Francis McGrew, "A Man and His Deeds," p. 206.

Illustrations for *Adventure,* 12 (September 1916).

177a. Proof.

177b. Illustration for heading of Contents, p. 1.

178a. Proof.

178b. Illustration for S. Carleton, "The Secret Wolf," p. 3.

179a. Proof.

179b. Illustration for Paul H. Harris, "Shep of the Wandering Foot," p. 86.

180a. Proof.

180b. Illustration for S. B. H. Hurst, "The Tide-Mating," p. 94.

181a. Proof.

181b. Illustration for W. C. Tuttle, "A Bull Movement in Yellow Horse," p. 101.

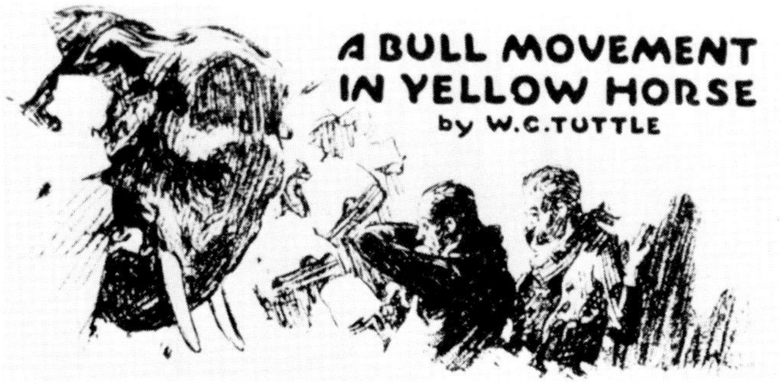

181a

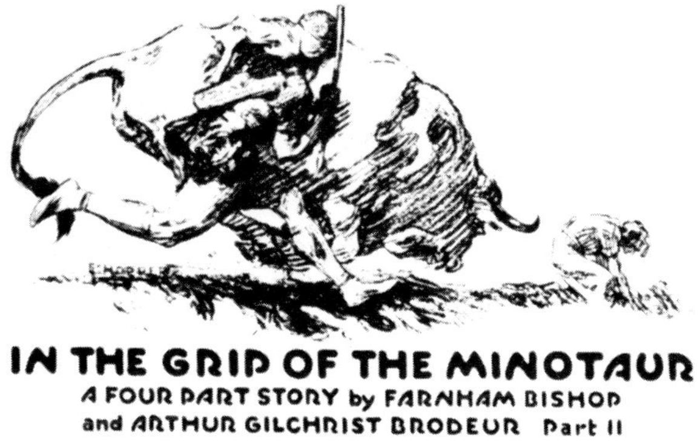

183a

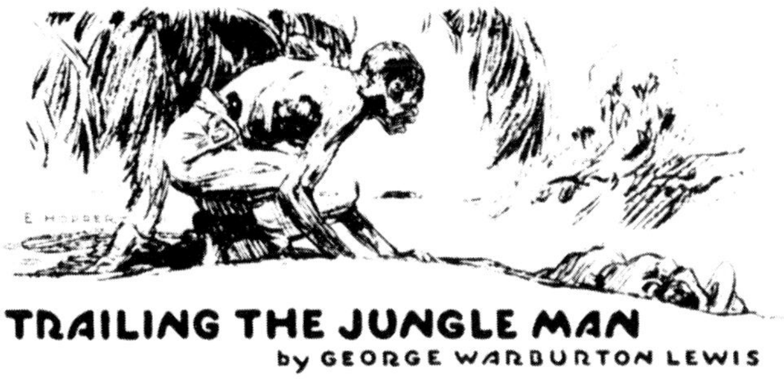

182a

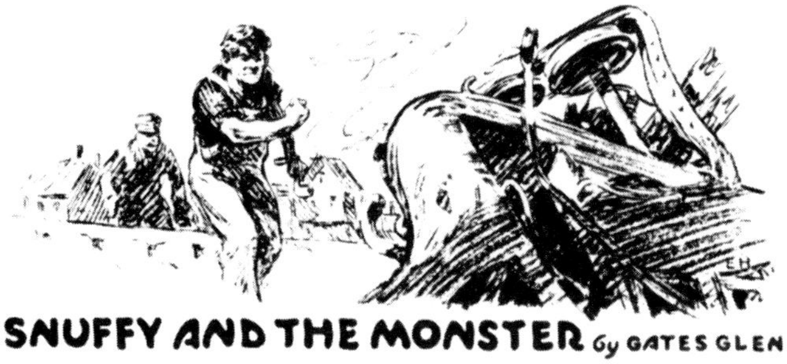

184a

182a. Proof.

182b. Illustration for George Warburton Lewis, "Trailing the Jungle Man," p. 112.

183a. Proof.

183b. Illustration for Farnham Bishop and Arthur Gilchrist Brodeur, "In the Grip of the Minotaur," part 2, p. 123.

184a. Proof.

184b. Illustration for Gates Glen, "Snuffy and the Monster," p. 148.

185a. Proof.

185b. Illustration for Douglas S. Watson, "The Unmudding of the Empire," p. 154.

186a. Proof.

186b. Illustration for Kathrene and Robert Pinkerton, "Guiding Clementine," p. 168.

187a. Proof.

187b. Illustration for Leland Ward Peck, "Fifty-Fifty," p. 180.

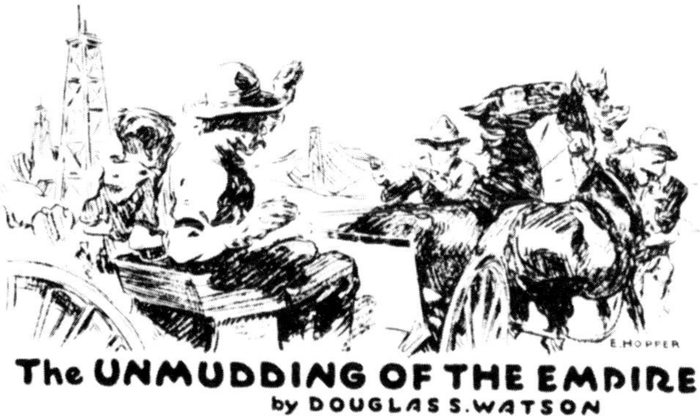

185a

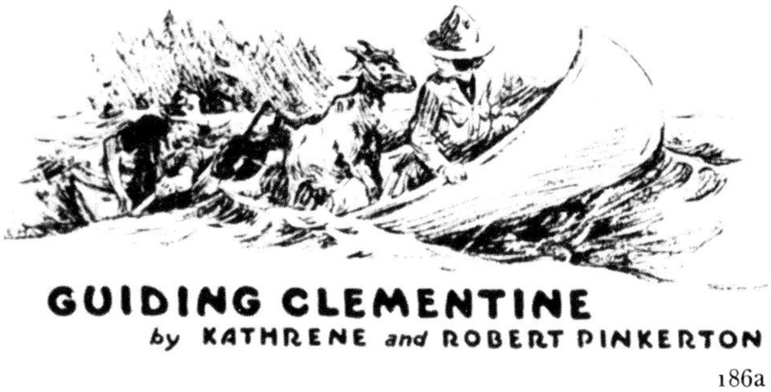

186a

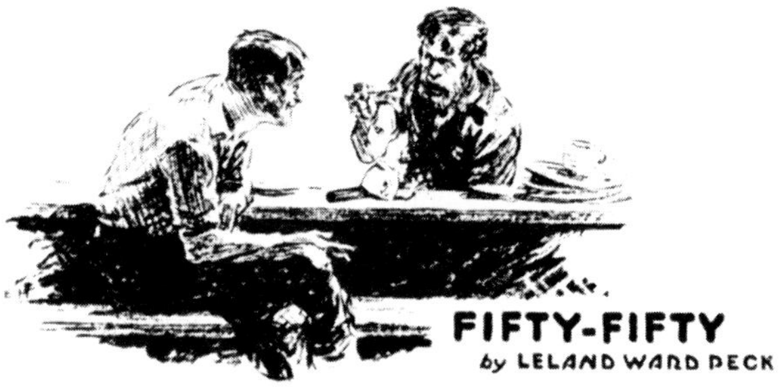

187a

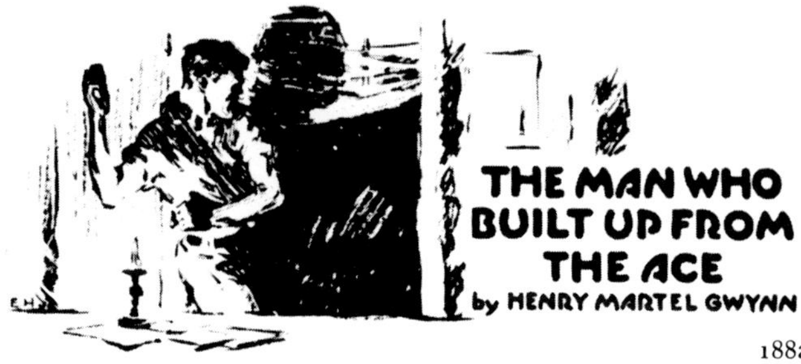

188a

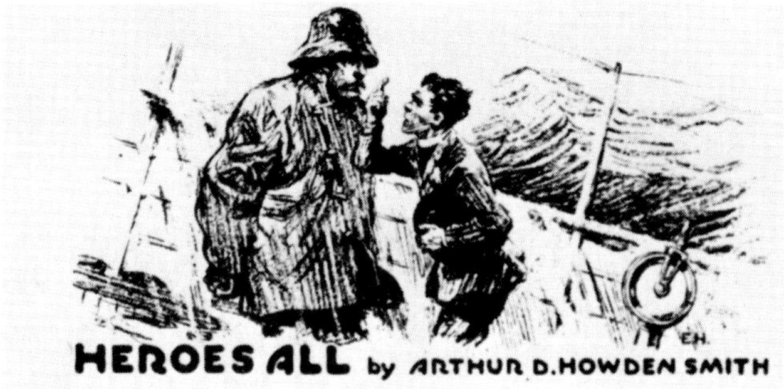

189a

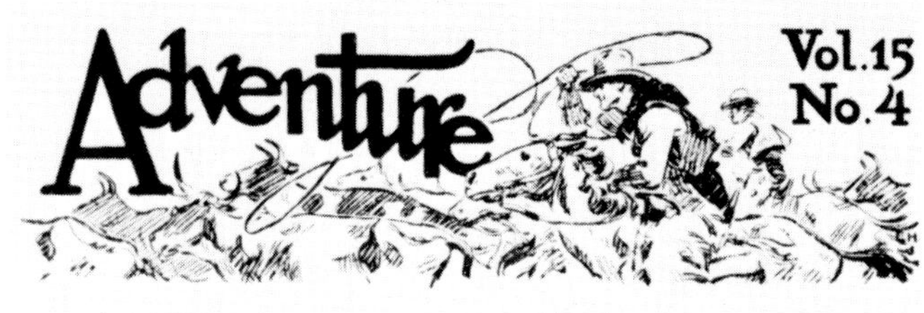

190a

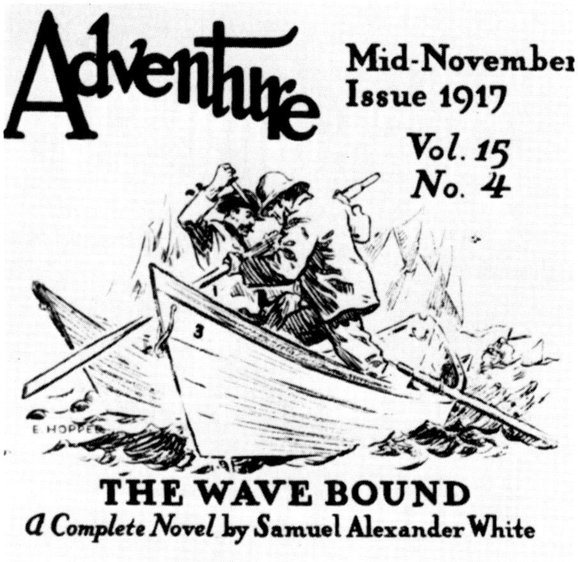

191a

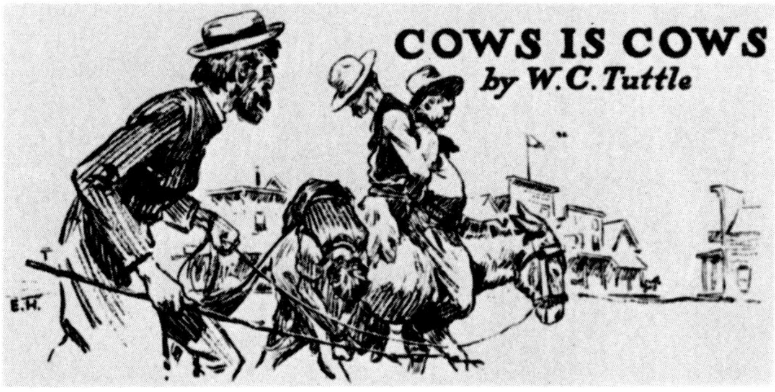

192a

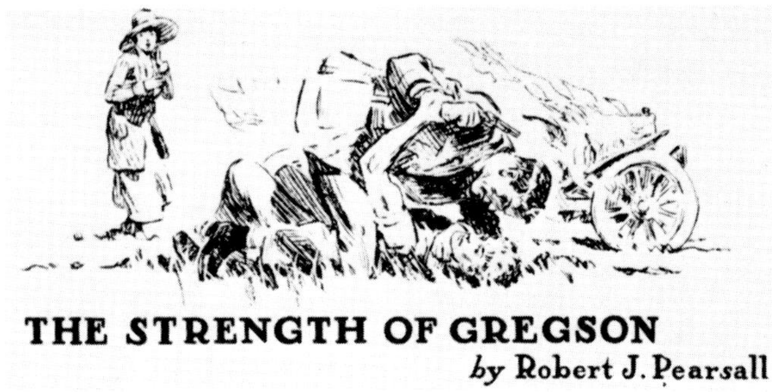

193a

188a. Proof.

188b. Illustration for Henry Martel Gwynn, "The Man Who Built Up from the Ace," p. 186.

189a. Proof.

189b. Illustration for Arthur D. Howden Smith, "Heroes All," p. 198.

Illustrations for *Adventure,* 15 (November 18, 1917).

190a. Proof.

190b. Illustration for heading of Contents, p. 1.

191a. Proof.

191b. Illustration for Samuel Alexander White, "The Wave Bound," p. 3.

192a. Proof.

192b. Illustration for W. C. Tuttle, "Cows Is Cows," p. 56.

193a. Proof.

193b. Illustration for Robert J. Pearsall, "The Strength of Gregson," p. 67.

194a. Proof.

194b. Illustration for Roy P. Churchill, "The High String," p. 73.

195a. Proof.

195b. Illustration for Hugh Pendexter, "A Bearer of Belts," p. 73.

196a. Proof.

196b. Illustration for Talbot Mundy, "Hira Singh's Tale," part 3, p. 79.

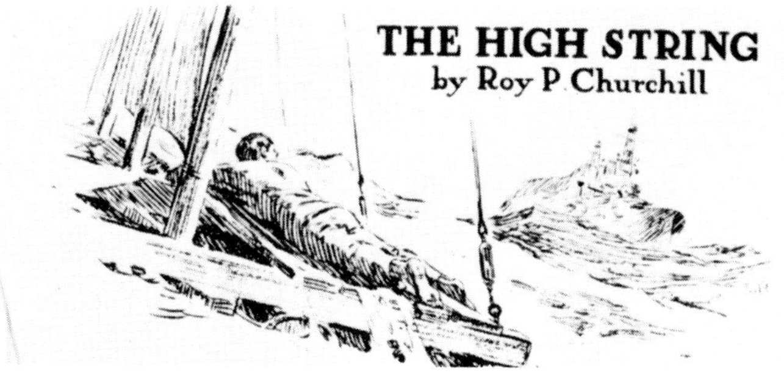

194a

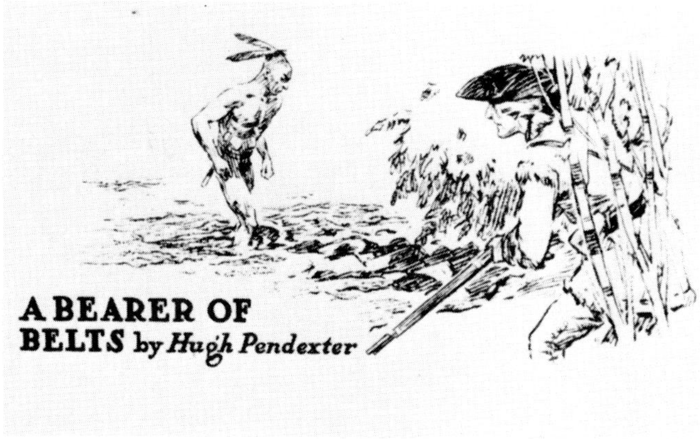

195a

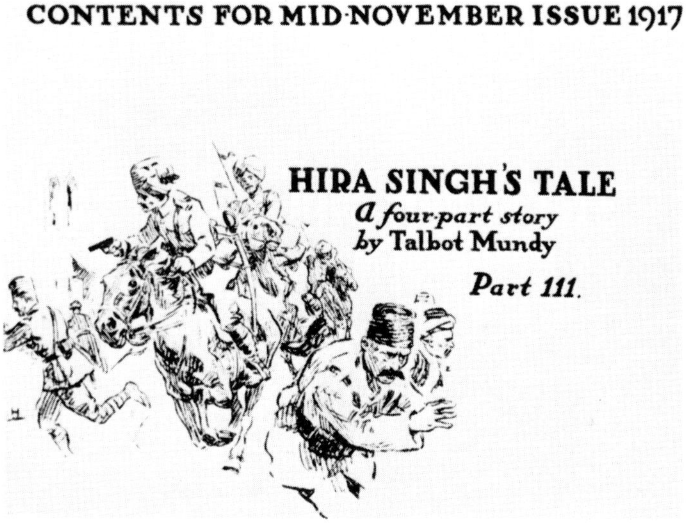

196a

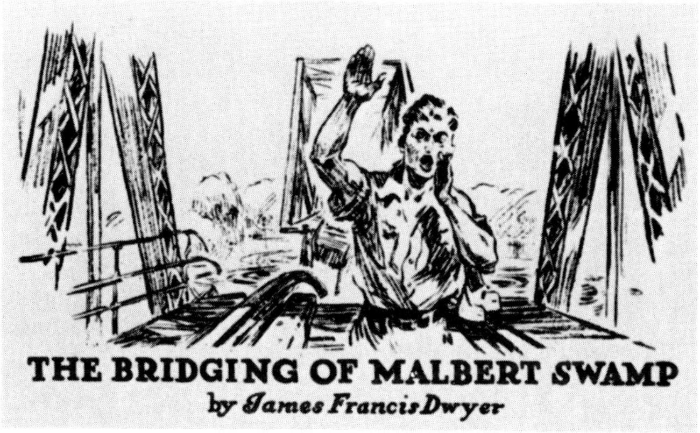

197a

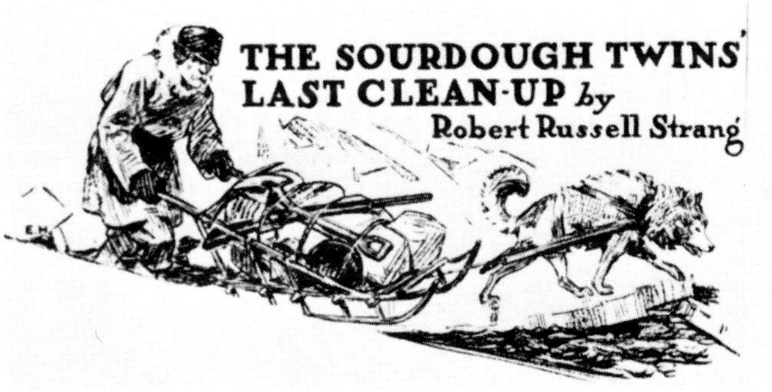

198a

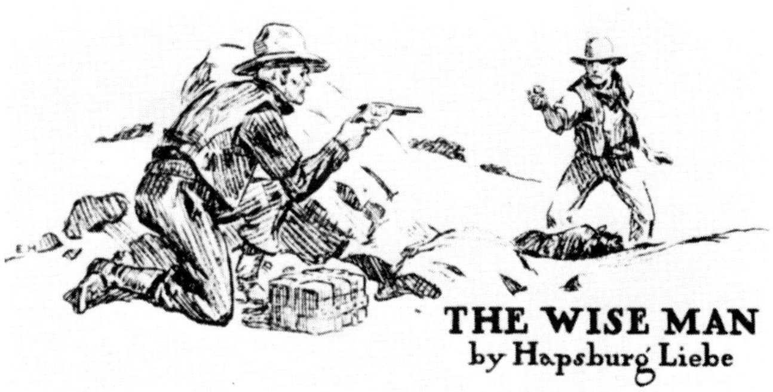

199a

197a. Proof.

197b. Illustration for James Francis Dwyer, "The Bridging of Malbert Swamp," p. 101.

198a. Proof.

198b. Illustration for Robert Russell Strang, "The Sourdough Twins' Last Clean-Up," p. 109.

199a. Proof.

199b. Illustration for Hapsburg Liebe, "The Wise Man," p. 116.

200a. Proof.

200b. Illustration for Vance Palmer, "The King of Carados," p. 123.

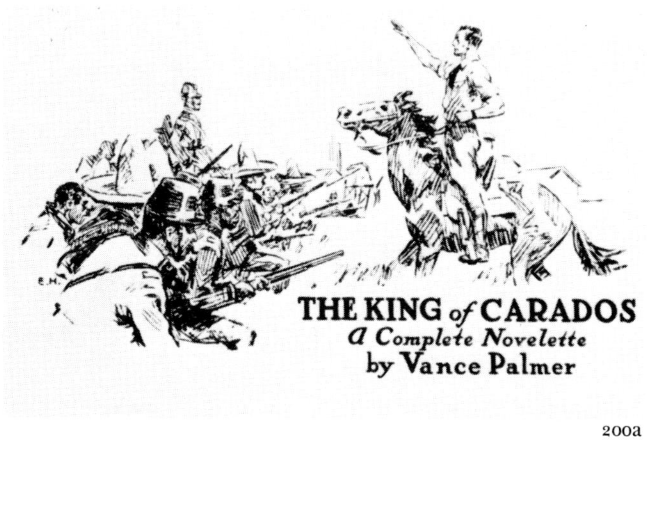

200a

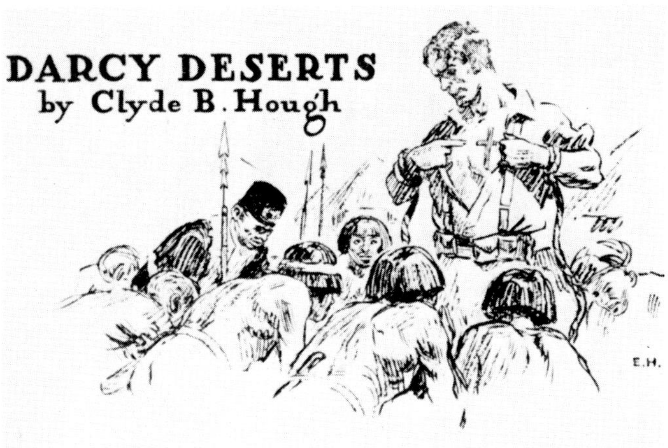

201a

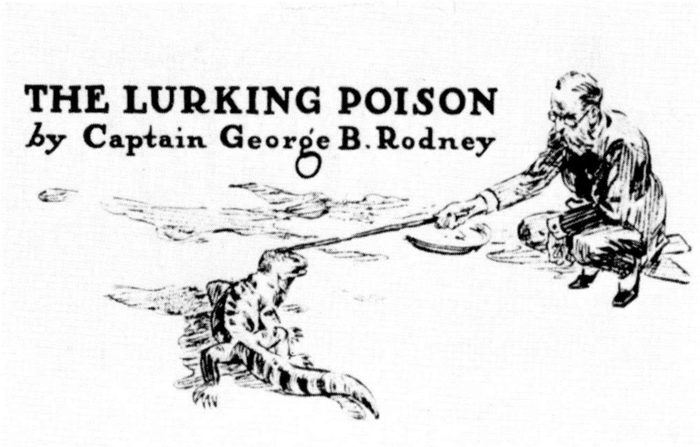

202a

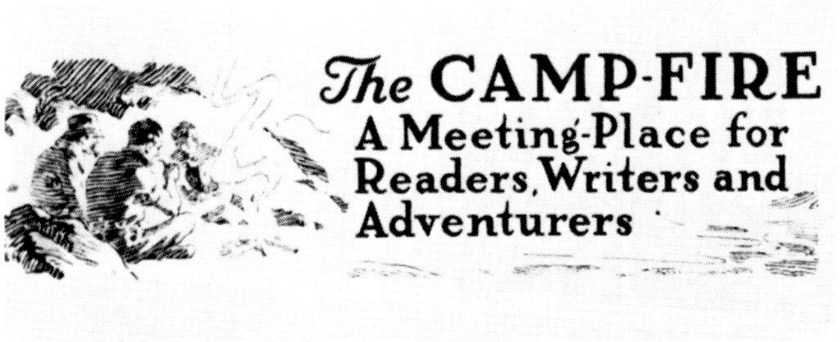

203a

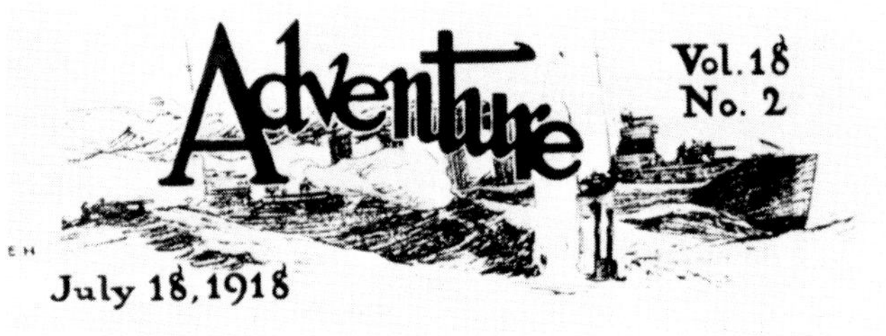

204a

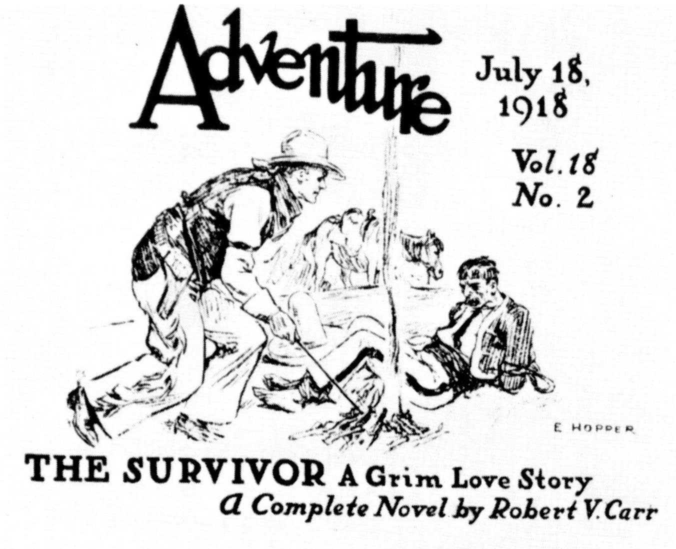

205a

201a. Proof.

201b. Illustration for Clyde B. Hough, "Darcy Derserts," p. 157.

202a. Proof.

202b. Illustration for Captain George B. Rodney, "The Lurking Poison," p. 161.

203a. Proof.

203b. Illustration for "The Camp-Fire: A Meeting-Place for Readers, Writers and Adventurers," p. 183.

Illustrations for *Adventure,* 18 (July 18, 1918).

204a. Proof.

204b. Illustration for heading of Contents, p. 1.

205a. Proof.

205b. Illustration for Robert V. Carr, "The Survivor: A Grim Love Story," p. 3.

206a. Proof.

206b. Illustration for Harold Titus, "A Fish Story About Love," p. 76.

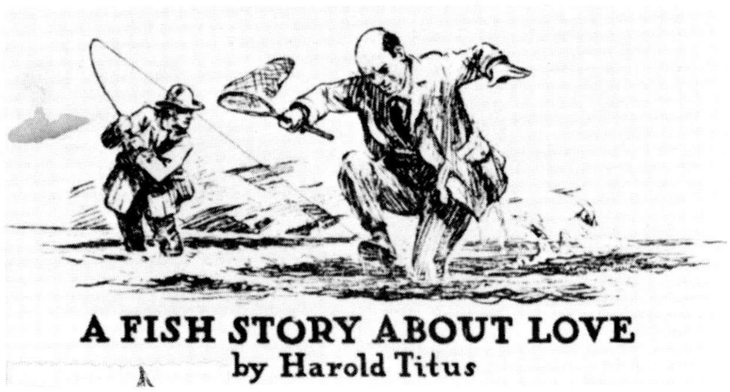

206a

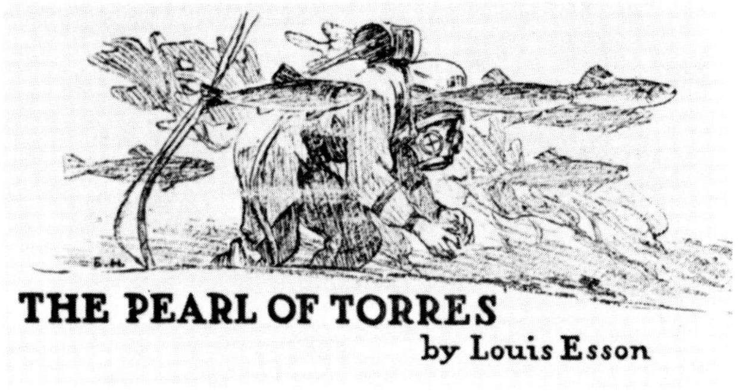

207a

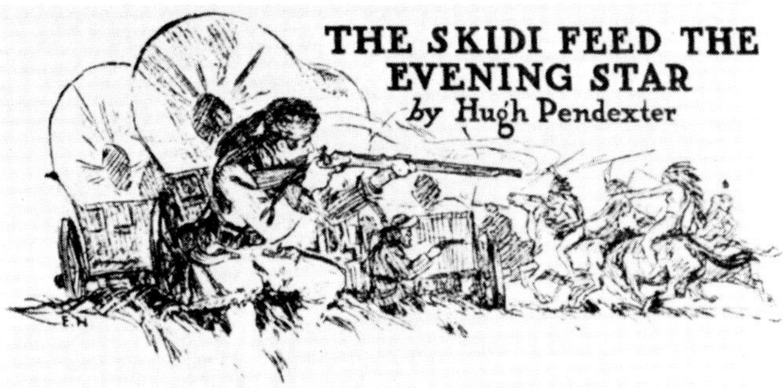

208a

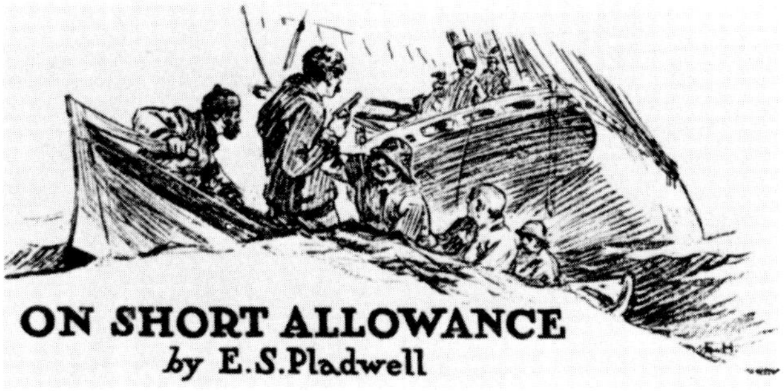

209a

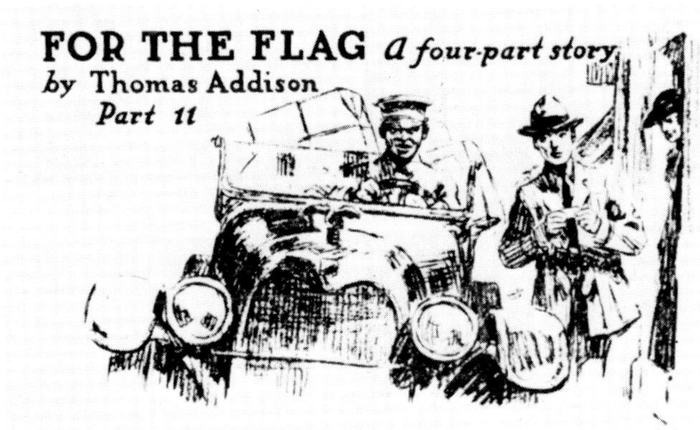

210a

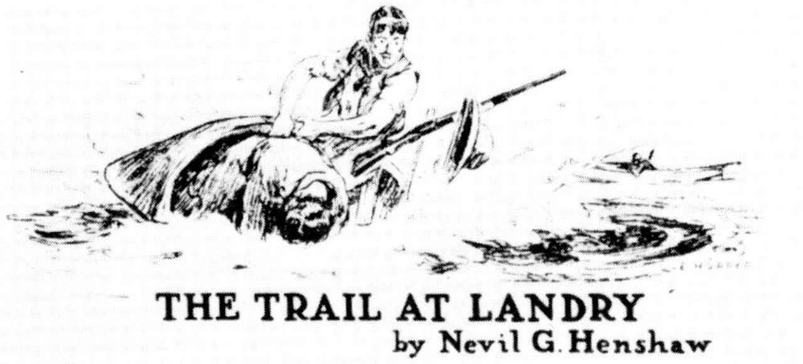

211a

207a. Proof.

207b. Illustration for Louis Esson, "The Pearl of Torres," p. 85.

208a. Proof.

208b. Illustration for Hugh Pendexter, "The Skidi Feed the Evening Star," p. 93.

209a. Proof.

209b. Illustration for E. S. Pladwell, "On Short Allowance," p. 104.

210a. Proof.

210b. Illustration for Thomas Addison, "For the Flag," part 2, p. 115.

211a. Proof.

211b. Illustration for Nevil G. Henshaw, "The Trail at Landry," p. 146.

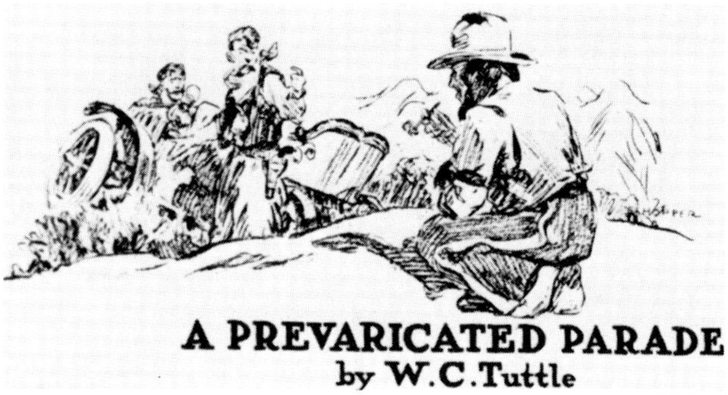

212a

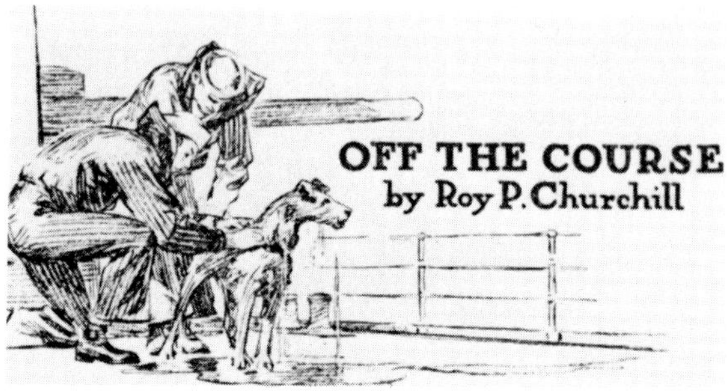

213a

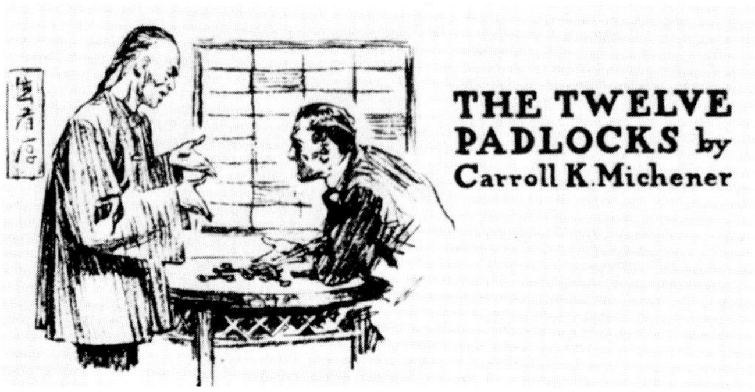

214a

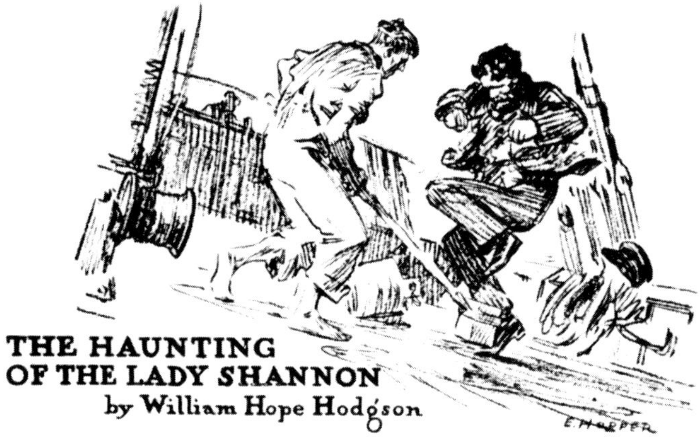

215

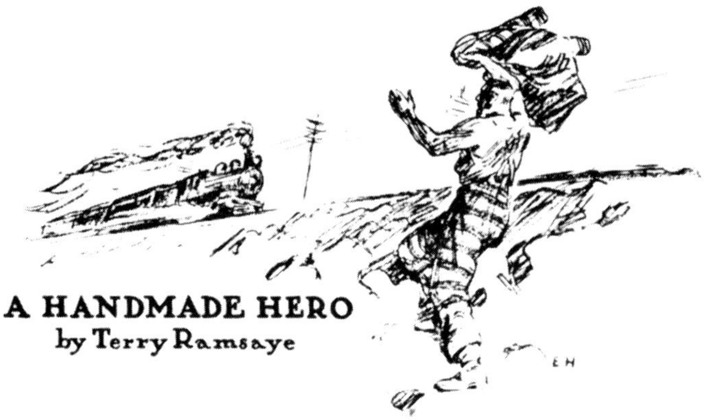

216

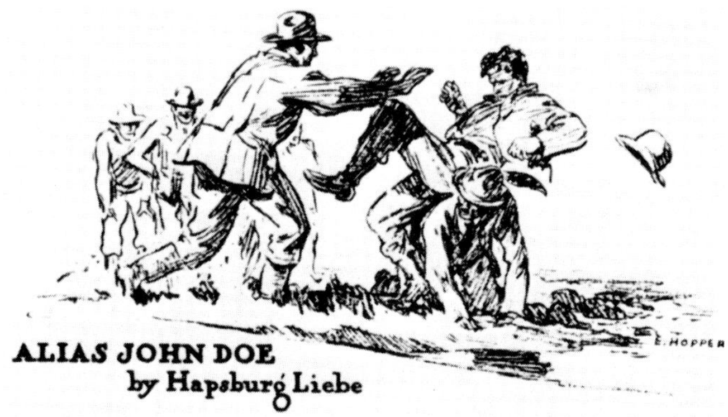

217

212a. Proof.

212b. Illustration for W. C. Tuttle, "A Prevaricated Parade," p. 154.

213a. Proof.

213b. Illustration for Roy P. Churchill, "Off the Course," p. 167.

214a. Proof.

214b. Illustration for Carroll K. Michener, "The Twelve Padlocks," p. 176.

215. Proof of illustration for William Hope Hodgson, "The Haunting of the Lady Shannon," probably *Adventure,* date unknown.

216. Proof of illustration for Terry Ramsaye, "A Handmade Hero," probably *Adventure,* date unknown.

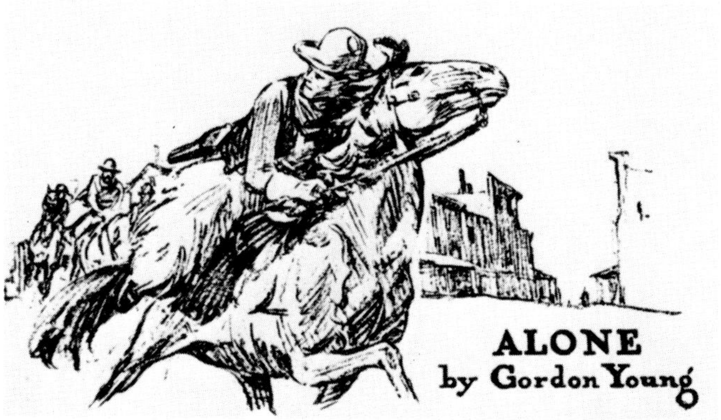

218

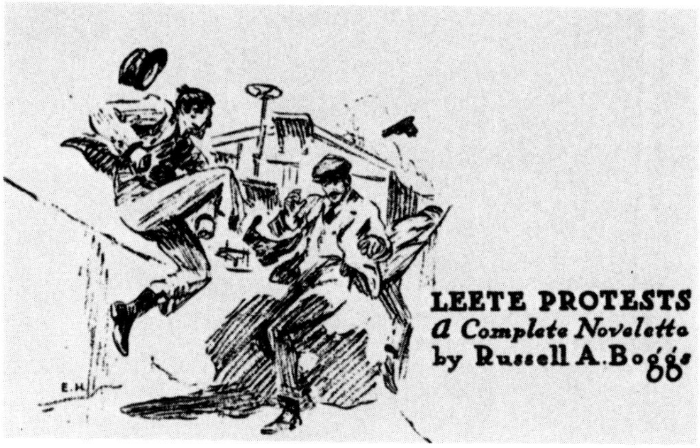

219

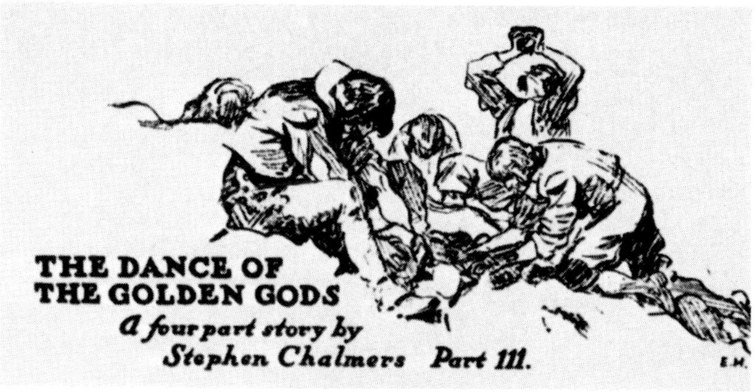

220

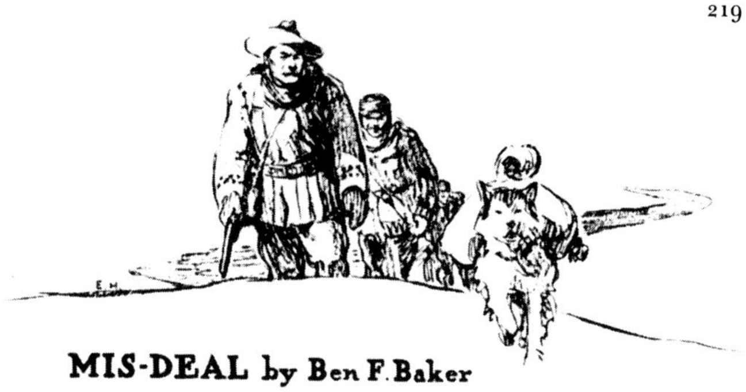

221

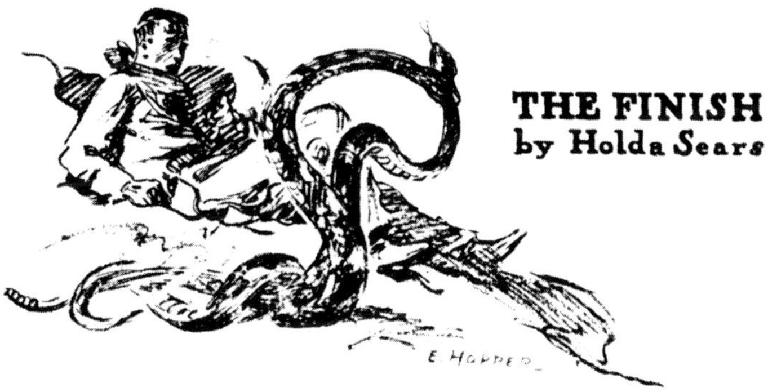

222

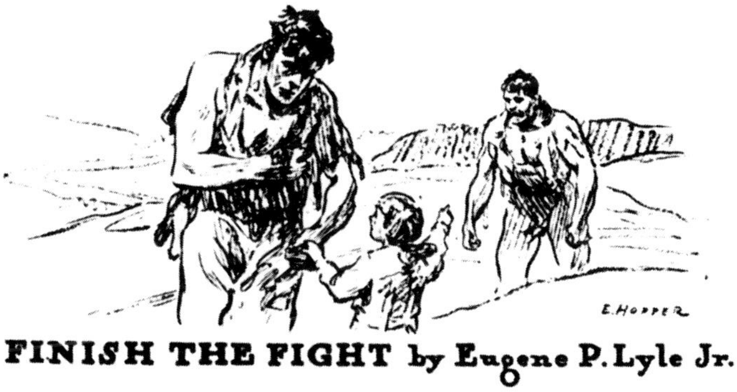

223

217. Proof of illustration for Hapsburg Liebe, "Alias John Doe," probably *Adventure,* date unknown.

218. Proof of illustration for Gordon Young, "Alone," probably *Adventure,* date unknown.

219. Proof of illustration for Russell A. Boggs, "Leete Protests," probably *Adventure,* date unknown.

220. Proof of illustration for Stephen Chalmers, "The Dance of the Golden Gods," part 3, probably *Adventure,* date unknown.

221. Proof of illustration for Ben F. Baker, "Mis-Deal," probably *Adventure,* date unknown.

222. Proof of illustration for Holda Sears, "The Finish," probably *Adventure,* date unknown.

223. Proof of illustration for Eugene P. Lyle, Jr., "Finish the Fight," probably *Adventure,* date unknown.

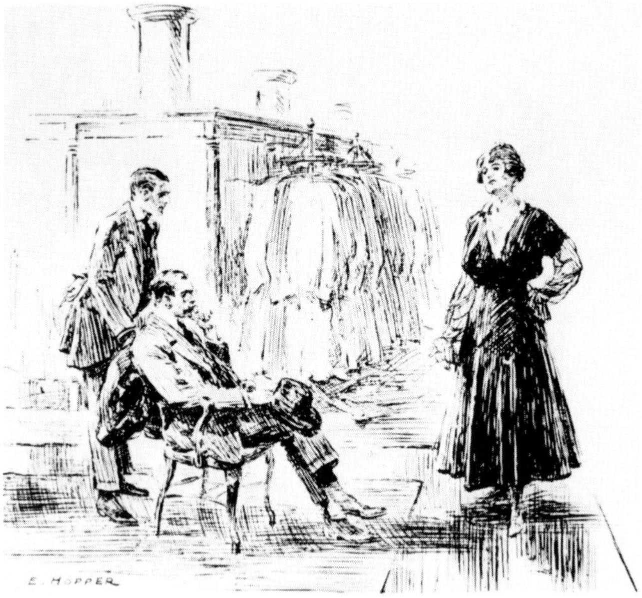

224a

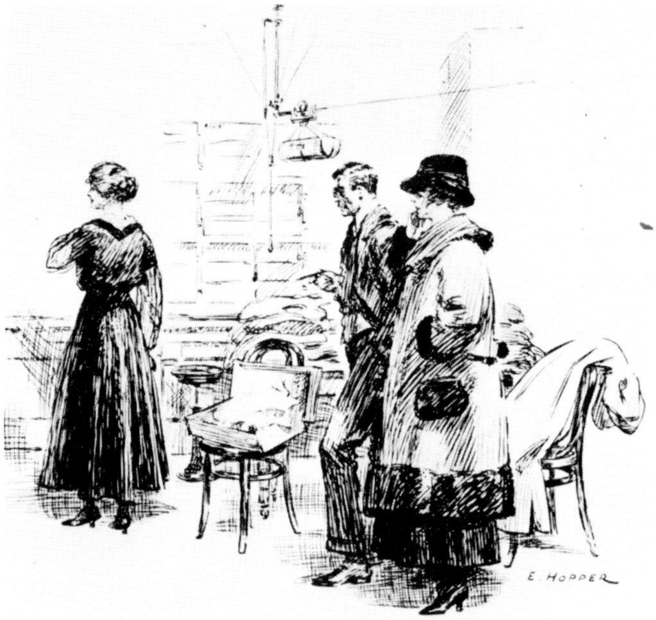

225a

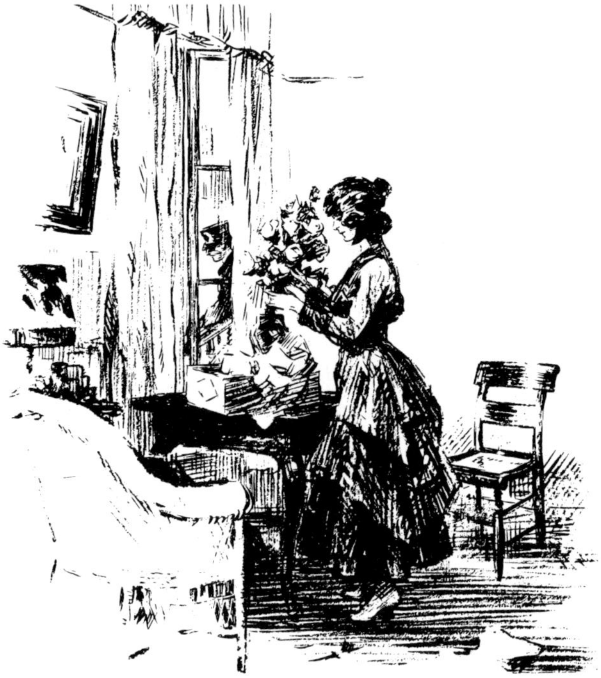

227

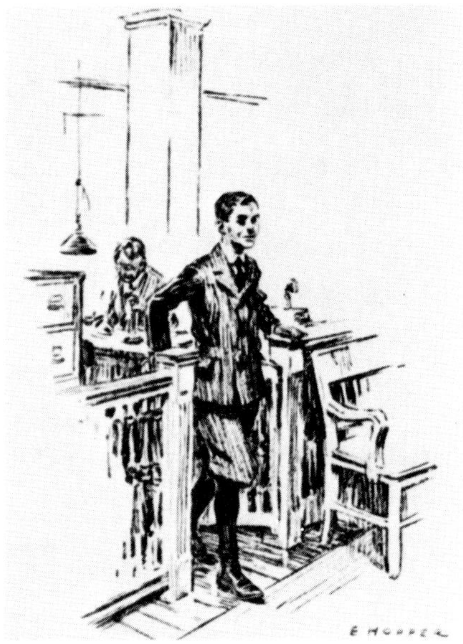

226

Illustrations for "How Style Rides the Express," *Wells Fargo Messenger,* 4 (April 1916).

224a. Proof.

224b. "In New York—the Paris of America—the Cosmopolis merchant inspects the latest styles in women's suits and gowns," p. 117.

225a. Proof.

225b. "Out in Cosmopolis, the customer is delighted with her gown, which has just arrived by express from New York," p. 118.

Illustration for H. E. Cartwright, "The Office Boy," *Wells Fargo Messenger,* 4 (June 1916).

226. "The office boy is a junior clerk," p. 155.

Illustrations for Cromwell Childe, "Flowers by Express," *Wells Fargo Messenger,* 5 (January 1917).

227. "When Love His message would impress / He sends her flowers by express," p. 73.

228. "Flowers handled the Fargo Way / Fresh and bright on New Year's Day," p. 74.

229. "The Wells Fargo 'Call Card'—An Automatic Signal." Commercial illustration for Wells Fargo & Co. Express, *Wells Fargo Messenger,* 5 (February 1917), inside front cover.

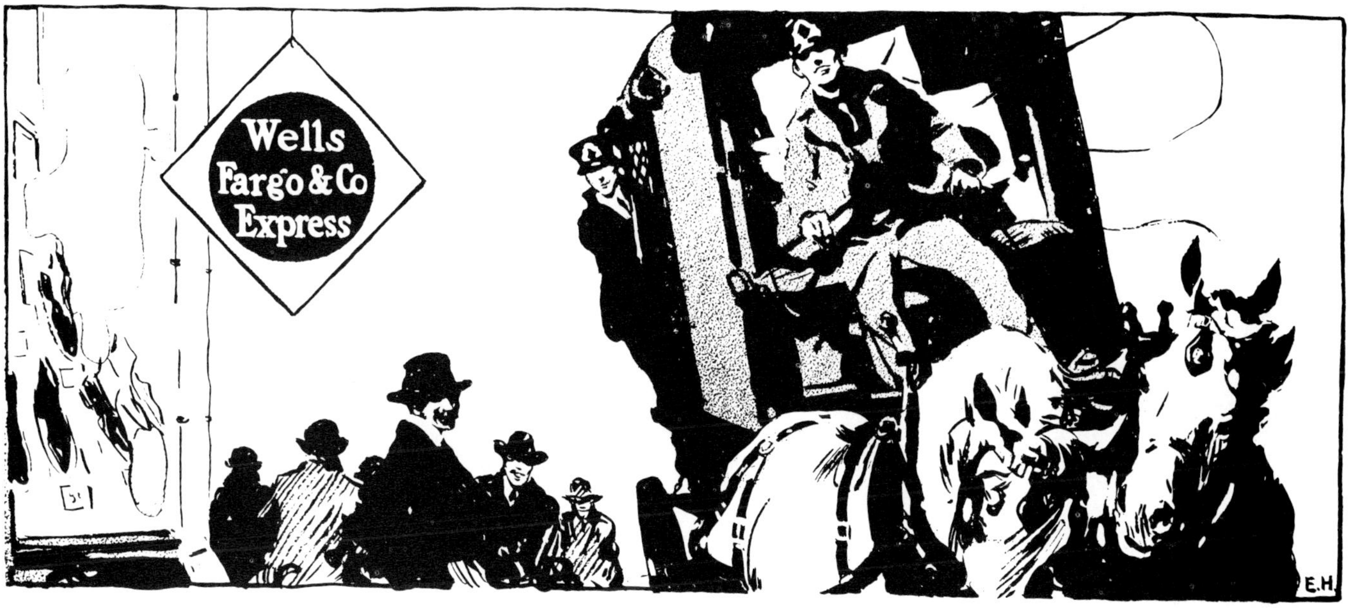

229

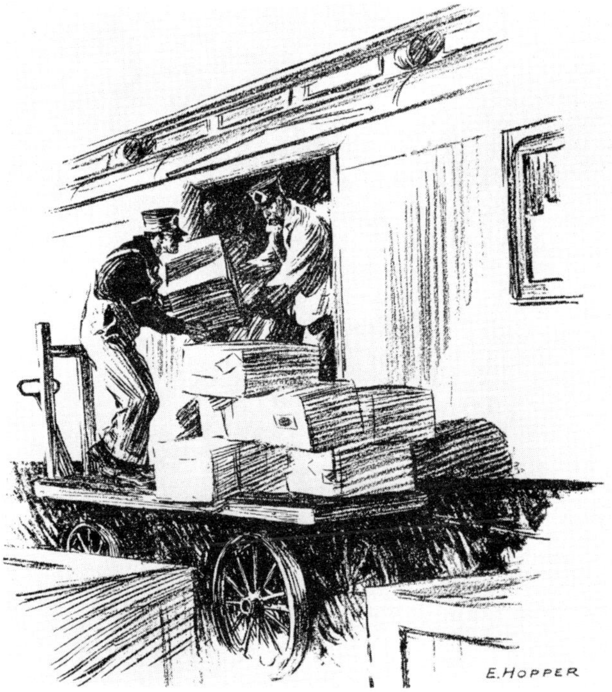

228

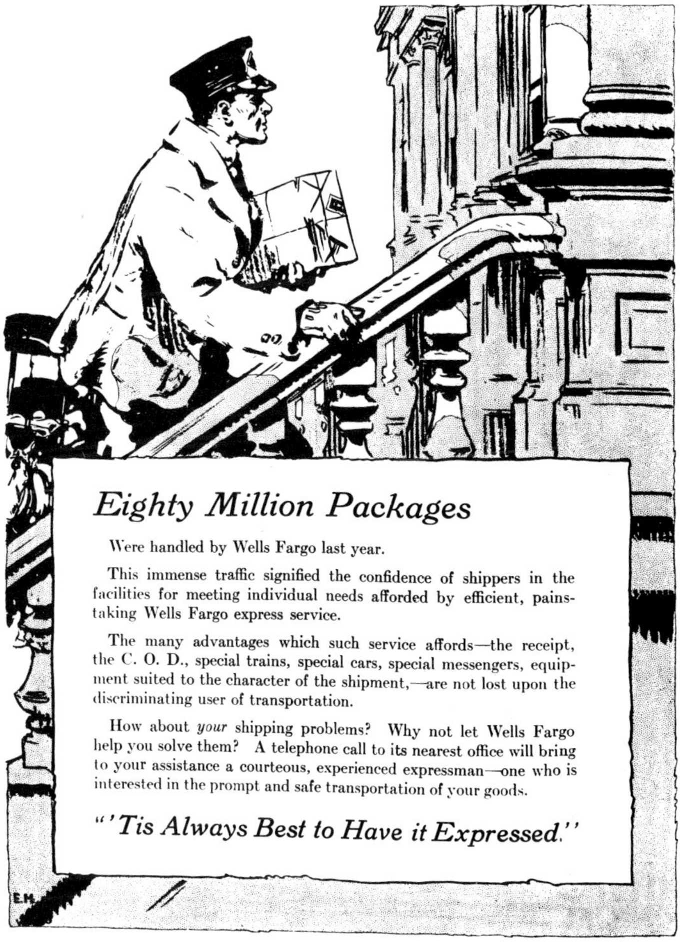

231

230a. Red progressive color proof from the Beck Engraving Co., 221 Fourth Ave., New York.

230b. Black progressive color proof.

230c. Final progressive color proof.

230d. Cover, *Wells Fargo Messenger,* 5 (March 1917). (Color plate, p. 67.)

231. "'Tis Always Best to Have it Expressed." Commercial illustration for Wells Fargo & Co. Express, *Wells Fargo Messenger,* 5 (March 1917), inside front cover.

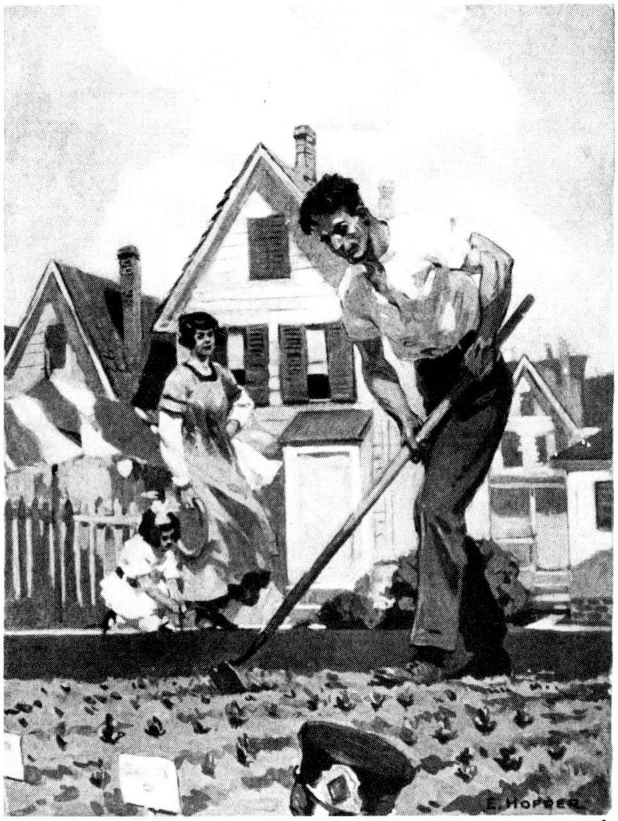

232b

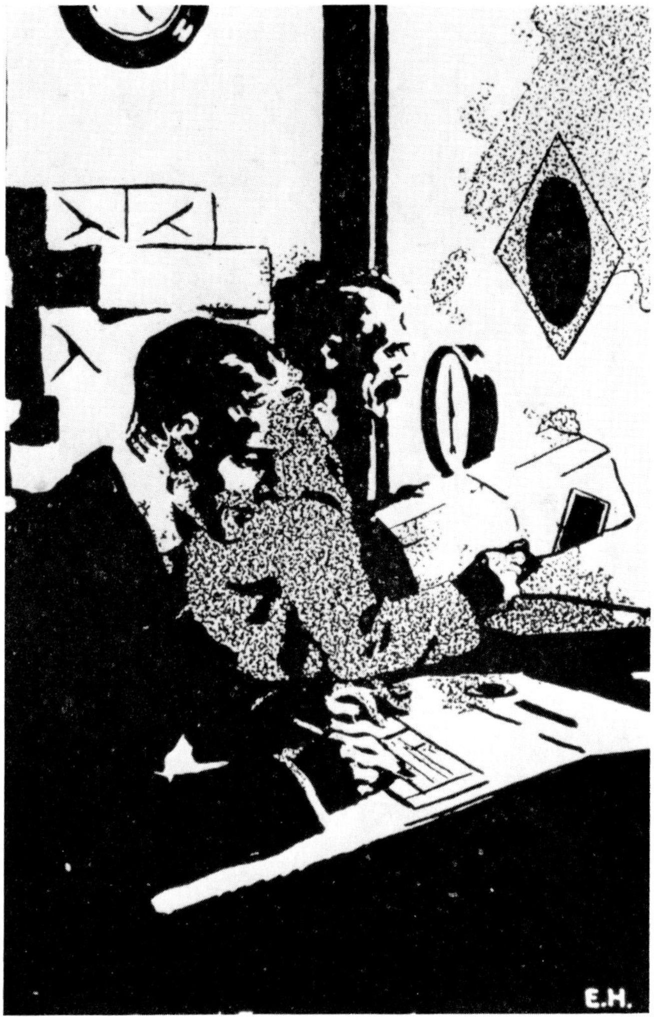

232a

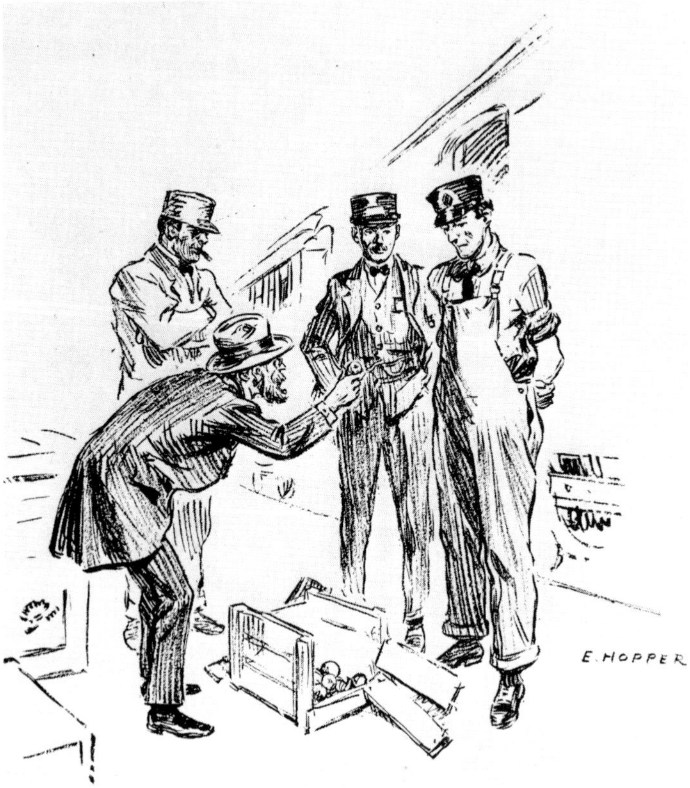

232a. "Suggestions Are Always In Order." Commercial illustration for Wells Fargo & Co., *Wells Fargo Messenger,* 5 (June 1917), inside back cover.

232b. "The Wells Fargo Man Does His Bit For Home and Country." Commercial illustration for Wells Fargo & Co., *Wells Fargo Messenger,* 5 (June 1917), back cover.

233. Cover, *Wells Fargo Messenger,* 6 (July 1917). (Color plate, p. 68.)

Illustration for C. W. Garrison, "Safe, Sure and Speedy Service," *Wells Fargo Messenger,* 6 (September 1917).

234. " 'Won't you save one?' he asks," p. 5.

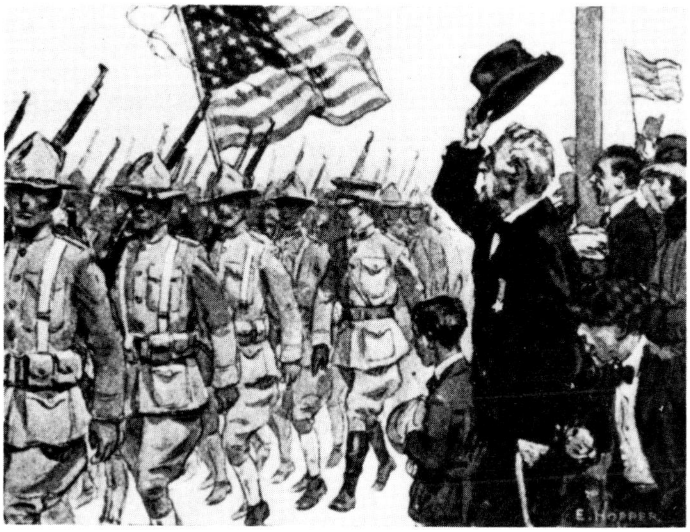

235a

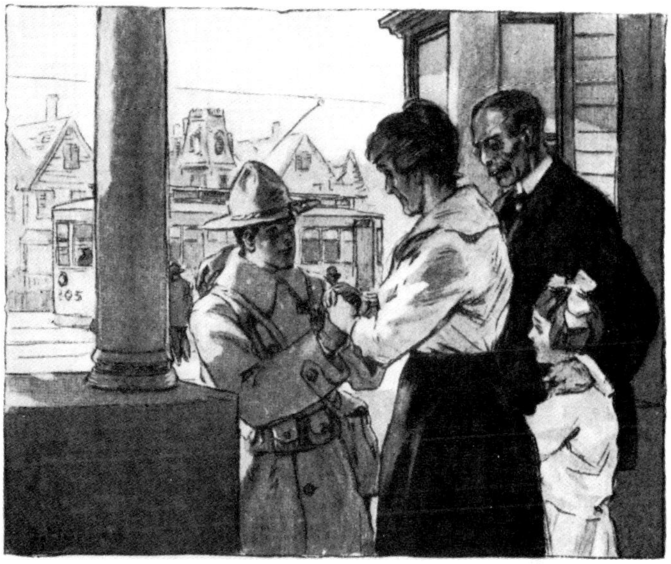

236

Illustration for E. A. Brininstool, "The Spirit of the Past," *Wells Fargo Messenger,* 6 (November 1917).

235a. Proof.

235b. P. 49.

236. Illustration for J. H. Horlock, "Your Boy and Mine," *Wells Fargo Messenger,* 6 (January 1918), p. 85.

237. "The folks back home sent me a Wells Fargo Money Order, the other day—and now I am going to return the compliment!" Commercial illustration for Wells Fargo & Co., *Wells Fargo Messenger,* 6 (January 1918), back cover.

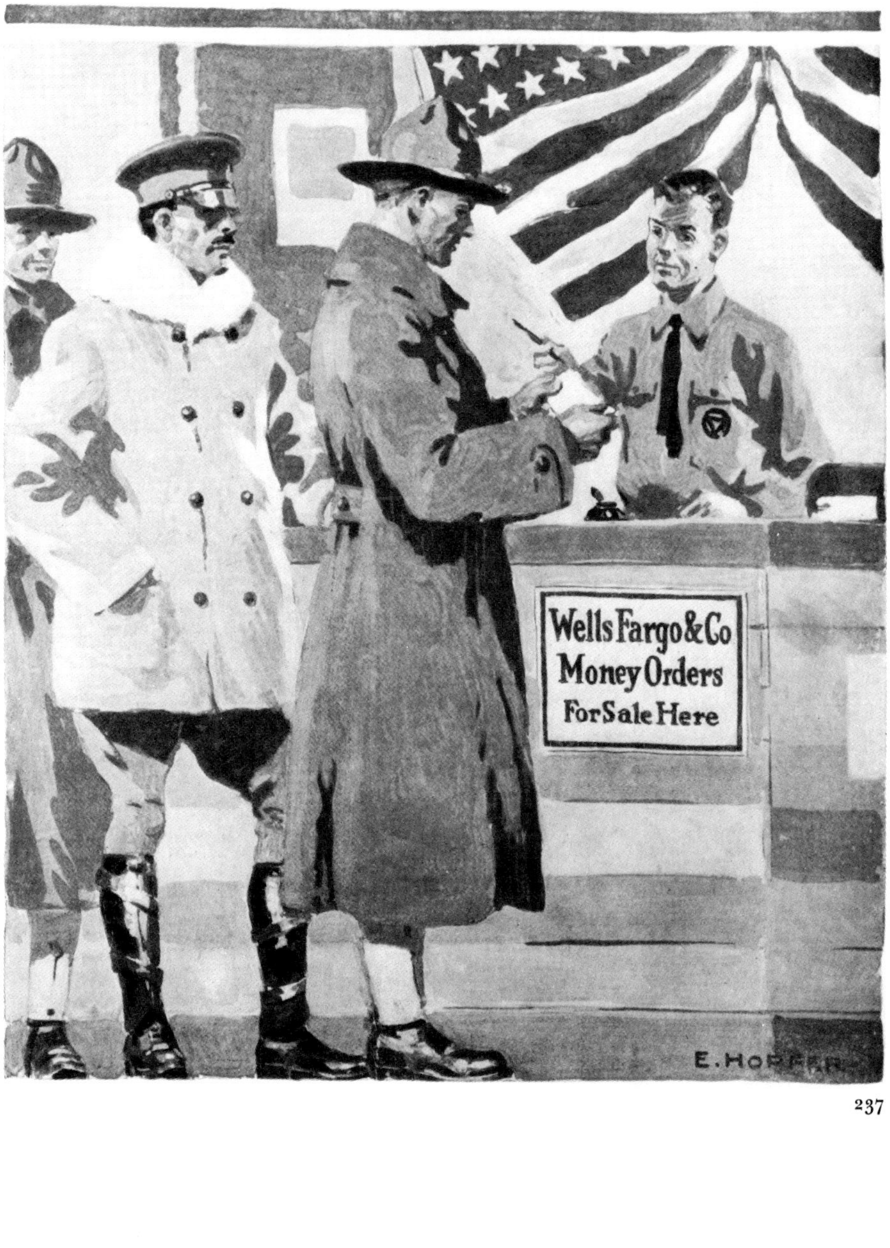

237

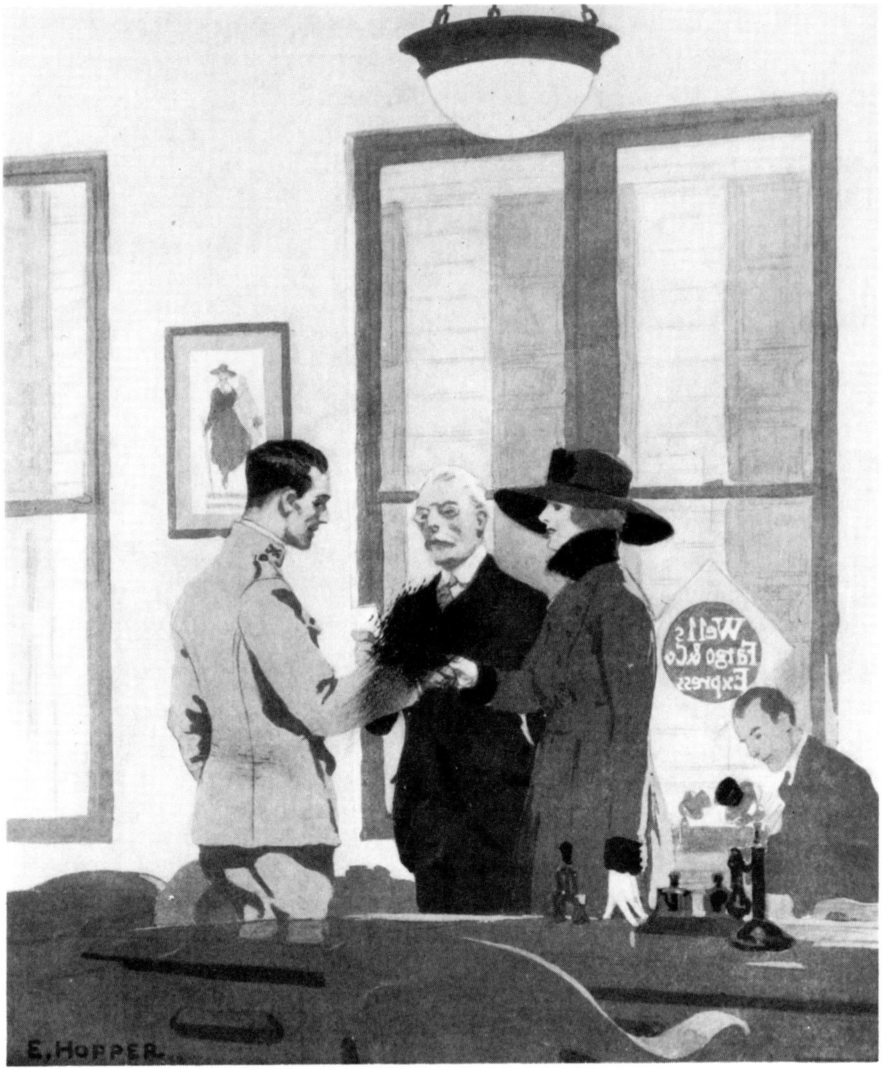

238

243a

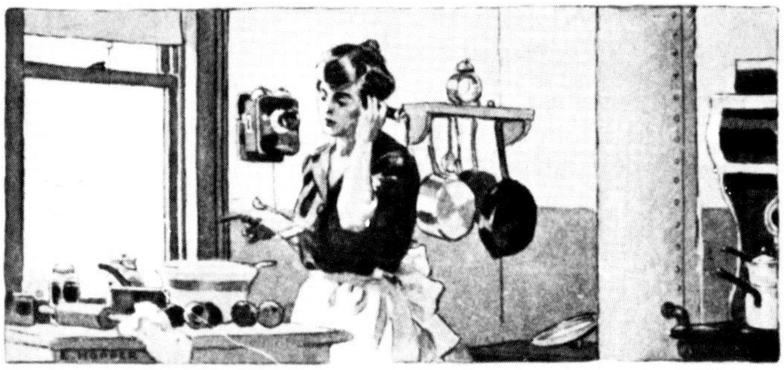

238. "Good bye and good luck! Don't worry about the office—that's my bit, now!" Commercial illustration for Wells Fargo & Co. Express, *Wells Fargo Messenger,* 6 (March 1918), back cover.

239. Cover, *Wells Fargo Messenger,* 6 (April 1918). (Color plate, p. 69.)

240. "See, my Thrift Card is almost filled! How is yours coming along?" / "The First of May is Thrift Stamp Day in the U.S.A." Commercial illustration for Wells Fargo & Co., *Wells Fargo Messenger,* 6 (May 1918), back cover. (Color plate, p. 70.)

241. Cover, *The Express Messenger,* 1 (July 1918). (Color plate, p. 71.)

242a. Proof.

242b. Cover, *The Express Messenger,* 1 (December 1918). (Color plate, p. 72.)

Illustration for "Lightening the Work," *Country Gentleman,* 81 (May 20, 1916).

243a. Proof.

243b. P. 1097.

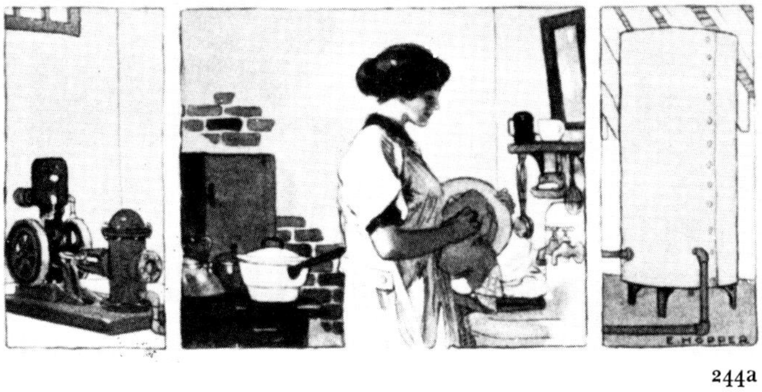

244a

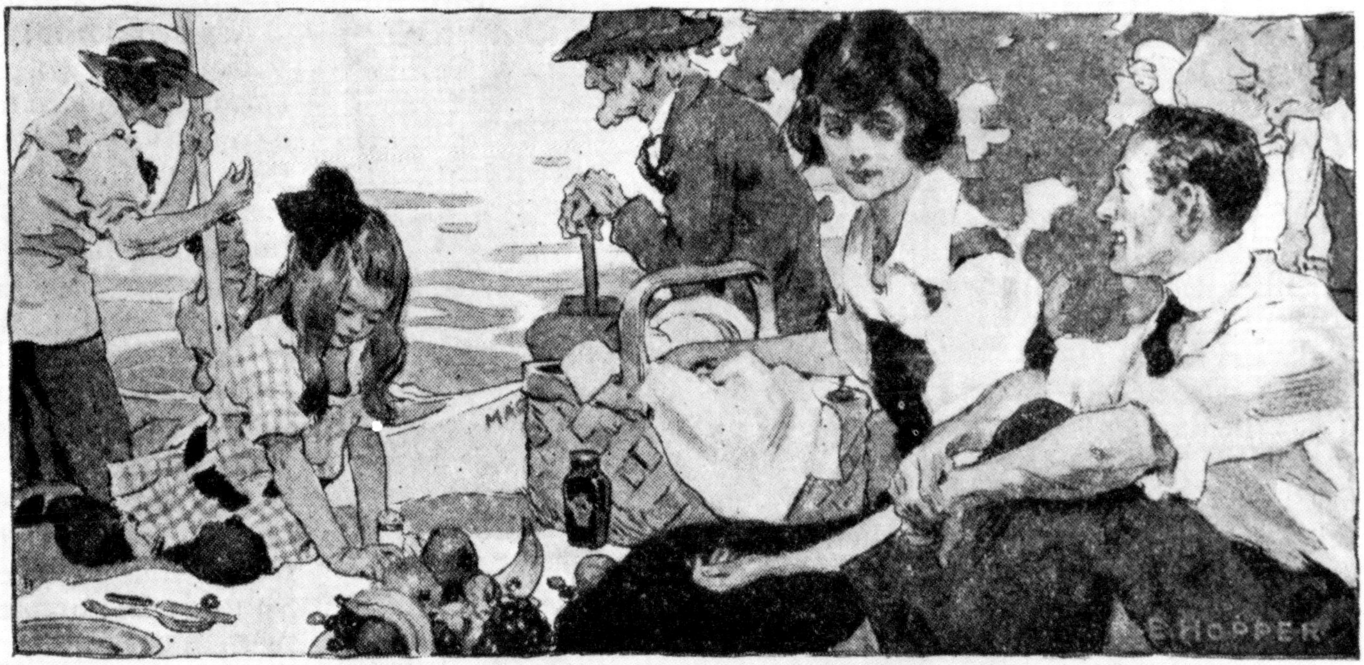

245

243c. Republished, *Country Gentleman,* 81 (October 14, 1916), p. 1855.

Illustration for Mrs. George L. Russell, "My New Farm Kitchen," *Country Gentleman,* 81 (June 3, 1916).

244a. Proof.

244b. P. 1174.

244c. Republished, *Country Gentleman,* 82 (January 27, 1917), p. 43.

244d. Republished, *Country Gentleman,* 82 (November 3, 1917), p. 50.

245. Illustration for "Good Times on the Farm: What to Do When You All Get Together," *Country Gentleman,* 81 (August 5, 1916), p. 1494.

246. Illustration for "Good Times on the Farm: All Sorts of Fun That Country Folks Enjoy," *Country Gentleman,* 81 (September 2, 1916), p. 1637.

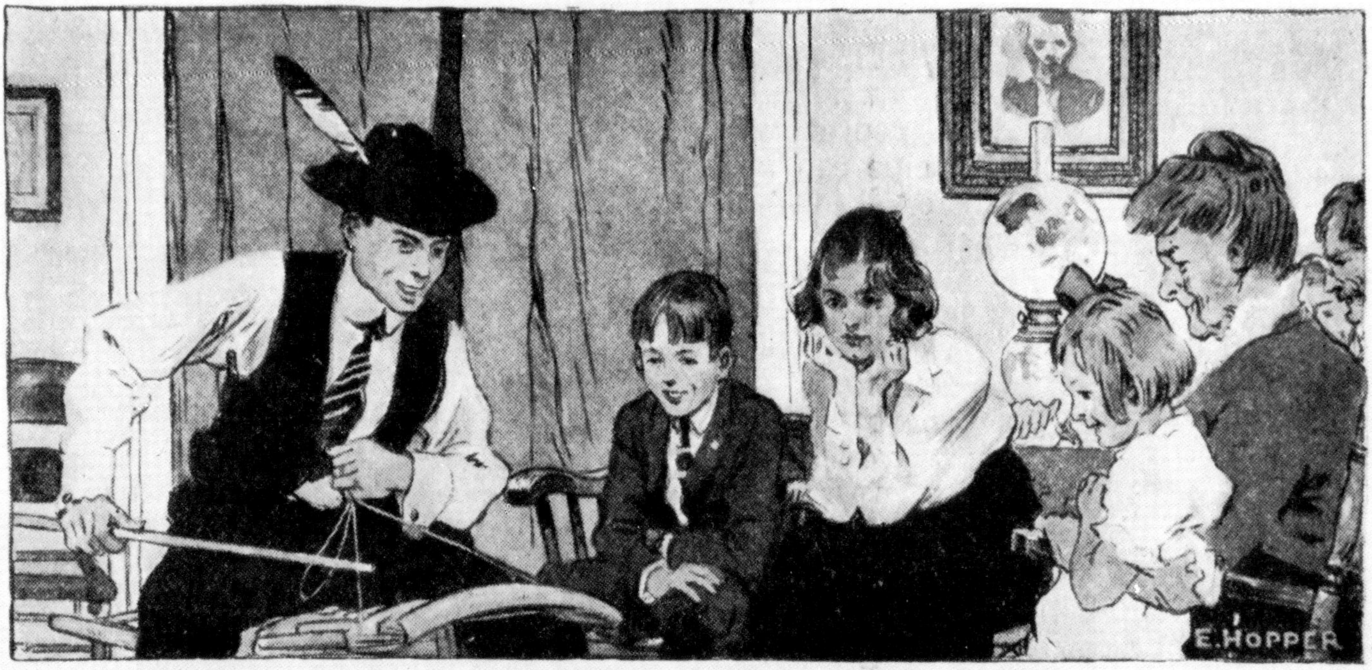

246

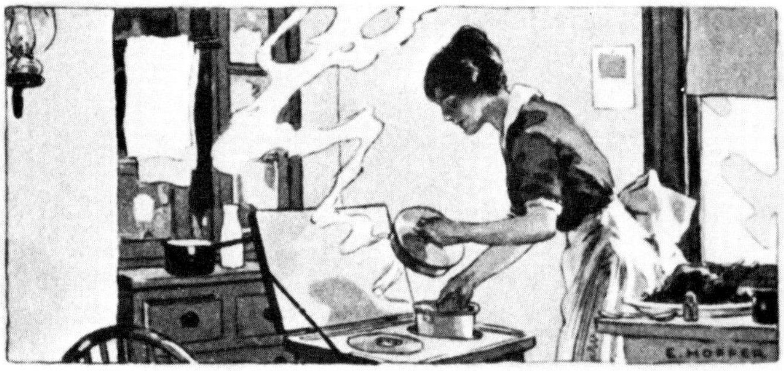

247a

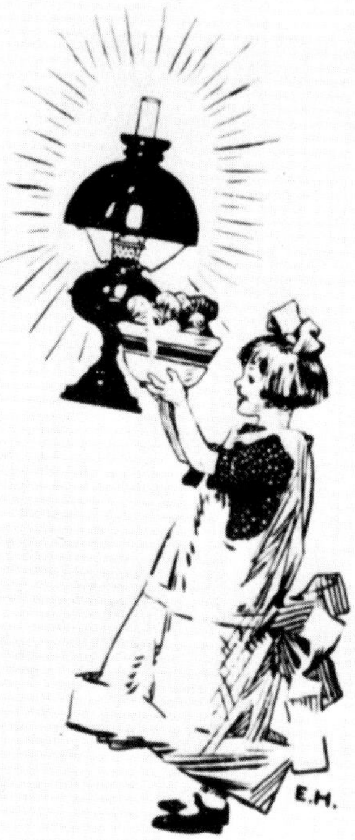

248a

249a

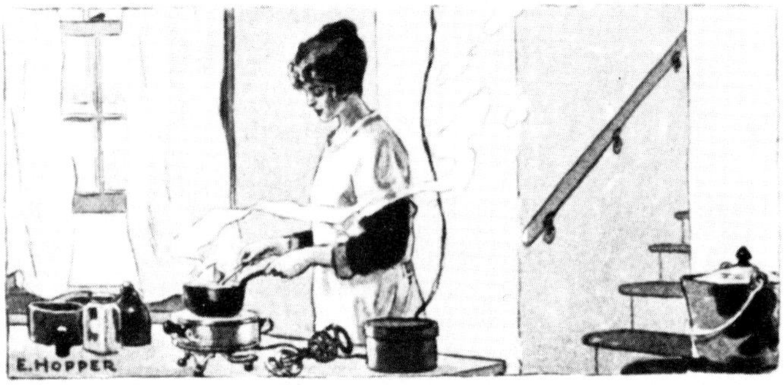

250a

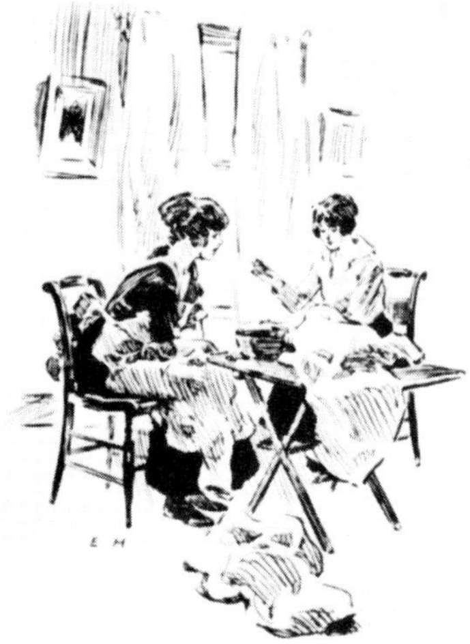

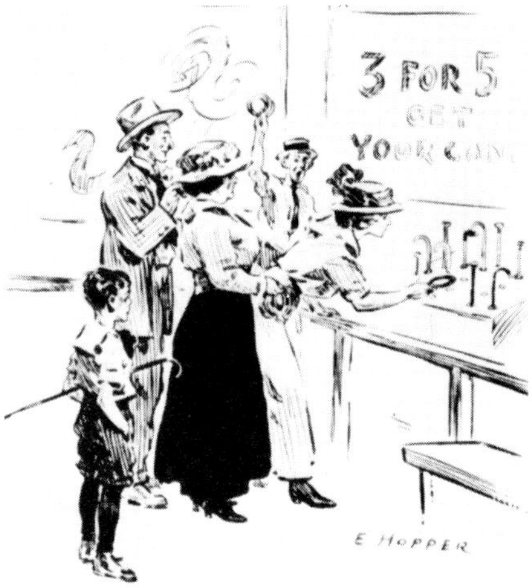

251a

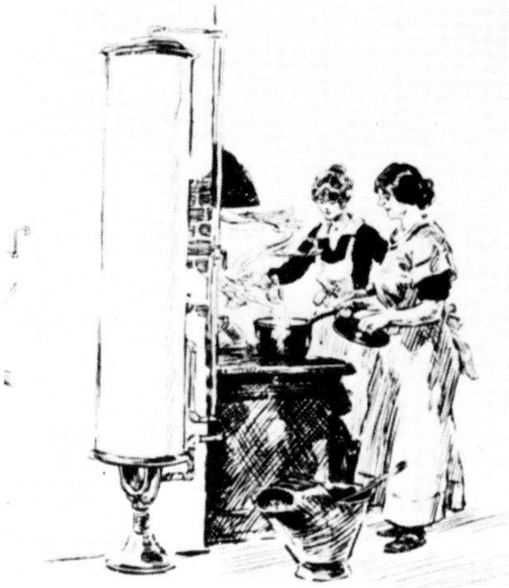

252a

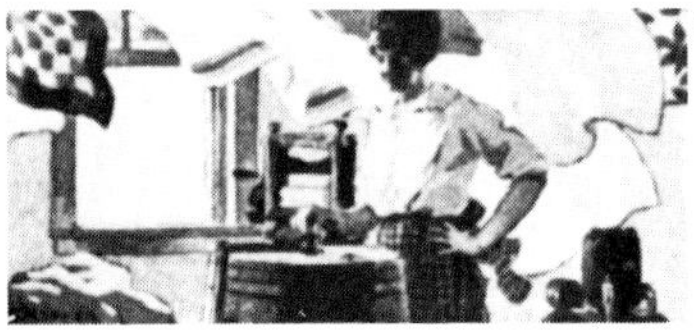

253a

Illustration for Mary H. Talbott, "Save the Tripe," *Country Gentleman,* 81 (September 23, 1916).

247a. Proof.

247b. P. 1740.

247c. Republished, *Country Gentleman,* 82 (April 21, 1917), p. 33.

247d. Republished, *Country Gentleman,* 82 (August 11, 1917), p. 25.

Illustration for Margaret Courtney, "The Slave of the Lamp," *Country Gentleman,* 81 (October 21, 1916).

248a. Proof.

248b. P. 1891.

Illustration for Grace Viall Gray, "Cut the Cooking Cost," *Country Gentleman,* 81 (November 4, 1916).

249a. Proof.

249b. P. 1955.

249c. Republished, *Country Gentleman,* 81 (November 18, 1916), p. 2027.

249d. Republished, *Country Gentleman,* 82 (May 26, 1917), p. 30.

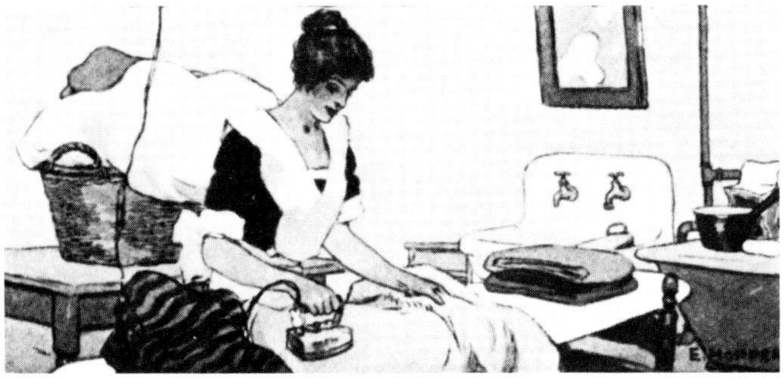

254a

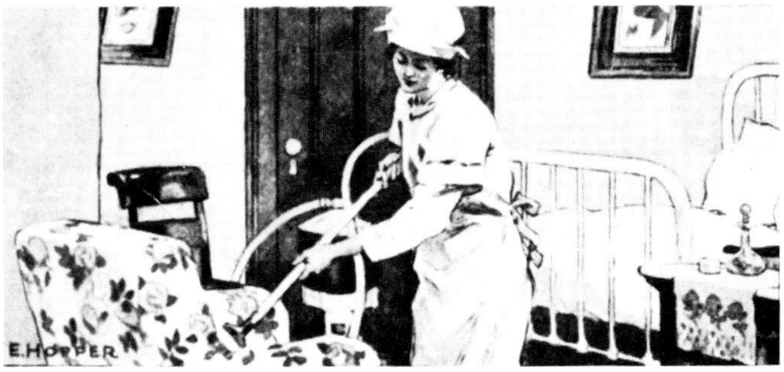

256a

Illustrations for Nellie Kedzie Jones, "Helping the Hired Girl," *Country Gentleman,* 81 (November 11, 1916).

250a. Proof.

250b. "Help her plan her clothes," p. 1987.

251a. Proof.

251b. "A hired girl is entitled to her fun," p. 1987.

252a. Proof.

252b. "Stand over her till she cooks it your way," p. 1987.

Illustration for Mary Kelley Dunne, "When Do You Live?" *Country Gentleman,* 81 (November 18, 1916).

253a. Proof.

253b. P. 2026.

253c. Republished, *Country Gentleman,* 82 (February 24, 1917), p. 49.

Illustration for "How a Home Grew," *Country Gentleman,* 81 (November 25, 1916).

254a. Proof.

254b. P. 2063.

254c. Republished, *Country Gentleman,* 82 (September 1, 1917), p. 31.

Illustration for "Looking After the Woman Speaker," *Country Gentleman,* 81 (December 2, 1916).

255a. Proof.

255b. P. 2099.

255c. Republished, *Country Gentleman,* 82 (December 1, 1917), p. 37.

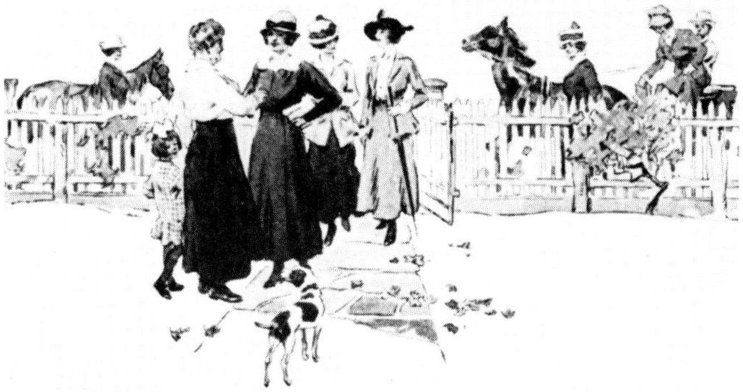

255a

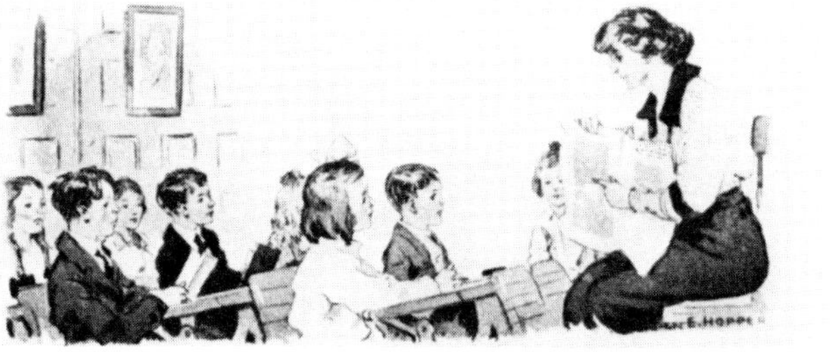

257a

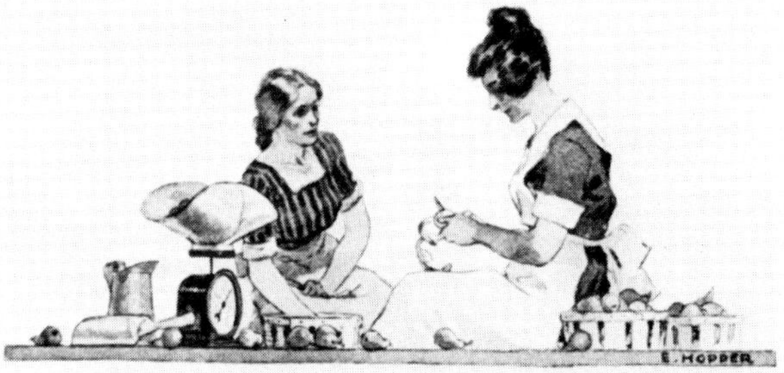

258a

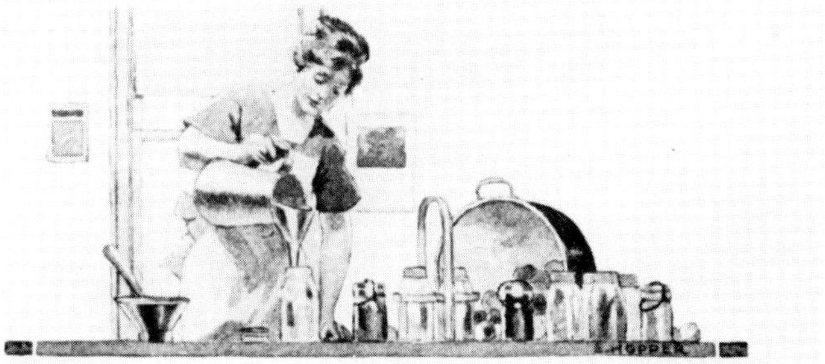

259a

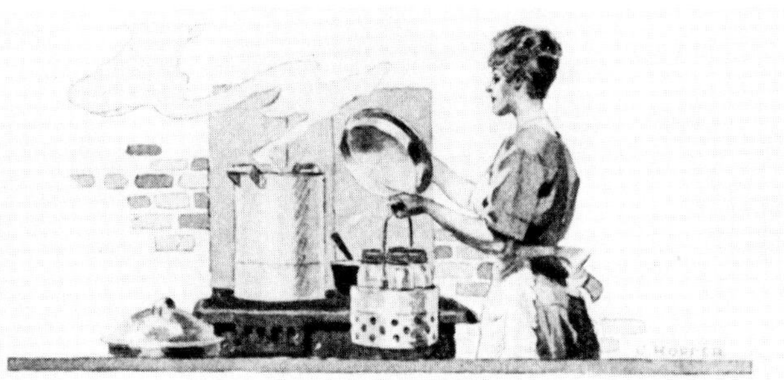

260a

Illustration for "Lightening the Work," *Country Gentleman,* 82 (February 3, 1917).

256a. Proof.

256b. P. 53.

256c. Republished, *Country Gentleman,* 82 (September 1, 1917), p. 31.

Illustration for "The Country Gentleman School," *Country Gentleman,* 82 (March 31, 1917).

257a. Proof.

257b. P. 44.

257c. Republished, *Country Gentleman,* 82 (April 7, 1917), p. 40.

257d. Republished, *Country Gentleman,* 82 (April 14, 1917), p. 44.

257e. Republished, *Country Gentleman,* 82 (April 21, 1917), p. 36.

257f. Republished, *Country Gentleman,* 82 (April 28, 1917), p. 32.

257g. Republished, *Country Gentleman,* 82 (May 12, 1917), p. 32.

257h. Republished, *Country Gentleman,* 82 (May 19, 1917), p. 32.

257i. Republished, *Country Gentleman,* 82 (June 2, 1917), p. 32.

257j. Republished, *Country Gentleman,* 82 (June 16, 1917), p. 32.

Illustration for Maud C. Hessler, "Our Club Diary," *Country Gentleman,* 82 (September 1, 1917).

258a. Proof.

258b. P. 30.

Illustration for "Home Canning," *Country Gentleman,* 82 (September 15, 1917).

259a. Proof.

259b. P. 34.

Illustration for Anna M. Johnson, "Home Canning," *Country Gentleman,* 82 (October 6, 1917).

260a. Proof.

260b. P. 35.

Illustrations for Will Levington Comfort, "The Black Frock Coat," *Every Week,* 2 (June 12, 1916).

261a. Proof.

261b. " 'We don't want to let that black frock get too far away. It's kind of been the hub of things the last few days,' " p. 13.

262. "He did not eat the scrap of food: he made his way to the pitiable figure crouched on the sand and holding the wailing child," p. 14.

263. "The woman screamed. 'God help us—did you drink? Did you drink?' the missionary cried," p. 14.

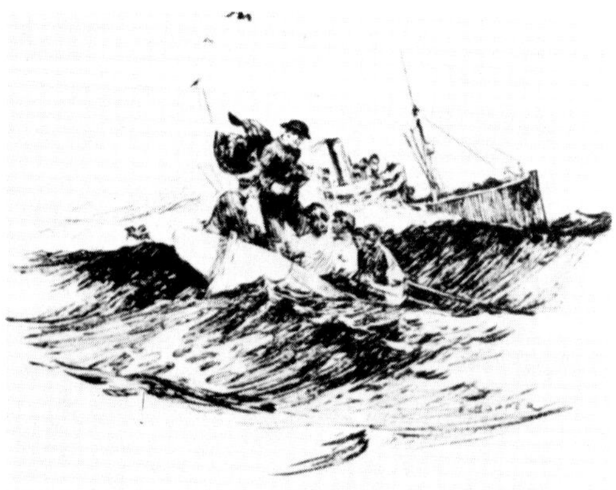

261a

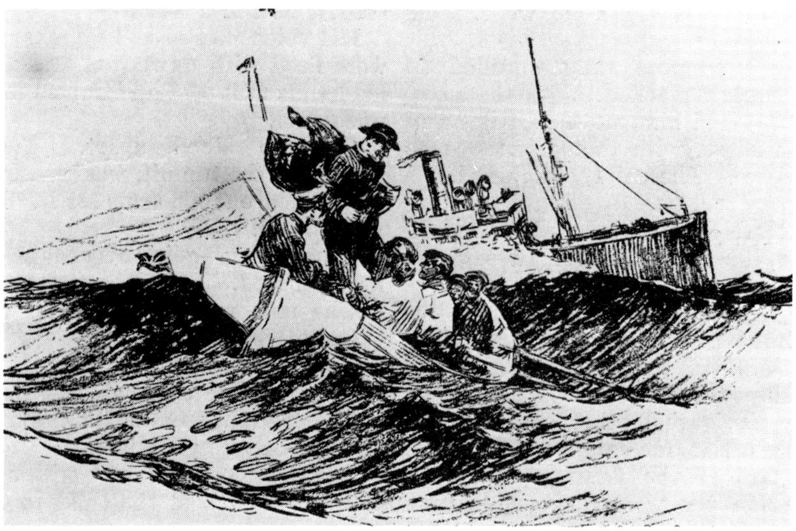

261b

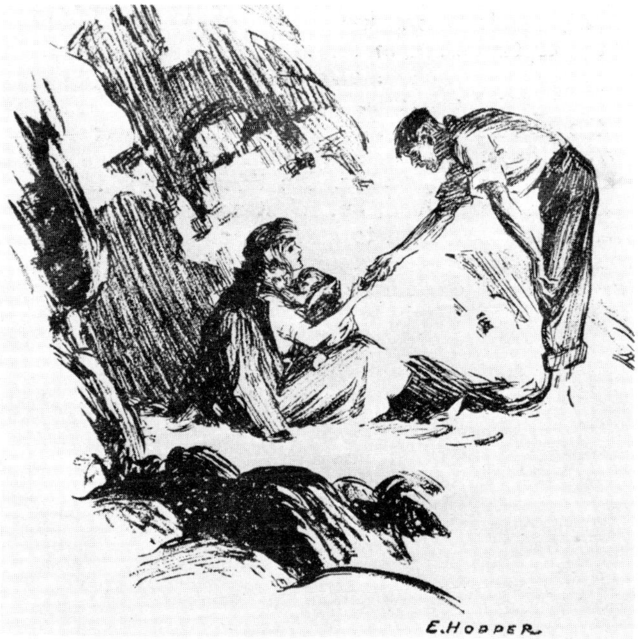

262

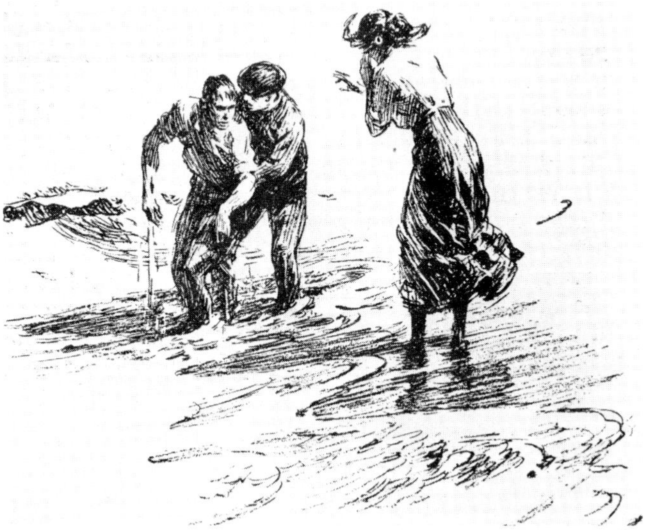

263

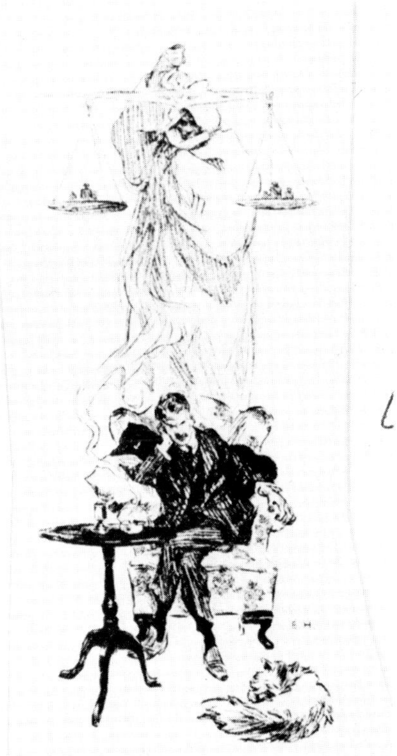

264a

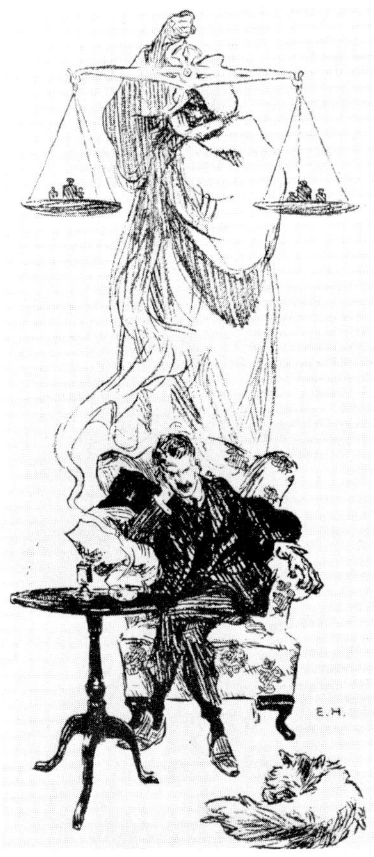

264b

Illustrations for H. Addington Bruce, "What Trivial Doubts Can Do to You," *Every Week,* 4 (April 16, 1917).

264a. Proof.

264b. P. 16.

265a. Illustration, 1917. Ink on illustration board, 22 × 15 inches. Whitney Museum of American Art, New York; Bequest of Josephine N. Hopper 70.1446.

265b. Proof.

265c. "They conjure up visions of possible mistakes in connection with the carrying of an umbrella," p. 16.

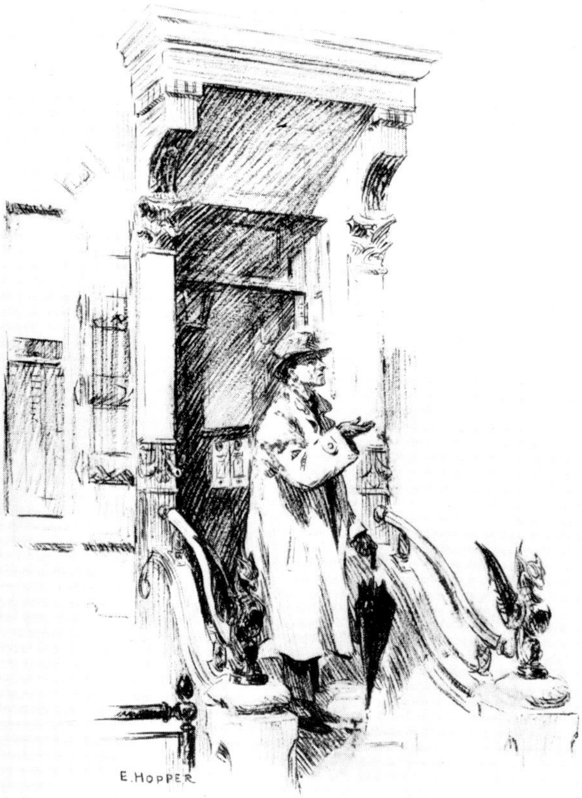

265a

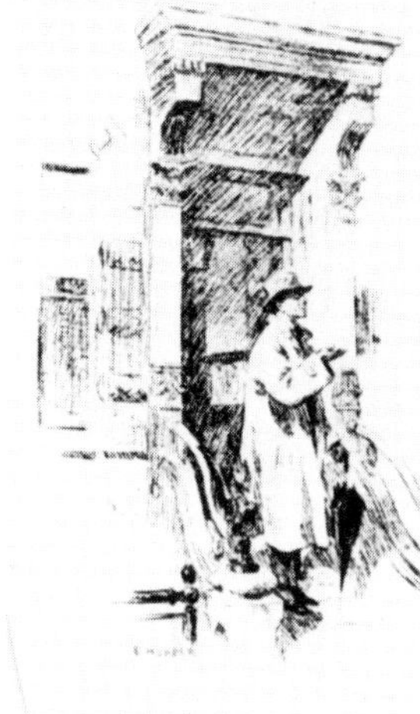

265b

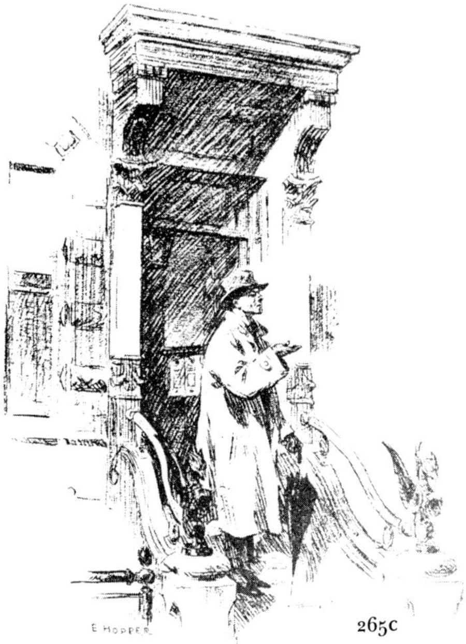

265c

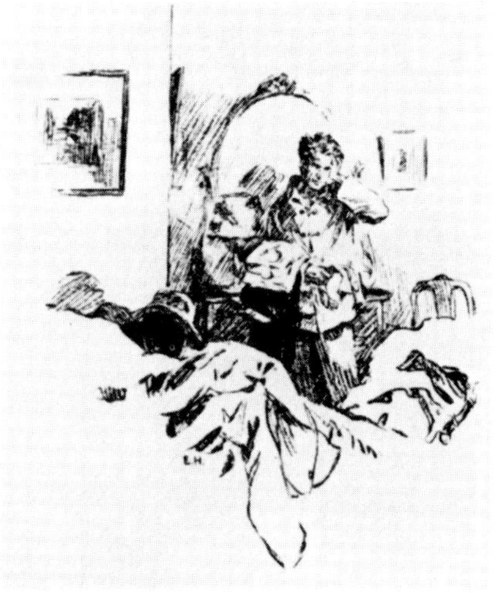

266b

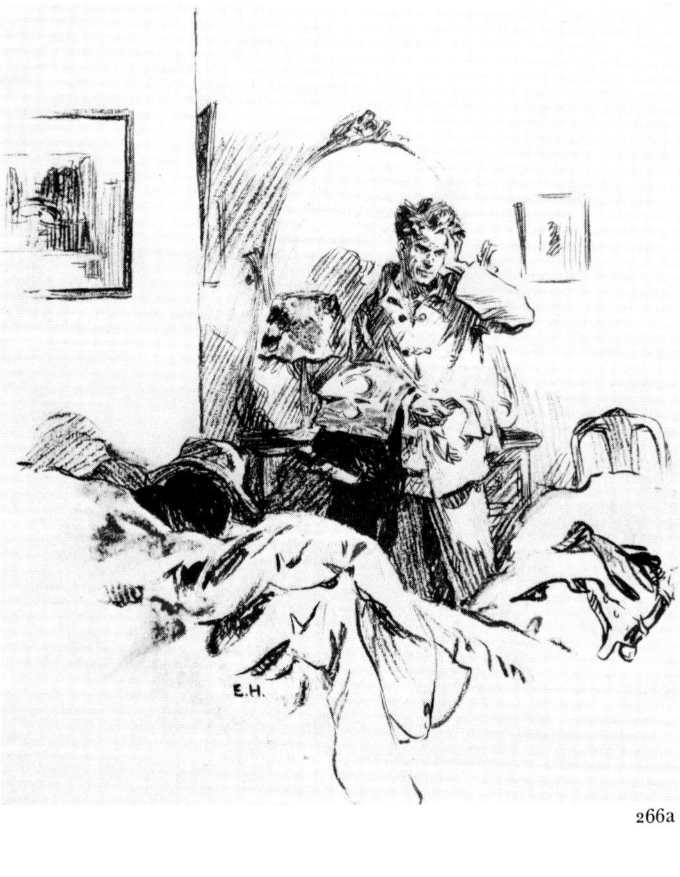

266a

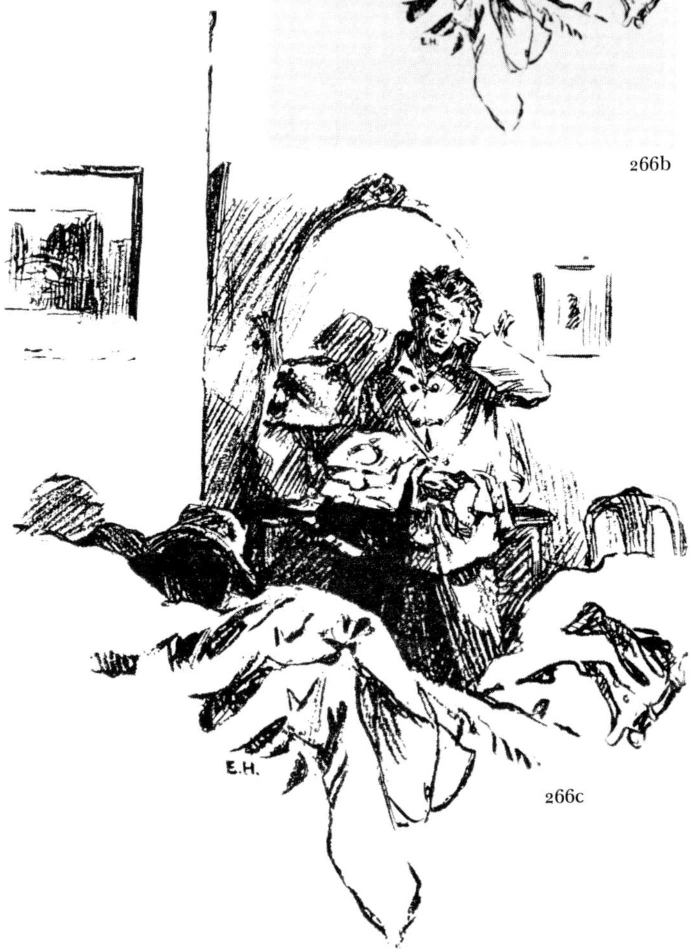

266c

266a. Illustration, 1917. Ink on illustration board, 22 × 15 inches. Whitney Museum of American Art, New York; Bequest of Josephine N. Hopper 70.1445.

266b. Proof.

266c. "The minute I get up a terrible conflict begins within me as to the clothes I should wear," p. 17.

Illustrations for James H. Collins, "Selling the Hard Ones," *Every Week*, 4 (May 28, 1917).

267. " 'Boss, did you hear about the brick-yard? It closes down Saturday,' " p. 10.

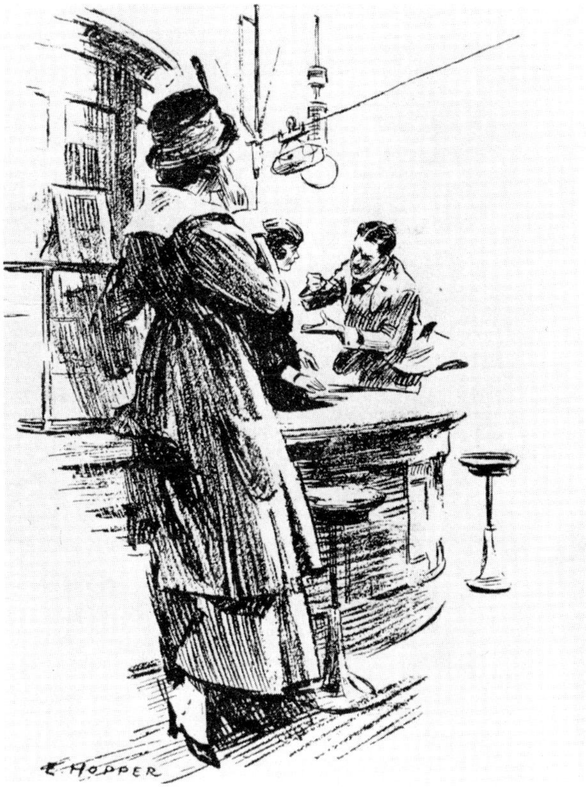

268

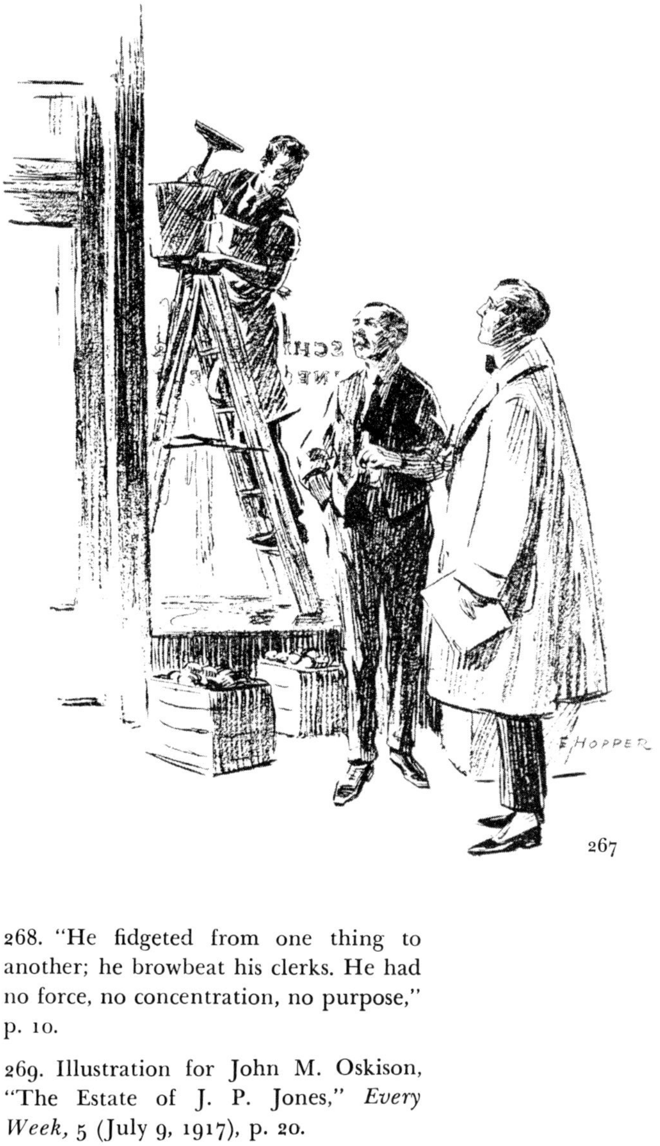

267

268. "He fidgeted from one thing to another; he browbeat his clerks. He had no force, no concentration, no purpose," p. 10.

269. Illustration for John M. Oskison, "The Estate of J. P. Jones," *Every Week*, 5 (July 9, 1917), p. 20.

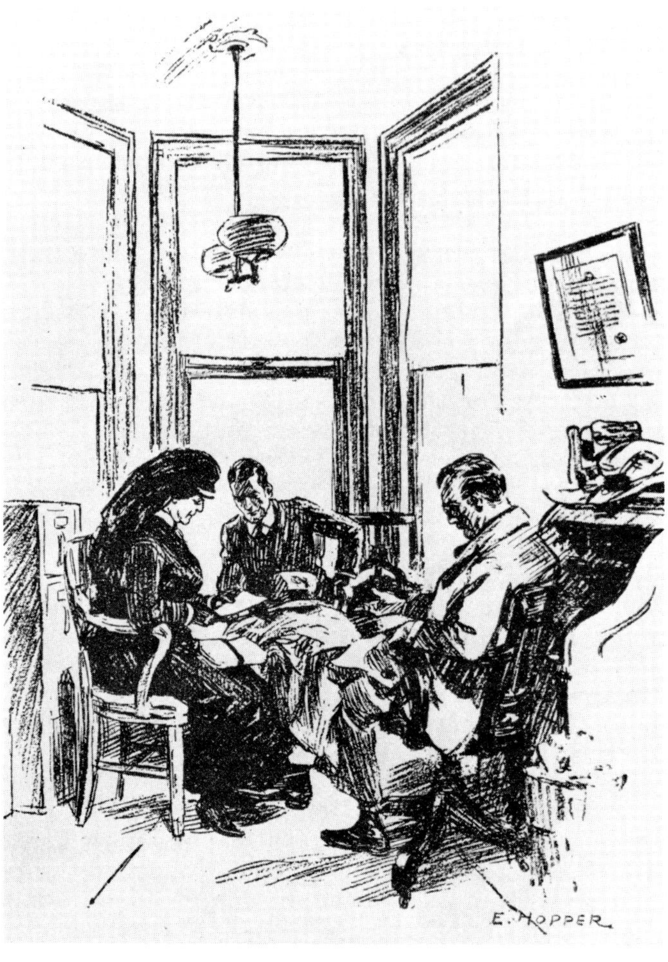

269

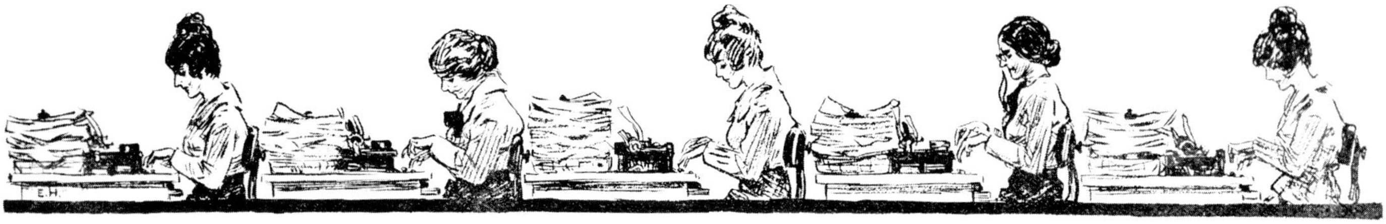

271

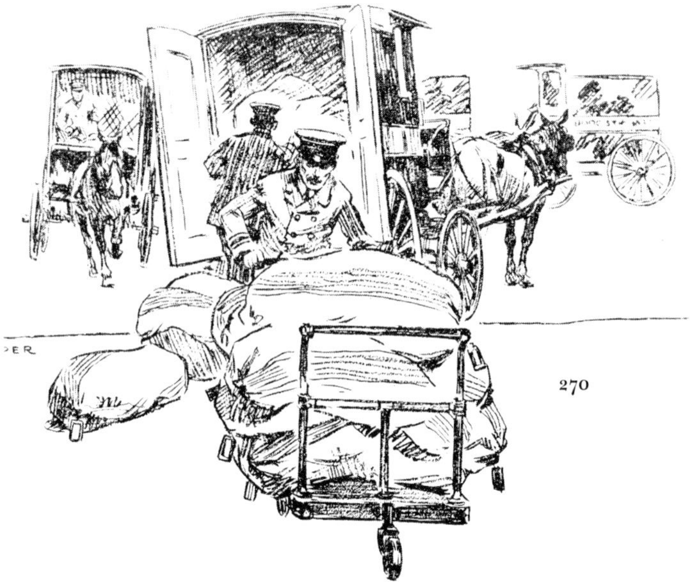

270

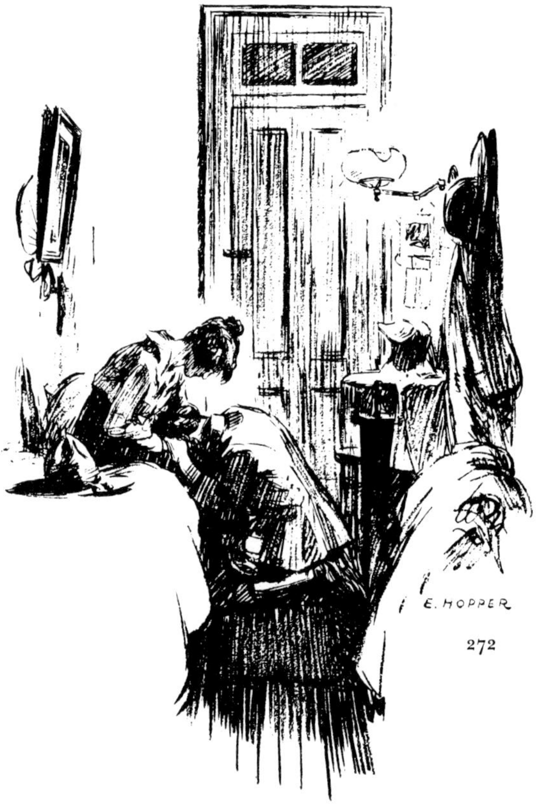

272

Illustrations for Fred C. Kelly, "A Fortune in the Day's Mail," *Every Week,* 5 (October 1, 1917).

270. P. 7.

271. P. 8.

Illustration for Bernadine Hilty, "In San Francisco," *Every Week,* 6 (March 9, 1918).

272. " 'Mag darlin', when I'm gone, I wisht at night you would say a little prayer fer me,' " p. 18.

---

273. Cover, *The Morse Dry Dock Dial,* 1 (January 1918). (Color plate, p. 73.)

274. Cover, *The Morse Dry Dock Dial,* 1 (February 1918). (Color plate, p. 74.)

275. Cover, *The Morse Dry Dock Dial,* 1 (March 1918). (Color plate, p. 74.)

276. Cover, *The Morse Dry Dock Dial,* 1 (April 1918). (Color plate, p. 74.)

277a. Proof.

277b. Cover, *The Morse Dry Dock Dial,* 1 (June-July 1918). (Color plate, p. 74.)

278a. Proof.

278b. Cover, *The Morse Dry Dock Dial,* 1 (August 1918). (Color plate, p. 75.)

279. Cover, *The Morse Dry Dock Dial,* 1 (September 1918). (Color plate, p. 76.)

280. Cover, *The Morse Dry Dock Dial,* 1 (October 1918). (Color plate, p. 76.)

281. Cover, *The Morse Dry Dock Dial,* 1 (November 1918). (Color plate, p. 76.)

282. Cover, *The Morse Dry Dock Dial,* 2 (January 1919). (Color plate, p. 76.)

283a. Study for poster *Smash the Hun,* 1918. Gouache on illustration board, 9½ × 6⅜ inches. The Charles Rand Penney Collection. (Color plate, p. 77.)

Poster exhibited at Gimbels department store, New York, with other entries in the competition of the National Service Section of the United States Shipping Board Emergency Fleet Corporation.

Reference: Reproduced in *The Sun* (New York), August 25, 1918.

283b. Cover, *The Morse Dry Dock Dial,* 2 (February 1919). (Color plate, p. 77.)

284a. First proof.

284b. Second proof.

284c. Third proof.

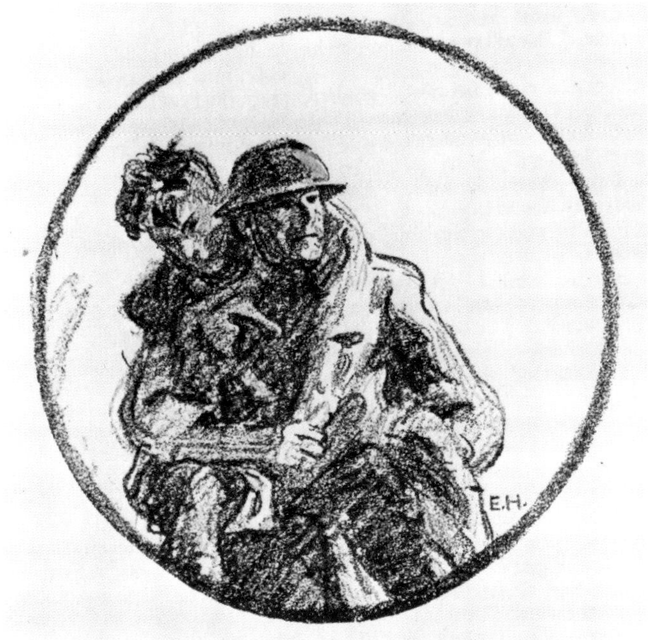

307

284d. Cover, *The Morse Dry Dock Dial,* 2 (March 1919). (Color plate, p. 78.)

285. Cover, *The Morse Dry Dock Dial,* 2 (May 1919). (Color plate, p. 79.)

286. Cover, *The Morse Dry Dock Dial,* 2 (July 1919). (Color plate, p. 80.)

287. Cover, *The Morse Dry Dock Dial,* 2 (September 1919). (Color plate, p. 81.)

288. Cover, *The Morse Dry Dock Dial,* 2 (October 1919). (Color plate, p. 81.)

289a. Proof.

289b. Cover, *The Morse Dry Dock Dial,* 2 (November 1919). (Color plate, p. 81.)

290. Cover, *The Morse Dry Dock Dial,* 2 (December 1919). (Color plate, p. 81.)

291. Cover, *The Morse Dry Dock Dial,* 2 (January 1920). (Color plate, p. 82.)

292. Cover, *The Morse Dry Dock Dial,* 3 (March 1920). (Color plate, p. 83.)

293. Cover, *The Morse Dry Dock Dial,* 3 (May 1920). (Color plate, p. 83.)

294. Cover, *The Morse Dry Dock Dial,* 3 (June 1920). (Color plate, p. 83.)

295. Cover, *The Morse Dry Dock Dial,* 3 (July 1920). (Color plate, p. 83.)

296. Cover, *The Morse Dry Dock Dial,* 3 (August 1920). (Color plate, p. 84.)

297. Cover, *The Morse Dry Dock Dial,* 3 (September 1920). (Color plate, p. 85.)

298. Cover, *The Morse Dry Dock Dial,* 3 (October 1920). (Color plate, p. 85.)

299. Cover, *The Morse Dry Dock Dial,* 3 (November 1920). (Color plate, p. 85.)

300. Cover, *The Morse Dry Dock Dial,* 3 (December 1920). (Color plate, p. 85.)

301. Cover, *The Morse Dry Dock Dial,* 4 (February 1921). (Color plate, p. 86.)

302. Cover, *The Morse Dry Dock Dial,* 4 (March 1921). (Color plate, p. 87.)

303. Cover, *The Morse Dry Dock Dial,* 4 (July 1921). (Color plate, p. 88.)

304. Cover, *The Morse Dry Dock Dial,* 4 (August 1921). (Color plate, p. 88.)

305. Cover, *The Morse Dry Dock Dial,* 4 (December 1921). (Color plate, p. 88.)

306. Cover, *The Morse Dry Dock Dial,* 5 (February 1922). (Color plate, p. 88.)

Illustrations for Henry Van Dyke, "The Hearing Ear," *Scribner's Magazine,* 64 (December 1918).

307. P. 670.

308. "I'm going to carry you in, 'spite of hell," p. 672.

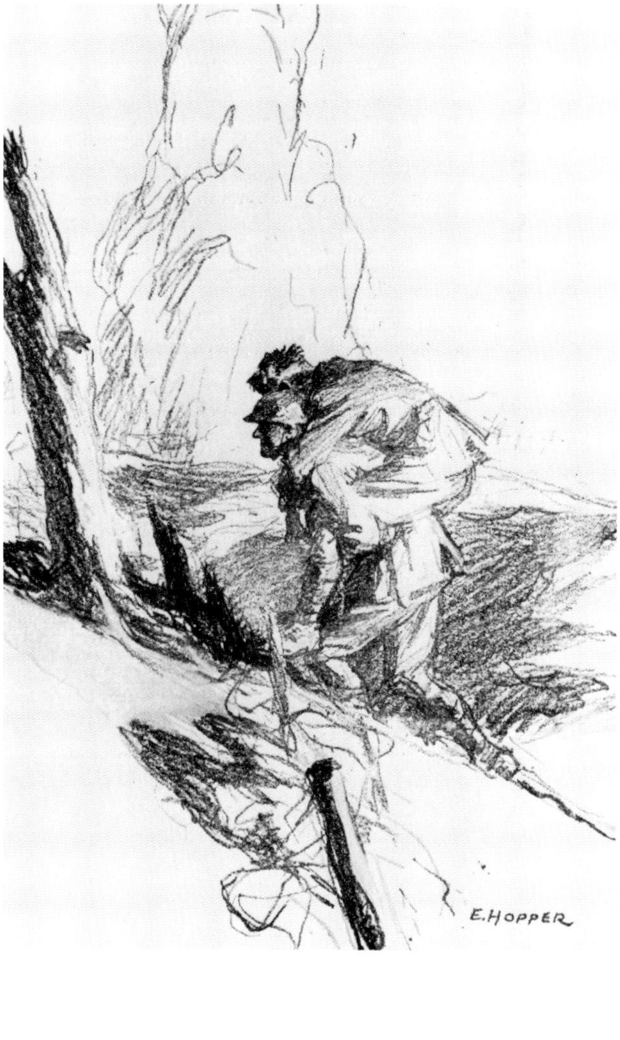

308

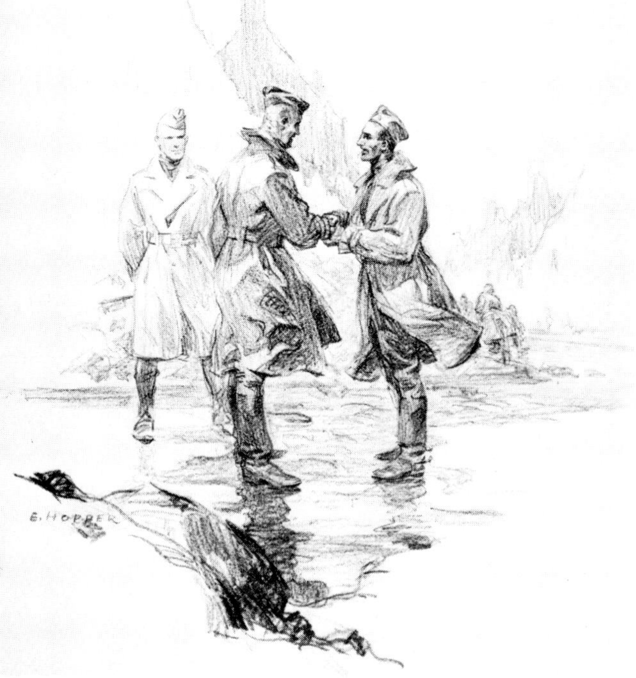

309a

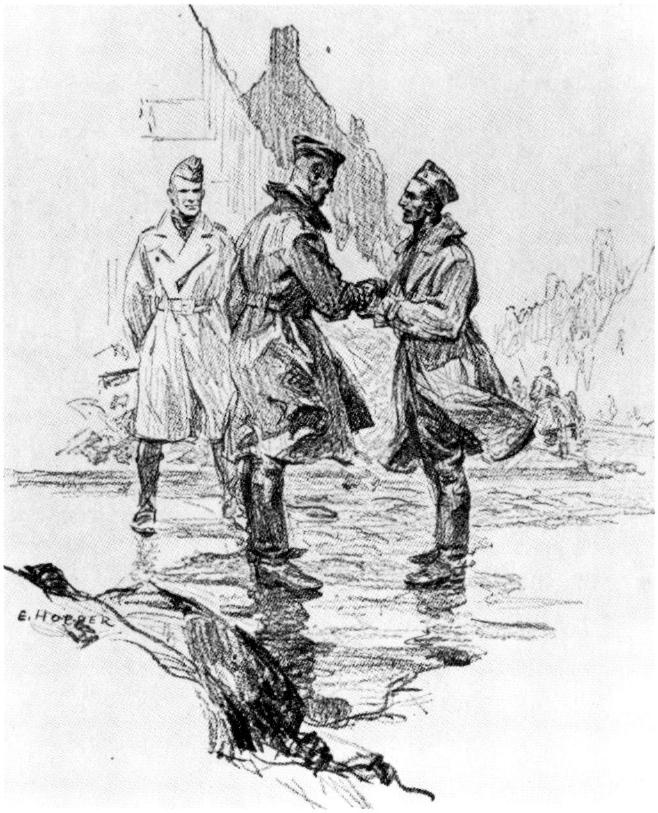

309b

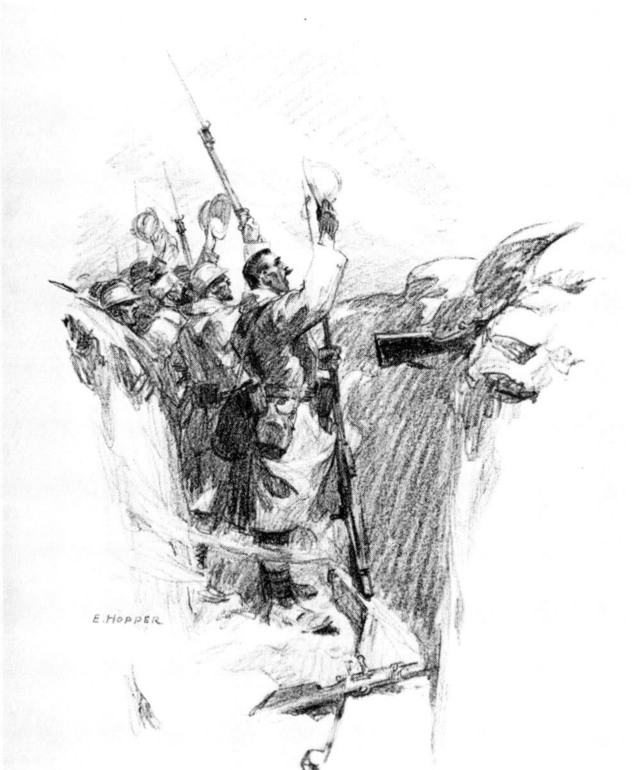

310a

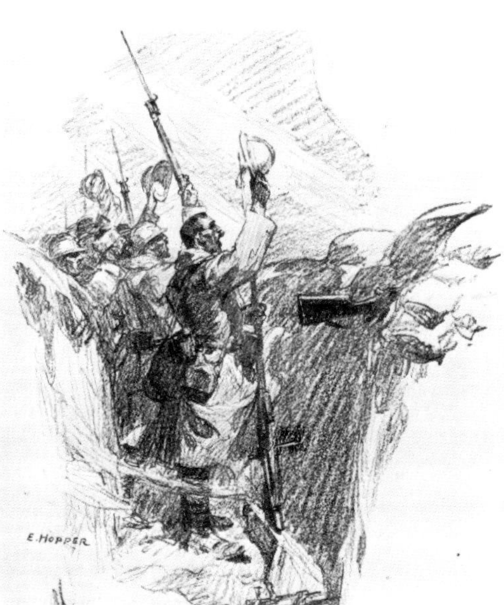

310b

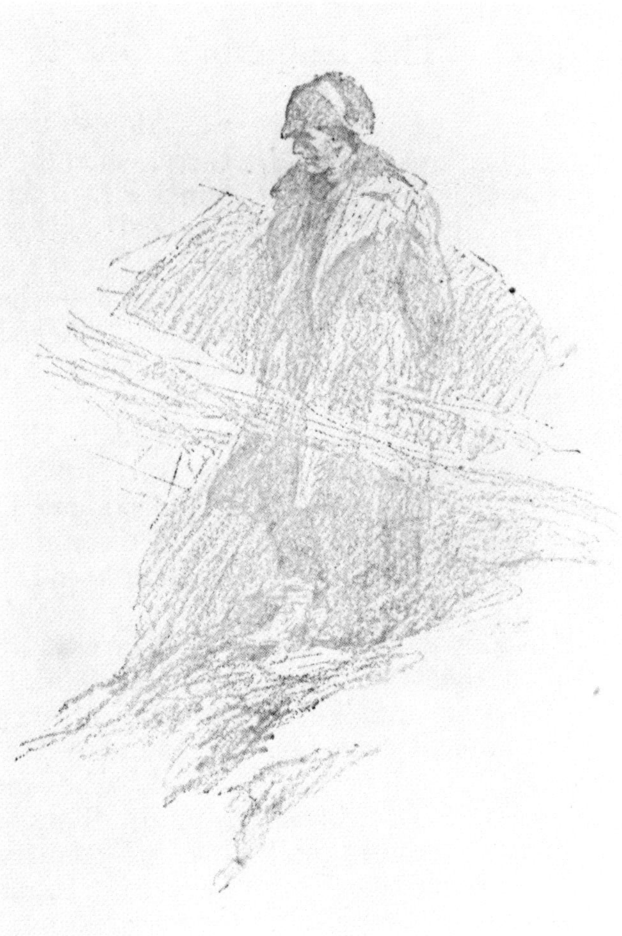

311

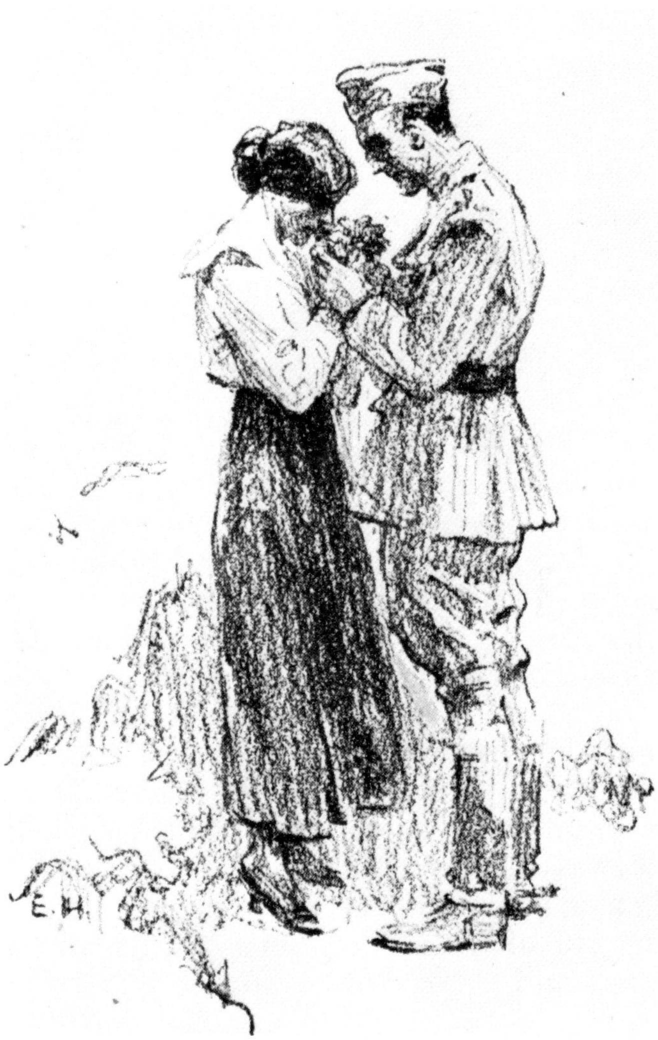

312a

Illustrations for Temple Bailey, "The Emperor's Ghost," *Scribner's Magazine,* 65 (February 1919).

309a. Illustration, 1918. Conte on illustration board, 27 × 19⅞ inches. Whitney Museum of American Art, New York; Bequest of Josephine N. Hopper 70.1456.

309b. "Good old MacDonald—at last!" p. 205.

310a. Illustration, 1918. Conte on illustration board, 27 × 20⅛ inches. Whitney Museum of American Art, New York. Bequest of Josephine N. Hopper 70.1457.

310b. "C'est l'Empereur! C'est l'Empereur! He returns to lead us," p. 206.

311. P. 207.

312a. "For love, mademoiselle, and truth and constancy," p. 208.

312b. Republished January 1937, *Scribner's Magazine*'s fiftieth anniversary issue.

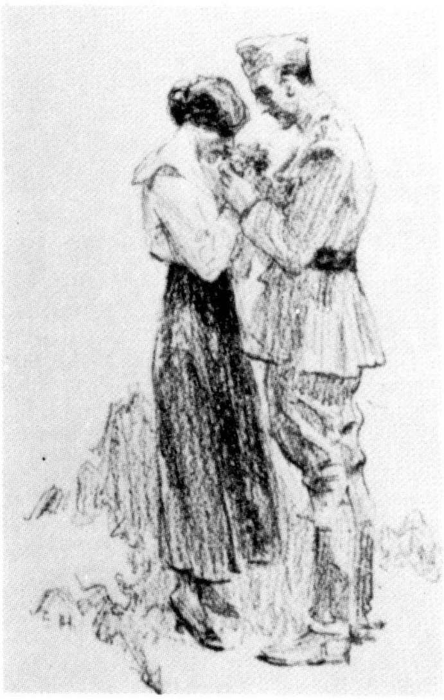

312b

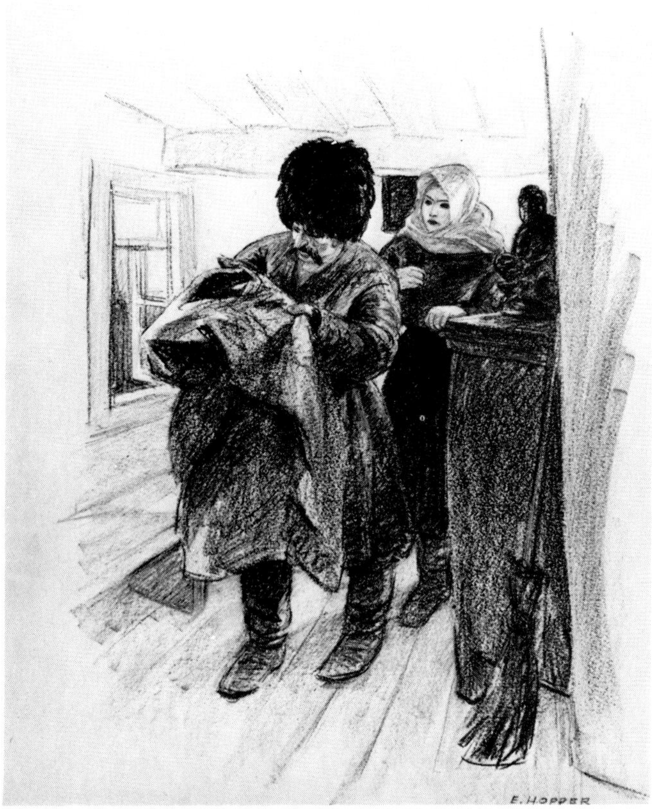

313a

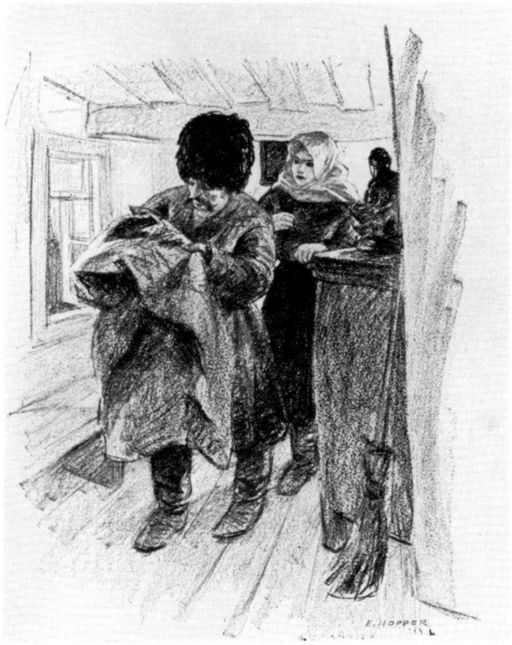

313b

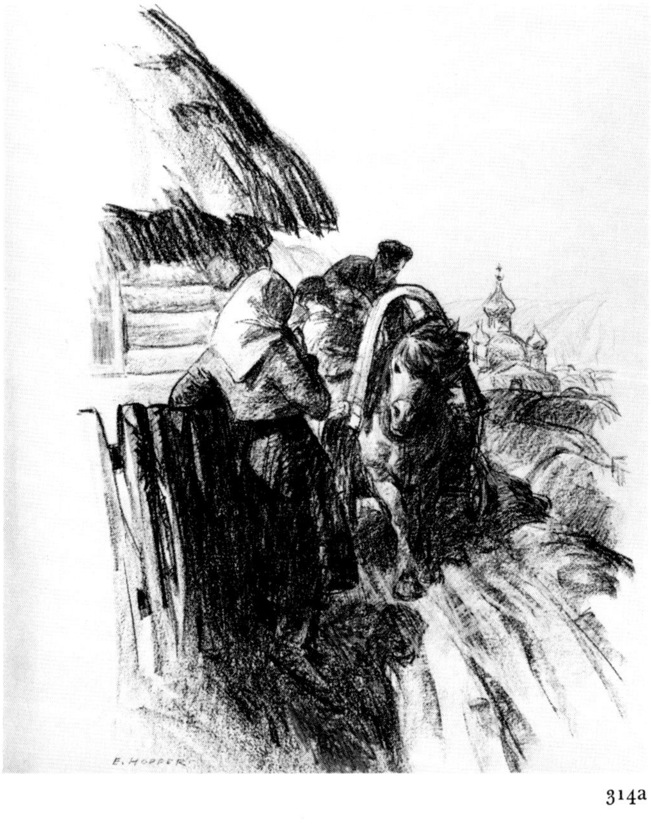

314a

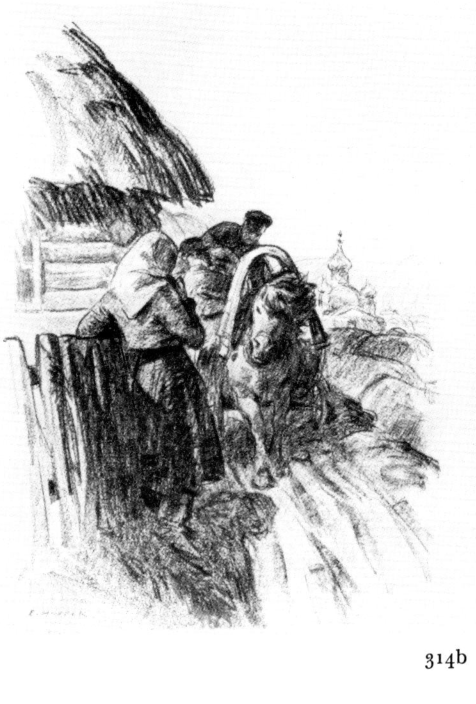

314b

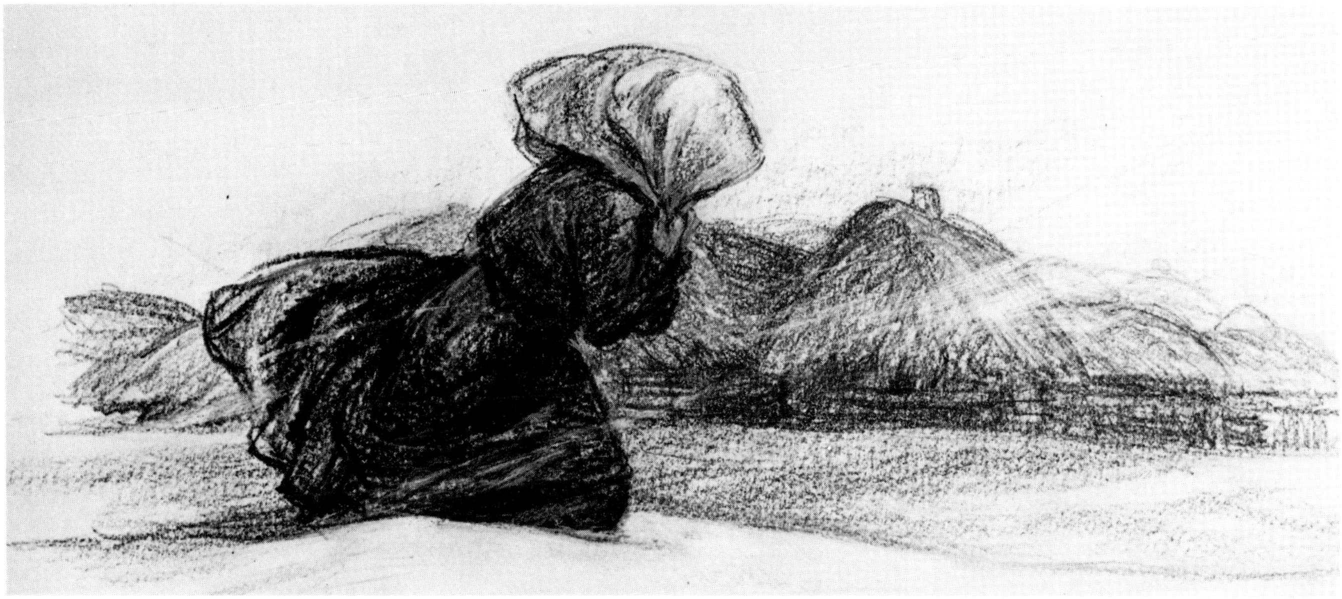

315a

Illustrations for Margharita Derfelden, "The Buddha," *Scribner's Magazine,* 74 (August 1923).

313a. Illustration, 1923. Conte and white paint on illustration board, 21⅝ × 19½ inches. Whitney Museum of American Art, New York; Bequest of Josephine N. Hopper 70.1447.

313b. "No amount of urging could persuade Selim to offer a price until he had given the coat a thorough inspection," p. 207.

314a. Illustration, 1923. Conte and white paint on illustration board, 21¾ × 19¼ inches. Whitney Museum of American Art, New York; Bequest of Josephine N. Hopper 70.1448.

314b. "Vladimir Romanovitch bundled his friend into a dilapidated victoria," p. 209.

315a. Illustration, 1923. Conte and white paint on illustration board, 15½ × 21¾ inches. Whitney Museum of American Art, New York; Bequest of Josephine N. Hopper 70.1438.

315b. P. 212.

Illustrations for Lawrence Reamer, "A Place with the Stars," *Scribner's Magazine,* 75 (January 1924).

316. "Lurline, in full costume, advanced into the illuminated zone," p. 32.

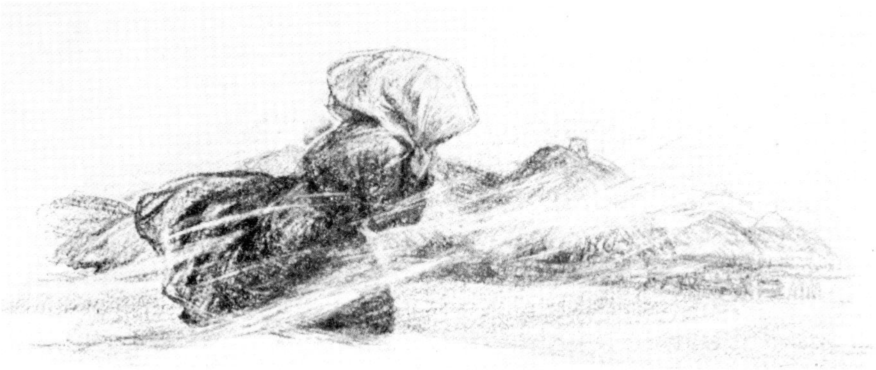

315b

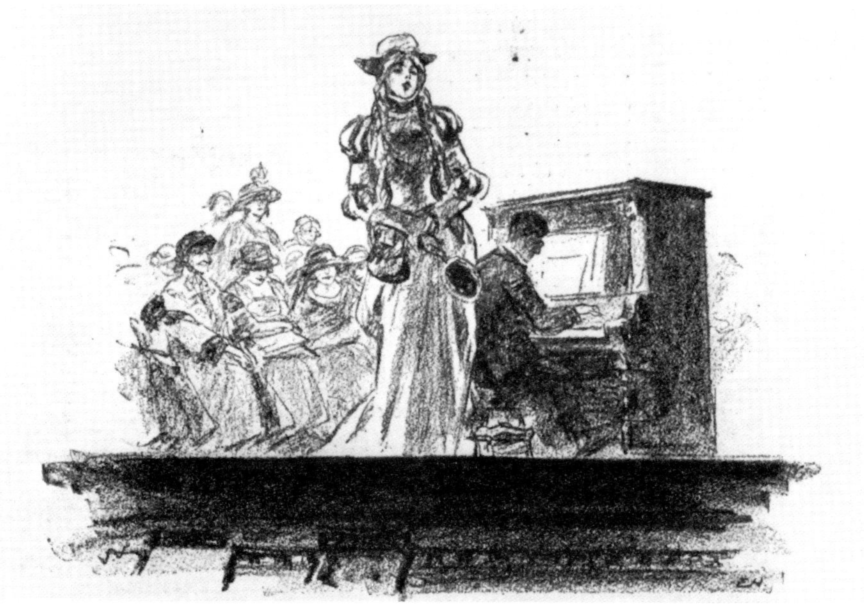

316

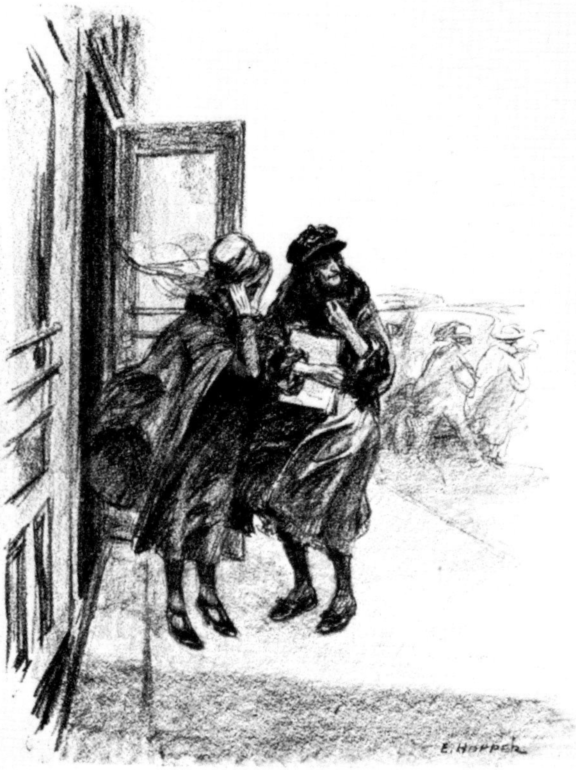

317

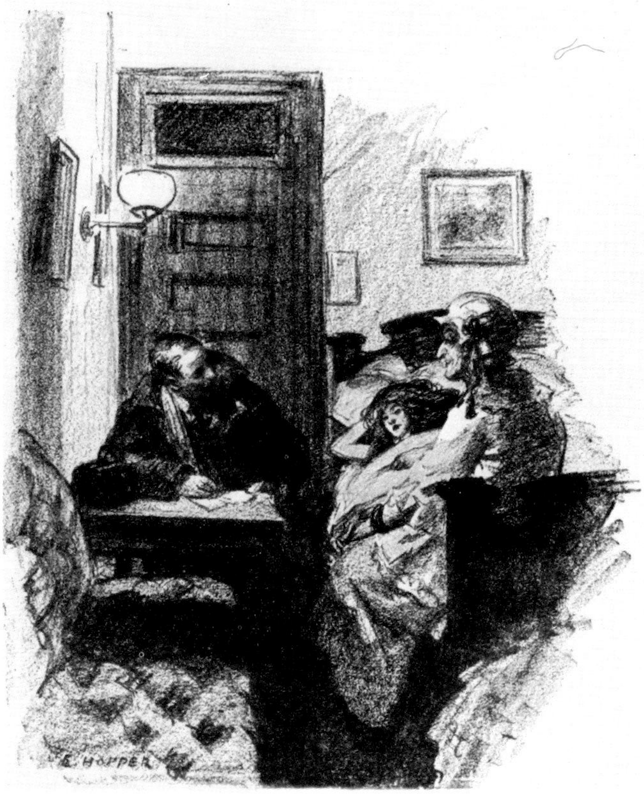

318

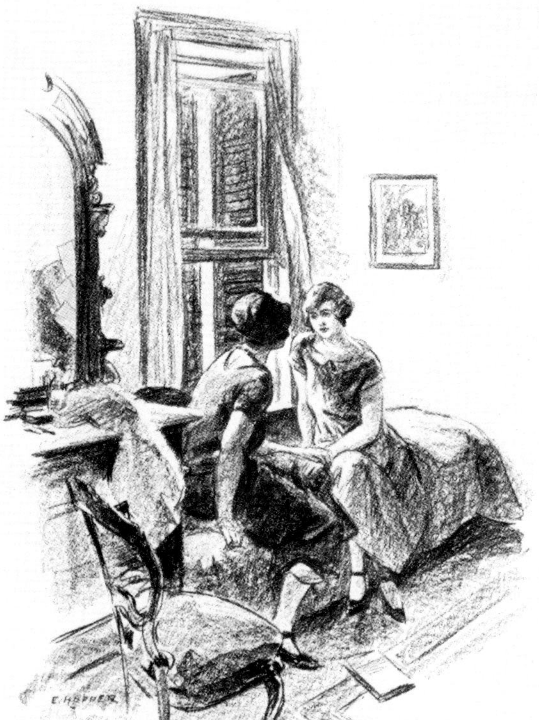

319a

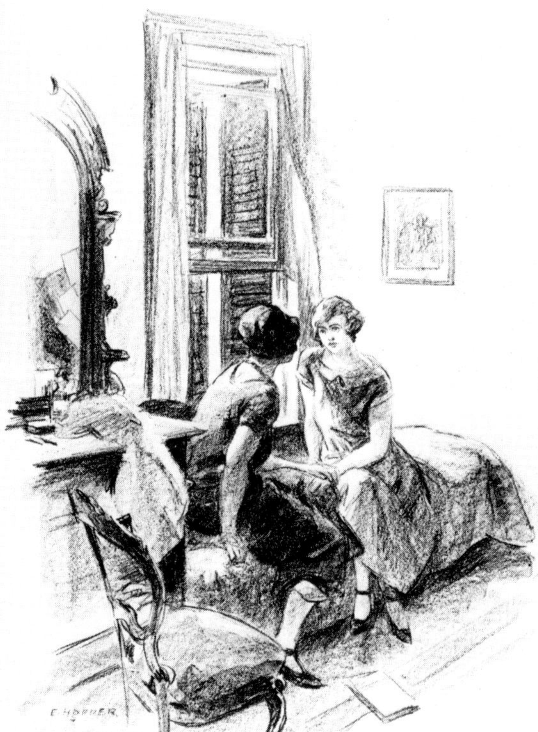

319b

317. "An east wind was sweeping through the street," p. 39.

318. "When could I travel, do you think?" p. 41.

Illustrations for Eva Moore Adams, "Shady," *Scribner's Magazine,* 76 (December 1924).

319a. Illustration, 1924. Conte and white paint on composition board, 30 × 21¾ inches. Whitney Museum of American Art, New York; Bequest of Josephine N. Hopper 70.1455.

319b. " 'I'm afraid,' she said, looking at me straightly now, 'that Shady's cough is more than just a cough,' " p. 627.

320. " 'Oh, Shady,' I said in dismay, 'she wanted to surprise you,' " p. 631.

321a. Illustration, 1924. Conte and white paint on illustration board, 18⅞ × 21¾ inches. Whitney Museum of American Art, New York; Bequest of Josephine N. Hopper 70.1439.

321b. "Then I proceeded to shed all the tears I'd been holding back for a year and a half," p. 632.

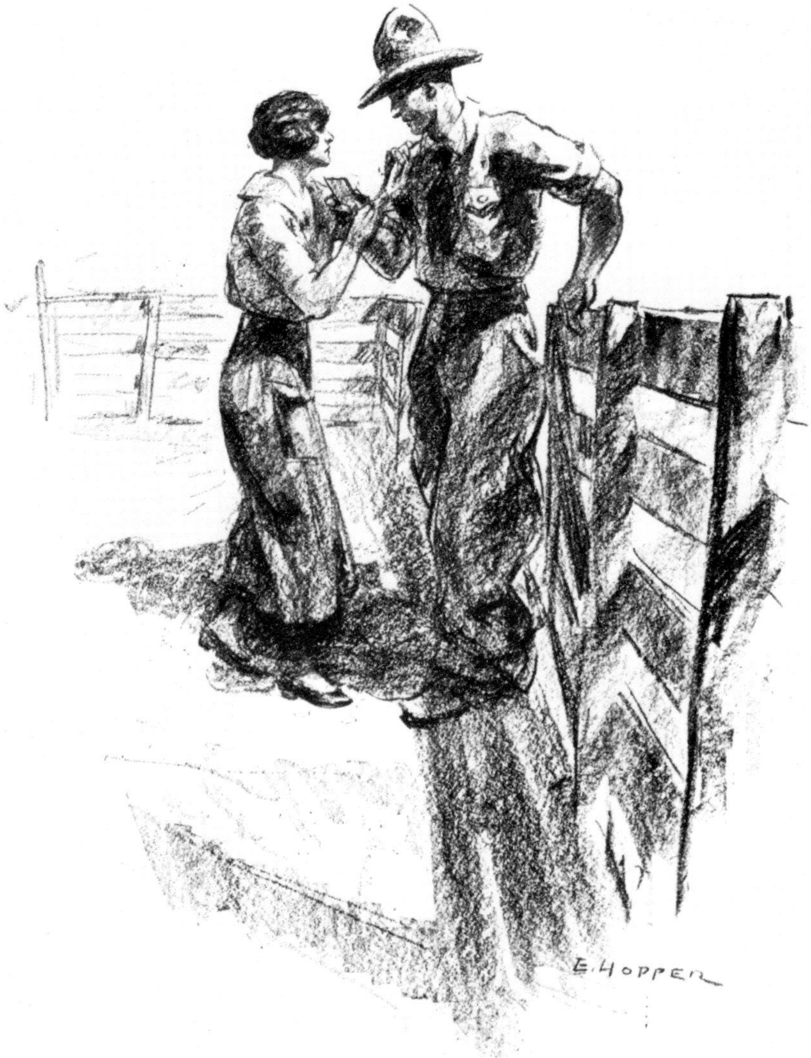

320

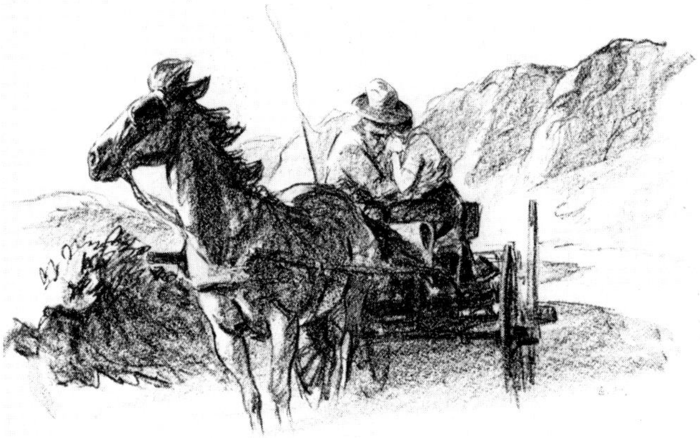

321a

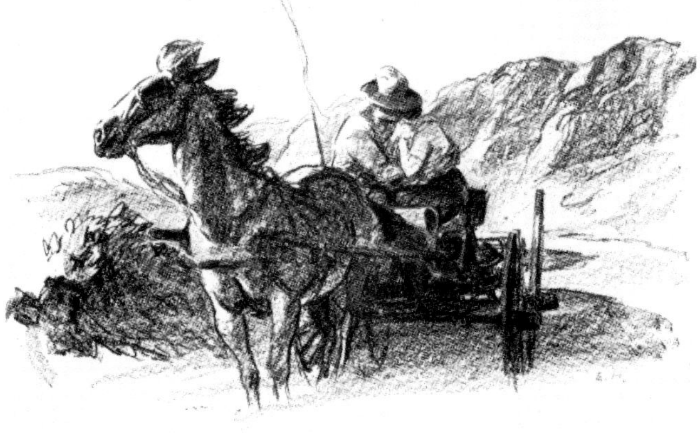

321b

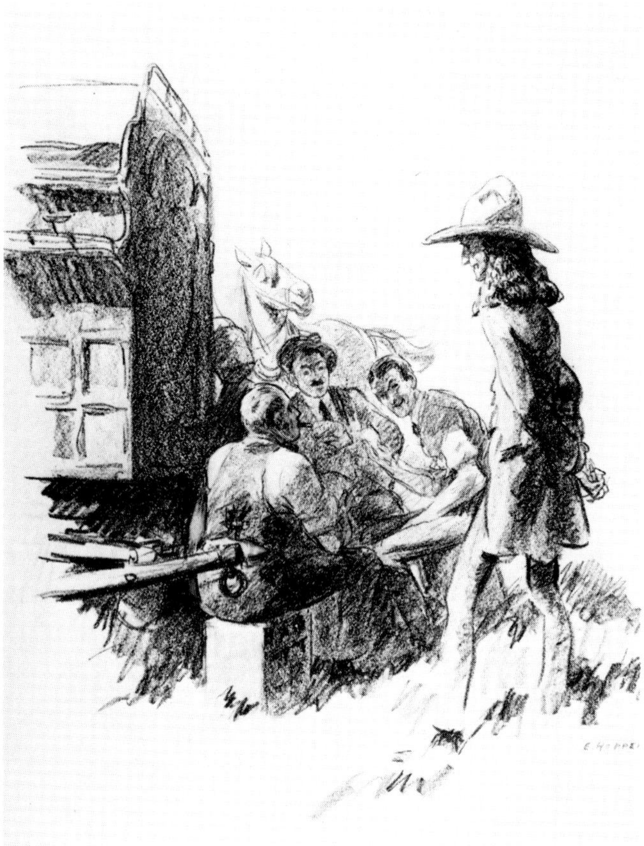

322a

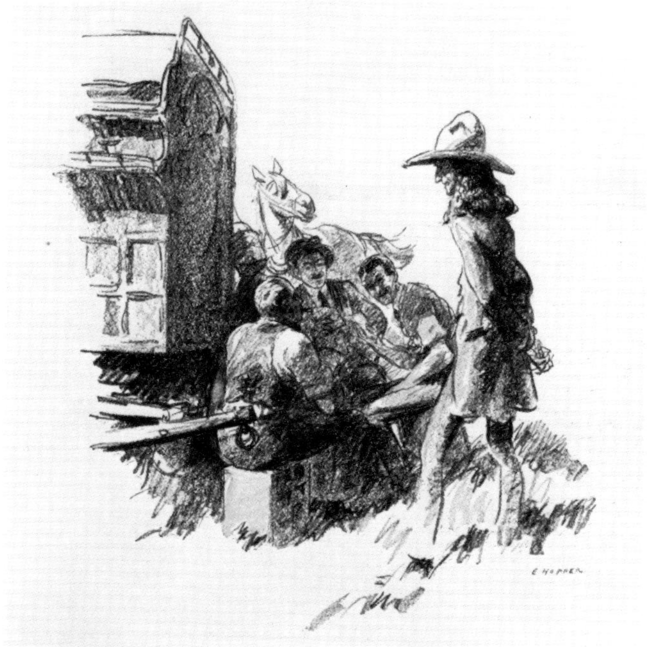

322b

Illustrations for Kyle S. Crichton, "For Sale: Med Show," *Scribner's Magazine,* 77 (February 1925).

322a. Illustration, 1924. Conte and white paint on illustration board, 30 × 21¾ inches. Whitney Museum of American Art, New York; Bequest of Josephine N. Hopper 70.1451.

322b. "The professor spoke kindly to his entertainers, who were sitting in the shade of the wagon playing cards," p. 179.

323a. Illustration, 1924. Conte and pencil on illustration board, 21½ × 30 inches. Whitney Museum of American Art, New York; Bequest of Josephine N. Hopper 70.1676.

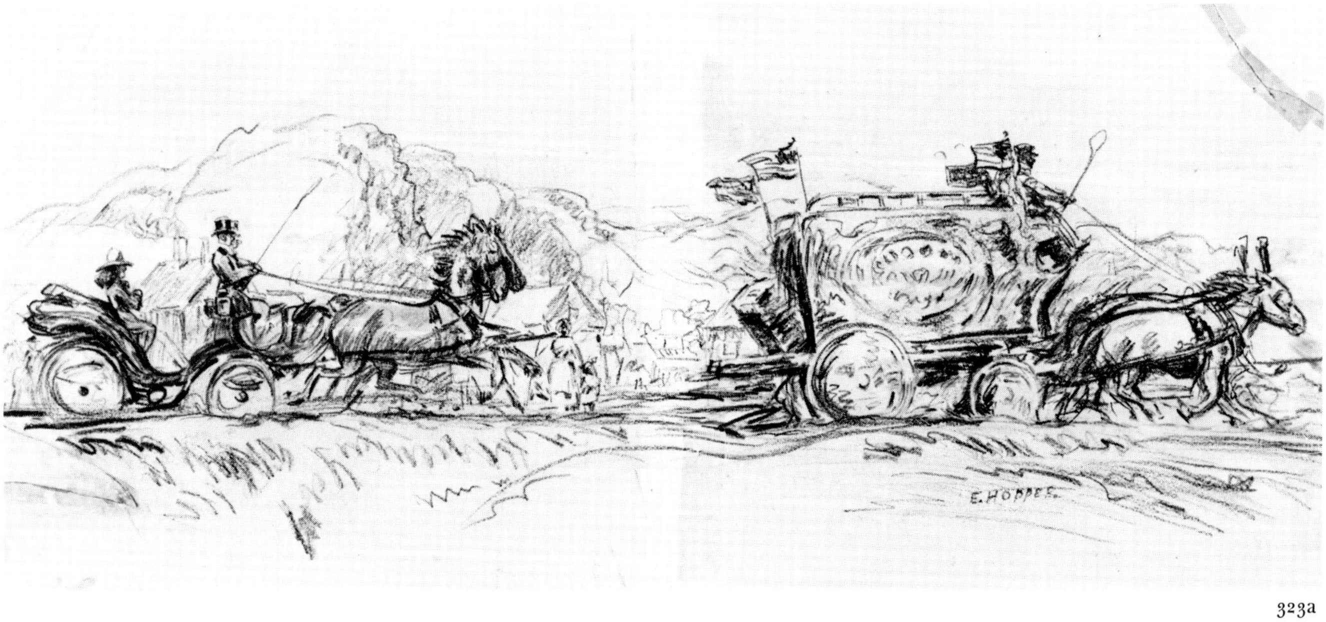

323a

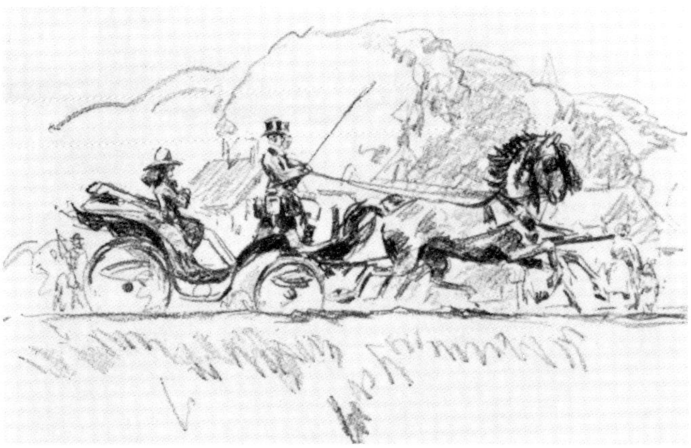

323b

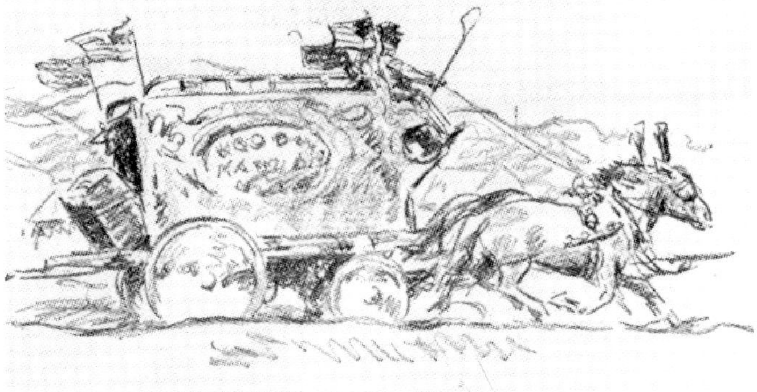

323b

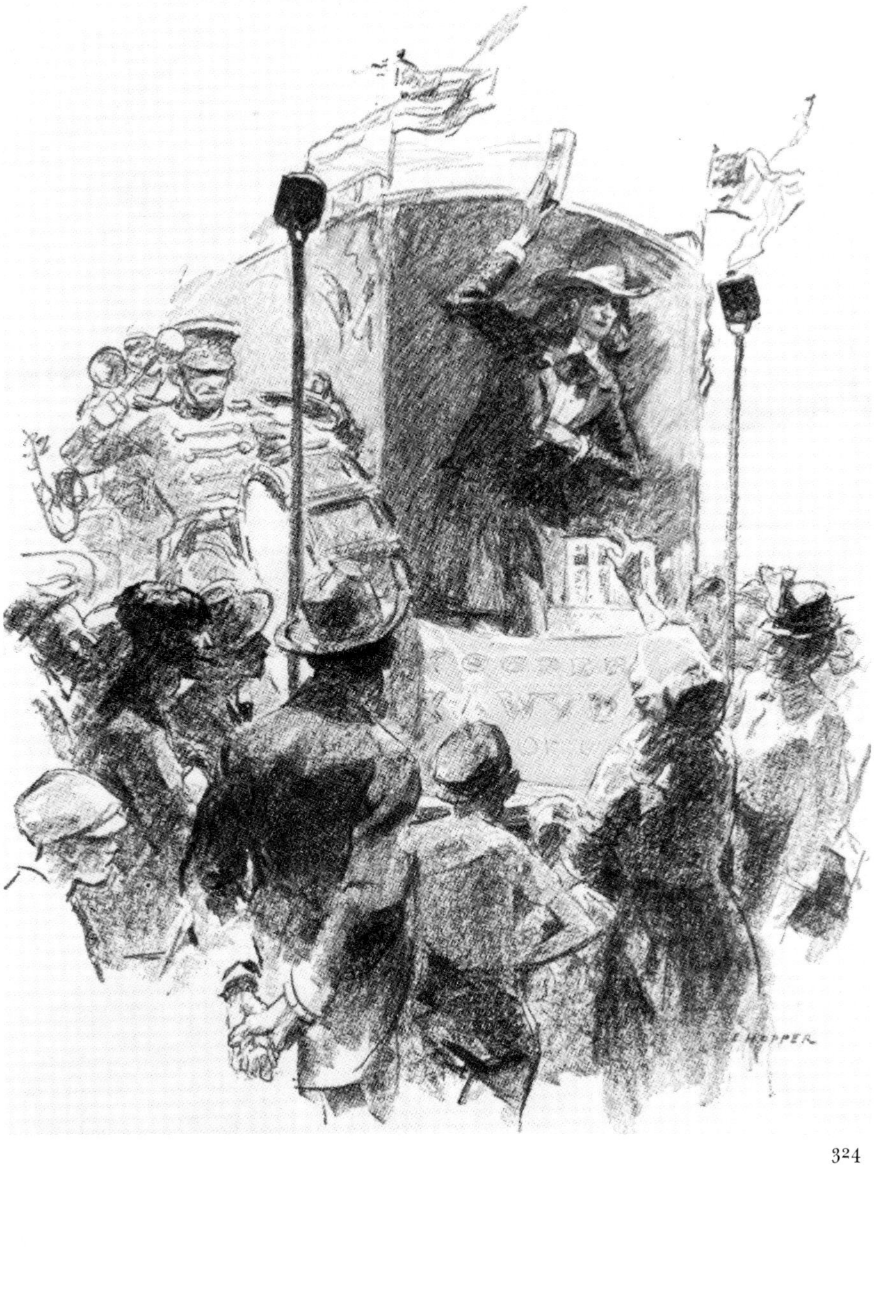

324

323b. "Behind the wagon at a respectable distance would come the professor himself in state, driven in a glistening carriage with two lively mares under the control of the driver's hand," pp. 180–81.

324. "Ah, madam, I am charmed to serve you again. It is the greatest joy of my life that I am enabled to bring relief to distraught mortals," p. 183.

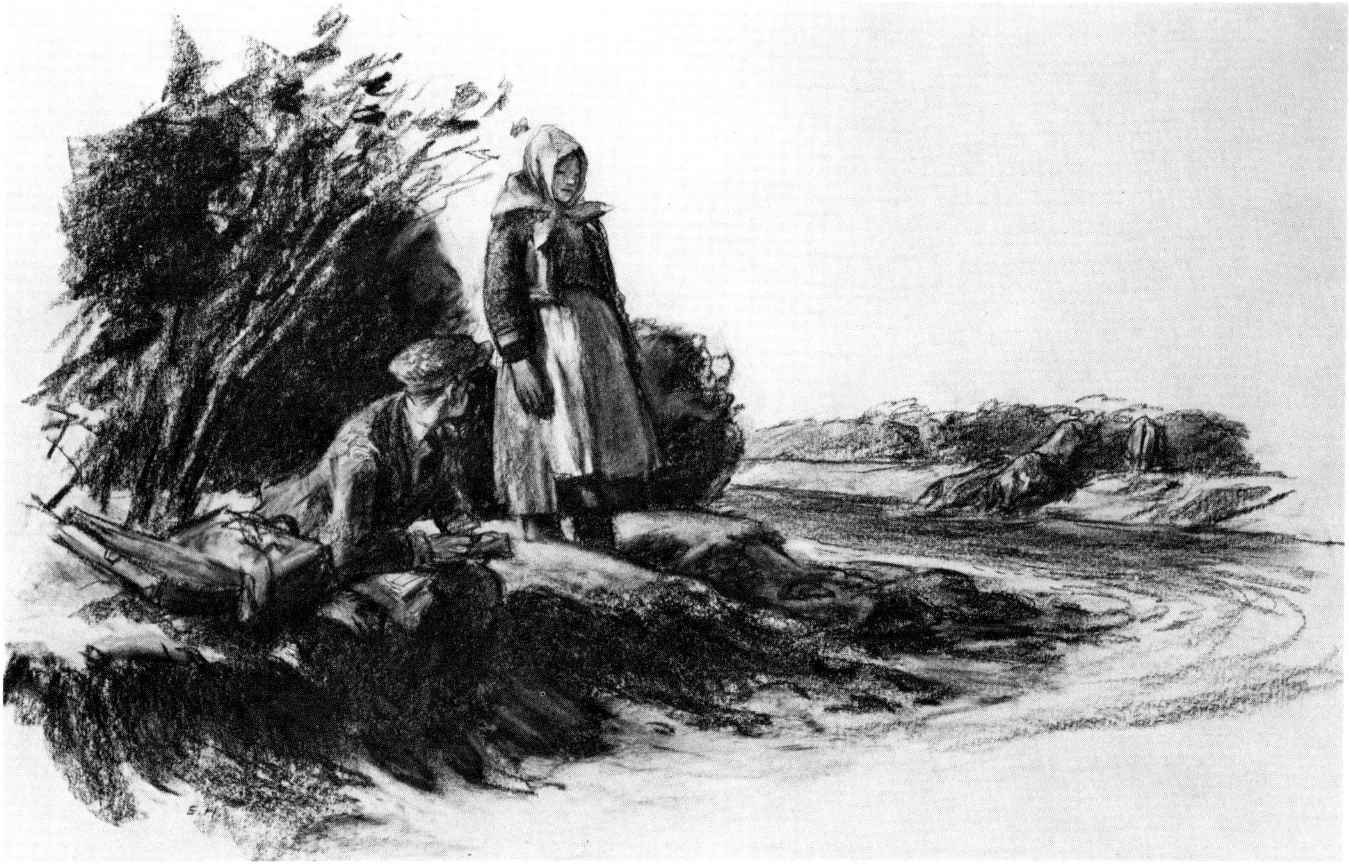

325a

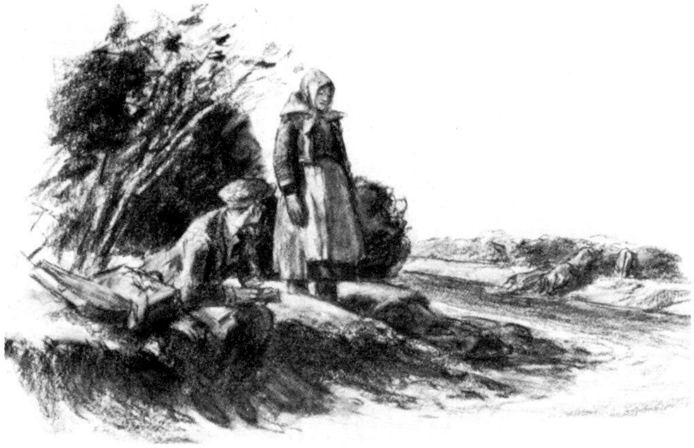

325b

Illustrations for Emerson Low, "The Man Who Had Been Away," *Scribner's Magazine,* 77 (May 1925).

325a. Illustration, 1925. Charcoal on illustration board, 16¾ × 27¼ inches. Kennedy Galleries, Inc., New York. Exhibited: Kennedy Galleries, Inc., New York, *Edward Hopper at Kennedy Galleries,* May 11—June 8, 1977 (no. 43).

325b. "Looking around, he saw the woman. She pretended not to notice him, and he kept on counting," p. 505.

326. "The stranger drew from his suitcase the doll, and gave it to the child," p. 507.

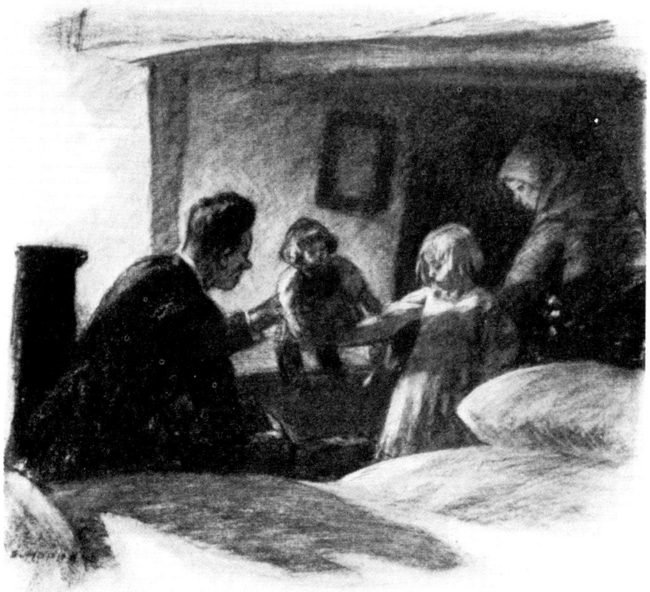

326

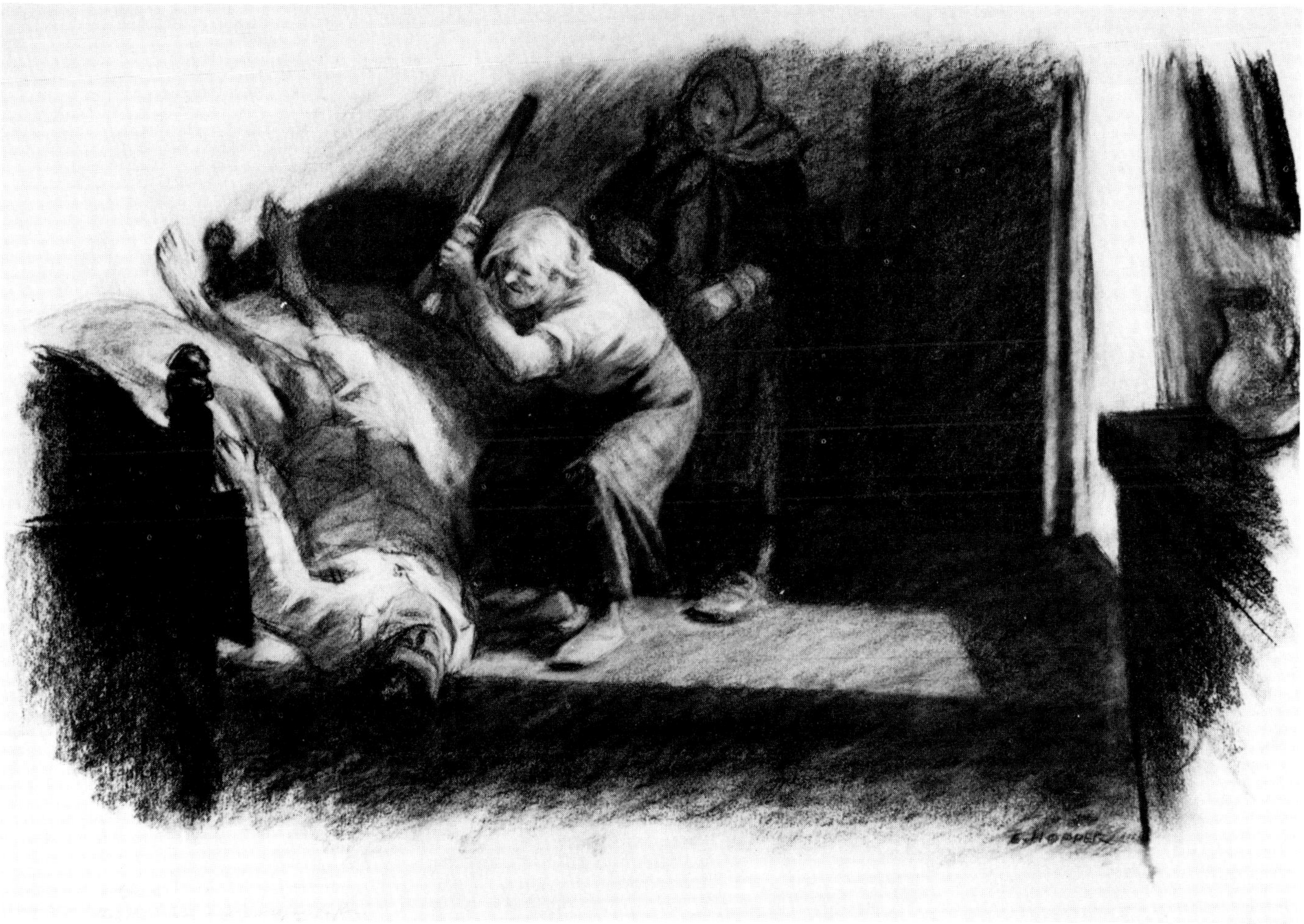

327a

327a. Illustration, 1925. Conte and white paint on illustration board, 20 × 30 inches. Whitney Museum of American Art, New York; Bequest of Josephine N. Hopper 70.1450.

327b. " 'What's this? . . . Don't, don't—Hannah!' " p. 514.

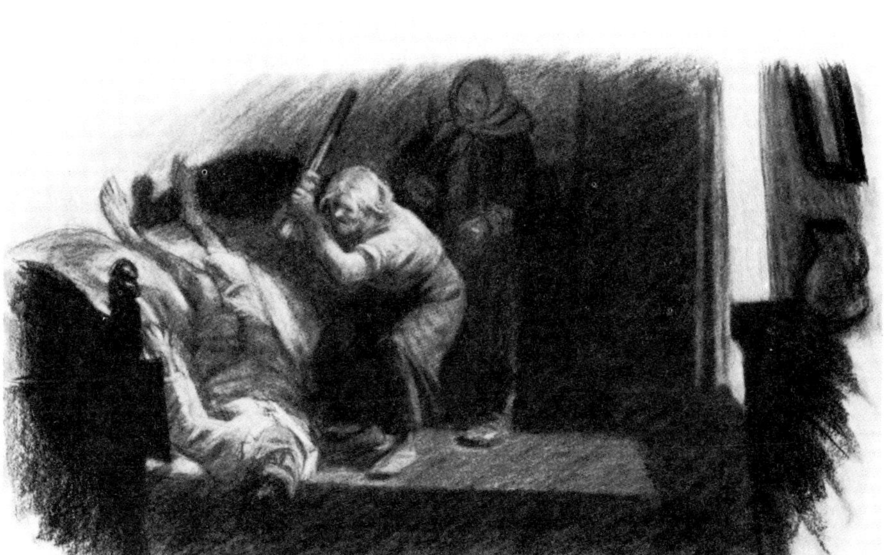

327b

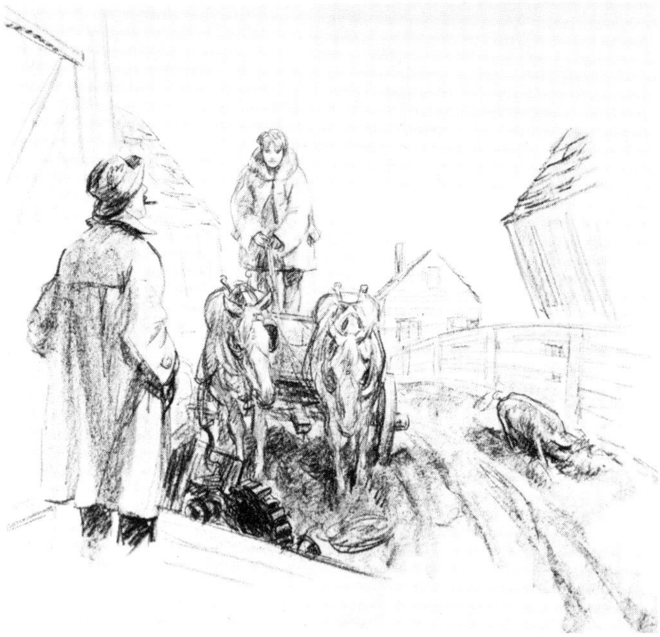

328a

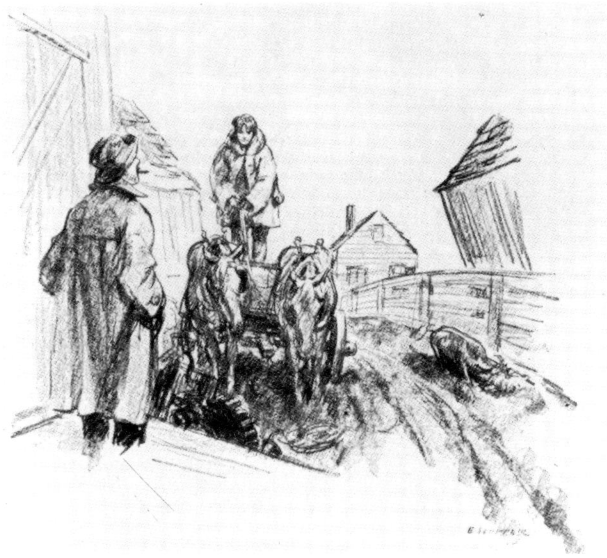

328b

Illustrations for J. Hyatt Downing, "Closed Roads," *Scribner's Magazine,* 78 (August 1925).

328a. Illustration, 1925. Conte and white paint on illustration board, 21¾ × 30 inches. Whitney Museum of American Art, New York; Bequest of Josephine N. Hopper 70.1453.

328b. " 'Son, you're going to lose money on that coat if you don't sell it pretty soon,' " p. 193.

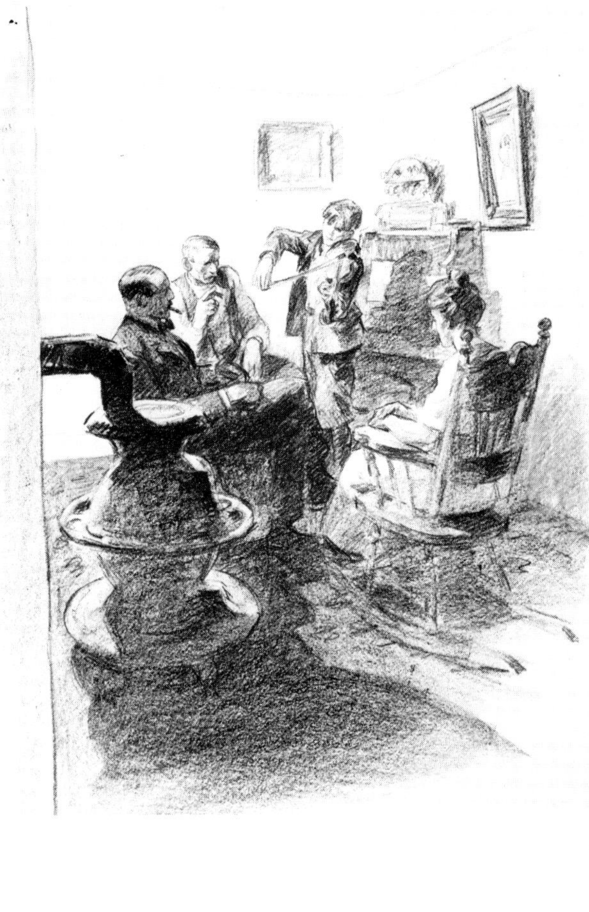

329a

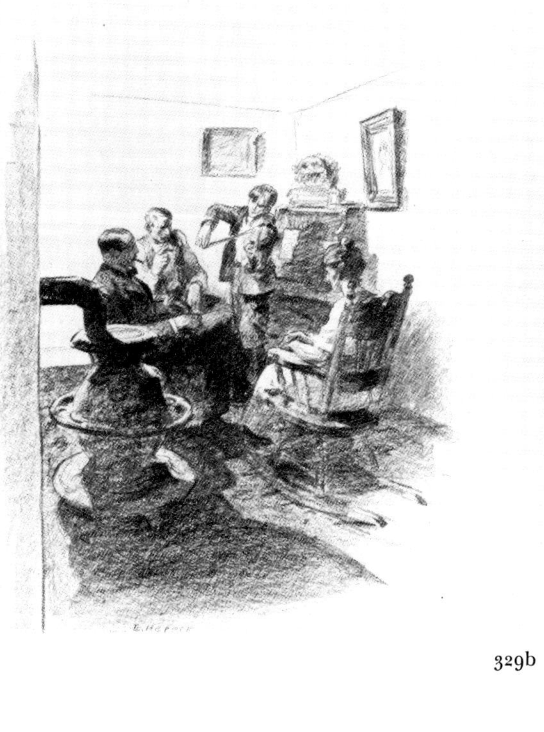

329b

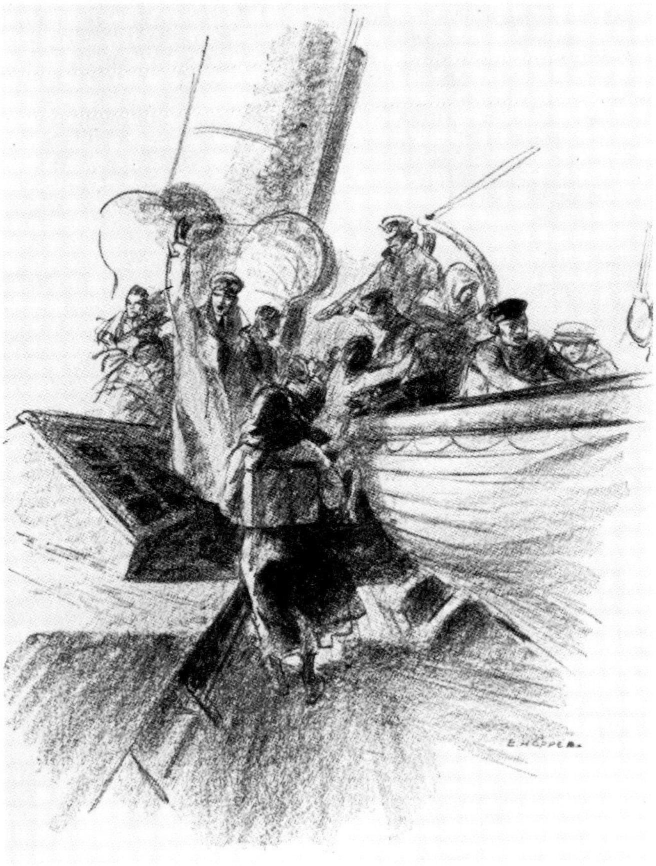

330

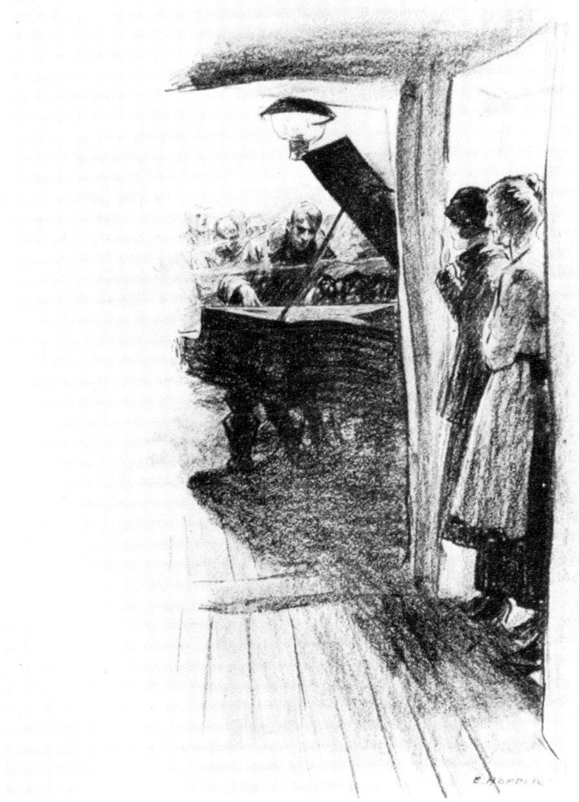

331

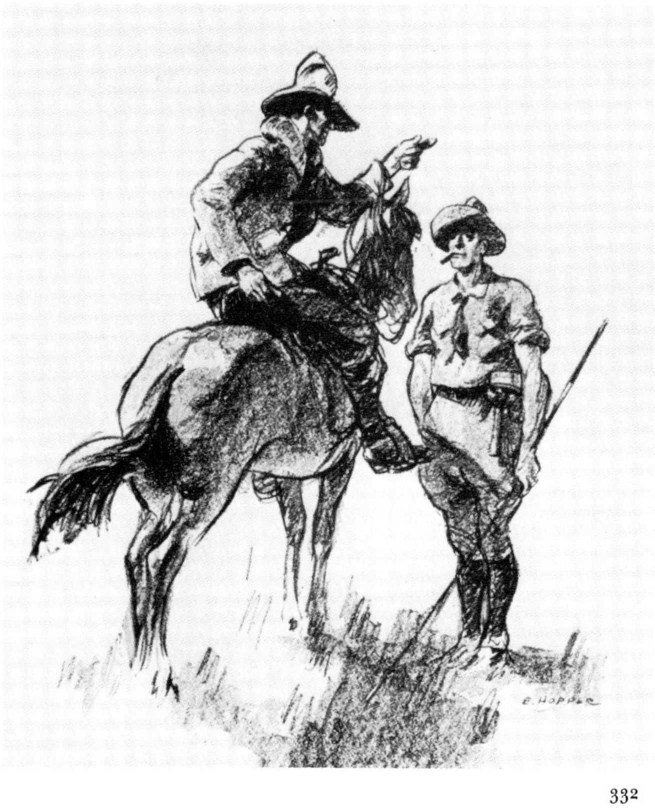

332

329a. Illustration, 1925. Conte on illustration board, 28¾ × 20¾ inches. Private collection.

329b. "With the first strain all Danny's nervousness left him . . . and the bare room was rich, filled with the most wonderful music I ever heard," p. 195.

330. ". . . swiftly the throb of music beat soothingly upon the ears of that fear-maddened crowd," p. 199.

Illustrations for J. Hyatt Downing, "The Distance to Casper," *Scribner's Magazine,* 81 (February 1927).

331. "At the piano was a man bent forward as in a listening attitude, his hands outspread upon the keyboard," p. 163.

332. "There is a government bench-mark under that rock cairn. I piled the stone around it myself, just to kill time," p. 167.

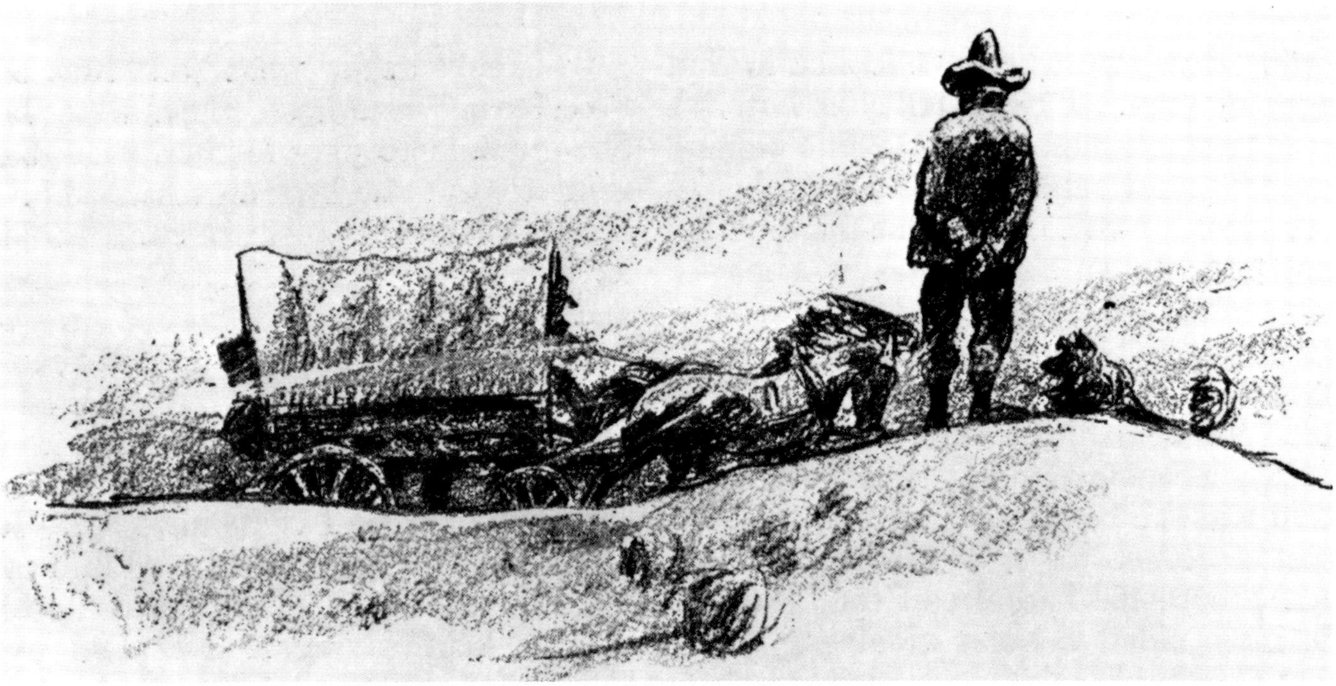

333

333. " 'Say, Old Timer,' yelled the teamster, . . . 'how far is it to Casper?' " p. 167.

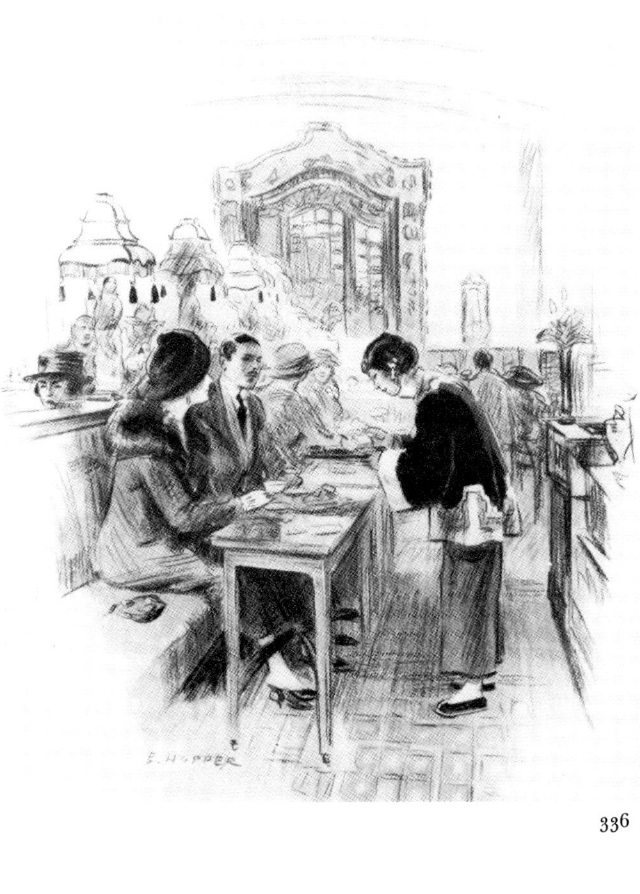

336

334a. Proof.

334b. Cover, *La France; An American Magazine,* 4 (November 1919). (Color plate, p. 89.)

335. Cover, *La France; An American Magazine,* 4 (April 1920). (Color plate, p. 90.)

Illustration for West Burden, "The New Sherry's" *Tavern Topics,* 1 (February 1920).

336. "In the McAlpin Shop deft and silent little Chinese maids serve ice cream sodas, afternoon tea, patisserie, and other delectable sweets," p. 6.

337. Cover, *Tavern Topics,* 1 (March 1920). (Color plate, p. 91.)

Illustration for West Burden, "Candies for the Captious: A Record Journey Through the Factory at Tiffin," *Tavern Topics,* 1 (March 1920).

338. "Speaking of sweets: Not all of them go out from Tiffin's big factory. Some of them stay there—right on the job," p. 2.

339. Cover, *Tavern Topics,* 1 (June 1920). (Color plate, p. 92.)

340. Cover, *Tavern Topics,* 1 (August 1920). (Color plate, p. 93.)

341. Cover, *Tavern Topics,* 2 (March 1921). (Color plate, p. 94.)

342. Cover, *Tavern Topics,* 4 (April 1923). (Color plate, p. 95.)

Illustration for Donald R. Richberg, "The Struggle for Prohibition," *Survey Graphic,* 2 (December 1922).

343. "The room seemed to have the air of carrying on the traditions of a long and honorable service," p. 284.

---

344. Cover, *Hotel Management,* 6 (July 1924). (Color plate, p. 96.)

345. Cover, *Hotel Management,* 6 (August 1924). (Color plate, p. 96.)

346. Cover, *Hotel Management,* 6 (September 1924). (Color plate, p. 96.)

347. Cover, *Hotel Management,* 6 (October 1924). (Color plate, p. 96.)

348. Cover, *Hotel Management,* 6 (November 1924). (Color plate, p. 97.)

349. Cover, *Hotel Management,* 6 (December 1924). (Color plate, p. 98.)

350. Cover, *Hotel Management,* 7 (January 1925). (Color plate, p. 99.)

351. Cover, *Hotel Management,* 7 (February 1925). (Color plate, p. 100.)

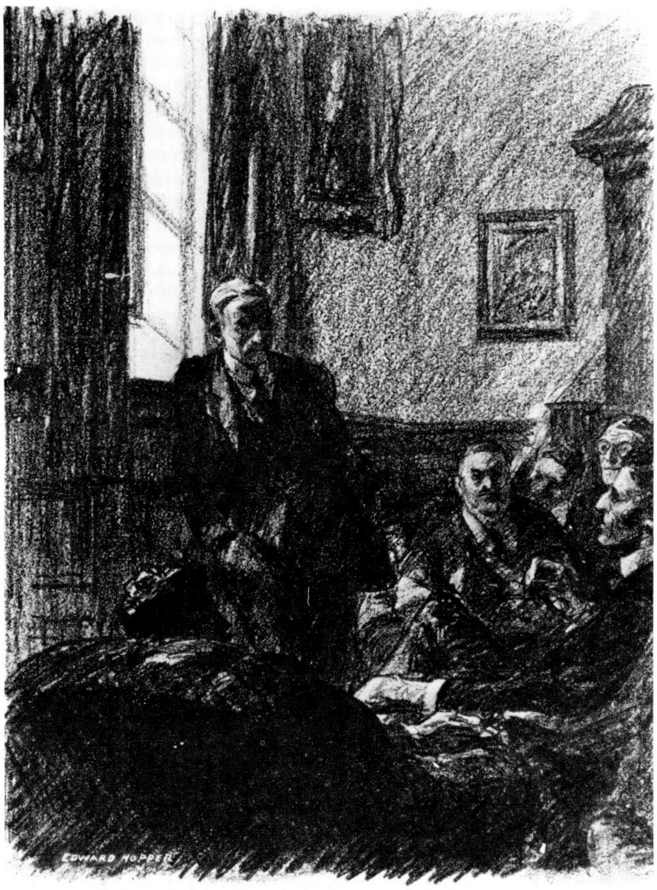

343

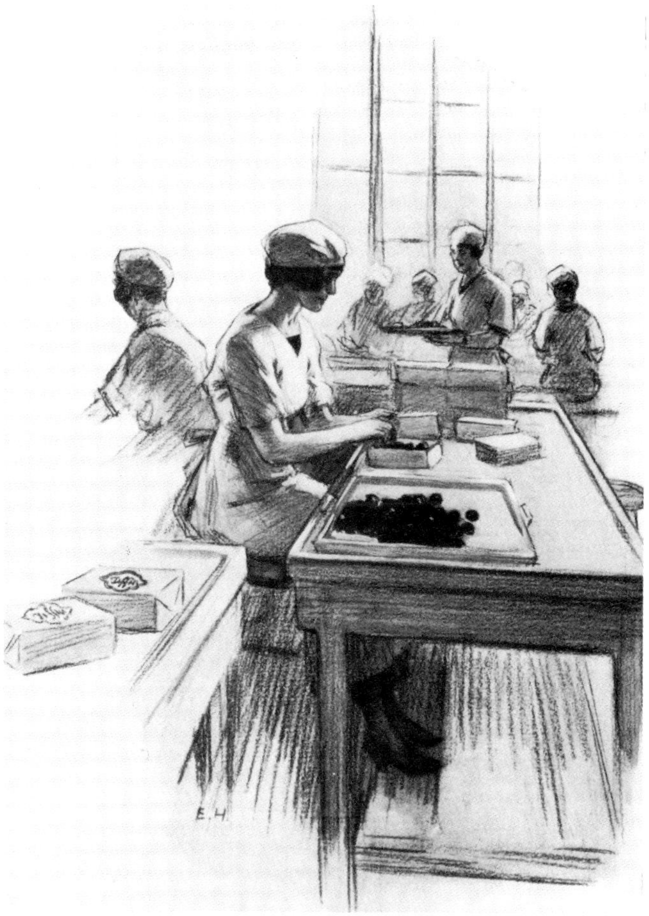

338

352. Cover, *Hotel Management,* 7 (March 1925). (Color plate, p. 101.)

353. Cover, *Hotel Management,* 7 (April 1925). (Color plate, p. 102.)

354. Cover, *Hotel Management,* 7 (May 1925). (Color plate, p. 103.)

355. Cover, *Hotel Management,* 7 (June 1925). (Color plate, p. 104.)

356. Cover, *Hotel Management,* 7 (July 1925). (Color plate, p. 105.)

357. Cover, *Hotel Management,* 7 (August 1925). (Color plate, p. 106.)

358. Cover, *Hotel Management,* 7 (September 1925). (Color plate, p. 107.)

359. Cover, *Hotel Management,* 7 (October 1925). (Color plate, p. 108.)

360. Cover, *Hotel Management,* 7 (November 1925). (Color plate, p. 109.)

361. Cover, *Hotel Management,* 7 (December 1925). (Color plate, p. 110.)

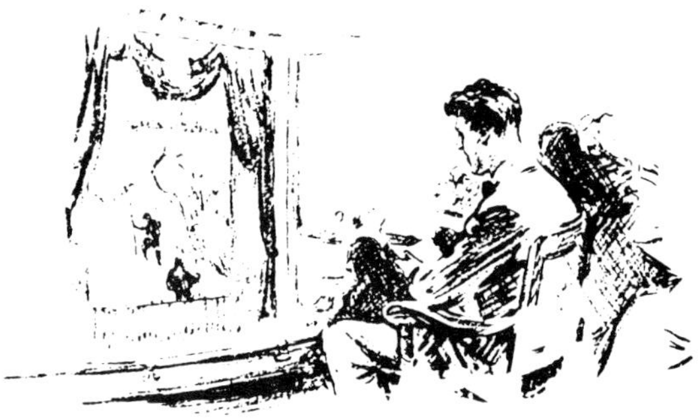

362

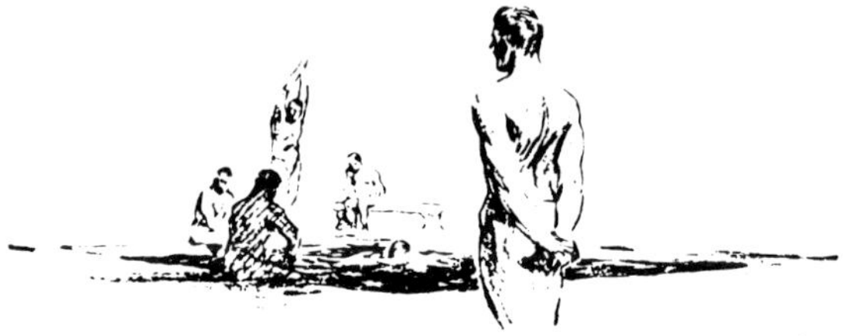

363

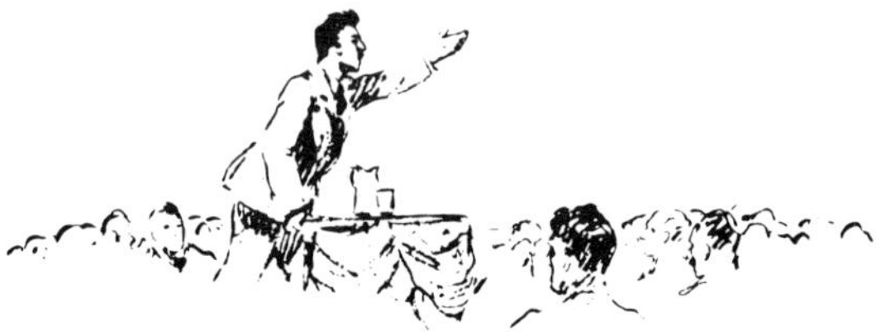

364

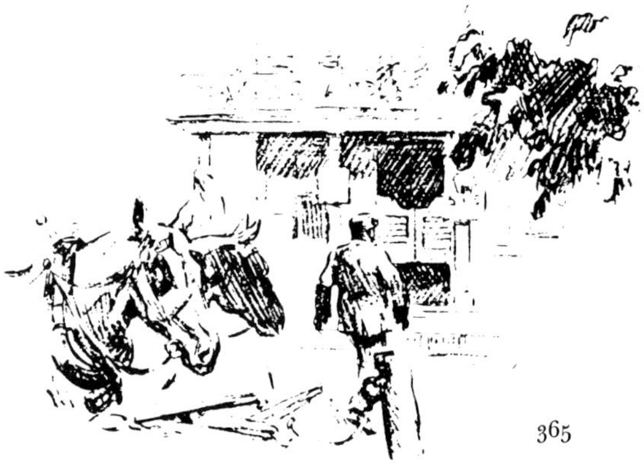

365

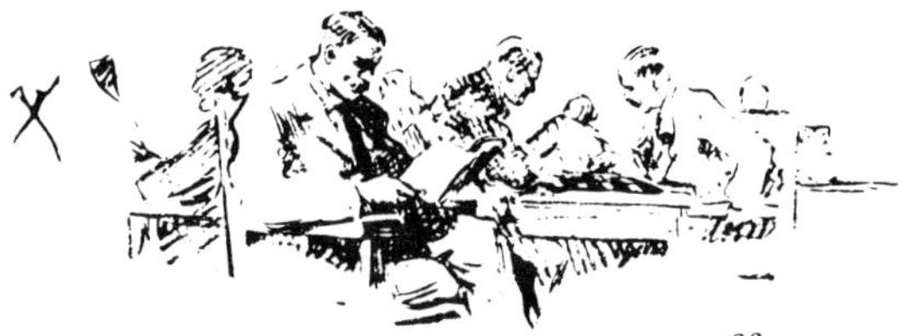

366

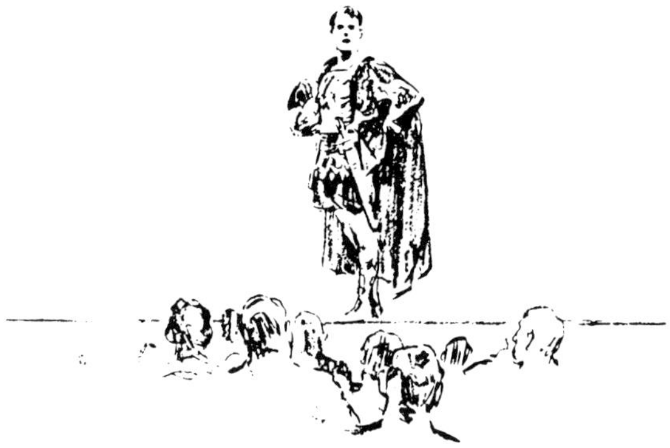

367

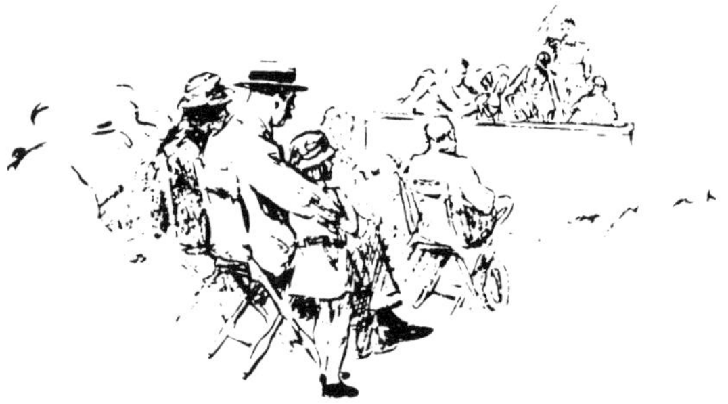

368

362. Proof, unidentified publication, c. 1912–18.
363. Proof, unidentified publication, c. 1912–18.
364. Proof, unidentified publication, c. 1912–18.
365. Proof, unidentified publication, c. 1912–18.
366. Proof, unidentified publication, c. 1912–18.
367. Proof, unidentified publication, c. 1912–18.

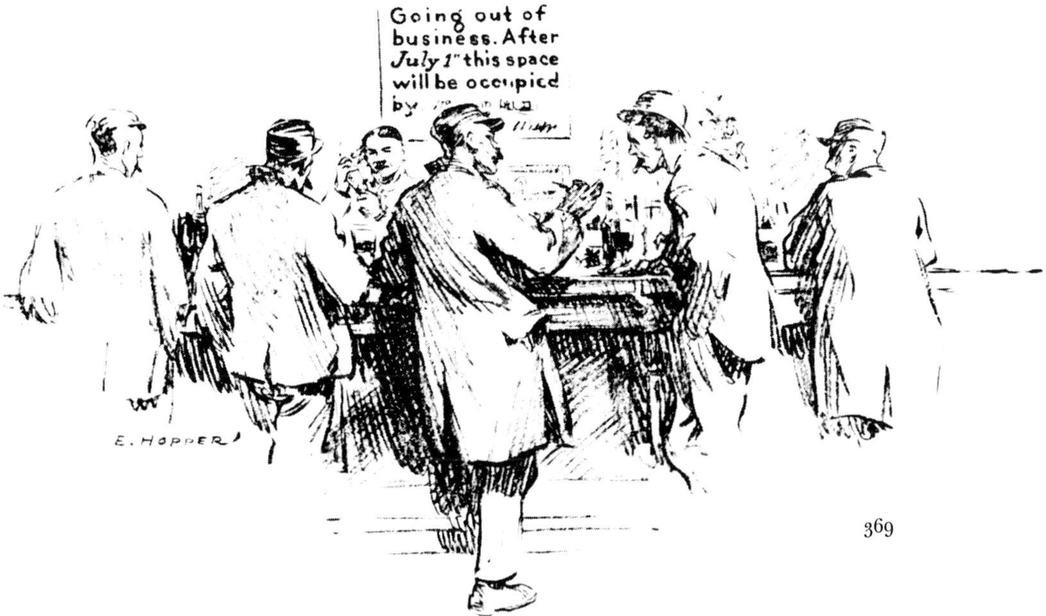

369

372

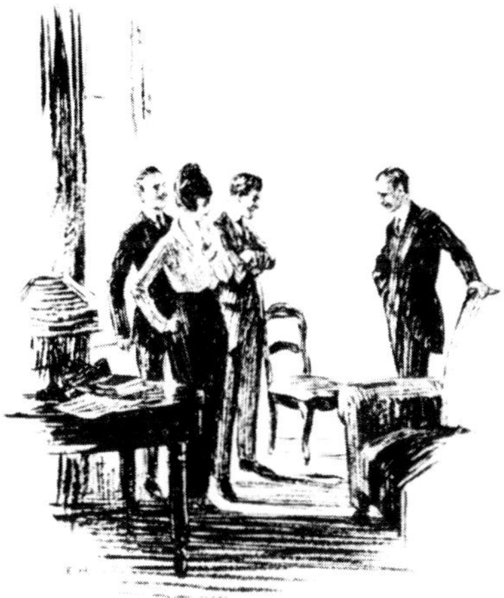

370

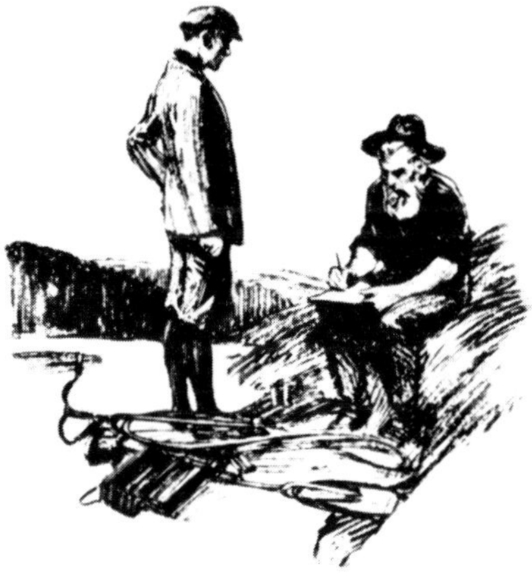

371

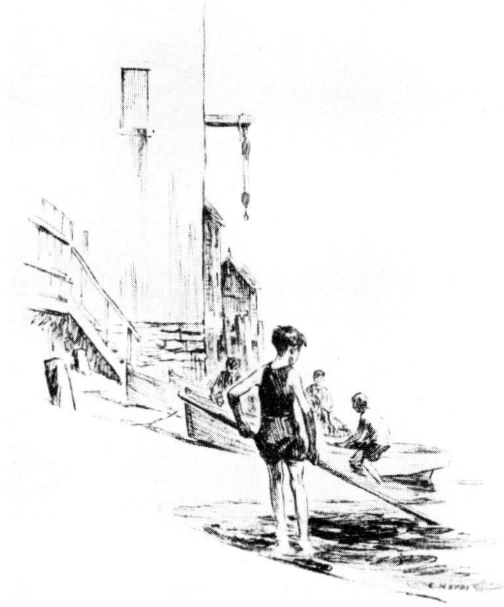

368. Proof, unidentified publication, c. 1912–18.
369. Proof, unidentified publication, c. 1912–18.
370. Proof, unidentified publication, c. 1912–18.
371. Proof, unidentified publication, c. 1912–18.
372. Proof, unidentified publication, c. 1912–18.
373. Proof, unidentified publication, c. 1912–18.

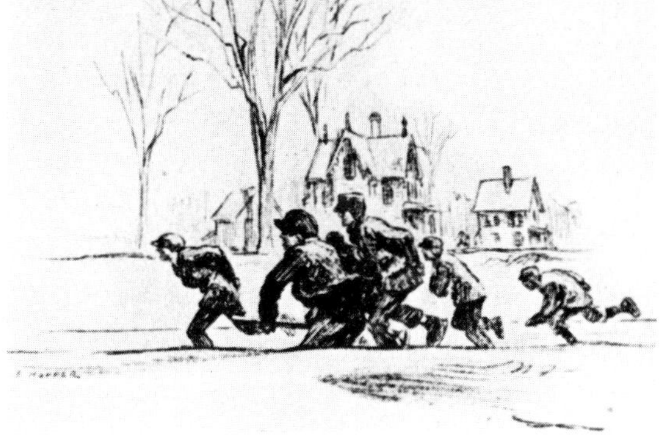

373

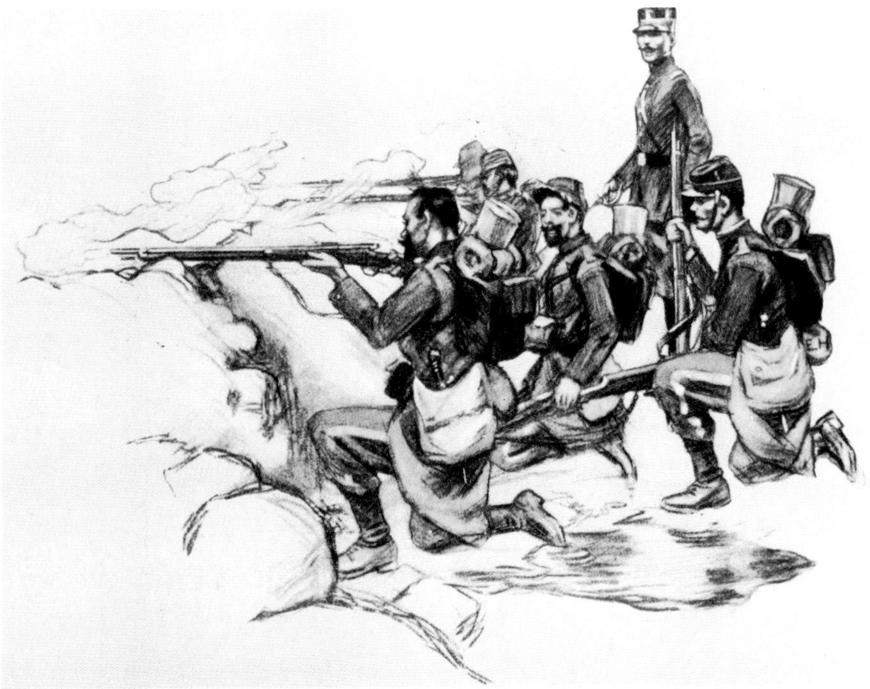

374

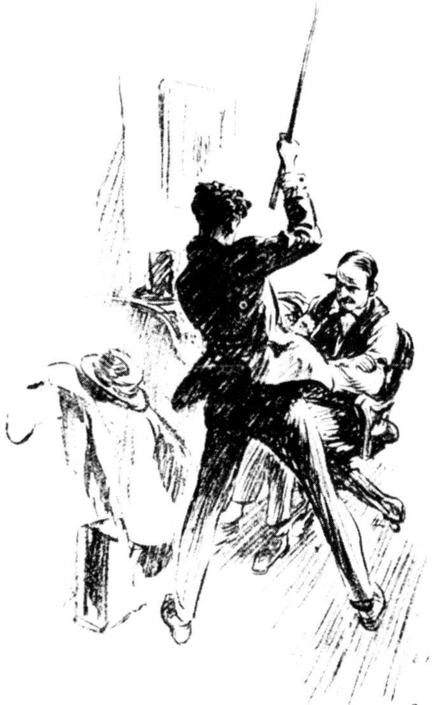

376

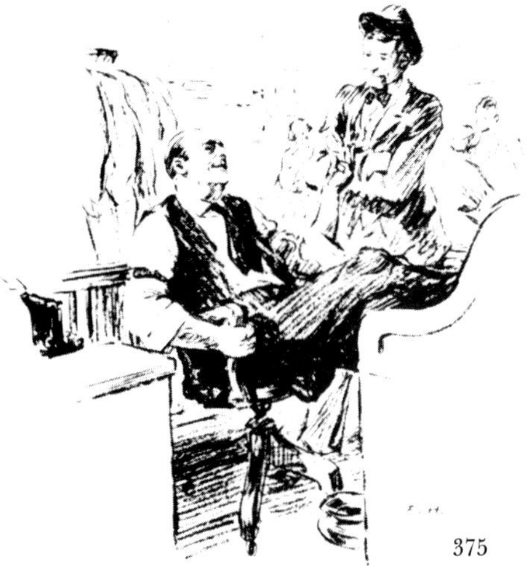

375

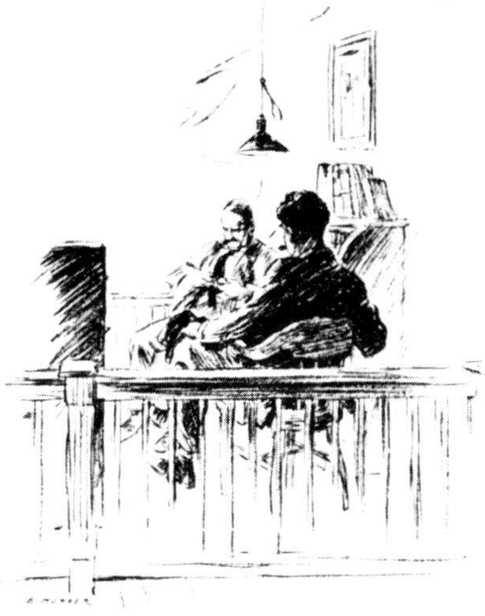

378

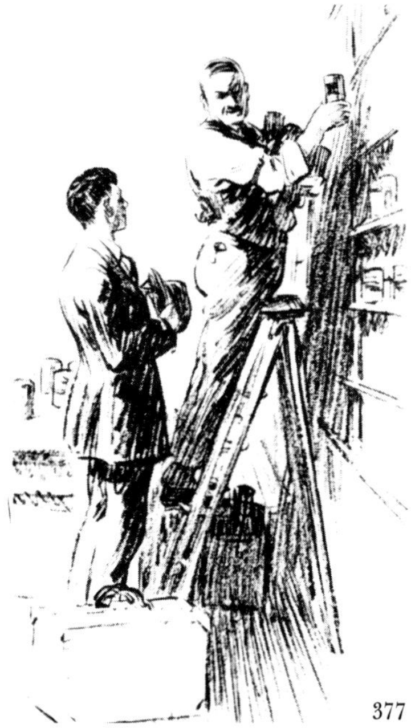

377

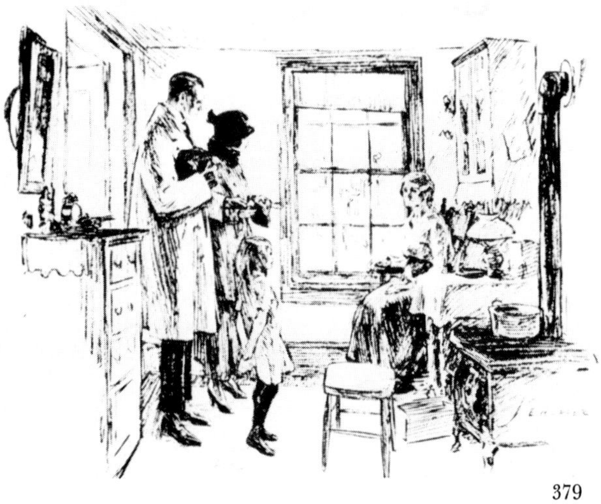

379

374. Proof, possibly unpublished illustration for "Frederick Palmer in Germany: My Day at the Front," *Everybody's,* 32 (January 1915).

375. " 'The salesmen I've been raving about have their politeness pasted onto their outsides, like shaving lotion or a bunion pad,' " tearsheet, unidentified publication, c. 1915–18.

376. Tearsheet, unidentified publication, c. 1915–18.

377. Tearsheet, unidentified publication, c. 1915–18.

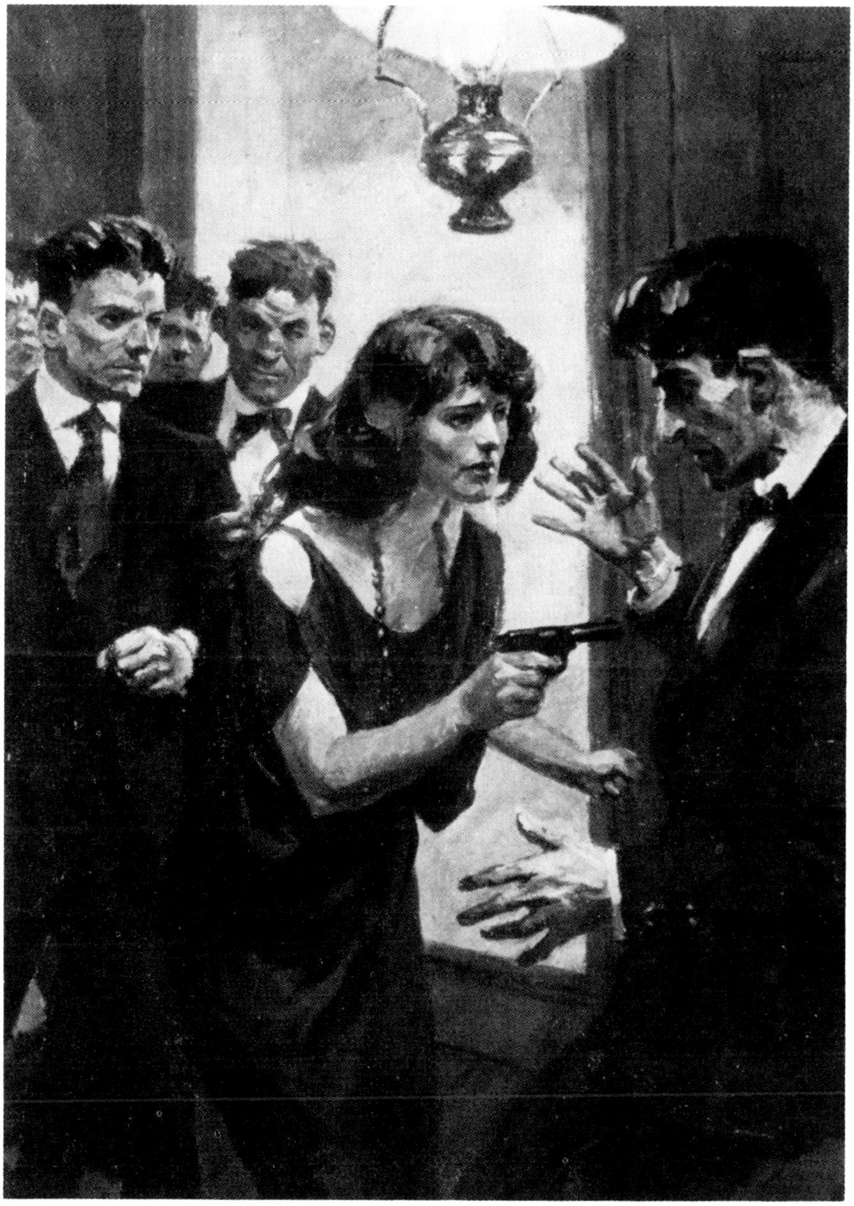

381

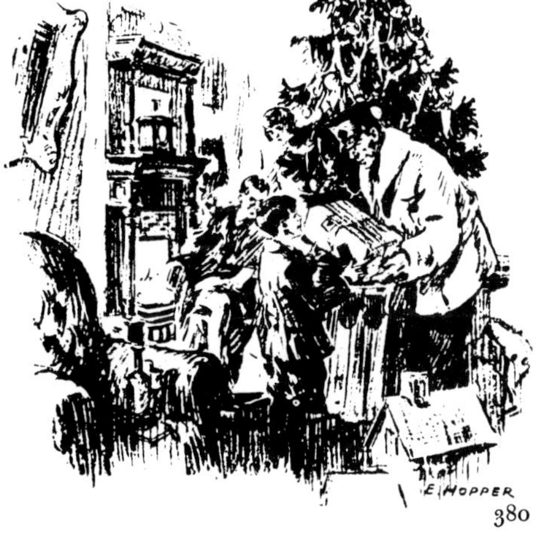

380

378. " 'Well-l-l,' he began, 'If you're really interested.' I assured him that I was," tearsheet, unidentified publication, c. 1915–18.

379. Proof, possibly illustration for *Farmer's Wife,* c. 1915–18.

380. Proof, possibly illustration for *Wells Fargo Messenger,* c. 1916–20.

381. Proof, possibly illustration for *Everybody's,* c. 1920–21.

382. Proof, possibly illustration for *Everybody's,* c. 1920–21.

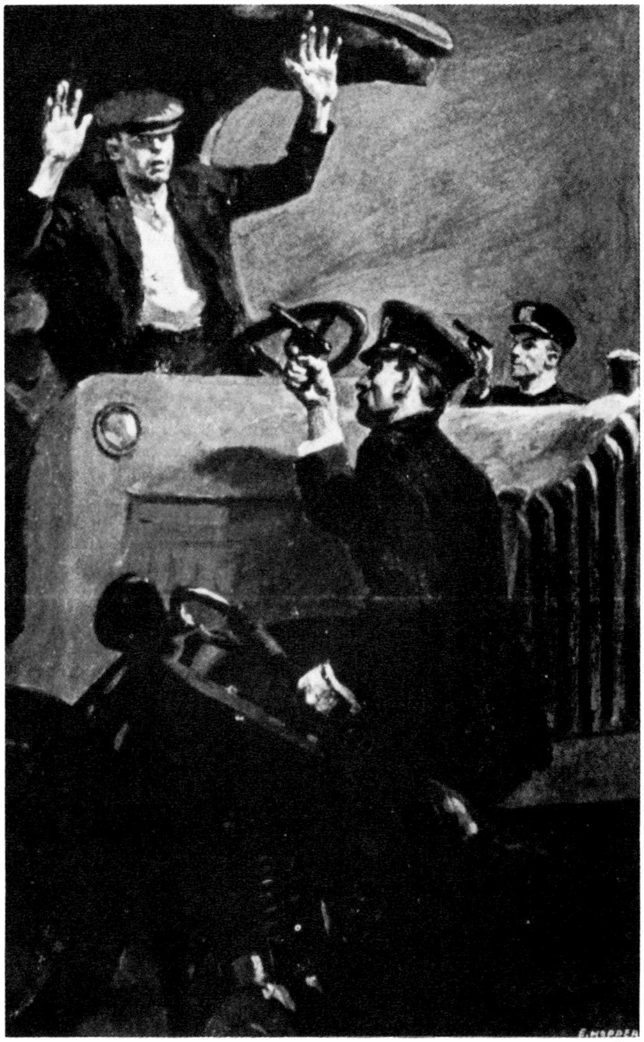

382

383b

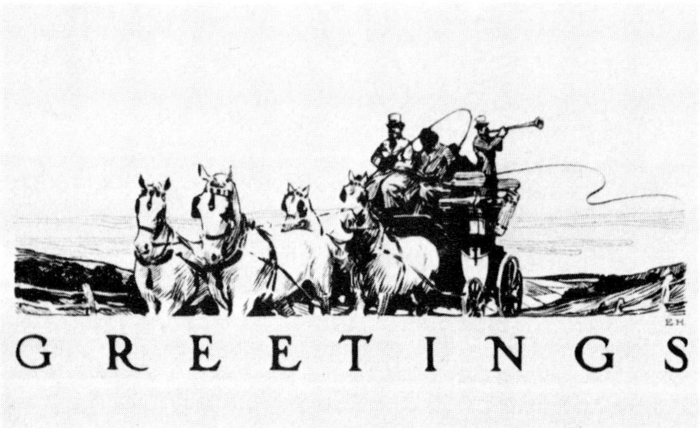

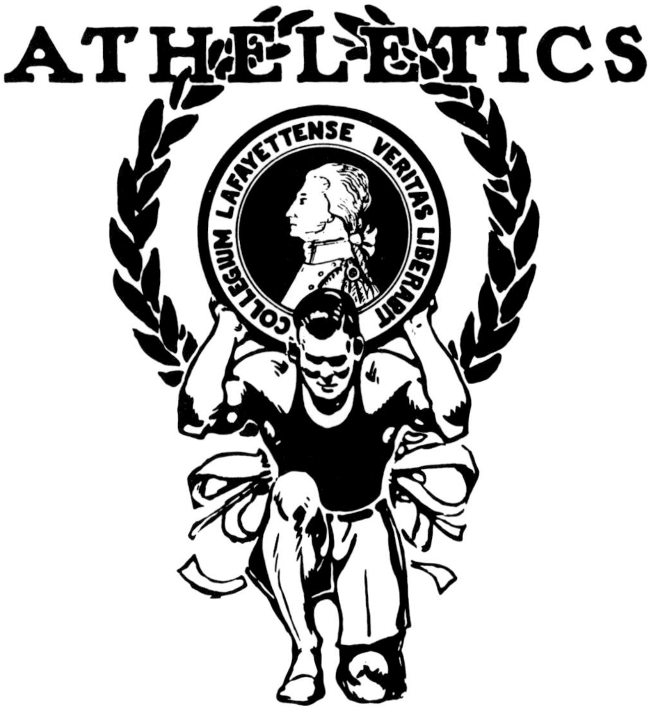

384b

Illustrations for *Melange,* 1912, yearbook of Lafayette College, Easton, Pennsylvania.

383a. Proof.

383b. "Greetings," p. 7.

384a. Proof.

384b. "Atheletics," p. 199.

385a. Proof.

385b. "Society," p. 245.

386. "Basket Ball," proof, publication unknown, c. 1911–12.

387. "Banjo Club," proof, publication unknown, c. 1911–12.

388. "Grinds," proof, publication unknown, c. 1911–12.

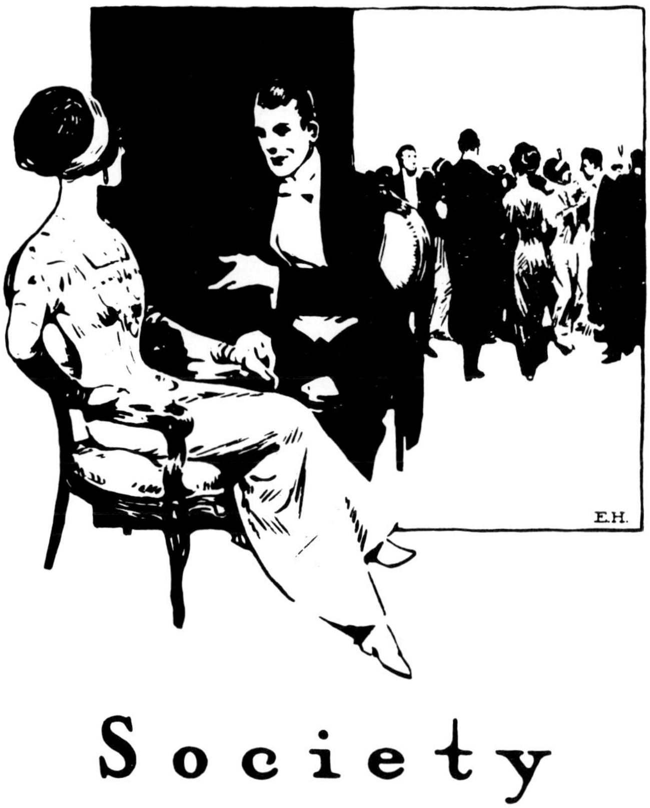

385b

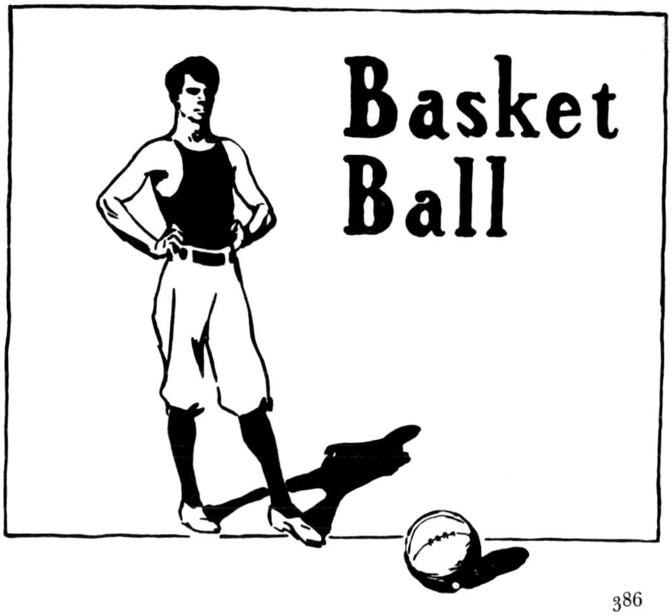

386

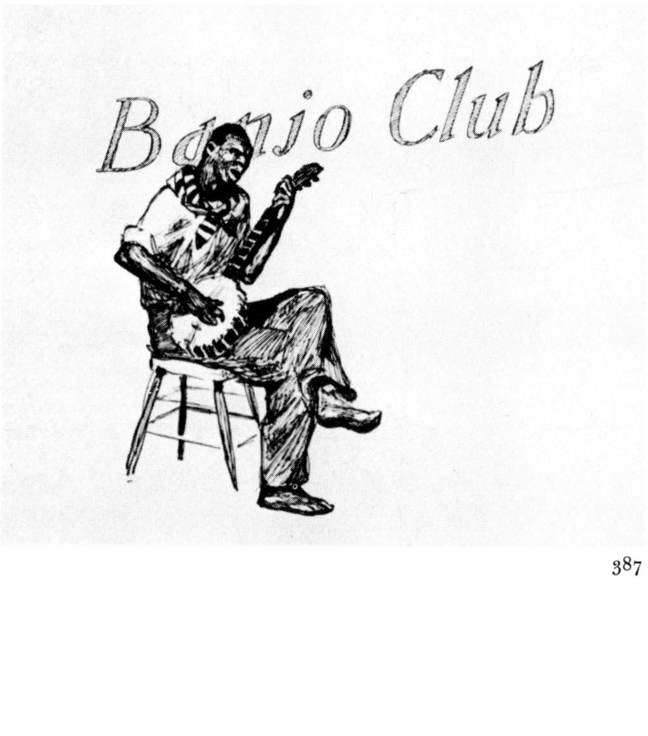

387

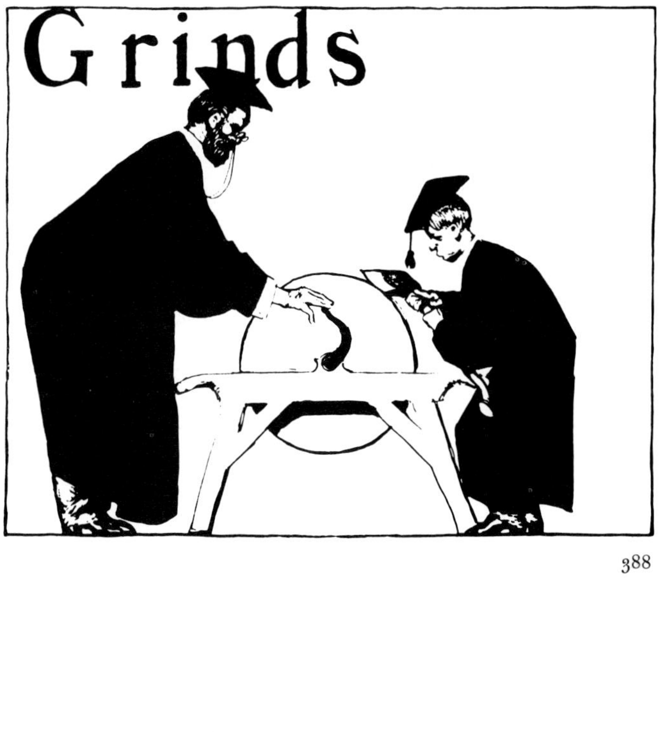

388

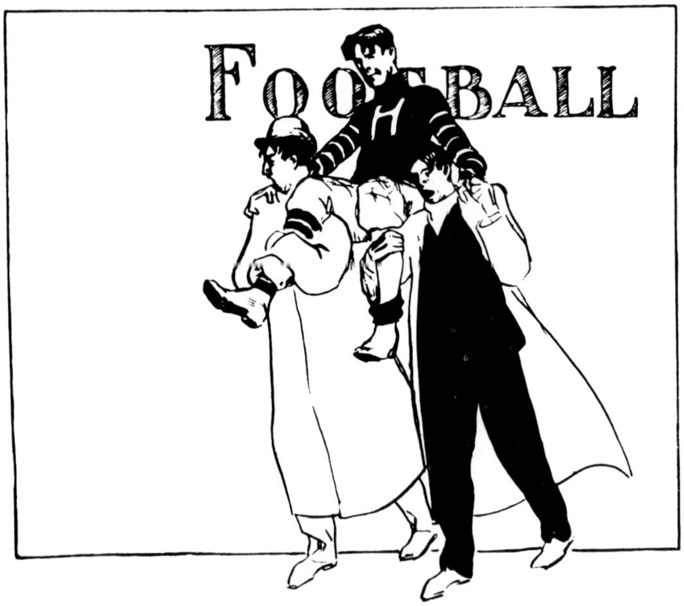

389

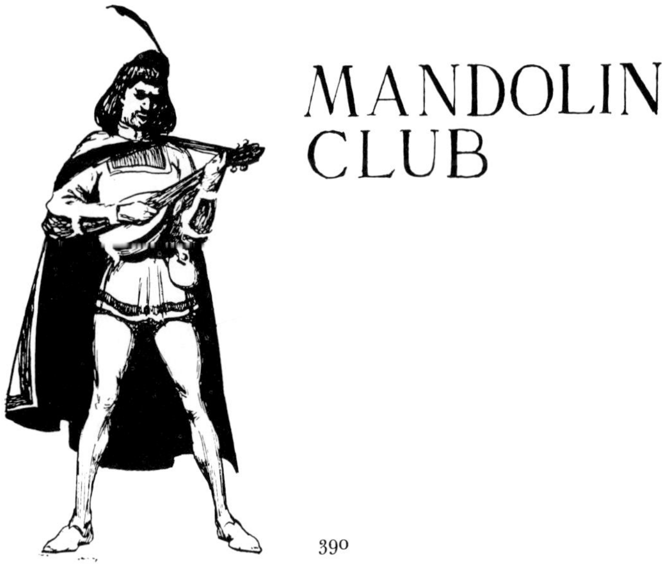

390

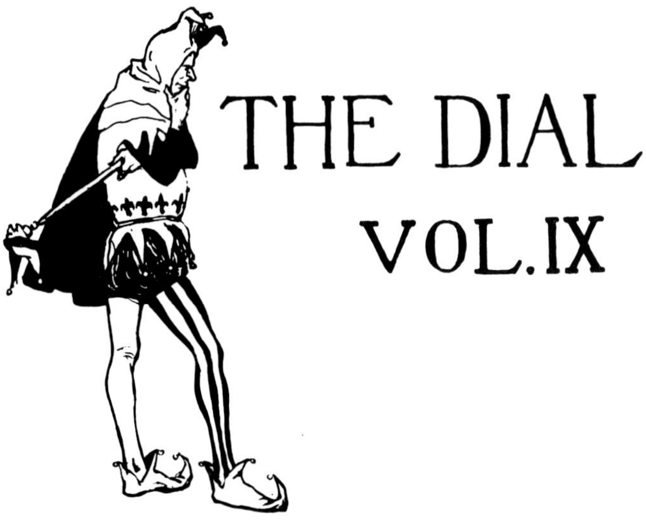

391

389. "Football," proof, publication unknown, c. 1911–12.

390. "Mandolin Club," proof, publication unknown, c. 1911–12.

391. "The Dial, Vol. IX," proof, publication unknown, c. 1911–12.

Brochure for Brigham, Hopkins Company, Baltimore and New York, c. 1908 (through Sherman & Bryan, Inc., advertising agency).

392. Front cover, silhouettes and display lettering by Hopper.

393. Inside spread, silhouettes and display lettering by Hopper.

394. Back cover, decorative border by Hopper.

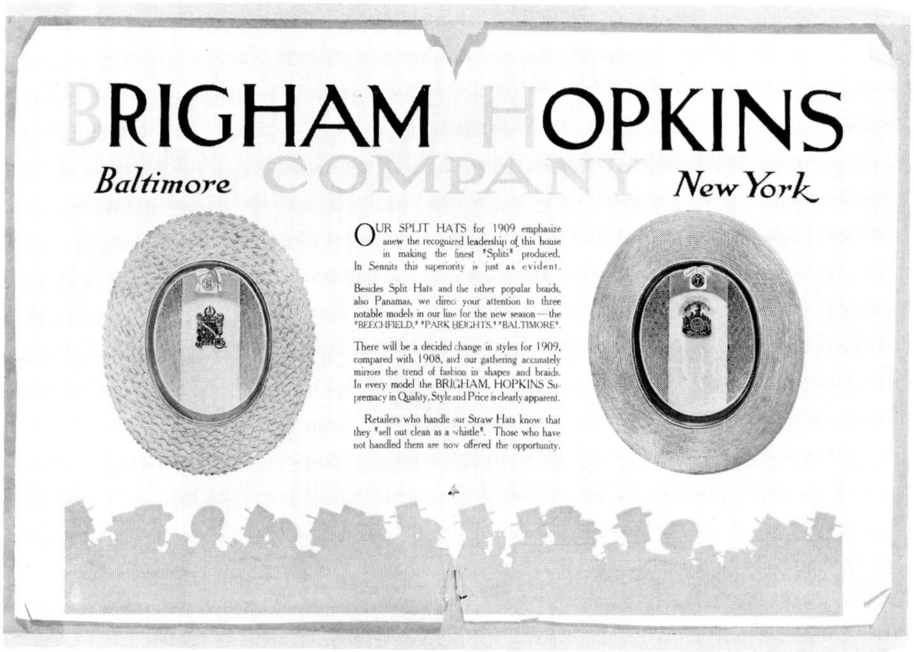
BRIGHAM HOPKINS
COMPANY
Baltimore
New York
OUR SPLIT HATS for 1909 emphasize anew the recognized leadership of this house in making the finest "Splits" produced. In Sennits this superiority is just as evident.
Besides Split Hats and the other popular braids, also Panamas, we direct your attention to three notable models in our line for the new season — the "BEECHFIELD," "PARK HEIGHTS," "BALTIMORE".
There will be a decided change in styles for 1909, compared with 1908, and our gathering accurately mirrors the trend of fashion in shapes and braids. In every model the BRIGHAM, HOPKINS Supremacy in Quality, Style and Price is clearly apparent.
Retailers who handle our Straw Hats know that they "sell out clean as a whistle". Those who have not handled them are now offered the opportunity.

393

392

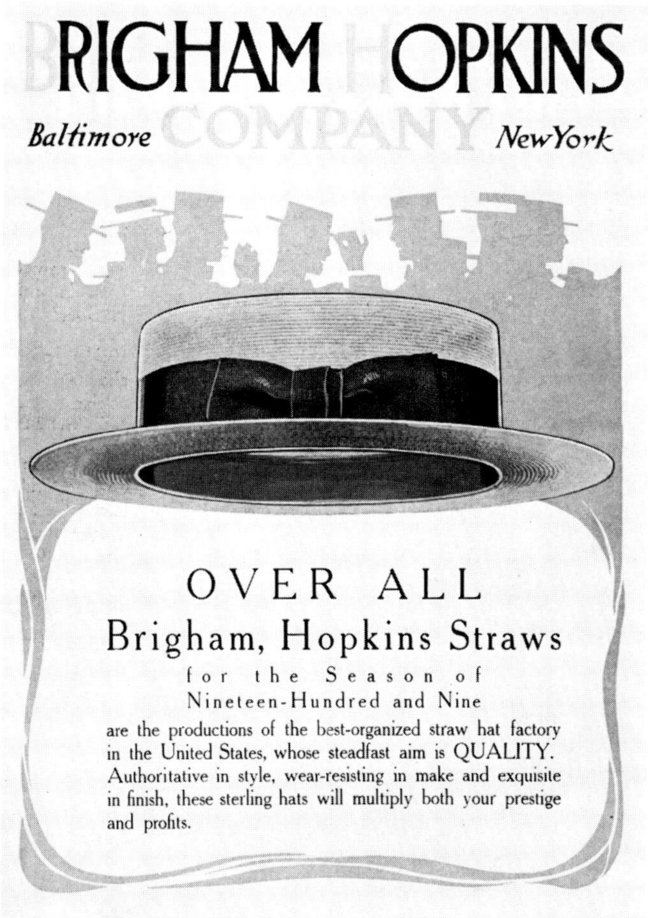
BRIGHAM HOPKINS
COMPANY
Baltimore
New York
OVER ALL
Brigham, Hopkins Straws
for the Season of
Nineteen-Hundred and Nine
are the productions of the best-organized straw hat factory in the United States, whose steadfast aim is QUALITY. Authoritative in style, wear-resisting in make and exquisite in finish, these sterling hats will multiply both your prestige and profits.

394

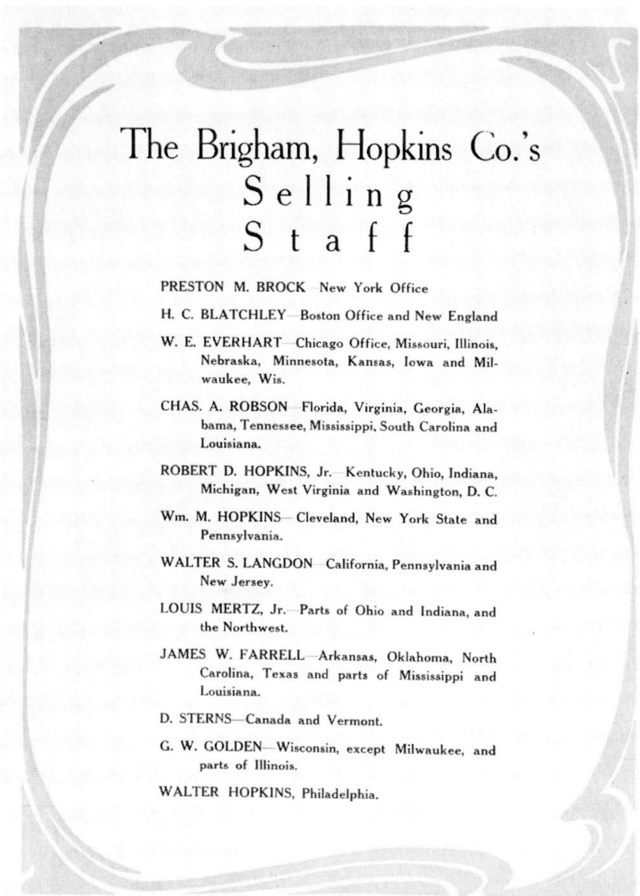
The Brigham, Hopkins Co.'s
Selling
Staff
PRESTON M. BROCK—New York Office
H. C. BLATCHLEY—Boston Office and New England
W. E. EVERHART—Chicago Office, Missouri, Illinois, Nebraska, Minnesota, Kansas, Iowa and Milwaukee, Wis.
CHAS. A. ROBSON—Florida, Virginia, Georgia, Alabama, Tennessee, Mississippi, South Carolina and Louisiana.
ROBERT D. HOPKINS, Jr.—Kentucky, Ohio, Indiana, Michigan, West Virginia and Washington, D. C.
Wm. M. HOPKINS—Cleveland, New York State and Pennsylvania.
WALTER S. LANGDON—California, Pennsylvania and New Jersey.
LOUIS MERTZ, Jr.—Parts of Ohio and Indiana, and the Northwest.
JAMES W. FARRELL—Arkansas, Oklahoma, North Carolina, Texas and parts of Mississippi and Louisiana.
D. STERNS—Canada and Vermont.
G. W. GOLDEN—Wisconsin, except Milwaukee, and parts of Illinois.
WALTER HOPKINS, Philadelphia.

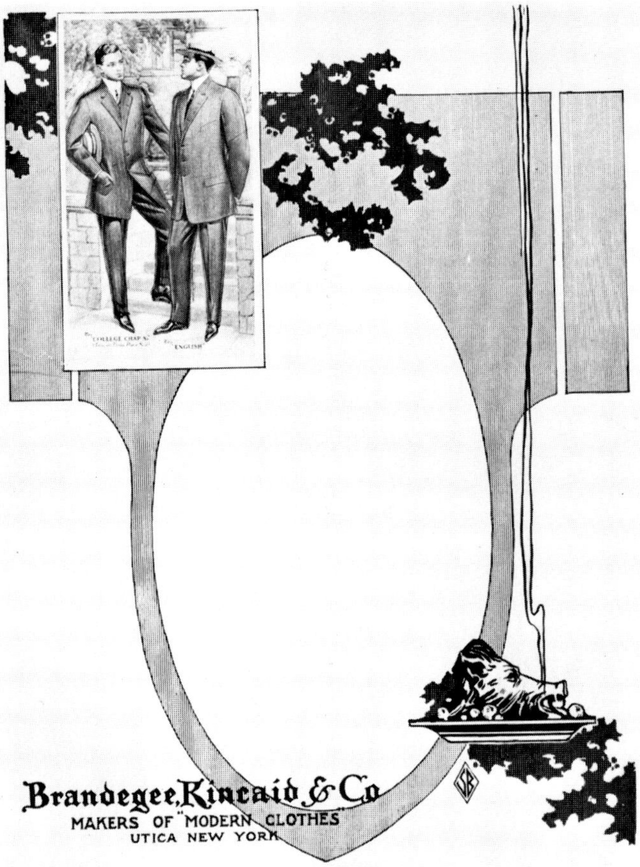

395

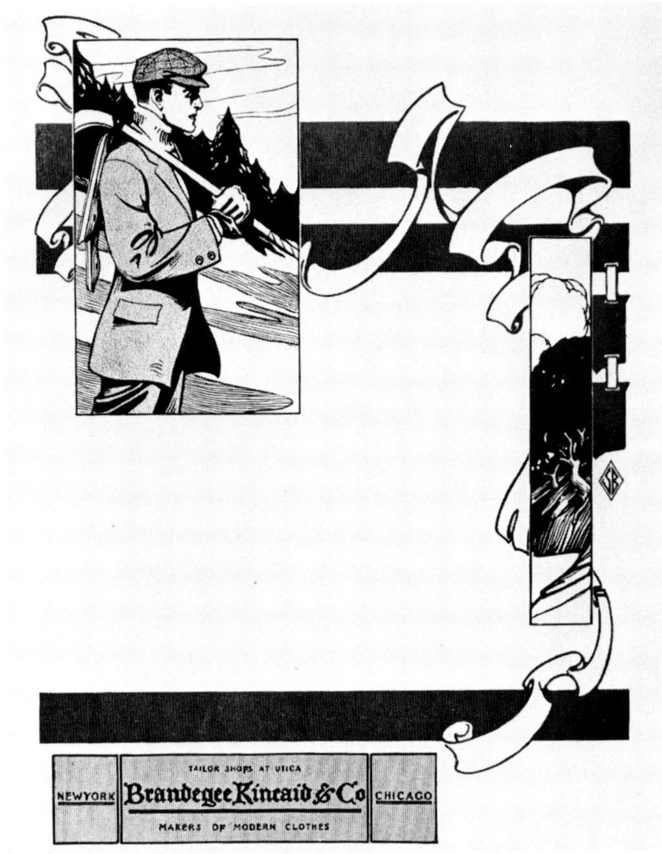

396

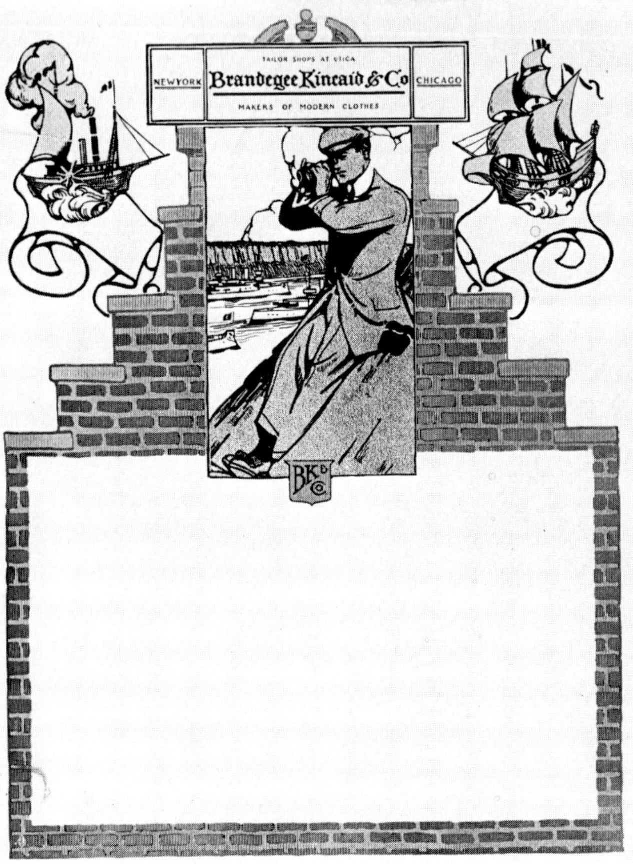

397

395. Proof, commercial illustration for Brandegee, Kincaid & Co., Utica, New York, c. 1909–11 (through Sherman & Bryan, Inc., advertising agency).

396. Proof, commercial illustration for Brandegee, Kincaid & Co., Utica, New York, c. 1909–11 (through Sherman & Bryan, Inc., advertising agency). Publication unknown.

397. Proof, commercial illustration for Brandegee, Kincaid & Co., Utica, New York, c. 1909–11 (through Sherman & Bryan, Inc., advertising agency). Publication unknown.

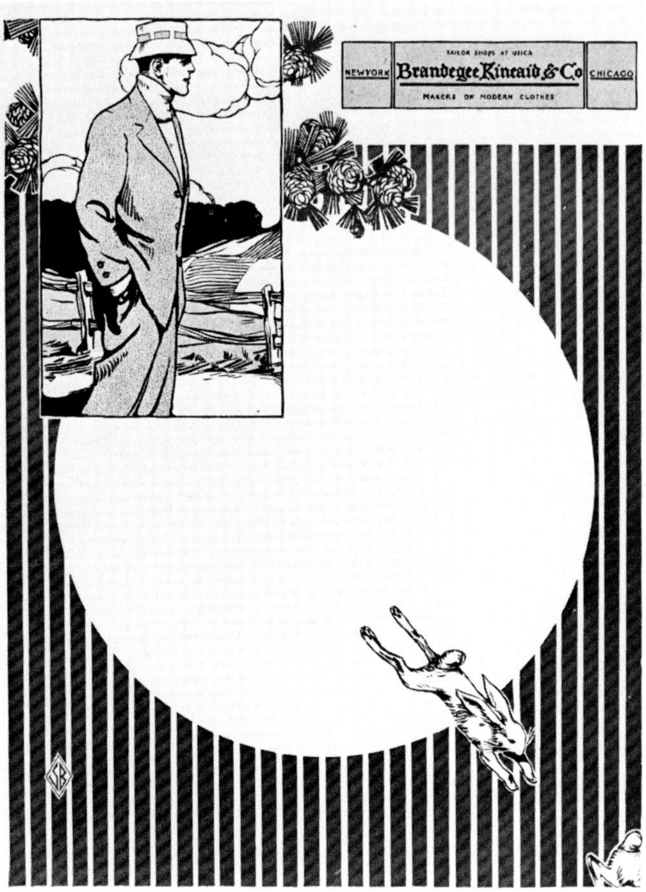

398

398. Proof, commercial illustration for Brandegee, Kincaid & Co., Utica, New York, c. 1909–11 (through Sherman & Bryan, Inc., advertising agency). Publication unknown.

399. Proof, commercial illustration for Brandegee, Kincaid & Co., Utica, New York, c. 1909–11 (through Sherman & Bryan, Inc., advertising agency). Publication unknown.

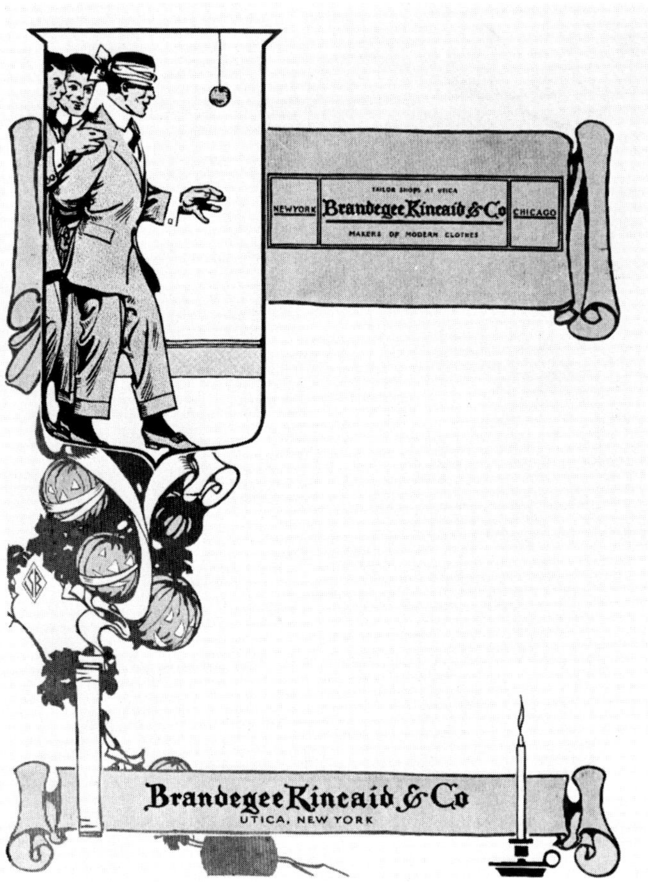

399

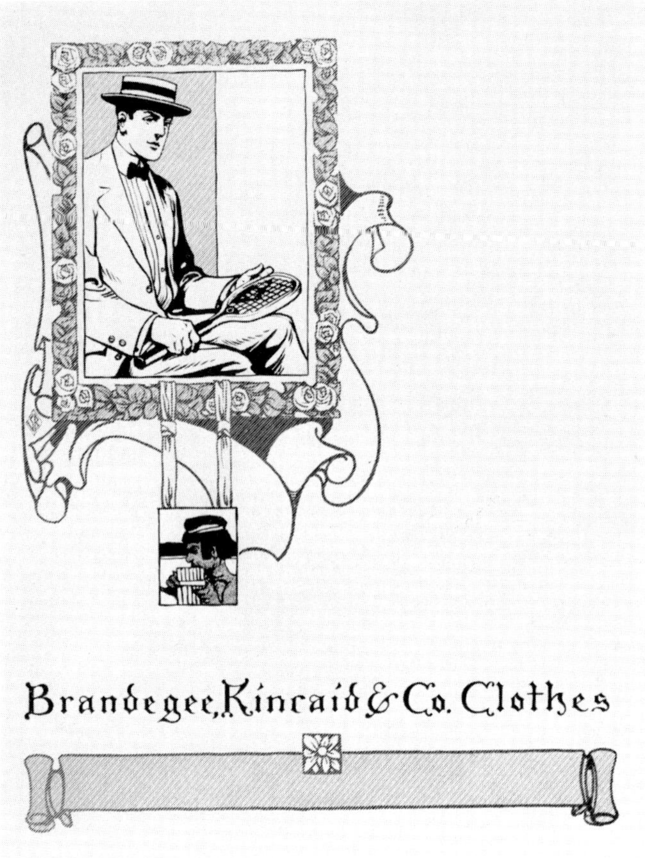
Brandegee, Kincaid & Co. Clothes

400

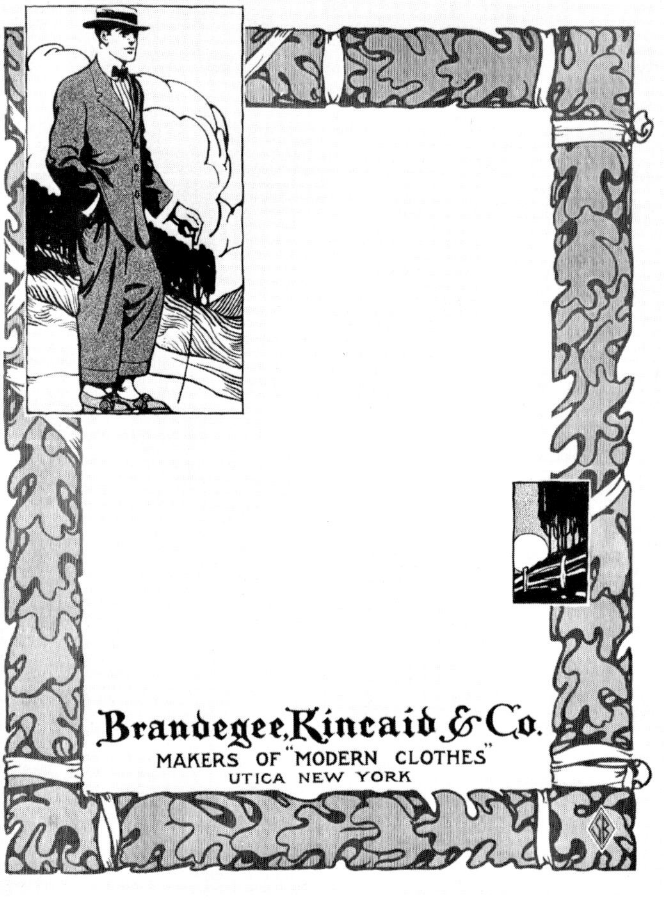
Brandegee, Kincaid & Co.
MAKERS OF "MODERN CLOTHES"
UTICA NEW YORK

401

400. Proof, commercial illustration for Brandegee, Kincaid & Co., Utica, New York, c. 1910–12 (through Sherman & Bryan, Inc., advertising agency). Publication unknown.

401. Proof, commercial illustration for Brandegee, Kincaid & Co., Utica, New York, c. 1910–12 (through Sherman & Bryan, Inc., advertising agency). Publication unknown.

402. Proof, commercial illustration for Brighton Flat Clasp Garters, c. 1909–11 (through Sherman & Bryan, Inc., advertising agency). Publication unknown.

403. Proof, commercial illustration advertising the Wearing Apparel Show Official Catalogue & Directory, Madison Square Garden, January 19–26, 1910, published by Sherman & Bryan, Inc., New York and Chicago. Two proofs known, one image smaller; publication unknown.

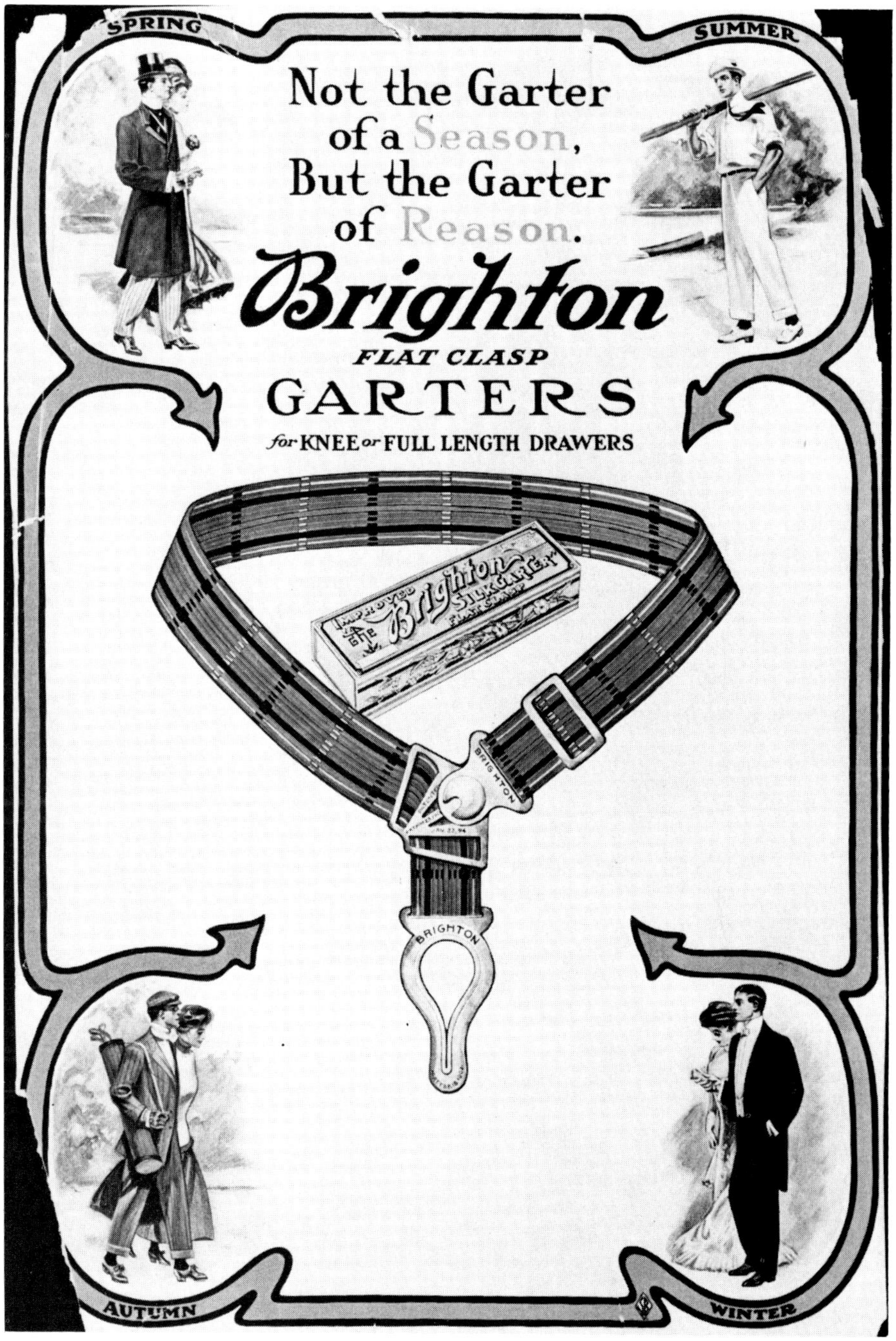

402

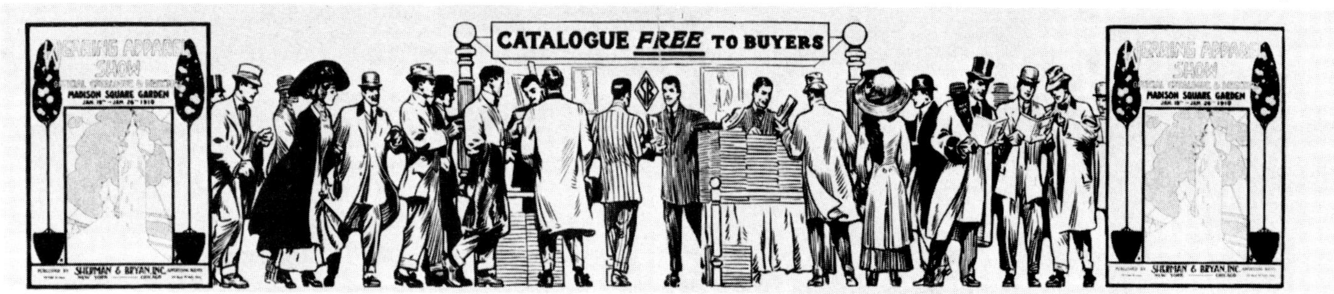

403

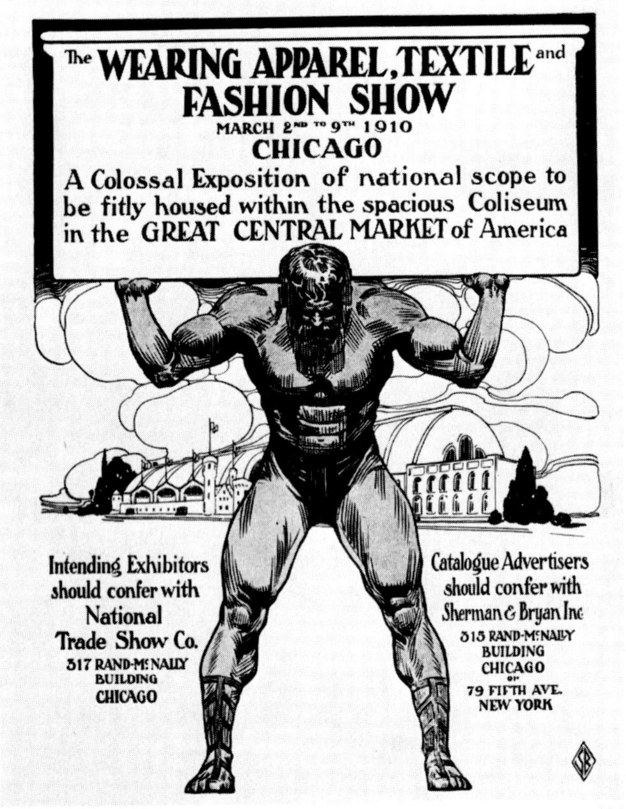

404

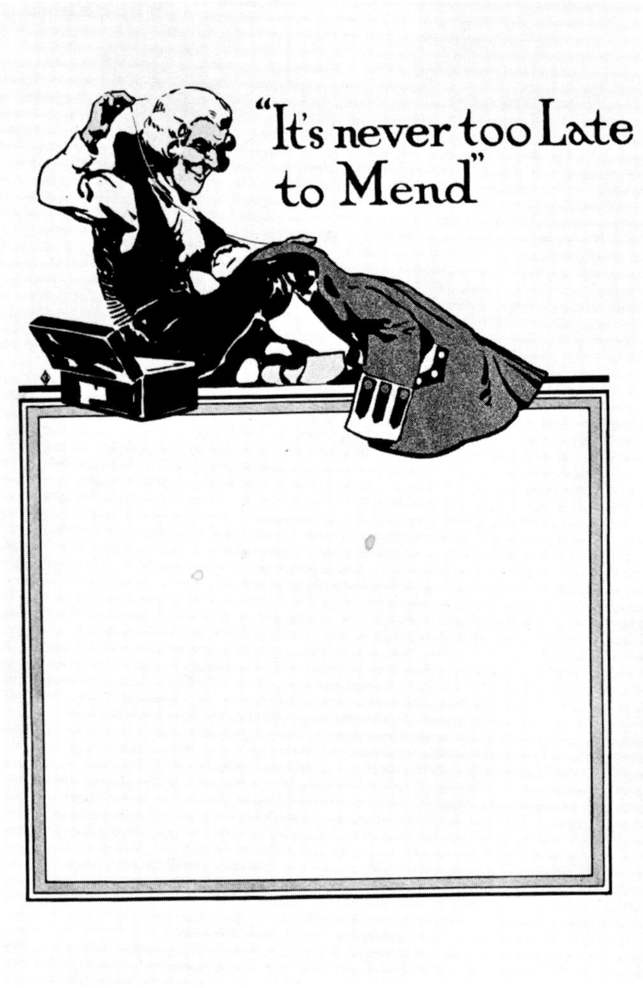

405

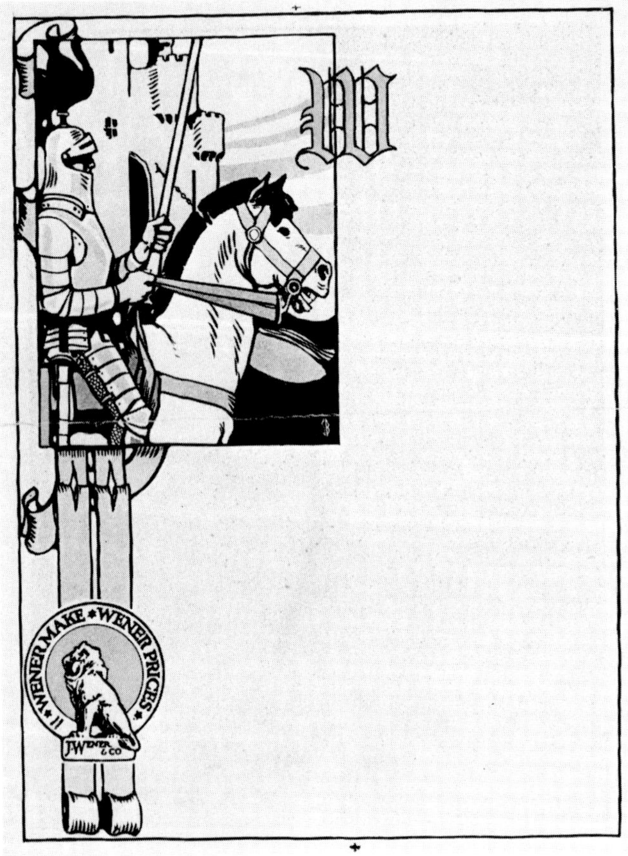

406

404. Proof, commercial illustration advertising the Wearing Apparel, Textile and Fashion Show, Chicago, March 2–9, 1910, organized by the National Trade Show Co., Chicago, and Sherman & Bryan, Inc., Chicago and New York. Publication unknown.

405. "It's never too Late to Mend," proof, commercial illustration, c. 1910–12 (through Sherman & Bryan, Inc., advertising agency). Publication unknown.

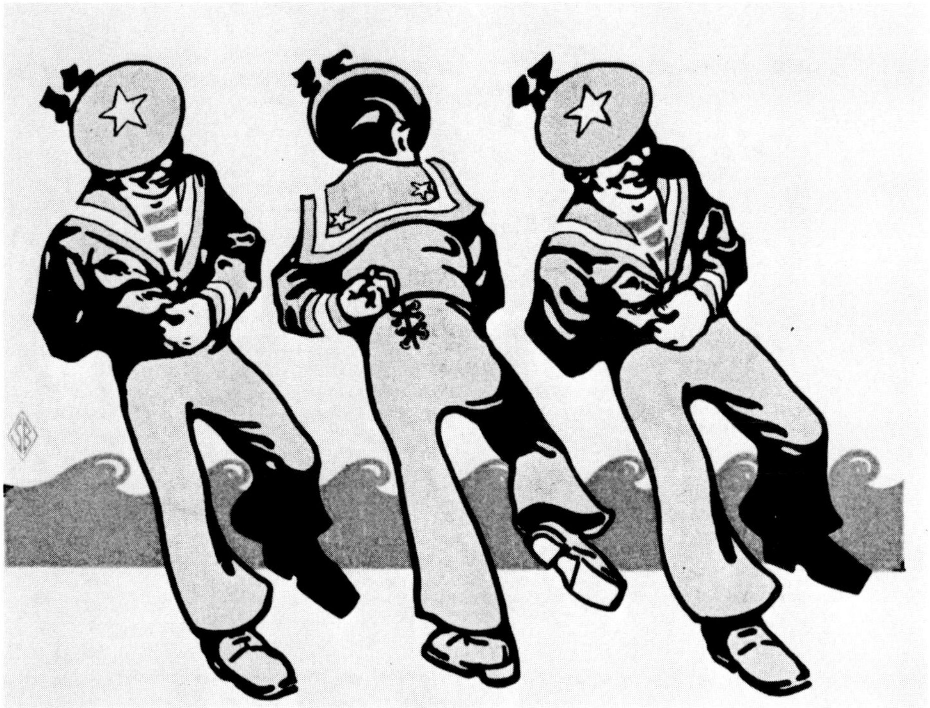

407

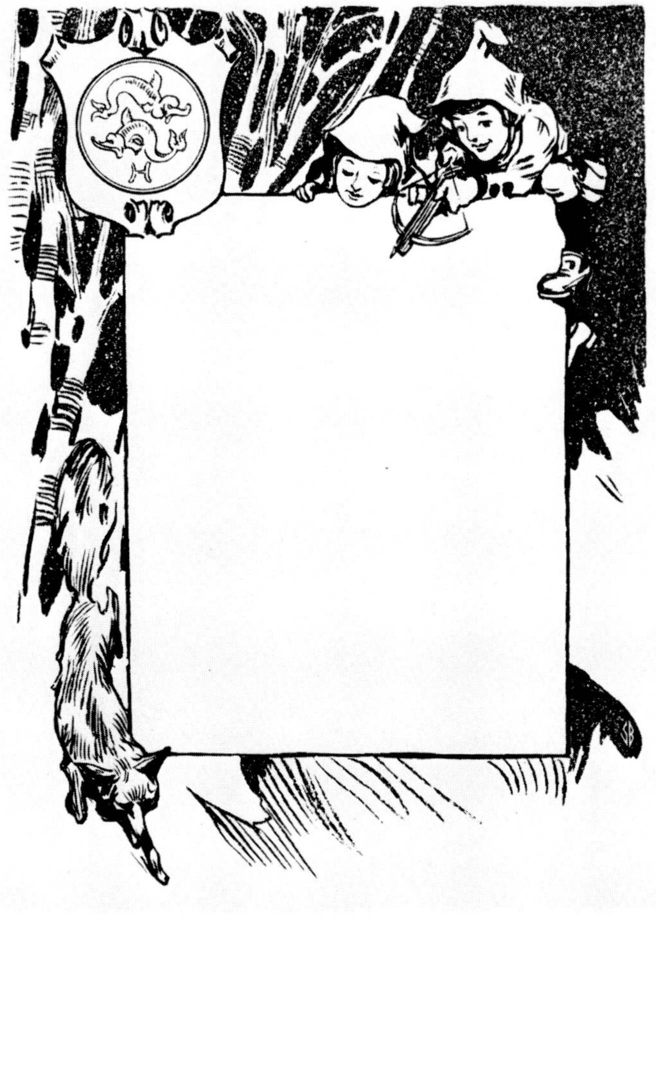

408

406. Proof, commercial illustration for J. Wener & Co., c. 1910–12 (through Sherman & Bryan, Inc., advertising agency). Publication unknown.

407. Proof, commercial illustration, c. 1910–12 (through Sherman & Bryan, Inc., advertising agency). Publication unknown.

408. Proof, commercial illustration, c. 1910–12 (through Sherman & Bryan, Inc., advertising agency). Publication unknown.

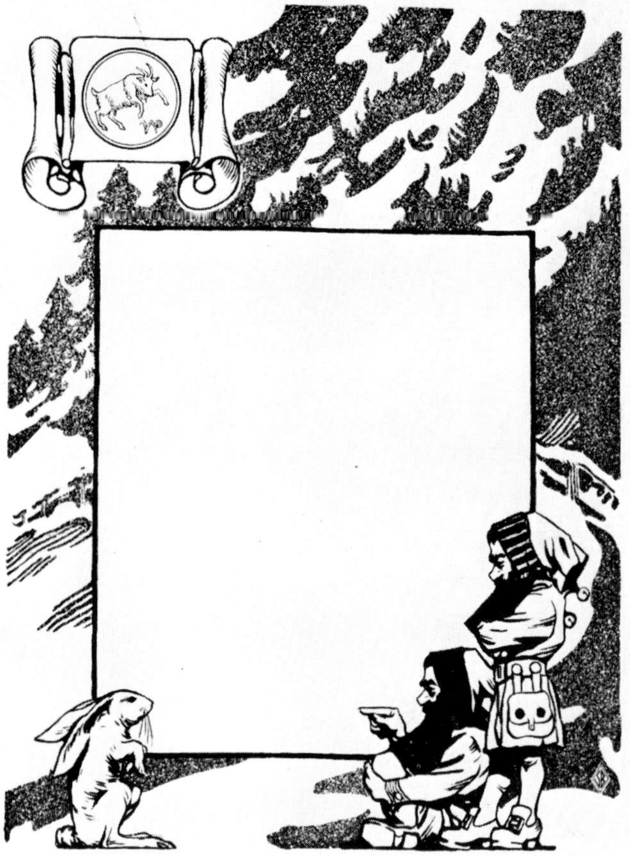

409

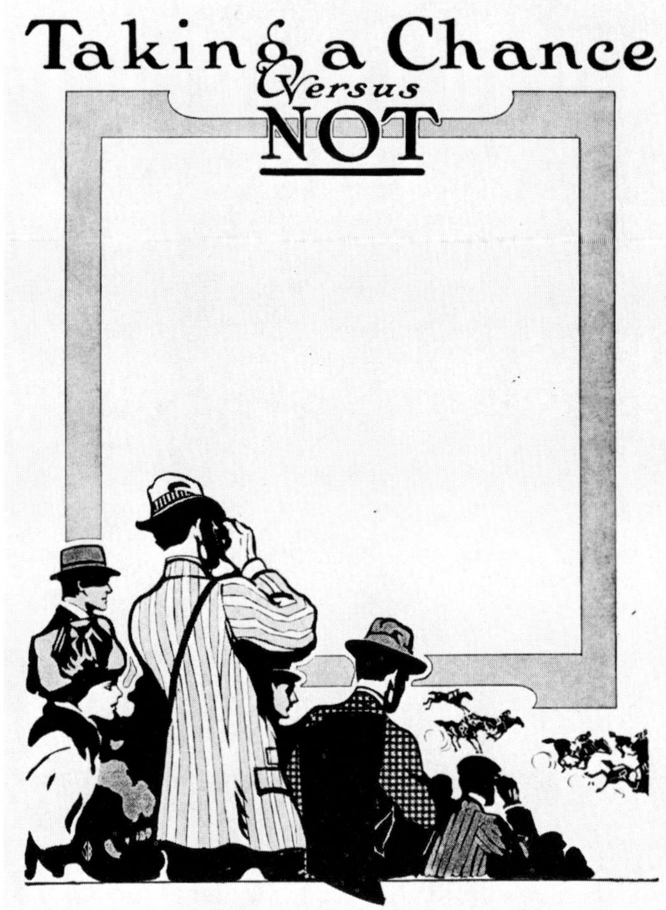

410

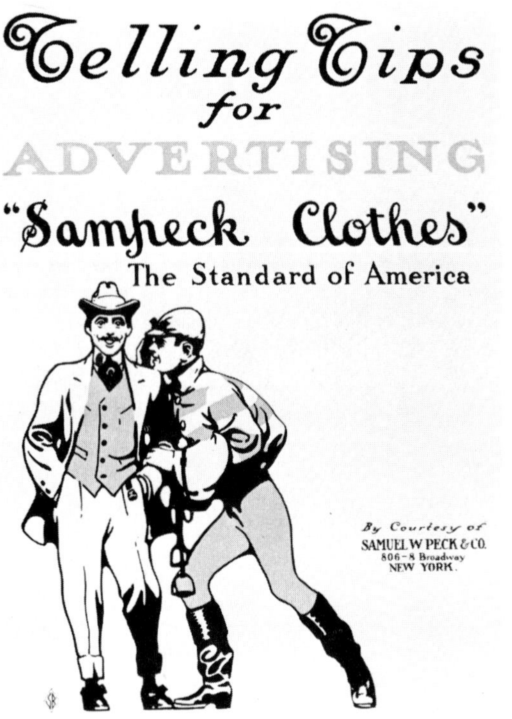

411

409. Proof, commercial illustration, c. 1910–12 (through Sherman & Bryan, Inc., advertising agency). Publication unknown.

410. "Taking a Chance Versus *NOT*," proof, commercial illustration, c. 1911–12 (through Sherman & Bryan, Inc., advertising agency). Publication unknown.

411. "Telling Tips for Advertising 'Sampeck Clothes' The Standard of America," proof, commercial illustration for Samuel W. Peck & Co., New York, c. 1911–12 (through Sherman & Bryan, Inc., advertising agency). Publication unknown.

412. "Litholin," proof, seven commercial illustrations, c. 1908–12. Publication unknown.

413. "Litholin," proof, six commercial illustrations, c. 1908–12. Publication unknown.

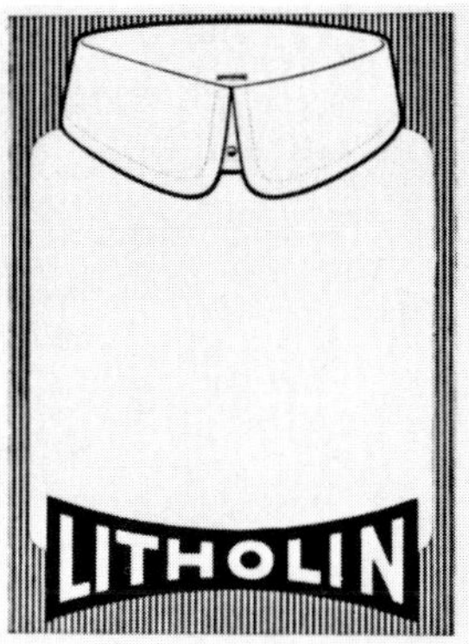
LITHOLIN
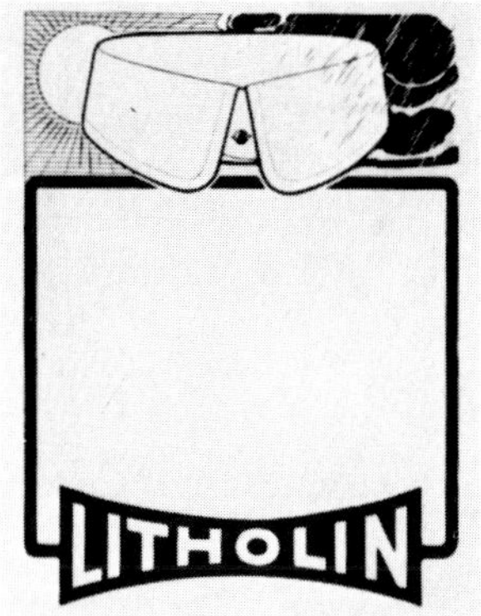
LITHOLIN
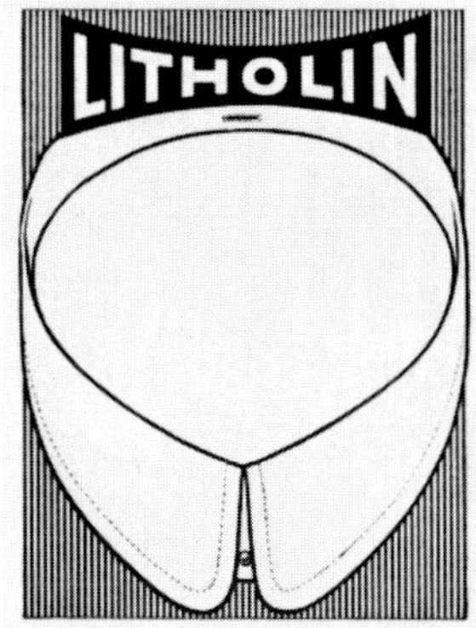
LITHOLIN
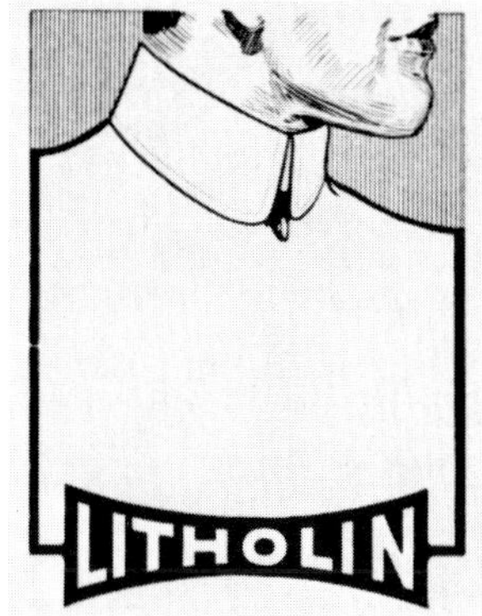
LITHOLIN

412

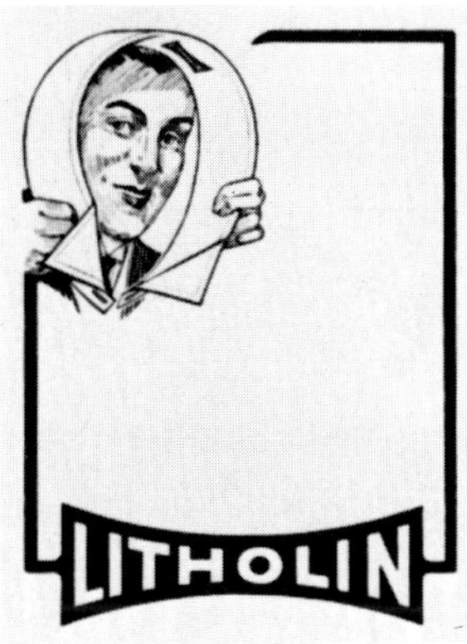
LITHOLIN
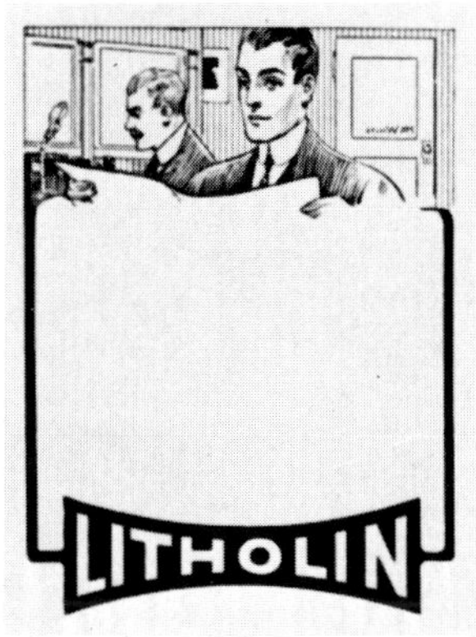
LITHOLIN
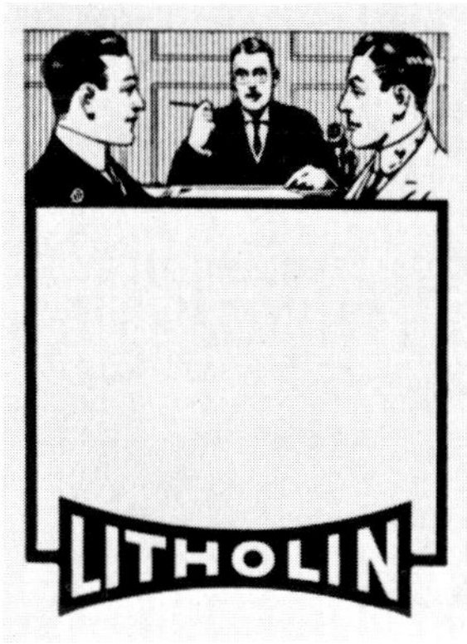
LITHOLIN
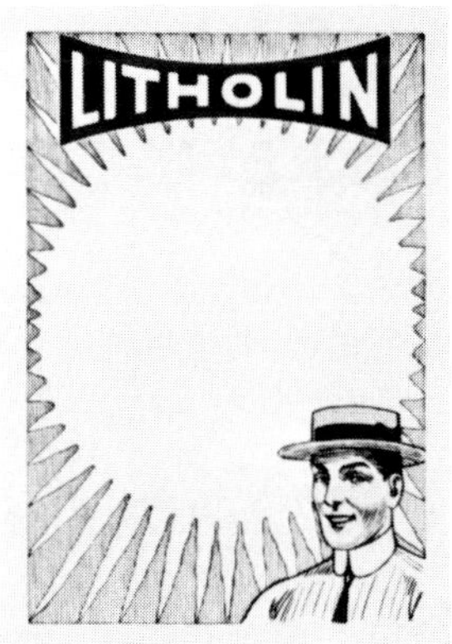
LITHOLIN
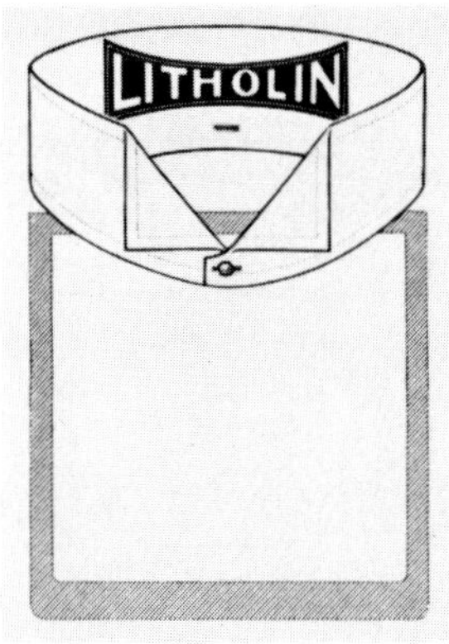
LITHOLIN
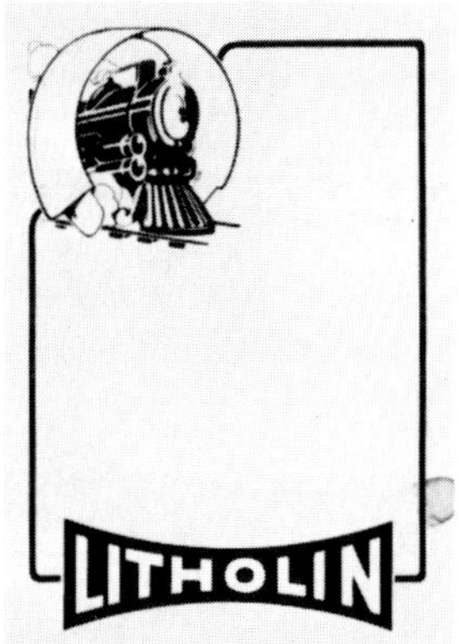
LITHOLIN
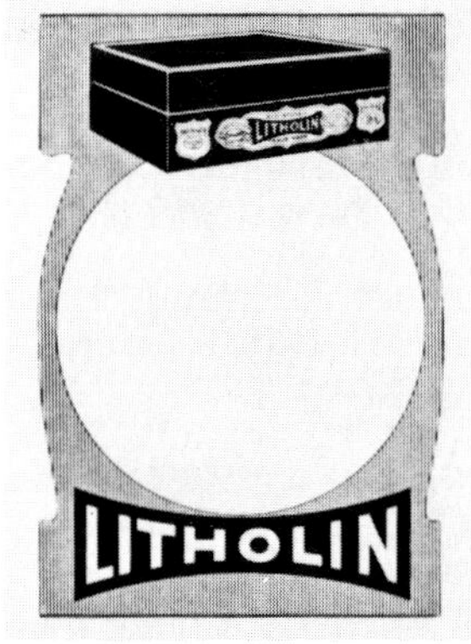
LITHOLIN
LITHOLIN

413

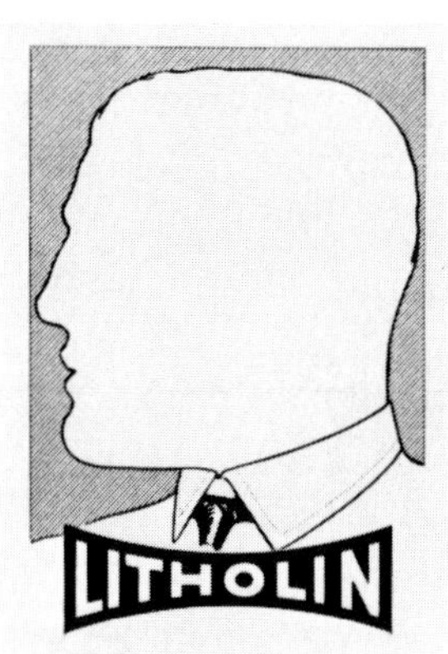
LITHOLIN
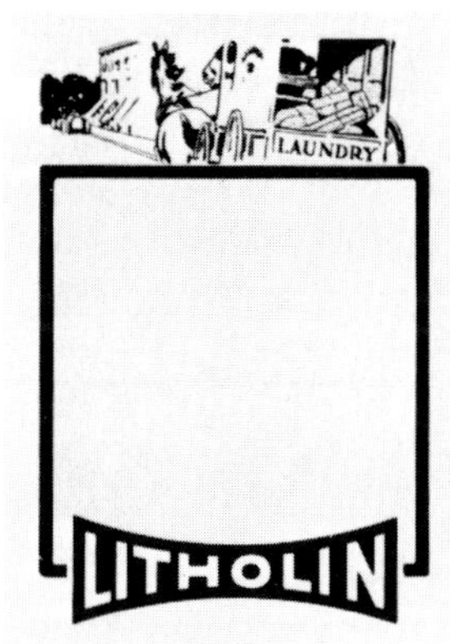
LAUNDRY
LITHOLIN

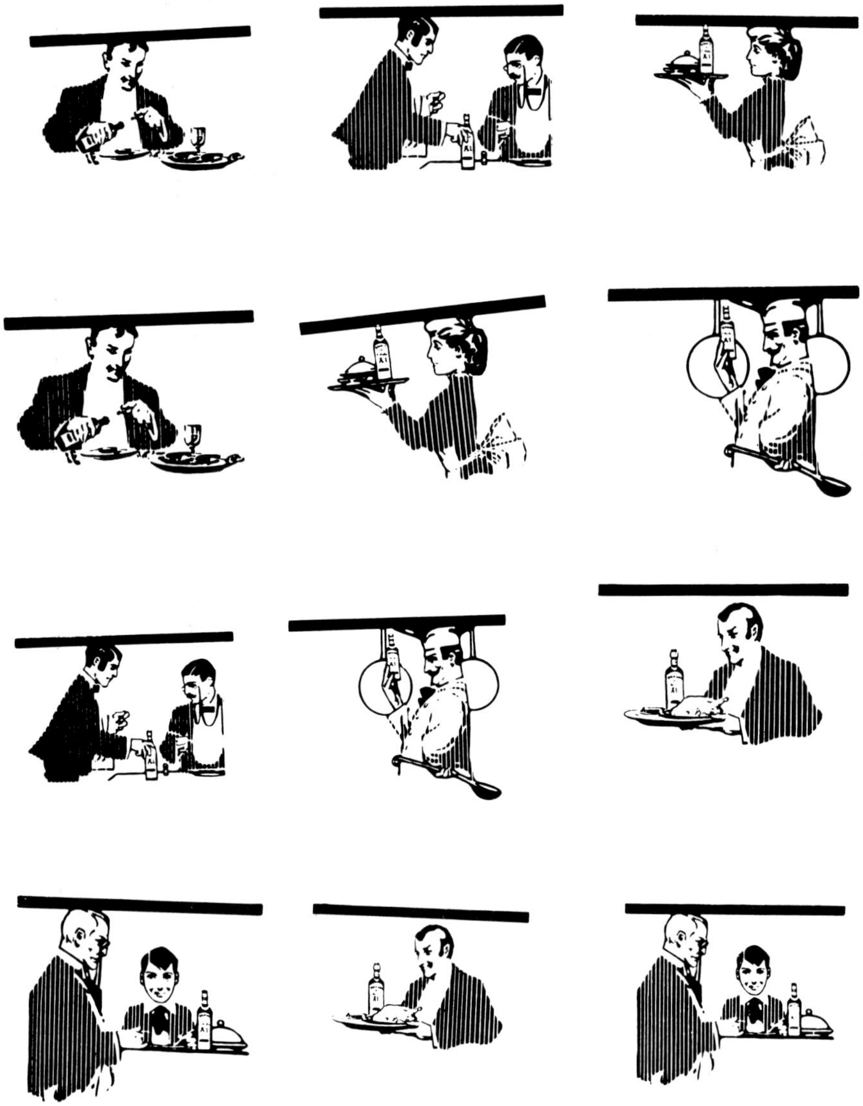

415

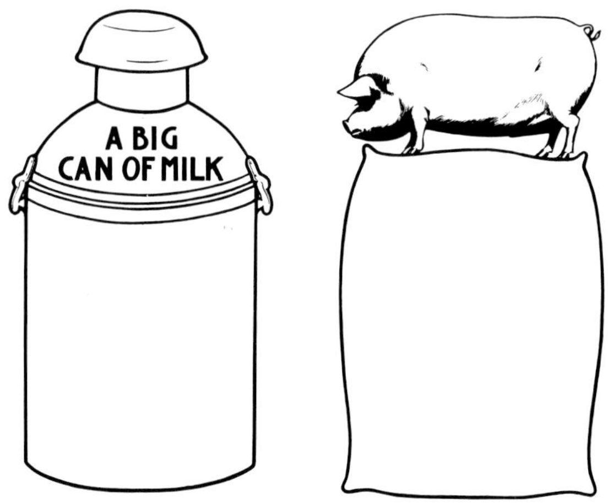

414

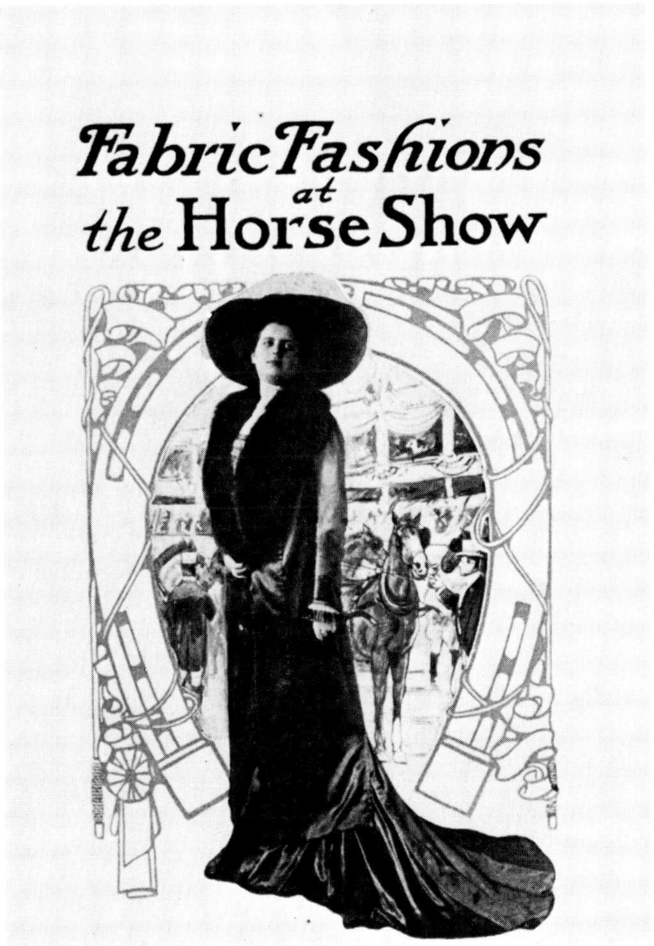

417

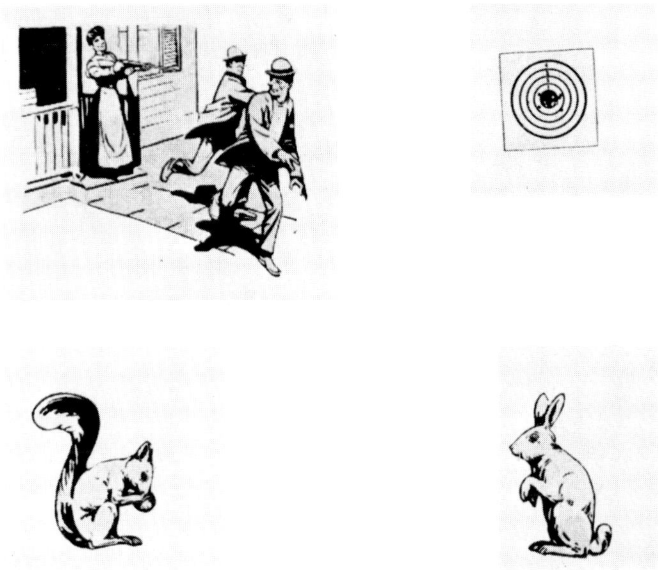

416

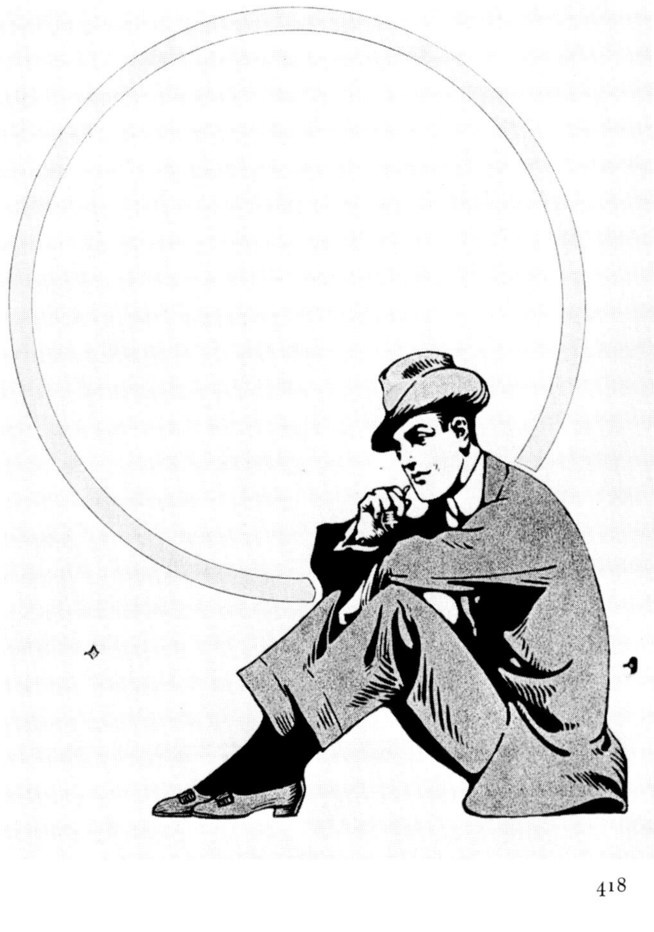

418

414. Proof, two commercial illustrations, c. 1908–12. Publication unknown.

415. Proof, six commercial illustrations for A-1 Steak Sauce, c. 1908–12. Publication unknown.

416. Proof, four commercial illustrations, c. 1908–12. Publication unknown.

417. "Fabric Fashions at the Horse Show," proof, commercial illustration, c. 1908–10. Publication unknown.

418. Proof, commercial illustration, c. 1908–12. Publication unknown.

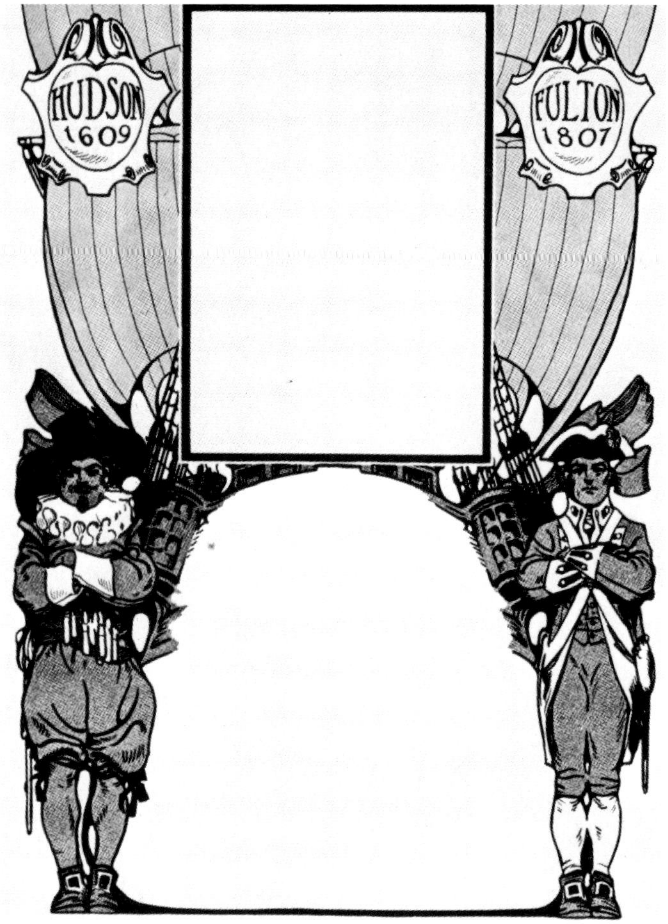

419

419. Proof, commercial illustration for Hudson (1609)—Fulton (1807), c. 1910–12. Publication unknown.

420. "Start Things Agoing," proof, commercial illustration, c. 1910–12. Publication unknown.

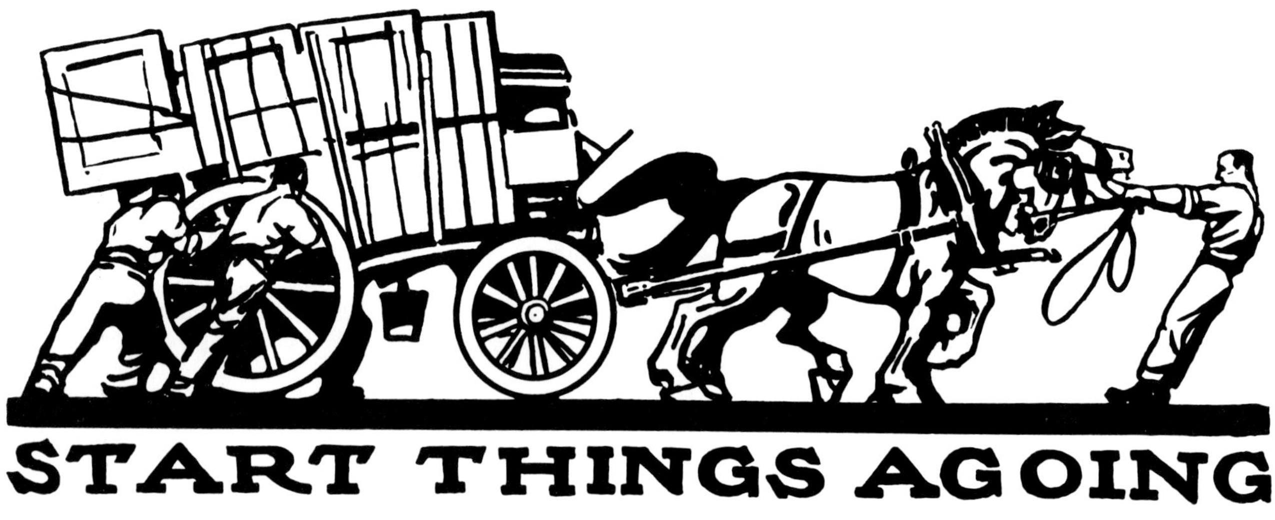

420

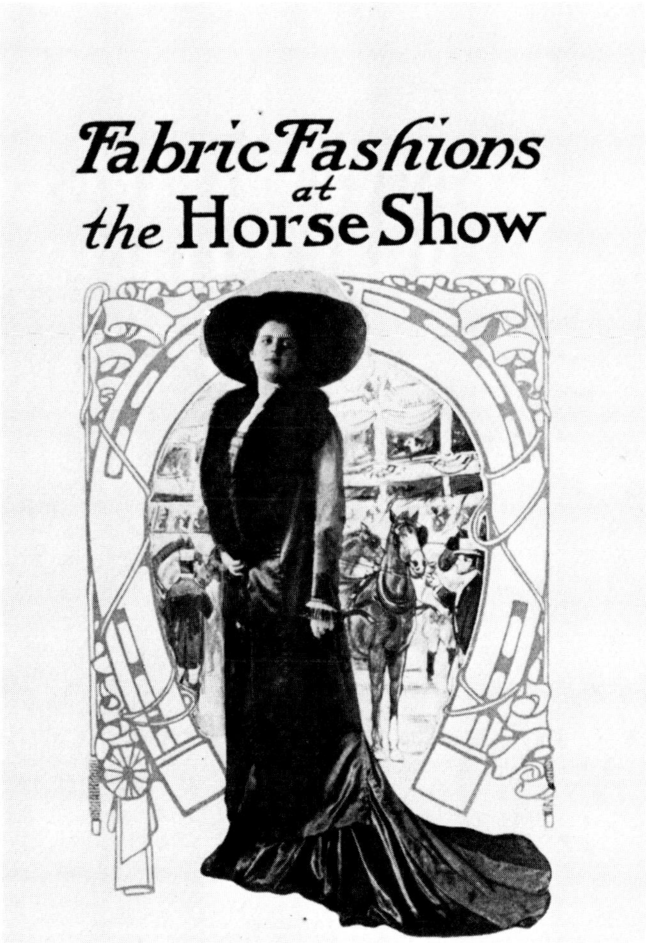

417

414. Proof, two commercial illustrations, c. 1908–12. Publication unknown.

415. Proof, six commercial illustrations for A-1 Steak Sauce, c. 1908–12. Publication unknown.

416. Proof, four commercial illustrations, c. 1908–12. Publication unknown.

417. "Fabric Fashions at the Horse Show," proof, commercial illustration, c. 1908–10. Publication unknown.

418. Proof, commercial illustration, c. 1908–12. Publication unknown.

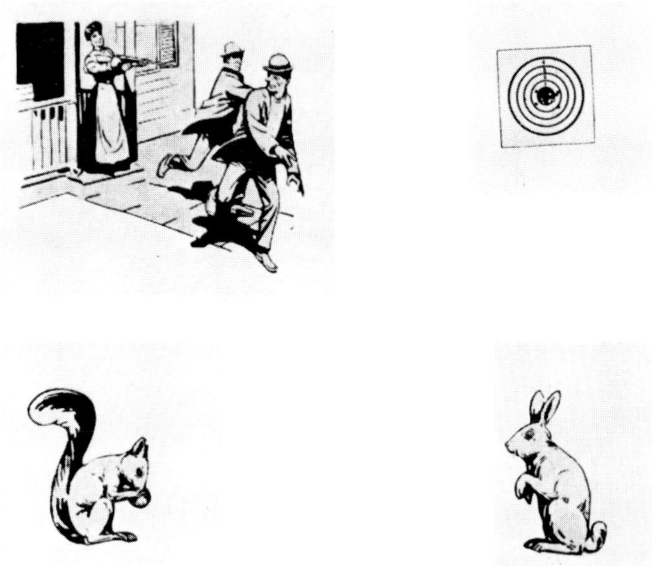

416

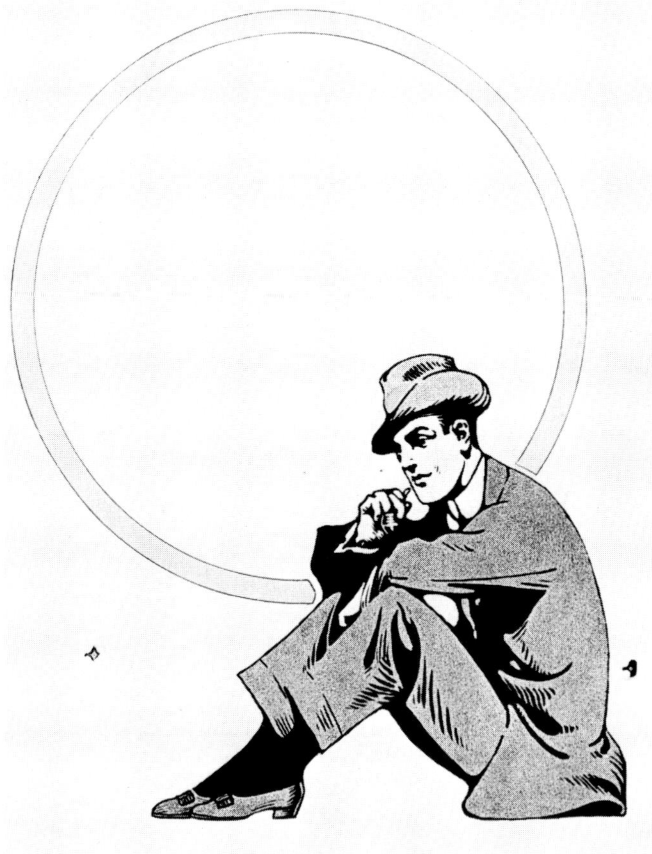

418

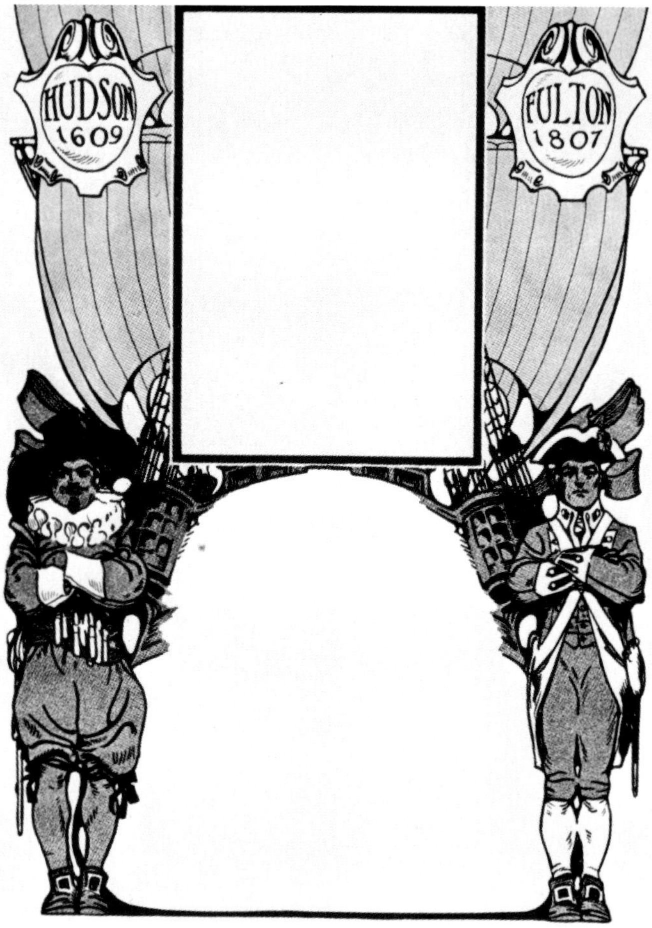

419

419. Proof, commercial illustration for Hudson (1609)—Fulton (1807), c. 1910–12. Publication unknown.

420. "Start Things Agoing," proof, commercial illustration, c. 1910–12. Publication unknown.

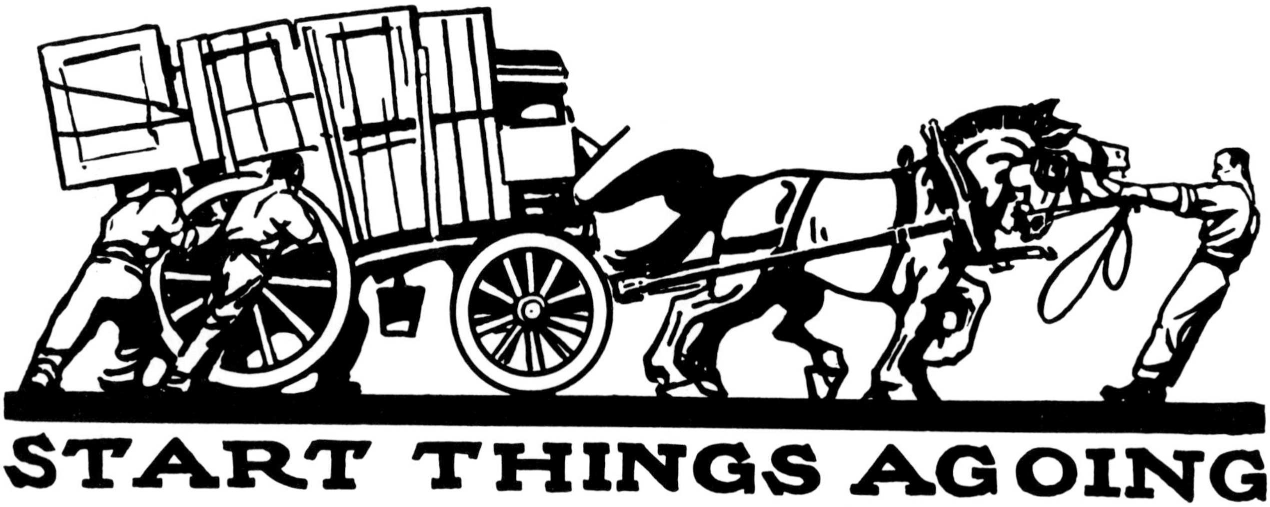

420

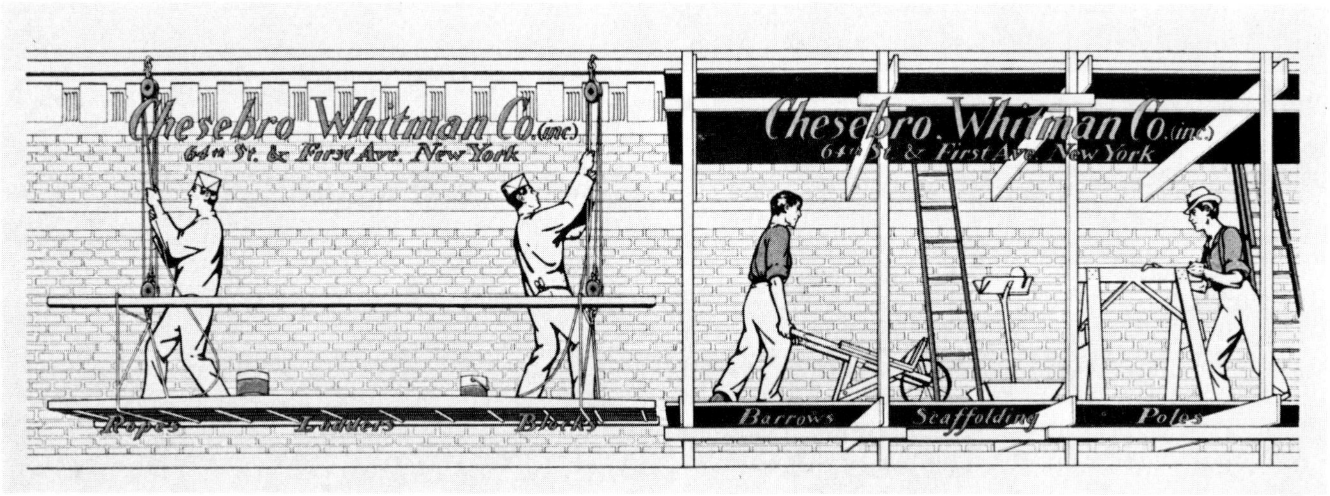

423

421. "Rubber & Waterproof Collars & Cuffs," proof, commercial illustration for the Arlington Company, c. 1910–12. Publication unknown.

422. "Variety Is The Spice Of Life," proof, commercial illustration for Fashion Clothes, c. 1911–12. Publication unknown.

423. "Ropes, Ladders, Blocks, Scaffolding, Poles," proof, commercial illustration for Chesebro Whitman Co., Inc., New York, c. 1911–12. Publication unknown.

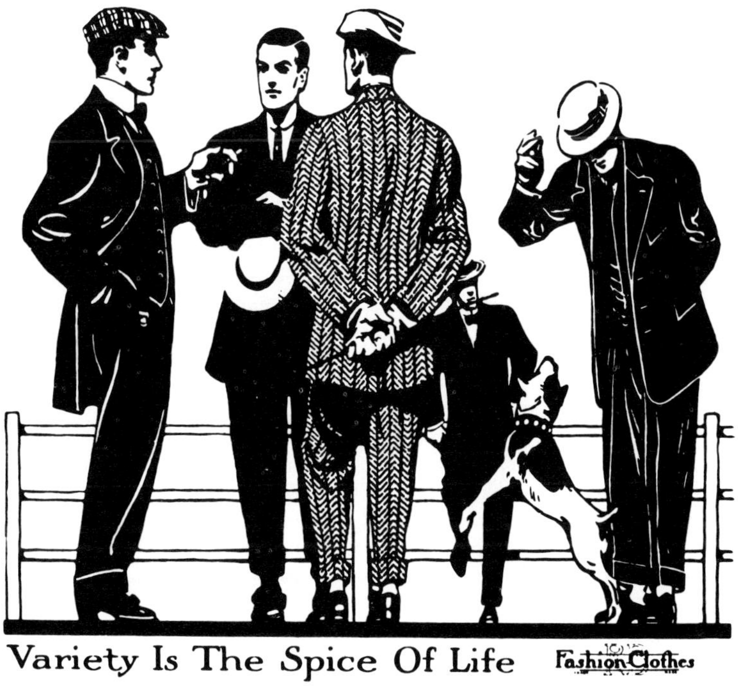

422

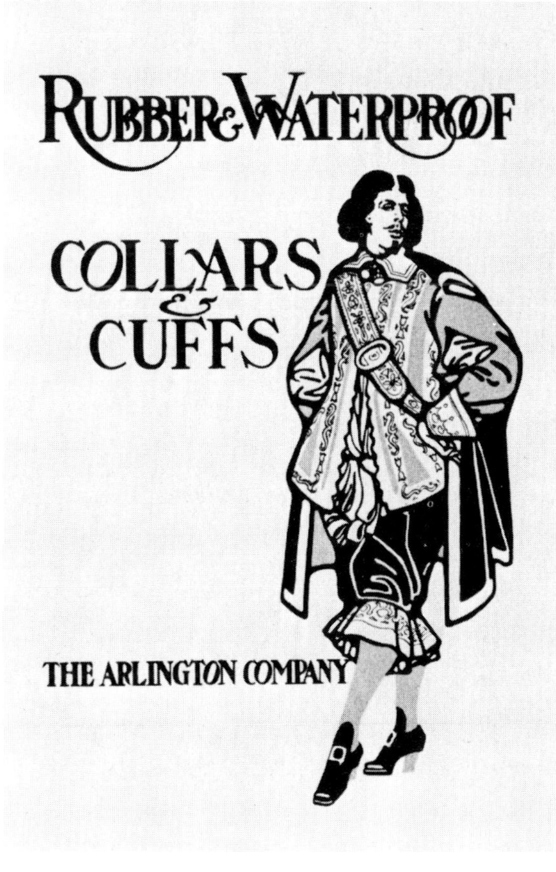

421

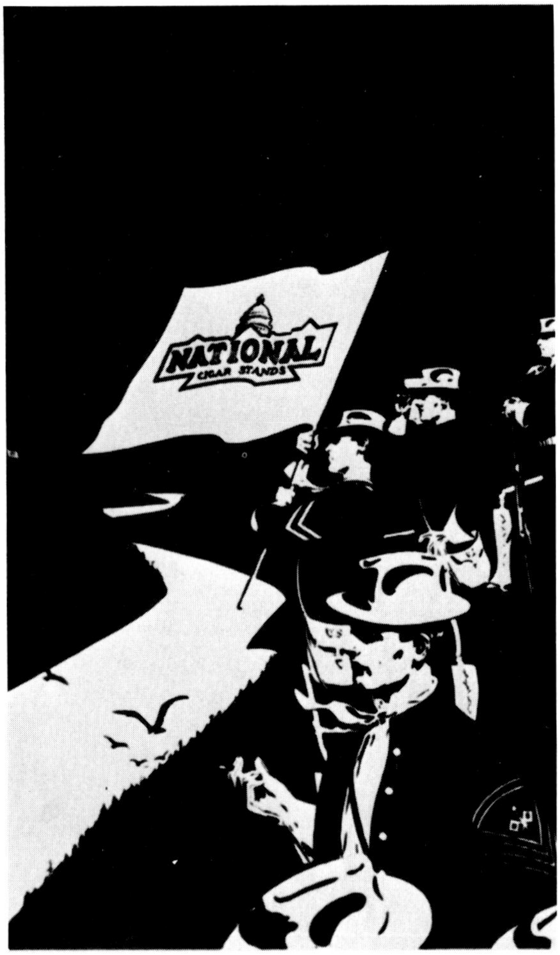

424

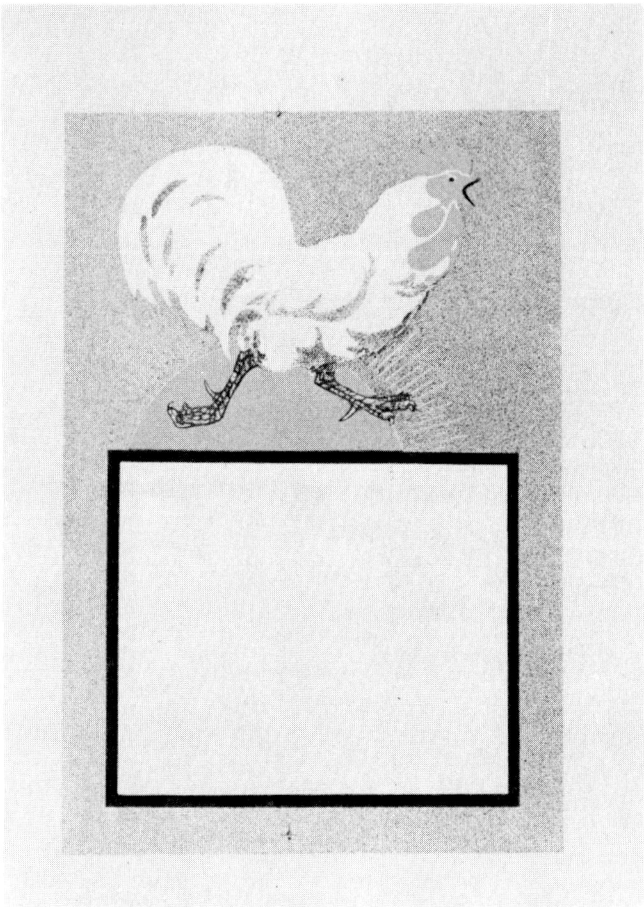

426

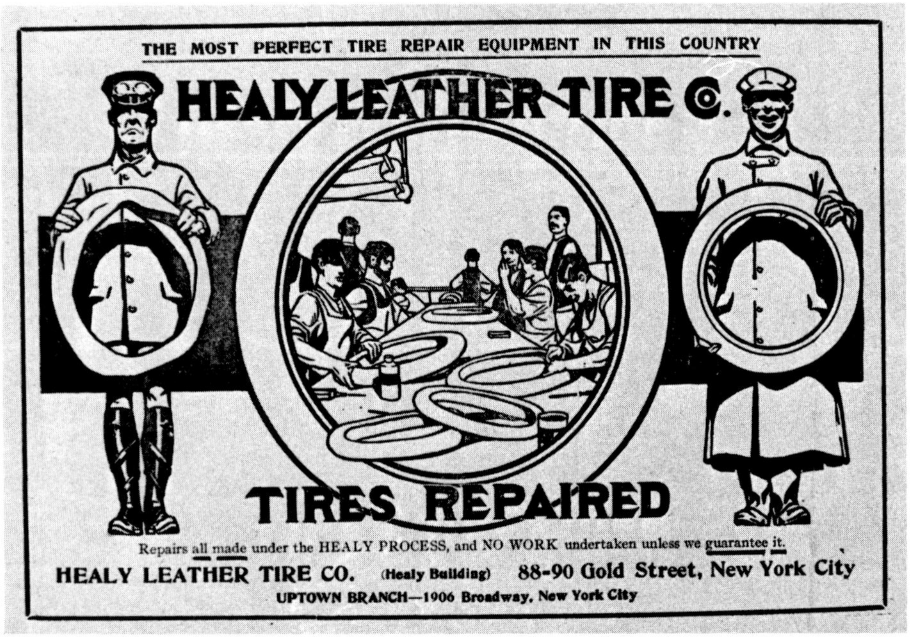

425

424. Proof, commercial illustration for National Cigar Stands, c. 1911–12. Publication unknown.

425. Proof, commercial illustration for Healy Leather Tire Co., New York, c. 1912. Publication unknown.

426. Proof, commercial illustration, c. 1912. Publication unknown.

427a. Illustration, c. 1917–20. Watercolor and wash on composition board, 18 × 7¾ inches. Whitney Museum of American Art, New York; Bequest of Josephine N. Hopper 70.1615.

427b. Proof, commercial illustration for Knothe Unseen Suspenders, c. 1917–20. Publication unknown.

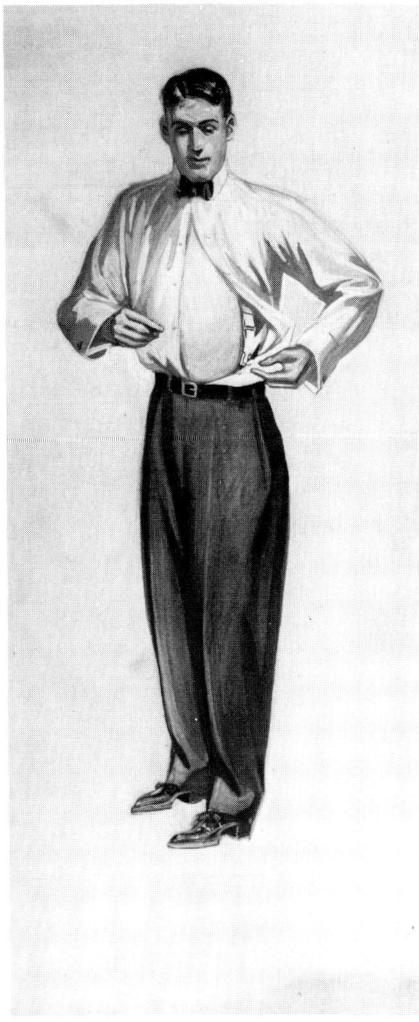

427a

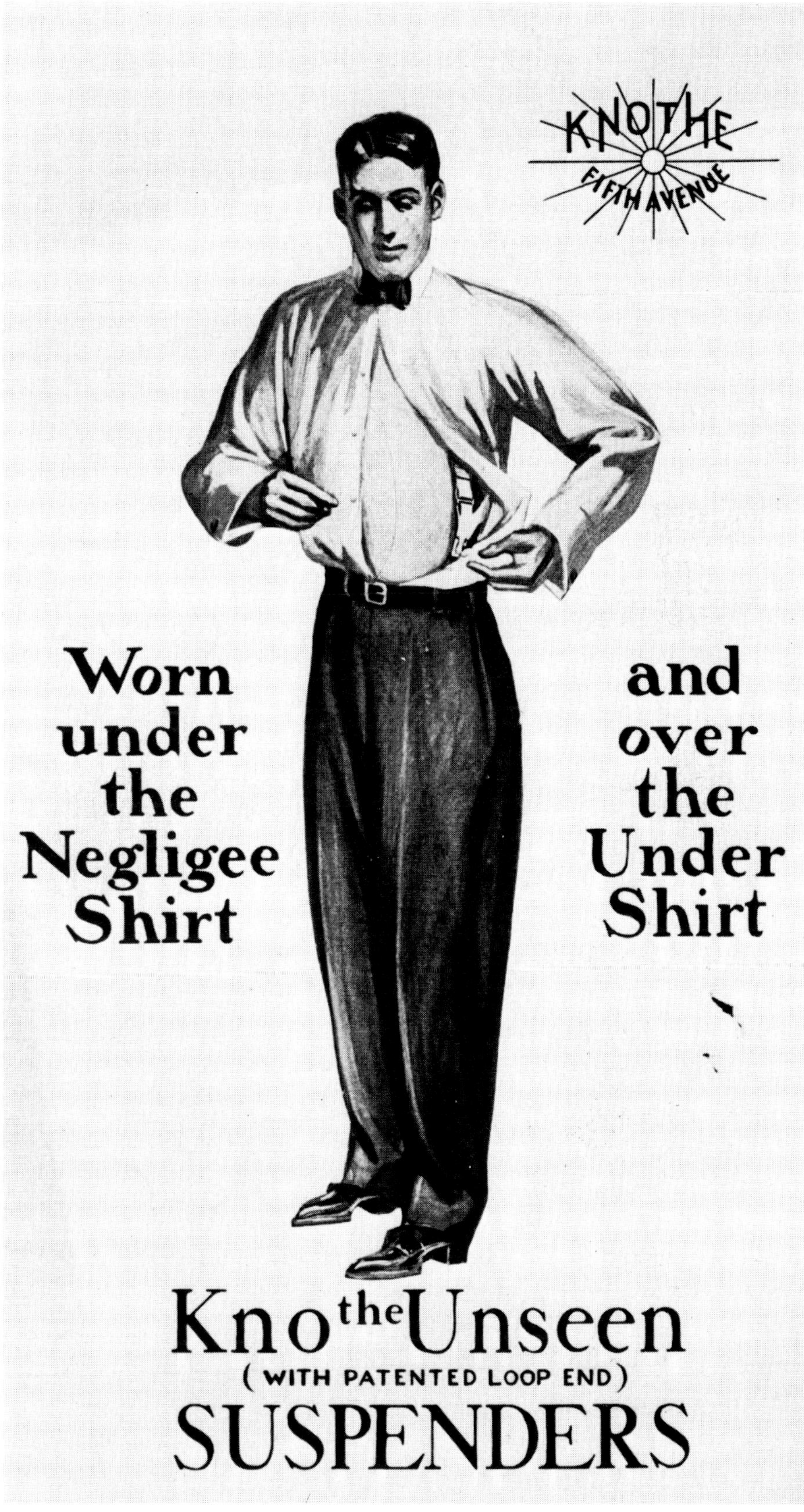

427b

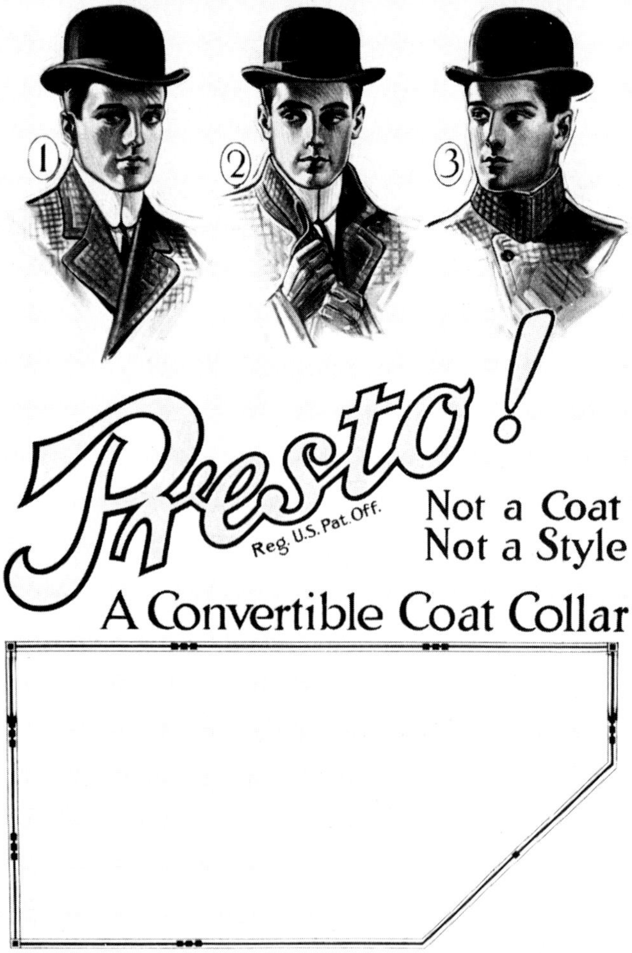

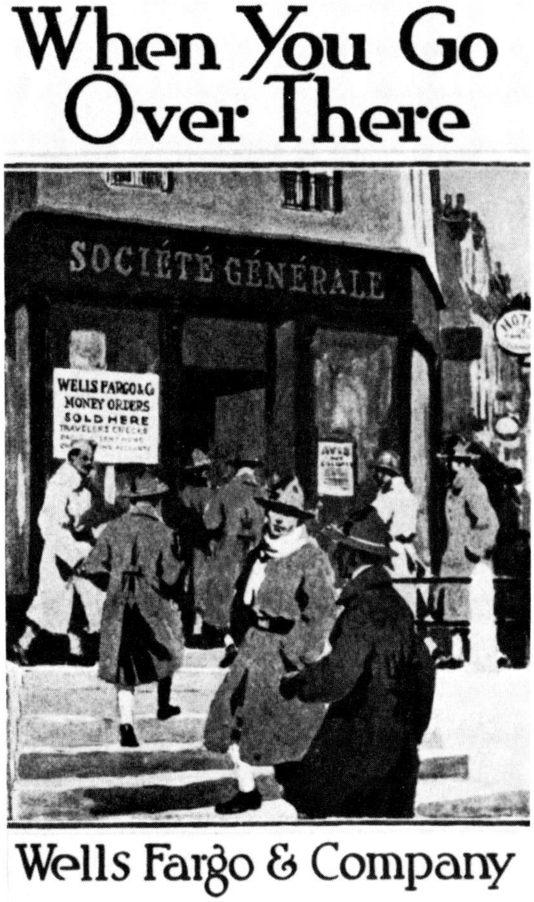

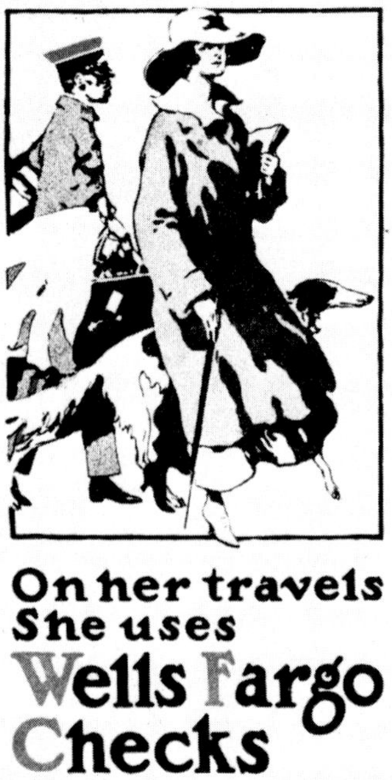

WELLS FARGO & COMPANY

Travelers Checks
Are SAFE

TRAVEL isn't completely enjoyable as long as you worry about losing your money or having it stolen. Make your journey care-free by taking Wells Fargo Travelers Checks.

If you lose cash there is no redress—it is gone. If you lose Wells Fargo Checks you get a refund. Your signature alone converts them into cash. In effect, Wells Fargo Travelers Checks insure your pocketbook against loss.

A party, roughing it in the mountains not long ago, actually was held up. But they carried Wells Fargo Checks and emerged from the experience with their funds intact. Brigands, burglars and "hold-up" men do *not* "accept" our travelers checks.

WELLS FARGO & COMPANY

Travelers Checks
Are CONVENIENT

WELLS FARGO TRAVELERS CHECKS in your purse establish and identify you. They are accepted at hotels, at shops—in railroad and steamship offices, and by all express companies.

Wherever your motor can take you, Wells Fargo Checks are good. Use

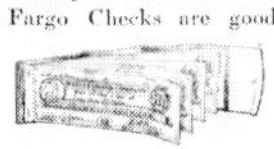

Wells Fargo Checks Insure Your Pocketbook

them to buy gasoline, tires, small parts and accessories.

The method of identification is simple. When you buy Wells Fargo Checks you are required to sign each one; when you need currency, or wish to pay a bill you countersign a check in the presence of the person who is to accept it. Thus your signature identifies you.

WELLS FARGO & COMPANY

Travelers Checks
Are ECONOMICAL

THE COST of Wells Fargo Checks is trifling, ten cents for ten dollars, fifty cents for a hundred. In addition, you avoid the payment of "exchange" often charged for cashing "out of town" checks.

The checks are bound in a neat leather case in one or assorted denominations, as you prefer—$10, $20, $50, $100, $200.

Wells Fargo Travelers Checks mean service, too. In each of Wells Fargo's ten thousand offices—it matters not whether it is located in the heart of New York or in far-distant Shanghai—you will find someone ready with information and assistance.

Wells Fargo men will care for your mail and telegrams—packages as well. Have them addressed in care of "Wells Fargo, Travelers Check Department." They will be held or forwarded as you wish.

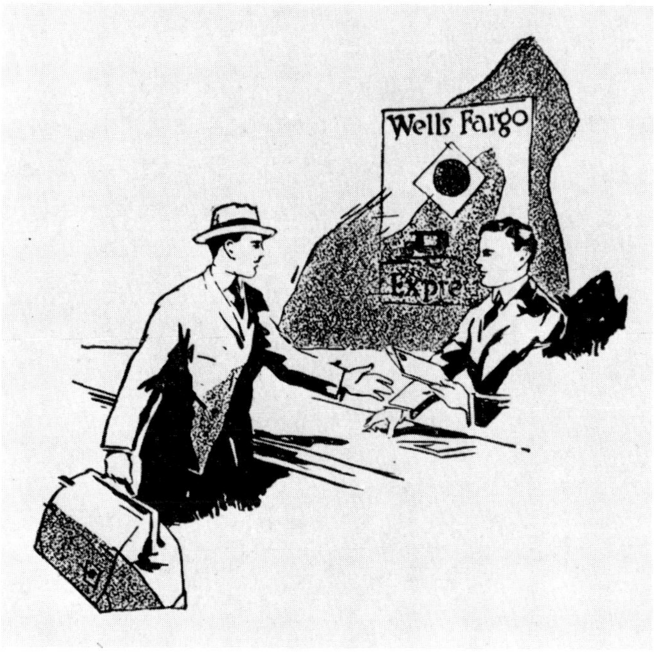

432

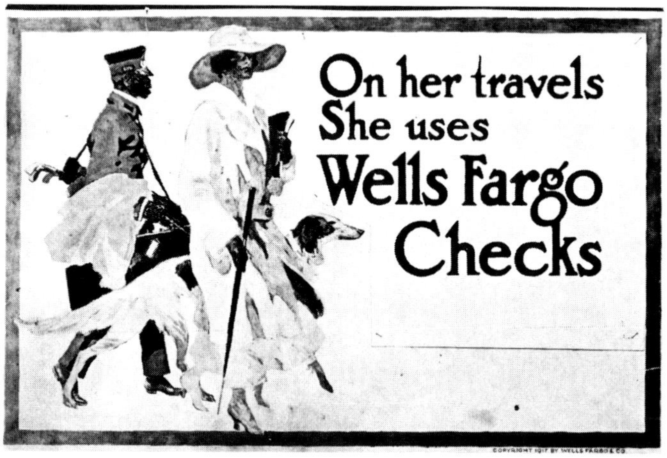

433

428. Proof, commercial illustration advertising Presto! Convertible Coat Collar, c. 1917–20. Publication unknown.

429. "When You Go Over There," illustration on front of fold-out brochure advertising Wells Fargo & Company office locations in Paris, 1917.

Fold-out brochure advertising Wells Fargo Checks for Wells Fargo & Company, 1917.

430. Illustration on front of brochure.

431. Four illustrations inside brochure.

432. Illustration on back of brochure.

433. Proof, commercial illustration advertising Wells Fargo Checks for Wells Fargo & Company, 1917. Publication unknown.

434. Proof, commercial illustration advertising Wells Fargo Checks for Wells Fargo & Company, 1917. Possibly used as a window-card display for the company.

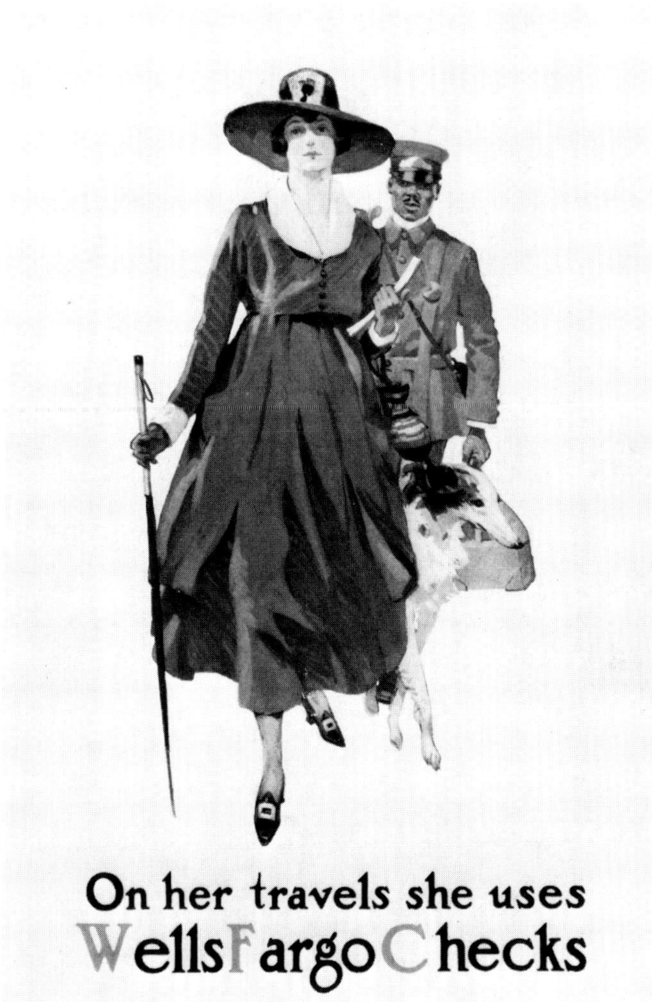

434

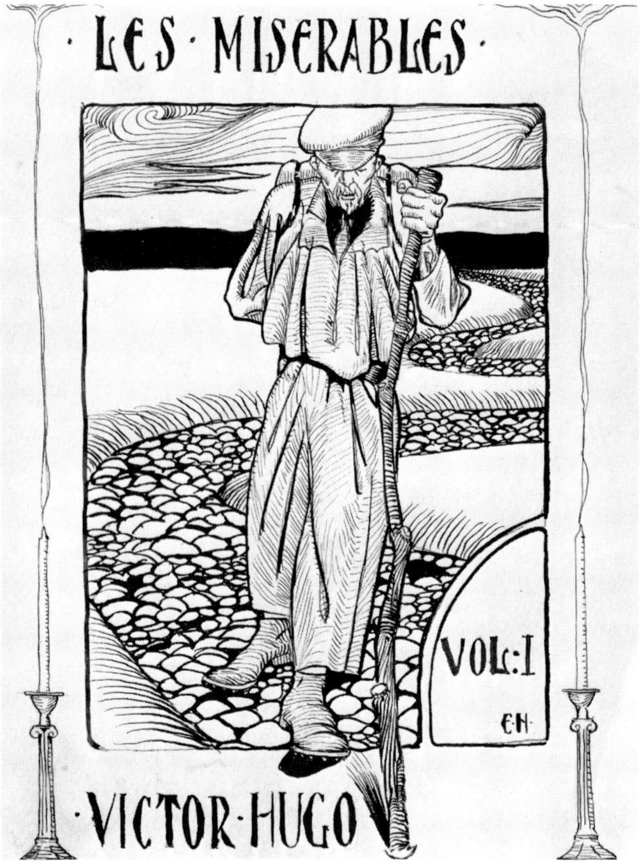

435a

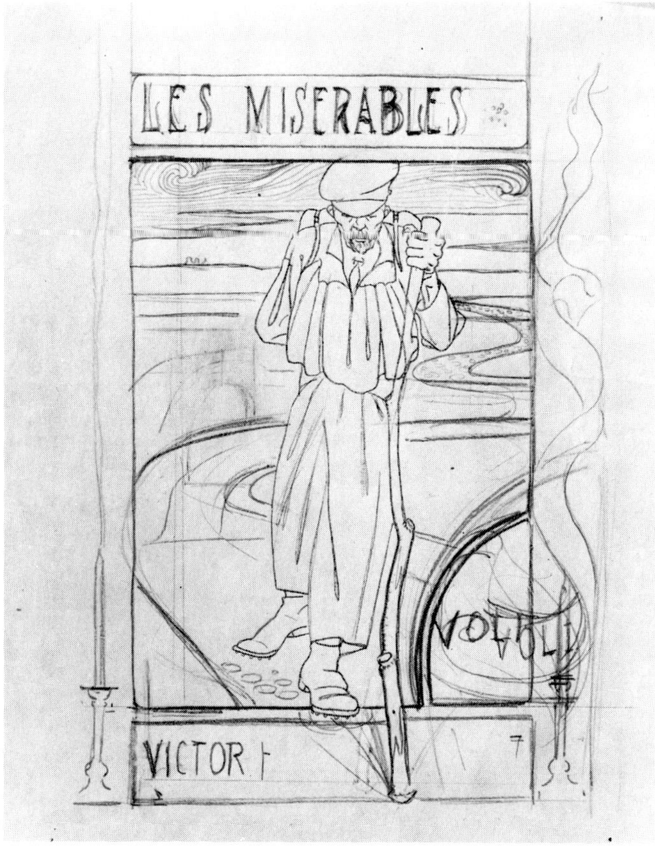

435b

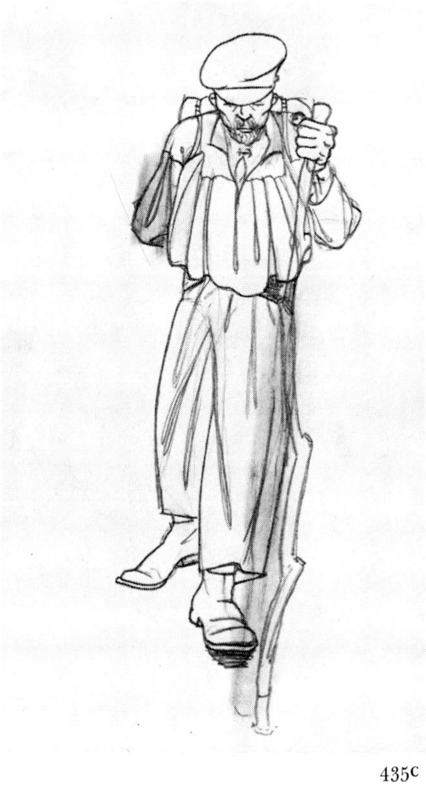

435c

435a. Illustration for Victor Hugo's *Les Misérables,* c. 1900–09. Pen and ink on paper, 8 1/16 × 6 1/4 inches. Whitney Museum of American Art, New York; Bequest of Josephine N. Hopper 70.1561.190.

435b. Drawing for illustration for Victor Hugo's *Les Misérables,* c. 1900–09. Pencil on paper, 8 × 5 3/4 inches. Whitney Museum of American Art, New York; Bequest of Josephine N. Hopper 70.1565.74.

435c. Drawing for Victor Hugo's *Les Misérables,* c. 1900–09. Pencil on paper, 8 × 5 inches. Whitney Museum of American Art; Bequest of Josephine N. Hopper 70.1563.63.

435d. Drawing for Victor Hugo's *Les Misérables,* c. 1900–09. Pencil on lined paper, 8 × 5 inches. Whitney Museum of American Art, New York; Bequest of Josephine N. Hopper 70.1605.63.

435e. Drawing for Victor Hugo's *Les Misérables,* c. 1900–09. Pencil on lined paper, 8 × 5 inches. Whitney Museum of American Art; Bequest of Josephine N. Hopper 70.1559.75.

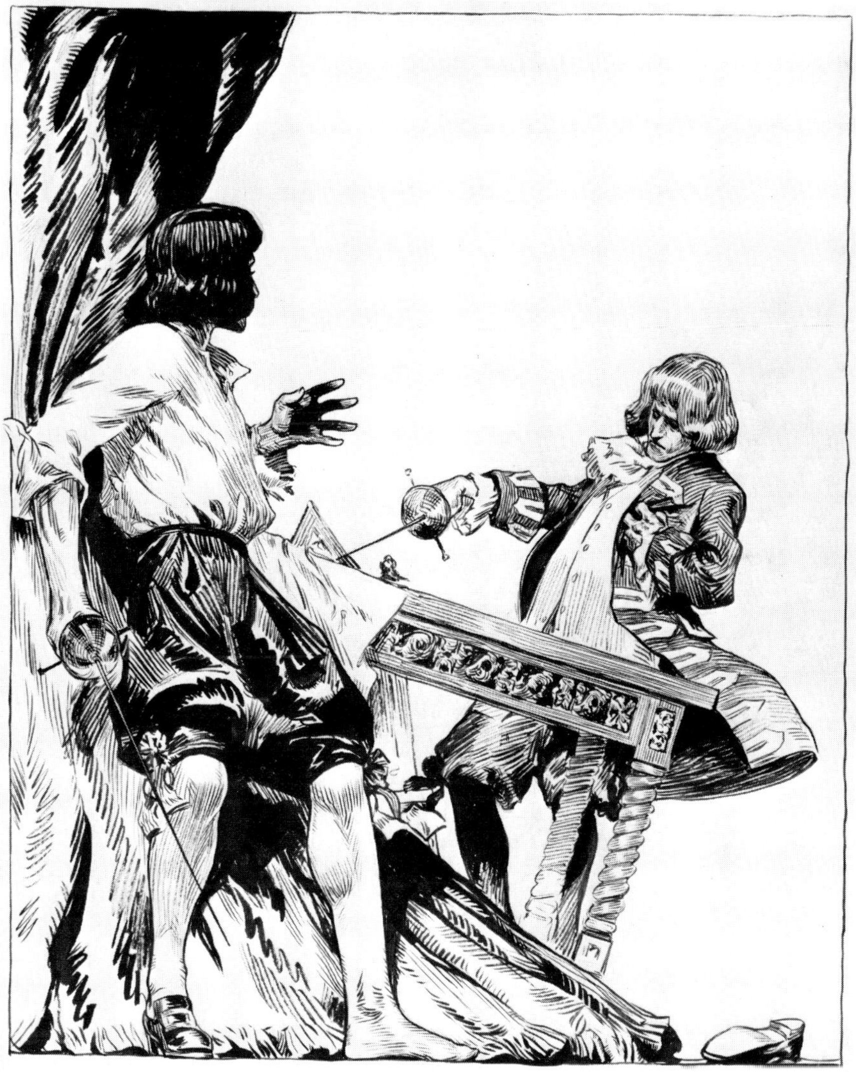

437

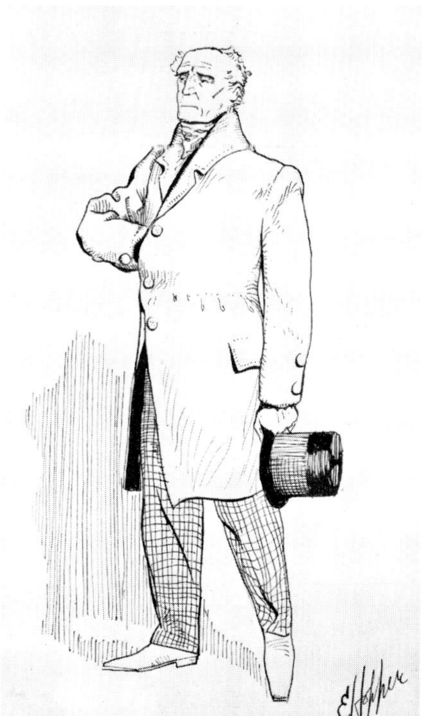

436

436. Jean Valjean from Victor Hugo's *Les Misérables,* c. 1900–09. Ink on paper, 7⅜ × 4¼ inches. Collection of Kennedy Galleries, Inc., New York.

437. [*The Duel*], c. 1900–10. Ink and white paint on illustration board, 21¾ × 13⅞ inches. Whitney Museum of American Art, New York; Bequest of Josephine N. Hopper 70.1363.

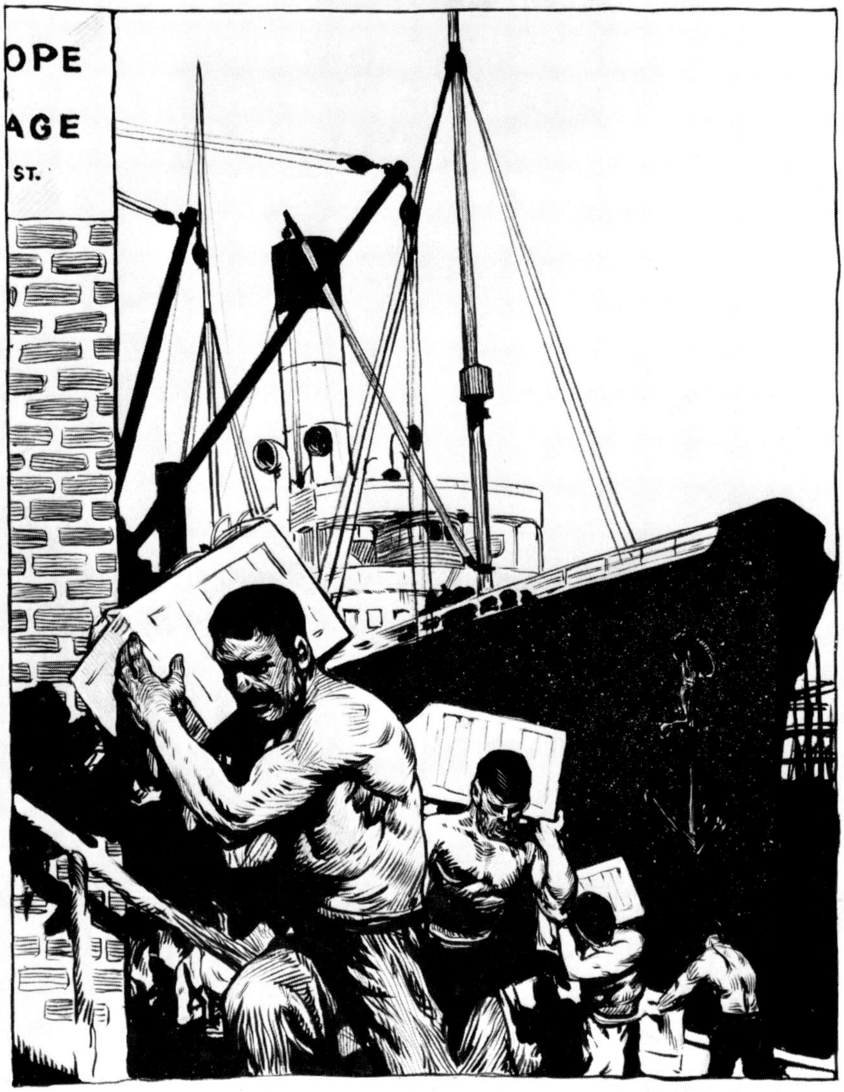

438

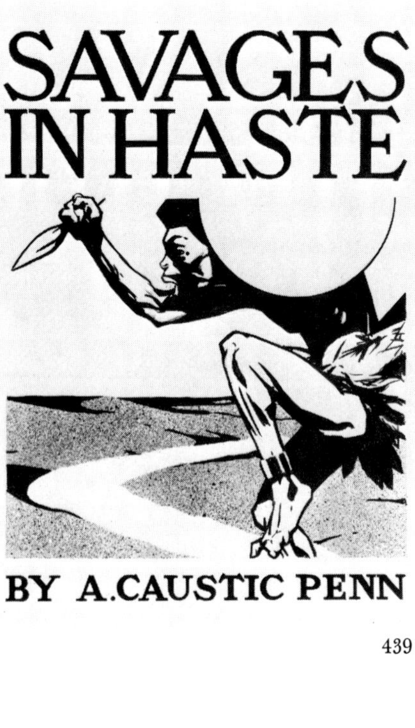

439

438. [*Stevedores Unloading Ship*], c. 1900–10. Ink and wash on illustration board, $21\frac{7}{8} \times 13\frac{15}{16}$ inches. Whitney Museum of American Art, New York; Bequest of Josephine N. Hopper 70.1341.

439. *Savages in Haste,* c. 1900–10. Ink and white paint on illustration board, $20 \times 14\frac{3}{4}$ inches. Whitney Museum of American Art, New York; Bequest of Josephine N. Hopper 70.1359.

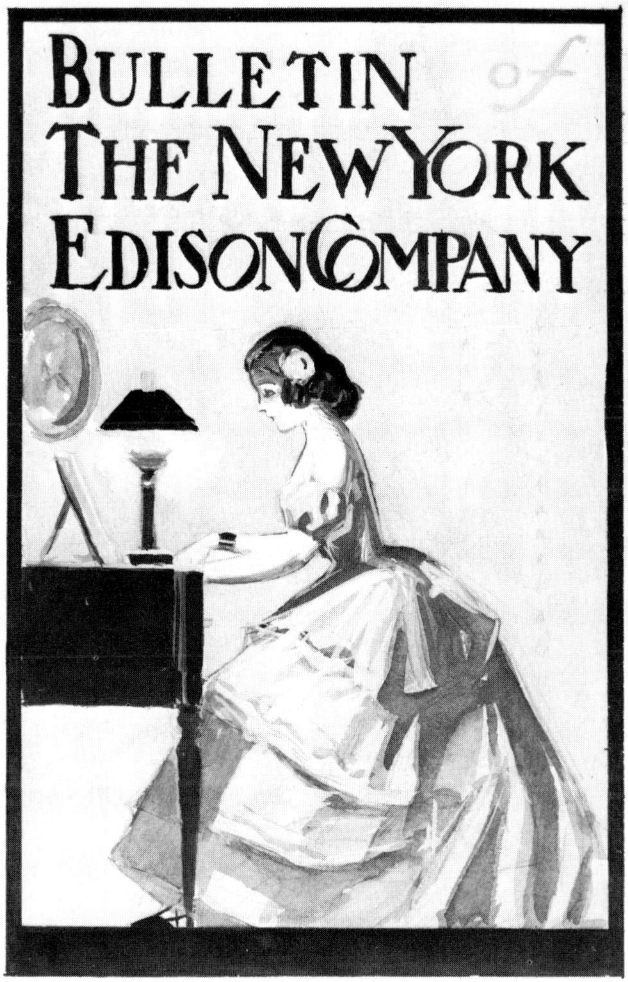

442

440. Cover for *Bulletin of The New York Edison Company,* 1906/07. Watercolor and ink on illustration board, 19⁹⁄₁₆ × 7¾ inches. Whitney Museum of American Art, New York; Bequest of Josephine N. Hopper 70.1607. (Color plate, p. 111.)

441. Cover for *Bulletin of The New York Edison Company,* 1906/07. Watercolor and ink on illustration board, 10½ × 7⅝ inches. Whitney Museum of American Art, New York; Bequest of Josephine N. Hopper 70.1608. (Color plate, p. 112.)

442. Cover for *Bulletin of The New York Edison Company,* 1906/07. Watercolor and ink on illustration board, 10⁹⁄₁₆ × 7¾ inches. Whitney Museum of American Art, New York; Bequest of Josephine N. Hopper 70.1609.

443. Cover for *Profitable Advertising,* c. 1906–08. Pencil and watercolor on illustration board, 15¼ × 11¼ inches. Whitney Museum of American Art, New York; Bequest of Josephine N. Hopper 70.1612.

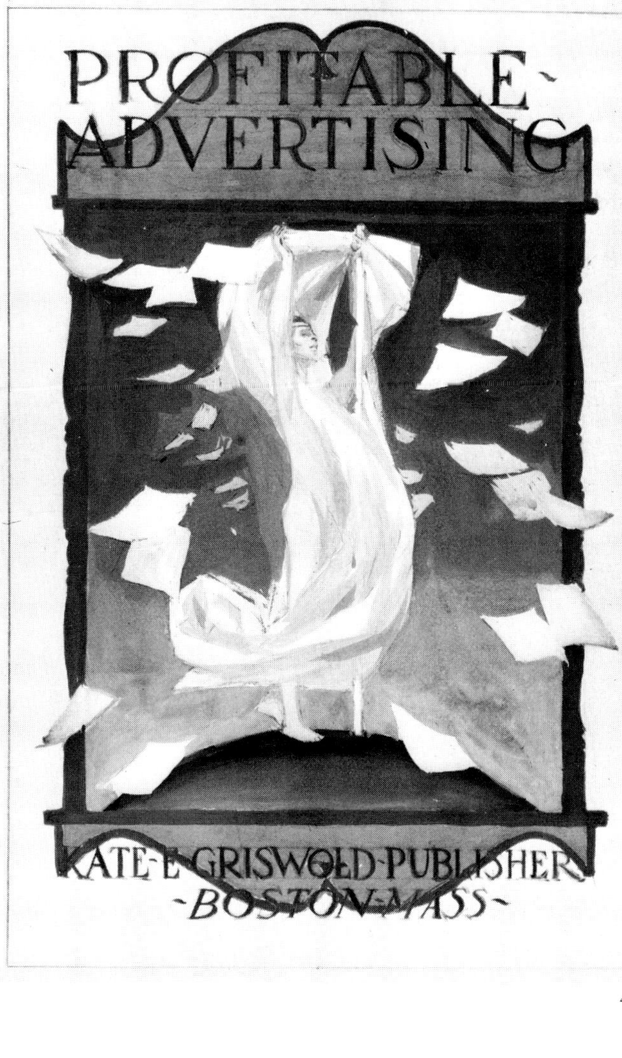

443

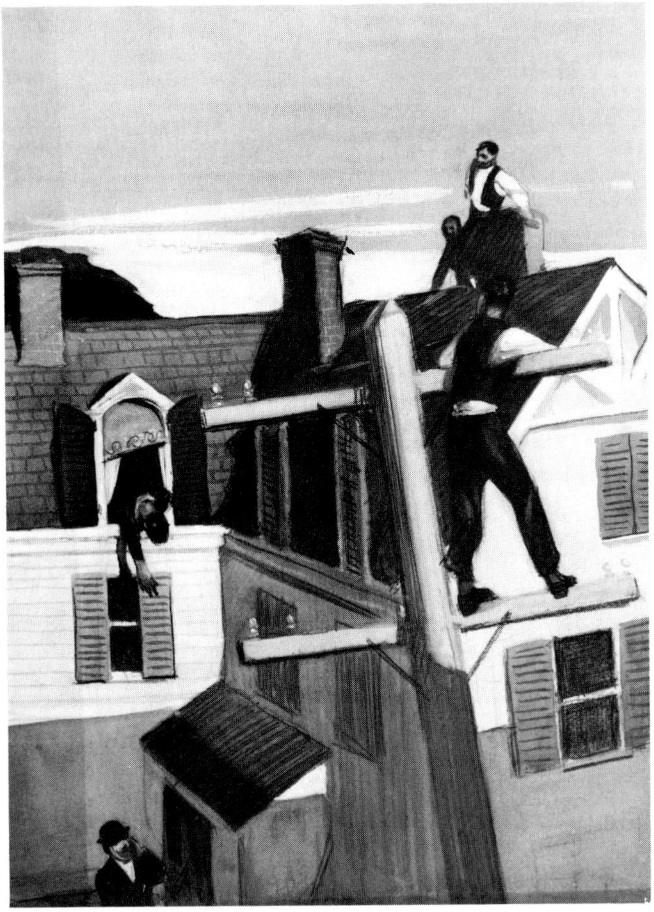

444

444. [*House with People*], 1906/07 or 1909. Gouache on illustration board, 20 × 15 inches. Whitney Museum of American Art, New York; Bequest of Josephine N. Hopper 70.1344.

445. Illustration for Victor Hugo's book of poems *L'Année Terrible,* 1906/07 or 1909. Watercolor and ink on paper, 19⁹⁄₁₆ × 14¾ inches. Whitney Museum of American Art, New York; Bequest of Josephine N. Hopper 70.1350. (Color plate, p. 113.)

Exhibited: Whitney Museum of American Art, New York, *Edward Hopper: Selections from the Hopper Bequest,* September 10–October 25, 1971 (no. 52). Downtown Branch, Whitney Museum of American Art, *Edward Hopper: Paintings, Prints, Drawings,* July 11–August 15, 1974.

446. *L'Année Terrible: At the Barricades,* 1906/07 or 1909. Watercolor and ink on paper, 21¾ × 14¹¹⁄₁₆ inches. Whitney Museum of American Art, New York; Bequest of Josephine N. Hopper 70.1337. (Color plate, p. 114.)

Exhibited: Whitney Museum of American Art, New York, *Edward Hopper: Selections from the Hopper Bequest,* September 10–October 25, 1971 (no. 53). Downtown Branch, Whitney Museum of American Art, *Edward Hopper: Paintings, Prints, Drawings,* July 11–August 15, 1974. *Edward Hopper,* traveling exhibition organized by the Whitney Museum of American Art, September 1974–December 1976.

Reference: Lloyd Goodrich, *Edward Hopper* (New York: Harry N. Abrams, 1971), p. 23.

447. *L'Année Terrible: On the Rooftops,* 1906/07 or 1909. Watercolor and ink on paper, 21¾ × 14¾ inches. Whitney Museum of American Art, New York; Bequest of Josephine N. Hopper 70.1338. (Color plate, p. 115.)

Exhibited: Whitney Museum of American Art, New York, *Edward Hopper: Selections from the Hopper Bequest,* September 10–October 25, 1971 (no. 54). Downtown Branch, Whitney Museum of American Art, *Edward Hopper: Paintings, Prints, Drawings,* July 11–August 15, 1974. Whitney Museum of American Art, New York, *The Whitney Studio Club and American Art 1900–1932,* May 22–September 3, 1975.

Reference: Lloyd Goodrich, *Edward Hopper* (New York: Harry N. Abrams, 1971), p. 22.

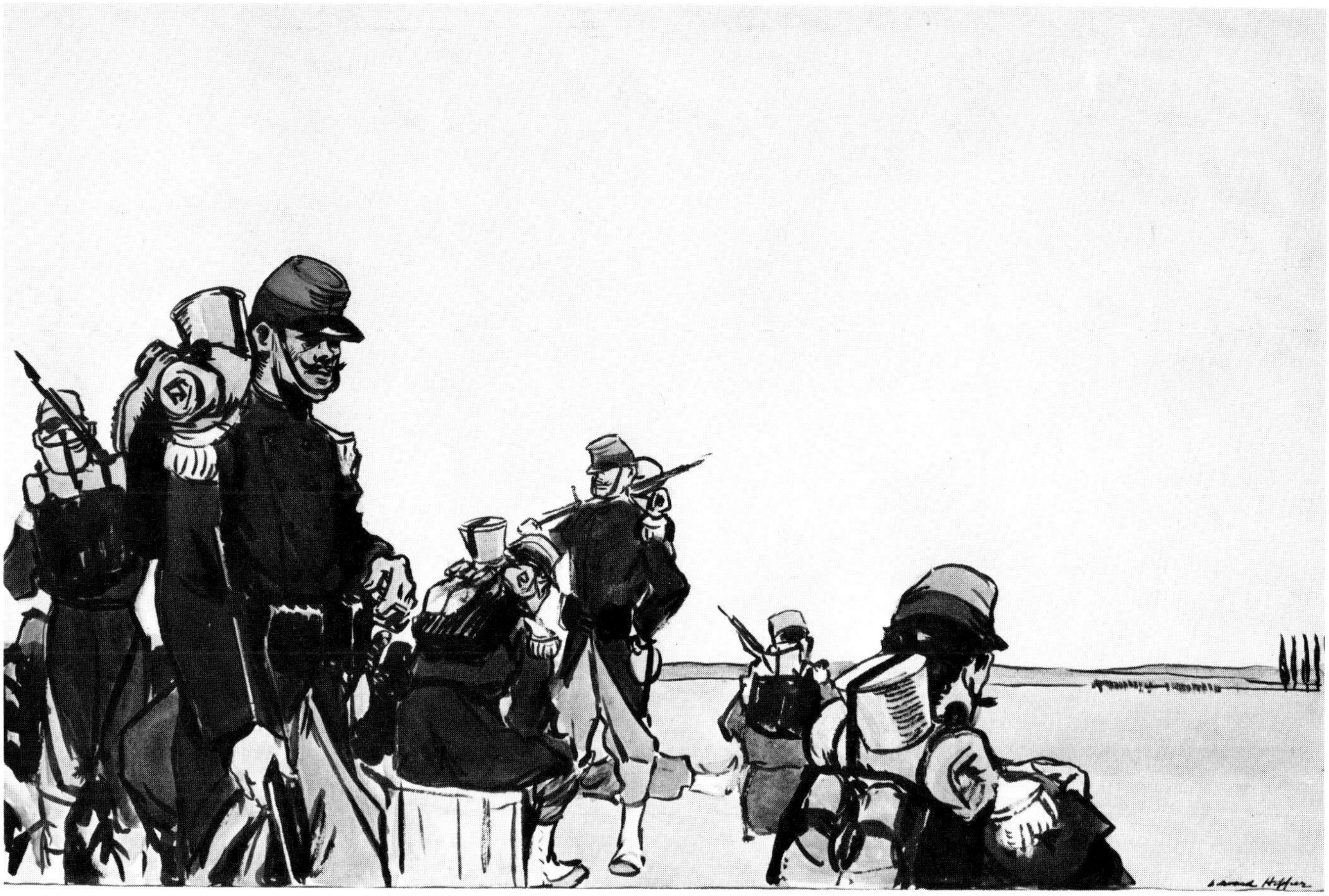

448

448. [*French Soldiers*], 1906/07 or 1909. Watercolor and ink on paper, 12 × 19 inches. Private collection.

449. *Jeanne d'Arc,* 1906/07 or 1909. Watercolor and ink on illustration board, 22 × 14⅞ inches. Whitney Museum of American Art, New York; Bequest of Josephine N. Hopper 70.1368. (Color plate, p. 116.)

450. *Don Quixote,* 1906/07 or 1909. Watercolor and ink on illustration board, 21¾ × 13¾ inches. Whitney Museum of American Art, New York; Bequest of Josephine N. Hopper 70.1346. (Color plate, p. 117.)

451. [*Boy and Moon*], 1906/07 or 1909. Watercolor and ink on paper, 21⅞ × 14$\frac{9}{16}$ inches. Whitney Museum of American Art, New York; Bequest of Josephine N. Hopper 70.1349. (Color plate, p. 118.)

Exhibited: Whitney Museum of American Art, New York, *Edward Hopper: Selections from the Hopper Bequest,* September 10–October 25, 1971 (no. 56). Downtown Branch, Whitney Museum of American Art, *Edward Hopper: Paintings, Prints, Drawings,* July 11–August 15, 1974. *Edward Hopper,* traveling exhibition organized by the Whitney Museum of American Art, September 1974–December 1976.

452. *Les Etudiants de Paris,* 1906/07 or 1909. Watercolor, ink, and pencil on illustration board, 19⅞ × 14¾ inches. Whitney Museum of American Art, New York; Bequest of Josephine N. Hopper 70.1345.

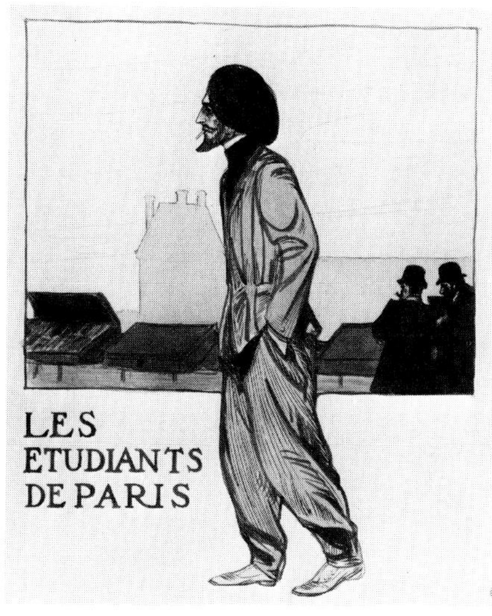

452

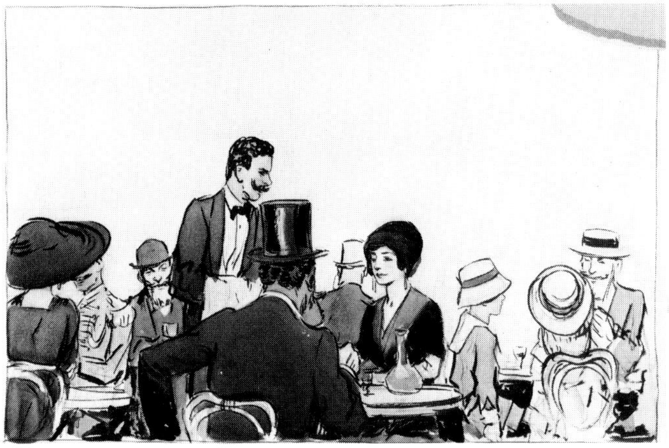

455

453. [*Men Seated at Cafe Table*], 1906/07 or 1909. Watercolor and ink on illustration board, 21⅞ × 14 inches. Whitney Museum of American Art, New York; Bequest of Josephine N. Hopper 70.1348. (Color plate, p. 119.)

454. [*Couple near Poplars*], 1906/07 or 1909. Watercolor and ink on illustration board, 21⅞ × 14⅞ inches. Whitney Museum of American Art, New York; Bequest of Josephine N. Hopper 70.1365. (Color plate, p. 120.)

455. [*Waiter and Diners*], 1906/07 or 1909. Watercolor and ink on illustration board, 14⅞ × 22 inches. Whitney Museum of American Art, New York; Bequest of Josephine N. Hopper 70.1443.

456. [*On the Deck*], 1906/07 or 1909. Watercolor and ink on illustration board, 14⅞ × 22 inches. Whitney Museum of American Art, New York; Bequest of Josephine N. Hopper 70.1444. (Color plate, p. 121.)

457. [*Along the River*], 1906/07 or 1909. Watercolor and ink on paper, 12½ × 19 inches. Frye Art Museum, Seattle, Washington.

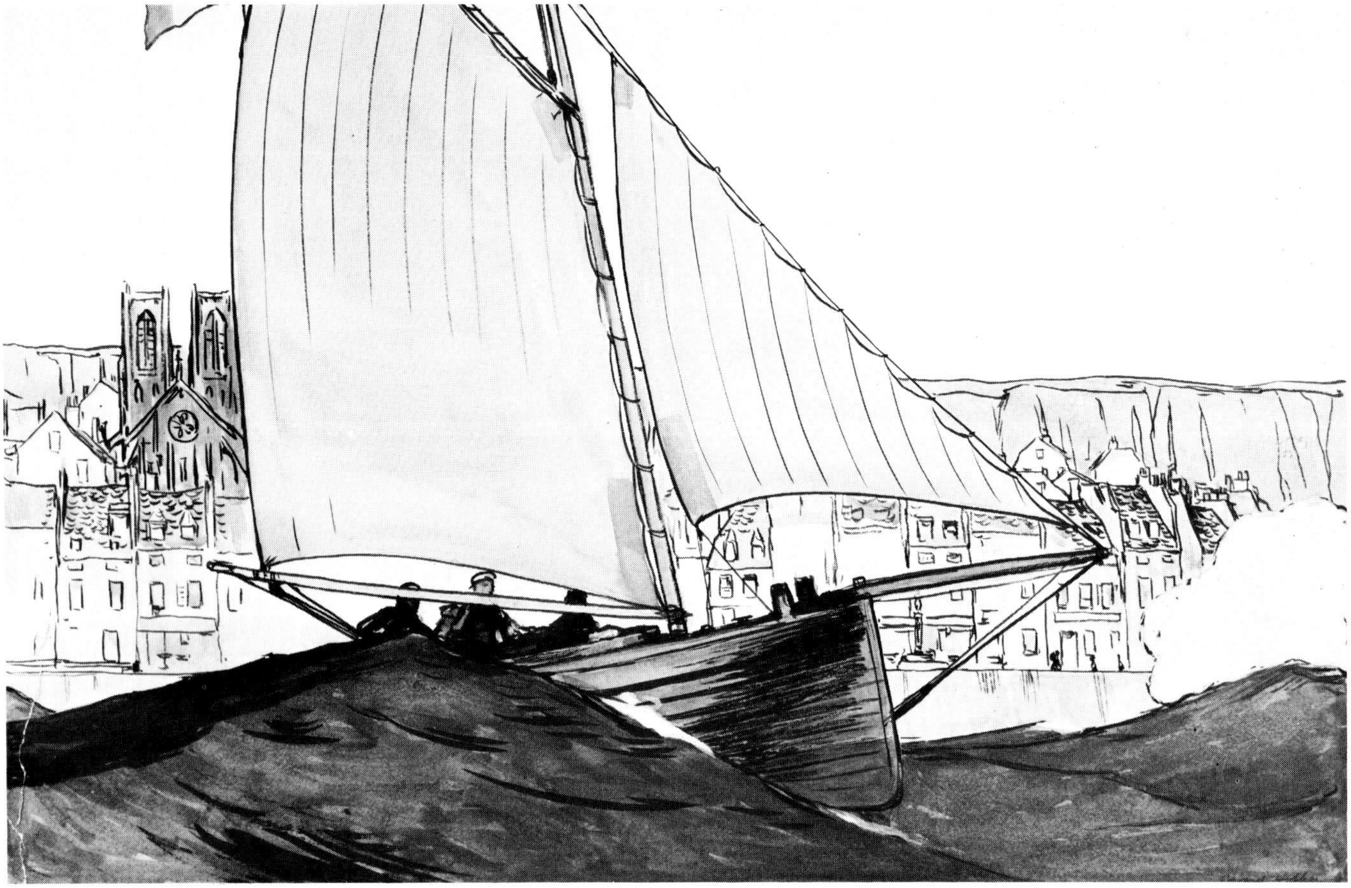

457

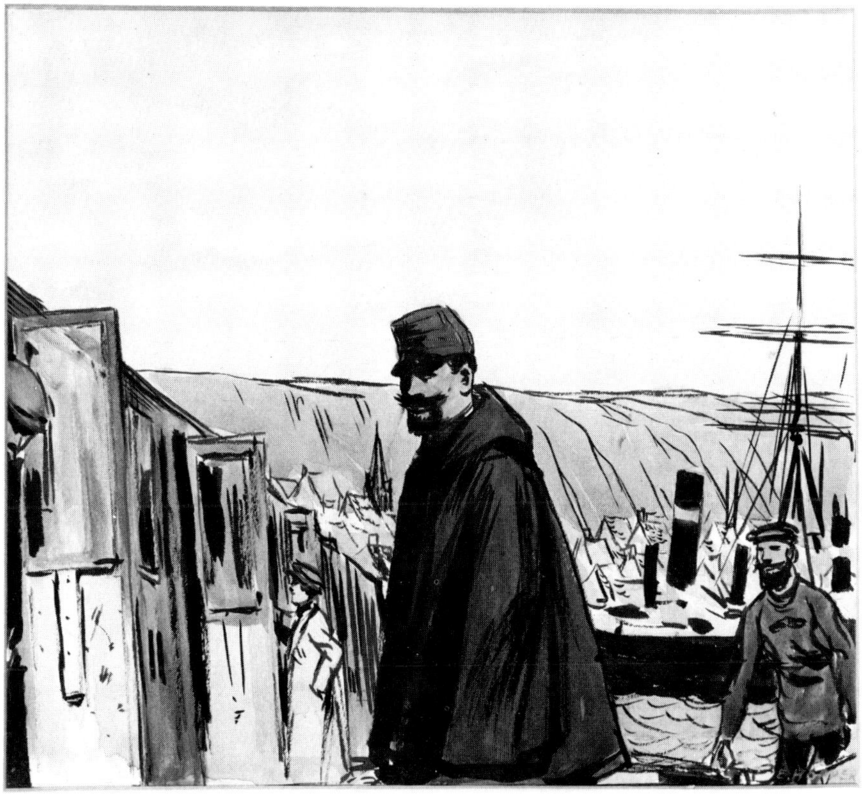

458

458. *The Port,* 1906/07 or 1909. Ink and watercolor on paper, $10\frac{1}{2} \times 11\frac{7}{8}$ inches. Whitney Museum of American Art, New York; Bequest of Josephine N. Hopper 70.1351.

Exhibited: National Arts Club, February 1920.

459. *New York and Its Houses,* c. 1906–10. Watercolor and ink on paper, $21\frac{13}{16} \times 14\frac{13}{16}$ inches. Whitney Museum of American Art, New York; Bequest of Josephine N. Hopper 70.1347. (Color plate, p. 122.)

Exhibited: Whitney Museum of American Art, New York, *Edward Hopper: Selections from the Hopper Bequest,* September 10–October 25, 1971 (no. 55). *Edward Hopper,* traveling exhibition organized by the Whitney Museum of American Art, September 1974–December 1976.

Reference: "The Guiding Light: The Paintings of the American Artist Edward Hopper," text by Robert Melville, research by Roger Law, *The London Sunday Times Magazine,* April 29, 1973, p. 61.

460. *Pow-wows,* c. 1906–10. Watercolor and ink on illustration board, $19\frac{13}{16} \times 14\frac{3}{4}$ inches. Whitney Museum of American Art, New York; Bequest of Josephine N. Hopper 70.1360. (Color plate, p. 123.)

461. [*A Dueling Death*], c. 1906–10. Watercolor and ink on illustration board, $19\frac{13}{16} \times 14\frac{5}{8}$ inches. Whitney Museum of American Art, New York; Bequest of Josephine N. Hopper 70.1369. (Color plate, p. 124.)

462. [*A Theater Entrance*], c. 1906–10. Ink and watercolor on illustration board, $19\frac{13}{16} \times 14\frac{13}{16}$ inches. Whitney Museum of American Art, New York; Bequest of Josephine N. Hopper 70.1378. (Color plate, p. 125.)

463. [*French Couple on Embankment*], c. 1906–14. Watercolor, ink, and conte on paper, $18\frac{7}{8} \times 15$ inches. Whitney Museum of American Art, New York; Bequest of Josephine N. Hopper 70.1343.

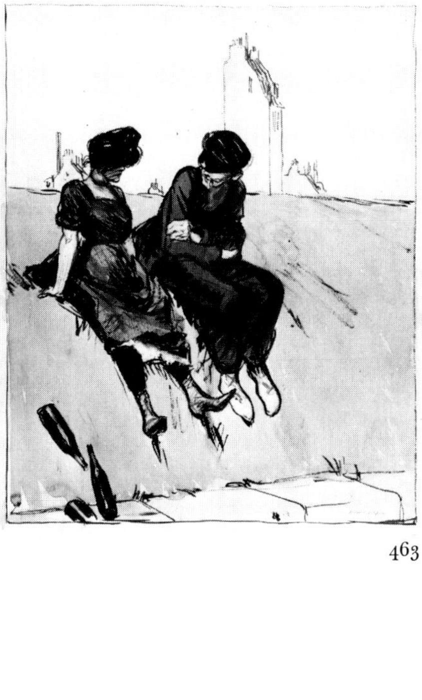

463

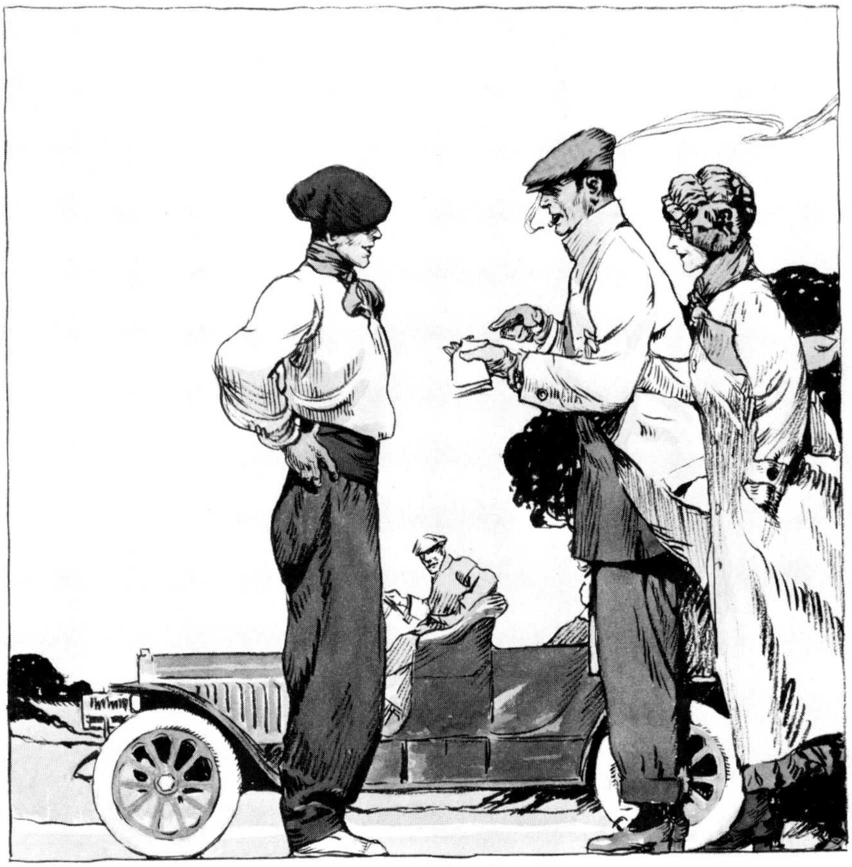

464

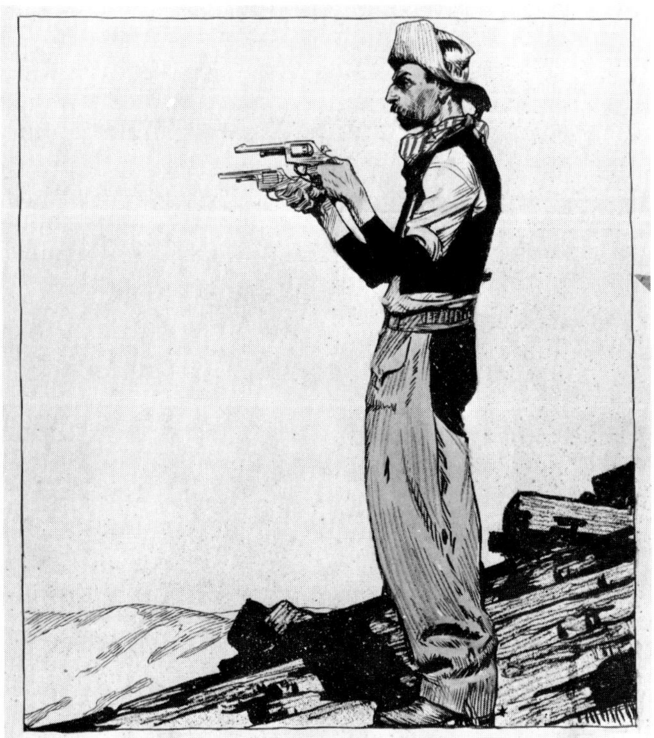

465

464. [*Group of Figures and Automobile*], c. 1906–14. Ink and wash on illustration board, 21⅞ × 14⅞ inches. Whitney Museum of American Art, New York; Bequest of Josephine N. Hopper 70.1371.

465. [*Cowboy*], c. 1906–14. Ink and wash on illustration board, 21^{13}⁄16 × 15 inches. Whitney Museum of American Art, New York; Bequest of Josephine N. Hopper 70.1356.

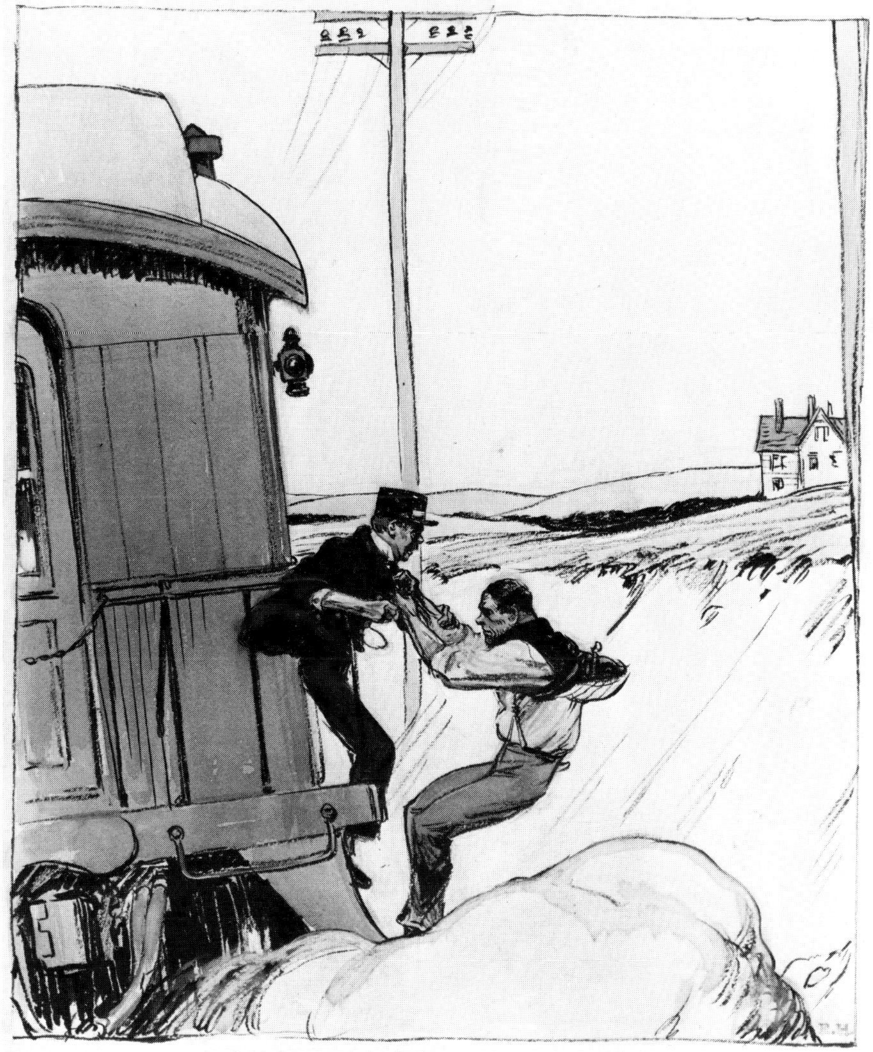

466

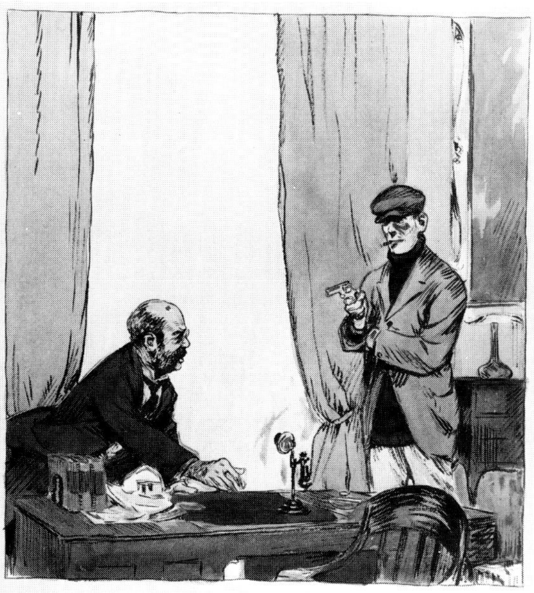

467

466. [*Jumping on a Train*], c. 1906–14. Ink and wash on illustration board, 18¾ × 15 inches. Whitney Museum of American Art, New York; Bequest of Josephine N. Hopper 70.1441.

467. [*Holdup*], c. 1906–14. Ink and wash on illustration board, 21$^{15}/_{16}$ × 15 inches. Whitney Museum of American Art, New York; Bequest of Josephine N. Hopper 70.1441.

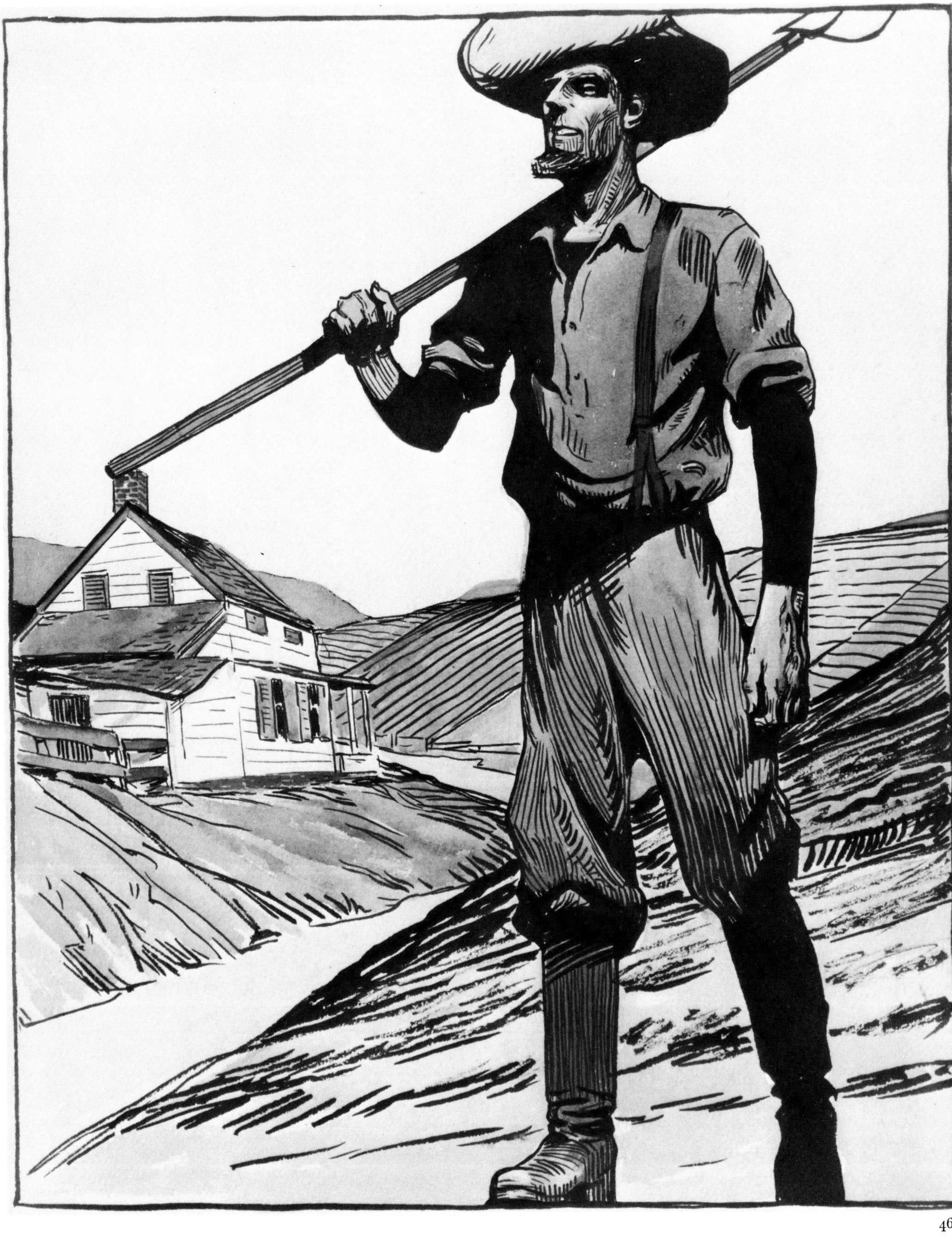

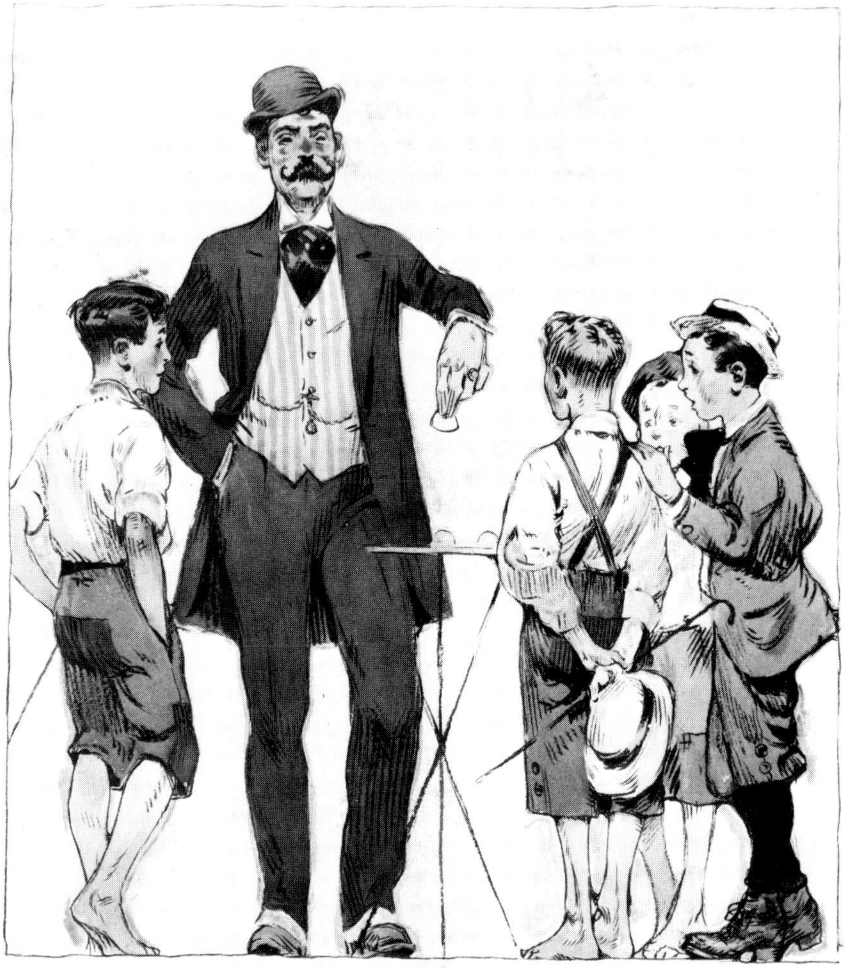

468

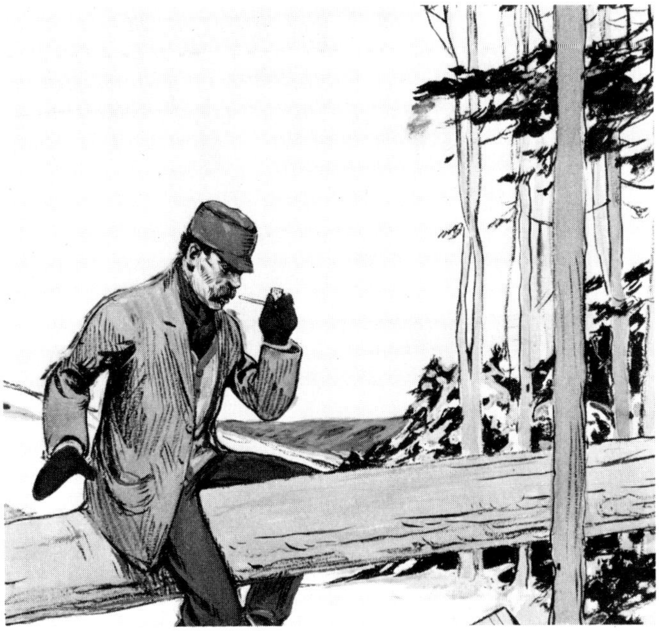

470

468. [*Magician and Boys*], c. 1906–14. Wash and ink on illustration board, 22 × 14⅞ inches. Whitney Museum of American Art, New York; Bequest of Josephine N. Hopper 70.1366.

469. [*Man with a Hoe*], c. 1906–14. Watercolor on illustration board, 16¾ × 13¾ inches. Collection of Mr. and Mrs. Frank Romano.

470. [*Man on Log*], c. 1906–14. Watercolor and ink on illustration board, 11 × 11½ inches. Collection of Anne E. Bach.

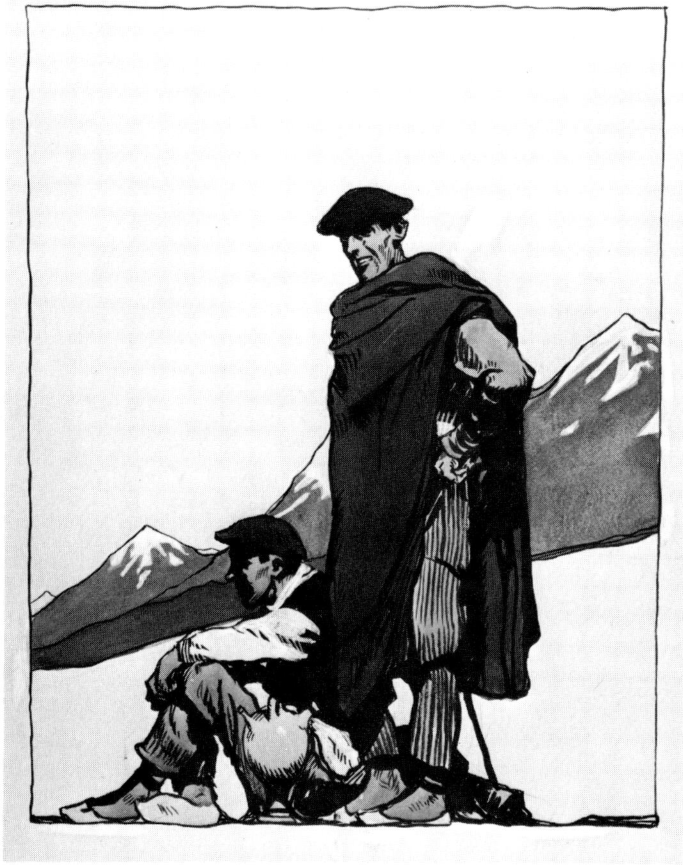

474

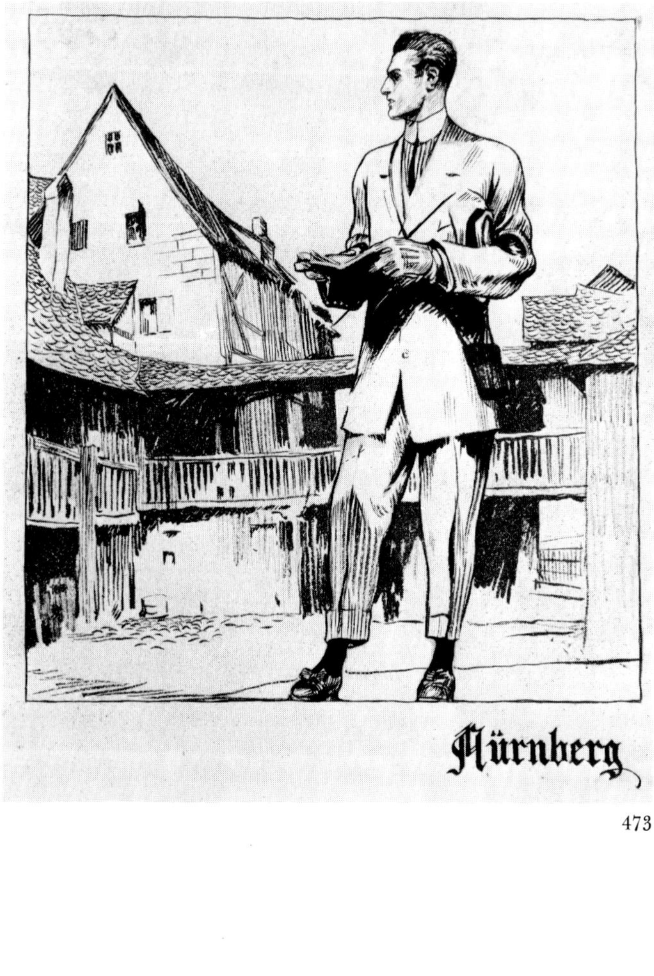

473

471. [*Man at Riverfront*], 1907. Watercolor and ink on paper, 19⅞ × 14$^{13}/_{16}$ inches. Whitney Museum of American Art, New York; Bequest of Josephine N. Hopper 70.1364. (Color plate, p. 126.)

472. [*Marching Bag-Pipers*], 1907. Watercolor on illustration board, 19⅞ × 14$^{13}/_{16}$ inches. Whitney Museum of American Art, New York; Bequest of Josephine N. Hopper 70.1377. (Color plate, p. 127.)

473. *Nürnberg*, c. 1907. Ink on illustration board, 22 × 15⅛ inches. Whitney Museum of American Art, New York; Bequest of Josephine N. Hopper 70.1367.

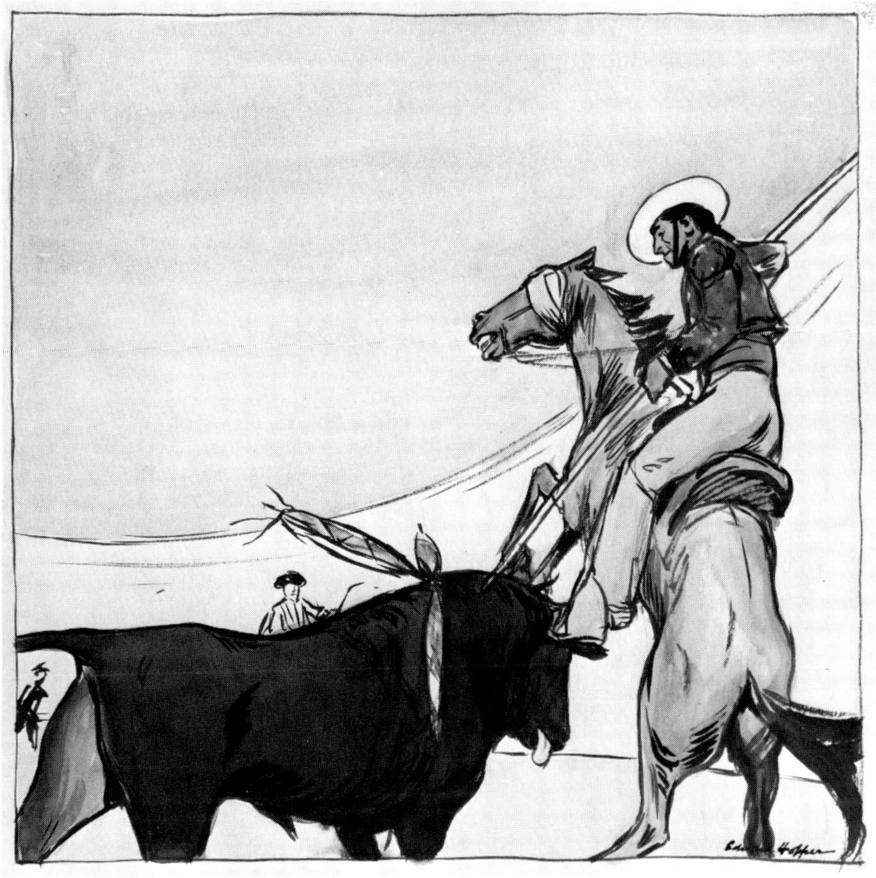

475

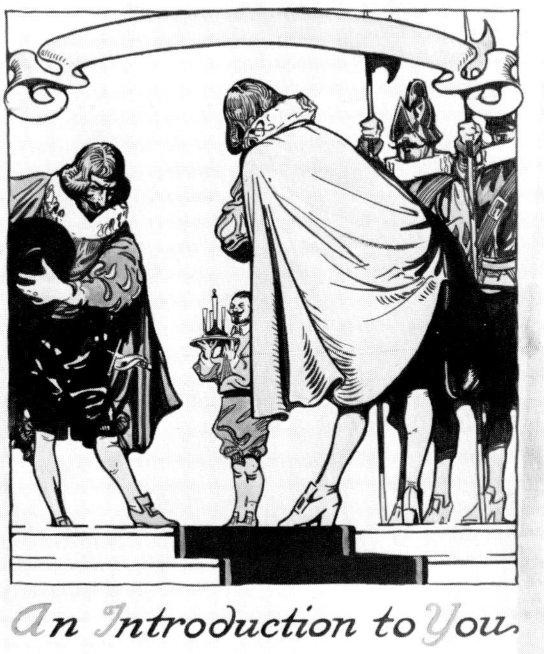

476

474. [*Two Men in the Pyrenees*], possibly an illustration for Victor Hugo's *En Voyage Alpes et Pyrénées* (1890), c. 1907–10. Watercolor on illustration board, 18½ × 13½ inches. Collection of Anne E. Bach.

475. [*Bull Fight*], c. 1907–10. Watercolor and ink on illustration board, 22 × 14 15/16 inches. Whitney Museum of American Art, New York; Bequest of Josephine N. Hopper 70.1442.

476. *An Introduction to You*, c. 1907–10. Ink and watercolor on illustration board, 20 × 14⅞ inches. Whitney Museum of American Art, New York; Bequest of Josephine N. Hopper 70.1358.

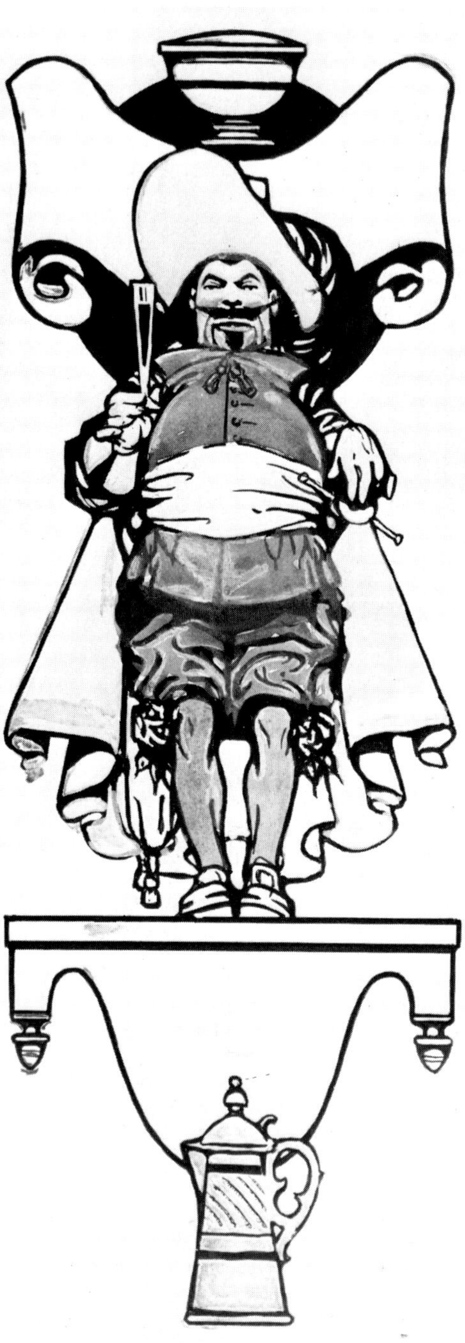

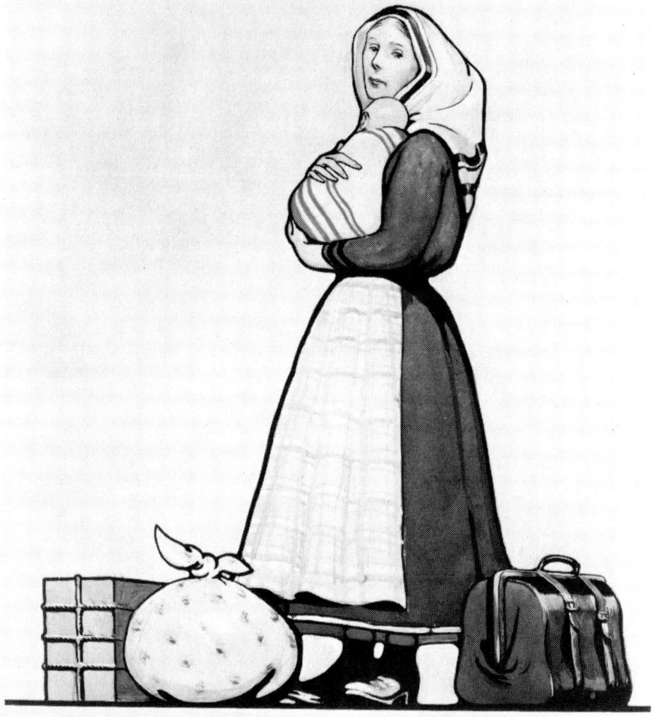

478

477. [*Beer-Drinking Burgher*], c. 1907–10. Ink and watercolor on illustration board, 14½ × 7⅜ inches. Whitney Museum of American Art, New York; Bequest of Josephine N. Hopper 70.1611.

478. [*Peasant Woman with Child*], c. 1907–10. Watercolor on illustration board, 16⅝ × 12½ inches. Kennedy Galleries, Inc., New York.

Exhibited: Kennedy Galleries, Inc., New York, *Edward Hopper at Kennedy Galleries,* May 11–June 8, 1977 (no. 8).

477

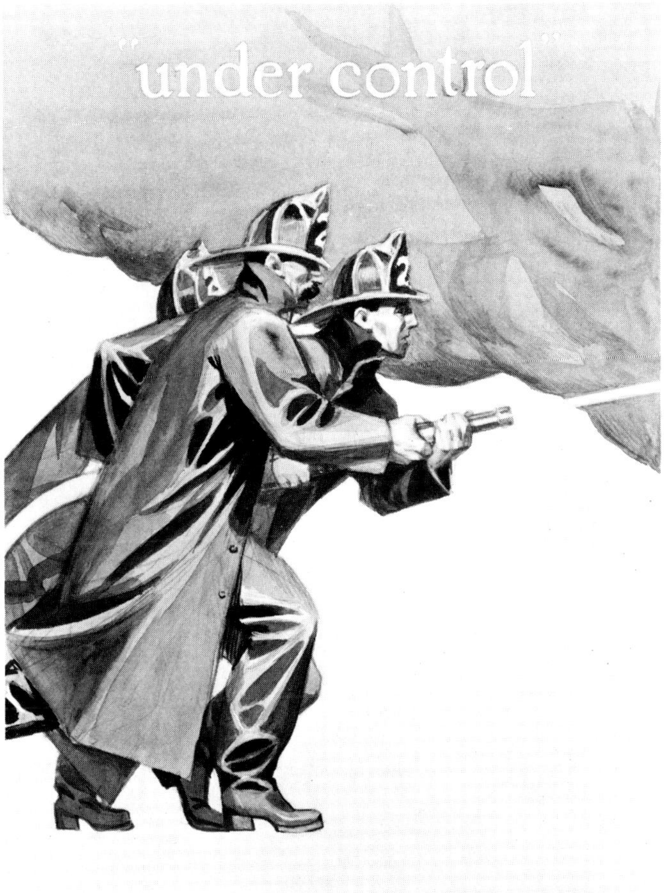

480

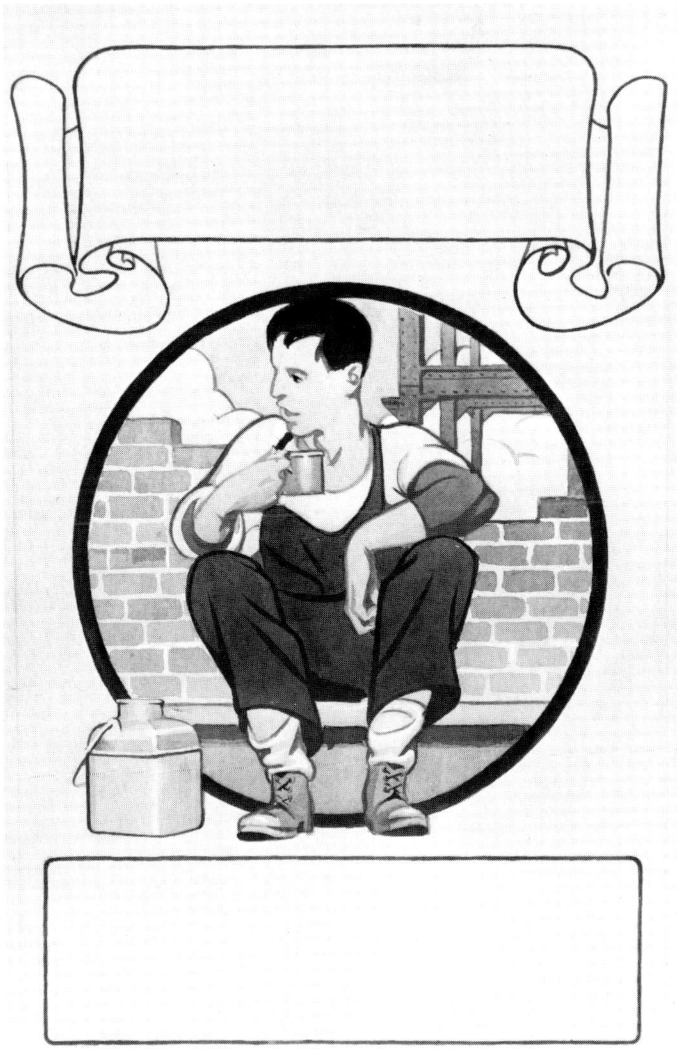

479. [*Brick-Layer's Coffee Break*], c. 1907–10. Watercolor on illustration board, 17¼ × 11⁷⁄₁₆ inches. Whitney Museum of American Art, New York; Bequest of Josephine N. Hopper 70.1614.

480. *Under Control,* c. 1907–10. Gouache on illustration board, 13 × 10 inches. Kennedy Galleries, Inc., New York.

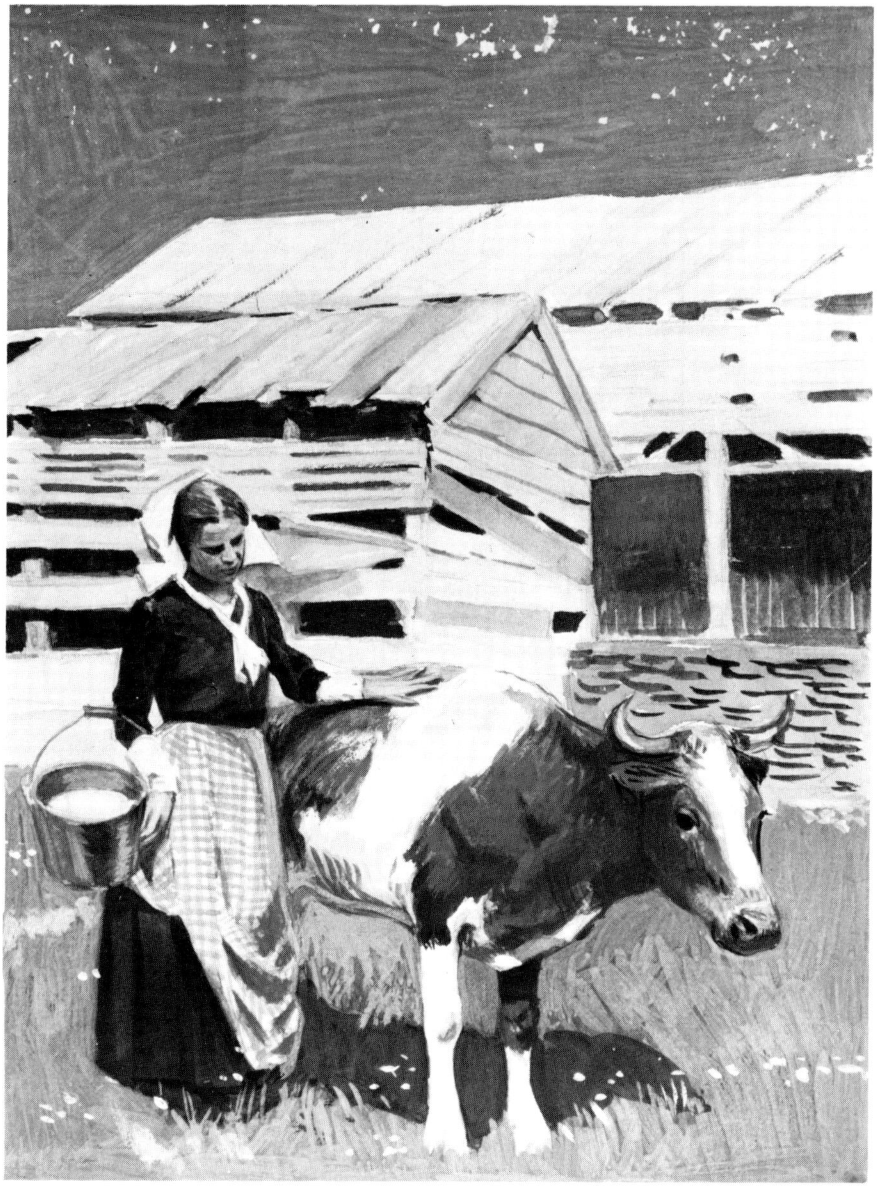

482

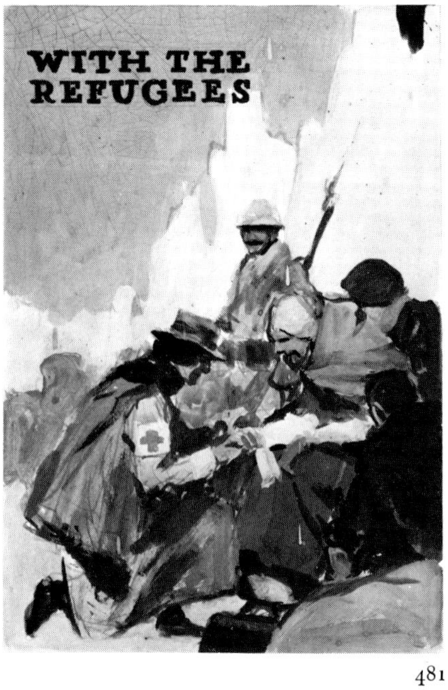

481

481. *With the Refugees,* c. 1919. Watercolor on illustration board, 10⅛ × 7 inches. Kennedy Galleries, Inc., New York. Study for a poster for the American Red Cross. Poster exhibited at The Penguin Club, 8 East Fifteenth Street, New York.

482. [*Milkmaid and Cow*], c. 1915–20. Gouache on illustration board, 14⁹⁄₁₆ × 9⅞ inches. Whitney Museum of American Art, New York; Bequest of Josephine N. Hopper 70.1610.

483. [*Workmen with Picks*], c. 1916–18. Watercolor and pencil on illustration board, 19¹³⁄₁₆ × 14⅞ inches. Whitney Museum of American Art, New York; Bequest of Josephine N. Hopper 70.1375. (Color plate, p. 128.)

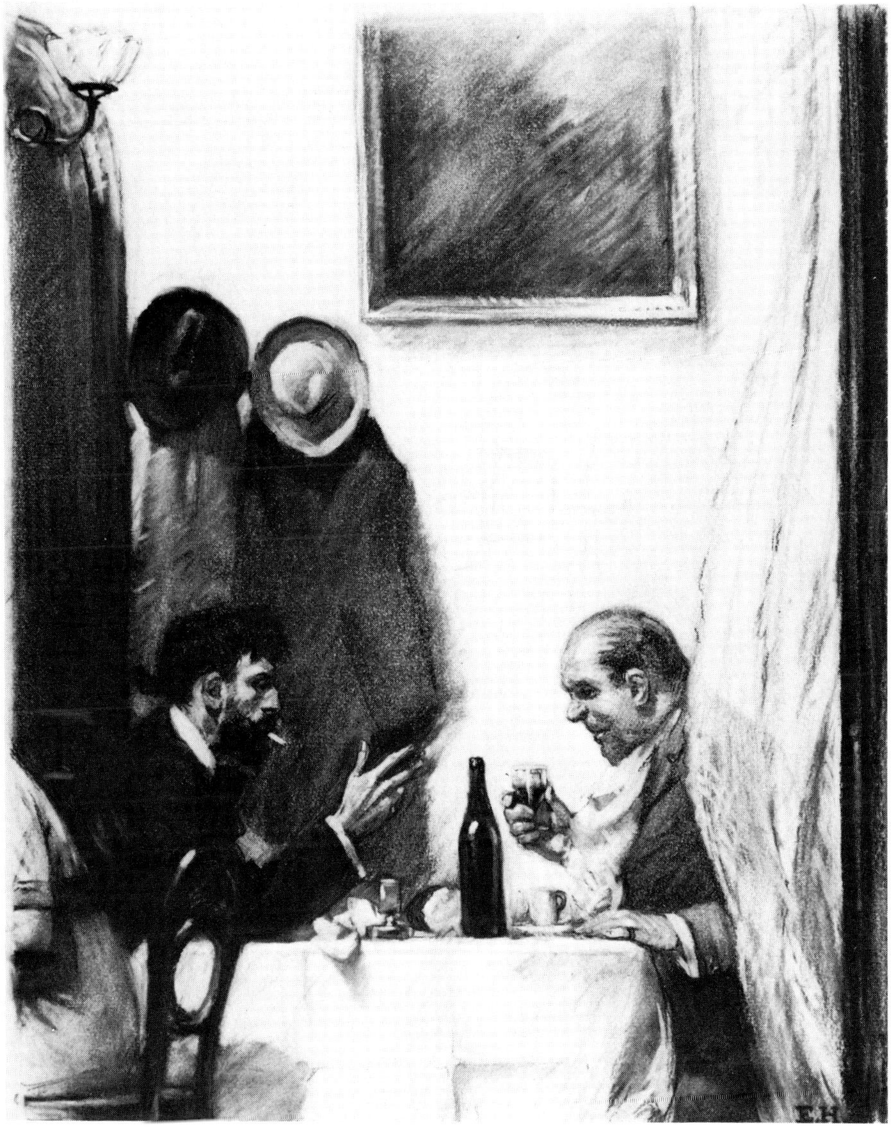

486

484. [*Tennis Players*], c. 1916–20. Gouache on illustration board, $14\frac{11}{16} \times 9\frac{7}{8}$ inches. Whitney Museum of American Art, New York; Bequest of Josephine N. Hopper 70.1613. (Color plate, p. 129.)

485. [*At the Theater*], c. 1916–22. Wash and ink on paper, $18\frac{5}{8} \times 15$ inches. Whitney Museum of American Art, New York; Bequest of Josephine N. Hopper 70.1440.

486. [*In a Restaurant*], c. 1916–25. Conte on illustration board, $26\frac{5}{8} \times 21\frac{11}{16}$ inches. Whitney Museum of American Art, New York; Bequest of Josephine N. Hopper 70.1449.

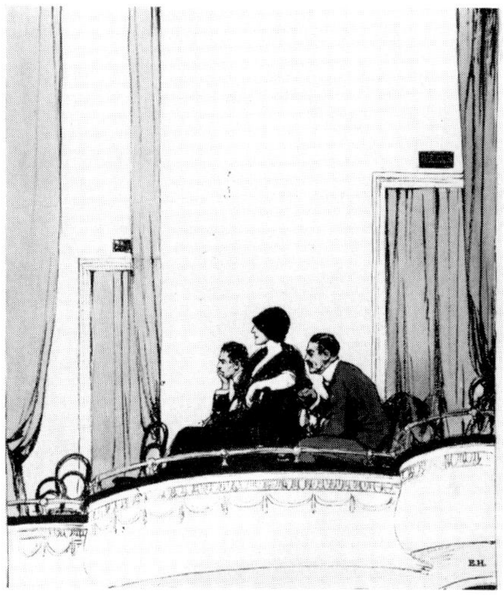

485

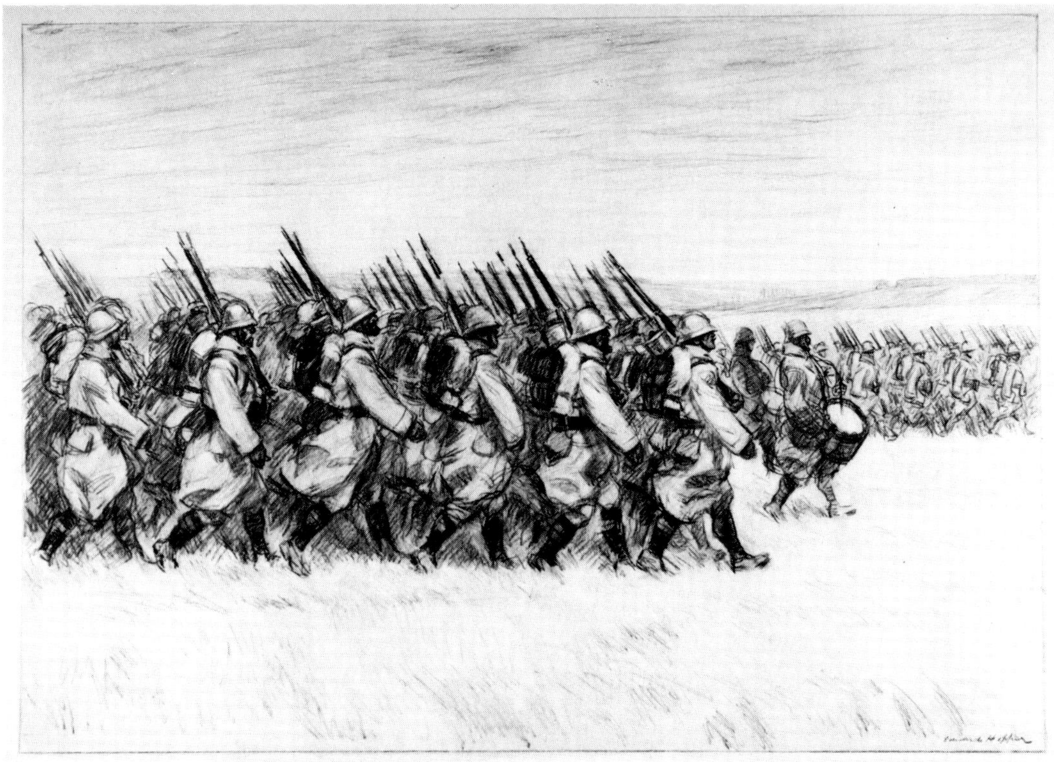

487

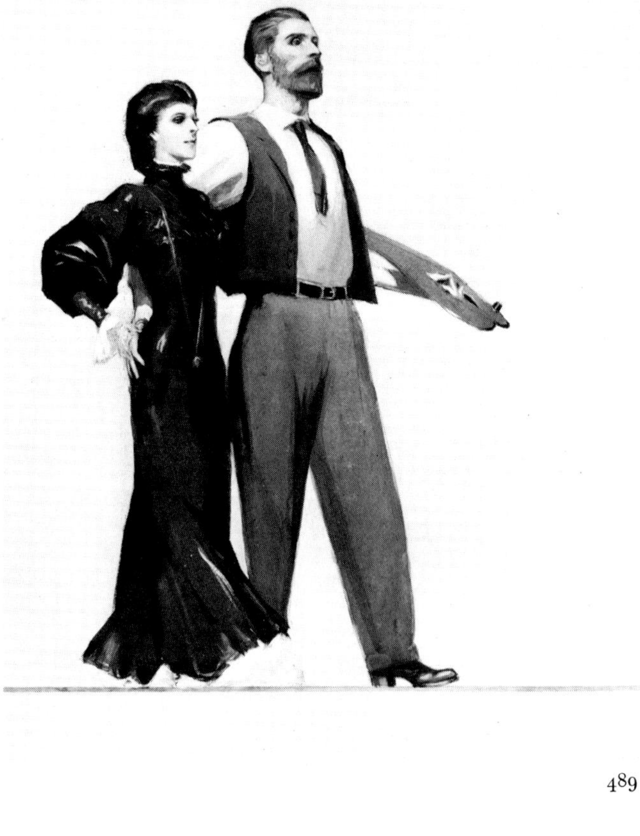

489

487. [*Troops on the March*], c. 1916–25. Wash and conte on illustration board, 20 × 30 inches. Whitney Museum of American Art, New York; Bequest of Josephine N. Hopper 70.1454.

488. [*Man Blowing Smoke Rings*], c. 1917–20. Watercolor and ink on illustration board, 18½ × 14$^{15}/_{16}$ inches. Whitney Museum of American Art, New York; Bequest of Josephine N. Hopper 70.1376. (Color plate, p. 130.)

489. [*A Couple Dancing*], c. 1917–20. Wash on illustration board, 20 × 15 inches. Whitney Museum of American Art, New York; Bequest of Josephine N. Hopper 70.1384.

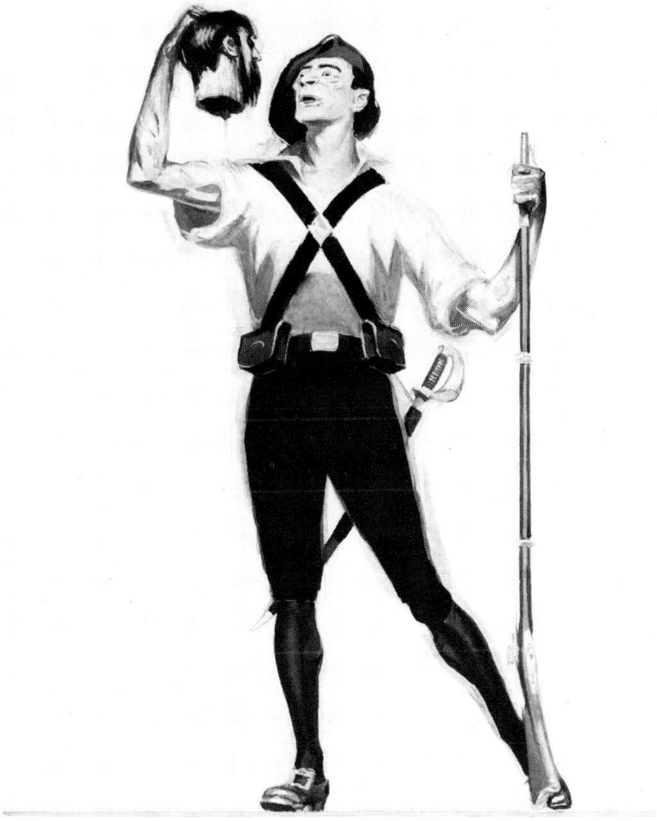

490

490. [*Rifleman Holding a Decapitated Head*], c. 1917–20. Wash on illustration board, 19⅞ × 15 inches. Whitney Museum of American Art, New York, Bequest of Josephine N. Hopper 70.1381.

491. [*Walking Man with Cape and Cane*], c. 1917–20. Watercolor on illustration board, 19⅞ × 15 inches. Whitney Museum of American Art, New York; Bequest of Josephine N. Hopper 70.1389.

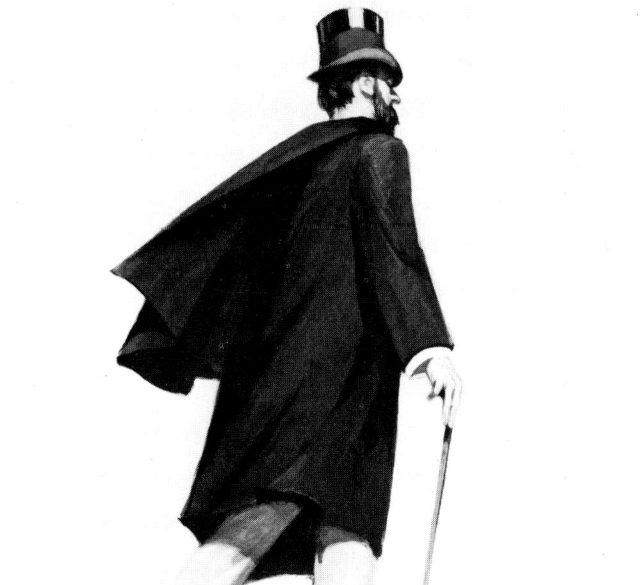

491

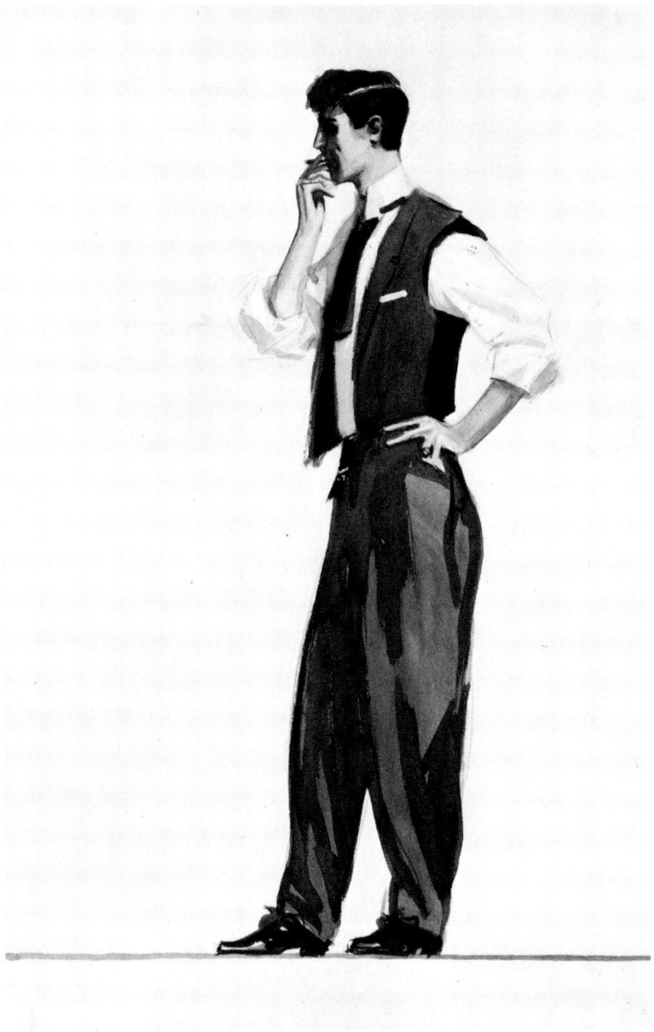

492

492. [*Standing Smoker*], c. 1917–20. Wash on illustration board, $19\frac{7}{8} \times 14\frac{7}{8}$ inches. Whitney Museum of American Art, New York; Bequest of Josephine N. Hopper 70.1387.

493. [*Standing Man in Evening Dress*], c. 1917–20. Wash on illustration board, $19\frac{7}{8} \times 12\frac{3}{8}$ inches. Whitney Museum of American Art, New York; Bequest of Josephine N. Hopper 70.1373.

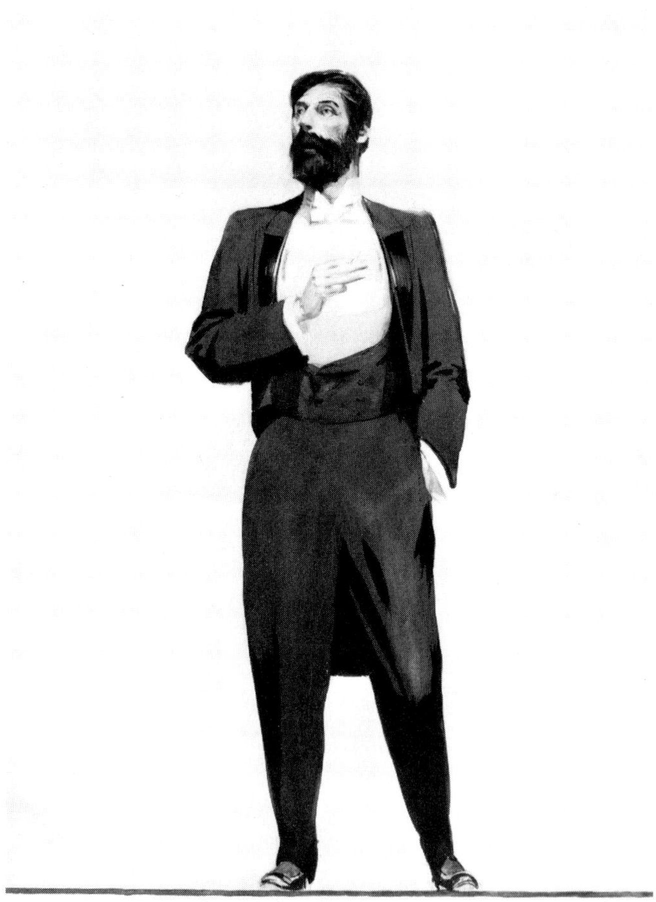

493

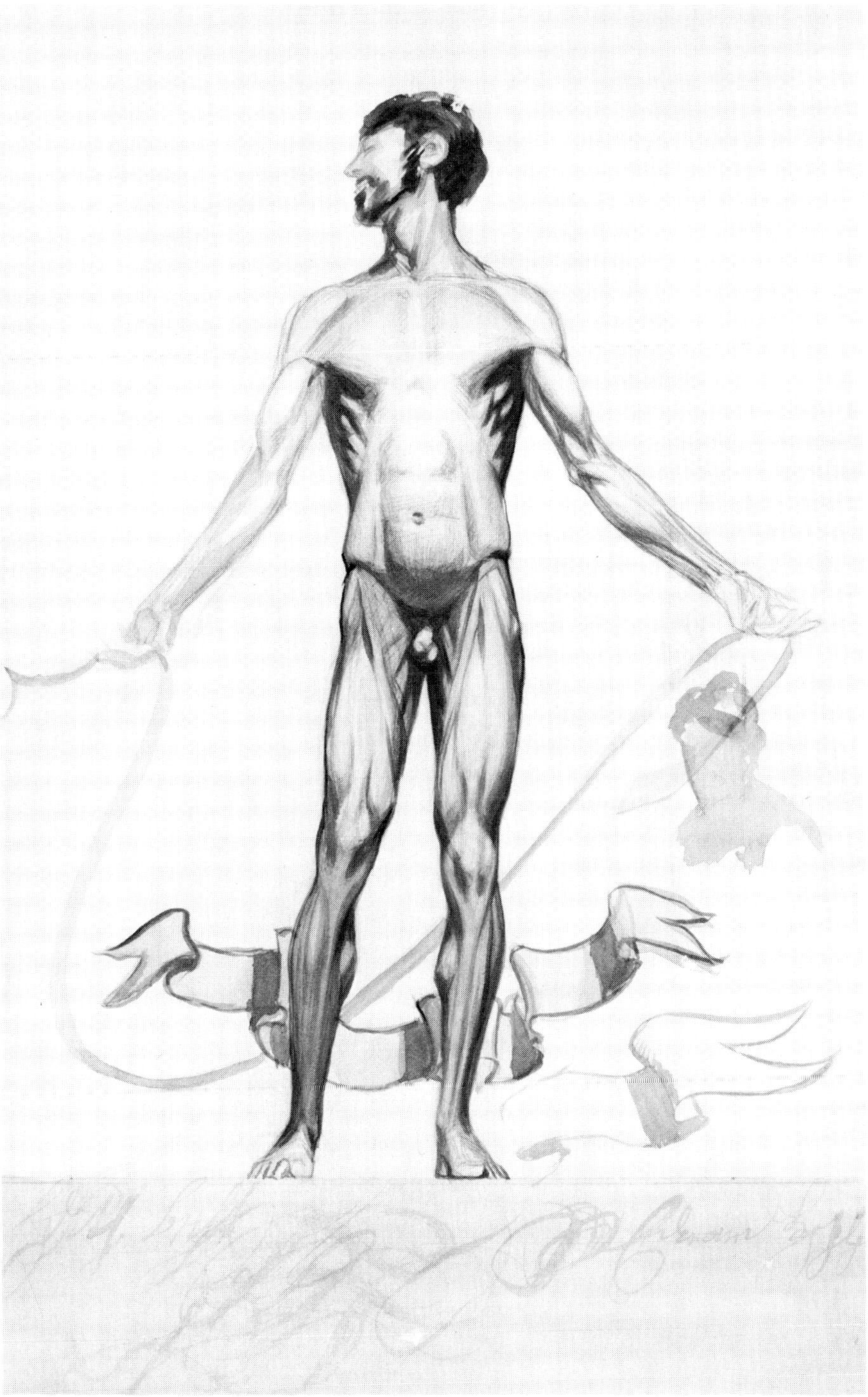

494

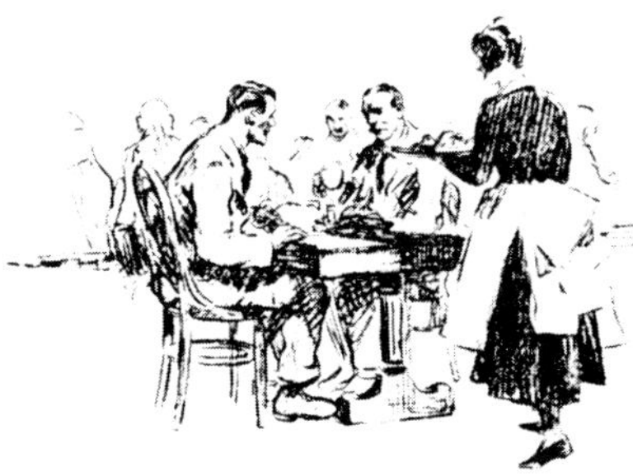

495

494. [*Male Nude*], c. 1917–20. Wash on illustration board, 19⅞ × 12¼ inches. Whitney Museum of American Art, New York; Bequest of Josephine N. Hopper 70.1370.

495. Proof, unidentified publication, c. 1915–18.

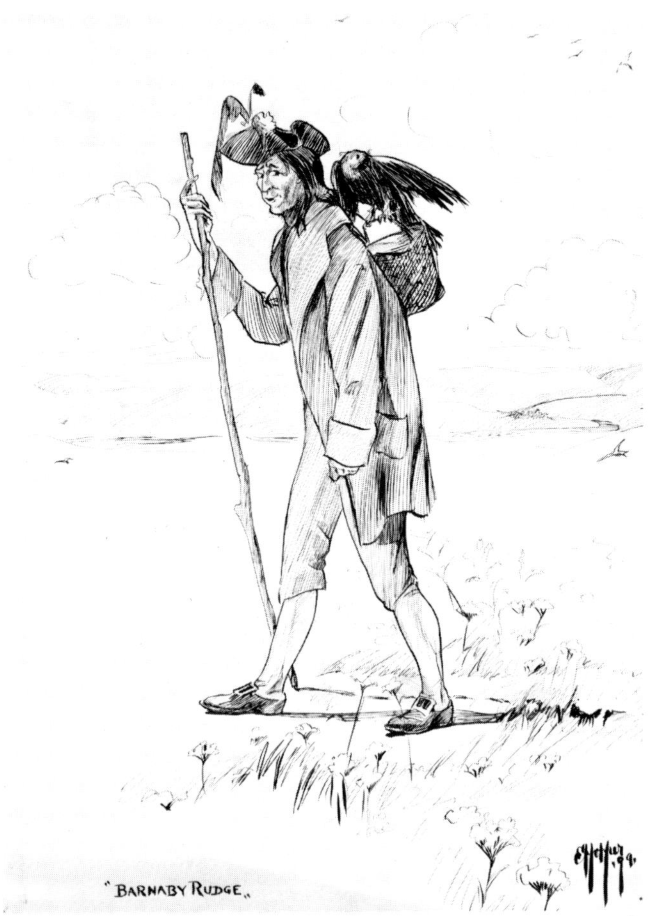

496

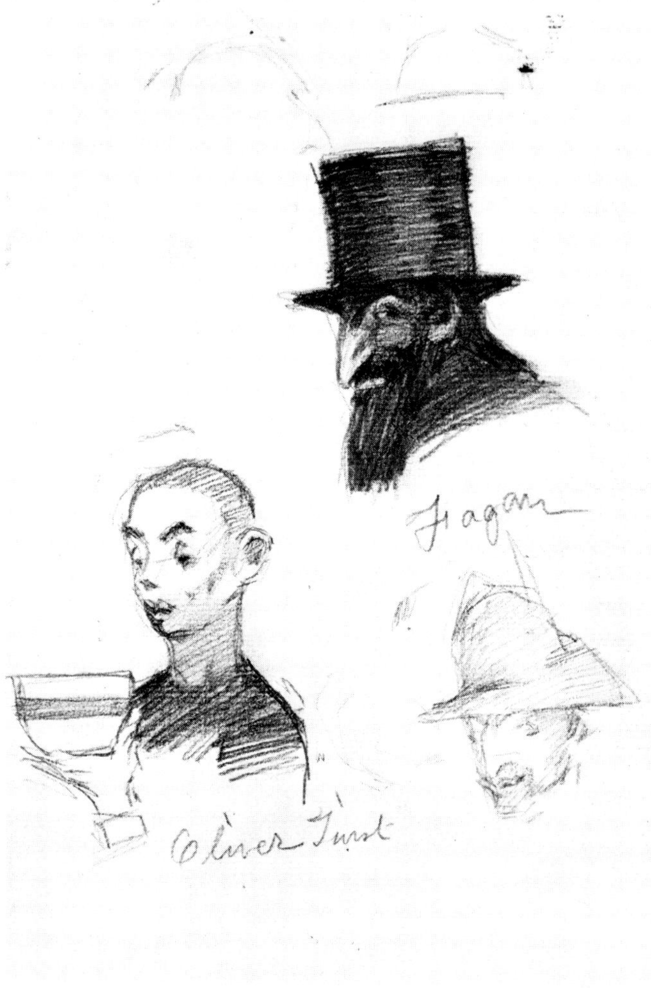

496. Illustration for Charles Dickens's *Barnaby Rudge* (1841), 1899. Pen and ink on paper, 12½ × 8⅝ inches. Whitney Museum of American Art, New York; Bequest of Josephine N. Hopper 70.1566.144.

497. Studies for Fagan and Oliver Twist from Charles Dickens's *Oliver Twist* (1838), c. 1899. Pencil on paper, 9⅝ × 6 inches. Whitney Museum of American Art, New York; Bequest of Josephine N. Hopper 70.1560.115.

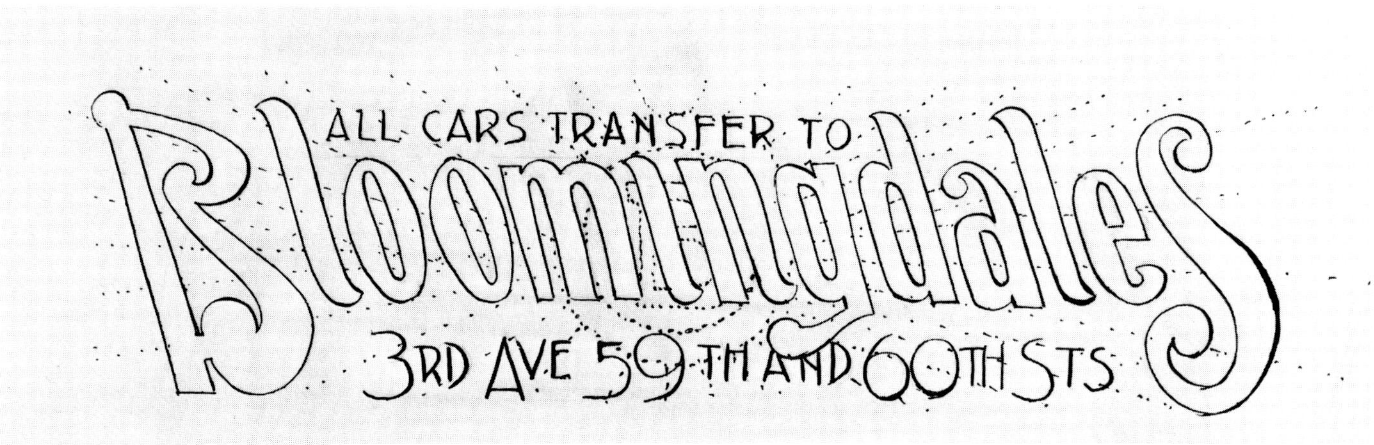

499

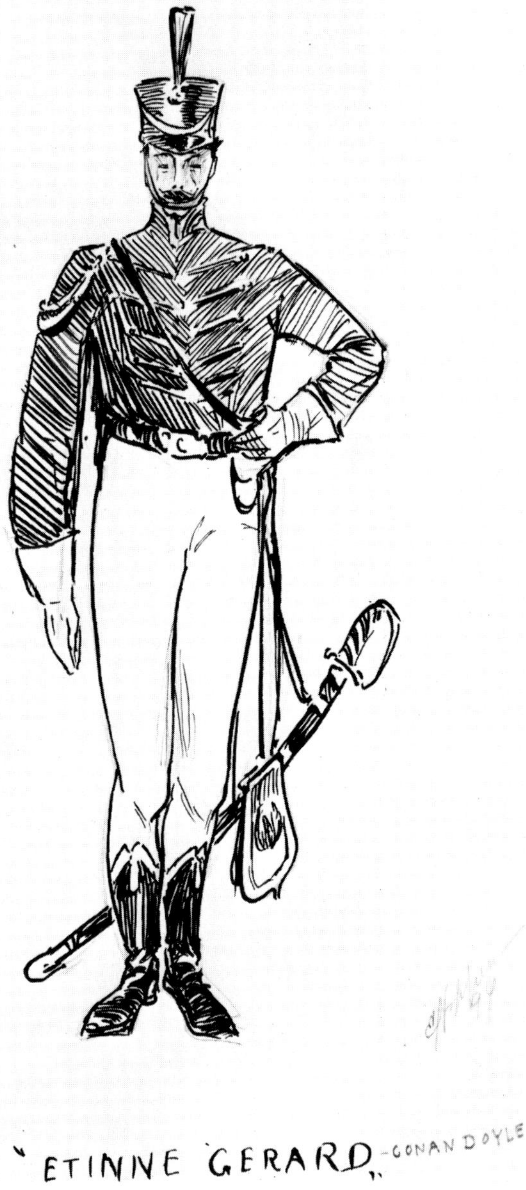

498

498. Illustration for Sir Arthur Conan Doyle's *The Exploits of Brigadier Gerard* (1899), 1899. Pen and ink on paper, $6\frac{7}{8} \times 4\frac{1}{2}$ inches. Whitney Museum of American Art, New York: Bequest of Josephine N. Hopper 70.1561.194.

499. Commercial illustration for Bloomingdales logo, c. 1900. Pen and ink on paper, $8\frac{5}{8} \times 12\frac{1}{2}$ inches. Whitney Museum of American Art, New York; Bequest of Josephine N. Hopper 70.1565.71.

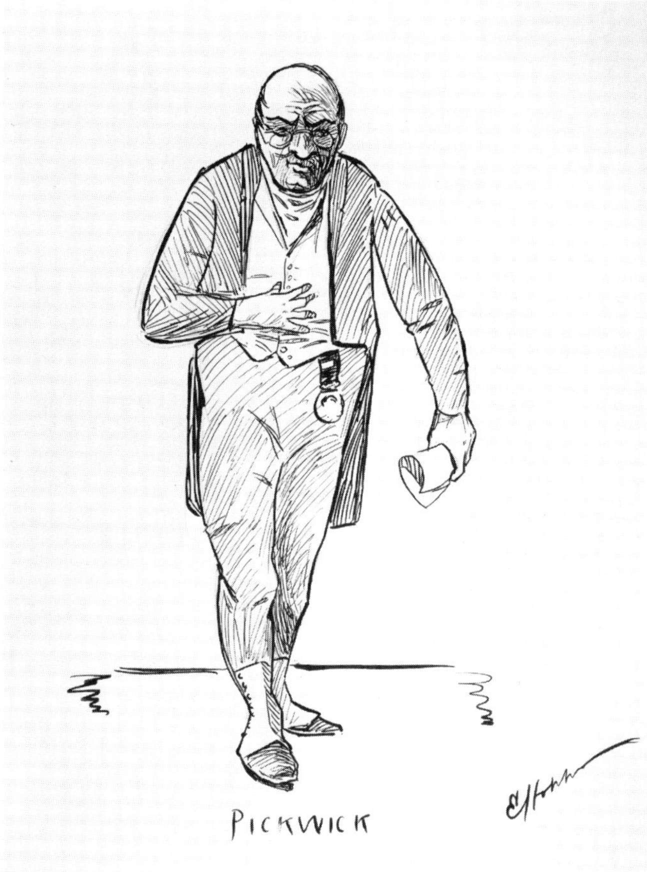

500

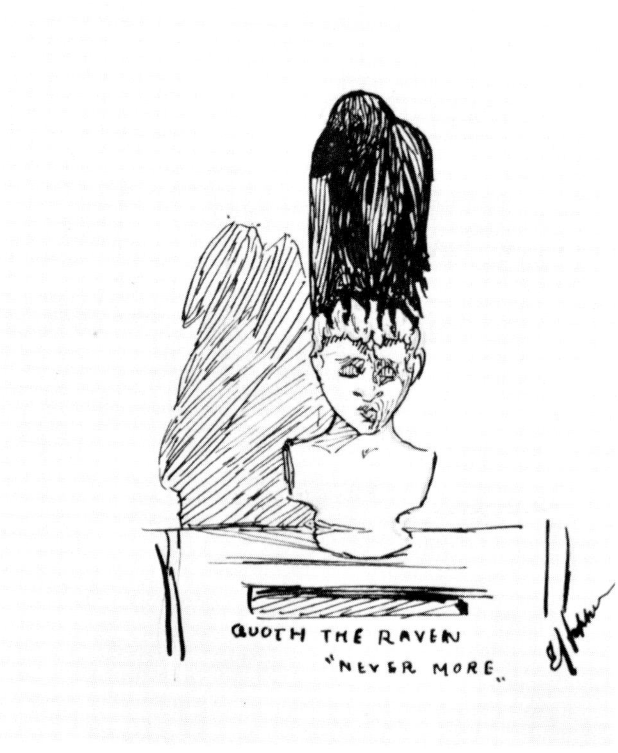

501

500. Illustration for Charles Dickens's *The Posthumous Papers of the Pickwick Club* (1836–37), c. 1900. Pen and ink on paper, 9⅞ × 7⅞ inches. Whitney Museum of American Art, New York; Bequest of Josephine N. Hopper 70.1562.82.

501. Illustration for Edgar Allen Poe's *The Raven* (1845), c. 1900–06. Ink on paper, 4⅜ × 3⅛ inches. Whitney Museum of American Art, New York; Bequest of Josephine N. Hopper 70.1561.13.

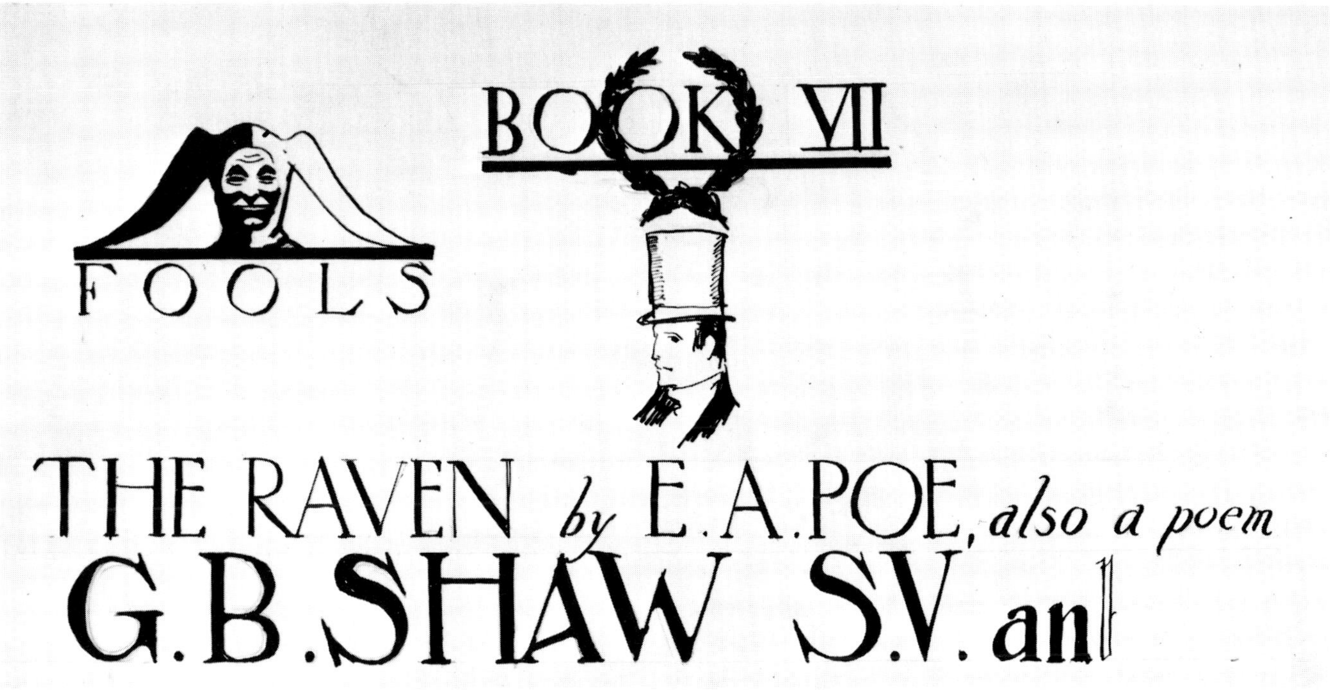

502

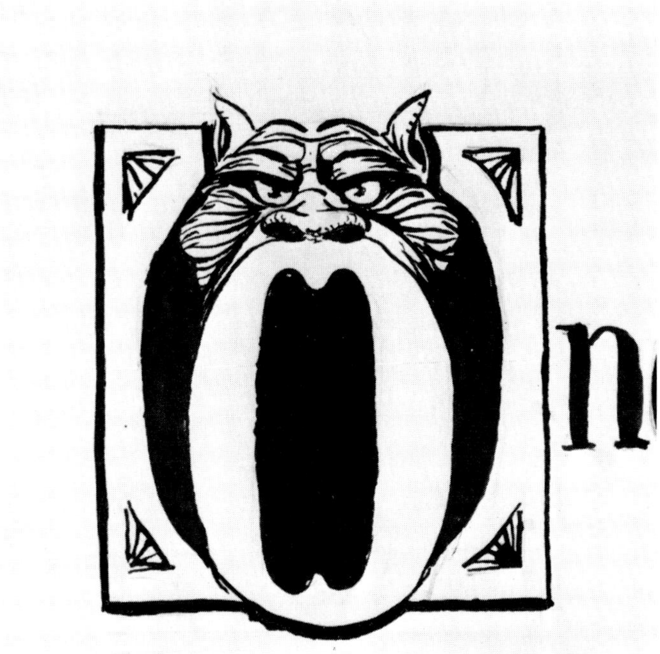

503

502. Miscellaneous illustration studies including lettering for *The Raven,* c. 1900–06. Ink on paper, 11¼ × 14⅛ inches. Whitney Museum of American Art, New York; Bequest of Josephine N. Hopper 70.1565.49.

503. Study for lettering for head piece, c. 1900–06. Ink on paper, 4¼ × 3⅜ inches. Whitney Museum of American Art, New York; Bequest of Josephine N. Hopper 70.1561.87.

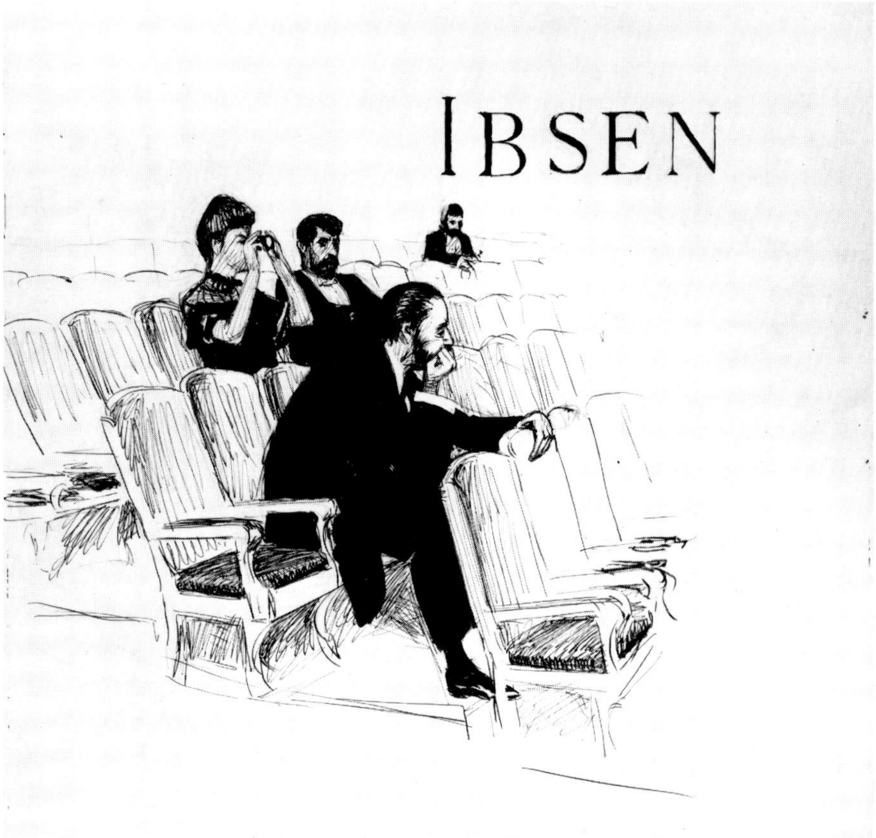

504

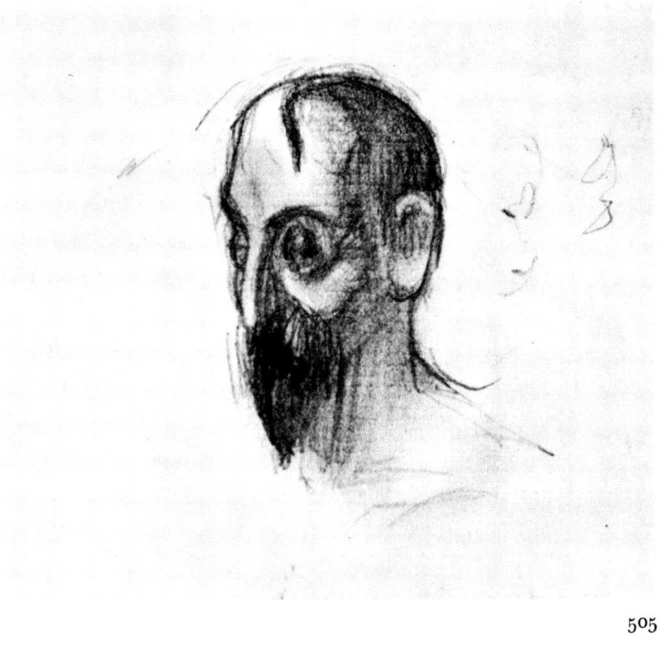

505

504. Study of illustration for Henrik Ibsen, c. 1900–06. Ink on paper, 14½ × 11⅝ inches. Whitney Museum of American Art, New York; Bequest of Josephine N. Hopper 70.1565.51.

505. Study for Gavroche from Victor Hugo's *Les Misérables* (1862), c. 1900–09. Pencil on paper, 12½ × 9⅝ inches. Whitney Museum of American Art, New York; Bequest of Josephine N. Hopper 70.1560.112.

506. Studies for Don Quixote and Sancho Panza from Miguel de Cervantes's *Don Quixote de la Mancha* (1605), 1906/07 or 1909. Pencil on paper, 9¾ × 6 inches. Whitney Museum of American Art, New York; Bequest of Josephine N. Hopper 70.1560.110.

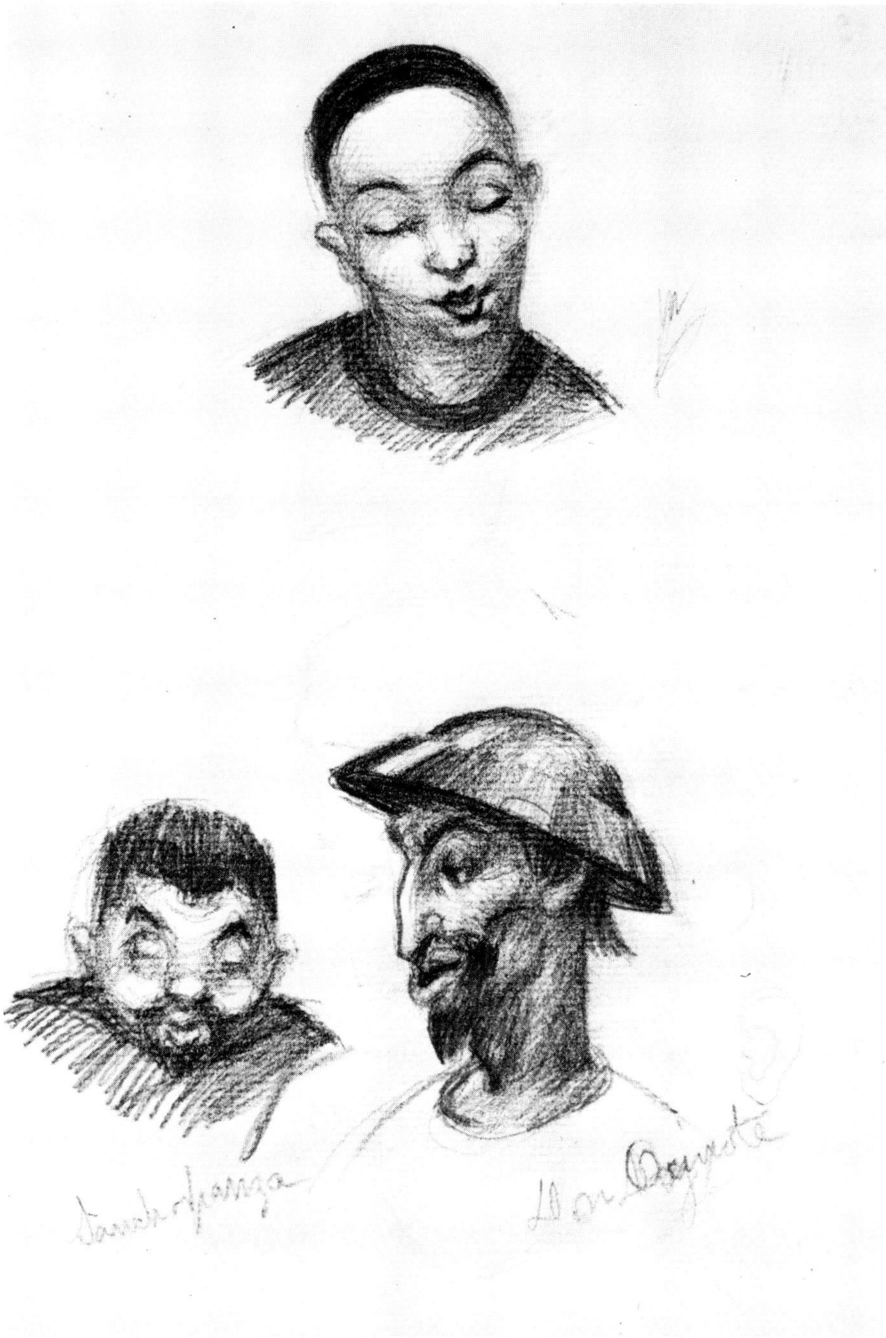
Sancho Panza
Don Quixote